*Major Problems
in the History
of the American South*

MAJOR PROBLEMS IN AMERICAN HISTORY SERIES

GENERAL EDITOR
THOMAS G. PATERSON

Major Problems in the History of the American South
Volume I: The Old South

DOCUMENTS AND ESSAYS

SECOND EDITION

EDITED BY

PAUL D. ESCOTT
WAKE FOREST UNIVERSITY

DAVID R. GOLDFIELD
UNIVERSITY OF NORTH CAROLINA, CHARLOTTE

SALLY G. McMILLEN
DAVIDSON COLLEGE

ELIZABETH HAYES TURNER
UNIVERSITY OF HOUSTON—DOWNTOWN

HOUGHTON MIFFLIN COMPANY   BOSTON   NEW YORK

For Lauren and David
Eleanor and Erik
Blair and Carrie
Meg and Laura
and to our students

Editor-in-Chief: Jean L. Woy
Senior Associate Editor: Frances Gay
Senior Project Editor: Janet Young
Editorial Assistant: Nasya Laymon
Associate Production/Design Coordinator: Jodi O'Rourke
Assistant Manufacturing Coordinator: Andrea Wagner
Senior Marketing Manager: Sandra McGuire

Cover image: *Big B Cotton Plantation* by William Aiken Walker. The Collection of Jay P. Altmayer.

Printed in the U.S.A.

Library of Congress Catalog Card Number: 98-72022

ISBN: 0-395-87139-5

789-CS-09 08 07 06

Contents

C H A P T E R   4
The Revolutionary South and Its Aftermath
Page 103

C H A P T E R   5
The Emergence of Southern Nationalism
Page 137

C H A P T E R   6
The Slaveholders' South
Page 173

C H A P T E R   7
The Slave and Free Black Experience
Page 208

CHAPTER 12
Emancipation and Reconstruction
Page 395

Preface

The historian David M. Potter once wrote that the South has been "a kind of Sphinx on the American land." Nothing in the two volumes of *Major Problems in the History of the American South* will challenge that description of a great American enigma. The documents and essays in these volumes demonstrate that the search to know what the South was and what it is remains at the core of southern history.

William Faulkner made the observation that in the South the past is not dead; it is not even past. Some students of southern history may well recognize this statement to be true; others will decide that the South has moved beyond its past, becoming more like the rest of the nation. Or, perhaps the rest of the nation has become more like the South. In any case, today the South is less a geographical entity than a state of mind, offering a panorama of almost bewildering diversity. Writers and historians have yet to agree on what makes the region's culture and history different. For all who have sought to discover its essence, the challenge has been in the pursuit and in the insights that come from what the scholar Fred Hobson has called "the southern rage to explain." We hope that the selections in this book will encourage readers to pursue that quest to understand the South's past.

Like the first edition of *Major Problems in the History of the American South,* this revised Volume I on the Old South follows a basically chronological tour of southern history, from pre-Columbian Indian settlements through the dislocations of Reconstruction. We have selected documents that evoke the atmosphere, personal experiences, and events of the times. In choosing the essays, we have provided historical perspective on some of the major issues that southerners confronted. We have included provocative interpretations of those key issues. We present, in both the documents and essays, a variety of viewpoints, inviting readers to reach their own conclusions about major interpretive problems in southern history.

After receiving guidance from instructors who teach southern history, in this second edition we have reduced the length of this volume by two chapters. Several chapters, including Chapters 5, 10, and 12, have been reorganized. Chapter 5 now covers southern political issues from the early national period through the Jacksonian period. Some of the divisive, often volatile political events from the 1850s through secession in 1861 are explored in Chapter 10. Chapter 12 combines both emancipation and federal Reconstruction.

In this edition we have also expanded our vision of the South as a varied, complex region by including more material on the Deep South and the southern frontier. Both documents and essays add additional background on southern women's experiences. Historians are engaging in instructive research to show how gender and class issues shape our interpretation of southern history. A shift in the study of slavery illuminates the reality and variety of slaves' oppression. Other new mater-

ial included here exposes readers to some of the exciting scholarship that has appeared since the first edition was published in 1990, without sacrificing some of
the classic literature that has stood the test of time. Despite pervasive myths that
continue to influence ideas about the region, this volume should make evident that
no single interpretation or image can reflect the rich variety of experiences in Old
South history.

This book follows the same general format as other volumes in the *Major
Problems in American History* series. Each chapter begins with a brief introduction
to its topic, followed first by documentary readings and then by essays that illumi-
nate the central theme. Headnotes that place the readings in historical and interpretive perspective introduce each chapter's primary sources and essays. A "Further
Reading" section, suggesting important books and articles for those who wish to
explore the subject in more depth, closes each chapter.

Many friends and colleagues have contributed to these volumes. For help with
the second edition, we want to thank Carlos Blanton, John B. Boles, Laura Edwards, Elna Green, Randal Hall, John Inscoe, Charles Israel, Paul Levengood,
Bruce McMillen, J. Russell Snapp, Randy Sparks, Pamela Tyler, and Marjorie
Wheeler.

Detailed and extremely helpful written reviews of draft tables of contents were
provided by Bradley G. Bond, University of Southern Mississippi; Jane Turner
Censer, George Mason University; Peter A. Coclanis, University of North Carolina, Chapel Hill; Elna C. Green, Sweet Briar College; John C. Inscoe, University
of Georgia; Lawrence N. Powell, Tulane University; Ann W. Ellis Pullen, Kenne-
saw State University; and Charles Reagan Wilson, University of Mississippi. And
we are grateful for the very helpful reviews of the first edition that were provided
by Clarence L. Mohr, Tulane University; Theodore Ownby, University of Mississippi; Christopher Phillips, Emporia State University; Joseph P. Reidy, Howard
University; J. B. Smallwood, Jr., University of North Texas; and Peter Wallenstein,
Virginia Polytechnic Institute.

We received documents and sound advice from the Library of Congress Prints
and Photographs Division, the Southern Baptist Historical Library and Archives,
the *Journal of Southern History,* and Rice University. Thomas G. Paterson, the editor of the *Major Problems in American History* series, provided timely assistance
and encouragement. And the editors at Houghton Mifflin, Jean Woy, Frances Gay,
and Janet Young, have kept us on track, even when part of the manuscript went
astray through the mail.

Without the unlimited support and patience of our families, this project would
not have been completed. This volume is dedicated to our children—all eight of
them—and to our students. May they always view the South with unclouded
vision.

P. E.
D. G.
S. M.
E. H. T.

Major Problems
in the History
of the American South

What Is the South?

Historian Michael O'Brien noted that *"no man's South is the same as another's."*
Although there is general agreement that the South is (or at least was, at some time)
distinct from other regions of the United States, there is no consensus on either the
nature or the duration of that difference. Definitions of the South have stressed
everything from the obvious (for example, climate and white supremacy) to the ob-
scure (the geographical line below which grits replace hash browns).

Part of the problem is that there are many Souths. Those who lived in the
South Carolina lowcountry were different in terms of ethnicity, accent, ideology, oc-
cupation, religion, music, and language from the people of the southern Appalachi-
ans. Distinctions exist within states—lowcountry versus upcountry, Piedmont versus
coastal plains, and Delta versus piney woods. These disparities have led some to con-
tend that the South is more a state of mind than a geographical region.

Yet some thing or things draw these disparate areas together, and observers
since the earliest settlements have tried to identify what constitutes "the South." The
task is more than a mere intellectual exercise. As with the study of any ethnic group,
distinction helps to define identity. And the study of the South has helped to define
our national identity as well. The South has often served as a counterpoint, both
good and bad, to the rest of the country. In learning what is special about the South
and how it became that way, we are learning about our national culture as well.

⚒ *E S S A Y S*

W. J. Cash's *The Mind of the South* is among the most eloquent and forceful statements
of a southern identity, though the Charlotte journalist's emphasis on the continuity of
southern history has provoked sharp responses from some historians, among them Yale
University's C. Vann Woodward. The first two essays present Cash's and Woodward's
differing views. Defining southern distinctiveness is a major academic industry and in
fact, as historian David L. Smiley notes in the next essay, has become a distinctive element in itself. Assuming the South's difference, the obvious question is, "Different
from what?" John B. Boles, professor of history at Rice University and managing editor of the *Journal of Southern History,* notes the complex task of identifying the
South's distinct character and how individuals continue to try to rediscover and embrace its uniqueness.

The Continuity of Southern History

W. J. CASH

There exists among us by ordinary—both North and South—a profound conviction that the South is another land, sharply differentiated from the rest of the American nation, and exhibiting within itself a remarkable homogeneity.

As to what its singularity may consist in, there is, of course, much conflict of opinion, and especially between Northerner and Southerner. But that it is different and that it is solid—on these things nearly everybody is agreed. Now and then, to be sure, there have arisen people, usually journalists or professors, to tell us that it is all a figment of the imagination, that the South really exists only as a geographical division of the United States and is distinguishable from New England or the Middle West only by such matters as the greater heat and the presence of a larger body of Negroes. Nobody, however, has ever taken them seriously. And rightly.

For the popular conviction is indubitably accurate: the South is, in Allen Tate's phrase, "Uncle Sam's other province." And when Carl Carmer said of Alabama that "The Congo is not more different from Massachusetts or Kansas or California," he fashioned a hyperbole which is applicable in one measure or another to the entire section.

This is not to suggest that the land does not display an enormous diversity within its borders. Anyone may see that it does simply by riding along any of the great new motor roads which spread across it—through brisk towns with tall white buildings in Nebraska Gothic; through smart suburbs, with their faces newly washed; through industrial and Negro slums, medieval in dirt and squalor and wretchedness, in all but redeeming beauty; past sleepy old hamlets and wide fields and black men singing their sad songs in the cotton, past log cabin and high grave houses, past hill and swamp and plain. . . . The distance from Charleston to Birmingham is in some respects measurable only in sidereal terms, as is the distance from the Great Smokies to Lake Pontchartrain. And Howard Odum has demonstrated that the economic and social difference between the Southeastern and Southwestern states is so great and growing that they have begun to deserve to be treated, for many purposes, as separate regions.

Nevertheless, if it can be said there are many Souths, the fact remains that there is also one South. That is to say, it is easy to trace throughout the region (roughly delimited by the boundaries of the former Confederate States of America, but shading over into some of the border states, notably Kentucky, also) a fairly definite mental pattern, associated with a fairly definite social pattern—a complex of established relationships and habits of thought, sentiments, prejudices, standards and values, and associations of ideas, which, if it is not common strictly to every group of white people in the South, is still common in one appreciable measure or another, and in some part or another, to all but relatively negligible ones.

It is no product of Cloud-Cuckoo-Town, of course, but proceeds from the common American heritage, and many of its elements are readily recognizable as being simply variations on the primary American theme. To imagine it existing outside this continent would be quite impossible. But for all that, the peculiar history of the South has so greatly modified it from the general American norm that, when viewed as a whole, it decisively justifies the notion that the country is—not quite a nation within a nation, but the next thing to it.

To understand it, it is necessary to know the story of its development. And the best way to begin that story, I think, is by disabusing our minds of two correlated legends—those of the Old and the New Souths.

What the Old South of the legend in its classical form was like is more or less familiar to everyone. It was a sort of stage piece out of the eighteenth century, wherein gesturing gentlemen moved soft-spokenly against a background of rose gardens and dueling grounds, through always gallant deeds, and lovely ladies, in farthingales, never for a moment lost that exquisite remoteness which has been the dream of all men and the possession of none. Its social pattern was manorial, its civilization that of the Cavalier, its ruling class an aristocracy coextensive with the planter group—men often entitled to quarter the royal arms of St. George and St. Andrew on their shields, and in every case descended from the old gentlefolk who for many centuries had made up the ruling classes of Europe.

They dwelt in large and stately mansions, preferably white and with columns and Grecian entablature. Their estates were feudal baronies, their slaves quite too numerous ever to be counted, and their social life a thing of Old World splendor and delicacy. What had really happened here, indeed, was that the gentlemanly idea, driven from England by Cromwell, had taken refuge in the South and fashioned for itself a world to its heart's desire: a world singularly polished and mellow and poised, wholly dominated by ideals of honor and chivalry and *noblesse*—all those sentiments and values and habits of action which used to be, especially in Walter Scott, invariably assigned to the gentleman born and the Cavalier.

Beneath these was a vague race lumped together indiscriminately as the poor whites—very often, in fact, as the "white-trash." These people belonged in the main to a physically inferior type, having sprung for the most part from the convict servants, redemptioners, and debtors of old Virginia and Georgia, with a sprinkling of the most unsuccessful sort of European peasants and farm laborers and the dregs of the European town slums. And so, of course, the gulf between them and the master classes was impassable, and their ideas and feelings did not enter into the makeup of the prevailing Southern civilization.

But in the legend of the New South the Old South is supposed to have been destroyed by the Civil War and the thirty years that followed it, to have been swept both socially and mentally into the limbo of things that were and are not, to give place to a society which has been rapidly and increasingly industrialized and modernized both in body and in mind—which now, indeed, save for a few quaint survivals and gentle sentimentalities and a few shocking and inexplicable brutalities such as lynching, is almost as industrialized and modernized in its outlook as the North. Such an idea is obviously inconsistent with the general assumption of the South's great difference, but paradox is the essence of popular thinking, and millions—even in the South itself—placidly believe in both notions.

These legends, however, bear little relation to reality. There was an Old South, to be sure, but it was another thing than this. And there is a New South. Industrialization and commercialization have greatly modified the land, including its ideology. . . . Nevertheless, the extent of the change and of the break between the Old South that was and the South of our time has been vastly exaggerated. The South, one might say, is a tree with many age rings, with its limbs and trunk bent and twisted by all the winds of the years, but with its tap root in the Old South. Or, better still, it is like one of those churches one sees in England. The facade and towers, the windows and clerestory, all the exterior and superstructure are late Gothic of one sort or another, but look into its nave, its aisles, and its choir and you find the old mighty Norman arches of the twelfth century. And if you look into its crypt, you may even find stones cut by Saxon, brick made by Roman hands.

The mind of the section, that is, is continuous with the past. And its primary form is determined not nearly so much by industry as by the purely agricultural conditions of that past. So far from being modernized, in many ways it has actually always marched away, as to this day it continues to do, from the present toward the past.

The Discontinuity of Southern History

C. VANN WOODWARD

Among the major monuments of broken continuity in the South are slavery and secession, independence and defeat, emancipation and military occupation, reconstruction and redemption. Southerners, unlike other Americans, repeatedly felt the solid ground of continuity give way under their feet. An old order of slave society solidly supported by constitution, state, church and the authority of law and learning and cherished by a majority of the people collapsed, perished and disappeared. So did the short-lived experiment in national independence. So also the short-lived experiment in Radical Reconstruction. The succeeding order of Redeemers, the New South, lasted longer, but it too seems destined for the dump heap of history.

Perhaps it was because Cash wrote toward the end of the longest and most stable of these successive orders, the one that lasted from 1877 to the 1950's, that he acquired his conviction of stability and unchanging continuity. At any rate, he was fully persuaded that "the mind of the section . . . is continuous with the past," and that the South has "always marched away, as to this day it continues to do, from the present toward the past." Just as he guardedly conceded diversity in advancing the thesis of unity, so he admits the existence of change in maintaining the thesis of continuity, change from which even the elusive Southern "mind" did not "come off scot-free." But it was the sort of change the French have in mind in saying. *"Plus ça change, plus c'est la même chose."* Tidewater tobacco, up-country cotton, rampaging frontier, flush times in Alabama and Mississippi, slavery, secession, defeat, abolition, Reconstruction, New South, industrial revolution—*toujours la même chose!* Even the Yankee victory that "had smashed the Southern world" was "almost entirely illusory," since "it had left the essential Southern mind and will . . . entirely unshaken. Rather . . . it had operated enormously to fortify and confirm that mind and will." As for Reconstruction, again, "so far from having reconstructed the Southern mind in the large and in its essential character, it was still this Yankee's fate to have strengthened it almost beyond reckoning, and to have made it one of the most solidly established, one of the least reconstructible ever developed."

The continuity upon which Cash is most insistent is the one he sees between the Old South and the New South. He early announces his intention of "disabusing our minds of two correlated legends—those of the Old and the New South." He promises in Rankean terms to tell us "exactly what the Old South was really like." He concedes that there was a New South as well. "Nevertheless, the extent of the change and of the break between the Old South that was and the New South of our time has been vastly exaggerated." The common denominator, the homogenizing touchstone is his "basic Southerner" or "the man at the center." He is described as "an exceedingly simple fellow," most likely a hillbilly from the backcountry, but fundamentally he is a petit bourgeois always on the make, yet ever bemused by his vision of becoming, imitating, or at least serving the planter aristocrat. Cash's crude Irish parvenu is pictured as the prototype of the planter aristocrat. Cash is confused about these aristocrats, mainly I think because he is confused about the nature and history of aristocracy. He admires their "beautiful courtesy and dignity and gesturing grace," but deplores their "grotesque exaggeration" and their "pomposity" and suspects that the genuine article should have been genteel. He grudgingly acknowledges their existence, but denies the legitimacy of their pretenses—all save those of a few negligible Virginians. He seems to be saying that they were all bourgeois, that therefore the Old South was bourgeois too, and therefore essentially indistinguishable from the New South. New and Old alike were spellbound by the spurious myth of aristocracy. This and the paradoxical fact that those parvenu aristocrats actually took charge, were a real ruling class, and the continuity of their rule spelled the continuity of the New South with the Old.

The masses came out of the ordeal of Civil War with "a deep affection for these captains, a profound trust in them," a belief in the right "of the master class to ordain and command." And according to Cash, the old rulers continued to ordain and command right on through the collapse of the old order and the building of the new. He detects no change of guard at Redemption. So long as the industrialists and financiers who stepped into the shoes of the old rulers gave the Proto-Dorian password and adopted the old uniforms and gestures, he salutes them as the genuine article. In fact they were rather an improvement, for they represent "a striking extension of the so-called paternalism of the Old South: its passage in some fashion toward becoming a genuine paternalism." Cash enthusiastically embraces the thesis of Broadus Mitchell's "celebrated monograph" that the cotton-mill campaign was "a mighty folk movement," a philanthropic crusade of inspired paternalists. The textile-mill captains were "such men as belonged more or less distinctively within the limits of the old ruling class, the progeny of the plantation." Indeed they were responsible for "the bringing over of the plantation into industry," the company town. Even "the worst labor sweaters" were "full of the ancient Southern love for the splendid gesture," fulfilling "an essential part of the Southern paternalistic tradition that it was an essential duty of the upper classes to look after the moral welfare of these people."

To the cotton mills the neopaternalists add the public schools for the common whites and thus "mightily reaffirm the Proto-Dorian bond." The common poverty acted as a leveler (back to the Unity thesis) and brought "a very great increase in the social solidarity of the South," a "marked mitigation of the haughtiness" of the old captains, now "less boldly patronizing," and "a suppression of class feeling that went beyond anything that even the Old South had known." The common white felt "the hand on the shoulder . . . the jests, the rallying, the stories . . . the confiding reminders of the Proto-Dorian bond of white men." That, according to Cash, was what did in the Populist revolt and the strikes of the lint-head mill hands as well. For from the heart of the masses came "a wide, diffuse gratefulness pouring out upon the cotton-mill baron; upon the old captains, upon all the captains and preachers of Progress; upon the ruling class as a whole for having embraced the doctrine and brought these things about."

Of course Cash professes not to be taken in by Progress like the rednecks and the lint-heads. He realizes that Progress and Success had their prices and he sets them down scrupulously in the debit column of his ledger. "Few people can ever have been confronted with a crueler dilemma" than the old planter turned supply merchant to his former huntin' and fishin' companion as sharecropper: "The old monotonous pellagra-and-rickets-breeding diet had at least been abundant? Strip it rigidly to fatback, molasses, and cornbread, dole it out with an ever stingier hand . . . blind your eyes to peaked faces, seal up your ears to hungry whines. . . ." And that sunbonnet, straw-hat proletariat of the paternalistic mill villages? By the turn of the century they had become "a pretty distinct physical type . . . a dead white skin, a sunken chest, and stooping shoulders. . . . Chinless faces, microcephalic foreheads, rabbit teeth, goggling dead-fish eyes, rickety limbs, and stunted bodies. . . . The women were characteristically stringy-haired and limp of breast at twenty, and shrunken hags at thirty or forty." Something admittedly was happening to the captains, too, what with "men of generally coarser kind coming steadily to the front." And in "all the elaborate built-up pattern of leisure and hedonistic drift; all the slow, cool, gracious and graceful gesturing of movement," there was a sad falling off, a decay of the ideal. "And along with it, the vague largeness of outlook which was so essentially a part of the same aristocratic complex; the magnanimity. . . ."

Admitting all that, "But when the whole of this debit score of Progress is taken into account, we still inevitably come back to the fact that its total effect was as I have said." *Plus ça change!* "Here in a word, was triumph for the Southern will . . . an enormous renewal of confidence in the general Southern way." In [Henry W.] Grady's rhetoric, "Progress stood quite accurately for a sort of new charge at Gettysburg." To be sure, Southern Babbitts eventually appeared, but even they were "Tartarin, not Tartuffe . . . simpler, more naïve, less analytical than their compatriots in Babbittry at the North. . . . They go about making money . . . as boys go about stealing apples . . . in the high-hearted sense of being embarked upon capital sport." Yet, like the planter turned supply merchant or captain of industry, "they looked at you with level and proud gaze. The hallmark of their breed was identical with that of the masters of the Old South—a tremendous complacency." And Rotary, "sign-manual of the Yankee spirit"? Granting "an unfortunate decline in the dignity of the Southern manner," it was but "the grafting of Yankee backslapping upon the normal Southern geniality. . . . I am myself," Cash wrote, "indeed perpetually astonished to recall that Rotary was not invented in the South." And does one detect "strange notes—Yankee notes—in all this talk about the biggest factory, about bank clearings and car loadings and millions"? Strange? Not for Jack Cash. "But does anybody," he actually asked, "fail to hear once more the native accent of William L. Yancey and Barnwell Rhett, to glimpse again the waving plume of, say, Wade Hampton?"

How could he? How could any historian? He sometimes reminds one of those who scribble facetious graffiti on Roman ruins. He betrays a want of feeling for the seriousness of human strivings, for the tragic theme in history. Looking back from mid-twentieth century over the absurd skyscrapers and wrecked-car bone piles set in the red-clay hills, how could he seriously say that the South believed it "was succeeding in creating a world which, if it was not made altogether in the image of that old world, half-remembered and half-dreamed, shimmering there forever behind the fateful smoke of Sumter's guns, was yet sufficiently of a piece with it in essentials to be acceptable." A great slave society, by far the largest and richest of those that had existed in the New World since the sixteenth century, had grown up and miraculously flourished in the heart of a thoroughly bourgeois and partly puritanical republic. It had renounced its bourgeois origins and elaborated and painfully rationalized its institutional, legal, metaphysical, and religious defenses. It had produced leaders of skill, ingenuity, and strength who, unlike those of other slave societies, invested their honor and their lives, and not merely part of their capital, in that society. When the crisis came, they, unlike the others, chose to fight. It proved to be the death struggle of a society, which went down in ruins. And yet here is a historian who tells us that nothing essential changed. The ancient "mind," temperament, the aristocratic spirit, parvenu though he called it—call it what you will, *panache* perhaps—was perfectly preserved in a mythic amber. And so the present is continuous with the past, the ancient manifest in the new order, in Grady, Babbitt, Rotary, whatever, *c'est la même chose.*

I am afraid that Cash was taken in by the very myth he sought to explode—by the fancy-dress charade the New South put on in the cast-off finery of the old order, the cult of the Lost Cause, the Plantation Legend and the rest. The new actors threw themselves into the old roles with spirit and conviction and put on what was for some a convincing performance. But Cash himself, even though he sometimes took the Snopeses for the Sartorises, plainly saw how they betrayed to the core and essence every tenet of the old code. "And yet," he can write,

> And yet—as regards the Southern mind, which is our theme, how essentially superficial and unrevolutionary remain the obvious changes; how certainly do these obvious changes take place within the ancient framework, and even sometimes contribute to the positive strengthening of the ancient pattern.
>
> Look close at this scene as it stands in 1914. There is an atmosphere here, an air, shining from every word and deed. And the key to this atmosphere . . . is that familiar word without which it would be impossible to tell the story of the Old South, that familiar word "extravagant."
>
> [Then, after a reference to the new skyscrapers in the clay hills:]
> Softly; do you not hear behind that the gallop of Jeb Stuart's cavalrymen?

The answer is "No"! Not one ghostly echo of a gallop. And neither did Jack Cash. He only thought he did when he was bemused.

After some years in the profession, one has seen reputations of historians rise and fall. The books of Ulrich Phillips and later Frank Owsley began to collect dust on the shelves, and one thinks of Beard and Parrington. In America, historians, like politicians, are out as soon as they are down. There is no comfortable back bench, no House of Lords for them. It is a wasteful and rather brutal practice, unworthy of what Cash would agree are our best Southern traditions. I hope this will not happen to Cash. The man really had something to say, which is more than most, and he said it with passion and conviction and with style. Essentially what he had to say is something every historian eventually finds himself trying to say (always risking exaggeration) at some stage about every great historical subject. And that is that in spite of the revolution—any revolution—the English remain English, the French remain French, the Russians remain Russian, the Chinese remain Chinese—call them Elizabethans or Cromwellians, Royalists or Jacobeans, Czarists or Communists, Mandarins or Maoists. That was really what Cash, at his best, was saying about Southerners, and he said it better than anybody ever has—only he rather overdid the thing. But in that he was merely illustrating once more that ancient Southern trait that he summed up in the word "extravagant." And, for that matter, his critic, poured in the same mold, may have unintentionally added another illustration of the same trait. If so, Jack Cash would have been the first to understand and not the last to forgive. Peace to his troubled spirit.

Quest for a Central Theme

DAVID L. SMILEY

In the history of Southern history in America the central theme has been the quest for the central theme. Local and state historians, students of regionalism and sectionalism, along with authors of American history surveys, have agreed in accepting the hypothesis that there is an American South and that it has had, historically, a unifying focus at its center. Furthermore, it has become customary among many historians to emphasize sectionalism as a key factor in American political history and to seek the causes for the apparent division of national patriotism. The man in the street, though his views may be hazy or overemotional, is confident that there are distinctive social and political patterns, perhaps traceable to a unique agricultural base, which combine to make the regions below the Potomac a recognizable entity, and most Americans at one time or another have engaged in the pursuit of a central theme in Southern history.

In its broadest sense the attempt to generalize regional folkways into an American South is part of the search for a national identity. Since the days of Noah Webster's early crusade for American English orthography and usage and Ralph Waldo Emerson's 1837 appeal for an American culture—Oliver Wendell Holmes called it "our intellectual Declaration of Independence"—Americans have earnestly sought to define the elusive qualities of their civilization and have squirmed uncomfortably

David L. Smiley, "The Quest for the Central Theme in Southern History." Reprinted with permission from *The South Atlantic Quarterly,* Vol. 71:3 (Summer 1972), pp. 307–325. Copyright 1972 by Duke University Press.

when critics such as Harriet Martineau or Charles Dickens ridiculed their efforts. There are interesting parallels between the national response to Dickens' *American Notes* and the Southern umbrage at the publication of Fanny Kemble's *Georgia Journal.* Still, the search for a national identity went on, and alongside it, as if in overt denial of a homogeneous national character, the search for Southern distinctiveness continued.

The reasons for the dichotomy in the national personality are complex and often obscure. At the same time that it served the purposes of American patriotism to sound a bold trumpet for a native civilization, it was politically advantageous to assent to the proposition that that civilization contained two "nations," opposites in fundamental aspects. The subsequent defeat of one "nation" by the other had the effect, on both sides, of inspiring each to glamorize its superior civilization and to denigrate that of the other as alien, un-American, and lacking in enduring and essential values. Especially was this activity prevalent among Southerners, where it took the form of reverence for the Lost Cause and allegiance to the cult of the Old South. In paying homage to a mythical past they were but acting out a characteristic common to peoples defeated by material or military force, i.e., the tendency to emphasize the superiority of less tangible qualities which their civilization allegedly produced in great quantity. This happened in the post–Civil War South at a thousand veterans' campfires, in political orations on days set aside to the memory of the dead, and in graduation addresses replete with scholarly appurtenances, and soon the emphasis began to appear in presumably objective histories and biographies of the Confederacy and its leaders.

In these expressions, down to the latest Rebel yell or defiant wave of the Confederate battle flag, there was the axiomatic acceptance of the belief that there was in fact an American South and that it possessed clearly defined traits which set it apart from the rest of the nation. In some instances, notably in the rhetoric of ambitious politicians and regional promoters, these assumptions conveyed overtones of immediate advantage to the author. A widely accepted central theme or distinguishing characteristic of the American South, for example, might affect a person's vote for or against a party, a personality, or a platform. On other occasions it might encourage or discourage decisions concerning the migration of industries and the choice of sites for capital investments, or the transfer of individual talents to sunnier climes or a more favorable labor situation.

At the same time, other statements of the central theme emerged from the labors of those committed to the highest obligations of scholarship: to sift the evidence and to generalize its meaning into an idea whose purpose is to enlarge understanding and to stimulate additional study and thought. In each case the motivation, though vastly different in purpose and effect, remains confused and unclear, and a study of the themes and forces which have attracted scholarly attention is significant in illuminating the problems and clarifying the objectives of the broader quest for national identity.

Basically and historically the effort to express the essence of the American South in a central theme has turned upon two related streams of thought. One has been to emphasize the causal effects of environment, while the other has put uppermost the development of certain acquired characteristics of the people called Southern. The work of the scholar Ulrich B. Phillips well illustrates the dual thrust of the endeavor. The South, he declared in a famous article, was a section dominated by racial conflict. It was "a land with a unity despite its diversity, with a people having common joys and common sorrows, and, above all, as to the white folk a people with a common resolve indomitably maintained—that it shall be and remain a white man's country." The "cardinal test of a Southerner and the central theme of Southern history," he said, was the desire to preserve the supremacy of the white race.

A few months after the article appeared, however, Phillips published *Life and Labor in the Old South,* in which he defined the South in terms of environmental causation. "Let us begin by discussing the weather," he wrote, "for that has been the chief agency in making the South distinctive." Behind the central theme of white supremacy Phillips could now discern a determinative meteorological pattern. Climate encouraged the production of staple crops, he declared, and staple crops promoted the plantation as the most efficient institution for their cultivation; the plantation's demand for large quantities of cheap labor led to slave importations; the presence of large numbers of Africans resulted in turn in a continuing race problem and the effort to maintain white supremacy. The acquired characteristic of racism now became a "house that Jack built" upon the foundation of a causative weather pattern.

Although critics have eroded much of Phillips' work, searchers for the central theme continued to follow the twin trails that he blazed. Generally they have undertaken to document either the theme of a dominant pattern of life or they have looked beyond the characteristic itself to seek geographical, meteorological, or psychological determinants of the significant traits. Sometimes a student has combined all of these in a single sentence. "The South," wrote Wendell H. Stephenson, "is a geographical location, a group of factors that differentiated the region and its inhabitants from other sections of the United States, and a state of mind to which these factors gave rise."

Thus, in one way or another, seekers for the central theme in Southern history have illustrated Phillips' observations that the South was either the home of a peculiar behavior pattern—all but universally present among people who considered themselves Southern and all but universally absent elsewhere in the land (the inheritance theory)—or a place where men's lives were molded by impersonal forces of climate or geography (the environmental view).

Perhaps the earliest assumption among those in quest of the central theme has been that the South is the product of a dictatorial environment. Phillips himself spoke of climate, in the form of heavy rainfall and an overheated sun, as causative factors in Southern life. Deluges eroded the topsoil, packed plowed lands, and ran off in floods, he said, and these rains conditioned the soils of the South. The sun was "bakingly hot"; it parched vegetation and enervated Europeans. Clarence Cason agreed that the South was a hot land. It was that part of the United States where the mercury reached 90 degrees in the shade at least one hundred afternoons a year. According to the climate theory, the tyrant sun slowed life to a languid crawl, impelled men to choose the shaded sides of streets, and induced cooks to concoct gastronomical delights to tempt heat-jaded appetites. It also dictated an emphasis upon staple crops, and as a consequence influenced the labor system of the South. Cason related with approval the Mississippi proverb that "only mules and black men can face the sun in July" in support of the comforting philosophy that only dark-skinned menials, presumably equipped by an all-wise Creator to endure the heat, should perform physical labor.

The idea that the central theme of Southern history may be found in the environment, in a causal relationship between a tropical climate and a peculiar way of life, has been a persistent one. in 1778 Judge William Henry Drayton told the South Carolina Assembly that "from the nature of the climate, soil and produce of the several states, a northern and southern interest naturally and unavoidably arise," and this view found ready acceptance. In his *Notes on Virginia* Thomas Jefferson remarked that "in a warm climate, no man will labor for himself who can make another labor for him." For this reason, he said, "of the proprietors of slaves a very small proportion indeed are ever seen to labor." Not only did the sun dictate a Southern interest and an aversion to toil; it also purified the Anglo-Saxon blood lines. In 1852 a newspaper editor pointed out that South Carolina lay in the same latitude as Greece and Rome, which was a "pretty good latitude for a 'breed of noble men.' " Six years later an observer commented that the "gentleman and lady of England and France, born to command, were especially fitted for their God given mission of uplifting and Christianizing the Negroes because they were softened and refined under our Southern sky." These views continued into the present century. Hamilton J. Eckenrode declared that in the warm climate of the American South a superior Nordic race became "tropicized" and thus improved in quality, and Francis B. Simkins also defined the South as the result of an adjustment of Anglo-Saxon peoples to a subtropical climate. He went on to deplore the modern preference for sun-tanned women and architectural styles that broke with the ante-bellum tradition, and—perhaps with tongue in cheek—he regarded all admiration for Southern temperatures as a form of Yankee carpetbaggery. "Because of the tyranny of books and magazines imported from strange climates," he said, Southerners had lost their fear of the sun, and in so doing had denied their birthright. They were "prompted to construct artificial lakes, treeless lawns, and low-roofed houses without porches or blinds."

Such is the environmental view—the causal effects of climate upon Southern folkways—and its inaccuracies are manifest. There is no unity in Southern climate, for the section includes startling variations in pattern and is wholly temperate rather than tropical in nature. William A. Foran pointed out that it was climate of opinion rather than climate in fact that influenced the configurations of life and thought among Europeans inhabiting the Southern regions of North America. "The Great South of 1860," Foran said, "began at Mason's and Dixon's line, just twenty-five miles south of the Liberty Bell on Independence Square, and ranged on through fifteen degrees of latitude." It encompassed almost every type of North American climate, "from pleasantly-tempered Virginia and magnolia-scented Charleston to the arctic blizzards of Texas. . . . Can historians speak glibly of a southern climate, much less of a tropical one," he asked, "of a land whose rainfall varies from zero to seventy inches a year?"

But the important question concerns the causal relationship between high temperatures and a distinctive life style. Even if there were a demonstrable meteorological unity to Southern weather, that would not of itself determine a particular social order, an agricultural pattern, or a way of life. That it did so in fact is the basic assumption of the advocates of the environmental theory. Yet climate neither forecast nor foreordained a staple crop-slave labor-race segregation cycle such as Phillips and others have described. Edgar T. Thompson explicitly rejected the Phillips thesis. "The plantation was not to be accounted for by climate," he said; the climate-plantation-slavery syndrome was instead a defense mechanism. "A theory which makes the plantation depend upon something outside the processes of human interaction, that is, a theory which makes the plantation depend upon a fixed and static something like climate," he declared, "is a theory which operates to justify an existing social order and the vested interests connected with that order."

Whatever forces produced the plantation—perhaps a complex combination of the English manorial tradition and the immediate need for a social unit that could provide a measure of economic independence and military defense—it has existed in low-country regions of the South as an important institution. Many seekers for the central theme have considered it, therefore, as the distinctive characteristic of Southern life. First used to describe a group of "planted" colonists, the word came to mean a system of farming with tenants, indentured servants, peons, or slaves working under the direction of proprietors who owned great estates and who used their wealth and social position to play active roles in their communities' affairs. As a close-knit social and political group, the planters exerted an influence that was indeed often predominant. In some regions they were able to define their interests as those of the entire population, and their way of life as typical of the whole. With the enthusiastic co-operation of nostalgic novelists, poets, song composers, and advertising agents, the plantation and its gentlemen of distinction became the epitome of the Southern ideal. For a generation prior to the Civil War its proponents were able to impose the "plantation platform" of opposition to national banks, internal improvements at federal government expense, and tariffs of protection upon the policies of the general government. At the same time, opponents of the Jeffersonian agricultural Arcadia and the Calhounian logic of dominant particularism came to view the plantation as the symbol of all that was evil or amiss about America. It represented wealth amassed by exploiting an immoral labor system, disunionist and antinationalistic sentiments, support for policies that tied the whole country to a humiliating economic colonialism, and political power resting upon a snobbish and superficial aristocracy. For these reasons, enemies of the plantation regarded it as "un-American." Still, it served as a definition of the South. The plantation system was an ancient one; in varying forms it antedated the rise of chattel slavery, and after emancipation it persisted in fact and fancy as a distinctive entity. It was also fairly well distributed over the coastal plains and river valleys, regions earliest settled and seat of preponderant voting strength, and it extended into a roughly similar topography as settlement advanced into the Southwest. The plantation pattern of production was therefore general enough to serve as an archetype, however superficial, of a recognizable Southern society.

The great estate, with its paternalistic Massa and Missus, and the values it allegedly conserved, has provided much of the romantic Southern tradition. "The plantation," said Sheldon Van Auken, "is central to any understanding of the South." Since before there were white men in New England, he declared, it has been the most significant aspect of a South differentiated by it from the rest of the nation. More than other forms of economic and social organization the plantation provided security to laborers and a satisfying way of life to its operators. It set the standards for the entire South, Van Auken concluded, and it has remained the ideal image of the South. Earlier, Francis P. Gaines studied the plantation as a Southern tradition and declared that "the supremacy of the great estate in the thinking of the South cannot be successfully challenged."

But despite the plantation's exalted place in tradition, at no time was it the typical pattern of life in the Southern regions. It was a hothouse flower that could not hold its own in the low country and could not survive the cooler breezes of the uplands. Many students, including both Gaines and Van Auken, pointed out that the plantation did not penetrate into the hilly regions where yeoman farmers predominated and where a different way of life prevailed; except for isolated regions in the Virginia tidewater and the South Carolina low country, it did not monopolize life anywhere. The Owsleys have demonstrated that the plantation was not typical even of the Alabama black belt and was becoming less important in the decade of the 1850's. And according to Avery Craven, by 1860 Virginia and Maryland had "come largely to the small farm and the small farmer." The governor of Virginia reported that the state was no longer characterized by the "large plantation system," but had developed into an agriculture of "smaller horticultural and arboricultural farming.". . .

The plantation was, presumably, the home of other significant factors in the Southern image—the planter and his code of honor, and the institution of slavery—and students turned to these as central characteristics. As Avery Craven put it, "Only two factors seem to have contributed to the making of anything Southern—an old-world country-gentleman ideal and the presence of negroes in large numbers." The small minority of well-to-do planters lived in conscious imitation of the old English squires, stocking their homes with books and musical instruments, importing furnishings and clothing, and providing tutors for their children. In their personal relationships the more refined among them practiced a gallant chivalry. "When you institute a comparison between the men of the North and the South, does it not result in favor of those of the South?" a speaker in the Kentucky constitutional convention of 1849 asked. "Has not the South acquired for itself a character for frankness, generosity, high-toned honor, and chivalry which is unknown in the North?"

This was the country-gentleman ideal as a characteristic of the South. Though many planters ignored the demands of the code, in theory it set Cavalier Southerner apart from Roundhead Yankee. It provided a theme for the Southern Agrarians, who saw in it a conservative civilization which had, in the words of John Crowe Ransom, come "to terms with nature." Living "materially along the inherited line of least resistance," the planters sought "to put the surplus of energy into the free life of the mind." But to emphasize the country-gentleman as the typical inhabitant of the Southern regions, and to pretend that he alone possessed a code of disinterested obligation to public service or polite manners, ignored a host of other types equally Southern and overlooked commendable contributions to statecraft made by men who lived in other quadrants of the country.

Much more common as a unifying factor was another by-product of the plantation system of production, slavery and the Negro. Thomas P. Govan declared that the South was that part of the United States in which slavery continued for sixty years after it was abandoned elsewhere, but was in all other respects similar to the rest of the country. The only important sectional conflict in America, he said, arose from the fact that Negroes were held as slaves; emancipation eliminated the single

Southern distinctive and removed the cause of its desire to be independent. The subsequent insistence upon white supremacy, Govan contended, merely meant that Southerners acted like other men of European origins when they confronted large numbers of people of differing ethnic types. To define the South as the land of white supremacy, he concluded, overlooked the very real racism among non-Southern Americans and incorrectly suggested that only Southerners were capable of bigotry and intolerance. Yet Charles S. Sydnor cited the presence of the Negro as the most popular of the monocausationist theories explaining the differences between Southerners and other Americans.

The plantation also fostered a rural environment with its strange mixture of the polished and the primitive, and some students have defined the South in terms of its folkways. Andrew N. Lytle stated the central theme as a "backwoods progression" of an agrarian Arcadia, and others of the Agrarian School have emphasized the essential "South-ness" of a slowed pace of life, enjoyment of living, and leisure for contemplation and meditation. John Hope Franklin saw a different product of a rural South. It was a land of violence whose peoples possessed a "penchant for militancy which at times assumed excessive proportions." The Southern reputation for pugnacity, he added, "did not always command respect, nor even serious consideration; but it came to be identified as an important ingredient of Southern civilization."

Another critique of the Agrarian School came from David Potter. Declaring that the agrarian formula fitted the South remarkably badly, he defined the section as a place where older folkways persisted. "The culture of the folk survived in the South long after it succumbed to the onslaught of urban-industrial culture elsewhere," he said. "It was an aspect of this culture that the relations between the land and the people remained more direct and more primal in the South than in other parts of the country." In addition, relationships of people to one another "imparted a distinctive texture as well as a distinctive tempo to their lives." Americans regarded the South with a kind of nostalgia, he noted; its basis was not an ideal utopian society that never existed, but a "yearning of men in a mass culture for the life of a folk culture which really did exist."

Thus the climate and its alleged offspring, the plantation, the planter, the staple crop, and the Negro, all set in a rural scene surrounded by primitive folkways, have provided students with the ingredients for a central theme. Another avenue into the character of the Southern regions has been to pursue the second of Phillips' hypotheses and to describe the South on the basis of social patterns. Charles S. Sydnor suggested both the problem and the possibilities. Southern historians, he pointed out, studied a region which had no definite boundaries and therefore faced the prior necessity of delimiting their subject. In doing so, they pioneered in the study of social history. They considered the distinctive traits of the people called Southern and then sought "to discover the geographical incidence of these characteristics." Thus the student of the South "was driven from the problem of area back to the prior problem of essence," Sydnor declared; "his initial task was to discover what the Old South was. From the nature of the case he was compelled to be a social historian."

Elaborating upon his own analysis, in another article Sydnor listed some distinctively Southern culture patterns. Among them he described an inherited way of life modeled after that of the English gentry, slavery, malaria, hookworm, lynching, farm tenancy, the advocacy of states' rights, mockingbirds, and a unique attitude toward law and order. Following Sydnor's suggestions, other South-seekers offered additional criteria: the South is the place where people celebrate Christmas but not the Fourth of July with fireworks; it is where cooks add salt pork to the extended boiling of green vegetables; it is the domain of hominy grits; it is the land of one-party politics, one-horse plowing, and one-crop agriculture. Charles F. Lane declared that "the preference for the mule as a draft animal is one of the least-considered traits characterizing Southern culture" and proposed a map showing the mule population of the country as a way of marking boundaries around the South.

Other observers defined the South as the center of Protestant evangelical fundamentalism. Edwin McNeill Poteat declared that "the South is religiously solid" in much the same way that it was, to him, politically solid. To most Southerners heresy remained heresy, he said, and "they still in the main submit readily to demagogy in the pulpit, and enjoy the thrill of denominational competition." The religious South exhibited a "more homogeneous quality than any other section," Poteat concluded. There was some agreement with this idea. "The distinctiveness of the Old South," said Francis B. Simkins, "is perhaps best illustrated by its religion. Historic Protestantism was reduced to the consistencies of the Southern environment without sacrificing inherent fundamentals." Charles W. Ramsdell noted that religious fundamentalism was a Southern characteristic, and pointed out its effects in the reaction to the biological discoveries of the evolution of species, the effort to prohibit the manufacture and sale of beverage alcohol by constitutional amendment, and the resurgence of the Ku Klux Klan.

Another proposal in the quest for cultural distinctives held that the South was a collection of "settlement characteristics." The geographer Wilbur Zelinsky catalogued these traits as the pattern in which men house themselves. "In the course of field observations of house types, urban morphology, farmsteads, and other settlement characteristics," he said, "I have discovered a constellation of traits that are apparently co-terminous with the South and function collectively as a regional label." Some of the traits he emphasized were houses placed well back from the street and from each other, low or nonexistent curbings, sidewalk arcades in front of town shops, a central location for courthouses in county seats, a large number of rural nonfarm homes, a lack of "spatial pattern" to farm buildings, and a high rate of building abandonment. "The observer can be reasonably certain that he is within the Southern culture area when the bulk of these traits recur with great frequency," Zelinsky concluded, "and particularly when they are assembled into one or another of the regional house types."

Related to the description of the South as a land of rather slovenly dwelling patterns is David Bertelson's idea that the distinguishing characteristic of Southerners is laziness. By his definition, however, they were afflicted not with a lack of energy but with a dearth of social unity. Southerners sought individual rather than social goals and were motivated by a desire for private gain, he said. They were prototypes of the "robber barons" who sought wealth without social responsibility, and were so thoroughly committed to economic motivation that the relatively un-self-seeking abolitionists baffled them. To Bertelson the South was an individualistic, chaotic economy in an America whose other inhabitants held some idea of community purpose, and this gave Southerners a sense of apartness and led both to the formation and to the failure of the Confederacy. Before and during the war, he said, the idea that labor meant liberty for private gain destroyed all efforts to create community and strengthened the view of outsiders that Southerners were lazy.

A similar view was that of Earl E. Thorpe, who also argued that freedom was a chief characteristic of Southerners. To Thorpe, however, its emphasis was upon sexual license. Easy access to black females who "desperately wanted displays of recognition and affection" meant that there was less repression in the South than elsewhere, and freedom led to romanticism, hedonism, and pugnacity. The Southern white male, confronting the criticism of a more inhibited outside world, became militant in the defense of his society and his frequently deceived womenfolk. Thorpe thus described a Freudian South lying just below the land of Id, a harem of sexual freedom rather than a place of economic individualism.

Another recent proposal, offered by C. Vann Woodward, held that the only distinguishing feature that may survive the social revolution of the post-1945 era is the memory of the Southern past. "The collective experience of the Southern people," he said, has made the South "the most distinctive region of the country." It was an experience that repudiated the most cherished aspects of the American self-image, for it was a record of poverty in a land of plenty, pessimism and frustration among a people wedded to optimism and unending success, and guilt complexes in a naively innocent America. Indeed, Woodward comes close to saying that the central theme of Southern history is Southern history. However helpful the idea may be in interpreting the dreary years after Appomattox, it ignores the peculiarities and events that caused such an aberrant history in the first place.

Another currently popular thesis, also based upon the harsh unpleasantness that surrounds much of Southern existence, contends that the Southerner is more inclined to romanticism than are other Americans. The Southerner is distinguished by his preference for fantasy and myth. "The quality that makes him unique among Americans," said T. Harry Williams, is his ability to conjure up "mind-pictures of his world or of the larger world around him—images that he wants to believe, that are real to him, and that he will insist others accept." George B. Tindall suggested the possibility that "we shall encounter the central theme of Southern history at last on the new frontier of mythology," and he listed some of the myths about the South that have at one time or another gained support: the Pro-Slavery South, the Confederate South, the Demagogic South, the States' Rights South, the Lazy South, and the Booster South. "There are few areas of the modern world," he declared, "that have bred a regional mythology so potent, so profuse and diverse, even so paradoxical, as the American South." Here again the searcher finds the results of an allegedly distinctive South, one of the inheritance family of character traits, but provides little illumination as to its cause.

The effort to locate the South by defining it as a single characteristic produced still another statement of the central theme. Outlined by Avery Craven and Frank L. Owsley and amplified by others, it argued that the South was the product of attacks from without. In this view the South was a state of mind, a conscious minority reacting to criticism by forging a unity as a defense mechanism. Opposition drew people together in defense of their peculiarities when their natural course would have been to fight among themselves. It began, according to Craven, with the tariff controversy in the 1820's and it became full grown in the abolition crusade.

Frank L. Owsley further developed the theme that the South came into being only when it became the victim of outside attack. "There was very little defense or justification of slavery until the commencement of a vigorous abolitionist assault from the North," he said. But "the attack upon slavery and the South resulted in the development of a philosophical defense of slavery. . . . So violent and dangerous did this new crusade appear to Southerners that a revolution in Southern thought immediately took place." Owsley declared that attacks upon the South had continued since the Civil War, but these merely succeeded in making the section more united than before. Charles W. Ramsdell, B. B. Kendrick, and A. B. Moore, along with others, defended the "outside attack" thesis, while Frank E. Vandiver emphasized an "offensive-defensive" pattern of Southern response to external criticism. Implicit in this argument is the assumption that a united South began as a Yankee invention.

The contention that the idea of a South grew out of external attacks produced its corollary—that the South was the result of a conscious effort to create a sense of unity among a diverse population with conflicting interests. In the effort, Southern leaders used all available arguments—climate, race, soil, staple-crop similarities, the agrarian philosophy with its country-gentleman ideal and the plantation as a romantic tradition, and slavery as a positive good. Some of them dramatized, if they did not actually invent, attacks from without as aids to their campaign for sectional unity. "If there is a central theme," said Robert S. Cotterill, "it is the rise of Southern nationalism." The study of the emergence of a divergent nationalism attracted many scholars. The South "was an emotion," Avery Craven wrote, "produced by an assumption on the part of outsiders of a unity there which did not exist, by propaganda within which emphasized likenesses rather than differences and created a unity of fear where none other existed."

In the conscious effort to create a South, every hint of attack from outside the section came as a godsend. William Lloyd Garrison and his abolition newspaper might well have passed unnoticed had not Southern publicists called attention to him by putting a price upon his head. Critics of the Southern system such as Elijah P. Lovejoy in Illinois and Cassius M. Clay in Kentucky found themselves the objects of violent mob resistance. In 1859 Edmund Ruffin, an energetic Southern unifier, expressed gratitude for the John Brown raid upon Harpers Ferry because of its beneficial effects upon "the sluggish blood of the South," and he took it upon himself to send samples of Brown's pikes to the governors of the slave states lest they forgot. After the war, Reconstruction again called forth a movement for white unity in the face of political and economic coercion—new attacks from without—and into the twentieth century there appeared leaders willing to evoke memories of the past as weapons against proposed changes in existing social or educational arrangements.

The flaw in the hypothesis of a movement to unify a people in the face of real or imaginary attacks from without has two aspects. First, as with all devil theories of historical motivation, it assumes almost magical powers of clairvoyance among promoters of the movement; and second, what it describes are but activities common to politicians practicing their profession wherever found, not uniquely Southern behavior at all. It was not surprising that Southern leaders should appeal for unanimity in support of their programs and candidacies; indeed, it would require explanation had any not done so. And that they could have foreseen the consequences of their conduct places a severe strain upon credulity.

From this confusing and sometimes contradictory survey of central themes in Southern history and life the suspicion emerges that the American South defies either location or analysis. It appears to be in fact an enigma challenging comprehension, "a kind of Sphinx on the American land." Its geographical boundaries are imprecise at best, and the characteristics of its population resist valid generalization. To say this is not to say that the South does not exist; it is to suggest that it exists only as a controlling idea or belief upon which men acted, risked, and died. The idea of the South is real; it is one of the most important ideas in American history, and that gives it significance.

The South idea has played a fundamental role in national development. In the early days of the Republic, as part of the debate between Thomas Jefferson and Alexander Hamilton which formed the basis of the first party divisions under the Constitution, the idea of a South contributed to the definition of public policy. As the internal dispute became more heated, it entered into the compromises that Americans made over the admission of Missouri, in the tariff settlement in 1833, and in the agreements of 1850. The idea appeared in party platforms and in the selection of candidates, and in 1860 it was an essential element in the division within the Democratic party.

The idea of a South produced an internal civil war whose outcome established the American nation. That result might have occurred in the absence of civil war, and also without the South idea, temporarily expressed as a Confederacy of states hostile to national union. But as it happened, the emergence of American nationality depended upon the idea of a South that posed a challenge to national citizenship and solidarity. In the postwar settlement—the constitutional amendments comprised in the peace treaty between the sections—the idea of the South profoundly affected the nature of the re-established Union upon national and pluralistic foundations. Later, when war emotions had cooled and industrial production expanded, it was the idea of the South that influenced the form and the content of the reactionary compromises of 1877. In the twentieth century the idea of a South re-emerged as men debated the meaning of national citizenship and the civil liberties the nation owed its citizens.

The American South is therefore not a place or a thing; it is not a collection of folkways or cultural distinctives. It is an idea. Those of whatever persuasion or tradition who believe themselves to be Southern are indeed Southern, and the South exists wherever Southerners form the predominant portion of the population. The study of the idea of Southness is thus a part of intellectual history, or, because it is an exercise in faith, it belongs among the academic offerings in the department of religion.

Perhaps a more fruitful question for students of the American South would be, not *what* the South is or has been, but *why* the idea of the South began, and *how* it came to be accepted as axiomatic among Americans. Whose interests were served when people spoke and thought of the South as an entity? How did the agents of the opinion-forming and opinion-disseminating institutions transmit the idea that allegiance to a section should transcend loyalty to the nation? What have been the effects upon American history of the belief in the idea of a South? Answers to these questions will go far to remove the study of the South from the realm of classifying and cataloguing to the tasks of probing causes and effects and the weighing of motivations. These are the true functions of the historian.

The Difficulty of Consensus on the South

JOHN B. BOLES

Any prospective reader of a book of essays on the modern South might expect a certain consensus of viewpoints, a commonly accepted definition of the region, even a general agreement about the South's past, if not its future. . . . No single conclusion, no mutually accepted point of view emerges. What the South is, whether it is persisting as a distinct region or vanishing into a great homogenous American culture, or whether that "loss" should be applauded, regretted, or prevented by some intellectual cardiopulmonary contraption, remains a riddle that different individuals answer differently. It has always been so with the South. Everyone has a ready image of the region, but the closer one comes to examine the South, the more the differences merge into similarities, and vice versa. Like a giant sphinx on the American land—as one historian called it—Dixie beckons investigators even as it resists explication. Therein of course lies its attraction.

The South is both American and something different, at times a mirror or magnifier of national traits and at other times a counterculture. That difference has been good, bad, and indefinable, but it has long been felt. . . . The South still challenges those who try to separate image from reality, stereotype from myth. Accepting the difficulty of consensus, wary of simple truths, adventurous readers will find here hard thinking, suggestive analysis, but ultimately no single key to understanding the South. And that makes the whole endeavor not futile but exciting. The southern character is too complex for easy answers, and southerners—at least the publishing kind—enjoy the perennial search for southern identity.

For at least two centuries Americans have recognized a distinctive South, and perhaps there is no more enduring regional image in the American mind than that of a Dixie different from the rest of the nation. In a famous letter to the Marquis de Chastellux, dated September 2, 1785, Thomas Jefferson compared the characteristics of northerners and southerners by listing their traits in parallel columns:

In the North they are	In the South they are
cool	fiery
sober	voluptuary
laborious	indolent
persevering	unsteady
independant [*sic*]	independant [*sic*]
jealous of their own liberties, and just to those of others	zealous for their own liberties, but trampling on those of others
interested	generous
chicaning	candid
superstitious and hypocritical in their religion	without attachment or pretensions to any religion but that of the heart

---

John B. Boles, "The Dixie Difference," introduction to *Dixie Dateline* (Houston: Rice University Studies, 1983).

Jefferson was so certain that these traits conformed to geographical setting that he wrote: "An observing traveller, without aid of the quadrant, may always know his latitude by the character of the people among whom he finds himself."

Jefferson ascribed the South's peculiarities to "that warmth of their climate," a judgment echoed almost a century and a half later by U. B. Phillips of Yale University. Georgia-born Phillips, the first great southern historian, commenced his classic account of the Old South with the sentence, "Let us begin by discussing the weather, for that has been the chief agency in making the South distinctive." We are less concerned here with the role of climate or the accuracy of Jefferson's classification than with the underlying assumption of southern distinctiveness. That idea grew slowly. Historians still debate when the South emerged as a self-consciously separate section, perceived as such also by the nation as a whole. Taking their cue from Jefferson and pronouncements made by delegates from several southern states during and shortly after the chaos of the American Revolution, some historians argue that the "South"—as distinct from the geographically southern colonies—existed as early as 1776, set apart even then by slavery.

Historians of course are no more likely to agree than are economists or theologians. Few scholars accept this early a date for the existence of full-blown southern identity. Instead, most view the long generation following the Treaty of Paris (1783) as the high-water-mark of southern Americanism, when southerners were at the liberal forefront of national decisionmaking and in fact controlled four of the first five presidential administrations. Washington, Jefferson, Madison, and Monroe were nation-builders, not dismantlers of the Union. For many twentieth-century southern liberals, these founding fathers represented the true South, the Great South, before slavery interests and John C. Calhoun led the region down the seductive path of sectionalism, then secession, Civil War, and Reconstruction, to sharecropping and colonial status within the nation.

There is a pleasing symmetry to this view, for it allows one to think of the history of southernness as a kind of long aberration, ended perhaps in 1976 when southerner Jimmy Carter became president. The great break occurred sometime between the War of 1812—when even John C. Calhoun was a fiercely nationalistic "war hawk"—and the early 1830s, by which time the nullification crisis in the South and the rise of modern antislavery activities in the North called forth a militant southern sectionalism. Perhaps the pivotal year was 1819, when the debate over the admission of Missouri as a state raised the critical question of the expansion of slavery. In that year also the deep economic depression—the Panic of 1819—highlighted profound economic differences between North and South. In retrospect it seems that a southern recognition of divergent values, contrasting social and economic systems, and an emerging distinctive culture began that eventful year, a full century and a half after the slavery-plantation system had developed.

Once the perception arose that the South had a unique destiny, events were interpreted to prove the perception. Old realities were observed in a new light. Many contemporaries saw the divisive issues and dilemmas of the next four decades as springing from the essential dichotomy between North and South. From this perspective the Civil War became necessary, even irrepressible, for a southern nation had arisen with manifold interests so different that continued union was impossible. Thus the Civil War, the apex of southern separateness, appears almost predetermined, with the long and often arduous century afterwards being merely the slow process by which the South was brought back into the Union, first legally in 1876, then politically in 1976, and not quite yet economically.

In this sense of the South's finally rejoining the nation, some commentators heralded Jimmy Carter's election to the presidency as ending the region's long sojourn as a separate province. How appropriate it seemed, on the nation's 200th birthday, for the great sectional rapprochement to occur. Yet those who thought that the nation was finally done with things distinctly southern were ill-prepared for the next few years. Punsters quickly labeled the Carter-Mondale team "Grits and Fritz," and Jimmy's brother Billy added a new dimension to the stereotype of the Good Ole Boy. With toe-tapping country music in the White House and recipes for catfish in the *New York Times,* southern fried chic seemed to suit the national taste. The subtitle of John Egerton's book, *The Southernization of America,* was perhaps more appropriate than its title, *The Americanization of Dixie.* The upshot of the matter was the question, with the South becoming more like the North, or vice versa, was there validity any more to the hoary concept of the distinctive South? Journalists vied with sociologists and historians to describe the death of Dixie. Their efforts proved premature.

Of course even an attempt to eulogize the South implies the assumption of regional distinctiveness, and the origin of that assumption lies intertwined with much of American history. For two centuries Americans North and South have felt a need to define the Dixie difference. In the antebellum days of slavery and plantations the South's economy and its labor system differentiated it from the rest of the nation, but southerners, feeling defensive about their peculiar institution and not a little guilty, sought to apotheosize their society. Real regional differences were exaggerated and elaborated upon. Like whistling in the dark to dispel fears and doubts, southerners tried, largely successfully, to persuade themselves that theirs was a higher form of civilization than the frenzied, industrial North. According to the plantation legend, the South produced gentlemen rather than vulgar businessmen; a leisurely life of manners and lofty thoughts rather than a hurried, pell-mell struggle for ever-higher profits; a working class of contented slaves, not sullen, unruly factory laborers. Thus the myth of the Old South emerged, but not entirely because it soothed southern consciences. Many northern intellectuals, dismayed by the social changes being wrought by the incipient Industrial Revolution, helped create the plantation legend and then used it to criticize the changing North. The Old South of moonlight and magnolias, of carefree hospitality and happy-go-lucky Sambos, served both regions as myths usually do, relieving social tensions and reconciling conflicting values.

During the generation before the Civil War both North and South conspired to create an image of the South, an illusion that never bore close resemblance to reality. For their contrasting needs Americans in the two regions constructed self-serving portraits of the Old South, an exotic, romantic "touched-up" portrait with the diversity, the conflict, the frontier aspects of the South removed. In the aftermath of Appomattox, white southerners, suffering a depression of both morale and money, sought to recoup some of their pride by romanticizing the Old South with a vengeance, constructing a never-never land of mess, magnolias, mansions, and mammies. Many southern clergy found meaning in Confederate defeat by arguing that God was thereby testing the South for a higher purpose, the reformation of the nation along the lines of evangelical Protestantism. Southern traditions were united with biblical themes to produce a religion of the Lost Cause, a faith that practically equated the heritage of Dixie with Holy Scripture.

Following Reconstruction, secular advocates of an urban, industrial "New South" of profits and progress helped sell their program, legitimate themselves as southern, and assuage vague guilt feelings about imitating the Yankees by piously glorifying the Old South. Joel Chandler Harris, for example, wrote booster editorials by day and Uncle Remus stories by night, seemingly without noticing the conflict. Ever since, students have labored under the heavy burden of myth and contradiction. In fact, much historical scholarship in the twentieth century has been an attempt to demythologize the popular notions of southern history. The list of myths debunked is long—the Lazy South, the Romantic South, the Cavalier South, the New South. Historians point out again and again, for example, that the large majority of southern whites in 1860 did not own slaves; that Reconstruction was not a "blackout of honest government"; that slaves were not happy Sambos; that Sunbelt notions to the contrary, the South is still the nation's poorest region. But the myths live on. Now historians are turning their attention to the function of myths, how they have helped shape southern history by forging unity, offering rationales for action, providing a common goal.

After acknowledging the prevalence of several mythical Souths and then trying to analyze the reality behind the facade, one quickly realizes that more riddles abound. Even defining the South quickly transcends geography to become a problem in cultural and intellectual history. Simple geography brings difficulties. The Mason-Dixon Line does not suffice as a boundary between North and South, for such a division would assign Delaware to the South. If we were to consider the former Confederate states as delimiting the South, we would be excluding Maryland and Kentucky, two important slave states, as well as Missouri. Some expansive Sunbelt theoreticians would lump the Southeast along with New Mexico, Arizona, and much of California and call the broad swath of geography "the southern rim," meanwhile searching in vain for parallels between southern California and South Carolina. In this century migrations of southerners northward and northerners southward have blurred the boundaries. Much of southern Illinois and Indiana have a southern cast, as do sections of Detroit; and Bakersfield, California, is a southern enclave in the West. The Virginia suburbs of Washington, D. C., the coastal areas of the Florida peninsula, and the cosmopolitan suburbs of Houston and Atlanta have been so penetrated by persons of northern birth as to lead to a proliferation of delicatessens and the easy availability—even home delivery—of the *New York Times.* Where does the South begin and end?

To make matters worse, any geographical concept of the South conveys the false impression of homogeneity. Expressions such as "the Solid South" have created the image of a monolithic region, a huge, warm, culturally flat region of slow-talking people who prefer grits with breakfast and their pork barbecued. Yet within the South there is variety of every kind: geological, climatic, cultural, ethnic. Even the favored styles of barbecue differ. The piedmont and mountain areas of Virginia, North Carolina, and Tennessee are as different from the coastal plains of Louisiana as Savannah is from Dallas. The Texas Germans and Czechs, the Louisiana Cajuns, and the North Carolina Moravians are people very different from the First Families of Virginia (the FFVs) and the aristocracies of Charleston and New Orleans. The mountain folk of the Appalachian valleys share little with Texas wildcatters or Georgia blacks. Yet all are southerners. One of the important roles of myth has been to create an illusion of unity out of this diversity. Similarly, students of the region, seeking to impose order on a crazy-quilt topic, have labored mightily to find a central theme of southern history with which to comprehend the whole. In many ways the search for a central theme has been the central theme of southern history; that quest now has added urgency because of the perception that the South is slowly, before our very eyes, disappearing as a definable entity.

Despite the historical uses and convenience of myths and stereotypes in characterizing or describing the region, most students of the South accept the truth that there really is something different about Dixie. From Jefferson's day the climate has frequently been interpreted as having played a major role in making the South distinctive. According to this view, a long growing season allowed the South to satisfy world demand for tobacco and cotton. The successful introduction of these crops led in turn to the rise of the broad-acred plantation system with its need for cheap labor, a need ultimately met by Negro slavery. Here then were the essential ingredients of southern history: a rural, agricultural region dominated by large planters, with a suppressed racial minority on the bottom. In tangible, measurable ways, the antebellum South was different from the antebellum North. From this fact emerged images of the romantic Old South, as well as the idea, expressed best in 1928 by U. B. Phillips, that the essence of southernism was "a common resolve indomitably maintained" that the South "shall be and remain a white man's country." Whether "expressed with the frenzy of a demagogue or maintained with a patrician's quietude," this was, according to Phillips, "the cardinal test of a Southerner and the central theme of Southern history." The myth of a planter aristocracy, the theme of an agrarian republic, the identification of the South with gracious living or white domination or rural-dominated Bible-Belt religion or one-party politics—all have evolved from the old assumption that environment shaped events.

The economy and society that were made possible and produced by the climate gave rise to a people who possessed certain characteristics, and many observers have shifted their attention away from the immediate consequences of climate and focused on those acquired human traits that seem to define southerners. Rather than its crops, it is its people and their character that distinguish the region. Because geography fails, we turn to defining the South as a region possessing a unique folk culture, or having experienced a history very unlike the rest of the nation. The South becomes a way of living, a sense of belonging, a state of mind. W. J. Cash's great book, *The Mind of the South,* is the classic of this genre, although in his emphasis on southerners' feeling instead of thinking, on their simple hedonism mixed with a rigid Puritanical streak, Cash came close to arguing that the South did not have a mind. Southerners, it seems, *are* more violent, more religious, more conservative, more fatalistic than nonsoutherners. Thinking does affect behavior. Statistics show that the southern death rate from tornadoes, for example, is significantly higher than elsewhere, and the best explanation is that southerners ignore warnings and neglect to build storm cellars in the belief that if your time has come, you can't escape, and if your time has not come, then why bother with precaution. Southerners also speak differently, whether with a Georgia drawl or an East Texas twang, and have an infatuation with words, a tendency to express themselves not in straightforward analytical prose but with detailed, richly textured stories. . . . The love affair with talk may explain the world-renowned outpouring of southern fiction, as well as the disproportionate number and influence of southern journalists and historians—people who, after all, mainly tell stories. Even that most southern of music, labeled "country," is peculiarly concerned with the stories that unfold in the lyrics.

In recent decades the quest to understand southern distinctiveness has produced more emphasis on the human dimension. David Potter, a Georgia-born historian who taught at Rice, Yale, and Stanford universities, argued that southern identity inhered in what he called a unique folk culture. In this folk society a sense of belonging, a relatedness of people to people and people to land, persisted amidst a national culture that was increasingly urban and technological. This identification with place and family seemed to be particularly true among rural southerners, and the South remained largely rural until after World War II. The urban areas in the South today are still peopled mostly by rural folk who have migrated to the cities in search of jobs. They have brought with them their tastes in food, music, sports, and religion. In subtle ways they have changed the cities, and certainly their urban residence has changed their expectations, even if it has not rendered them completely urbane. During the decade of the 1970s, Dixie was the only region of the nation in which urban growth outpaced rural growth. The rising generation of city-born southerners will determine whether the South can survive urbanization and remain recognizably southern. If southernness is merely an artifact of rurality, then it will soon be gone with the winds of change and growth. Sociological data shows, however, that educated, urban southerners continue to attend church far more regularly than their counterparts nationally and identify themselves with their homeplaces with greater intensity than northerners—an indication that southern values will persist in the cities.

Realizing that the bulldozer revolution of urban sprawl and industrialization would eventually end the South's rural isolation, and that the Supreme Court's desegregation decision in *Brown* v. *Board of Education of Topeka* in 1954 would ultimately end the white South's intransigence on race, C. Vann Woodward sought the essence of southernness in the region's peculiar historical experience. According to Woodward, what had made the South different was not its relative absence of cities, its agrarian traditions, its inordinate concern with race, or its political practices, but rather the way it had been treated by time itself.

Writing a generation ago, Woodward contrasted the nation's history of prosperity—being the people of plenty—with the South's long travail of poverty, stretching from the rise of sharecropping to the trough of the Great Depression, when President Franklin D. Roosevelt called the region the nation's number one economic problem. Moreover, although no nation in all history had succeeded like the United States, winning all its wars and spreading its banner from sea to shining sea, the South had failed, and failed utterly, in its one great attempt to have a separate national destiny. And while the nation—born in liberty, protector of the Union, and emancipator of the slaves—basked in innocence, the South had to live with the guilt of slavery and secession bearing heavily on its soul. Thus, Woodward concluded, in a nation marked by success, prosperity, and innocence, the South was set apart by its failure, poverty, and guilt. That collective experience, shared by all southerners, gave them a sense of identity, a common heritage apart from the national norm. The South's history, a past that was not dead, defined the southern character. A sense of tragedy, a recognition of frailty and limits to endeavor marked the regional psyche. Because the southern experience has been more akin to the world experience than the northern experience has been, southern literature both fictional and historical attracts an enormous audience abroad. Moreover, two quintessential southern musical forms, jazz and country, enjoy a global acceptance. The southern encounter with history has ironically produced an intensely localistic people with universal dilemmas and international appeal.

Of course, in the years since Woodward made his influential analysis, the nation has undergone a series of shocks. In the aftermath of Vietnam, Watergate, and the discovery of poverty in the land of plenty—what Michael Harrington called "The Other America"—the national experience no longer seems so different from that of the South. And with the South solving its racial problems arguably more satisfactorily than the North, with Sunbelt prosperity narrowing the regional income gap, and with a recent southern president, one might even argue that the regions have flip-flopped. Such of course is not the case, but southerners now feel much freer of that scorn once directed their way, and are finding "Snowbelt" envy much more gratifying.

The southern folk culture that has experienced a history unlike the rest of the United States is in many ways biracial. In the South blacks and whites have lived together, cheek by jowl, for more than three hundred years. Nothing and no one in the South has escaped the mutual influences of the two races. Black values and styles have helped shape the white culture, and vice versa, to such an extent that today it is impossible to separate the strands. Southerners are truly both the white and black inhabitants of the region. Hearing Elvis Presley borrow from black vocal traditions or Charlie Pride singing Hank Williams, or eating southern home cooking, or listening to southern preachers or gospel singers, who can deny that we truly are one at the same time that we are two people?

But the question remains: where is and what is the South today? Efforts to reappraise the South seem to proliferate shortly after every period of change. At the end of the 1950s, Arkansas journalist Harry Ashmore wrote a perceptive book entitled *An Epitaph for Dixie,* but historian Francis B. Simkins of Virginia countered with *The Everlasting South.* Parallel titles could be supplied down to the present, with concern ever being raised about *The Americanization of Dixie,* then laid aside with reflections on *The Enduring South.* As change erodes the characteristics that were once thought to define the South—poverty, rurality, educational and "cultural" backwardness, segregation, Democratic hegemony—the South's separate existence seems threatened. With that threat of loss, writers of every sort start examining the region, hunting for surviving fossils of the past or subtle new forms of southern identity, and lo, that very concern with self-identity betrays a very southern habit of wanting to know who you are and from whence you came. That concern with family, with place, with "relatedness" that so epitomizes the southerner produces a spate of regional analysis and nostalgia and, yes, even pious self-congratulation that keeps the South alive. Whether one assumes that there is still a tangible essence that sets the region apart or that one must, in the face of modernization and homogenization, "Dixiefy Dixie" . . . to keep the image alive artificially, the search for southern identity has continued for at least two centuries and shows no signs of faltering or concluding.

With the South, as with much else, a great deal lies in the eye of the beholder. High technology, interstate highways, and industrial growth may threaten one vision of the South, but recorded country music, fast food outlets for fried chicken and biscuits and sausage, C-B radios in eighteen-wheelers crackling with good-ole-boy talk from their drivers, and the working poor who have moved from the fields to the factories keep alive memories of the past. Southern speech patterns and that signal form of ethnic identification, gastronomic preferences, show sure signs of resisting change. While the architecture and form of southern cities appear as standardized as American cities elsewhere, . . . in human terms the texture of life in them reveals surprising continuity with the rural past. Yet popular images often lag behind changing reality, and the myth of southern distinctiveness may ultimately be more tenacious, and more significant, than actuality. Perceptive journalists . . . can document that southern universities are more than holding their own and subscribing to national standards for research, tenure, and curricula. Yet a "manual" like *The Insiders' Guide to the Colleges* (1971) stereotypically includes most southern universities under the category "Hard Playin', Hard Drinkin', Hard Lovin' Southern Schools." How do myth, perception, and reality merge in the popular mind? The acceptance of diversity, real or imagined, can make a real difference. As long as southerners believe in, fear, or desire a regional identity, or worry about whether one exists, there will be a South. What that South is, precisely speaking, no one can say.

And surely few will not admit that the loss of many "southern characteristics" is a great blessing. The South's long heritage of spirit-breaking poverty, of ignorance and religious prejudice, of savage racism and brutal violence, of irrelevant politics and undemocratic control, took a heavy toll on all southerners. To the extent that *that* South has died, humanity has triumphed. Better schools and improved job opportunities have freed thousands from poverty and given them immeasurably better lives. While city dwellers acknowledge a twinge of nostalgia for life back on the farm, the higher pay, greater scope of entertainment, and educational and medical advantages of urban life keep them in town. Even so, many still identify with their rural homeplaces and intend to retire and be buried there. For the huge majority of southerners, black and white, the South today is certainly a much better place to live than it was a generation ago. The beneficial changes in race relations alone represent a fundamental reshaping of the social, cultural, and political landscape, and give promise of improving relations in the future. The tide of black migration has turned back toward the South, and southern blacks are finding new purpose and meaning in their original American homeland. Even today one is surprised, driving into Montgomery from Atlanta, to see overhead the large green interstate sign proclaiming the "Martin Luther King, Jr., Expressway," but what could be a better symbol of the changing South?

In one sense this whole endeavor of defining and making predictions about the continuity of southernness has an abstract, ersatz quality about it. Most southerners take their sense of regional identity for granted even if they cannot articulate its nature. Perhaps one even has to be a southerner to know really what it is. For southerners, after all, grew up with a perception of differentness that had its roots in that long-ago time when slavery gave a concreteness that has since evaporated to the idea of separate cultures. That folk memory of distinction, imbibed with their mothers' milk, predisposes southerners to assume their distinctiveness, even when tangible evidence is wanting. And for generations, except when threatened by or contrasted to outsiders, the search for regional self-identity was what kept novelists and historians and journalists in business; the folk simply were southerners. The magnitude of the change in recent years, however, has brought urgency, a sense of potential loss, not only to aspiring authors but to average persons who can instinctively sense that they are drifting away from their old world. Often loss brings reflection and renewed appreciation, and exactly that seems to be happening with southernness.

People are suddenly eating homestyle cooking and saying "y'all," purposely being southern as a personal statement of identity. People are no longer ashamed to be southerners. A perception that the South might be disappearing in a cultural sense has led to a discovery of its importance in personal and national terms. Ninety years ago the census revealed that the American frontier was closed; three years later a great historian discovered "The Significance of the Frontier." . . . [S]omething similar might be happening in the South's largest and most rapidly changing city. Houston's phenomenal growth in population and prosperity has changed its motto from the "Magnolia City" to the "Urban West." A new culture is emerging, neither completely southern nor western. But as Houston becomes less like the Texas of old, with its heritage of openness and individuality, native Houstonians (and transplanted rural Texans) eagerly try to recapture that old ethic. Cowboy chic began not as a movie gimmick but as a grassroots attempt to recapture and hold on to a way of life and a mythical identity that was rapidly disappearing. Moreover, the thousands of mobile Americans from California, Michigan, and New York who have moved to Houston—rootless searchers for economic opportunity and advancement—seize upon the cowboy image in an attempt to legitimate their residence and show that they "belong." While the western cowboy seems to have conquered the southern cavalier in Texas, partly because of the more favorable popular associations of the cowpoke with freedom and "good" and partly because the cowpuncher is a more national hero, Houston's cowboy renaissance may suggest the future of southernness.

As the South disappears in demographic, economic, and political terms, there seems to be a corresponding effort to rediscover and revivify at least certain components of the southern way of life. Opinion molders sense the popular concern, and thus symposia, books, clothing, musical fads, and even college curricula—witness the proliferation of "southern institutes"—speak to that concern. In a very real sense, southerners did not exist until about 1819, when they began to perceive themselves as an identifiable group. The underlying socioeconomic factors that gave substance to the perception existed for more than a century before the perception arose. Self-identification as "southern" was the essence of southernness, and that perception has acquired a life of its own, in large part independent of material reality. Southernness is now almost an intellectual construct, "the flesh made word,". . . . Having a distinctiveness to lose makes possible a recognition of loss, and that triggers a process of retrospection and nostalgia that bodes well to keep the South alive and thriving. The South will continue to exist, if only by an act of the will. After all, . . . they aren't having symposia in Phoenix to discuss the everlasting West.

✦ *F U R T H E R   R E A D I N G*

David Bertelson, *The Lazy South* (1967)

John B. Boles, ed., *The Dixie Difference* (1983)

———, *Dixie Dateline* (1983)

———, *The South Through Time* (1995)

James Branch Cabell, *Let Me Lie* (1947)

W. J. Cash, *The Mind of the South* (1941)

James C. Cobb, *The Most Southern Place on Earth: The Mississippi Delta and the Roots of Regional Identity* (1992)

Albert E. Cowdrey, *This Land, This South: An Environmental History* (1983)

F. Garvin Davenport, *Myth and Southern History* (1970)

Carl N. Degler, *Place over Time: The Continuity of Southern Distinctiveness* (1977)

———, "Thesis, Antithesis, Synthesis: The South, the North, and the Nation," *Journal of Southern History* 53 (1987), 3–8

Paul D. Escott, ed., *W. J. Cash and the Minds of the South* (1992)

John Hope Franklin, *The Militant South* (1956)

Patrick Gerster and Nicholas Cords, eds., *Myth and Southern History* (1974)

Larry J. Griffin and Don H. Doyle, eds., *The South as an American Problem* (1995)

Fred C. Hobson, *Tell About the South: The Southern Rage to Explain* (1983)

C. Hugh Holman, *The Immoderate Past: The Southern Writer and History* (1977)

Lewis M. Killian, *White Southerners* (1970)

Florence King, *Southern Ladies and Gentlemen* (1975)

Jack Temple Kirby, *Media-Made Dixie* (1978)

A. Cash Koeniger, "Climate and Southern Distinctiveness," *Journal of Southern History* 54 (1988), 21–44

Bill C. Malone, *Southern Music, American Music* (1979)

Sharon McKern, *Redneck Mothers, Good Ol' Girls, and Other Southern Belles* (1979)

Grady McWhiney, *Southerners and Other Americans* (1973)

U. B. Phillips, "The Central Theme of Southern History," *American Historical Review* 34 (1928), 30–43

David M. Potter, "The Enigma of the South," *Yale Review* 51 (1961), 142–151

John Shelton Reed, *One South: An Ethnic Approach to Regional Culture* (1982)

John Herbert Roper, ed., *C. Vann Woodward: A Southern Historian and His Critics* (1997)

Francis Butler Simkins, *The Everlasting South* (1963)

William R. Taylor, *Cavalier and Yankee* (1961)

Frank E. Vandiver, ed., *The Idea of the South: Pursuit of a Central Theme* (1964)

Charles Reagan Wilson and William Ferris, eds., *Encyclopedia of Southern Culture* (1989)

C. Vann Woodward, *The Burden of Southern History,* 3rd ed. (1993)

———, *The Future of the Past* (1989)

Howard Zinn, *The Southern Mystique* (1964)

CHAPTER

2

Settlement of Red, White,

and Black

Historians of the colonial South have discovered that whites—Spanish, French, and English—did not happen on an empty wilderness in the New World. Along the South Atlantic and Gulf coasts and as far into the interior as the Appalachian Mountains, Native American tribes and confederations had built towns, and they farmed and hunted vast territories. Most of what we know of the first southern civilizations consists of indirect evidence gleaned from accounts of whites, from archaeological sites, and from transcribed comments of descendants. The Indians who inhabited the South in the sixteenth century were nonliterate people, and their numbers dwindled rapidly once whites interacted with them and introduced previously unknown diseases and customs into the New World environment.

The earliest white explorers and settlers in this part of the New World encountered numerous, often enormous problems and, in the process of colonization, experienced high mortality rates, both in the Chesapeake region and along the Gulf South. Unfamiliar diseases, strange plants and animals, idealistic and often unrealistic expectations about settlement, extreme weather, lazy colonists, and a host of other problems made initial European exploration and colonization extremely difficult. Whites often came to depend on Native Americans for both sustenance and trade.

The introduction of blacks from Africa and the West Indies, beginning in 1619, added to the diversity of the southern colonial population. The growth of the slave population, especially after 1680, has enabled historians to develop a deeper cultural portrait of uprooted Africans than has been possible for Native Americans. Through their research, historians are trying to discover the extent of cultural interaction between black, Indian, and white southerners during the colonial era and how this varied from colony to colony. It is important to understand when and how slavery developed as a labor system and when and why racial attitudes hardened.

☀ D O C U M E N T S

Much of what little we know about the southeastern Indians comes from contemporary whites' perceptions. Usually the prejudices of sixteenth- and seventeenth-century Euro-

29

peans encountering a culture different from their own influenced these observations. Nevertheless, several firsthand accounts provide valuable insights. Document 1, from Jamestown, Virginia, presents Captain John Smith's descriptions of Native Americans. Though somewhat of an autocrat in his dealings with his fellow colonists, Captain Smith had a keen appreciation for Indian culture and for the meaning of the Indian-white encounter. Document 2 relates to an episode known as Bacon's Rebellion, 1675–1676. The power-hungry Nathaniel Bacon led an armed rebellion against the governor of Virginia, who many felt was unresponsive to the growing uneasiness between Indians and European settlers. Virginia statutes, in Document 3, show the growing importance of slave labor and the gradual hardening of race lines due in part to increasing slave imports and white fears over the growing number of slaves. The House of Burgesses began to enact laws specifically based on race that circumscribed Africans' lives, including a law that made the children of slaves follow the legal status of their mother. The journals of a French Canadian explorer, d'Iberville, in Document 4, describe his journey into the interior of the Gulf South. He reveals the potential conflict between competing European cultures and Europeans' dependence on Native Americans for both staples and valuable trade. The South Carolina statute of 1740 in Document 5 was a direct response to a brief, but bloody, slave revolt in 1739 in the Stono River district, 20 miles outside of Charleston.

1. Captain John Smith Describes the Natives of Virginia, 1612

The land is not populous, for the men be fewe; their far greater number is of women and children. Within 60 miles of James Towne there are about some 5000 people, but of able men fit for their warres scarse 1500. [The Indian population figures for Smith's day are under review, but no consensus seems to have been reached as yet.] To nourish so many together they have yet no means because they make so smal a benefit of their land, be it never so fertill. 6 or 700 have beene the most hath beene seene together, when they gathered themselves to have surprised Captaine Smyth at Pamaunke, having but 15 to withstand the worst of their furie. [This maximum show of fighting men (probably exaggerated by Smith) only confirms Smith's conviction that the land of Virginia was not populous. England's second city, Norwich, then had twice as many inhabitants as Powhatan's entire "empire."] As small as the proportion of ground that hath yet beene discovered, is in comparison of that yet unknowne, the people differ very much in stature, especially in language, as before is expressed. Some being very great as the Sesquesahamocks; others very little, as the Wighcocomocoes: but generally tall and straight, of a comely proportion, and of a colour browne when they are of any age, but they are borne white. Their haire is generally black, but few have any beards. The men weare halfe their heads shaven, the other halfe long; for Barbers they use their women, who with 2 shels will grate away the haire, of any fashion they please. The women are cut in many fashions agreeable to their yeares, but ever some part remaineth long. They are very strong, of an able body and full of agilitie, able to endure to lie in the woods under a tree by

This document is from John Smith, *A Map of Virginia* (Oxford, England: Joseph Barnes, 1612), citied in Philip L. Barbour, ed., *The Complete Works of Captain John Smith, 1580–1631,* vol. I (Chapel Hill: University of North Carolina Press), pp. 160–163, 164–165, 169–171, 173–174.

the fire, in the worst of winter, or in the weedes and grasse, in Ambuscado in the Sommer. They are inconstant in everie thing, but what feare constraineth them to keepe. Craftie, timerous, quicke of apprehension and very ingenuous. Some are of disposition fearefull, some bold, most cautelous [wary and wily], all Savage. Generally covetous of copper, beads, and such like trash. They are soone moved to anger, and so malitious, that they seldome forget an injury: they seldome steale one from another, least their conjurers should reveale it, and so they be pursued and punished. That they are thus feared is certaine, but that any can reveale their offences by conjuration I am doubtfull. Their women are carefull not to bee suspected of dishonesty without the leave of their husbands. Each household knoweth their owne lands and gardens, and most live of their owne labours. For their apparell, they are some time covered with skinnes of wilde beasts, which in winter are dressed with the haire, but in sommer without. The better sort use large mantels of deare skins not much differing in fashion from the Irish mantels. Some imbrodered with white beads, some with copper, other painted after their manner. But the common sort have scarce to cover their nakednesse but with grasse, the leaves of trees, or such like. We have seen some use mantels made of Turky feathers, so prettily wrought and woven with threeds that nothing could bee discerned but the feathers. That was exceeding warme and very handsome. But the women are alwaies covered about their midles with a skin and very shamefast [modest] to be seene bare. They adorne themselves most with copper beads and paintings. Their women some have their legs, hands, brests and face cunningly imbrodered [tattooed] with diverse workes, as beasts, serpentes, artificially wrought into their flesh with blacke spots. In each eare commonly they have 3 great holes, whereat they hange chaines bracelets or copper. Some of their men weare in those holes, a smal greene and yellow coloured snake, neare halfe a yard in length, which crawling and lapping her selfe about his necke often times familiarly would kisse his lips. Others wear a dead Rat tied by the tail. . . .

Their buildings and habitations are for the most part by the rivers or not farre distant from some fresh spring. Their houses are built like our Arbors of small young springs [saplings] bowed and tyed, and so close covered with mats, or the barkes of trees very handsomely, that notwithstanding either winde, raine or weather, they are as warme as stooves, but very smoaky, yet at the toppe of the house there is a hole made for the smoake to goe into right over the fire.

Against the fire they lie on little hurdles of Reedes covered with a mat borne from the ground a foote and more by a hurdle of wood. [Smith refers to the rectangular frames lifting the Indian beds slightly from the ground.] On these round about the house they lie heads and points one by th'other against the fire, some covered with mats, some with skins, and some starke naked lie on the ground, from 6 to 20 in a house. Their houses are in the midst of their fields or gardens which are smal plots of ground. Some 20, some 40. some 100. some 200. some more, some lesse, some times from 2 to 100 of those houses togither, or but a little separated by groves of trees. Neare their habitations is little small wood or old trees on the ground by reason of their burning of them for fire. So that a man may gallop a horse amongst these woods any waie, but where the creekes or Rivers shall hinder.

Men women and children have their severall names according to the severall humor of their Parents. Their women (they say) are easilie delivered of childe, yet doe they love children verie dearly. To make them hardy, in the coldest mornings they wash them in the rivers and by painting and ointments so tanne their skins, that after a year or two, no weather will hurt them.

The men bestowe their times in fishing, hunting, wars and such manlike exercises, scorning to be seene in any woman-like exercise, which is the cause that the women be verie painefull and the men often idle. The women and children do the rest of the worke. They make mats, baskets, pots, morters, pound their corne, make their bread, prepare their victuals, plant their corne, gather their corne, beare al kind of burdens and such like.

Their fire they kindle presently [quickly] by chafing a dry pointed sticke in a hole of a little square peece of wood, that firing it selfe, will so fire mosse, leaves, or anie such like drie thing, that will quickly burne. In March and Aprill they live much upon their fishing weares, and feed on fish, Turkies and squirrels. In May and June they plant their fieldes and live most of Acornes, walnuts, and fish. But to mend their diet, some disperse themselves in small companies and live upon fish, beasts, crabs, oysters, land Torteyses, strawberries, mulberries, and such like. In June, Julie, and August they feed upon the rootes of *Tocknough* berries, fish and greene wheat. It is strange to see how their bodies alter with their diet, even as the deare and wilde beastes they seeme fat and leane, strong and weak. Powhatan their great king and some others that are provident, rost their fish and flesh upon hurdles as before is expressed, and keepe it till scarce times. . . .

For fishing and hunting and warres they use much their bow and arrowes. They bring their bowes to the forme of ours by the scraping of a shell. Their arrowes are made some of straight young sprigs which they head with bone, some 2 or 3 inches long. . . .

In their hunting and fishing they take extreame paines; yet it being their ordinary exercise from their infancy, they esteeme it a pleasure and are very proud to be expert therein. And by their continuall ranging, and travel, they know all the advantages and places most frequented with Deare, Beasts, Fish, Foule, Rootes, and Berries. At their huntings they leave their habitations, and reduce themselves into companies, as the Tartars doe, and goe to the most desert places with their families, where they spend their time in hunting and fowling up towards the mountaines, by the heads of their rivers, where there is plentie of game. . . .

When they intend any warres, the Werowances usually have the advice of their Priests and Conjurers, and their Allies and ancient friends, but chiefely the Priestes determine their resolution. Every Werowance, or some lustie fellow, they appoint Captaine over every nation. They seldome make warre for lands or goods, but for women and children, and principally for revenge. They have many enimies, namely all their westernely Countries beyond the mountaines, and the heads of the rivers. . . .

For their ordinary burials they digge a deep hole in the earth with sharpe stakes and the corpes being lapped in skins and mats with their jewels, they lay them upon sticks in the ground, and so cover them with earth. The buriall ended, the women being painted all their faces with black cole [charcoal, soot, burned wood] and oile, doe sit 24 howers in the houses mourning and lamenting by turnes, with such yelling and howling as may express their great passions.

In every Territory of a werowance is a Temple and a Priest 2 or 3 or more. Their principall Temple or place of superstition is at Uttamussack [site of the principal

Pamunkey temple] at Pamaunke, neare unto which is a house Temple or place of Powhatans.

Upon the top of certaine redde sandy hils in the woods, there are 3 great houses filled with images of their kings and Divels and Tombes of their Predecessors. Those houses are neare 60 foot in length built arbor wise after their building. This place they count so holy as that but the Priestes and kings dare come into them; nor the Savages dare not go up the river in boats by it, but that they solemnly cast some peece of copper, white beads or *Pocones* into the river, for feare their *Oke* should be offended and revenged of them. . . .

Although the countrie people be very barbarous, yet have they amongst them such governement, as that their Magistrats for good commanding, and their people for du subjection, and obeying, excell many places that would be counted very civill. The forme of their Common wealth is a monarchicall governement, one as Emperour ruleth over many kings or governours. Their chiefe ruler is called Powhatan, and taketh his name of the principall place of dwelling called Powhatan. But his proper name is Wahunsonacock. Some countries he hath which have been his ancestors, and came unto him by inheritance, as the countrie called Powhatan, Arrohateck, Appamatuke, Pamaunke, Youghtanund, and Mattapanient. All the rest of his Territories expressed in the Map, they report have beene his severall conquests. In all his ancient inheritances, hee hath houses built after their manner like arbours, some 30 some 40 yardes long, and at every house provision for his entertainement according to the time. . . .

He hath as many women as he will, whereof when hee lieth on his bed, one sitteth at his head, and another at his feet, but when he sitteth, one sitteth on his right hand and another on his left. As he is wearie of his women, hee bestoweth them on those that best deserve them at his hands. When he dineth or suppeth, one of his women before and after meat, bringeth him water in a woden platter to wash his hands. Another waiteth with a bunch of feathers to wipe them instead of a Towell, and the feathers when he hath wiped are dryed againe. His kingdome descendeth not to his sonnes nor children, but first to his brethren, whereof he hath 3. namely Opitchapan, Opechancanough, and Catataugh, and after their decease to his sisters. First to the eldest sister then to the rest and after them to the heires male and female of the eldest sister, but never to the heires of the males.

2. Nathaniel Bacon's Rebellion in Virginia, 1675–1676

The Opinion of the Council of Virginia Concerning Nathaniel Bacon's Proceedings, May 29, 1676

We being required, by the right honorable his Majesty's Governor and Captain-General of Virginia, as his Majesty's Council here to declare our judgments concerning the proceedings of Mr. Bacon by beating of drums, raising of men, and marching with them, not only without commission but contrary to the Governor's commands; we being all knowing of his Honor's divers admonitions and

From Nathaniel Bacon, *Foundations of Colonial America,* edited by W. Keith Kavenaugh. © 1973 Chelsea House Publishers. Reprinted by permission.

commands to the said Mr. Bacon to forebear his rash and unlawful proceedings, and of his gracious pardons for what had been passed upon his acknowledgment; all which the said Bacon has slighted and condemned and does still continue in opposition to his most sacred Majesty's government and the laws to the great endangering the utter ruin of this his Majesty's country and all the inhabitants here. We cannot, out of duty to God, his most sacred Majesty, and his country, but declare, and it is our unanimous opinions, that the said Mr. Bacon's proceedings are and always have been rash, illegal, unwarrantable, and most rebellious and consequently destructive to all government and laws, he having not only endeavored to seduce and draw his most sacred Majesty's good subjects from their duty and allegiance, but by divers scandalous papers by him sent about the country endeavoring to traduce his Majesty's Governor here with many false and scandalous imputations when we and all his majesty's good subjects in the whole country are sensible of the integrity, constant care, and diligence which have manifestly been found in him at all times in discharging his duties to his most sacred Majesty and the welfare and preservation of his country which, without divine assistance, had proved insupportable to him in this unfortunately troublesome conjuncture of affairs. We do, therefore, humbly conceive that it is necessary that his Majesty's Governor and Captain-General of Virginia by his declaration to all the inhabitants of this his majesty's colony do declare the said Mr. Bacon, his aiders, assisters, and abetters, rebels to his most sacred Majesty and his country and we hope and doubt not but with his sacred Majesty's Governor and us, his Majesty's Council, all his Majesty's loyal subjects within this colony will join in the prosecution of him and them according to the nature of their offenses. Dated under our hands the 29th day of May *anno. dom.* 1676.

Phill Ludwell   *Henry Chichley*
James Dray   *Nathaniel Bacon*
William Cole   *Thomas Swann*
Thomas Ballard

Declaration of Nathaniel Bacon in the Name of the People of Virginia, July 30, 1676

1. For having, upon spacious pretences of public works, raised great unjust taxes upon the commonalty for the advancement of private favorites and other sinister ends, but no visible effects in any measure adequate; for not having, during this long time of his government, in any measure advanced this hopeful colony either by fortifications, towns, or trade.
2. For having abused and rendered contemptible the magistrates of justice by advancing to places of judicature scandalous and ignorant favorites.
3. For having wronged his Majesty's prerogative and interest by assuming monopoly of the beaver trade and for having in it unjust gain betrayed and sold his Majesty's country and the lives of his loyal subjects to the barbarous heathen.
4. For having protected, favored, and emboldened the Indians against his Majesty's loyal subjects, never contriving, requiring, or appointing any due or proper means of satisfaction for their many invasions, robberies, and murders committed upon us.

5. For having, when the army of English was just upon the track of those Indians, who now in all places burn, spoil, murder and when we might with ease have destroyed them who then were in open hostility, for then having expressly countermanded and sent back our army by passing his word for the peaceable demeanor of the said Indians, who immediately prosecuted their evil intentions, committing horrid murders and robberies in all places, being protected by the said engagement and word past of him the said Sir William Berkeley, having ruined and laid desolate a great part of his majesty's country, and have now drawn themselves into such obscure and remote places and are by their success so emboldened and confirmed by their confederacy so strengthened that the cries of blood are in all places, and the terror and consternation of the people so great, are now become not only a difficult but a very formidable enemy who might at first with ease have been destroyed.

6. And lately, when, upon the loud outcries of blood, the assembly had, with all care, raised and framed an army for the preventing of further mischief and safeguard of this his Majesty's colony.

7. For having, with only the privacy of some few favorites without acquainting the people, only by the alteration of a figure, forged a commission, by we know not what hand, not only without but even against the consent of the people, for the raising and effecting civil war and destruction, which being happily and without bloodshed prevented; for having the second time attempted the same, thereby calling down our forces from the defense of the frontiers and most weakly exposed places.

8. For the prevention of civil mischief and ruin amongst ourselves while the barbarous enemy in all places did invade, murder, and spoil us, his Majesty's most faithful subjects.

Of this and the aforesaid articles we accuse Sir William Berkeley as guilty of each and every one of the same, and as one who has traitorously attempted, violated, and injured his Majesty's interest here by a loss of a great par. of this his colony and many of his faithful loyal subjects by him betrayed and in a barbarous and shameful manner exposed to the incursions and murder of the heathen. And we do further declare these the ensuing persons in this list to have been his wicked and pernicious councillors, confederates, aiders, and assisters against the commonalty in these our civil commotions.

Sir Henry Chichley	*Nicholas Spencer*
Lt. Col. Christopher Wormeley	*Joseph Bridger*
Phillip Ludwell	*William Claiburne, Jr.*
Robt. Beverley	*Thomas Hawkins*
Ri: Lee	*William Sherwood*
Thomas Ballard	*John Page Clerke*
William Cole	*John Cluffe Clerk*
Richard Whitacre	

John West, Hubert Farrell, Thomas Reade, Math. Kempe.

And we do further demand that the said Sir William Berkeley with all the persons in this list be forthwith delivered up or surrender themselves within four days after the notice hereof, or otherwise we declare as follows.

That in whatsoever place, house, or ship, any of the said persons shall reside, be hid, or protected, we declare the owners, masters, or inhabitants of the said places to be confederates and traitors to the people and the estates of them is also of all the aforesaid persons to be confiscated. And this we, the commons of Virginia, do declare, desiring a firm union amongst ourselves that we may jointly and with one accord defend ourselves against the common enemy. And let not the faults of the guilty be the reproach of the innocent, or the faults or crimes of the oppressors divide and separate us who have suffered by their oppressions.

These are, therefore, in his Majesty's name, to command you forthwith to seize the persons abovementioned as traitors to the King and country and them to bring to Middle Plantation and there to secure them until further order, and, in case of opposition, if you want any further assistance you are forthwith to demand it in the name of the people in all the counties of Virginia.

Nathaniel Bacon
General by consent of the people.

Vera Copy Test.

William Sherwood

3. Virginia's Statutes, 1630–1705

"September 17th, 1630. Hugh Davis to be soundly "whipped, before an assembly of Negroes and others "for abusing himself to the dishonor of God and "shame of Christians, by defiling his body in lying "with a negro; which fault he is to acknowledge "next Sabbath day."

1660–1661, Act XXII.

English running away with negroes.

BEE itt enacted That in case any English servant shall run away in company with any negroes who are incapable of makeing satisfaction by addition of time, *Bee itt enacted* that the English so running away in company with them shall serve for the time of the said negroes absence as they are to do for their owne by a former act.

1662, Act XII.

Negro womens children to serve according to the condition of the mother.

WHEREAS some doubts have arrisen whether children got by any Englishman upon a negro woman should be slave or ffree, *Be it therefore enacted and declared by this present grand assembly,* that all children borne in this country shalbe held bond or free only according to the condition of the mother, *And* that if any christian shall commit ffornication with a negro man or woman, hee or shee soe offending shall pay double the ffines imposed by the former act.

The Statues at Large; Being a Collection of all the Laws of Virginia, from the First Session of the Legislature, in the year 1619, Volumes I, II, III by William Waller Hening, © 1823.

1662, Act XIII.

Women servants whose common imployment is working in the ground to be accompted tythable.

WHEREAS diverse persons purchase women servants to work in the ground that thereby they may avoyd the payment of levies, *Be it henceforth enacted by the authority aforesaid* that all women servants whose common imployment is working in the crop shalbe reputed tythable, and levies paid for them accordingly; and that every master of a family if he give not an accompt of such in his list of tythables shalbe fined as for other concealments.

1668, Act VII.

Negro women not exempted from tax.

WHEREAS some doubts, have arisen whether negro women set free were still to be accompted tithable according to a former act, *It is declared by this grand assembly* that negro women, though permitted to enjoy their ffreedome yet ought not in all respects to be admitted to a full fruition of the exemptions and impunities of the English, and are still lyable to payment of taxes.

1705, Chap. XLIX.

IV. *And also be it enacted, by the authority aforesaid, and it is hereby enacted,* That all servants imported and brought into this country, by sea or land, who were not christians in their native country, (except Turks and Moors in amity with her majesty, and others that can make due proof of their being free in England, or any other christian country, before they were shipped, in order to transportation hither) shall be accounted and be slaves, and as such be here bought and sold notwithstanding a conversion to christianity afterwards. . . .

VII. *And also be it enacted, by the authority aforesaid, and it is hereby enacted,* That all masters and owners of servants, shall find and provide for their servants, wholesome and competent diet, clothing, and lodging, by the discretion of the county courts and shall not, at any time, give immoderate corrections neither shall, at any time, whip a christian white servant naked, without an order from a justice of the peace: And if any, notwithstanding this act, shall presume to whip a christian white servant naked, without such order, the person so offending, shall forfeit and pay for the same, forty shillings sterling, to the party injured: To be recovered, with costs, upon petition, without the formal process of an action, as in and by this act is provided for servants complaints to be heard, provided complaint be made within six months after such whipping. . . .

X. *And be it also enacted,* That all servants, whether, by importation, indenture, or hire here, as well feme coverts, as others, shall, in like manner, as is provided, upon complaints of misusage, have their petitions received in court, for their wages and freedom, without the formal process of an action; and proceedings, and judgment, shall, in like manner, also, be had thereupon.

XI. And for a further christian care and usage of all christian servants, *Be it also enacted, by the authority aforesaid, and it is hereby enacted,* That no negros, mulattos, or Indians, although christians, or Jews, Moors, Mahometans, or other infidels, shall, at any time, purchase any christian servant, nor any other, except of their own complexion, or such as are declared slaves by this act: And if any negro, mulatto, or Indian, Jew, Moor, Mahometan, or other infidel, or such as are declared slaves by this act, shall, notwithstanding, purchase any christian white servant, the said servant shall, *ipso facto,* become free and acquit from any service then due, and shall be so held, deemed, and taken: And if any person, having such christian servant, shall intermarry with any such negro, mulatto, or Indian, Jew, Moor, Mahometan, or other infidel, every christian white servant of every such person so intermarrying, shall, *ipso facto,* become free and acquit from any service then due to such master or mistress so intermarrying, as aforesaid. . . .

XIII. And whereas there has been a good and laudable custom of allowing servants corn and cloaths for their present support, upon their freedom; but nothing in that nature ever made certain, *Be it also enacted, by the authority aforesaid, and it is hereby enacted,* That there shall be paid and allowed to every imported servant, not having yearly wages, at the time of service ended, by the master or owner of such servant, viz: To every male servant, ten bushels of indian corn, thirty shillings in money, or the value thereof, in goods, and one well fixed musket or fuzee, of the value of twenty shillings, at least: and to every woman servant, fifteen bushels of indian corn, and forty shillings in money, or the value thereof, in goods: Which, upon refusal, shall be ordered, with costs, upon petition to the county court, in manner as is herein before directed, for servants complaints to be heard. . . .

XV. *And also be it enacted, by the authority aforesaid, and it is hereby enacted,* That no person whatsoever shall buy, sell, or receive of, to, or from, any servant, or slave, any coin or commodity whatsoever, without the leave, licence, or consent of the master or owner of the said servant, or slave: And if any person shall, contrary hereunto, without the leave or licence aforesaid, deal with any servant, or slave, he or she so offending, shall be imprisoned one calender month, without bail or main-prize; and then, also continue in prison, until he or she shall find good security, in the sum of ten pounds current money of Virginia, for the good behaviour for one year following; wherein, a second offence shall be a breach of the bond; and moreover shall forfeit and pay four times the value of the things so bought, sold, or received, to the master or owner of such servant, or slave: To be recovered, with costs, by action upon the case, in any court of record in this her majesty's colony and dominion, wherein no essoin, protection, or wager of law, or other than one imparlance, shall be allowed. . . .

XVII. *And also be it enacted, by the authority aforesaid, and it is hereby enacted, and declared,* That in all cases of penal laws, whereby persons free are punishable by fine, servants shall be punished by whipping, after the rate of twenty lashes for every five hundred pounds of tobacco, or fifty shillings current money, unless the servant so culpable, can and will procure some person or persons to pay the fine; in which case, the said servant shall be adjudged to serve such benefactor, after the time by indenture, custom, or order of court, to his or her then present master or owner, shall be expired, after the rate of one month and a half for every hundred pounds of tobacco; any thing in this act contained, to the contrary, in any-wise, notwithstanding.

XVIII. And if any women servant shall be delivered of a bastard child within the time of her service aforesaid, *Be it enacted, by the authority aforesaid, and it is hereby enacted,* That in recompence of the loss and trouble occasioned her master or mistress thereby, she shall for every such offence, serve her said master or owner one whole year after her time by indenture, custom, and former order of court, shall be expired; or pay her said master or owner, one thousand pounds of tobacco; and the reputed father, if free, shall give security to the church-wardens of the parish where that child shall be, to maintain the child, and keep the parish indemnified; or be compelled thereto by order of the county court, upon the said church-wardens complaint: But if a servant, he shall make satisfaction to the parish, for keeping the said child, after his time by indenture, custom, or order of court, to his then present master or owner, shall be expired; or be compelled thereto, by order of the county court, upon complaint of the church-wardens of the said parish, for the time being. And if any woman servant shall be got with child by her master, neither the said master, nor his executors administrators, nor assigns, shall have any claim of service against her, for or by reason of such child; but she shall, when her time due to her said master, by indenture, custom or order of court, shall be expired, be sold by the church-wardens, for the time being, of the parish wherein such child shall be born, for one year, or pay one thousand pounds of tobacco; and the said one thousand pounds of tobacco, or whatever she shall be sold for, shall be emploied, by the vestry, to the use of the said parish. And if any woman servant shall have a bastard child by a negro, or mulatto, over and above the years service due to her master or owner, she shall immediately, upon the expiration of her time to her then present master or owner, pay down to the church-wardens of the parish wherein such child shall be born, for the use of the said parish, fifteen pounds current money of Virginia, or be by them sold for five years, to the use aforesaid: And if a free christian white woman shall have such bastard child, by a negro, or mulatto, for every such offence, she shall, within one month after her delivery of such bastard child, pay to the church-wardens for the time being, of the parish wherein such child shall be born, for the use of the said parish fifteen pounds current money of Virginia, or be by them sold for five years to the use aforesaid: And in both the said cases, the church-wardens shall bind the said child to be a servant, until it snall be of thirty one years of age.

XIX. And for a further prevention of that abominable mixture and spurious issue, which hereafter may increase in this her majesty's colony and dominion, as well by English, and other white men and women intermarrying with negros or mulattos, as by their unlawful coition with them, *Be it enacted, by the authority aforesaid, and it is hereby enacted,* That whatsoever English, or other white man or woman, being free, shall intermarry with a negro or mulatto man or woman, bond or free, shall, by judgment of the county court, be committed to prison, and there remain, during the space of six months, without bail or mainprize, and shall forfeit and pay ten pounds current money of Virginia, to the use of the parish, as aforesaid.

XX. *And be it further enacted,* That no minister of the church of England, or other minister, or person whatsoever, within this colony and dominion, shall hereafter wittingly presume to marry a white man with a negro or mulatto woman; or to marry a white woman with a negro or mulatto man, upon pain of forfeiting and paying, for every such marriage the sum of ten thousand pounds of tobacco; one half to our sovereign lady the Queen, her heirs and successors, for and towards the support of the government, and the contingent charges thereof; and the other half to the informer: To be recovered, with costs, by action of debt, bill, plaint, or information, in any court of record within this her majesty's colony and dominion, wherein no essoin, protection, or wager of law, shall be allowed.

4. Chevalier d'Iberville Explores the Gulf South, 1699

December 22nd. At seven o'clock in the morning, I sailed from Havre Français in company with the *Gironde* and set the course for Cape San Antonio, which we doubled on the 30th at eight o'clock in the morning, having observed nothing unusual on that part of the voyage.

From Cape San Antonio I steered for the Biloxy Bay anchorage, at which we arrived on January 8, 1700, and moored with two anchors in 21 feet of water.

The 9th. In the morning, M. de Sauvolle came aboard. I learned from him that the garrison was in good health, although four men had died, among them two Canadians, one buccaneer, and one enlisted man from La Rochelle.

He told me that an English corvette of ten guns, commanded by Captain Louis Banc, had entered the Mississipi and gone 25 leagues upstream, where my brother, De Bienville, with five men in two bark canoes, had come across the corvette at anchor, awaiting favorable winds to go higher upstream. My brother sent two men to tell him to immediately leave the country, which was the possession of the king, and that, if he did not leave, he would force him to. With this he complied after talking with my brother, whom he knew from having seen him with me at Hudson Bay, where I captured this captain.

He told my brother that three ships had departed from London in October [1698] to come and establish a settlement on the Mississipi, acting on information they had received that I had put back into Brest, being unable to continue my voyage. He had gone by way of Carolina, where the majority of their men and women intended for the colony had remained, as they found it to be a fine country. One of their ships returned to London; the other two, of twenty-six twelve-pounders, set out again from Carolina in May 1699 to carry out their plans, not having dared to do so during winter because of the foul weather. He said that he had gone looking for the Mississipi 30 and 40 leagues [east] of where the relations about Louisiana written by the Recollect Father and Tonty locate it; there he found nothing but poor harbors and a Spanish post about 90 leagues west of this river. They believe, as I do, that it is St. Louis Bay. From there they returned along the coast, taking soundings with some big pirogues. They say they found no good harbor except about 40 leagues west from here, among some sandy islands, in a bay into which no river empties. And the country is a sandy coast. Chancing to be at the mouth of the river, he had sounded the three passes, finding only the East Pass to have 11 to 12 feet of water. Through it he went in, as he had no doubt that this was the Mississipi, for it was the biggest river he had come to along this coast. . . .

Those ships were sent out on behalf of a company formed at London by some Englishmen and French refugees. On this ship was a man representing the interests

---

"The Journal of the Renommée," by Chevalier d'Iberville from *Iberville's Gulf Journals,* Gaillard McWilliams, ed. and trans., University of Alabama Press, © 1981.

of those two groups; the Frenchman was greatly distrusted by the English; he told my brother about it and testified that he wished with all his heart, as did every single one of the French refugees, that the king would permit them to settle in this country, under his rule, with liberty of conscience. He guaranteed that many would soon be here who were unhappy under English rule, which could not be sympathetic to the French temperament, and he begged my brother to ask me to bear their petition to the king; and he left for me his address in Carolina and in London, so that I can write them the king's will about it. This Frenchman showed great disappointment over our forestalling them, saying that they were losing this country, which his associates would not wish to contest with the French. This English captain, on parting company with my brother on the lower part of the river, where they spoke with each other for the third time, threatened to come back and settle this river with ships having bottoms better constructed for the purpose; there was land for them and land for us, one on one side, and the other on the other side; they had discovered this river several years before, and it was as much theirs as ours. Here is a threat that can have no important consequences; it will always be easy to keep them from carrying it out.

The Sieur de Sa[u]volle tells me also that two missionary priests from Quebec, one of them named Montigny, descended the Mississipi and came to the fort on July 4th with fourteen men; they set out again to establish their missions at the Taensas, who are 150 leagues from the sea, and at the Tonicas, who are 170 leagues. One of these missionaries, named Davion, had gone overland from the Tonicas to the Chicachas on horseback, along with an Englishman, who had come from the Chichachas to the Tonicas to see whether the French would not carry on a trade in beaver with them. I later learned that this Englishman tried to make the Indians kill this missionary, but they would not do so. For several years this Englishman has been among the Chicachas, where he does a business in Indian slaves, putting himself at the head of Chicacha war parties to make raids on their enemies and friends and forcing them to take prisoners, whom he buys and sends to the islands to be sold. . . .

February 1st. I set out from the ships in the smack to go and establish a post on the Mississipi, in order to take possession of it, for fear the English might come and put a post on it, having noticed that we had no posts closer than 30 leagues from the river, and might use that as a pretext for holding on there. With me I am carrying along at the same time enough supplies to make a journey inland and look over the country as well as the River Marnes, near the upper part of which the Senis live and, on my way, to make peace between the Bayogoulas and the Oumas and force the Nadezés to sue for peace and hand over to me the murderers of M. de Montigny. All the Indians assure me that he was killed by that nation. I have thought it important, at the beginning of a settlement, not to permit the Indians to kill any Frenchman without making a show of preparation to avenge his death, in order to avoid making ourselves contemptible to every nation in the area; moreover, it seemed to me of the utmost importance to go among that nation, which is the strongest of all the nations that are on the bank of the river, but not strong enough to resist eighty men whom I am taking with me, they being enough for me to compel that nation to disown the men who did it and to make them unwilling to side with them. They will be in hiding, and I shall not be hampered by having to make a search; I shall be satisfied with showing them that we are not men that are to be given an affront; thereby I shall make safe all Frenchmen who may come and go in small groups from one nation to another, wherever we shall need to send them. . . .

The disease diarrhea, which had been in this village for five months, had killed more than half the people. In this village were about forty Little Taensas, who had come to see them and to offer their services against the Bayogoulas. These Taensas are rovers; usually they dwell three days west of this village. They are well-built men that live on the deer, the bear, and the game they hunt; in their district they have few buffalo. My intention was to obtain guides in this village and go up the River Marne, or Sablonnière River. These Indians spoke to me about it last year, leading me to believe that it was fine, and told me about the nations that live on it, saying that they had been there; but today they assured me that it is not navigable, being obstructed by logs. No matter what I did, they would not consent to guide me up it to the Cadodaquios. They told me that the only route they knew to get there was by way of the Big Taensas, who are above the Chéloëlles, or Nadchés, which is the route they commonly take, making the trip overland. Although this river seems fine to me, I did not dare undertake to go up it without a guide, since it makes several forks, and I thought it better to go to the Taensas and from there by land to the Nadchitoes and the Cadodaquios, by whose village this river flows. There I shall get some canoes, or shall have some made, to go down the river and explore it well. . . .

The 14th. In the morning we reached the shore of the lake, where we came upon four Indians, who were bringing us some canoes, having heard our musket-shots. On the lake we made about 2 leagues and reached the village at noon. Here I found M. de Montigny, a missionary, who had two Frenchmen with him. He has had a house built there for himself and is preparing to build a church. In this nation there are about 120 huts stretched out over a distance of 2 leagues along the lake shore. In this place there is a rather fine temple. Once this was a large nation, but now they are no more than three hundred men. They have very big fields and a very fine location along the shore of this lake, which is not at all subject to inundation. The lake may be a fourth of a league wide and $4\frac{1}{2}$ leagues [long], coming from the northeast and making a bend to the west. The main part of this village is about 2 leagues from the end, as one comes from the Mississipi River, and facing a small river, 100 yards wide, along the bank of which are a few Indian huts.

I interrogated these Indians about the nations west of them and along the River Marne, questioning particularly a Ouatchita Indian who had been to the Cadodaquios and to some Spanish posts. He reports the roads as being very difficult, the whole route being overland. I asked him whether he would guide us there, and he agreed to do so after I had promised to pay him well. M. de Montigny, acting as my interpreter, induced them to do what I wanted them to do. . . .

The 16th and 17th. It rained and thundered a great deal. The night of the 16th–17th lightning struck the Taensas' temple, set it on fire, and burned it up. To appease the Spirit, who they say is angry, these Indians threw five little infants-in-arms into the temple fire. They would have thrown several others into it had it not been for three Frenchmen, who rushed up and prevented them from doing so. An old man, about sixty-five years old, who played the role of a chief priest, took his stand close to the fire, shouting in a loud voice, "Women, bring your children and offer them to the Spirit as a sacrifice to appease him." Five of those women did so, bringing him their infants, whom he seized and hurled into the middle of the flames. The act of those women was considered by the Indians as one of the noblest that could be performed; accordingly, the Indian women followed that old man, who led them ceremoniously to the hut of the Indian who was to be made chief of the nation, for the chief had died a short time before. At the death of their chief, they observed the custom of killing fifteen or twenty men or women to accompany him, they say, into the other world and serve him. According to what they say, many are enraptured to be of that number. I have strong doubts about that. That old man whom I mentioned above was saying that the Spirit had become angry because, at the death of the last chief, no one had been killed to accompany him and that the chief himself was angry and had had the temple burned. The old man accused the French of being the ones that had caused this calamity, because M. de Montigny, who happened to be in the village when the chief died, had prevented any one from being killed—with which everybody in the nation seemed highly pleased except this high priest. When these women, sanctified and consecrated to the Spirit by the deed they had just done (that is how several of these Indians speak of them), were brought to the house of the claimant to the throne, they were caressed and highly praised by the old men; and each of them was clothed in a white robe made from mulberry bark, and a big white feather was put on the head of each. All day they showed themselves at the door of the chief's hut, seated on cane mats, where many brought presents to them. Everybody in the village kept busy that day, surrounding the dead chief's hut with a palisade of cane mats, reserving the hut to be used as a temple. In it the fire was lighted, in keeping with their custom. . . .

The 25th. In the morning I started for the Bayogoulas. The Jesuit Father [is] leaving his servant at the Oumas to build a church. M. de Tonty is going back to the Illinois. I entrusted to him several presents to give to the Tonicas and to the chief of the Chicachas who are to come to the Tonicas, as I want him to talk to them there through M. Davion, a missionary. I instructed M. de Tonty to tell them that we have settled on the Mississipi—friends of all the nations nearby, with whom we are doing business in everything; that is rested entirely with them to do as much and become friends of ours by ceasing to make war on the Nadchés and the Colapissas and the Chaquitas; that, if they did not make peace with them, I would arm those nations with guns like the ones they had, because of which they would be unable to hold out against so many Indians equipped to fight them; whereas, if they made peace with those nations, we would all be friends, making one nation. This would be advantageous to them on account of the trade they would have with us, who would give them merchandise at one-fourth less than the English were giving, who take from them only deer skins, whereas we would take buffalo skins, which they have in great quantity without doing anything with them.

5. South Carolina Restricts the Liberties of Slaves, 1740

I. *And be it enacted,* . . . That all negroes and Indians, (free Indians in amity with this government, and negroes, mulattoes and mustizoes, who are now free,

---

This document can be found in Thomas Cooper and David J. McCord, eds., *The Statutes at Large of South Carolina,* vol. 7 (Columbia, SC: 1836–1841), pp. 397–417.

excepted,) mulattoes or mustizoes who now are, or shall hereafter be, in this Province, and all their issue and offspring, born or to be born, shall be, and they are hereby declared to be, and remain forever hereafter, absolute slaves. . . .

XXIII. *And be it further enacted* by the authority aforesaid, That it shall not be lawful for any slave, unless in the presence of some white person, to carry or make use of fire arms, or any offensive weapons whatsoever, unless such negro or slave shall have a ticket or license, in writing, from his master, mistress or overseer, to hunt and kill game, cattle, or mischievous birds, or beasts of prey, and that such license be renewed once every month, or unless there be some white person of the age of sixteen years or upwards, in the company of such slave, when he is hunting or shooting, or that such slave be actually carrying his master's arms to or from his master's plantation, by a special ticket for that purpose, or unless such slave be found in the day time actually keeping off rice birds, or other birds, within the plantation to which such slave belongs, lodging the same gun at night within the dwelling house of his master, mistress or white overseer. . . .

XXXII. *And be it further enacted* by the authority aforesaid, That if any keeper of a tavern or punch house, or retailer of strong liquors, shall give, sell, utter or deliver to any slave, any beer, ale, cider, wine, rum, brandy, or other spirituous liquors, or strong liquor whatsoever, without the license or consent of the owner, or such other person who shall have the care or government of such slave, every person so offending shall forfeit the sum of five pounds, current money, for the first offence. . . .

XXXIV. And *whereas,* several owners of slaves have permitted them to keep canoes, and to breed and raise horses, neat cattle and hogs, and to traffic and barter in several parts of this Province, for the particular and peculiar benefit of such slaves, by which means they have not only an opportunity of receiving and concealing stolen goods, but to plot and confederate together, and form conspiracies dangerous to the peace and safety of the whole Province; *Be it therefore enacted* by the authority aforesaid, That it shall not be lawful for any slave so to buy, sell, trade, traffic, deal or barter for any goods or commodities, (except as before excepted,) nor shall any slave be permitted to keep any boat, perriauger or canoe, or to raise and breed, for the use and benefit of such slave, any horses, mares, neat cattle, sheep or hogs, under pain of forfeiting all the goods and commodities which shall be so bought, sold, traded, trafficked, dealt or bartered for, by any slave, and of all the boats, perriaugers or canoes, cattle, sheep or hogs, which any slave shall keep, raise or breed for the peculiar use, benefit and profit of such slave. . . .

XXXVII. And *whereas,* cruelty is not only highly unbecoming those who profess themselves christians, but is odious in the eyes of all men who have any sense of virtue or humanity; therefore, to refrain and prevent barbarity being exercised towards slaves, *Be it enacted* by the authority aforesaid, That if any person or persons whosoever, shall wilfully murder his own slave, or the slave of any other person, every such person shall, upon conviction thereof, forfeit and pay the sum of seven hundred pounds, current money, and shall be rendered, and is hereby declared altogether and forever incapable of holding, exercising, enjoying or receiving the profits of any office, place or employment, civil or military, within this Province. . . .

XXXVIII. *And be it further enacted* by the authority aforesaid, That in case any person in this Province, who shall be owner, or shall have the care, government or charge of any slave or slaves, shall deny, neglect or refuse to allow such slave or slaves, under his or her charge, sufficient cloathing, covering or food, it shall and may be lawful for any person or persons, on behalf of such slave or slaves, to make complaint to the next neighboring justice, in the parish where such slave or slaves live or are usually employed. . . .

XLIII. And *whereas,* it may be attended with ill consequences to permit a great number of slaves to travel together in the high roads without some white person in company with them; *Be it therefore enacted* by the authority aforesaid, That no men slaves exceeding seven in number, shall hereafter be permitted to travel together in any high road in this Province, without some white person with them. . . .

XLV. And *whereas,* the having of slaves taught to write, or suffering them to be employed in writing, may be attended with great inconveniences; *Be it therefore enacted* by the authority aforesaid, That all and every person and persons whatsoever, who shall hereafter teach, or cause any slave or slaves to be taught, to write, or shall use or employ any slave as a scribe in any manner of writing whatsoever, hereafter taught to write, every such person and persons, shall, for every such offence, forfeit the sum of one hundred pounds current money.

XLVI. And *whereas,* plantations settled with slaves without any white person thereon, may be harbours for runaways and fugitive slaves; *Be it therefore enacted* by the authority aforesaid, That no person or persons hereafter shall keep any slaves on any plantation or settlement, without having a white person on such plantation or settlement.

⋏ E S S A Y S

Kathleen Brown, an associate professor at the University of Pennsylvania, explores racism and slavery in an excerpt from her book *Good Wives, Nasty Wenches and Anxious Patriarchs.* She argues that the legal distinctions made between English and African females helped to determine and transform attitudes about slavery and the planter elite in Virginia. Daniel Usner, a professor at Cornell University, looks beyond traditional Anglo-Atlantic settlements by examining early colonization in the Gulf South. He reveals a multicultural society of Indians, Europeans, and Africans. Colonial Louisiana floundered for years, in part because of European nations' limited commitment to providing supplies and reinforcements, but also because of widespread diseases, apathetic colonists, high mortality, and inadequate food sources. Europeans had to depend on Native Americans for sustenance, trade, and protection. Like colonists in the Chesapeake, Lower Mississippi settlers gradually turned to African labor to survive.

Gender and Race in Colonial Virginia

KATHLEEN M. BROWN

English racial attitudes of the early seventeenth century are perhaps best described as an increasingly coherent construction of racial difference to communicate desires for domination. Interactions between the English and Indians in Virginia contributed to these early perceptions of difference, recasting the English national identity that had emerged from contact with the Irish. During the seventeenth century, English attitudes toward Africans shifted with the growing need for African labor and the initiation of an overseas trade in slaves. Although the concepts of racial difference elaborated in the literature of the early seventeenth century did not lead inevitably to the slave labor system of the century's final quarter, they did inform the legal and intellectual framework within which slavery emerged. The establishment of slavery as the primary labor system in Virginia subsequently ushered in a new age of racism in which legal constructions of race weighed more heavily upon the social relations of Africans and English than they had previously.

The social meaning the English attached to racial difference during the 1620s and 1630s derived from and overlapped with their attitudes toward non-English nations and laboring people. The similarity between perceptions of ethnic differences and those of race appear in colonial musters of residents, with the treatment of Africans forming one end of a continuum of English discomfort with non-English peoples. Although Mary Johnson's official listing as "Mary a Negro Woman" distinguished her from English settlers who were listed with surnames, this expression was not inherently racial. Like "Choupouke an Indian," "James a Frenchman," James and John, "Irishmen," "Anthony a Portugall," and "Epe the Dutchman," imported Africans endured the disadvantage of non-English heritage in a colony settled by the ethnocentric English who may have been unable to spell, pronounce, or remember unfamiliar surnames. Unlike most non-English New World residents, however, the children of imported Africans continued to receive the designation "negar," while the offspring of Dutch, French, and Irish individuals eventually lost their ethnic labels.

The bound condition of imported Africans also influenced the status-conscious middling and genteel English. Men and women of England's own lower class, for example "Mary, a maid," were sometimes identified by only first names. The combination of non-English heritage and servility created a double jeopardy for enslaved Africans who were rarely dignified with more than a first name and the tag "negre." The crucial element in English constructions of racial difference during the 1630s and 1640s may not have been the physical appearance of Africans, but the context in which English people witnessed that appearance: nearly all Africans were slaves when they arrived in Virginia, and, before 1644, nearly all slaves in Virginia were Africans.

The development of slavery in the Caribbean affected the servile treatment of Africans in Virginia, and, to a lesser degree, may have influenced the pattern of some early slave laws. Before 1630, Africans came to the European outposts of the Caribbean incidentally and in small numbers. With Dutch entry into both the slave trade and the sugar industry of Curaçao and Brazil, sugar technology and slavery spread throughout the region. Caribbean planters turned to slavery quickly, developing slave laws piecemeal. As early as 1636, Barbadian planters may have been holding Africans and their children in perpetual bondage. In Antigua, laws discouraging sexual intimacy between Africans and Europeans appeared by 1644, whereas, in Bermuda, legislators prohibited interracial marriages in 1663. Although before 1660 there was no clear legal template for slavery in the Caribbean upon which Virginia could rely, laws restricting sexual contact and marriage between African and English laborers revealed the subordinate status of Africans in other New World colonies.

Ship captains, merchants, wealthy landowners, and enslaved Africans themselves acted as vectors for African, Dutch, and Caribbean culture in Virginia, influencing a cosmopolitan notion of slavery to take root in the colony before midcentury. As early as the 1630s, ship captains traded slaves to wealthy Norfolk and York County residents, often the same men who served as justices and burgesses. Dutch vessels carrying cloth, liquor, and slaves sailed to Virginia ports at the height of their nation's dominance of the slave trade. Like other colonial commodities, slaves became international currency for Dutch merchants in the colony. Some, like Rotterdam merchant William Moseley of Norfolk, settled debts with customers through exchanges of African laborers. By the mid-1640s, even English merchants were beginning to traffic in slaves. Frequent contact with travelers from Barbados and New England brought still other Norfolk residents into slave trade networks.

Despite constituting only a small proportion of the colonial population before 1660—probably never more than 5 percent—Africans themselves had an important impact on slavery in the colony. Virginians with overseas connections enjoyed access to a small but steady supply of incoming slaves whom they hired out, sold to other colonists, or bequeathed to their children. By midcentury, enough Virginians owned slaves that it was no longer unusual for a colonist to attach the slaves of a wealthy debtor. Enslaved Africans raised cattle, shot wolves, and escorted strangers to their destinations. In Lancaster County, an African named Grasher even served as a beadle (parish official) in charge of whipping offenders, although he was not permitted to attend the court. As the international traffic in humans began to surround Virginia by the 1630s, Africans became a part of the daily lives of an English population much larger than the actual number of slaveowners.

Although the foreign birth and slave status of Africans were important to English definitions of racial difference, Christianity also played a crucial role in shaping English attitudes toward Africans. Already convinced that the syncretic Catholicism of the Gaelic Irish indicated paganism, the English easily adapted this Protestant criterion for civility to reach a similar conclusion about Chesapeake Indians. Traveling among Africans who practiced totemic religions, witchcraft, and, allegedly, cannibalism, the uneasy English believed themselves surrounded by savages and barbarians. Even those Africans christened by the Portuguese before being transported across the Atlantic did not pass muster but provoked the English to denigrate papism. Christianity ultimately provided a highly adaptable means by which Europeans designated native populations—especially those whose lands, markets, and peoples they wished to appropriate—uncivilized.

Slave status was not simply a symbolic brand marking Africans as outsiders. It carried with it several legal, economic, and social disadvantages that distinguished Africans and a tiny handful of captive Indians from other populations the English deemed alien. Masters who hoped to extract long (if not life) terms from African slaves were willing from as early as the 1630s to pay more for these laborers. The greater initial investment undoubtedly complicated individual African efforts to gain freedom through self-purchase, legal petition, and enforcement of indentures. In 1659, to take one instance, a Norfolk slave with Portuguese connections sued his master for his freedom, pleading that he had lived in England and should serve only as long as other servants coming from that country. The papers "fardinando a negro" produced to back his case were written in a language the court could not decipher; justices rejected his plea and ordered him to serve for life. For Africans like Fardinando who lacked the protection afforded by English indentures and custom, appeals for freedom could be easily circumvented by masters who sought to exploit their laborers' status as outsiders.

Enduring domestic ideals for English female labor also may have affected the reception of Africans in Virginia. In contrast to their plans for their own women, English settlers perceived African women as an exploitable new source of agricultural labor, an exception to the gender division of labor but compatible with the vision of domestically employed English women. English accounts of women in West Africa as heavily burdened drudges—a staple of most English colonial literature by the second quarter of the seventeenth-century—may have influenced the predominantly cosmopolitan owners of African labor to set their female slaves to work in the fields. Many English masters also may have been aware that African women were being used interchangeably with men to grow sugar in Brazil. Few paused to contemplate the dairying, meal preparation, and child care that women from several West African societies performed. That West African women themselves viewed field work, not as indicative of servility or nastiness, but as gender-appropriate labor, may only have facilitated their exploitation at the hands of English masters.

African women's significance in the population of bound female laborers may have been one reason why they became the subjects of Virginia's earliest legal discriminations. By the 1660s, as Carole Shammas has shown, enslaved women slightly outnumbered English servant women in several Virginia counties. Bound African women also outnumbered their Indian servant counterparts for most of the century. If such patterns prevailed before 1660—and the absence of a marked shift in female slave and servant importations before that date makes such an assumption plausible—African women's demographic significance among the colony's female laborers may have contributed to the early legal focus upon them.

All of these factors—English predispositions to view African women as drudges, the usefulness of English women's domesticity for colonial promoters, and the colony's peculiar demography—combined with the demands of the tobacco economy to transform the meaning of African women's labor. In a colony in which the public acknowledgment of English women's domestic traditions did not protect them from sweating in tobacco fields, African women's domestic traditions were easily ignored and quickly eroded. Bondage and legal constraints on African families similarly altered the context of African women's agricultural labor. It was this subordination of African women to the needs of English labor and family systems that ultimately provided the legal foundation for slavery and for future definitions of racial difference.

The tax levied on African women in 1643 was the earliest distinctive and clearly unfavorable treatment of African people to be enshrined in law in Virginia. Although English precedents, colonial economic pressures, and gendered definitions of productivity and citizenship all contributed to Virginia's haphazard tax practices during the seventeenth century, the critical factor leading to the categorization of

African women as "tithables" (individuals who performed taxable labor) was planter assumptions about African women's role in the colony as laborers. . . .

Driven by their need for soldiers and military fortifications, colonial legislators adopted Virginia's first tax on individual men in the aftermath of the 1622 Indian attack led by Opechancanough. The Assembly required each household head either to send a man to the military compound or to contribute five pounds of tobacco per person for himself and each of the servants (implicitly male) in his household. As an alternative to military service, Virginia's first poll (or per person) tax thus targeted only men. Throughout the 1630s and 1640s, this definition of tithable appears to have determined local decisions about the individuals liable to serve and the compensation for their lost labor.

The overwhelmingly male character of the tobacco-growing population in Virginia and the lucrative potential of production for an expanding European market also encouraged lawmakers to view each individual laboring man, rather than the household, as a taxable unit. Markets that gave each man's labor a definable monetary value in Virginia were only just beginning to transform agricultural production along London's grain-trade routes and other farm regions. Undoubtedly hoping to maximize its revenues from this predominantly male population of tobacco producers, the Governor's Council ordered all "male hed" above the age of sixteen to contribute tobacco and corn toward the support of the minister in 1624 and defined "tithable[s]" in 1629 to include masters of families, all free men, and people "working the ground."

Until the late 1620s, Virginia lawmakers never seriously entertained the notion of taxing English women. Military contributions underpinning male liability for taxes traditionally did not apply to women. English women were not only exempt from military service but also classified as dependents in need of protection. Defense plans in the colony were thus devised to minimize the dangers to this vulnerable portion of the population, as they did in 1627 when the governor and Council ordered "woemen and children and unserviceable people" to take cover at "Mathews Mannor" while the men made a stand against the Indian enemy. . . .

In 1643, the Virginia Assembly's new definition for "tithable" created a legal distinction between English and African women for the first time and revealed very different expectations for their future roles in the colony. Tithables who were chargeable for the minister's allowance now included "youths of sixteen years of age [and] upwards, as also for all negro women at the age of sixteen years." In practice, this definition meant that the masters of African women were forced to contribute to the support of the colony's ministers just as they did for all the men, African and English, in their employ. By including African women in the category of male tithables, Virginia lawmakers classified them as field laborers with a productive capacity equivalent to that of men. For the first time, the divergence in planters' attitudes toward English and "negro" laborers appeared openly, encoded in law. . . .

The laws defining tithability divided laborers into two groups. English women, servant and free, children, and old men were deemed too weak to produce as much as prime male hands and were categorized as dependents. Productive laborers—English men, African men, and African women—were judged capable of making their own living based on the market value of the tobacco they cultivated. The distinction between English and African women created a legal fiction about their different capacities for performing agricultural labor. Linking the productive capability of African women to that of all male laborers, lawmakers assumed that the English gender division of labor—the one they continued to hope would take hold in the colony—did not and need not apply to Africans. Although West African women's own traditions of agricultural labor may have had some influence upon English colonists' assessments of their economic value, from the English perspective such work roles connoted low social position and an absence of civility. . . .

Forced to pay extra taxes for an African wife, a free man might have thought twice about marrying her. Perhaps that was why so many free African men on the Eastern Shore married English women even though a nearly equal sex ratio would have allowed them to find African wives. Of the ten black male householders in Northampton between 1664 and 1677, five appear to have been married to women of English descent. Richard Johnson, son of Anthony, fathered four children by his white wife Susan. Richard's son also married a white woman in the 1680s. Francis Payne married Amye, a white woman, soon after securing the freedom of his children and first wife in 1655. Emmanuel Driggus fathered a child by a woman named Elizabeth, whom he married in 1661. Philip Mongan married a white widow named Martha Merris in 1651. Likewise, Anthony Longo's first wife, Hannah, seems to have been white.

Some African men may have believed that white partners would enhance their ability to function within a predominantly white society, while others may have married these women because nothing stood in their way. In Northampton County, white residents whose racial attitudes had been shaped by the presence of a small but relatively successful group of free black men voiced little public dissent against interracial relationships until later in the century. Still other free black men may have chosen white mates because free black women were themselves involved in interracial unions and unavailable for marriage. For women like Ann Skiper, the black wife of white Norfolk County resident Francis Skiper, marriage to a man of English descent offered opportunities to join white planter social and economic networks.

Throughout the seventeenth century, marriage provided opportunities for white men to become respected members of their communities and may similarly have enhanced the lives of free black men. No matter what his race, a married man who headed a household in Virginia was expected to rule over his dependents. The authority of being a husband, father, and master brought social and political advantages and material benefits to the lives of planters, including recognition as an adult, the ability to persist in one locale, and networks of kin and friends. In addition, white planters who married may have improved their chances of being considered for local offices. Although as a free black man, Johnson likely would not have been eligible for such political advantages, his good fortune in being a married man in the 1630s undoubtedly contributed to his success, making him remarkable, not just in the community of free Africans but in the larger pool of immigrant males scrambling to find wives among the women they outnumbered by three or four to one.

The significance of marriage for community standing and security, however, was not simply a feature of New World settlements or English culture. Most Africans arriving in the colony came from societies in which marriage was one means of creating long-standing lineages, community ties, and wealth. Although marriage in West Africa took a very different form from its counterpart in Virginia, it still conveyed power and status. Obstacles impeding free black people from forming unions thus impinged upon their abilities to function in a colonial society, both in the Anglo-Virginian sense in which marriage offered opportunities for upward mobility and in the West African sense of constituting families, alliances, and wealth.

The difficulties many African men faced in trying to accumulate property also may have impeded their opportunities for marriage. As late as 1675, no laws *prohibited* a free black man like Anthony Johnson from owning land, livestock, or even slaves, but, realistically, his chances of amassing a comfortable estate were considerably lower than those of his white peers. Self-purchase, the key to the freedom of many of Northampton's free black residents, swallowed the small estates of several aspiring free men even before they had a chance to begin their lives outside their master's household. As open as Northampton society may have been for Africans before 1675, white men on the make occasionally stooped to harassment and chicanery to improve their own fortunes. None of these factors helped black men to attract spouses or maintain independent households.

For free black women, the tithe's potential to impede marriage only compounded the moral stigma of racial slavery and field labor. Pamphleteers such as Hammond and English women themselves continued to predicate female morality upon domestic employment and marriage. In his efforts to encourage English women to migrate to the colony, for example, Hammond suggested that a woman's failure to marry well in Virginia was usually caused by her own moral corruption rather than by other circumstances. Such reasoning was, as we have already noted, similar to many English women's own reckonings of female status in the colony. It left little doubt that an enslaved African woman would automatically be judged morally dissolute by English settlers. Even if she was lucky enough to escape the confines of slavery, moreover, an African woman faced an additional obstacle—the tax upon her labor—to achieving the status of a good wife.

The tax on the labor of African and Afro-Virginian women was one of the first obstacles black people faced if they wished to achieve the patriarchal family forms that conferred social standing upon white people. These taxes similarly made the large family lineages of West Africa more costly and difficult to attain. Like the moral failings of English "nasty wenches," detailed by Hammond, the tax liability of free black women also may have dimmed their prospects of marriage.

In responding to the three problems inherent in their ambiguously defined tax laws—English women's doing field work, the classification of free African women, and the criteria for female exemption—seventeenth-century Virginia lawmakers began to define the social meaning of racial difference by reserving the privileges of womanhood for the masters and husbands of English women. In a colony where many English women worked regularly in tobacco fields, creating a legal identity that would distinguish them from enslaved women was crucial to maintaining traditional English family roles. The legal discourse of womanhood that emerged during the seventeenth century enshrined the domesticity and economic dependence of English women, giving husbands and masters sole claim to the fruits of female labor.

The taxation of African women was the cornerstone of a concept of womanhood that became less class-specific and increasingly race-specific throughout the seventeenth century, laying the groundwork for subsequent distinctions between Afro- and Anglo-Virginian families. In contrast to English women, African women were presumed capable of and naturally suited to strenuous field work. African men, moreover, were denied the right to the tax-free labor of wives and daughters. By 1688, as questions arose about the labor of African women who had escaped slavery, racial distinction became its own goal. Lawmakers relegated all African women and their daughters to the status of "negroes," making possible a more exclusive definition of English womanhood. . . .

In the colonies, illegitimate children threatened not only the budgets of parish and county but the system of indentured labor. Early statutes forbidding secret marriages of women servants had originally been designed to protect masters from the expense of pregnancy and childrearing, but they also prevented conflicts between husbands and masters over claims to the economic services of a particular woman. Once presented to a local court by a minister or churchwarden, the offending couple was expected to appear to answer the charge against them. A mother might make another trip to court after she gave birth to declare her claim against the father. On occasion, a woman might bring the child to court with her, adding theater to the courtroom identification of the father of the "child in her armes." The court verified the truth of the woman servant's claim by requiring her to swear to the father's identity under oath or by summoning the midwife to testify to the mother's words during labor.

Although statutes specified that the father of an illegitimate child was supposed to pay all expenses of the birth and maintenance of the child except for the lost time of the mother, justices crafted individual solutions in cases where the father was poor or in service himself. The main concern of most local courts was to ensure that the woman's master and the parish were well compensated for the expenses of her lost service, her lying-in, and the care of her child. After Joanne Ragged identified servant James Collings as the father of her child, the court ordered her to support the child until Collings became a free man and could provide for it himself. The justices also may have encouraged the couple to marry. When servant Elizabeth Tomlyn bore a child fathered by Thomas Mannaugh, the Lancaster court ordered him to leave a hogshead of tobacco with Tomlyn's master for the child's upkeep. A year later, Tomlyn requested that her child live with Roger Haris and his wife until the age of eighteen and be taught to read and write.

When a master fathered a child by his servant woman, justices seem to have followed the rule of paternal responsibility as they did in all other cases where a father could be identified. Masters occasionally tried to obscure the paternity charge by consenting to their female servants' marriage to other men or by encouraging them to accuse others. Presented to the Norfolk court in 1656 for fornication committed before her marriage to William Norwood, Mary Roche, for example, named Thomas Allen, her former master, as the father of her child. The court ordered him to maintain the child "according to the law in the case" and pay court charges. The case of Clement Theobalds and his servant Elizabeth Hall proved more complicated. Hall claimed that John Powis, son of a Norfolk minister, was the father of her child. Theobalds may have encouraged this deceit, hoping to escape the charge himself. After a married woman offered her testimony, presumably concerning Theobalds's involvement with his servant, Theobalds and Hall agreed to marry.

If the father and mother could not maintain the child, the court often ordered the offending male to pay compensation to the parish. Daniel Grisley thus paid his Lancaster County parish twelve hundred pounds of tobacco in 1654 for having a child by Margaret Mealey, who apparently could not raise the infant herself. The parish sometimes placed the child in a household of a third party who was paid to keep it, an arrangement similar to that for poor or orphan children. By custom, these children served until age eighteen or marriage if they were girls and age twenty-one or twenty-two if they were boys. . . .

The real test for the applicability of English family law to enslaved Africans was, not interracial fornication, however, but cases where women serving life terms became pregnant. Here the usual remedy for pregnant English servants—extra time served by the mother to compensate the master for the loss of her labor and expense of giving birth—did not apply if the mother was already understood to be serving for life. The ambiguities surrounding the legal status of enslaved men and women and their relationships, moreover, forced African parents who wanted to enjoy legal rights over their children to make arrangements as if their children were illegitimate. John Graweere, an African "servant," successfully arrived at such an agreement with his own and his enslaved lover's masters in 1641. William Evans permitted Graweere to keep hogs and half their increase, the profits from which Graweere used to pay Lieutenant Robert Sheppard, who owned the African mother of Graweere's child. Graweere wanted the child to "be made a christian and be taught and exercised in the church of *England,* by reason whereof he the said negro did for his said child purchase its freedom." The General Court ordered that the child should be free from Sheppard and Evans to "remain at the disposing and education of the said *Graweere* and the child's godfather." Agreements such as Graweere's were similar to arrangements made by the courts for bastard children, but the use of the terms "freedom" and "purchase" to describe the father's maintenance of the child would not have been part of an English father's settlement.

In situations where the father was English and either incapable of or uninterested in keeping his child by [an] enslaved woman, the courts presumed as early as the 1650s that the child also belonged to the mother's master. In 1657, Thomas Twine, servant to Captain Daniel Parke, was brought before the York court for fathering a child by an African servant of Parke's. In this case, the court appears to have responded as it would have in any other fornication case, ordering Twine to perform public penance at Marston church. The court, however, specified no fine, no arrangements for the upkeep of the child, and no punishment for the African woman. In cases such as Twine's, county court justices provided creative solutions for a situation that statutes had not considered: the damages suffered by a master whose pregnant slave was already serving for life. Twine's record is unclear, but the absence of any of the usual arrangements for damages or maintenance of the child points suspiciously in the direction of a different treatment of this case. The justices retained an interest in the paternity of the child, as they did in all bastardy cases involving English women, yet that knowledge seemed almost irrelevant if a man like Twine paid no damages to a master. . . .

Most striking was the contrast between lawmakers' treatment of African women in 1662 and their new approach to English servant fornication. Even as the new irrelevance of paternity in cases of slave pregnancy made African women more vulnerable to sexual exploitation, the Assembly was busy strengthening existing fornication laws, making it more difficult for lecherous masters to take advantage of English female servants. Servant women convicted of fornication faced two additional years of service and the possibility of another half-year if their masters paid their fine instead of allowing them to be whipped. The parish would care for the child of a male servant during the father's term of service, but, once the father was free, he was expected to reimburse the parish and resume maintenance of the child himself. Addressing the issue of "dissolute masters" who impregnated their female servants and then claimed additional service, the Assembly ordered these women to be sold by the churchwardens to serve additional time. The funds from the sale were to go to the parish rather than to the master.

Rendering the condition of slavery inheritable through the mother, the 1662 statute resolved the most pressing problem from the point of view of white masters: how to balance masters' claims to the agricultural labor of enslaved women with the sometimes incapacitating or even deadly physical risks of their reproductive lives as women. There was legal precedent in Virginia for compensating masters for the lost work time of pregnant English servant women. Female servants who bore illegitimate children had traditionally served their masters for an additional year to repay them for lost labor and the expense of lying-in, the assumption being that time spent in pregnancy and childbirth was time lost to work in the tobacco fields. Even though most masters were undoubtedly pushing their pregnant servants to work as hard as possible for as long as possible, the legal equation was clear: production and reproduction could not take place at the same time, as long as it was on the master's time.

Although the courts treated the pregnancy and childbirth of English women, free and servant, as serious and life-threatening events, they held enslaved women to a different standard. As a consequence, masters *never* sought tax exemptions for pregnant slave women who might have been incapacitated for work during the year they gave birth. There are several possible explanations for this difference. As courts moved toward requiring greater verification of disability by the late seventeenth century, the reproductive complaints of enslaved women may have been too difficult to prove. The state was willing to uphold the authority and investment of the master by extending the service of pregnant English servants; such generosity cost them nothing. It was not willing to acknowledge losses to masters of enslaved women by waiving the annual tax on tobacco producers, however, in part because such an exemption would reduce state revenues. As long as the children of slaves remained slaves, capable of compensating masters for expenses incurred by enslaved mothers, neither the state nor the slaveowners would lose. After 1662, no legal discourse, economic motive, or cultural tradition provoked concern for the well-being of pregnant slave women. And no masters tried to use such a concern to avoid paying their taxes.

The difference in the legal treatment of English women's and enslaved women's reproduction lay primarily in the configuration of their lives as laborers, wives, and mothers. While servitude and marriage theoretically divided English women's lives into two distinct phases of economic dependence, one in which masters owned their labor and the second in which husbands owned both their labor and reproductive capacity, enslaved women found both their production and reproduction owned by the same man in perpetuity. The statute of 1662 confirmed slave women's status as productive and reproductive property, a condition that reflected significant innovations in English traditions for marriage, family, and parental authority. African women, whose reproductive capacity presented the most serious challenge to the integrity of slave property, had become the means by which that property would be sustained and increased. They had also become a means for naturalizing slave status with a concept of race. If being a slave was something one became at birth, rather than as a consequence of military defeat or indebtedness, certain groups of people could be seen as being inherently suited to slavery. The notion that enslaved women could pass their bound condition on to their children strengthened the appearance that slavery was a natural condition for people of African descent.

Slaves for Their Lives

The Virginia colony's movement toward a concept of slavery in which race conferred an aura of naturalness to bondage was nowhere more apparent than in two laws of the late 1660s that limited the means of escaping servitude for life. Christianity had long been a part of the discourse of difference, appearing in the earliest English accounts of Africans, Gaelic Irish, and Indians. It was crucial to the way the English defined themselves and legitimized their attempts to conquer, settle, and appropriate valuable commodities through trade. Throughout the seventeenth century, the word "Christian" surfaced in the laws of Virginia when the English wanted a self-referential term to distinguish their own powers, privileges, and rights from the burdens, punishments, and legal disabilities of the peoples they hoped to dominate. It also helped them define who the "other" people were. Difficulties arose when Africans and Indians became Christians and when English settlers were Virginia-born. By 1667, Christianity was still crucial to legal concepts of difference but no longer adequate for the purposes of slaveholding Anglo-Virginians.

In that year, Virginia lawmakers restricted the legal meaning of "Christian" to conform to the demands of slavery. Legislators decided that baptism would no longer free "slaves by birth." Cutting off an important avenue by which African slaves had demanded release from bondage, Virginia's lawmakers resolved the conflict between property interests and Christian mission, declaring "the conferring of baptisme doth not alter the condition of the person as to his bondage or freedome." With this law, the colony reinforced the notion that slavery could not be renegotiated during an individual's lifetime.

Three years later, the Virginia Assembly resurrected the concept of Christianity to sharpen distinctions between English laborers and those non-English peoples who seemed most alien: Indians and Africans. Noting the difficulty of determining terms of service for Indians captured in war, the Assembly concluded that

> all servants not being christians imported into this colony by shipping shalbe slaves for their lives; but what shall come by land shall serve, if boyes or girles, untill thirty years of age, if men or women twelve yeares.

This law made two crucial distinctions. The first separated Christian (English and other Europeans) and non-Christian (Indian, African, and Moorish) peoples, with the latter group forming the potential pool of slaves. The second distinguished between "slaves" imported to the colony in ships and sold (African) and "servants" captured during wartime (Indian). With this measure, the colony effectively refined its definitions of slavery, limiting bondage to imported Africans. Together, the two statutes culminated thirty years of legal measures defining Africans as slaves and excluding them from the family, gender, and religious privileges enjoyed by the English.

Tax laws, hereditary slavery, and attempts to refine the legal meaning of "Christian" offered a measure of protection to Anglo-Virginian families from the radical economic and social changes threatened by women's work and female indentured servitude in the colony. The project of defining English families as Christian and white and privileging white patriarchs was intimately connected to the legal denial of English-style families to be enslaved.

These early laws were among the most important of all slave statutes in Virginia. They created a legal discourse of slavery rooted in the sexual, social, and economic lives of African laborers and effectively naturalized the condition of slavery by connecting it to a concept of race. Slavery and freedom, like race, became under colonial law conditions that could not be easily altered during one's own lifetime, or, if one was an enslaved woman, during the lifetime of one's children. Grounded in English class-based notions of women's proper role in an economy of commercial agriculture and in the family, "womanhood" began to take on a race-specific meaning in the colony.

Trade and Settlement in the Lower Mississippi Valley

DANIEL H. USNER, JR.

Like other North American colonies, Louisiana floundered during its earliest years. Under economic stress at home and overextended in other parts of the world, Louis XIV failed to support his latest colonial venture with adequate supplies and reinforcements. "The King seemed to be maintaining a small garrison there," Bienville recalled, "only to preserve for himself the possession of such a vast extent of country." Hunger and fever afflicted the small number of men stationed on the Gulf Coast, making them almost entirely dependent upon food provided by local Indian villagers. By 1708 the colonial population of Louisiana numbered only 122 soldiers and sailors, 80 Indian slaves, and 77 settlers, or habitants (24 men, 28 women, and 25 children). "Everybody," according to special commissioner Martin d'Artaguette, was asking for gunpowder "to trade with the Indians for the things we need." The few colonists willing to consider developing this isolated outpost into a productive colony saw their only hope in acquiring African slaves "to clear the land." Bienville proposed that since the Indians being captured by Frenchmen and their allies deserted too easily, although "very good for cultivating the earth," settlers be allowed to "sell these slaves in the American islands in order to get negroes in exchange." Aware of the disorder and animosity incurred by the English slave trade in Indians from Carolina, the French minister of Marine prohibited this practice in 1710. Meanwhile, Bienville and a Monsieur Chateaugue managed to acquire at least six of Louisiana's first black slaves from the plunder captured by Iberville from the English island of Nevis during the War of Spanish Succession.

Beginning principally as an avenue to food for settlers, trade with Indians quickly became an important means of both military protection and commercial development in Louisiana. Access to trade goods and the protocol employed to distribute them, therefore, were critical issues in French-Indian relations. In 1711 Bienville, governing the colony since his brother Iberville had died of yellow fever at Havana five years earlier, declared that the Choctaws "are the key to this country" and that they must be provided with "cloth to clothe them and weapons to defend themselves." The Chickasaws, however, had already made it clear that "not being able to obtain from us their needs which have become indispensable to them they find themselves obliged to take them from the English." According to exchange customs that extended widely across North America, Indians in the Lower Mississippi Valley required that presents be distributed to them whenever any agreement or transaction was made. They traded among themselves, and now with Europeans, not only to acquire scarce products or ritual items but, as importantly, to demonstrate a willingness to maintain peaceful political relations. Gift-giving, smoking the calumet, and other hospitable acts served as symbolic expressions of sociable ties between host and guest parties. As one early French official keenly observed, Louisiana Indians would be conciliated only by "the presents that are given them, the justice that is done them and even more the food that one must not let them lack when they come on visits, together with caresses and evidences of friendship."

Through fixed prices and gift exchange, Indians hoped to make colonial commerce fit their political customs as well as their immediate needs. Presents distributed annually to each tribe served as a kind of tribute from the colony for occupying and using native land, as suggested in various speeches and negotiations, but more fundamentally displayed to the Indians the peaceful intentions of the colonial populace. An absence of trade goods and of gifts signaled potential disruption and often resulted in conflict between colonial and native groups. Although Bienville hoped "to put them on another basis" after 1706, Indians in Louisiana received more than six thousand livres worth of presents from Louis XIV during the hunting season of 1706–1707. Despite repeated complaints over cost from officials on both sides of the Atlantic Ocean, the Choctaws along with other Indian nations in the Lower Mississippi Valley received an increasing amount of gift merchandise throughout the century, reaching twenty thousand livres per year by 1732.

When the company of Antoine Crozat took over Louisiana in 1712, the mercantile interests of company officials immediately clashed with frontier economic relationships that were being forged in the colony. Settlers and soldiers still depended heavily upon trade with Indian villagers for both subsistence and security. Many purchased food directly from Indians, and some acquired peltry from them that they then exchanged for imported grains and meats. Deer, bear, and even raccoon skins were essential export commodities. Early colonists used Indian-produced furs, along with planks sawed from coastal timber, to purchase products like sugar, wine, and wheat from the nearby Spanish garrison at Pensacola or from the French ships that occasionally arrived. In order to establish a monopoly over Louisiana commerce, Crozat prohibited trade with Pensacola and other Spanish colonial bases and marked up the prices of merchandise as much as 300 percent. The company also refused to buy deerskins at more than one livre apiece, but managed to sell them in France at nearly double this price. In pursuit of their own strategies of survival and gain, settlers resorted to now illegal trade practices, bartering independently with Indians and diverting products from company channels. The eight thousand livres worth of bear- and deerskins that did manage to fall into the hands of Crozat's Louisiana agent in 1713 resulted from innumerable social and economic exchanges occurring between colonial residents and native villagers beyond the company's control.

With deerskins fast becoming the colony's major export commodity, an extensive network of trading posts developed over the next decade. Outposts established along interior waterways facilitated the movement of peltry to company warehouses on the coast but functioned more instantly as marketplaces for personal exchange, especially of food, between colonists and Indians. In 1714 the French built a storehouse on the east bank of the Mississippi at Natchez, located some 250 miles above the mouth of the river, in order to acquire deerskins from upcountry villages and to counteract English intrigue and commerce at a most propitious moment. Joining the Atlantic coastal Yamasees in a pan-tribal war against South Carolina, the Alibamons, Tallapoosas, and Abehkas ousted English traders from their villages. In 1715 these Upper Creek Indians began to carry their deerskins to Mobile and in 1717 allowed Bienville to build Fort Toulouse near the junction of the Coosa and Tallapoosa rivers.

In 1716 Fort Rosalie was constructed among the Natchez Indians, a highly centralized and densely populous nation whose several villages occupied mixed pine and hardwood bluffs overlooking the east bank of the Mississippi. For some time, Canadian voyageurs and missionaries had been visiting the Natchez, whose gatherings around French camps looked to Father Du Ru "like one of our ports in France, or like a Dutch fair." Frequent contact with Europeans exposed the Natchez and neighboring tribes, particularly the Taensas and Tunicas, to a high rate of epidemics and wars. So the positioning of Fort Rosalie at this strategic location occurred under volatile circumstances. In the fall of 1715, Natchez leaders were insulted by Antoine de La Mothe Cadillac, the disreputable founder of Detroit and governor of Louisiana during most of the Crozat years, when on a downriver voyage he refused to stop and smoke their calumet. Interpreting this negligence as a sign of hostility, a Natchez war party assassinated four traders and pillaged ten thousand livres worth of merchandise from the Crozat company's local warehouse. In the following spring Bienville led a small army of thirty-five men upriver to the Indian town of Tunica. There he negotiated with a group of Natchez leaders, took some of them hostage, and demanded the heads of all persons responsible for the deaths. The brother of the grand chief, called Petit Soleil by the French, returned with only three heads, pleading that he was unable to impose any more police power over his people. Bienville then had four of the hostages, including two apparent leaders of the revolt, tomahawked to death in a brash effort to assert his dubious strength. As many as a thousand Natchez warriors were available against the commandant's small army, but the execution worked. The Natchez agreed to settle the matter by building a new fortified post to be occupied by a French garrison and to facilitate trade relations. In 1719 Fort St. Pierre was established up the Yazoo River, extending Louisiana's trade sphere among the Ofogoulas, Chachiumas, and other northern neighbors of the Natchez. . . .

By the 1720s the contour of Louisiana's network of Indian trade alliances was firmly established. Carolina traders resumed their commerce with the Chickasaws and some Upper Creek towns, but henceforth trade in the Lower Mississippi Valley flowed mainly from the Indian villages around the interior French posts to the Gulf Coast ports of Mobile and New Orleans. French control of the central valley was reinforced in 1721 when a small detachment of soldiers from the Yazoo River garrison joined a group of settlers at the lower Arkansas River, where the Quapaw Indians had allowed Henri de Tonti to situate his short-lived trade house back in 1686. Most of the peltry exported from Louisiana, numbering "fifty thousand deerskins every year" Bienville estimated in 1726, originated among tribes situated within a 350-mile radius of New Orleans. The outer limits, or periphery, of this network included the Upper Creeks to the northeast, the Quapaws due north, and the Caddoes to the northwest. The Choctaws and most of their neighbors in the region formed a relationship with French Louisiana similar to that existing between the Iroquois nations and the English colony of New York. Previous conflicts with one colony, Canada in the case of the Iroquois and Carolina in the case of the Choctaws, greatly influenced their decision to ally and trade with another European colony.

The formation of this regional network of Indian trade occurred mainly while Louisiana remained a deprived and isolated satellite of the French empire. As of 1718 the colonial populace consisted of "no more than three hundred and fifty to four hundred people," most of them soldiers, officers, and other royal employees scattered among six administrative posts: Dauphin Island, Mobile, and Pascagoula on the Gulf Coast, Fort Toulouse at the forks of the Alabama River, Natchitoches on the Red River, and New Orleans just being constructed on the Mississippi. A drastic change in the size and composition of Louisiana, however, was already under way. France ceded the colony to John Law's Company of the Indies in August 1717, after Crozat relinquished his title. Amid the surging commercial activity generated initially by Law's Company of the West and other assorted schemes, several financial and landed families in France invested in the colonization of the Mississippi Valley. Through the Company of the Indies, which unlike Law's bank and other projects survived the collapse of 1720 and his exile from France, investors hoped to receive a return from the colony in the form of tobacco, indigo, or some other agricultural staple.

Between 1717 and 1721 the Company of the Indies transported in forty-three shipments seven thousand Europeans to the Gulf Coast, and eight vessels brought two thousand slaves from West Africa. Among the European immigrants there were 977 soldiers and 122 officers. The company itself employed 302 workers and 43 clerks, warehouse keepers, and artisans. Only 119 immigrants, known as *concessionaires,* had been granted land concessions, while 2,462 laborers, or *engagés,* had contracted to serve them for an average term of three years. Illicit salt dealers, tobacco smugglers, army deserters, and other criminals taken from the streets and prisons of French cities constituted another 1,278 of the people transported to Louisiana by the company. In addition to this male population of 5,303 immigrants, 1,215 women and 502 children traveled aboard the ships. Although most of these people were natives of France, some 1,300 of them had been recruited from various parts of Germany. The Negro slaves of diverse nationalities who reached Louisiana during the same period came from entrepôts at Gorée, on the coast of the Senegal region, and Juida, farther south and east on the West African coast at the Bight of Benin. Most were people called Bambara, Malinke-speaking captives from the interior, but slaves exported from Senegambia also included such coastal ethnic groups as the Wolof and Sereer.

Although at a lower rate than that experienced by Indians, death overcame many of these different migrants to Louisiana. "Numbers died of misery or disease," remarked Father Pierre de Charlevoix, "and the country was emptied as rapidly as it had filled." Of the seven thousand whites who entered the Lower Mississippi Valley from 1717 to 1721, at least half of them either perished or abandoned the colony before 1726. The approximately seven thousand blacks transported to Louisiana on slave ships between 1718 and 1731 experienced a similar rate of diminution. Removed from their homelands where they had inherited or developed substantial immunities to the common maladies of the region, these newcomers found their health threatened by the deprivations of oceanic transportation and the unfamiliar viruses of a different disease environment. European immigrants to the Gulf Coast and other parts of the coastal South were particularly vulnerable to malarial fevers caused by infectious transmission from the anopheles mosquito. West Africans, like the residents of Sicily and other traditionally malarious regions, had developed through genetic selection a sickle cell trait in some blood cells that provided substantial hereditary immunity to malaria. But if Africans usually avoided the debilitating "fevers and ague" experienced by their white counterparts, other contagious and chronic illnesses had a fatal effect upon these enslaved colonial workers. Respiratory and intestinal viruses contracted from Europeans, in addition to sicknesses caused by the conditions of their enslavement and transportation, took a heavy toll upon the lives of African-Louisianians. . . .

In addition to the general food crisis encountered on the Gulf Coast, other specific factors contributed to a high rate of mortality among enslaved black immigrants. Whereas immigration of European settlers virtually halted after 1721, the Company of the Indies shipped additional cargoes of African slaves to Louisiana for another decade. Information regarding the fifteen known shipments of slaves between June 1719 and March 1729 indicates that about 20 percent of these Africans destined for Louisiana died in transit. After months of imprisonment in such slave warehouses as Gorée near the mouth of the Senegal River, blacks were crowded into ships each carrying as many as 450 people. Unhealthy confinement, mistreatment, and malnutrition killed many passengers. Those who reached the pilot's station at the mouth of the Mississippi, known as Balize, still had to withstand several ailments. In 1727, for example, the *Prince de Conti* "arrived at the Balize on the twelfth of September *with 266 blacks,* rather fine, but a good part of these blacks were attacked on their arrival by two diseases, some by dysentery with a bloody flux and others by an inflammation on the eyes by which many have been left one-eyed and blind." The latter malady was probably trachoma, a contagious infection inside the eyelids and on the cornea easily contracted aboard unsanitary and crowded slave ships.

Because of inadequate supplies of food, especially the lack of ascorbic acid found in citrus fruits, scurvy struck most slave ships during and after passage to Louisiana. The *Galatée* reached the mouth of the Mississippi on January 18, 1729, with only 260 of the 400 Africans who had boarded three months earlier at Gorée. "On account of the bad condition in which its crew and its negroes were," this ship had left 45 sick slaves, 9 sailors, and 1 officer at the port of La Caye on St. Domingue. Shortly after their arrival at Louisiana, 25–30 more Negroes died, "all of scurvy." Characterized by bleeding gums and loosening teeth, this disease accounted for a large percentage of deaths among African immigrants. Of the 450 men, women, and children boarded on the *Venus* in 1729, 87 died during the voyage. En route from the mouth of the river to New Orleans, another 43 perished. Finally, 320 people reached the capital, but according to Governor Étienne Boucher de Périer and Commissioner Jacques de La Chaise, "they were so violently attacked by the scurvy that more than two-thirds of those who were sold at auction into the hands of the inhabitants have died." Principally concerned with the financial effects of this terrible mortality, the two officials reported on August 26, 1729, that settlers "outbid each other for the scurvied, consumptive and ulcerated and raise the price for them as high as one thousand livres. We saw some in this last auction as well as in the preceding ones die half a quarter of an hour after they had been awarded to them, and that in great numbers; others were not able to get them out of New Orleans; others remained with them only two days, and finally there are inhabitants who have taken as many as six or seven of them who have all died on their hands in less than a week."

By the late 1720s Louisianians who endured ocean travel, disease, and hunger found themselves living in a stabilizing environment. They acquired greater immunity to infectious viruses and became acclimated to conditions in the Lower Mississippi Valley. Many colonists owed their survival to Indian villagers who provided food during the hard times. Settlers and slaves began to produce sufficient crops of grain and vegetables, and the quantity of hogs, cattle, and poultry slowly increased. Health hazards nonetheless persisted. Smallpox, dysentery, yellow fever, and typhus always threatened, especially young and elderly inhabitants. Overwork and mistreatment, although prohibited by the Code Noir, condemned slaves frequently to sickness and occasionally to death. Situated mostly below sea level and surrounded by mosquito-breeding waters, New Orleans was a promising site for commerce but potentially fatal to residents. A malignant fever "spread through the entire town" in the summer of 1723, attributed by La Chaise to "the stagnation of the water since it [the Mississippi River] did not retire until the beginning of July." Until the 1790s, however, the population of New Orleans remained small enough to avoid epidemic levels of contagious fever. Only then did yellow fever, and later cholera, become endemic in the Crescent City.

The nearly two thousand settlers and four thousand slaves inhabiting Louisiana by 1731 represented only about half of the number of people actually transported by the Company of the Indies. As distressing as this tragic rate of migrant mortality was in itself, company officials were equally concerned about the character of those who survived. Showing little eagerness to commit themselves to planting a commercial crop, colonial inhabitants constituted a weak population base for developing an agricultural export economy. As in other colonial regions, the Louisiana economy was evolving in a direction sharply divergent from the hopes and expectations of colonial planners and investors in France. During the 1720s the Company of the Indies promoted tobacco production through a series of measures: sending experienced tobacco workers to the colony, paying artificially high prices for the harvests, and even offering bounties to concession directors who chose to plant the crop. But before the wave of immigration began, officials such as General Commissioner Marc-Antoine Hubert had detected a strong reluctance among settlers to till the soil, predicting in 1716 that they "will never be satisfied with this infallible resource, accustomed as they are to the trade with the Indians the easy profit from which supports them, giving them what they need day by day like the Indians who find their happiness in an idle and lazy life." Unable to control effectively the behavior of settlers and soldiers, much less of native villagers, promoters of Louisiana and of other colonial projects usually disparaged Indian life while reluctantly accepting patterns of trade and settlement very different from original schemes.

Many Europeans arriving in Louisiana between 1717 and 1721 were unemployed and underemployed laborers or deported salt smugglers, prostitutes, and other illicit dealers who had moved freely across the countryside and in cities. *Rouleurs* (traveling workers) and *colpoteurs* (peddlers) carried small quantities of merchandise from place to place, in what one historian of eighteenth-century France has called a "makeshift subeconomy," and the practice of itinerant peddling proved useful and persistent in America. One official of the Company of the Indies observed that New Orleans by 1724 consisted of many "common people [*petites gens*] who were engaged in a commerce detrimental to the Colony and even to the interests of the Company." As soon as a ship landed at the levee, these "common people" petitioned the Superior Council for the orders needed to obtain merchandise from the company warehouse, quickly emptied it of all kinds of goods, and resold them at much higher prices. In March of 1725 the council restricted the distribution of these permits, declaring that the "number of little inhabitants who carry on no other business here than of trading" made it impossible to "find a servant or a workman to work in the fields that are in cultivation." One observer more sympathetic to those immigrants who did not want to work the land for someone else or could not begin their own farms described the importance of frontier exchange to them: "On their return from the Indians they disperse in the city their peltries or produce, which they bring in payment to those from whom they have borrowed in order to carry on their trade. This causes each one to share this commerce instead of it belonging exclusively to three or four persons who grow wealthy while the others die from hunger inside a settlement."

The importation of several thousand African slaves and the establishment of successful plantations during the 1720s helped reduce tensions between the *petits habitants* wanting to trade independently and the concessionaires demanding a tractable labor force. But few settlers could afford to purchase slaves, even on credit, from the company. Furthermore, the enslaved black workers themselves quickly adapted their own traditional economic practices to colonial life, turning to small-scale farming and frontier exchange to mitigate their bondage in America. Open interaction between Indians, settlers, and slaves—characteristic of most North American colonies during their early years—had already taken its course in other plantation societies, where governments turned exclusively to African-American slavery as a source of labor and took advantage of cultural differences to control social relations. This process, however, did not unfold without intense conflict. Nor did it completely eliminate the strategies of exchange preferred by the people who struggled hardest to survive in a colonial region.

ᚼ F U R T H E R　　R E A D I N G

James Axtell, *The Invasion Within: The Contest of Cultures in Colonial North America* (1985)

T. H. Breen and Stephen Innes, *"Myne Owne Ground": Race and Freedom on Virginia's Eastern Shore, 1640–1676* (1980)

Kathleen M. Brown, *Good Wives, Nasty Wenches, and Anxious Patriarchs* (1996)

Lois Green Carr, Russell R. Menard, and Lorena S. Walsh, *Robert Cole's World: Agriculture and Society in Early Maryland* (1991)

Catherine Clinton and Michele Gillespie, eds., *The Devil's Lane: Sex and Race in the Early South* (1997)

Wesley Frank Craven, *The Southern Colonies in the Seventeenth Century* (1949)

Philip D. Curtin, *The Atlantic Slave Trade: A Census* (1969)

David Brion Davis, *The Problem of Slavery in Western Culture* (1966)

David Hackett Fischer, *Albion's Seed: Four British Folkways in America* (1989)

David W. Galenson, *Traders, Planters, and Slaves* (1986)

Gary C. Goodwin, *Cherokees in Transition: A Study of Changing Culture and Environment Prior to 1775* (1977)

Charles M. Hudson, *The Southeastern Indians* (1976)

Charles M. Hudson and Carmen Chaves Tesser, eds., *The Forgotten Centuries: Indians and Europeans in the American South, 1521–1704* (1994)

Francis Jennings, *The Invasion of America: Indians, Colonialism, and the Cant of Conquest* (1975)

Winthrop D. Jordan, *White over Black: American Attitudes Toward the Negro, 1550–1812* (1968, 1987)

Winthrop D. Jordan and Sheila L. Skemp, eds., *Race and Family in the Colonial South* (1987)

Karen O. Kupperman, *Roanoke, the Abandoned Colony* (1984)

Daniel R. Mannix, *Black Cargoes: A History of the Atlantic Slave Trade, 1518–1865* (1962)

James H. Merrell, *The Indians' New World: Catawbas and Their Neighbors* (1989)

Edmund S. Morgan, *American Slavery, American Freedom* (1975)

Gerald W. Mullin, *Flight and Rebellion: Slave Resistance in Eighteenth-Century Virginia* (1972)

Abraham P. Nasatir, *Borderland in Retreat: From Spanish Louisiana to the Far Southwest* (1976)

Gary B. Nash, *Red, White, and Black: The Peoples of Early America* (1974, 1982)

Theda Perdue, *Slavery and the Evolution of Cherokee Society, 1548–1866* (1979)

James R. Perry, *The Formation of a Society on Virginia's Eastern Shore, 1615–1655* (1990)

David B. Quinn, *Set Fair for Roanoke: Voyages and Colonies, 1584–1606* (1985)

Helen C. Rountree and Thomas E. Davidson, *Eastern Shore Indians of Virginia and Maryland* (1997)

Bernard W. Sheehan, *Savagism and Civility: Indians and Englishmen in Colonial Virginia* (1980)

Timothy Silver, *A New Face on the Countryside: Indians, Colonists, and Slaves in South Atlantic Forests, 1500–1800* (1990)

Thad W. Tate and David L. Ammerman, eds., *The Chesapeake in the Seventeenth Century: Essays on Anglo-American Society* (1979)

Daniel H. Usner, Jr., *Indians, Settlers and Slaves in a Frontier Exchange Economy* (1992)

Clarence L. Ver Steeg, *Origins of a Southern Mosaic: Studies of Early Carolina and Georgia* (1975)

Lorena S. Walsh, *From Calabar to Carter's Grove: The History of a Virginia Slave Community* (1997)

Betty Wood, *Slavery in Colonial Georgia, 1730–1775* (1984)

Peter H. Wood, *Black Majority: Negroes in Colonial South Carolina from 1670 Through the Stono Rebellion* (1974)

Peter H. Wood, Gregory A. Waselkov, and M. Thomas Hatley, eds., *Powhatan's Mantle: Indians in the Colonial Southeast* (1989)

J. Leitch Wright, Jr., *Anglo-Spanish Rivalry in North America* (1971)

CHAPTER
3

The Maturing of the Colonial South

More than three decades ago, colonial historians began a systematic study of New England towns. Borrowing the methods of European social scientists, they explored such concepts as community and culture and such institutions as the family, the church, and politics. Within the past couple of decades, studies of southern communities have paralleled and expanded upon the scholarship of New England historians. Even though the colonial South rarely offered the discrete community structure exemplified by New England settlements, scholars have discovered that the absence of specific geographic boundaries is not an obstacle to creative community studies.

This work has led historians to see the eighteenth century as a crucial period in the colonial's South's maturation—a time when its social structure, political ideology, and economic institutions first emerged in recognizable form. Scholars have identified at least five elements in this maturation process: the increasing separation of black and white worlds, the growing economic distance among whites, the development of cash-crop agriculture based on slave labor, changes in family structure and relationships, and the emergence of a coherent set of political beliefs. These elements did not evolve without challenge—from slaves, landless whites, dissenting political and religious movements, and ultimately the British. In turn, the challenges resulted in a constant shaping and reshaping of these basic features of eighteenth-century southern life and eventually influenced the American Revolution and the society that emerged from that conflict.

Historians continue to explore how the southern colonies differed from one another; how dependent each was on others; and what values and experiences they had in common, such as slavery, demographic makeup, and cash crops. As coastal areas filled with settlers, many individuals and families began to move inland, transferring their culture and values to frontier areas and creating new pressure for land and additional conflict with Native Americans. Even by the mid-eighteenth century, the colonies did not see themselves as unified, nor did southern colonies regard themselves as a unified region.

⋏ *D O C U M E N T S*

Document 1 suggests the harsh conditions often endured by white indentured servants. Here, a young, repentant woman pours out her woes to her father. By the early eighteenth century, slaves had replaced white indentured servants as the principal laborers in the

65

colonies, though indenture remained in use into the nineteenth century. Document 2, by Eliza Lucas, reveals a remarkable teenage girl who not only managed her father's properties in his absence but successfully introduced indigo cultivation into South Carolina. These excerpts from her letterbook show the importance of family relations and her ability to couch her observations within the feminine linguistic conventions of the time. As an initial holdout against slave labor, Georgia was the last southern colony to grapple with slavery. As Document 3 reveals, pressure mounted and the colony eventually repealed its laws prohibiting slavery. The advertisements concerning runaway slaves from the *South-Carolina Gazette* in Document 4 show that slaves openly resisted their oppression and also reveal owners' attitudes toward their slaves. Document 5 comes from the letterbook of Robert Pringle, a successful Charleston merchant. It reveals the extensive trade among merchants in the West Indies, Europe, and the colonies, and a wealthy man's preoccupation with crop prices, fashionable clothing, and urban disasters. Document 6, by the Anglican minister Charles Woodmason, presents a lively vignette on the Carolina backcountry on the eve of the American Revolution. Woodmason performed missionary work in the interior and had anything but flattering comments to make about its inhabitants. However, he was determined to uplift and convert those whom he regarded as hopelessly heathen. The Regulators, as backcountry dissenters were called, directed their charges, reprinted here in Document 7, at lowcountry legislators.

1. Elizabeth Sprigs Describes Harsh Conditions of Servitude, 1756

MARYLAND Sept'r 22'd 1756.

Honred Father

My being for ever banished from your sight, will I hope pardon the Boldness I now take of troubling you with these, my long silence has been purely owing to my undutifullness to you, and well knowing I had offended in the highest Degree, put a tie to my tongue and pen, for fear I should be extinct from your good Graces and add a further Trouble to you, but too well knowing your care and tenderness for me so long as I retaind my Duty to you, induced me once again to endeavour if possible, to kindle up that flame again. O Dear Father, belive what I am going to relate the words of truth and sincerity, and Ballance my former bad Conduct [to] my sufferings here, and then I am sure you'll pitty your Destress [ed] Daughter,   What we unfortunat English People suffer here is beyond the probibility of you in England to Conceive, let it suffice that I one of the unhappy Number, am toiling almost Day and Night, and very often in the Horses druggery, with only this comfort that you Bitch you do not halfe enough, and then tied up and whipp'd to that Degree that you'd not serve an Annimal, scarce any thing but Indian Corn and Salt to eat and that even begrudged nay many Neagroes are better used, almost naked no shoes nor stockings to wear, and the comfort after slaving dureing Masters pleasure, what rest we can get is to rap ourselves up in a Blanket and ly upon the Ground, this is the deplorable Condition your poor Betty endures, and now I beg if you have any Bowels of Compassion left show it by sending me some Relief, C[l]othing is the principal thing wanting, which if you should condiscend to, may easely send them to me by

As found in Isabel M. Calder, *Colonial Captivities, Marches and Journeys* (New York: Macmillan, 1935). Reprinted by permission of the National Society of Colonial Dames of America.

any of the ships bound to Baltimore Town Patapsco River Maryland, and give me leave to conclude in Duty to you and Uncles and Aunts, and Respect to all Friends

> Honred Father
> Your undutifull and Disobedient Child
>
> Elizabeth Sprigs

Please to direct for me at Mr. Rich'd Crosses to be left at Mr. Luxes Merc't in Baltimore Town Patapsco River Maryland

2. Eliza Lucas Writes on Love and Business, 1740, 1741

March [?] 1740

[To Colonel Lucas]
Hond. Sir

Your letter by way of Philadelphia which I duly received was an additional proof of that paternal tenderness which I have always Experienced from the most Indulgent of Parents from my Cradle to this time, and the subject of it is of the utmost importance to my peace and happiness.

As you propose Mr. L. to me I am sorry I can't have Sentiments favourable enough of him to take time to think on the Subject, as your Indulgence to me will ever add weight to the duty that obliges me to consult what best pleases you, for so much Generosity on your part claims all my Obedience, but as I know tis my happiness you consult [I] must beg the favour of you to pay my thanks to the old Gentleman for his Generosity and favourable sentiments of me and let him know my thoughts on the affair in such civil terms as you know much better than any I can dictate; and beg leave to say to you that the riches of Peru and Chili if he had them put together could not purchase a sufficient Esteem for him to make him my husband.

As to the other Gentleman you mention, Mr. Walsh, you know, Sir, I have so slight a knowledge of him I can form no judgment of him, and a Case of such consiquence requires the Nicest distinction of humours and Sentiments. But give me leave to assure you, my dear Sir, that a single life is my only Choice and if it were not as I am yet but Eighteen, hope you will [put] aside the thoughts of my marrying yet these 2 or 3 years at least.

You are so good to say you have too great an Opinion of my prudence to think I would entertain an indiscreet passion for any one, and I hope heaven will always direct me that I may never disappoint you; and what indeed could induce me to make a secret of my Inclination to my best friend, as I am well aware you would not disaprove it to make me a Sacrifice to Wealth, and I am as certain I would indulge no passion that had not your aprobation, as I truly am

> Dr. Sir, Your most dutiful and affecte. Daughter
>
> E. Lucas

This document can be found in Elise Pinckney, ed., *The Letterbook of Eliza Lucas Pinckney* (Chapel Hill: University of Carolina Press, 1972), pp. 5, 15–16.

To my Father.

Hon'd Sir   June the 4th, 1741

. . . We expect the boat dayly from Garden Hill when I shall be able to give you an account of affairs there. The Cotton, Guiney corn, and most of the Ginger planted here was cutt off by a frost. I wrote you in [a] former letter we had a fine Crop of Indigo Seed upon the ground, and since informed you the frost took it before it was dry. I picked out the best of it and had it planted, but there is not more than a hundred bushes of it come up—which proves the more unluckey as you have sent a man to make it. I make no doubt Indigo will prove a very valuable Commodity in time if we could have the seed from the west Indias [in] time enough to plant the latter end of March, that the seed might be dry enough to gather before our frost. I am sorry we lost this season. We can do nothing towards it now but make the works ready for next year. The Lucern is yet but dwindlering, but Mr. Hunt tells me 'tis always so here the first year.

3. The Debate over Slavery in Georgia, 1735–1750

Minutes of the Georgia Privy Council, 1735

April 3, 1735.

An Act for rendering the Colony of Georgia more Defencible by Prohibiting the Importation and use of Black Slaves or Negroes into the same.

Whereas Experience hath Shewn that the manner of Settling Colonys and Plantations with Black Slaves or Negroes hath obstructed the Increase of English and Christian Inhabitants therein who alone can in case of a War be relyed on for the Defence and Security of the same, and hath Exposed the Colonys so settled to the Insurrections Tumults and Rebellions of such Slaves and Negroes and in Case of a Rupture with any Foreign State who should Encourage and Support such Rebellions might Occasion the utter Ruin and loss of such Colonys, For the preventing therefore of so great inconveniences in the said Colony of Georgia. We the Trustees for Establishing the Colony of Georgia in America humbly beseech Your Majesty That it may be Enacted And be it Enacted that from and after the four and twentieth day of June which shall be in the Year of Our Lord One Thousand Seven hundred and thirty five if any Person or Persons whatsoever shall import or bring or shall cause to be imported or brought or shall sell or Barter or use in any manner or way whatsoever in the said Province or in any Part or Place therein any Black or Blacks Negroe or Negroes such Person or Persons for every such Black or Blacks Negroe or Negroes so imported or brought or caused to be imported or brought or sold Bartered or used within the said Province Contrary to the intent and meaning of this Act shall forfeit and lose the Sum of fifty pounds Sterling Money of Great Britain. . . .

These documents can be found in Allen D. Candler and Lucian Lamar Knight, eds., *Colonial Records of the State of Georgia* (Atlanta, GA.: 1904–1916), vol. I, pp. 50–52, 56–62; vol. XXIV, pp. 434–444; and in Memorial to the Trustees, December 9, 1738, Edgemont Papers, pt. 2, 330–335, University of Georgia Library.

Remonstrance of the Inhabitants of Savannah, 1738

SAVANNAH, 9th December, 1738.

To the Honorable the Trustees for Establishing the Colony of Georgia in America.

May it please your Honors: We whose names are underwritten, being all set-tlers, freeholders and inhabitants in the province of Georgia, and being sensible of the great pains and care exerted by you in endeavoring to settle this colony, since it has been under your protection and management, do unanimously join to lay before you, with the utmost regret, the following particulars. . . . Timber is the only thing we have here which we might export, and notwithstanding we are obliged to fall it in planting our land, yet we cannot manufacture it for a foreign market but at double the expense of other colonies; as for instance, the river of May, which is but twenty miles from us, with the allowance of negroes, load vessels with that commodity at one half of the price that we can do; and what should induce persons to bring ships here, when they can be loaded with one half of the expense so near us; therefore the timber on the land is only a continual charge to the possessors of it, though of very great advantage in all the northern colonies, where negroes are allowed, and conse-quently, labor cheap. We do not in the least doubt but that in time, silk and wine may be produced here, especially the former; but since the cultivation of the land with white servants only, cannot raise provisions for our families as before men-tioned, therefore it is likewise impossible to carry on these manufactures according to the present constitution. It is very well known, that Carolina can raise every thing that this colony can, and they having their labor so much cheaper will always ruin our market, unless we are in some measure on a footing with them. . . . Your honors, we imagine, are not insensible of the numbers that have left this province, not being able to support themselves and families any longer. . . .

The want of the use of negroes, with proper limitation; which, if granted, would both occasion great numbers of white people to come here, and also render us capable to subsist ourselves, by raising provisions upon our lands, until we could make some produce fit for export, in some measure to balance our importation. We are very sensible of the inconveniences and mischiefs that have already, and do daily arise from an unlimited use of negroes; but we are as sensible that these may be prevented by a due limitation, such as so many to each white man, or so many to such a quantity of land, or in any other manner which your Honors shall think most proper.

The Reverend John Martin Bolzius to the Reverend George Whitefield, 1745

EBENEZER Dec. 24th 1745.

Revd. and Dear Sir, Besides the Blessings, the Lord was pleased to impart to my Soul in your and Mrs. Whitefield's Conversation, I felt many Griefs and troubles in my heart Since my Return from Bethesda and Savannah, arising from the unhappy News, I heard at Savannah and from your Self, that you are induced to petition the Honble. Trustees for giving their Consent to the Introduction of Negroes into this our Colony, for which you think to be Under Necessity with Respect to the Main-tainance of the Orphan House. Dont be amazed, Sir at my Boldness to write to you in this Secular Affair, in which I would not meddle at all, if not the Love to your Worthy person, to my Congregation and to this Colony Obligded me to it. For the Introduction of Negroes inconsistent with the prayseworthy Scheme of the Honble. Trustees our Lawful and Bountiful Superiours, will be very Mischievous to the happy Settling of this Colony, and Especially to the poor white Labouring people in many Respects, and the Sighs of them would be unprofitable for you or any other, who joins with the principles and aims of the Wishers for Negroe Overseer. A Common white Labourer white Man of the meaner Sort can get his and his Family's Livelyhood honestly in Carolina, except he embraces the Sorry Imploy of a Negroe Overseers. A Common white Labourer in Charles-Town (I am told) has no more Wages, than a Negroe for his work *Viz.* 7 *s.* Cur. or 12 *d.* Sterl. a Day, for which it is in my Opinion impossible to find Victuals, Lodging and washing, much less Cloaths. In case he would Settle and Cultivate a plantation, is not all good and Convenient Ground at the Sea Coasts and Banks of the Rivers taken up in Large Quantities by the Merchants and Other Gentlemen? Consequently the poor white Inhabitants are forced to possess Lands, remote from the Conveniencys of Rivers and from Town to their great Disappointment to Sell their produce. Being not inclined to give their Produce of their Plantations or Other Sort of Work for Such a Low price, as Negroes can afford, they find no market, then they are discouraged and Obliged to Seek their Livelihood in the Garrisons, Forts, Scout-Boats, Trading Boats or to be imploy'd amongst the Negroes upon a Gentleman's Plantation, or they are forced to take Negroes upon Credit, of which they will find in Process of time the Sad Consequences on Account of their Debts. I hear the Negroes in Carolina learn all Sorts of trade, which takes away the bread of a poor white trades' man Like wise.

I have Considered the Strength of your Arguments by which you seem to be induced to promote the Introduction of Negroes, as far as it lyes in your power.

First you think the Providence of God has Appointed this Colony rather for the work of black Slaves than for Europians, because of the hot Climate, to which the Negroes are better used than white people.

But, Dear Sir, give me Leave to say, that every honest Labourer amongst us will testify the Contrary and that in some parts of Germany in the Middle of the Summer being the Only Season there to make Hay, and to bring in their Crop, is as hot as here. And if it be so, that in the 3 Months of the Summer it is too hot for white people to work with the hoe in the field, is it so with the plow Can they not Chuse the Morning and Afternoon Hours for Labouring in the Field? Have they not 9 Months in the Year time Enough to prepare the Ground for Europian and Countrey Grain? Which preference they enjoy not in the Northern Parts, by Reason of the Deep Snow and the Exceeding Cold Weather. . . .

II. Your Second Argument for the Introduction of Negroes was, that the Trustees have laid out about 250,000 Pounds Sterl. for Establishing this Colony, and almost to no purpose. . . . There are so many Thousands of Protestants in Germany, who would embrace eagerly an Invitation to this Colony, if they could meet with Encouragement, as they will in time, and it is a Thousand pity, that you will help to make this Retirement and Refuge for poor persecuted or Necessitous Protestants, a Harbour of Black Slaves, and deprive them of the benefit to be Settled here. . . .

IV. Your Last Argument for Negroes was, as I remember, that you intended to bring them to the Knowledge of Christ.

But, Sir, my Heart wishes, that first the White people in the Colony and Neighbourhood may be brought to the Saving and Experimental Knowledge of Christ. As long as they are for this World, and take Advantage of the poor black Slaves, they will increase the Sins of the Land to a great Heighth. If a Minister had a Call to imploy his Strength and time to Convert Negroes, he has in Carolina a Large Field. Dont believe, Sir, the Language of those persons, who wish the Introduction of Negroes under pretence of promoting their Spiritual Happiness, as well as in a Limited Number and under some Restrictions. I am sure, that if the Trustees allow'd to one thousand White Settlers so many Negroes, in a few Years you would meet in the Streets, So as in Carolina, with many Malattoes, and many Negroe Children, which in process of time will fill the Colony. The Assembly in Carolina have made good Laws and Restrictions in favour of the White people, but how many are, who pay regard and Obedience to them? not better would fare the Restrictions and Good Laws of the Trustees. I will not mention the great Danger, to which we are exposed by the Introduction of Negroes with Respect to the Spaniards, and it is a Groundless thing, to say, that one of the Articles of Peace with Spain must be not to give Shelter to the Negroes at Augustine, who would run away.

Repeal of the Act Excluding Negroes, 1750

May it please Your Majesty, . . .

Whereas an Act was passed by his Majesty in Council in the Eighth Year of his Reign Intituled (an Act for rendering the Colony of Georgia more defensible by prohibiting the Importation and Use of Black Slaves or Negroes into the same) by which Act the Importation and Use of Black Slaves or Negroes in the said Colony was absolutely prohibited and forbid under the Penalty therein mentioned and whereas at the time of passing the said Act the said Colony of Georgia being in its Infancy the Introduction of Black Slaves or Negroes would have been of dangerous Consequence but at present it may be a Benefit to the said Colony and a Convenience and Encouragement to the Inhabitants thereof to permit the Importation and Use of them into the said Colony under proper Restrictions and Regulations without Danger to the said Colony as the late War hath been happily concluded and a General Peace established. Therefore we the Trustees for establishing the Colony of Georgia in America humbly beseech Your Majesty that it may be Enacted And be it enacted That the said Act and every Clause and Article therein contained be from henceforth repealed and made void and of none Effect and be it Further Enacted that from and after the first day of January in the Year of Our Lord One thousand seven hundred and fifty it shall and may be lawful to import or bring Black Slaves or Negroes into the Province of Georgia in America and to keep and use the same therein under the Restrictions and Regulations hereinafter mentioned and directed to be observed concerning the same And for that purpose be it Further Enacted that from and after the said first day of January in the Year of Our Lord One thousand seven hundred and fifty it shall and may be lawful for every Person inhabiting and holding and cultivating Lands within the said Province of Georgia and having and constantly keeping one white Man Servant on his own Lands capable of bearing Arms and aged between sixteen and sixty five Years to have and keep four Male

Negroes or Blacks upon his Plantation there and so in Proportion to the Number of such white Men Servants capable of bearing Arms and of such Age as aforesaid as shall be kept by every Person within the said Province.

4. Runaway Slave Advertisements from South Carolina, 1743–1784

South-Carolina Gazette *(Timothy), October 31, 1743.*

WHEREAS a Negro Boy belonging to Mr. William Bissett at Hobkaw, named Tom, about 15 Years of Age, went away on Thursday Night, (having been sent to carry to a Gentleman, a super fine Scarlet Cloth Coat, with Scarlet Basket Buttons, and a Lanthorn). Whoever brings the said Boy to my Coffee house in Elliott Street, shall have Twenty Shillings reward. Any Person stopping the said Boy or Cloak, shall have the like Reward. But Persons receiving, buying or bartering the same, may depend upon being punish'd.

William Menat.

South-Carolina Gazette *(Timothy), November 14, 1743.*

RUN away the 5th of October, 1743, from the Subscriber, in the Upper District of St. James Parish, Santee; two Mustee Fellows, one call'd Tom, Twenty one Years of Age, about six Feet nine Inches high; the other call'd Billey, Eighteen Years of Age, and more of an Indian Colour than the former, both of them pretty slim for their highth [sic], speaks tolerable good English, and neither of them had the Mark of a Lash when they went away. Whoever takes them up and brings them safe to me, or to the Work house in Charles-Town, shall have 10 1. Currency Reward, for each, and if any will inform where they are to be found, so that they may be had, they shall have 5 1. for each, paid by

Rene Peyre.

South-Carolina Gazette *(Timothy), April 2, 1744.*

RUN AWAY about the 18th of March last, a young Negro Wench, known by the Name of Akin's Moll, of a middle Stature, and very black, had on when she went away a Garlix Gown, she is this Country born, and formerly belonged to the Estate of Anthony Poitevine, deceased. Whoever brings the said Negro Wench to me in Tho. Elliott's Alley, Charlestown, shall have 5 1. reward.

James Bremar.

South-Carolina Gazette *(Timothy), July 11, 1774.*

RUN AWAY on Wednesday 29th of June last, a Negro Fellow names JAMES, about 25 Years old; had on when he went away, a blue Jacket, Shoes and Stockings;

This material can be found in Lathan A. Windley's *Runaway Slave Advertisements,* published by Greenwood Press.

he is a likely Fellow, and has a small Impedient [sic]. Whoever gives Information to the Warden of the Work-House in Charles-Town, so that he may be apprehended, or delivered into his Custody, shall receive Ten Pounds Reward.

N. B. All Masters of Vessels are hereby forewarned from carrying the said Fellow off the Province, as it is very probable he may endeavour to get a Passage to some Part of the West-Indies.

South-Carolina Gazette *(Timothy), July 11, 1774.*

RUN away from my plantation at Ashepoo, about the end of May last, two country born NEGRO MEN named July*and Cupid*: July is a squat well made fellow, about thirty years of age, very artful and sensible, and is well known in Charles-Town, and in many other parts of the province, being formerly a boatman; Cupid is a slim young fellow of about eighteen years of age. As they are particularly known at the Indian-Land, it is supposed they are concealed or harboured there. I hereby offer a reward of TEN POUNDS currency for each, with all lawful charges, to any person delivering them, either to the Warden of the Work-house in Charles-Town, to my Overseer at Horse-Savannah, or at my said Plantation at Ashepoo; and I do hereby offer a further reward of FIFTY POUNDS currency to any person that will inform me of their being harboured, if by a white person, or if by a negro, TWENTY POUNDS, on conviction of the offender or offenders.

ROBERT LADSON.

Charleston South-Carolina and American General Gazette, *October 2, 1777. Supplement.*

RUN away Sept. 14, from the subscriber, a Negro Boy named Saunders*, 13 or 14 years of age, of the Guinea country, about 4 feet 8 inches high, had on an osnaburg shirt and breeches, is rather of the yellowish complexion, is pitted a little with the small pox, and is very artful. Whoever delivers him to me or the Warden of the Work-house, shall have Five Pounds reward, Ten Pounds if harboured by a negro, and Twenty Pounds if by a white person, on conviction; if he is taken in the country all reasonable charges will be paid by

WILLIAM LAWRENCE.

Charleston South-Carolina and American General Gazette, *October 9, 1777.*

RUN away from the subscriber the 21st of June last, a Negro Fellow named DUKE, about 5 feet 6 inches high; also a Negro Wench named LUCY, pretty stout, about eight months gone with child, bought at the sale of Zachariah Villepontoux, Esq; and supposed to be harboured there or thereabouts. A reward of Ten Pounds will be given for the fellow, and Five Pounds for the wench, to any person who apprehends and delivers them to me or the Warden of the Work-house. Twenty-five Pounds will be given to any person that can prove their being harboured by a negro, and Fifty by a white person, which will be paid on conviction.

SAMUEL BONNEAU.

Charleston South-Carolina Gazette and General Advertiser, *January 3 to January 6, 1784.*

RUN AWAY,

In the month of April last, a Negro Woman named CATE, about 4 feet 10 inches, or 5 feet high, of a yellowish complexion, middle aged, was formerly the property of — Whitesides's estate, but lately belonged to Capt. Andrew Quelch, deceased, of Hobcaw, at the sale of the whole estate I purchased him. She has numerous connections in the Parish of Christ-Church, and is very well known. As I have reason to believe she was persuaded to elope by some persons residents in said Parish, I do hereby offer a reward of Ten Guineas to any white person who will prove her being harboured by a white person; and if by a negro, Five Guineas, to be paid on conviction of the offender or offenders. Whoever apprehends said Negro Woman, and delivers her to the Warden of the Sugar-House, in Charlestown, or to the Subscriber in said Parish, shall be entitled to a reward of Two Guineas. If she will return shortly of her own accord, her past offence shall not be noticed.

JOHN H. W. D. SMITH.

Christ-Church Parish,
Dec. 30.

5. Merchant Robert Pringle Observes Life and Trade in Charleston, 1739–1743

TO DAVID GLEN

London

Charles Town, 22nd January 1738/9

SIR:

The above of the 2nd Instant is copy of my Last to which please be Refferr'd & this serves to Convey you the 2nd Bill of Exchange for Twelve pounds Sterling also 2nd Letter of advice. As under you have a List of what Cloaths I have Occasion of from you which I am to Desire may be made in the best manner you can & am in a particular manner to take notice to you they may not be made Scanty but every way Large & full & if too Large may be Remedied, but if too Little or too Scanty can never be made Large. All the Cloaths you have hitherto sent me having been too Little & Scanty for me which hope you'll take Care to prevent for the future. I am also to desire you may send me some Odd Buttons of each Coat you send me, as also what of the Stuff remains as there is no such thing as matching them here & Let all be shipt as soon as Conveniently you can in a Box Directed for me taking a bill of Loading for same vizt. 1. a Horseman's Riding Coat of the Best superfine Drabb of a fashionable Middling Colour, not Light & the Cape not of Velvet, but of the

From Walter B. Edgar, ed., *The Letterbook of Robert Pringle,* © 1972. Reprinted by permission of the University of South Carolina Press.

same Drabb with good neat strong Buttons of Horse hair & send some spare Buttons. 2. a Best superfine Scarlett Broad Cloath Jackett or Waist Coat, full trimm'd & pretty Deep or Long with gold Buttons & a full Lace with Best Gold Lace or gold arras & fashionable, & Lin'd with Scarlett Alepine, & am to desire you'll please send me what Remains of the Lineing to mend same. 3. a Banyan morning gown and made in the same manner as the last you sent me, to weave both sides alike of a very fashionable worsted Damask of the finest & best sort, of a middling Colour not Light, or a gown of any other handsome stuff fashionable & full for a gown butt the two sides be of Different Colours & send me some spare Buttons & Stuff that Remains. 4. A superfine fashionable broad Cloth Fly Coat & Breeches of a Dark Colour Lin'd with deep Bleue Alepine & neat Buttons & please send some spare Button's & the Lineing that remains. 5. Two finest India Dimitty Jacketts Larger & Longer than the two sent me. I hope you'll take particular care in providing me with the above things & send them with your Conveniency so as they may be here toward next fall of the year at least in Eight or nine Months hence at furthest & shall take Care to Remitt your money as soon as I receive your Account. . . .

TO EDWARD & JOHN MAYNE & CO.

Lisbon

Charles Town, 19th September 1740

GENTLEMEN:

The Last I did myself the pleasure to write you was of the 29th April to which please be refferr'd, Since have not the pleasure of any of your favours.

This will be delivered you by Capt. Robert Thompson, Commander of the Snow *Dorsett,* & please receive Inclosed Bill of Loading for a Negro Girl nam'd Esther, which I take the Liberty to Consign to your address by said Capt. Thompson for Sale & Desire you'll please receive her & dispose of her to my best advantage in Case you have not Occassion for her your Self at your House. She is a Very Likely Young Wench & can doe any House Work, such as makeing Beds, Cleaning Rooms, Washing, attending at Table, &c. & talks good English being this Province Born, & is not given to any Vice, & have always found her honest. The only Reason of my sending her off the Province is that she had a practice of goeing frequently to her Father and Mother, who Live at a Plantation I am Concern'd in about Twenty Miles from Town from whence there was no Restraining her from Running away there, & Staying every now & then, which determin'd me to send her off & hope may sell her to good Advantage. She is valued at Twenty pounds Sterling here & hope may be worth as many Moydores with you. However desire you may Sell her Off for the Most you Can. Capt. Thompson has been so Good as to give me Her passage free. He tells me that she is Lyable to a Duty at Lisbon, which he will Likewise Endeavour to Save me and the Neat proceeds of whatever She Sells for, you'll please to Remitt on my Account to my Brother in London.

The Gunpowder you ship'd here per Capt. Trimble on my Brother's Account proves but very indifferent in Quality, which renders it unsaleable haveing as yet been able to Dispose of but very Little of it & what I have is Complain'd of.

We have had fine Seasonable Weather all this Summer, which has produc'd a very Large Crop of Rice & is Reckon'd will be full as much if not more than Last

Crop, which is not yet all Exported and our Planters are now upon their Harvest Cutting down the Rice. There are a pretty many Shipping here at present, especially for this Season of the year, insomuch that Rice has gott up to 45/ per Ct. & Likely to be higher as Shipping arrive. Freight to London at £4 per ton.

A few Days agoe Two of our Privateers brought in here a Spanish prize Value about £2,000 Sterling. . . .

TO WILLIAM PRINGLE

   Antigua

Charles Town, 10th November 1740

SIR:

The last I did myself the pleasure to write you, was of the 19th April last per Capt. Watson, to which please be refferr'd, since have not any of your favours. In my Last I sent you the Account Sales of your Five hhds. Rum, which hope you receiv'd, Neat Proceeds being £275.14.6 this Currency, & not being able to procure a Bill of Exchange for said sum, I sometime agoe order'd my Brother Capt. Andrew Pringle now of London, Merchant to pay to Mr. James Douglass on your Account as you Order'd £32.17.0 Sterling, Exchange being at £800 per 100 Sterling which doubt not will be punctually Comply'd with, & hope you'll soon hear from Mr. Douglas advising of Same being received accordingly. Please receive Inclosed your account Current, Ballance in my favour being 4/3 this Currency which hope you'll find Right & which you'll please to note accordingly.

Rum is pretty high here & also Muscovado Sugar & has been so for sometime past being at 26/ Currency or 2/ Sterling per Gallon & Sugar from £9 to £12 per Ct. & Likely to Continue high if the War Continues.

[335] We have again a large Crop of Rice this Year & are afraid we shall want Shipping to Carry it off.

You have heard no Doubt before this of our very unsuccessfull expedition against St. Augustine which miscarried entirely thro' Generall Oglethorpes bad Conduct in the Affair.

We have no material News here at present all being pretty quiet & no Vessels from Europe for sometime. Shall always be very Glad to have the pleasure of hearing from you & to render you any agreeable Service as will Likewise My Brother in London in Case you may have any Commands there & I remain most respectfully &c.

ADDRESSED: "Per Capt. Drummond"

TO ANDREW PRINGLE

   London

Charles Town, 22nd November 1740

SIR:

My last to you was of the 7th Inst. to which please be refferr'd, & two days ago receiv'd yours very agreeably per Capt. Collcock.

I am now with the utmost Grief & anguish of mind to advise you of the most melancholly & fatal Calamity that has befallen this Town of Charles Town on tuesday the 18th Inst. by fire which broke out about two a Clock afternoon by accident & the wind blowing fresh at North West, it spread it self with that astonishing violence & fierceness that in four hours Time it Consum'd about three hundred dwelling Houses besides a great [338] many stores, some of the Wharfs, & an Immence quantity of Goods & merchandize and if it had not happened to be flowing water most of the Shipping in the Harbour had been likewise destroyed. In the number I am one of the unhappy sufferrers, the top of my House having Catch'd fire, the first in my neighbourhood, about an hour after it first began, altho' then at a great distance from me, & in less than half an hour after it Catch'd was obliged to Quitt it being all in flames, as were then a great part of the Houses on the Bay & all about mine, & by which am a Considerable Sufferer having lost a great part of my houshold furniture, as well as other goods & am likewise heartily Concern'd for yours & Capt. Sanders Share therein but Cannot yet advise what is lost & what not. This much is Certain that a great part of the Cargoe per the *Susannah,* unsold is missing, altho in Endeavouring to save the Goods in the Store, I thereby lost a great part of my Houshold Goods.

My Wife arriv'd from Boston about a fortnight ago, in perfect health & greatly recovered, & desires to be kindly remembered to you. It was owing to her presence of mind that we sav'd any of our household Goods we have, I being below stairs in the Store, seeing the Goods taken out there, my wife run a very great risque, her Cloaths having Catch'd fire before we left the House, & what goods were sav'd, being put on board a Vessel, very narrowly Escap'd being again burnt there with our Lives, before she gott off from the Wharf. I have had the good fortune to save all my Books & papers most of what little plate we had, & Cloaths.

It is inexpressible to relate to you the dismal schene which much surpassed anything I ever saw of that nature & is a vast loss & Calamity to this Province, the best part of this Town being laid in Ashes. But there is now no reflecting. We must Endeavour to look forward & not Backward & if it pleases God to spare me a few Years doubt not of recovering both for you & myself, & am a good deal better off than a great many here, and as there will be a great deal of Building here, Nails of all sorts will be much in demand & Iron Ware of all sorts for Houses & Stores & if you can Indent Two House Carpenters as Servants for four years may be of good Service here. . . .

ADDRESSED: "Per Capt. Langdon & Copie per Capt. Hunt Via Bristoll"

6. Reverend Charles Woodmason Decries the "Wild Peoples" of the Carolina Backcountry, 1768

Sunday, August 7 It is impossible that any Gentleman not season'd to the Clime, could sustain this—It would kill 99 out of 100—Nor is this a Country, or place where I would wish any Gentleman to travel, or settle, altho' Religion and the State requires a Number of Ministers—Their Ignorance and Impudence is so very high,

This document can be found in Richard J. Hooker, *The Carolina Backcountry on the Eve of the Revolution: The Journal and Other Writings of Charles Woodmason, Anglican Itinerant* (Chapel Hill: University of North Carolina Press 1953), pp. 52; 60–61.

as to be past bearing—Very few can read—fewer write—Out of 5000 that have attended Sermon this last Month, I have not got 50 to sign a Petition to the Assembly. They are very Poor—owing to their extreme Indolence for they possess the finest Country in America, and could raise but ev'ry thing. They delight in their present low, lazy, sluttish, heathenish, hellish Life, and seem not desirous of changing it. Both Men and Women will do any thing to come at Liquor, Cloaths, furniture, &c. &c. rather than work for it—Hence their many Vices—their gross Licentiousness Wantonness, Lasciviousness, Rudeness, Lewdness, and Profligacy they will commit the grossest Enormities, before my face, and laugh at all Admonition.

Last Sunday I distributed the last Parcel of Mr. Warings Tracts on Prayer. It is very few families whom I can bring to join in Prayer, because most of them are of various Opinions the Husband a Churchman, Wife, a Dissenter, Children nothing at all. My Bibles and Common Prayers have been long gone, and I have given away to amount of £20 of Practical Books, besides those I received of the Society—Few or no Books are to be found in all this vast Country, beside the Assembly, Catechism, Watts Hymns, Bunyans Pilgrims Progress—Russells—Whitefields and Erskines Sermons. Nor do they delight in Historical Books or in having them read to them, as do our Vulgar in England for these People despise Knowledge. . . .

Saturday, September 3 Many of these People walk 10 or 12 Miles with their Children in the burning Sun—Ought such to be without the Word of God, when so earnest, so desirous of hearing it and becoming Good Christians, and good Subjects! How lamentable to think, that the Legislature of this Province will make no Provision—so rich, so luxurious, polite a People! Yet they are deaf to all Solicitations, and look on the poor White People in a Meaner Light than their Black Slaves, and care less for them. Withal there is such a Republican Spirit still left, so much of the Old Leaven of Lord Shaftsbury and other the 1st principal Settlers still remains, that they seem not at all disposed to promote the Interest of the Church of England—Hence it is that above 30,000£ Sterling have lately been expended to bring over 5 or 6000 Ignorant, mean, worthless, beggarly Irish Presbyterians, the Scum of the Earth, and Refuse of Mankind, and this, solely to ballance the Emigrations of People from Virginia, who are all of the Established Church. . . .

It will require much Time and Pains to New Model and form the Carriage and Manners, as well as Morals of these wild Peoples—Among this Congregation not one had a Bible or Common Prayer—or could join a Person or hardly repeat the Creed or Lords Prayer—Yet all of 'em had been educated in the Principles of our Church. . . .

It would be (as I once observ'd before) a Great Novelty to a Londoner to see one of these Congregations—The Men with only a thin Shirt and pair of Breeches or Trousers on—barelegged and barefooted—The Women bareheaded, barelegged and barefoot with only a thin Shift and under Petticoat—Yet I cannot break [them?] of this—for the heat of the Weather admits not of any [but] thin Cloathing—I can hardly bear the Weight of my Whig and Gown, during Service. The Young Women have a most uncommon Practise, which I cannot break them off. They draw their Shift as tight as possible to the Body, and pin it close, to shew the roundness of their Breasts, and slender Waists (for they are generally finely shaped) and draw their Petticoat close to their Hips to shew the fineness of their Limbs—so that they might as well be in Puri Naturalibus—Indeed Nakedness is not censurable or indecent here, and they expose themselves often quite Naked, without Ceremony—Rubbing themselves and their Hair with Bears Oil and tying it up behind in a Bunch like the Indians—being hardly one degree removed from them—In few Years, I hope to bring about a Reformation, as I already have done in several Parts of the Country.

7. "We Are *Free-Men* . . . Not Born Slaves": Grievances from the Backcountry, 1767

Thus situated and unreliev'd by Government, many among Us have been obliged to punish some of these Banditti and their Accomplices, in a proper Manner—Necessity (that first Principle) compelling them to Do, what was expected that the Executive Branch of the Legislature would *long ago,* have Done.

We are *Free-Men*—British Subjects—Not Born *Slaves*—We contribute our Proportion in all Public Taxations, and discharge our Duty to the Public, equally with our Fellow Provincials Ye[t] We do not participate with them in the Rights and Benefits which they Enjoy, tho' equally Entituled to them.

Property is of no Value, except it be secure: How Ours is secured, appears from the foremention'd Circumstances, and from our now being obliged to defend our Families, by *our own Strength:* As *Legal Methods* are beyond our Reach—or not as yet *extended* to Us.

We may be deem'd too bold in saying *"That the present Constitution of this Province is very defective, and become a Burden, rather than being beneficial to the Back-Inhabitants"*—For Instance—To have but *One* Place of Judicature in this Large and Growing Colony—And that seated *not Central,* but *In a Nook* by the SeaSide—The Back Inhabitants to travel Two, three hundred Miles to carry down Criminals, prosecute Offenders appear as Witnesses (tho' secluded to serve as Jurors) attend the Courts and Suits of Law—The Governour and Court of Ordinary—All Land Matters, and on ev[e]ry Public Occasion are Great Grievances, and call loudly for *Redress* For 'tis not only *Loss of Time* which the poor Settlers sustain therefrom, but the *Toil of Travelling,* and *Heavy-Expences* therefrom arising. Poor Suitors are often driven to Great Distresses, Even to the spending their Last Shilling or to sell their *Only* Horse for to defray their traveling and Town Costs; After which, they are oblig'd to trudge home on foot, and beg for Subsistence by the Way. . . .

Nor can We be said to possess our Legal Rights as Freeholders, when We are so unequally represented in *Assembly*—The South Side of Santee River, electing 44 Members, and the North Side, with these Upper Parts of the Province (containing 2/3 of the White Inhabitants) returning but Six—It is to this Great Disproportion of Representatives on our Part, that our Interests have been so long neglected, and the Back Country disregarded. But it is the Number of *Free Men,* not *Black Slaves,* that constitute the Strength and Riches of a State.

The not laying out the Back Country into Parishes, is another most sensible Greivance. This Evil We apprehend to arise from the Selfish Views of those,

---

This document can be found in Richard J. Hooker, *The Carolina Backcountry on the Eve of the Revolution: The Journal and Other Writings of Charles Woodmason, Anglican Itinerant* (Chapel Hill: University of North Carolina Press 1953), pp. 215; 221–222.

whose Fortune and Estates, are in or near *Charlestown*—which makes them endeavour, That all Matters and Things shall center there, however detrimental to the Body Politic, Hence it arises, That Assemblies are kept setting for six Months, when the Business brought before them might be dispatch'd in six Weeks—to oblige us (against Inclination) to chuse such Persons for Representatives, who live in or contiguous to *Charlestown;* and to render a Seat in the Assembly too heavy a Burden, for any Country Planter, of a small Estate, for to bear. From this our Non-Representation in the House, We conceive it is; That Sixty thousand Pounds Public Money, (of which we must pay the Greater Part, as being levy'd on the Consumer) hath lately been voted, for to build an *Exchange* for the Merchants, and a *Ball-Room* for the Ladies of Charlestown; while near *Sixty thousand* of Us Back Settlers, have not a Minister, or a place of Worship to repair too! As if We were not worth even the Thought off, or deem'd as *Savages,* and not *Christians!*

To leave our Native Countries, Friends, and Relations—the Service of God—the Enjoyment of our Civil and Religious Rights for to breathe here (as We hop'd) a Purer Air of Freedom, and possess the *utmost Enjoyment* of *Liberty,* and *Independency*—And instead hereof, to be set adrift in the Wild Woods among *Indians,* and *Out Casts*—To live in a State of Heathenism—without Law, or Government or even, the *Appearance of Religion*—Expos'd to the Insults of Lawless and Impudent Persons—To the Depredations of *Theives* and *Robbers*—and to be treated by our Fellow Provincials who hold the Reins of Things, as Persons hardly worthy the Public Attention, Not so much as their Negroes:—These Sufferings have broken the Hearts of Hundreds of our New Settlers—Made others quit the Province, some return to *Europe* (and therefrom prevent others coming this Way) and deterr'd Numbers of Persons of Fortune and Character (both at Home, and in *America*) from taking up of Lands here, and settling this our Back Country, as otherwise they would have done.

⅃ E S S A Y S

Historian Lorena Walsh, who has written extensively on the colonial Chesapeake, shows in the first essay how crop cultivation shaped the lives of slaves. Planters purchased slaves to perform demanding labor and concentrated them where they were most needed. Because slave imports tended to be heavily male, it took decades to create a gender balance and for slaves to form families and for their population to increase through reproduction. Seasonal demands affected slaves' daily lives and the type of work they performed. Walsh also argues that the addition of a second system of agriculture based on grain production affected slavery. In the second essay, Jack Greene reminds us that colonies developed at different paces and that not all were fully mature by the mid-eighteenth century. As the last and largest colony to be settled, Georgia was founded with high expectations. It seemed to be a land of promise where settlers could avoid a frivolous pursuit of wealth and self-interest. Despite its ordered settlement and efforts to avoid earlier problems elsewhere, initial euphoria was dampened by malcontents who wanted Georgia to be on an equal footing with other colonies. Making a commitment to slave labor sacrificed the initial ideals but promised economic success for the colony.

How Tobacco Production Shaped
Slave Life in the Chesapeake

LORENA S. WALSH

Tobacco shaped the seventeenth- and early eighteenth-century Chesapeake. "Tobacco is our meat, drinke, cloathing and monies," Hugh Jones wrote in 1699. Thirty years later Benedict Leonard Calvert affirmed, "Tobacco, as our staple, is our all, and Indeed leaves no room for anything else." The requirements of tobacco culture influenced everything from agricultural techniques and the yearly agricultural calendar, to types of housing, to settlement patterns and urban development (or the lack thereof), to the occupational structure and networks of trade and credit. Scholars have paid much attention to the links between the staple and white society, economy, and even mentality. However, although tobacco and slaves have been judged sufficiently intertwined to serve as the title of a recent book on the Chesapeake between 1680 and 1800, the intimate connections between the staple and slave society have been less intensively studied. The original sources, moreover, tell the story from the viewpoint of slaveowners—and mostly large ones at that. Shifting the perspective to that of the slaves is thus a challenging task.

Tobacco, more than anything else, brought black people to the Chesapeake. Planters by and large turned slaveholders when the supply of white indentured servants dwindled, providing too few new field hands for a revolving-door labor system that required a constant influx of workers. Once slavery was established, the price of tobacco determined the shape of the slave trade. Surges in slave imports tended—especially in the first half of the eighteenth century—to coincide with booms in the tobacco market, as had earlier peaks in migration of indentured servants. When the tobacco market was good, planters wanted to expand production and had the cash or could get credit to purchase new workers. As Norfolk merchant Charles Stewart noted early in the 1750s, "Our planters have had great prices for their Tobacco these late years, and are full of Cash, which nothing but Negroes will draw forth, . . . the planters having left room in their Crops" for additional slaves.

Since tobacco also influenced where slaves would live once they entered the region, it eventually determined the racial demography of the Chesapeake. There was less need for extra field hands in places like the lower Delmarva peninsula and the southside of the lower James River that had little good tobacco land. In addition, planters in these areas tended to be poorer, making them an unpromising market for human chattels. Slave ships therefore disgorged their merchandise in the places where rich planters who were expanding their labor forces were most numerous. As a result, slaves were concentrated in prime tidewater tobacco areas in the first quarter of the eighteenth century. By mid-century, most large tidewater planters no longer needed to buy additional workers; natural increase among their slaves supplied any extra hands they required. Then, as westward expansion into the piedmont accelerated, slaves migrated to or were sold at the outset in areas of expanding tobacco culture. After the Revolution, slavery expanded chiefly in the western

"Slave Life, Slave Society, and Tobacco Production in the Tidewater Chesapeake, 1620–1820," by Lorena Walsh from *Cultivation and Culture: Labor and the Shaping of Slave Life in the Americas,* edited by Ira Berlin and Philip D. Morgan © 1993. Reprinted with permission of the University Press of Virginia.

piedmont of Virginia where—unlike in much of the tidewater, the Shenandoah valley, and western Maryland—tobacco remained the mainstay of the regional economy. A combination of slave migration westward and white out-migration resulted by 1810 in high concentrations of black people in those areas of the Chesapeake that remained most committed to tobacco.

That many slaves lived alone or in small residential groups resulted from several circumstances, including the disease environment, sex ratios among imported slaves, and slaveowners' purchasing patterns and inheritance practices. In the seventeenth and early eighteenth centuries slaves encountered a harsh disease environment and suffered high rates of mortality. Among imported slaves men outnumbered women by roughly two to one, so that many men were unable to find wives and form families. African-born slave women were generally too sick or too alienated to begin bearing children until some time after they arrived in the Chesapeake. And, while a handful of grandees bought dozens of slaves at a time, most tobacco planters wealthy enough to buy slaves could afford to purchase only one or two per year. As the slave population in older areas changed from largely immigrant to native born and—in the second quarter of the eighteenth century—began to grow by natural increase, its demography became more normal. Still, residence groups remained small, in part because slaveholders tended to divide slaves among several heirs and in part because of the dispersed settlement pattern dictated by the requirements of tobacco culture.

The persistence of small work and residence units into the nineteenth century resulted directly from the nature of the staple. Good tobacco soils occur in small plots scattered over the Chesapeake landscape. In order to make the most of the best soils and to maintain the long fallows necessary to restore soil fertility, small slaveholders tended to limit work forces in keeping with the long-term capacity of their farms. Large landowners, who were usually also some of the largest slaveowners, dispersed laborers among outlying quarters near the home farm or else on more distant holdings.

In addition to the limitations imposed by soil properties, there were few economies of scale in tobacco culture. Two or three workers could tend and harvest the crop more efficiently than one. Beyond this, however, successful tobacco culture required careful attention to a host of details throughout the growing season and during the subsequent harvesting and processing. Ordinarily overseers could supervise no more than ten working hands, and even the most skillful laboring slaveowners or estate agents no more than twenty. Consequently, while the size of slave work and residential units increased over time, with small quarters of one to five slaves becoming rarer, only at the great houses of the rich, were laborers pursued a variety of craft and diversified agricultural activities, could slaves expect to live together in large groups. Over time, too, as the numbers of slaves in older areas increased, the chances for socialization between and family formation among adjacent plantations multiplied. Nonetheless, tobacco culture continued to impose a high degree of residential isolation.

Tobacco cultivation gave rise to a pattern of work both familiar and unfamiliar. Many features of early Chesapeake agriculture—especially hoe culture and long fallows—would have been familiar to farming peoples in any place where men and women were few and land plenty. The marked emphasis on production of a cash crop for distant, international markets, however, was probably less familiar. In most traditional societies, people use the labor time saved in raising sufficient food by extensive rather than intensive cultivation techniques for home manufactures and for various leisure activities—whereas Chesapeake planters devoted most of the extra labor time to producing tobacco.

Seventeenth-century Chesapeake planters—both slaveless farmers and those with bound laborers, whether servants or slaves— exploited land, which was abundant and cheap, and sought to make the most of labor, which was scarce and dear. In the process of learning how to survive in an often hostile environment and finding a staple that they could exchange for imports, colonists developed a new system of husbandry. Abandoning most European agricultural practices, planters adopted girdling or slash-and-burn clearing, long fallows, and hoe culture from local native Americans, as well as embracing maize and tobacco. The Europeans' main innovations were the introduction of domestic livestock and the use of metal tools. At first they concentrated on maximum production of tobacco from fresh lands. The annual work cycle was almost wholly shaped by the seasonal demands of tobacco, which required constant attention throughout most of the year. Production of food crops— primarily maize—was usually limited to the requirements of self-sufficiency, and almost all essential manufactured items imported. Until the last quarter of the seventeenth century, small farmers, who often owned a few indentured servants, were the major producers. Then, as the supply of European servants dwindled, richer planters turned to slaves as the primary source of bound labor. Large plantations (by Chesapeake standards) became more common, and wealth among whites more concentrated. Slaves produced an increasing proportion of the region's cash crop.

This initial system of Chesapeake agriculture, modified and diversified as settlements matured, would be repeated throughout the region as frontiers expanded. Although condemned as wasteful and inefficient, it saved labor, the scarcest resource, while exploiting the richness of virgin land in the short run. Planters rotated fields rather than crops, working only a small amount of land each year. Long fallows of about twenty years that followed six to eight years of cultivation preserved much of the long-term fertility of the soil, while hill and hoe culture prevented serious erosion. As a result, there was little resource depletion before 1775, although abandoned old fields that reverted to natural vegetation made the landscape unsightly to European eyes. For Africans, native Americans, and creole planters, though, these cultivation practices simply reflected common sense.

The system was successful, and everywhere tobacco output per laborer increased through 1690. The amount of tobacco one worker could produce in a single growing season rose from around three hundred pounds in the 1620s to over a thousand by the 1650s and 1660s, and in some places over two thousand pounds in the 1670s and 1680s. . . . Output rose because, over the first three quarters of the century, planters learned how to handle more tobacco plants per worker and developed improved plant strains. They also made improvements in curing and packing the crop. Through 1675 these increases in output were accompanied by decreasing costs for food, clothing, and tools, and for transportation and distribution of the crop. These savings allowed planters to continue to make a profit despite falling tobacco prices. But in order to profit handsomely, planters needed more workers. As the supply of European servants dwindled, they turned increasingly to slaves to remedy the labor shortage.

The productivity of tobacco slaves was related to the ways workers resisted enslavement, their health, the weather, local natural resources, the managerial skills of owners and overseers, and differing techniques of crop management. In the late seventeenth and early eighteenth centuries output per laborer varied widely from farm to farm. A spate of bad growing seasons and, in some places, experiments with high-quality but lower-yielding strains caused drops of output per worker that had little to do with the composition of the labor force. But slave sickness, resistance, and alienation also lowered productivity on occasion. African slaves had little incentive to work diligently for their captors, and many planters and overseers did not know how to motivate them. From the outset Africans in the Chesapeake certainly resisted enslavement, but little evidence survives about the particular means they employed. Methods of resistance may have included refusing to work, running away, real or feigned misunderstanding of commands given in English, or simply denying the authority of their owners. Some slaves resisted the new regime strenuously; others could not or would not work hard. Some suffered harsh punishments as a result, while others—who appeared too sickly ever to become useful workers—were left to do whatever work they would, with minimal supervision and minimal care. Many black men and women perished in an unhealthy environment and climate colder than that to which they were accustomed, and many more were periodically or chronically ill. Some of the early tidewater plantations were located in particularly disease-prone places. The histories of individual farms show a link between low productivity per worker in both the cash crop (tobacco) and the subsistence crop (maize) on the one hand, and an unhealthy location, heightened slave resistance, and unsatisfactory performance and frequent turnover among overseers on the other.

Nonetheless, the switch from predominantly servant to predominantly slave labor did raise productivity on the majority of plantations, just as slave buyers had hoped. Output per worker peaked during the years in which the proportion of slaves in the bound labor force rose to half or more. More general estimates of output per worker that aggregate information from the entire region do not show this rise, but estimates broken down by subregions, or better yet, by country, confirm this pattern. . . . Black slaves, not white servants, made most of the largest individual crops recorded, and most of these efficient workers were Africans, not creoles. African slaves arrived in the right places at the right time to exploit fresh lands for their owners. Planters could get new fields cleared more readily and thus expand their scale of operation. The initial preponderance of men among new slaves raised the proportion of prime laborers in the agricultural work force, and hence average crop sizes.

Planters also found new ways to exploit the strange new workers. So long as white servants made up most of the labor force, English work customs tended to prevail in the Chesapeake, customs that had evolved where there was a surplus of workers and a shortage of work. A climate in which summers were hotter and winters colder than in Britain also encouraged rest breaks in heat and slack times in cold. In the seventeenth-century Chesapeake, the workday ran from sunrise to sunset, but even during the growing season field laborers were permitted a rest in the heat of the day and given Saturday afternoon and various traditional holidays off. Little work was done in winter, aside from hunting, cutting firewood, preparing meals, and packing tobacco. So long as African slaves were few and intermingled with European servants, work rules designed for white laborers probably also applied to black ones.

But once slaves came to dominate the bound labor force late in the seventeenth century, the experiences of slaves and servants diverged. Slaves had no claim to English workers' customary rights: food of reasonable quantity and quality, adequate clothing and shelter, and a certain amount of rest and leisure. Granted, slaveowners were unlikely to starve their expensive workers or to provide insufficient clothing or shelter, and planters frequently condemned those who failed to meet certain generally agreed upon standards, realizing that heightened slave resistance was a likely consequence. In 1732 William Byrd II encountered some badly provisioned slaves: "The poor Negroes upon [Colonel Jones's plantations] are a kind of Adamites, very scantily supplied with clothes and other necessaries. . . . However, they are even with their master and make him but indifferent crops, so that he gets nothing by his injustice but the scandal of it." Nonetheless, in order to raise profits, slaveholders economized wherever possible with rations, clothing, bedding, and housing. They made little attempt to understand or to accommodate the blacks' preferences in diet or clothing, and they housed their slaves in small, insubstantial, and exceedingly cheap huts.

More significantly, planters began imposing new, more stringent work routines. First, the number of workdays was increased. By about 1730 holidays were reduced to three a year—Christmas, the duration of this holiday being left to the master's discretion, and three days each at Easter and Whitsuntide. In addition, for almost all slaves Saturday became a full workday, and the same rule began to be applied to servants. Even Sundays were far from inviolate, although, with time, slaveowners found it prudent to compensate slaves for Sunday work with extra food or a little cash. (In the early eighteenth century slaveowners seem to have regarded a Sunday free of work as enjoined merely by their own religious sensibilities, but by mid-century the slaves had converted that practice into a right that could not be violated arbitrarily.) Slaves also had to respond to any situation the master declared to be an emergency. The slaves' workday, furthermore, was often extended into the night. Night work probably originated with the need to beat corn into meal with mortars and pestles daily. In the 1650s the Maryland provincial court ruled that a master could not keep his white servants in the fields so long that they must beat corn for their victuals at night. By the late 1670s, as slaves became more numerous, a traveler noted that "the servants and negroes after they have worn themselves down the whole day, and come home to rest, have yet to grind and pound the grain, which is generally maize, for their masters and all their families as well as themselves, and all the negroes, to eat."

Slave women in the Chesapeake performed the same field labor as did slave men. In the seventeenth century, labor-short planters were also putting some white servant women to work at the hoe, albeit with a certain ambivalence about the types of work proper for servant women. Once slaves predominated in the labor force, however, white women servants all but disappeared from the fields. In contrast, every able-bodied slave woman and most slave girls aged twelve or more did regular field labor. Men and women toiled together at the same tasks in a single work group, and work requirements were the same for both sexes. When rating laborers as full or partial hands, planters made allowances for youth, disability, or advanced age but made no distinctions by sex. Most planters had too few slaves to divide their work force into men's and women's gangs, but even those who could divide their workers did not, at least until the middle of the eighteenth century. Before that time, any productivity increases that a division of the work force by sex might have created—an intensification of the pace of work in men's gangs, for example—were insufficient to offset the extra cost of supervising two gangs, or, more likely, to offset the drop in efficiency that would certainly occur when one overseer had to divide his attention between two groups.

New customs evolved that governed work relations between masters and slaves, but these were specific to individual plantations. Slaves had no legal rights, as did servants, that courts might enforce. Plantation custom still defined the amount of work expected, the standard weekly food ration, and the kind and amount of new clothing to be provided each year. The work requirements might be harsh and the provisions scanty, but once minimums and maximums were set, slaves had some hedge against further exploitation. They could protest increased work demands, lack of sufficient food and clothing, or curtailment of privileges by appealing to their owners' or former owners' past practices or to current practices on neighboring plantations. If these arguments failed, they had to resort to work slowdowns, feigned illness, or running away. A few resisted violations of custom through direct, sometimes violent, confrontation with the offending owner or overseer, almost invariably suffering punishment as a result.

Whenever a new overseer attempted to change current privileges or work routines, the importance of customary practice became evident. Slaves resisted unfavorable changes, while the overseers' complaint was almost always that the slaves had become accustomed to doing too little work or were accustomed to working as they pleased. There was, then, a continuing contest about work requirements and about who would set the pace and determine the intensity of that work. Some slaveowners recognized that the more they allowed custom to define plantation work relations, the less their flexibility to make changes. Accordingly, they attempted to limit their slaves' ability to develop customary privileges and to control the work pace by changing overseers frequently—although incompetence on the part of the overseers or the irascibility of the slaveowners themselves sometimes produced the same result. Plantation records demonstrate that this was bad policy. Slaves usually expressed less open discontent and consistently made bigger crops on those quarters where overseers had long tenures. Indeed, by the early nineteenth century a candidate for a vacant overseer's post would solicit the job by promising not to interfere with whatever privileges the slaves had enjoyed under the previous overseer.

Planters who owned bound laborers in the early eighteenth century sought to cut costs and to intensify labor requirements because they faced growing economic difficulties. They were caught between trade disruptions, rising costs of production, and diminishing tobacco yields. After the 1690s in all the older settled areas, tobacco output per laborer—and thus income from the major cash crop—began to fall, since tobacco prices remained low. The decline, which occurred well after slaves predominated in the unfree labor force, was a consequence of the interaction of changing populations with natural resources. Nonslaveowners, who generally had a growing number of dependent children in their households and who often farmed poorer quality land, experienced the same decline as did slaveowners. Some drop in tobacco output per full-time worker was an inevitable result of diminishing returns to available natural resources. Even prime fields, recultivated after a long fallow, failed to yield as well as virgin clearings, and over time, if they did not move somewhere else, planters began cropping more marginal, lower-yielding lands. As settlements matured, limits were soon reached on the amount of tobacco a worker—slave or free—could tend and consequently the size of crop he or she could produce. Only in the twentieth century, when chemical fertilizers became available, did tidewater tobacco growers achieve higher outputs per worker than they had between 1670 and 1700. Moreover, once slaves began to form couples and have offspring, more black women and children joined the labor force. Women and teenagers, although counted as full field hands, could not produce as much tobacco as prime-aged men, which again [led] to a drop in average crop size.

During the eighteenth century tobacco planters adopted several strategies to counter diminishing returns. When they could farm fresh land extensively, planters realized high outputs per person-hour. Once output per hour declined, ever more labor had to be expended in order to maintain returns. Farmers without slaves had either to work harder or accept a lower standard of living. Slaveowners sought to extract more work from their slaves. Since they could no longer expand tobacco output per worker, they added other kinds of activities that cut costs or generated additional revenues. These strategies included some on-farm production or local purchase of goods like coarse shoes, cloth, and basic tools to replace costly imports. In some parts of Virginia tobacco was further processed before export, adding to its value but increasing off-season work. Most slaveowners also added maize and wheat as major revenue crops. By making these changes, planters realized relatively stable revenues per worker, in constant value, across the whole colonial period. Evidence from individual farms suggests that the annual gross revenue per hand from the major field crops was roughly £15 sterling constant value from the 1640s to the early 1680s, then probably fell to about £10 from about 1680 to 1740, but rose again to around £15 in the third quarter of the eighteenth century. Slaves suffered disproportionately, since it was primarily their leisure that was sacrificed in the planters' drive to counter diminishing returns to the staple. . . .

While tobacco remained the regional staple in all the parts of the Chesapeake except the lower James basin and lower Delmarva peninsula, grains became a more significant part of the agricultural mix. Beginning in some places in the 1720s and more generally by the 1730s, planters—especially large and middling slaveowners—responded to growing markets for grain in Europe and the West Indies by producing surpluses of corn and wheat. Throughout the Chesapeake grain production per worker rose from the 1730s onwards. . . . Everywhere maize crops reached ten or more barrels per hand, a level of deliberate market production where about half of the crop was marketable surplus. Wheat output per laborer varied greatly between regions, reflecting the low yields per acre most planters could effect with poor plows, weak draft animals, and on acid soils. The labor demands of corn and tobacco also limited the amount of land planters could cultivate in wheat. However, even small crops of wheat raised market income since, unlike maize (much of which was consumed on the plantation), about 90 percent of the wheat crop net of seed was sold.

The addition of grains to the crop mix was, however, not easily accomplished. A major constraint on increased grain production throughout the period was inadequate livestock forage. If planters were to raise more grain per hand, they had to make greater use of plows, and they also needed more manure for fertilizer. And if they were going to pen stock and employ draft animals, they had either to grow or buy extra maize, fodder, hay, or cultivated grasses to feed the penned and especially the working animals. Many planters managed nothing beyond collecting and storing corn fodder more assiduously. Pasture improvement required a lot of extra work and hay a delicate meshing of seasonal schedules, since the wheat and hay harvests conflicted. Because of these constraints, many planters were slow to substitute plows for hoes. In a number of areas plows were far from universal farm equipment until the 1790s, and scarcity of forage remained a serious problem even in 1820. Plow culture supplanted the hoe more quickly in the piedmont than in the tidewater. There planters often succeeded in negotiating agreements with overseers, whereby the planters retained an extra share of corn and wheat crops in return for supplying plow teams.

Scholars have generally failed to appreciate the forage constraint and have concluded in consequence that Chesapeake cultivation techniques were backward because slaves were poor workers who abused draft animals and who were unwilling or unable to use plows properly. Plantation records and planter correspondence do suggest that slaves were often careless with their owners' tools and that they appropriated part of the corn that was supposed to feed the stock. But planters and overseers generally agreed that draft animals performed poorly because they had insufficient food, and there is little to suggest that slaves consistently mistreated them. Neither did planters trust only native, more acculturated slaves with plows and carts. In two very old tidewater counties—York, Virginia, and St. Mary's, Maryland—only about half of all planters who left inventories owned plows in the 1770s. While slaves had arrived in number in both counties by the 1660s and had become self-reproducing around 1700, planters in both areas concentrated on hand-cultivated tobacco and made minimal use of plows, even when they grew extra corn or wheat. In contrast, in Kent and Talbot counties on Maryland's upper eastern shore, planters began to shift into wheat culture in the late 1720s. By the 1730s the majority of inventoried farmers and almost all the big slaveowners employed plows, although these counties developed later than either York or St. Mary's. Few planters acquired slaves until the 1690s, and large numbers of Africans were sold on the eastern shore in the 1710s and 1720s. Slaves, whatever their origins, began using plows consistently when and where planters began raising wheat as a major cash crop.

In short, planters developed a second system of agriculture that depended on the plow to produce surplus corn and wheat. Albeit gradually in many places, these alterations to the Chesapeake system of husbandry had profound implications for slave work routines. Work patterns changed most on large plantations, for it was big slaveowners who took the lead in adopting the plow. So long as laborers employed hoes alone to prepare land for planting, the possibility of expanding grain production was limited: no more crops could be grown than hills to grow them on could be prepared. Plowing released labor time by speeding planting in spring and weeding during the growing season, thus enabling planters to double the production of corn.

The extra corn could in turn be fed to the animals that pulled the plows and, when penned, produced manure for fertilizing, again increasing yields of corn and tobacco. Plowing was also essential for the expanded production of wheat, a crop that interfered less with the seasonal requirements of tobacco than did corn. The land could be prepared in off-seasons, and the grain seeded and plowed or harrowed in after the tobacco was harvested and before the corn needed gathering. Planters required extra labor only for the short harvest, and wheat growers had no difficulty hiring free whites or slaves belonging to planters who did not grow much grain. Consequently, slaves on large plantations cultivated more acres per worker and spent more time plowing and raising grains than did slaves on small plantations where hoe-cultivated tobacco remained the major crop.

In addition to increased use of plows and manure, a second source of greater productivity came from greater exploitation of the work force. In the first three quarters of the seventeenth century, most bound laborers did not usually work after dark, and only sporadically in winter. As planters increased total crop output, they first eliminated a number of holidays and free Saturday afternoons. Gradually they increased requirements for night work, until by the middle of the eighteenth century slaves were often made to strip tobacco or husk corn by firelight, and planters sometimes whipped those who failed to complete their allotted task. Winter work intensified as well. As markets for timber and casks in the West Indies and the Wine Islands expanded and localized urban demand for firewood and lumber developed, more timber was cut and carted in winter. Small grains, threshed out immediately after harvest if possible, remained to be winnowed and the seed picked over in the off-season. Some began harvesting early spring runs of shad and herring with seines. Planters who wished to improve their lands found this an optimal period for grubbing swamps and cleaning pastures. The agricultural year was filled, with slaves fully employed the year round.

When planters first ventured into diversification at the turn of the eighteenth century, the work patterns of laboring whites changed much more than did those of slaves. Initially, white men and women undertook most of the new or expanded skilled tasks, while slave men and women were kept at work in the fields. Free or indentured white men did almost all the artisanal work, such as shoemaking, coopering, smithing, and wagon making. The planter's wife, along with white women servants, did most of the domestic work and dairying. Around the middle of the century, however, the level of home industry increased markedly, and work patterns changed for everyone. With few European servant women entering the colonies, the planter's wife and his daughters—at least in slaveowning families—spent more time at the domestic production of fibers and at sewing, candle molding, butter making, and the like for their own families.

Slaves, especially those on large plantations, also began to experience a marked increase in the sexual division of labor. The new crops and routines required new tasks that were both varied and often involved some degree of skill—sowing and mowing grain, plowing, harrowing, carting, ditching, lumbering, fishing, and milling, for example. These new jobs fell primarily to slave men. By the end of the century men were thus performing a greater variety of tasks, and even on large plantations they sometimes worked on special projects by themselves or with only one or two mates, and not always under constant supervision. The great majority of slave women, however, did not share in the new opportunities, and probably lost considerably from agricultural change. A few became more involved in textile production and house service than in earlier years. However, poor free white women, especially spinsters and widows, did much of the spinning, weaving, and sewing that slaveowners needed done, while others worked as waged housekeepers. The great majority of black women continued to perform unskilled manual field labor, such as hand hoeing and weeding, and more often without the help of their menfolk. The new jobs assigned to slave women (or the old jobs formerly shared with men) included many of the least desirable chores: building fences, grubbing swamps, cleaning winnowed grain, breaking up new ground too rough or weedy to plow, cleaning stables, and loading and spreading manure. On large plantations, the work of slave women was less varied than that of the men, and they often labored together in gangs under the direct supervision of an overseer.

Planters who adopted these practices considered themselves to be improving farmers. Some acknowledged that they had developed a new system of Chesapeake agriculture; others believed that they had adopted a course of "English husbandry," although this was far from the case. For a time, plow technology, the use of manure, and intensified grain culture—grafted onto traditional, long-fallow tobacco growing—raised total agricultural productivity. In part, farmers were responding to the harsh critiques of both European observers and native agrarian reformers of their supposedly primitive system of agriculture. In larger measure, they were also responding to changing market incentives. Between 1750 and 1775, while relative prices of wheat and tobacco oscillated, there was no clear trend in favor of one crop over the other, and most large planters raised both, but by 1775 planters had to make new choices, as the second system of Chesapeake agriculture was losing its viability. Population densities in the tidewater had reached a level at which there was not enough land available to rotate crops in long fallow, allowing for the forty to fifty acres required for each laborer. Diminishing yields were inevitable without some change in either crop mix or cultivation techniques. Shifts in the relative prices of tobacco and grain after 1775—accompanied by European wars which closed major continental markets and made tobacco an exceedingly risky market crop—also encouraged a shift from tobacco to grain. Even if the American Revolution had not occurred, population growth would have forced basic alterations in agricultural practices. The nature of that war and the economic depression that followed pushed planters into particularly destructive kinds of change.

Georgia's Attempt to Become a Viable Colony

JACK P. GREENE

In contrast to many other early modern British-American colonies, the settlers of Georgia from its very beginning had an unusually clear sense of what they hoped to do. Indeed, it is probable that no other early modern British colony began with a

From *Imperatives, Behaviors, and Identities* by Jack Greene, © 1992, pp. 113–142. Reprinted with permission of the University Press of Virginia.

more fully articulated set of goals. These goals were revealed in an extensive promotional literature that in volume probably exceeded that for any of the earlier
colonies, except possibly Virginia and Pennsylvania. Georgia was the first entirely
new British colony founded in America since Pennsylvania almost fifty years before and the last until the establishment of East and West Florida and several new island colonies in the West Indies at the close of the Seven Years' War. Not since the
founding of England's first colony in Virginia at the beginning of the seventeenth
century had the establishment of any colony attracted so much public attention in
Britain or such wide public support, the extent of which was indicated not only by
large private contributions but by an unprecedented outlay of government funds.

In some ways, the initial projections for Georgia do not appear very different
from those for most other colonies. Like most of its predecessors, Georgia was intended to enhance the power and wealth of the British nation and to provide an outlet
and a field of opportunity for the unfortunate, the persecuted, and the adventurous of
the Old World. Its specific strategic role as a barrier to render the increasingly valuable but black colony of South Carolina "safe from Indians and other enemies," particularly the Spanish in Florida, was not unlike that foreseen for Jamaica in the 1650s
and New York and the Carolinas in the 1660s. Ever since the establishment of Virginia, moreover, colonies had been seen as "Asylum[s] to receive the Distressed,"
and, especially since the founding of the Carolinas, New Jersey, and Pennsylvania
during the last half of the seventeenth century, they had been promoted as places of
religious refuge, where besieged and "distressed Protestants" from the continent of
Europe could find "Liberty of Conscience and a free Exercise of Religion."

Similarly, Georgia's depiction in the promotional literature as a land of
promise, a new Eden, was not significantly different from the early portraits of
other colonies in regions south of New England. With a warm, temperate climate
and rich soil, which required "slight" husbandry and little work to yield a rich abundance, Georgia was presented as a place where the settlers could easily achieve both
prosperity and contentment. Not only would its "fertile lands" and generous climate
yield up all of the crops and other commodities produced in South Carolina, including corn, grains, rice, livestock, naval stores, and deerskins, it also promised to be
suitable for the production of flax, hemp, and potash, which Britain then imported
in substantial quantities from Russia. Most important, because it occupied "about
the same latitude with part of China, Persia, Palestine, and the Made[i]ras," it was
"highly probable," Georgia's promoters predicted, that as soon as the new colony
was "well peopled and rightly cultivated," it would supply Britain with many of the
exotic products—"raw silk, wine, [olive] oil, dies, drugs, and many other materials"—which it then had to purchase at vast expense from other "Southern Countries." Because it already had "white mulberry-trees [growing] wild, and in great
abundance," silk, the production of which was "so Easy a work that Every Person
from Childhood to old Age can be Serviceable therein," would, it was thought, be to
Georgia what sugar was to Barbados and Jamaica, tobacco to Virginia and Maryland, and rice to South Carolina. Georgians at the same time would grow prosperous through such easy and potentially profitable productions and contribute to the
prosperity and power of the entire Anglophone world.

Nor until they had succeeded in such enterprises would Georgians have to
worry much about either sustenance or defense, "difficulties" that had frequently

"attended the planting" of earlier colonies. Just across the Savannah River, South Carolina abounded with cattle, grain, and other provisions that would be easily and cheaply available to feed the settlers of the new colony until they could support themselves. And although they would have to be on guard against the treacherous Spaniards, they had little to fear from Indians. Unlike both Virginians and Carolinians in their early days, Georgians would be "in no danger" from the Indians, whose numbers had so "greatly decreased" over recent decades that they "live[d] in perfect amity with the English." Such a safe and "fine Land . . . in a Temperate Climate" that would yield "a vast variety of Productions fit for the Benefit of Trade and Comfort of Life" was obviously "capable of great improvements." The colony's promoters assured potential supporters and settlers that the newcomers "must in a few Years be a flourishing and happy People." Like Pennsylvania, which a mere fifty years earlier had been "as much a forest as Georgia is now, and in those few years, by . . . wise economy . . . now gives food to 80,000 Inhabitants, and can boast of as fine a City as most in Europe," Georgia could not fail to grow into "a mighty Province."

But the trustees had no intention of permitting this extraordinary promise to be frittered away in the egocentric pursuit of wealth. They knew that many earlier colonies had been undertaken with the best of intentions and the most elaborate plans and that in every one, with the possible exceptions of the orthodox Puritan colonies of New England, the plans of the organizers had quickly given way before the uncontrollable pursuit of self-interest. Placing their own welfare over all social concerns, the colonists had settled in a pell-mell and dispersed fashion, monopolized as much land as they could, and done everything possible to enhance their own private wealth. With their small white populations, legions of dangerous and discontented slaves, and large concentrations of land in the hands of a few proprietors, South Carolina and Jamaica were exactly what Georgia's organizers were determined that it would never become. Having learned from the mistakes of earlier promoters, the trustees were determined that Georgia would be "founded upon Maxims different from those on which other Colonies have been begun."

The Georgia plan as devised by the trustees was less a throwback to seventeenth-century ventures than a preview of the later doctrines of "systematic colonization" advocated by Edward Gibbon Wakefield and others for the settlement of Australia and New Zealand in the 1830s and 1840s. In contrast to such places as Jamaica and South Carolina, Georgia was to be "a regular Colony," by which its promoters meant "methodical; orderly," "agreeable to rule," "instituted . . . according to established forms of discipline," "constituent with the mode prescribed," and "governed by strict regulations." . . .

As one looks more deeply into the Georgia plan, it becomes obvious that it was designed to avoid not only the mistakes of earlier colonies but the contemporary social evils of Britain as well. As is well known, Georgia was conceived as a charitable trust that would employ a combination of lightly occupied land between the Savannah and the Altamaha rivers, the private contributions of the benevolent in Britain, and public funds to relieve the nation's growing population of the impoverished and the imprisoned. Hence the founding of the colony was widely heralded in Britain as an act of beneficence by which "many families who would otherwise starve" would "be provided for & made masters of houses and lands," and many other unfortunates then languishing in prison would be once again rendered useful to the nation. That this charitable assistance would also free the British public from some of the economic burdens of poor relief was also a consideration. Contemporary cynics could dismiss this aspect of the Georgia enterprise as a clever device to get the poor and the imprisoned out of the country and off the public charge: to rephrase the old aphorism, out of sight, out of mind—and not out of pocket.

But the impulse behind the founding of Georgia obviously went far deeper than such expedient calculations. Established during what one contemporary social critic called "the very age of retention, [an age] in which every man's benevolence is centered in himself, and publick spirit is absorbed by private interest," Georgia was to be not just a model colony but a model society for Britain, a mirror or counterimage that would stand as both a reaffirmation of old values and a repudiation of the baser tendencies then rampant in British life. For throughout the first half of the eighteenth century, one social commentator after another sounded the theme that Britain's rising wealth and growing involvement in an expanding and volatile money economy were the primary sources of the blatant social miseries that Georgia was in part designed to relieve. These developments, critics asserted, had produced not only a decline in virtue and other traditional English values but social evils unknown to earlier generations. As the rich grew ever richer and wallowed in more and more luxury, it seemed, the gap between rich and poor grew ever wider, poverty increased, the number of poor in workhouses, poorhouses, and prisons rose dramatically, and private virtue and public spirit fell victim to a deluge of possessive individualism and a riot of self-indulgence. . . .

Georgia may thus have become a great national undertaking not only because of the growing appreciation of the worth of colonies and a desire to enhance the wealth and power of the nation but also because it spoke directly—and positively— to some of the British elite's deepest social anxieties. If Georgia could prove that the habits and character of such "miserable objects" as the poor and the indebted could, under proper regulations, be reformed and such people given a new sense of purpose and self-worth, there was still hope for Britain itself. The "example of a whole Colony" behaving "in a just, moral and religious manner" would, it was hoped, strike a blow against profligacy throughout the entire Anglophone world. Georgia could become a model, indeed, the inspiration, for Britain's own social salvation. As the patrons and promoters of such a glorious enterprise, the trustees became national social heroes, and James Oglethorpe was lionized for his selfless patriotism and public spirt. "That a Gentleman of his Fortune possessed of a Large and Valuable Acquaintance[,] a Seat in Parliament, with the Genius to make a Figure in any Senate in the World, Should renounce all these Pleasures to cross a perilous Ocean for the Sake of establishing a few distressed families undone by Idleness, Intemperance, Sickness, with other ill habits and all Oppressed with Poverty, to Found a Colony in a Wilderness wholly uncultivated," was, declared one observer, "one of the greatest pieces of Self Denial this Age has afforded."

For more than a decade, people hoped that this ambitious enterprise would succeed in its original design. Indeed, for the first few years, reports from the colony were largely encouraging. "A very pleasant country" with a "good . . . climate" that, one visitor noted, would produce, "with God's blessing, everything which grows in the

West Indies" and afforded "the opportunity of cultivating olives, grapes, and silk," Georgia seemed to be a "great success." Despite some sickness and predictable intemperance and disobedience on the part of a few of the settlers, Oglethorpe reported to the trustees eleven months after the arrival of the first settlers that the colony had "increased and flourished." Savannah had been laid out and contained fifty houses; several necessary public works had been begun; the population was approaching five hundred. During the next year, the number of houses in Savannah almost doubled, and many additional settlers swelled population figures. By June 1735 one new arrival claimed that people were flooding in so rapidly "from all parts of America as well as from England" and the Continent that "the builders and brickmakers cannot make and build [houses] fast enough for [all] the [new] inhabitants." "Trade and planting" were developing "very fast"; cattle exceeded two thousand head; naval stores, corn, and peas were being produced in abundance; oranges were coming "on finely"; and silk culture appeared so promising that, it was said, "the name of it fills the colony so full [of hope] that if it goes on so for seven years," Savannah would "be the largest city or town in all the Continent of America."

Although a few lazy and improvident people among the new settlers neglected "to improve their Lands," got into debt, and were "generally discontented with the Country," the "Industrious ones," another visitor told his London readers, "have throve beyond Expectation" and "made a very great Profit" out of provisions and cattle. Obviously, remarked the young Baron Philipp Georg Friedrich von Reck, who conducted the first transport of Salzburger immigrants to Georgia, God had "so far . . . blessed" the enterprise as to permit industry, justice, and good order to triumph over "[self-]indulgence and idleness," "Discord and disorder." . . .

Although Georgia continued into the late 1730s to receive glowing reports in the British press, the initial euphoria gave way to doubt as the settlers slowly began to come to terms with the questions of what kind of a place Georgia was and what could or ought to be done there. Reports began to filter back across the Atlantic that all was not well in the new Eden. Within two years, there were complaints about a variety of problems, including incompetent magistrates, ethnic antagonisms, political contention, social dissipation, and the engrossment of trade by a handful of Scottish merchants. Most important were the complaints that, despite all the money being poured into the colony, it was making but "small progress." Contrary to the "extravagant representations . . . in favour of this settlement" circulated in the London press, John Brownfield wrote the trustees from Georgia in May 1737, a little over four years after the initial settlement, Georgians could not yet feed themselves, few settlers could "subsist independent of" public support, and there was no credit and almost no foreign trade. Instead of becoming the prosperous, well-regulated, regenerated, and contented people initially projected by the trustees, some significant part of them were slowly falling into an "indolent and dejected" state, and many of the "best workmen" were "beginning to leave the place in order to get employment in Carolina and by that means prevent their families from starving." Far from being "so flourishing as our public papers would persuade us," Georgia was, Brownfield noted, "never yet so low as at this time," and all the inflated reports of its "great improvements" were nothing more than "great chimerical idea[s]" designed to deceive the trustees and the British public. . . .

In opposition to [the trustees'] rosy projections, a rising chorus from people the trustees tried to dismiss as "clamorous malcontents" argued that the colony was an abysmal failure. The first history of Georgia—entitled *A True and Historical Narrative of the Colony of Georgia,* published in Charleston and London in 1741 and composed by three of the trustees' most vehement critics, Patrick Tailfer, Hugh Anderson, and David Douglas—provided a detailed account of that failure. The promotional literature, these critics complained, had depicted Georgia "as an *Earthly Paradise,* the soil far surpassing that of England; the air healthy, always serene, pleasant and temperate, never subject to excessive heat or cold, nor to sudden changes." Such reports had led the early immigrants to expect a "Land of Promise, overflowing with the abundance of all good things necessary and desirable for the comfortable support of life, and those to be obtained with half the labour, industry and application" required in the Old World "for the lowest subsistence." Instead, the settlers found an excessively hot and, by European standards, inhospitable climate in which sickness and disease were rife and people could feed themselves only with the most debilitating labor without hope of ever achieving more than simple subsistence. Despite the large sums poured into the colony, its critics contended, Georgia during its first decade remained a poor, "miserable colony," a place, indeed, that did not even deserve "the *Name* of a Colony."

The reasons for this failure, according to the malcontents, did not lie in the place. Just across the Savannah River, in South Carolina, people were prospering in the same climate and with the same soil. Nor was the problem in the settlers themselves, most of whom had worked hard, and many of whom, having given up on Georgia, had succeeded elsewhere. Rather, Georgia's desolate state was entirely traceable to its initial design and to the implementation of that design by the trustees and their subordinates in Georgia. Specifically, the restrictions on land acquisition and inheritance had "extinguish[ed] every Incitement to Industry and Improvement" and had been *"a great Means of de-peopling the Colony, as fast as you can people it."* In their passion for system and regularity, the trustees had assigned lands without regard to fertility or worth and had thus left many people both with inferior plots and at a serious disadvantage. Most important, by excluding black slavery, the trustees had deprived the colonists of the means by which to develop lands in a hot climate. "It has hitherto been a received maxim in all owr southerne setlements, not only in the West Indies, but also in Carolina," one discontented Georgian noted, "that negroes are much more profitable to the planter (as being naturalisled to the extreame heats) than any European servants," who were both less reliable and more expensive. . . .

Finally, as if these difficulties were not enough, the malcontents charged that the interior government of the colony had been conducted in an arbitrary manner that was wholly inconsistent with the customary rights of Britons and was utterly "unexampled under any *British* Government." "While the nation at home was amused with the fame of the happiness and flourishing of the colony, and of its being *free from lawyers of any kind,*" the malcontents reported, "the poor miserable settlers and inhabitants were exposed to as *arbitrary* a government as Turkey or Muscovy ever felt. Very looks were criminal, and the grand sin of *withstanding,* or any way *opposing* authority, (as it was called, when any person insisted upon his just rights and privileges) was punished without mercy." The result was that "for some time there were more imprisonments, whippings, &c. of white people, in that *colony of liberty,* than in all British America besides." Instead of the silkworm, the "Georgia stocks, whipping-post, and logg-house" came to symbolize the colony "in Carolina and every where else in America, where the name of the Province was heard of, and the very thoughts of coming to the colony became a terror to the people's minds." "By all appearance[s]," Georgia thus seemed "to have been calculated and prepared" not as a settlement of British subjects but as "a colony of vassals, whose *properties* and *liberties* were, *at all times,* to have been disposed of at the discretion or option of their superiors." "Not even the flourishing of wine and silk," the malcontents declared, could "make a colony of British subjects happy if they" were "deprived of the liberties and properties of their birthright."

Although first set forth in a conciliatory, even deferential, tone, the criticisms of the malcontents represented a demand for precisely what the trustees were determined to avoid: placing Georgia on the same "foot of the other American Colonies." In demanding liberty for individuals to acquire as much land as they wished, to dispose of their possessions without restraint, to settle where they liked, to have as many slaves as they saw fit, and, ultimately, to enjoy a government that provided the benefits of British law and assured that they would neither be deprived of liberty and property without due process of law nor governed by laws passed without their consent, they were asking that Georgia be permitted to follow the time-tested pattern of British colonization—the "ancient Custom of sending forth Colonies, for the Improvement of any distant Territory, or new Acquisition," as it had been "continued down to ourselves." . . .

This frontal assault upon virtually every element that had given the Georgia plan its distinctive character stimulated an increasingly strident and uncompromising verbal battle that lasted for the five years from 1738 to 1743 and produced a continuous round of petitions, counterpetitions, and pamphlets. At first, the trustees and their supporters held fast to all aspects of their initial plan, and, although they eventually agreed to modify the restrictions on inheritance and land distribution, they refused to abandon the prohibition on slavery on the grounds that it was thoroughly "inconsistent" with "the first Design of the Establishment." Not only, they argued, were slaves unnecessary for the production of "Silk, Cotton, Cochineal, [wine,] and the other designed Products of the Colony," all of which were "Works rather of Nicety than Labour," but they were "absolutely dangerous." Recent "Insurrections of Negroes in *Jamaica* and *Antigua*" had revealed that slaves were "all secret Enemies" who were "apt . . . to rise against their Masters, upon every Opportunity." For that reason, they were wholly inappropriate for a frontier colony such as Georgia. Much more important, however, slavery was a primary source of most of the evils that were present in the other colonies and that the trustees were determined to avoid in Georgia. Slaves, they argued, citing South Carolina and the West Indies as examples, discouraged white immigration, led to the concentration of wealth and the engrossment of lands in the hands of those who could afford them, destroyed the industry of poor whites, who invariably "disdain[ed] to work like Negroes," and ultimately drove even the slaveholders "to absent themselves, and live in other Places, leaving the Care of their Plantations and their Negroes to Overseers."

Pointing out that "none of our most beneficial Colonies have yielded an early Profit," the trustees admitted in their counterattacks that Georgia's progress had been slow. But they attributed that slowness not to the prohibition of slaves or to any of the other regulations called into question by the malcontents but to the quality of the early immigrants, many of whom were "low and necessitous People" who had been difficult "to form . . . into Society, and reduce . . . to a proper Obedience to the Laws." The colony's recent problems, the trustees professed, resulted from the activities and example of the malcontents, those profligate lovers of Negroes, who had fomented a spirit of idleness, dissipation, and contention that discouraged the entire colony. . . .

Participants on both sides of this long and bitter public debate agreed on two points: first, that Georgia had not made as much progress in its first decade as had been originally hoped, and second, that it was still a place of extraordinary promise. Their disagreement was over the means by which that promise could best be achieved. When the trustees continued "their inflexible Adherence to" their "pernicious and impracticable Schemes and Maxims of Government," the malcontents appealed twice to Parliament for redress, in 1742 and 1743. During the second appeal, one member of Parliament indicated in debate that he had "always thought the affair of Georgia a jobb" and averred that the trustees, though honest men, must have been "misled and misinformed of the [true] state of the colony, or they would [have] change[d] their measures of proceeding." On both occasions, however, Parliament sided with the trustees on the major issues. Thereafter, the controversy gradually became less intense. Some Georgians continued to press for slavery, but the trustees resisted their demands until later in the decade.

In the meantime, Georgia continued to grow slowly. By the mid–1740s Savannah may have had three hundred houses, its famous public garden was still "in a very thriving Way," and in its immediate vicinity were "several very pretty Plantations," including Wormsloe, the seat of the trustees' treasurer Noble Jones and a place with many "extraordinary" improvements. Nearby was the Reverend George Whitefield's famous orphan house, a large "Superstructure . . . laid out in a neat and elegant Manner" with rooms that were "very commodious, and prettily furnished." Except for Savannah, Ebenezer, and a few other small, scattered settlements, however, the Salzburger spiritual leader Johann Martin Boltzius reported in the early 1750s, Georgia was mostly "still forests" with "small plantations . . . established only here and there." Between 1740 and 1750 population had increased at a rate of less than two hundred per year, and many settlers, who preferred to "run around rather than work," were primarily hunters with no permanent abode. . . .

But the truth was that the old design no longer had any vigor. Through their intensive public campaign, the malcontents had undermined its appeal, if not its credibility, and that battle had taken much of the enthusiasm for the project out of the trustees. As a result, Georgia during the 1740s was left without any clear sense of direction. Between an old design that was no longer fully in operation and the alternative model of the ordinary British colony that had not yet been tried, Georgia had no agreed-upon set of goals and priorities, no coherent sense of place, no acceptable collective sense of self. Oldmixon, Kimber, and Harris to the contrary notwithstanding, by the mid–1740s it was clear that Georgia would never become the well-regulated, egalitarian yeoman utopia initially envisioned by the trustees. Whether it could by another route achieve an equality with other British colonies remained to be seen. . . .

Once the trustees had surrendered their charter, and Georgia, now "new modelled," was finally put upon "the same footing with Carolina," the colony was at last to have a new—the malcontents would have said, a proper—beginning. Following the removal of the restrictions on slavery, [German engineer William Gerard] De Brahm remembered, "many rich Carolina Planters . . . came with all their Families and Negroes to settle in Georgia in 1752," and "the Spirit of Emigration out of South Carolina into Georgia became so universal that year, that this and the following year near one thousand Negroes were brought in Georgia, where in 1751 were scarce above three dozen." Formal establishment of royal government under the first crown governor, John Reynolds, in late 1754 seemed at last, as one older resident declared, to bring the colony "the greatest prospect to being . . . happy." "People were then crowding in every day, fill'd with expectations of being Settled in a Country which" had "all the Advantages of Air & Soil and was [finally] founded upon liberty"—a country that at last, in [New England historian William] Douglass's terms, had been "colonized." But Reynolds turned out to be a disaster, "a lawless tyrant" whose "iron rod" created so much "Discord" and faction that migration once again flowed out rather than in and Georgia, one disappointed inhabitant lamented, seemed likely to "be reduced to as low as ebb as it was under the Late unhappy Constitution under the Trustees." Several more years would have to elapse before the colony would achieve an identity as a free and flourishing place. . . .

For the last fifteen years of the colonial period Georgia rapidly acquired a reputation for having an abundance of rich land and a growing population, animated by a building "spirit of industry" that was putting the colony into a "happy" and "most flourishing Condition." Because the "Climate & Soil is at least equal, the Spirit of Industry very Great, and the People beginning to have Property & Foundation Sufficient to Enable them to make Considerable Progress," Governor James Wright, who, as Ellis's successor, presided over Georgia during these boom years, observed in early 1763 that "the only thing now wanting to make this in a few years a Province of as much Consequence to Great Britain as some others in our Neighbourhood" was "a great Number of Inhabitants."

The close of the Seven Years' War brought peace to the colony and, by placing Florida under British control, removed all apprehension of danger from the Spaniards. Wright negotiated a series of treaties with Indians that brought at least seven million more acres under British jurisdiction. Spurred by these inducements, inhabitants poured into Georgia. The number of whites tripled between 1761 and 1773, rising from just over six thousand in 1761 to ten thousand in 1766 and eighteen thousand in 1773. At the same time, the number of blacks, virtually all of whom were slaves, more than quadrupled, increasing from thirty-six hundred in 1761 to seventy-eight hundred in 1766 and fifteen thousand in 1773. With these growing numbers, the face of the landscape changed. The Savannah River and other areas near the coast now were described as having an "abundance of very fine Settlements and Plantations." But the most dramatic change occurred in the backcountry, where by 1772 the number of whites substantially exceeded that of the lowcountry. By 1773 the colony was "well laid out with Roads," and "the many

Plantations and Settlements" along them made "travelling very convenient and easy." "Increasing . . . extreamly fast" since 1760, Savannah had many new houses which were spreading west to the new suburbs of "Yamacraw" and the "Trustees Garden," while Savannah Bay was already "nearly fronted with contiguous Wharfs," all built to handle Georgia's expanding volume of trade.

Indeed, Georgia increased not only in population and settledness during these years but also in production, credit, shipping, and wealth. Its rising production can best be measured by the growing value of its exports, which jumped from around £40,000 in 1761 to almost £85,000 in 1766 to over £100,000 in 1773. The expansion of credit was revealed by the adverse balance of trade. The annual value of imports often exceeded that of exports by nearly £50,000, and much of that difference went for the purchase of slaves, who, in a remark that showed how far Georgia had departed from the trustees' initial plan, Governor Wright described as the "wealth & strength of the Southern American Colonies" and the "chief means of their becoming Opulent & considerable.". . .

Georgia's new prosperity was based almost entirely upon the same commodities that had been so successful in South Carolina: rice, indigo, naval stores, provisions, lumber, and wood products. "Without Exception," one author proclaimed, all of these commodities could be produced "to the same Perfection, and in every respect equal to South Carolina," and they "arrived at the markets in Europe [and the West Indies] in equal excellence and perfection, and, in proportion to its strength, in equal quantities with those of its more powerful and opulent neighbours in Carolina." Alexander Hewatt claimed that because it contained "more good River Swamp," Georgia was actually "a better rice Colony than South Carolina." As proof, several "planters of Carolina, who had been accustomed to treat their poor neighbours with the utmost contempt," had "sold their estates in that colony, and moved with their families and effects to Georgia." Cotton, which was reported to agree "well with the soil and climate of Georgia" and in a few decades would be Georgia's premier staple, was only beginning to be produced in small quantities.

. . . With the implementation of royal government in 1754 and the immediate establishment of a representative assembly and a regular judicial system, Georgians appeared finally to have obtained those "English freedom[s]" enjoyed by "all English Colonies"—except Georgia under the trustees. Once Reynolds was removed as governor, it would be accurate to say, as did a contemporary, that Georgia contained "no trace of a despotic government." But the conversion to a royal colony occurred just when colonial authorities in Britain were strongly advocating limiting the autonomy of all of the older colonies and bringing them under much tighter metropolitan control. The officials who designed and oversaw the establishment of royal authority in Georgia had no intention of permitting Georgians to exercise the same autonomy then enjoyed by the other colonies. Once again, Georgia, along with contemporary Nova Scotia, was to be a model colony, this time a model royal colony, a place where "Royal Government" would be "settled in it's greatest purity" and the errors of other governments would be corrected. Georgians were indeed to be "intitled to British Liberty," but their "Mode of Government," as Henry Ellis later declared, was to be "the freest from a Republican Mixture, and the most conformable to the British Constitution of any that obtains amongst our Colonies in North America." In practical terms, this meant that metropolitan officials in the colony—the royal governor and the council—were to have more authority and the representative assembly less than was the case in the other colonies. Even as a royal colony, Georgia would be swimming against the mainstream of British colonial development. . . .

As Georgians, through their economic, social, and political behavior, were establishing during the 1760s and early 1770s the credibility of their claims to the positive attributes of abundance, strength, and liberty forecast by their seal, they also came to a new understanding of their history, of their collective experiences as a people. "Few countries," one commentator remarked during the American Revolution, had "undergone so many changes as Georgia has, in the course of fifty years." But the most dramatic of these changes was the colony's sudden rise to prosperity: "Under the long administration of Sir James Wright . . . it made such a rapid progress in population, agriculture, and commerce, as no other country ever equalled in so short a time." From the perspectives supplied by that change, on the basis of the observable fact that Georgia did not begin "to flourish" until after "the original Constitution framed by the trustees" had been altered, Georgians and other observers could only conclude that the colony's difficulties under the trustees were not attributable to the character of the settlers, who with some exceptions had worked hard enough to ensure that Georgia, as De Brahm declared, had been "a Place of Industry ever since its very Beginning." Rather, Georgia's "Backwardness seemed only to be owning, first to the Prohibition of introducing African Servants, [and] . . . secondly for not being governed in a manner as other Provinces [with] . . . Representatives, with the Liberty to make their own Laws." As soon as the colony had been "freed from those Prohibitions, and invested with Privileges and Liberties, as other Provinces," as soon as its "planters," as another writer put it, "got the strength of Africa to assist them" (and it might be said that the planters enjoyed the abundance and liberty forecast by the seal while the Africans supplied the strength), they immediately began to labor "with success, and the[ir] lands every year yielded greater and greater increase.". . .

Notwithstanding the anxieties that slavery brought to the colony, Georgia during the royal period finally achieved a positive sense of itself as a place and as a people. Some areas were unhealthy; indeed, disease seemed to increase with prosperity, population, and trade. As a "young new settled Country," Georgia society was still crude and culturally undeveloped. "We have no Plays, Operas, or public Exhibitions, either in point of Literature or Amusements, to animadvert upon," wrote [Savannah merchant James] Habersham in 1772. Or, to put the matter more positively, although Georgia had "some brilliant . . . [public] Assemblys" and at least five "fine [private] Libraries" and there was talk of turning George Whitefield's orphanage into the first college south of Williamsburg, Georgia, in De Brahm's words, had "not as yet [been] debauched by European Luxuries, such as Balls, Masquerades, Operas, Plays, etc.," and Georgians who sought cultural enrichment had little choice but to apply "themselves to reading good Authors."

In spite of these deficiencies in health and culture, Georgia obviously was becoming a place of which its free white inhabitants could be proud. With large amounts of unoccupied land that, especially in the interior, was said to be "the finest in all America," Georgia was rapidly becoming known and was usually depicted as a "rich and plentiful country" with great opportunity not just for rich slave owners but even for "people of small fortunes" who did "not dislike retirement" in a place of rural delights. As it became increasingly clear that Georgia was "Making a very Rapid Progress towards being an Opulent & Considerable Province" and that that progress finally afforded Georgians "a Prospect of . . . soon becoming a rich, commercial People," and even outsiders began to suspect that Georgia would "become one of the richest, and most considerable provinces in British America, and that[,] in a very few years," Georgians gradually acquired a positive sense of themselves as a demonstrably prosperous and liberty-loving people.

At the same time, their home and their society—their country—was gaining an increasingly flattering reputation as a place of opportunity, freedom, and ease. Like all of the other new plantation societies at a comparable point in their development, Georgians had not been together long enough to articulate any very well developed sense of whether as individuals they were acquiring in common any distinctive characteristics, that is, a collective identity. Georgians were just beginning to attribute special defining qualities to themselves—"a Volatile, but kind people," in the estimation of Habersham; a people who were, "in general of very elevated Spirits," according to De Brahm; a people who, not caring "for a small profit" or a modest way of living, were prone, in the words of Boltzius, to "abuse . . . [their] freedom." But their sense of self was primarily expressed through their understanding of their physical and social landscapes. . . .

That Georgia's success in achieving a positive sense of self in the 1760s and 1770s was so heavily dependent upon the massive adoption of black slavery was thoroughly consistent with its entire colonial history. For one of the most interesting facets of the history of colonial Georgia, one that provides some consistency over the entire period, was that it seemed forever to be destined to go against history. Started as a place that would be free of the social evils of other British-American colonies, it had been reconstituted as an entity that would be as free as possible from the centrifugal impulses toward autonomy that, at least to metropolitan authorities, had seemed to make the colonies politically fragile and increasingly difficult to control. By managing to subvert both of these designs, Georgians had succeeded in placing themselves on an equal footing with the other colonies. But in thus thrusting themselves into and thereby showing that they belonged in the mainstream of British-American colonial history, they were at the same time once again going against much larger currents in Western history. For at the very time Georgia was moving so heavily into slavery, that institution was beginning—for the first time—to be widely condemned in western Europe as a moral evil that was inappropriate for civilized societies. Although this movement seems to have created no problems for Georgians during the colonial period, the rapid triumph of the point of view it represented, which was nearly as sudden as, and far more revolutionary than, Georgia's rise to prosperity, would soon put Georgians at the same point where they had repeatedly found themselves on the defensive. No doubt the earl of Egmont and the other authors of the trustees' Georgia plan would have found this development disquieting, as they would have found almost everything else that happened to their colony. But they might also have gained a certain amount of satisfaction in the knowledge that their early forebodings about slavery had not been without foundation.

⅄ *F U R T H E R   R E A D I N G*

Ira Berlin and Philip D. Morgan, eds., *Cultivation and Culture: Labor and the Shaping of Slave Life in the Americas* (1993)

Warren M. Billings, John E. Selby, and Thad W. Tate, *Colonial Virginia: A History* (1986)

T. H. Breen, *Tobacco Culture: The Mentality of the Great Tidewater Planters on the Eve of Revolution* (1985)

Carl Bridenbaugh, *Myths and Realities: Societies of the Colonial South* (1952)

Joyce E. Chaplin, *An Anxious Pursuit: Agricultural Innovation and Modernity in the Lower South, 1730–1815* (1993)

Paul G. E. Clemens, *The Atlantic Economy and Colonial Maryland's Eastern Shore: From Tobacco to Grain* (1980)

Peter A. Coclanis, *The Shadow of a Dream: Economic Life and Death in the South Carolina Low Country, 1670–1920* (1989)

Kenneth Coleman, *Colonial Georgia: A History* (1976)

Verner W. Crane, *The Southern Frontier, 1670–1732* (1928)

Harold E. Davis, *The Fledging Province: Social and Cultural Life in Colonial Georgia* (1976)

Richard Beale Davis, *Intellectual Life in the Colonial South, 1585–1763,* 3 vols. (1978)

A. Roger Ekirch, *"Poor Carolina": Politics and Society in Colonial North Carolina, 1729–1776* (1981)

Jack P. Greene, *The Quest for Power: The Lower Houses of Assembly in the Southern Royal Colonies, 1689–1776* (1963)

Gwendolyn Midlo Hall, *Africans in Colonial Louisiana: The Development of Afro-Creole Culture in the Eighteenth Century* (1992)

Rhys Isaac, *The Transformation of Virginia, 1740–1790* (1982)

Allan Kulikoff, *Tobacco and Slaves: The Development of Southern Cultures in the Chesapeake, 1680–1800* (1986)

Aubrey C. Land, *Colonial Maryland: A History* (1981)

Kenneth A. Lockridge, *The Diary and Life of William Byrd of Virginia, 1674–1744* (1987)

D. W. Meinig, *The Shaping of America: A Geographical Perspective on 500 Years of History,* vol. 1: *Atlantic America, 1492–1800* (1986)

Philip D. Morgan, *Slave Counterpoint: Black Culture in the Eighteenth-Century Chesapeake and Lowcountry* (1998)

Theda Perdue, *Cherokee Women: Gender and Culture Change 1700–1835* (1998)

Jacob M. Price, *Capital and Credit in British Overseas Trade: The View from the Chesapeake, 1700–1776* (1980)

Darrett B. Rutman and Anita H. Rutman, *A Place in Time: Middlesex County, Virginia, 1650–1750* (1984)

Marylynn Salmon, *Women and the Law of Property in Early America* (1986)

Daniel Blake Smith, *Inside the Great House: Planter Family Life in Eighteenth-Century Chesapeake Society* (1980)

Mechal Sobel, *The World They Made Together: Black and White Values in Eighteenth-Century Virginia* (1987)

Julia Cherry Spruill, *Women's Life and Work in the Southern Colonies* (1938)

Wilcomb E. Washburn, *The Governor and the Rebel: A History of Bacon's Rebellion in Virginia* (1957)

Robert M. Weir, *Colonial South Carolina: A History* (1983)

———, *"The Last of American Freemen": Studies in the Political Culture of the Colonial and Revolutionary South* (1986)

CHAPTER
4

The Revolutionary South and

Its Aftermath

Early in this century, historian Carl Becker suggested that the American Revolution involved two conflicts: home rule and who should rule at home. This was an especially accurate characterization of the Revolution in the South, where much of the war took place, as colonists fought against both the British and one another. A significant percentage of the southern population remained loyalists, dedicated to the mother country. White southerners feared that the conflict might excite their slave population, a concern that became all too real when in 1775 Lord Dunmore granted freedom to slaves who would join the British. White patriots who were determined to overthrow the yoke of Britain used language that sounded all too familiar (and ironic) in demanding their freedom from enslavement by Parliament. The South produced more than its share of patriots, including George Washington, Thomas Jefferson, James Madison, and Patrick Henry.

Many historians who have examined the Revolutionary War in the South have shown that it was far more than a struggle for independence; it was also an event that began to solidify and define a distinctive region. In the aftermath of the conflict, southern representatives to Philadelphia in 1787 insisted upon a constitutional protection of slavery. Postwar debates on the meaning of liberty along with a temporary economic downturn encouraged a few southerners to manumit their slaves, but this proved a temporary and extremely limited opportunity for slaves to gain their freedom.

⋏ DOCUMENTS

Document 1 shows the serious concern that arose with respect to the situation in the Carolina backcountry. The South Carolina Assembly dispatched three men, including two ministers, Baptist Oliver Hart and Presbyterian William Tennent, to persuade key individuals on the frontier to support, or at least remain neutral during, the war. Their accounts reveal a troubled region where long-standing animosities evidently spilled over into the new Revolution. Few measures infuriated southern white colonists, especially Virginians, more than Royal Governor Lord Dunmore's emancipation proclamation in November 1775. This proclamation, reprinted as Document 2, conjured up images of rapacious blacks wreaking vengeance on the region. Although no wholesale defections occurred, as whites had feared, some blacks participated in a few military campaigns. However, many blacks who ran away to the British endured poor treatment or died from diseases. In his Farm Book, Document 3, amid notations of crops and livestock, Thomas Jefferson listed the names of his slaves who escaped to the British. During this period, Jefferson was also active in the Virginia state assembly, sponsoring numerous measures designed to put some of the Revolution's ideals into practice. His bill on religious freedom, reprinted as Document 4, was drafted in 1777 but not passed until 1786 (the italicized words in the selection were not included in the final version). Document 5 shows the exhilarating and terrifying impact of the war on civilians. This is an excerpt from the letters of Eliza Wilkinson, a young widow who resided on Yonge's Island, some thirty miles south of Charleston. While the Revolution brought danger into the relatively placid lives of elite women like Wilkinson, it also offered them an opportunity to break out of their accustomed roles. Colonel David Fanning, a prominent North Carolina loyalist who single-mindedly pursued patriots for seven years before he was forced into exile in Canada, offers a soldier's perspective on the war in Document 6. Finally, Document 7 presents sections of the Constitution that protected and perpetuated slavery. While the issue never monopolized constitutional debates, the outcome assured the new nation's acceptance of slavery.

1. Two Attempts at Converting the Carolina Backcountry, 1775

Reverend William Tennent Records Some Difficult Conversions, 1775

[August] 6th.—. . . Finding some disaffected among the soldiers, Mr. Drayton harangued them and was followed by myself; until all seemed well satisfied, and we returned to Mr. Chestnut's, about two miles. About midnight were alarmed by an officer from the camp, who, informed us that they had mutinied and were determined to go off in the morning. We agreed to let matters rest until then. Ordered the companies to come to us.

7th.—Discovered that the mutiny arose from some words dropped by some officers concerning their pay and tents.

We dealt plainly with the corps of officers, and addressed the men at the head of the Regiment in such a manner as that they all went away happy. . . .

[8th.] Crossed Congaree river and rode five miles to an election for the Congress, where they refused to proceed unless we should enlighten them. We found persons had come a great way to oppose the election. Harangued the meeting in turns until every man was convinced, and the greatest opposer signed the Association and begged pardon for the words he had spoken to the people. . . .

[14th.] . . . It seems as though nothing could be done here, as they have industriously taught the people that no man from Charleston can speak the truth, and that all the papers are full of lies. . . .

20th.— . . . Set off at half after eight for King creek, to a muster of Capt. Robert McAfee's company, after a hard and rough ride of twenty miles, in which crossed King

These documents can be found in Robert W. Gibbes, ed., *Documentary History of the American Revolution* (New York, 1853–1857), vol. I, pp. 225–239 and in the Diary of Oliver Hart in the Oliver Hart Papers, South Carolina Library, University of South Carolina.

creek at a beautiful rocky ford; found about one hundred people assembled, among whom were some of the most obstinate opposers of the Congress. Spoke to the people at large on the state of America. They seemed much affected towards the close, but afterwards aided by two gainsaying Baptist preachers, they all refused to sign the Association except ten. After their refusal which proceeded from the grossest ignorance and prejudice, spoke again to their heads, who, upon renewing the charge, seemed quite softened, and only asked a little time. They proposed to obtain some powder to defend themselves from the Indians who are troublesome; told them it was impossible; knew they would not use it properly; told them as soon as they would associate and let us know it, we would try to do something for them. This I hope will have its influence.

Reverend Oliver Hart Encounters Resentment and Failure, 1775

[Thurs. Aug. 10] . . . Upon discoursing with Mr. Mulkey, found that He rather sides with ministerial Measures, and is agt. those adopted by the Country. Altho' He profess Himself difficulted about these Things; The People, in general, are certainly (as they say) for the King; ie, for the Minister, & his Measures; one Man, with whom we conversed, fairly trembled through Madness. Friday Augt. ye 11th: Rose in Health, but somewhat fatigued; Some of the Neighbors came to see us, with whom we had much Conversation about the present States of the Times; found them so fixed on the Side of the Ministry, that no argument on the contrary Side seemed to have any Weight with them. . . . One of them wish'd 1000 Bostonians might be kill'd in Battle—One wish'd there was not a grain of Salt in any of the sea Coast Towns on the Continent. On the whole they appear to be obstinate and irritated to an Extreme. Saturday Augt. 12th: . . . After Sermon had some Conversation with Col: Fletchal, who declar'd that He had no Intention of fighting against his Country Men, but at the same Time highly disapproved of the Measures fallen upon to preserve our Rights, and complain'd of sundry Threats which He says are given out against Himself, and the Inhabitants of the Frontiers. A number of People gathered round us while we were conversing together, who seem'd almost universally, by Words & actions to applaud every Thing the Col: said. Upon the Whole there appears but little Reason, as yet, to hope that these People will be brought to have a suitable Regard to ye interest of America. . . . Lords Day Augt: 13th: . . . Went home with Mr: Mulkey, Mr: Newton in Company, who gave us an account of the distracted State of the frontier Inhabitants, which at present wears the most alarming Face; insomuch that there is the greatest appearance of a civil War; unless God, by some remarkable Interposition of Providence prevent.

2. Lord Dunmore's Proclamation Freeing Virginia's Slaves, 1775

As I have ever entertained Hopes that an Accommodation might have taken Place between *Great Britain* and this Colony, without being compelled, by my Duty, to this most disagreeable, but now absolutely necessary Step, rendered so by a Body

---

This document can be found in Francis Berkley, ed., *Dunmore's Proclamation of Emancipation* (Charlottesville, VA.: 1941).

of armed Men, unlawfully assembled, firing on his Majesty's Tenders, and the For-mation of an Army, and that Army now on their March to attack his Majesty's Troops, and destroy the well-disposed Subjects of this Colony: To defeat such trea-sonable Purposes, and that all such Traitors, and their Abetters, may be brought to Justice, and that the Peace and good Order of this Colony may be again restored, which the ordinary Course of the civil Law is unable to effect, I have thought fit to issue this my Proclamation, hereby declaring, that until the aforesaid good Purposes can be obtained, I do, in Virtue of the Power and Authority to me given, by his Majesty, determine to execute martial Law, and cause the same to be executed throughout this Colony; and to the End that Peace and good Order may the sooner be restored, I do require every Person capable of bearing Arms to resort to his Majesty's STANDARD, or be looked upon as Traitors to his Majesty's Crown and Government, and thereby become liable to the Penalty the Law inflicts upon such Offences, such as Forfeiture of Life, Confiscation of Lands, &c. &c. And I do hereby farther declare all indented Servants, Negroes, or others (appertaining to Rebels) free, that are able and willing to bear Arms, they joining his Majesty's Troops, as soon as may be, for the more speedily reducing this Colony to a proper Sense of their Duty, to his Majesty's Crown and Dignity. I do farther order, and re-quire, all his Majesty's liege Subjects to retain their Quitrents, or any other Taxes due, or that may become due, in their own Custody, till such Time as Peace may be again restored to this at present most unhappy Country, or demanded of them for their former salutary Purposes, by Officers properly authorized to receive the same.

3. Thomas Jefferson on the Defection of His Slaves to the British, 1781

Slaves who went off with the British & died

Hannibal	Nanny
Patty	Fanny
Prince	Nancy
Sam 9, years old	Flora
Sally	Quomina

Went off with the British & was never more heard of.
Sam.
Went off with the British, returned & died of the camp fever Lucy. Black Sall. Jane 10. years old.
Lost for want of cultivation by loss of the hands
   about 80 barrels of corn
     130. lb of cotton
       7. hogshead of tobacco

This document can be found in Julian P. Boyd, ed., *The Papers of Thomas Jefferson* (Princeton Univer-sity Press, 1952), vol. VI, pp. 224–225.

4. Thomas Jefferson's Bill for Establishing Religious Freedom in Virginia, 1777

Well aware that the opinions and belief of men depend not on their own will, but follow involuntarily the evidence proposed to their minds; that Almighty God hath created the mind free, *and manifested his supreme will that free it shall remain by masking it altogether insusceptible of restraint;* that all attempts to influence it by temporal punishments, or burthens, or by civil incapacitations, tend only to beget habits of hypocrisy and meanness, and are a departure from the plan of the holy author of our religion, who being lord both of body and mind, yet chose not to propagate it by coercions on either, as was in his Almighty power to do, *but to extend it by its influence on reason alone;* that the impious presumption of legislators and rulers, civil as well as ecclesiastical, who, being themselves but fallible and uninspired men, have assumed dominion over the faith of others, setting up their own opinions and modes of thinking as the only true and infallible, and as such endeavoring to impose them on others, hath established and maintained false religions over the greatest part of the world and through all time: That to compel a man to furnish contributions of money for the propagation of opinions which he disbelieves *and abhors,* is sinful and tyrannical: that even the forcing him to support this or that teacher of his own religious persuasion, is depriving him of the comfortable liberty of giving his contributions to the particular pastor whose morals he would make his pattern, and whose powers he feels most persuasive to righteousness; and is withdrawing from the ministry those temporary rewards, which proceeding from an approbation of their personal conduct, are an additional incitement to earnest and unremitting labours for the instruction of mankind; that our civil rights have no dependance on our religious opinions, any more than our opinions in physics or geometry; that therefore the proscribing any citizen as unworthy the public confidence by laying upon him an incapacity of being called to offices or trust and emolument, unless he profess or renounce this or that religious opinion, is depriving him injuriously of those privileges and advantages to which, in common with his fellow citizens, he has a natural right; that it tends also to corrupt the principles of that *very* religion it is meant to encourage, by bribing, with a monopoly of worldly honours and emoluments, those who will externally profess and conform to it; that though indeed these are criminal who do not withstand such temptation, yet neither are those innocent who lay the bait in their way; *that the opinions of men are not the object of civil government, nor under its jurisdiction;* that to suffer the civil magistrate to intrude his powers into the field of opinion and to restrain the profession or propagation of principles on supposition of their ill tendency is a dangerous falacy, which at once destroys all religious liberty, because he being of course judge of that tendency will make his opinions the rule of judgment, and approve or condemn the sentiments of others only as they shall square with or differ from his own; that it is time enough for the rightful purposes of civil government for its officers to interfere when principles break out into overt acts against peace and good order; and finally,

---

This document can be found in the Revisal of the Laws, Drafts of Legislation, A Bill for Establishing Religious Freedom. Report on the Committee of Revisors Appointed by the General Assembly of Virginia in MDCCLXXVII. Richmond, Virginia, 1784, pp. 58–59. Virginia State Library, Richmond, microfilm.

that truth is great and will prevail if left to herself; that she is the proper and suffi-cient antagonist to error, and has nothing to fear from the conflict unless by human interposition disarmed of her natural weapons, free argument and debate; errors ceasing to be dangerous when it is permitted freely to contradict them.

We the General Assembly of Virginia do enact that no man shall be compelled to frequent or support any religious worship, place, or ministry whatsoever, nor shall be enforced, restrained, molested, or burthened in his body or goods, nor shall other-wise suffer, on account of his religious opinions or belief; but that all men shall be free to profess, and by argument to maintain, their opinions in matters of religion, and that the same shall in no wise diminish, enlarge, or affect their civil capacities.

And though we well know that this assembly, elected by the people for the or-dinary purposes of legislation only, have no power to restrain the acts of succeeding Assemblies, constituted with powers equal to our own, and that therefore to declare this act irrevocable would be of no effect in law; yet we are free to declare, and do declare, that the rights hereby asserted are of the natural rights of mankind, and that if any act shall be hereafter passed to repeal the present or to narrow its operation, such act will be an infringement of natural right.

5. Eliza Wilkinson's Thoughts on Women and War, 1779

Never were greater politicians than the several knots of ladies, who met together. All trifling discourse of fashions, and such low little chat was thrown by, and we commenced perfect statesmen. Indeed, I don't know but if we had taken a little pains, we should have been qualified for prime ministers, so well could we discuss several important matters in hand. . . .

Well, now comes the day of terror—the 3d of June. (I shall never love the an-niversary of that day.) In the morning, fifteen or sixteen horsemen rode up to the house; we were greatly terrified, thinking them the enemy, but from their behavior, were agreeably deceived, and found them friends. They sat a while on their horses, talking to us; and then rode off, except two, who tarried a minute or two longer, and then followed the rest, who had nearly reached the gate. One of the said two must needs jump a ditch—to show his activity I suppose; for he might as well, and better, have gone in the road. However, he got a sad fall; we saw him, and sent a boy to tell him, if he was hurt, to come up to the house, and we would endeavor to do some-thing for him. He and his companion accordingly came up; he look'd very pale, and bled much; his gun somehow in the fall, had given him a bad wound behind the ear, from whence the blood flowed down his neck and bosom plentifully: we were greatly alarmed on seeing him in this situation, and had gathered around him, some with one thing, some with another, in order to give him assistance. We were very busy examining the wound, when a negro girl ran in, exclaiming—"O! the king's people are coming, it must be them, for they are all in red." Upon this cry, the two men that were with us snatched up their guns, mounted their horses, and made off; but had not got many yards from the house, before the enemy discharged a pistol at them. Terrified almost to death as I was, I was still anxious for my friends' safety; I

This document can be found in Caroline Gilman, ed., *Letters of Eliza Wilkinson During the Invasion and Possession of Charlestown, South Carolina by the British in the Revolutionary War,* (New York: Samuel Coleman, 1839), pp. 17, 27–31, 61.

tremblingly flew to the window, to see if the shot had proved fatal: when, seeing them both safe, "Thank heaven," said I, "they've got off without hurt!" I'd hardly utter'd this, when I heard the horses of the inhuman Britons coming in such a furious manner, that they seemed to tear up the earth, and the riders at the same time bellowing out the most horrid curses imaginable; oaths and imprecations, which chilled my whole frame. Surely, thought I, such horrid language denotes nothing less than death; but I'd no time for thought—they were up to the house—entered with drawn swords and pistols in their hands; indeed, they rushed in, in the most furious manner, crying out, "Where're these women rebels?" (pretty language to ladies from the *once famed Britons!*) That was the first salutation! The moment they espied us, off went our caps, (I always heard say none but women pulled caps!) And for what, think you? why, only to get a paltry stone and wax pin, which kept them on our heads; at the same time uttering the most abusive language imaginable, and making as if they'd hew us to pieces with their swords. But it's not in my power to describe the scene: it was terrible to the last degree; and, what augmented it, they had several armed negroes with them, who threatened and abused us greatly. They then began to plunder the house of every thing they thought valuable or worth taking; our trunks were split to pieces, and each mean, pitiful wretch crammed his bosom with the contents, which were our apparel, &c. &c. &c.

I ventured to speak to the inhuman monster who had my clothes. I represented to him the times were such we could not replace what they'd taken from us, and begged him to spare me only a suit or two; but I got nothing but a hearty curse for my pains; nay, so far was his callous heart from relenting, that, casting his eyes towards my shoes, "I want them buckles," said he, and immediately knelt at my feet to take them out, which, while he was busy about, a brother villain, whose enormous mouth extended from ear to ear, bawled out "Shares there, I say; shares." So they divided my buckles between them. The other wretches were employed in the same manner; they took my sister's ear-rings from her ears; hers, and Miss Samuells's buckles; they demanded her ring from her finger; she pleaded for it, told them it was her wedding ring, and begged they'd let her keep it; but they still demanded it, and, presenting a pistol at her, swore if she did not deliver it immediately, they'd fire. She gave it to them, and, after bundling up all their booty, they mounted their horses. But such despicable figures! Each wretch's bosom stuffed so full, they appeared to be all afflicted with some dropsical disorder; had a party of rebels (as they called us) appeared, we should soon have seen their circumference lessen.

They took care to tell us, when they were going away, that they had favored us a great deal—that we might thank our stars it was no worse. But I had forgot to tell you, that, upon their first entering the house, one of them gave my arm such a violent grasp, that he left the print of his thumb and three fingers, in black and blue, which was to be seen, very plainly, for several days after. I showed it to one of our officers, who dined with us, as a specimen of British cruelty. If they call this *favor,* what must their cruelties be? It must want a name. To be brief; after a few words more, they rode off, and glad was I. "Good riddance of bad rubbish," and indeed such rubbish was I never in company with before. One of them was an officer too! a sergeant, or some such, for he had the *badge of honor on his shoulders!* After they were gone, I began to be sensible of the danger I'd been in, and the thoughts of the vile men seemed worse (if possible) than their presence; for they came so suddenly up to the house, that I'd no time for thought; and while they staid, I seemed in amaze! Quite stupid! I cannot describe it. But when they were gone, and I had time to consider, I trembled so with terror, that I could not support myself. I went into the room, threw myself on the bed, and gave way to a violent burst of grief, which seemed to be some relief to my full-swollen heart. . . .

I do not love to meddle with political matters; the men say we have no business with them, it is not in our sphere! and Homer . . . gives us two or three broad hints to mind our domestic concerns, spinning, weaving, &c. and leave affairs of higher nature to the men; but I must beg his pardon—I won't have it thought, that because we are the weaker sex as to *bodily* strength, my dear, we are capable of nothing more than minding the dairy, visiting the poultry-house, and all such domestic concerns; our thoughts can soar aloft, we can form conceptions of things of higher nature; and have as just a sense of honor, glory, and great actions, as these "Lords of the Creation." What contemptible *earth worms* these authors make us! They won't even allow us the liberty of thought, and that is all I want. I would not wish that we should meddle in what is unbecoming female delicacy, but surely we may have sense enough to give our opinions to commend or discommend such actions as we may approve or disapprove; without being reminded of our spinning and household affairs as the only matters we are capable of thinking or speaking of with justness or propriety. I won't allow it, positively won't.

6. Colonel David Fanning's Memoirs of a Loyalist, 1781

In the 19th year of my age, I entered into the War; and proceeded from one step to another, as is herein mentioned, and at the conclusion thereof, was forced to leave the place of my nativity for my adherence to the British Constitution; and after my sore fatigues, I arrived at St. John River; and there with the blessing of God, I have hitherto enjoyed the sweets of peace, and freedom under the benevolent auspices of the British Government. . . .

    King's County,
      Long Beach,
        New Brunswick.
    June 24th, 1790.

. . . After a little while some of us had assembled at a friend's house, where we were surrounded by a party of 14 Rebels under the command of Capt. John Hinds; we perceived their approach and prepared for to receive them; when they got quite near us, we run out of the door of the house, fired upon them, and killed one of them; on which we took three of their horses, and some firelocks—we then took to the woods and unfortunately had two of our little company taken, one of which the Rebels shot in cold blood, and the other they hung on the spot where we killed the man a few days before. We were exasperated at this, that we determined to have satisfaction, and in a few days I collected 17 men well armed, and formed an ambuscade on Deep River at Coxe's Mills, and sent out my spies. In the course of two hours, one of my spies gave me information of a party of Rebels plundering his house, which was about three miles off. I instantly marched to the place and discovered them in a field near the house. I attacked them immediately, and kept up a smart fire for half an hour, during which time we killed their Captain, and

---

This document can be found in Lindley Butler, ed., *The Narrative of Colonel David Fanning* (Davidson, NC.: Briarpatch Press, 1982), pp. 35–36, 63.

one private, on the spot—wounded three of them, and took two prisoners besides eight of their horses well appointed, and several swords. This happened on the 11th of May, 1781. The same day, we persued another party of Rebels, and came up with them the morning following; we attacked them smartly and killed four of them on the spot, wounded 3 dangerously and took one prisoner with all their horses, and appointments. In about an hour after that, we took two men of the same party, and killed one more of them; the same evening we had intelligence of another party of Rebels, which were assembling about 30 miles off in order for to attack us; as I thought it best to surprise them where they were collecting, I marched all night and about 10 o'clock next morning, we came up with them; we commenced a fire upon each other, which continued for about 10 minutes when they retreated; we killed two of them, and wounded 7, and took 18 horses well appointed; we then returned to Deep River again. . . .

. . . One evening, I had assembled thirty men, at a friend's house, and sent out spies. They soon returned with the account of a party of rebels within four miles of us, distressing and plundering our friends. We immediately set forward to render our assistance, and got within a half a mile of them; I, then, sent out to get information how they were situated, and by break of day came upon them. We retook seven horses which they had carried off, with a large quantity of baggage. We wounded two of them mortally, and several of them slightly; we came off without injury except two horses wounded. The day following, we pursued them, to Cumberland county, and on my way, I burnt Capt. Coxe's house, and his Father's. I had also two skirmishes and killed two of the rebel party. On my return to Little River, I heard of a Capt. Golson; who had been distressing the Loyalists; and went in search of him, myself; but unfortunately I did not meet him; but fell in, with one of his men, who had been very assiduous, in assisting the rebels. I killed him. I mounted a man of my own on his horse, and returned back. I then took Capt. Currie and the man of my own before mentioned, and I went with a design of burning Capt. Golson's house; which I did; and also two others. In my way, I fell in, with a man, who had been very anxious for to have some of my men executed. I sent him word for to moderate and he should have nothing to fear, but if he persisted, I would certainly kill him. He took no notice of this; but persisted, for several months, and on observing me that day, he attempted to escape; but I shot him.

7. Constitutional Clauses Referring to Slavery, 1787

Article I

Section I.   All legislative powers herein granted shall be vested in a Congress of the United States, which shall consist of a Senate and a House of Representatives.

Section 2.   The House of Representatives shall be composed of members chosen every second year by the people of the several States, and the electors in each State shall have the qualifications requisite for electors of the most numerous branch of the State Legislature.

These clauses are part of the Constitution of the United States of America.

No person shall be a Representative who shall not have attained to the age of twenty-five years, and been seven years a citizen of the United States, and who shall not, when elected, be an inhabitant of that State in which he shall be chosen.

Representatives and direct taxes shall be apportioned among the several States which may be included within this Union, according to their respective numbers, *which shall be determined by adding to the whole number of free persons, including those bound to service for a term of years and excluding Indians not taxed, three-fifths of all other persons.* The actual enumeration shall be made within three years after the first meeting of the Congress of the United States, and within every subsequent term of ten years, in such manner as they shall by law direct. The number of Representatives shall not exceed one for every thirty thousand, but each State shall have at least one Representative, *and until such enumeration shall be made, the State of New Hampshire shall be entitled to choose three, Massachusetts eight, Rhode Island and Providence Plantations one, Connecticut five, New York six, New Jersey four, Pennsylvania eight, Delaware one, Maryland six, Virginia ten, North Carolina five, South Carolina five, and Georgia three.* . . .

Section 9.   *The migration or importation of such persons as any of the States now existing shall think proper to admit shall not be prohibited by the Congress prior to the year 1808; but a tax or duty may be imposed on such importation, not exceeding $10 for each person.*

The privilege of the writ of habeas corpus shall not be suspended, unless when in cases of rebellion or invasion the public safety may require it.

No bill of attainder or ex post facto law shall be passed.

No capitation, or other direct, tax shall be laid, unless in proportion to the census or enumeration herein before directed to be taken.

No tax or duty shall be laid on articles exported from any State. . . .

Article IV . . .

Section 2.   The citizens of each State shall be entitled to all privileges and immunities of citizens in the several States.

A person charged in any State with treason, felony, or other crime, who shall flee from justice, and be found in another State, shall on demand of the executive authority of the State from which he fled, be delivered up, to be removed to the State having jurisdiction of the crime.

No person held to service or labor in one State, under the laws thereof, escaping into another, shall, in consequence of any law or regulation therein, be discharged from such service or labor, but shall be delivered up on claim of the party to whom such service or labor may be due.

⚔ E S S A Y S

Sylvia Frey, professor of history at Tulane University, insists in a selection from her book *Water from the Rock: Black Resistance in a Revolutionary Age* that one cannot consider the American Revolution in the South without looking at the impact of slavery. Whites had to prevent possible insurrection among their slaves while fighting the British and one another. Chaos and dislocation could easily have unleashed major resistance on the home front. As Frey argues, the British had no desire to create a social revolution and free all slaves, and Lord Dunmore's proclamation was a pragmatic gesture, intended to enlist the sympathy and support of slaves but not infuriate southern whites. Adopting a different approach in the second essay, Rachel Klein, an associate professor at the University of California, San Diego, explores the complexities of backcountry affiliations, stressing the importance of local leaders and the misfiring of British strategies there.

The Impact of African American Resistance During the War

SYLVIA R. FREY

The era of the American Revolution was a time of violent and unpredictable social, economic, and political change. The dislocations of that period were most severely felt in the South. Although historians have tended to view the war in the South in military terms as a bipolarity, in fact it was a complex triangular process involving two sets of white belligerents and approximately four hundred thousand slaves. The environment in which the revolutionary conflict developed in the South was shaped not only by British policies or white southern initiatives but also by African-American resistance.

Actual or potential resistance was a main factor in the development of Britain's southern strategy. Influenced in part by slaves' combative and aggressive behavior, British military leaders and Crown officials seized upon the idea of intimidating independence-minded white southerners with the threat of a slave rising without, however, actually inciting one. In the end the British strategy of manipulating conflict between the races became a rallying cry for white southern unity and impelled the South toward independence. The need to weaken slaves' zeal for service with the British, which threatened to expose the moral absurdity of a society of slaveholders proclaiming the concepts of natural rights, equality, and liberty, formed part of the complex interaction of events that constituted the revolutionary war in the South. To that extent, the American Revolution in the South was a war about slavery, if not a war over slavery.

Before the outbreak of the American Revolution, there were relatively few overt slave conspiracies or uprisings in the thirteen British mainland colonies. Historians have, therefore, concluded that American slaves were not prone to revolt. It is, however, clear from records of the revolutionary period that slaves posed a real, not imaginary, threat to the very existence of the plantation colonies of the South. The list of conspiracies and other overt acts of resistance is impressive, especially when one takes into account the tendency of slaveowners to suppress all news of revolts or plots. As historians of slavery have suggested, patterns of resistance were, by and large, influenced by internal or motivational factors and by external factors, which limited the parameters of choice and forced slaves to act within circum-scribed boundaries. Slave reactions were also influenced by behavior inherited from the African past, specifically from African systems of slavery from which thousands of New World slaves were drawn, and from traditional patterns of war-fare. To be sure, African-American slaves had a different set of disabilities than African slaves, but they operated in the same way to produce similar patterns of resistance.

Although research on the subject is just beginning, it appears that slave revolts were relatively rare in Africa. For such revolts to occur, anthropologists maintain, a large number of slaves must have formed "a self-conscious stratum," that is, a group that was conscious of itself. The formation of a self-conscious stratum is a necessary preliminary to group solidarity, which alone makes collective action pos-sible. The complex nature of African slavery militated against such formation. . . .

During the two decades beginning in 1765, slave unrest was more intensive and widespread than in any previous period. In the gathering intensity of the decade beginning in 1765, white Americans in the thirteen English colonies were passing resolutions denouncing Parliament's attempt to "enslave" them by regulating and taxing their property without their consent. In discussing the scope and powers of Parliament, colonists inevitably relied upon the ideology of natural rights, which rested upon the fundamental assumption that all humans are born with the inalien-able right to be free. Apart from James Otis and Benjamin Rush, who publicly ac-knowledged the anomaly in colonial cries for freedom and the existence of chattel slavery, and Benjamin Franklin, who for a quarter-century had denounced slavery as unconstitutional, most political leaders preferred to ignore the relationship be-tween political slavery and chattel slavery. The connection was not, however, en-tirely lost on black slaves who, like their white owners, responded to the political ferment of the revolutionary years.

Blacks, slave and free, urban and rural, artisan and field hand, literate and illit-erate, were swept up by the force of ideological energy. Northern blacks, who were disproportionately urban, mostly native-born and English speaking, were generally more conversant with the ideology of the Revolution. When asserting their claims to freedom, they frequently invoked the philosophical arguments that white revolu-tionaries were making in their own fierce struggle against oppression. In the South, where revolutionary ideology was as sincerely affirmed as in the North though the commitment to slavery was much more thorough, the large slave population per-ceived a change in the coherence and ideology of the master class and tried to take advantage of it.

Although the mass of southern slaves were illiterate, there is every reason to suppose that they had access to revolutionary ideology, particularly in a period of history when written communication was still hindered by undependable mail ser-vice and a paucity of printers and publishers. As late as 1775 more people probably heard the news of Lexington and Concord from riders on horseback relaying the news than read about it in newspapers. Newspaper advertisements for runaways in-dicate that most fugitives spoke English, some fluently.

The slave community had, moreover, the means to maintain a vital oral tradi-tion. The close physical proximity and the communality, which had disappeared among the white upper classes by the late eighteenth century, continued in a modified form among poor whites and slaves, most of whom lived in communal quarters of ten or more people. With the development of larger slave quarters and the creation of a common language, a complex communication system emerged. Table talk listened to by domestic slaves, conversations overheard by slave attendants or musicians, was quickly carried back to the slave quarters and was rapidly disseminated through the cross-quarter underground to other plantations, even to other colonies. Indeed, as Archibald Bullock and John Houston, two of Georgia's delegates to the Continental Congress, confided to John Adams, the slave network could carry news "several hundreds of miles in a week or fortnight."

Whether or not slaves were impelled by the subsuming power of the ideas of liberty and equality, their actions show that they did follow the progress of the war, and they fully appreciated its implications for their own lives. Slaves tried, for example, to take advantage of the confusion generated by the Stamp Act crisis in 1765 to make good their own understanding of revolutionary ideology. In Charleston, South Carolina, they watched with interest as white crowds protested the Stamp Act by parading around the homes of suspected stamp officers shouting "Liberty! Liberty and stamp'd paper." Shortly after, in a move clearly calculated to call attention to their own clanking chains, a group of blacks threw white citizens into panic as they chanted the same cry, "Liberty." In recounting the incident Henry Laurens dismissed the slaves' behavior as a "thoughtless imitation" of whites. But time and events leave no doubt that this show of consciousness and activism was no [aberration]. . . .

The changing political situation after 1773 exposed the slave population to new motives and greater opportunities for overt resistance. Early in 1773 a group of Boston slaves presented three petitions for freedom to the general court and to General Thomas Gage, British commander in chief in America and governor of Massachusetts Bay. A year later, Gage was presented with two more petitions from "a grate Number of Blacks," as they styled themselves, offering to fight for him if he would arm them and set them free once victory was achieved. In November a group of Virginia slaves met together secretly to select a leader, "who was to conduct them when the English troops should arrive—, which they foolishly thought would be very soon and that by revolting to them they should be rewarded with their freedom." Their plans were, however, discovered and "proper precautions taken to prevent the Infection." In reporting the incident to William Bradford, James Madison cautioned that "it is prudent such things should be concealed as well as suppressed." . . .

In the meantime, British military leaders and Crown officials viewed with intense interest the aggressive behavior of slaves and the apprehension it excited in their owners. Although the motives of the London government were complex, from the beginning of the conflict the North ministry was tempted by the idea of using the slave population in some capacity to crush southern resistance. Early in January 1775, news reached the southern colonies that an extraordinary proposal had been recently introduced into the House of Commons. Aimed at "humbling the high aristocratic spirit of Virginia and the southern colonies," it called for the general emancipation of slaves. The measure failed to win the necessary support in the Commons, but the idea of recruiting slaves as a disruptive tactic gained support as war with the colonies became imminent. Soon afterwards, Gage, whose own experience with Boston slaves clearly heightened his appreciation of the intense psycho-logical repercussions a war of nerves might produce, expressed interest in the idea. In what was apparently a private letter written in February or March to John Stuart, British Indian superintendent in the Southern District from 1762 to 1779, Gage warned that unless South Carolina moderated its opposition to British policies "it may happen that your Rice and Indigo will be brought to market by negroes instead of white People."

The complex triangularity of events is increasingly apparent in the events lead-ing up to independence. In April 1775, shortly after John Murray, fourth earl of Dunmore and royal governor of Virginia, seized the colony's store of gunpowder from the magazine at Williamsburg, "some Negroes (by one of his servants) had of-fered to join him and take up arms," thus anticipating by several months Dunmore's famous proclamation. Dunmore ordered them "to go about their business," and "threatened them with his severest resentment, should they presume to renew their application." Slaveholders were, however, suspicious. Convinced that Dunmore "designed, by disarming the people to weaken the means of opposing an insurrec-tion of the slaves," a group of citizens armed themselves and demanded that the powder be returned to the magazine. "Exceedingly exasperated," Dunmore threat-ened to "declare freedom to the slaves and reduce the City of Williamsburg to ashes" and boasted that in the event of war "he should have . . . people and all the Slaves on the side of Government."

The situation grew steadily more explosive following the actual commence-ment of hostilities at Lexington and Concord on April 19, 1775. On May 1, Dun-more wrote to William Legge, second Earl of Dartmouth and secretary of state for the colonies, informing him of his plan "to arm all my own Negroes and receive all others that will come to me whom I shall declare free." Properly armed, he boasted, his force would soon "reduce the refractory people of this colony to obedience." Dunmore's threat to recruit slaves and the arrival on May 3 of a letter from Arthur Lee, the American correspondent in London, to Henry Laurens, confirming "that a plan was laid before Administration, for instigating the slaves to insurrection," brought the racial issue to the forefront of public consciousness and gave an entirely new character to the conflict in the South. "This was the more alarming," William Drayton, a member of the South Carolina Committee of Intelligence, remembered, "because it was already known, [the slaves] entertained ideas that the present con-test was for obliging us to give them their liberty."

The growing [identification] of slave militancy and British plots to incite slaves as part of its American policy—always a factor in the relations of Britain and her southern colonies—became increasingly important in the spring of 1775. The "dread of instigated Insurrections," a popular euphemism for a British-inspired slave revolt, was particularly acute in South Carolina because of its unique racial demography. In May, a report that slaves would be set free on the arrival of the new governor, Lord William Campbell, and that the sloop of war carrying Campbell was also bearing fourteen thousand stand of weapons became "common talk" among slaves throughout the province and "occasioned impertinent behaviour in many of them." The discovery of an insurrection plot, planned to coincide with the British arrival, threw the white citizenry of Charleston into panic. "The newspapers were full of Publications calculated to excite the fears of the People—Massacres and Instigated Insurrections, were words in the mouth of every Child—," recalled John Stuart, who was forced to flee the city after he was implicated in the plan to employ Indians. . . .

By the end of the critical summer of 1775 British authority had been significantly undermined by the series of crises in the low country. In South Carolina escalating violence and the patriot decision to capture Fort Johnson led to open confrontation between Governor Campbell and the Council of Safety. On September 15, Campbell dissolved the assembly, closed his offices and fled to the *Tamar* in Charleston harbor, thus suspending royal government in South Carolina until the British capture of Charleston in 1780 restored royal control.

The waves of unrest that swept the South during the tumultuous summer of 1775 crested in Virginia with the so-called Dunmore rising. Dunmore's military activities in Virginia in the following months have been so frequently described and at such length, that a detailed account here is unnecessary. For nearly a year he ordered spoiling operations among Virginia's waterways, causing considerably more fear than damage. After several minor clashes with militiamen, Dunmore declared martial law and on November 7, 1775, issued his proclamation from on board the *William,* which he had seized from local merchants and fitted out for war.

Although it was viewed on both sides of the Atlantic as a threat to the very foundations of slavery, Dunmore's intention was neither to overthrow the system nor to make war on it. Directed principally at "all indented servants, Negroes, or others, (appertaining to Rebels), that are able and willing to bear Arms," the proclamation was designed to encourage the defection of useful blacks without provoking a general rebellion and to disrupt the psychological security of whites without unleashing the full military potential of blacks. Practical rather than moral, it was rooted in expediency rather than humanitarian zeal. That is not, however, how it was perceived in the South.

The Continental Congress meeting in Philadelphia represented Dunmore's offer of freedom to slaves as "tearing up the foundations of civil authority and government" in Virginia, and called on the colony to establish a government that would produce happiness and secure peace. In a vain effort to prevent word of it from reaching Maryland's slave population, the provisional government there prohibited all correspondence with Virginia, either by land or water. But in Dorchester County on Maryland's Eastern Shore, an area already troubled by persistent rumors of insurrectionist activities among slaves and lower class whites, the committee of safety reported new signs of slave militancy: "The insolence of the Negroes in this county is come to such a height, that we are under a necessity of disarming them which we affected [sic] on Saturday last. We took about eighty guns, some bayonets, swords, etc." In neighboring North Carolina, Howe's Continentals and the Edenton Minute Men were ordered to Pasquotank and Currituck to prevent a rumored attempt by Dunmore to march into North Carolina and to apprehend agents of Dunmore who were allegedly working to incite slaves in the Albemarle region. . . .

The defection of hundreds of slaves produced a powerful defensive response from white leaders. When Colonel Stephen Bull arrived with reinforcements from South Carolina early in March, he learned that some two hundred black fugitives were massed on Tybee Island. Reasoning that if they were successful in joining the

British it would "only enable an enemy to fight against us with our own money or property," Bull recommended to Henry Laurens, president of the Council of Safety of Charleston, a campaign of eradication: "It is far better for the public and the owners, if the deserted negroes on Tybee Island . . . be shot, if they cannot be taken." To "deter other negroes from deserting," and to "establish a hatred or aversion between the Indians and negroes," Bull asked permission to employ a party of Creek Indians to carry out the distasteful mission.

Laurens expressed personal horror at the "awful business contained in your letter," but he conceded that it was necessary, perhaps because South Carolina was also losing "many hundreds" of slaves by desertion to British coastal cruisers. "We think," he wrote for the Charleston Council, that "the Council of Safety in Georgia ought to give that encouragement which is necessary to induce proper persons to seize and if nothing else will do to destroy all those Rebellious Negroes upon Tybee Island or wherever else they may be found." He approved as well the classic slaveholder policy of pitting hostile ethnic groups against one another: "If Indians are the most proper hands let them be employed on this Service but we would advise that Some discreet white Men be encorporated with or joined to lead them." Because Bull and Laurens agreed that the information be selectively circulated, it is not known whether the general massacre that was planned actually occurred. Nevertheless, the event stands as a stark dramatization of the extreme brutality necessary to maintain the slave system.

Even without access to interministerial discussions it seems clear that the slaveholders' fear of a servile rising and the groundswell of slave resistance that both preceded and accompanied the development of Dunmore's experiment with armed blacks were precipitating factors in the shaping of Britain's Southern strategy. On October 15, 1775, one month before Dunmore's Proclamation, Lord North had recommended to the King an "immediate expedition against the Southern Provinces in North America." The claims of crown officials there that loyalist forces could be raised to restore royal government and pacify the South were "the more to be credited," North told the King, "as we all know the perilous situation of three of them from the great number of their negro slaves, and the small proportion of white inhabitants." Although the strategy was several years away from implementation, the North ministry continued to advance the idea of employing slaves as an ingredient of military policy.

On October 26, 1775, William Henry Lyttleton, former royal governor of South Carolina (1755–1760) and of Jamaica (1760–1766) and a consistent supporter of Lord North, introduced into the House of Commons "something like a proposal for encouraging the negroes in that part of America to rise against their masters, and for sending some regiments to support and encourage them, in carrying the design into execution." Lyttleton's comparison of America to a chain, the upper part, or northern colonies, of which was strong, populous, and capable of resistance, the lower part, or southern colonies, of which was weak "on account of the number of negroes in them," reveals a keen awareness of southern vulnerability. If a few regiments were sent to the South, Lyttleton predicted, "the negroes would rise, and embrue their hands in the blood of their masters." In an acrimonious debate that continued until 4:30 A.M., Lyttleton was "most severely reprehended from the other side, and the scheme totally reprobated, as being too black, horrid and wicked, to be heard of, much less adopted by any civilized people." Lyttleton's motion was defeated by a vote of 278 to 108. One month later Dunmore issued his proclamation.

Impressed by reports coming from southern refugees and exiled governors of the material advantages to be gained by the employment of slaves, British officials were reluctant to cast aside the weapon of a black force. Several of the proposals urged the home government to ride the wave of fear created in the Chesapeake by the active hostility of slaves during Dunmore's operations and by the seething discontent of the lower classes, particularly on Maryland's Eastern Shore. In a daring proposal designed to capitalize on local fears of united action by Maryland's slaves and poor whites, Sir John Dalrymple recommended that levies of indentured servants be raised on the Pennsylvania side of the Delaware Bay and in major cities, such as Alexandria, Fredericksburg, Baltimore, and Annapolis, along with "the bravest and most ingenious of the black Slaves whom He may find all over the Bay of Chesapeake." The effect, Dalrymple confidently predicted, would be "to throw the Estates on the Delaware Bay in waste, because the Masters will carry off the Servants from their Estates upon hearing what is happening in Chesapeake Bay."

Rather more remarkable because it came from a prominent Anglican cleric noted for his sermons on civil obedience and passive resistance, was a similar proposal from the Reverend Jonathan Boucher of Maryland. Government should, Boucher maintained, "keep their Fears perpetually awake, either by apprehensions of having their Slaves armed against them, or their savage Neighbours let loose on their Frontiers." Besides their slaves, Maryland and Virginia had in their indentured servants other "enemies in their bowells." As white servants they were generally better treated than were slaves and stood above slaves in social status. Nonetheless, they harbored latent hostility over social and political inequities, which sometimes erupted into open revolt, making them, Boucher insinuated, a force "not a little to be dreaded." . . .

Proposals to arm slaves and the actual attempt to do so in the Chesapeake provoked an outburst of indignation in and out of Parliament. Merchants and traders in London and Bristol, where the British slave trade was centered, resolutely condemned the idea. In a petition to the Crown a group of London merchants expressed "indignation and horror" at the prospect of slaves in arms against "our *American* brethern." "Very long representations" from the cities of London and Bristol were also presented to Parliament in protest of the "improper manner of carrying on the war and burning towns, savage invasions, and insurrections of negroes." In a letter to a friend in Philadelphia one Londoner denounced the North ministry as "worse than barbarians" for its "thoughts of declaring all your negroes free, and to arm them."

The emotional response to the various proposals for the arming of slaves sprang from several concerns. First, the measure was viewed as a radical departure from civilized practice. Historical precedents for using slaves in a military capacity reach back to ancient societies. Normally, however, slaves played a secondary and subordinate role in the military, serving as galley slaves in ancient fleets or as fatigue men to relieve the land forces of onerous duties. Even in ancient societies the arming of slaves was a highly exceptional measure resulting usually from a desperate emergency. In part this was due to the fear that armed slaves would turn their weapons against their masters. It was also due to ideological factors. Beginning in classical antiquity, the rule obtained that military duties were proportional to social status, with the highest classes being assigned the greatest obligations; the slaves generally were excluded from military [service]. Although the equivalence of political and military functions changed over the centuries, the ancient practice of exempting slaves persisted.

The use of slave labor in a military capacity was also common among European powers since the seventeenth century, particularly in the Caribbean and Brazil, where shortages of manpower forced colonial nations to recruit slaves for various military functions. The dangerous expedient of arming slaves was, however, generally eschewed until 1795, when the problem of West Indian defense forced the British government to organize black companies. The fact that the government's efforts to arm slaves ran counter to the weight of tradition caused concern in many quarters that the national honor would be impugned. It was their anxiety to "vindicate the national honour" that moved a group of London merchants to plead with the Crown to repudiate the reports circulating of "slaves incited to insurrection." Britain's violation of the time-honored rule against inciting foreign slaves against their masters had, Edmund Burke lamented in Commons, "deeply wounded" the national honor and debased "our character as a people" in the estimation of foreigners. Burke's claim that the arming of slaves had served only "to embitter the minds of all men" resonated through the *Annual Register's* account of Dunmore's activities in the Chesapeake: "This measure of emancipating the negroes," the *Register* regretfully reported on July 8, 1776, has been "received with the greatest horror in all the colonies, and has been severely condemned elsewhere."

Critical to British concern over world reaction was the fear of retaliation. Should "the Ministry act in that way," one Londoner predicted, "the *Americans* would march (the slaves) back, and perhaps arm them all that they could trust." Driven by the same fear, Burke warned the Commons that "when we talk of enfranchisement, do we not perceive that the American master may enfranchise too; and arm servile hands in defense of freedom?" Although American slaveowners proved to be more reluctant than the British to put weapons into the hands of slaves, a few, including the diplomat Silas Deane, recognized that considerable psychological advantages were to be gained by threatening to do so: "*Omnia tendanda* is my motto," Deane wrote to his friend John Jay in Paris, "therefore I hint the playing of their own game on them, by spiriting up the *Caribs* in *St. Vincents,* and the negroes in *Jamaica,* to revolt." . . .

The most important argument against the arming of slaves as a war measure was that it involved a social revolution that went far beyond the aim of disciplining the rebellious colonies. "This measure of emancipating the negroes," the *Annual Register* grimly warned its readers, had momentous implications. It threatened the existing social order. Whereas the conventional practice of relegating slaves to menial tasks had confirmed the validity of the social order, the plan to encourage "African negroes" to appear in arms against white men and to encounter them upon an equal footing in the field, weakened the traditional system of social relations, which turned on social discrimination and a sense of race. Furthermore, the *Register* broadly hinted, the full participation of slaves in the revolutionary crisis, with promises of freedom, endangered existing arrangements of property and wealth and the cluster of privileges and rights associated with it. Throughout the South the slave was regarded by whites as property. A capital asset, the slave was subject to taxation and was attachable for debt. From ancient times the protection of property was regarded as a fundamental obligation of the state. Now, the *Register* objected, by advancing the offer of freedom to slaves, "those who were the best friends of government" were exposed "to the same loss of property, danger, and destruction, with the most incorrigible rebels."

But the gravest risk was to the slave system itself. Prior to the American Revolution the military employment of slaves was usually aimed at preserving the institution of slavery. The various proposals for arming slaves during the revolutionary war generally implied its destruction, an issue few English leaders were prepared to debate in 1776. Since the seventeenth century, Englishmen, like other Europeans, had considered black peoples different. That perception of difference formed the basis for the traditional justification for slavery: a belief in the Negroes' cultural and racial inferiority, often interwoven with arguments for the utility of slave labor. Reinforced by Christian theology, which continued to distinguish between the spiritual equality of God's children and worldly enslavement, slavery enjoyed general acceptance. . . .

It is highly doubtful that the North ministry ever intended to effect a general emancipation of slaves. More likely the policy represented an effort to exploit slave militancy and coerce support from their owners. Had Dunmore's efforts to crush the South with an army of blacks been successful, it is difficult to assess what public reaction might have been. Burke believed that had Chesapeake slaves "reduced the province to their obedience, and made themselves masters of the houses, goods, wives, and daughters of their murdered lords," then "Another war must be made with them, and another massacre ensue; adding confusion to confusion, and destruction to destruction." At any rate, clearly on the defensive, North weakly defended Dunmore's Proclamation on the grounds that "it did not call on them to murder their masters . . . but only to take up arms in defense of their sovereign." Hoping to lay the matter to rest, he volunteered that "Lord Dunmore's proclamation should be laid on the table, that, if reprehensible, it might be attended to." Despite North's public disavowal of attempts to incite a slave insurrection, the temptation to employ slaves in some capacity remained, particularly in the South, whose huge black population made slaves a potentially powerful political, psychological, and military weapon.

Aware of the dangers inherent in such a plan, and with the memory of the public controversy still fresh in mind, the government proceeded cautiously. But the British path toward the military employment of slaves was smoothed by the decision of Americans to accept volunteered slaves for military service. Until the late seventeenth century blacks served in colonial militias, but only in a limited capacity and usually in noncombative roles. Fear of mutiny and the widely held belief that mustering slaves among freeholders was inappropriate, eventually led to their exclusion during peacetime in the mature plantation colonies of the upper South. In periods of war the scarcity of manpower forced most colonies to accept slaves and free blacks for military service in exchange for the promise of freedom. Blacks fought in mixed companies in all of the colonial wars. In the lower South, frontier warfare allowed blacks to play a major role, often as combat troops. Black soldiers fought in the Tuscarora War of 1711–1712 and played an active part in the Yamasee

War of 1715. As late as 1755 a shortage of white manpower and imperial rivalries along the vulnerable southern frontier forced the Georgia assembly to authorize the recruitment of blacks into the militia.

At the outbreak of the American Revolution several colonies, all of them in the North, accepted blacks in militia units. Blacks were with the patriot forces at Lexington and Concord and at Bunker Hill. Several served with Connecticut units during the Boston campaign. At the time of the Lexington engagement, however, rumors that slaves were mobilizing to massacre the citizens left defenseless when the militia marched off to fight caused such panic among white citizens that the Massachusetts Committee of Safety decided in May to prohibit the enlistment of slaves in any of the colony's armies. Five days after he was appointed commander in chief of the Continental Army, George Washington, the Virginia slaveholder, issued orders against enlisting blacks, although those already in the army were allowed to remain. In a move that suggests the degree to which white attitudes toward slavery had hardened as a result of British "tampering" and escalating slave resistance, Edward Rutledge, who represented South Carolina at the Continental Congress, moved that all blacks, whether slave or free, be discharged from the Continental Army; although the motion was "strongly supported" by southern delegates, it failed. The actuality of black insurrection in Virginia, however, gave the delegates second thoughts and on November 12, 1775, the Continental Congress formally declared all blacks, slave or free, ineligible for military service. Similar policies were subsequently approved by the other northern states.

But the weight of common sense and military necessity compelled the abandonment of the policy. Despite his own repugnance for using slaves as soldiers, Washington was among the first to recognize that slavery had become a military weakness because of the willingness of slaves to fight for the enemy. Dunmore must be crushed instantly, he earnestly urged his countrymen, "otherwise, like a snowball, in rolling, his army will get size." Convinced that the outcome of the war hinged "on which side can arm the Negroes the faster," Washington publicly advocated the recruitment of blacks into the Continental Army, otherwise "they may seek employ in the ministerial army." His great influence in support of the military employment of blacks persuaded the cautious Continental Congress to agree to allow the enrollment of free blacks, although the exclusion of slaves from American armies continued.

Although Dunmore had not created slave rebellion but merely exploited it, the crisis created by his reception and use of black soldiers worked by no means entirely to the disadvantage of America. By blaming Dunmore for inciting slaves to rebellion, colonists found a strong stick with which to beat their opponents. The "dread of instigated Insurrections" combined with the hardening of attitudes after Lexington and Concord were, even to a moderate like Henry Laurens, "causes sufficient to drive an oppressed People to the use of Arms." Paradoxically, white Americans found as well a rationalization for their own incorporation of slaves, rendered necessary by a rapidly developing manpower shortage. When in 1777 Congress began to impose troop quotas on the states, a number of New England towns and state governments began quietly enrolling blacks, although their enlistment was not yet legally sanctioned. Following the military disasters at Forts Washington and Lee and Washington's shameful retreat across New Jersey, the

Continental Army dissolved like a morning fog, and Congress was forced to approve the raising of eighty-eight battalions, which were assigned to the several states on the basis of population. Rhode Island, with a population of little better than fifty-one thousand whites and the British in possession of most of the state, including the capital city of Newport, had difficulty in filling its quota of two battalions. Prompted by the seeming hopelessness of the situation, the legislature approved slave enlistments. Promised freedom in return for service during the duration of the war, some two hundred and fifty slaves joined Rhode Island's black battalion. Similar problems in completing continental quotas led Connecticut to form an all-black company, the Second Company of the Fourth Regiment. By the end of 1777 free blacks and slaves were serving in mixed regiments in a number of states, most of them in the North.

Eager to escape blame for having first resorted to the use of slaves, Lord North later claimed that it was the American decision to enlist blacks that forced Britain to follow suit. In fact the precipitating factor was the decision made in 1778 to shift the seat of the war to the South. During the revolutionary war, Britain pursued a variety of strategies for ending the rebellion: by subduing New England; by securing the Middle Colonies; by pacifying the South. Although the shifting strategies were often marked by confusion, by 1778 operations in the southern colonies clearly occupied the principal place in British planning. Britain's Southern strategy finally emerged with three crucial components: to enlist the help of loyalists to defeat the rebels and to hold territory once it was liberated by British regular forces; to weaken rebel resistance by depriving the South of its labor force and by cutting off southern resources, such as tobacco, rice and indigo, the exportation of which helped attract foreign capital and thus sustained the rebellion; to exploit pro-British Indian tribes along the southern frontiers and the tens of thousands of slaves concentrated in the tidewater and the low country. The groundswell of slave resistance that both preceded and accompanied the gradual crystallization of that strategy, played an instrumental role in Britain's decision to gamble on the dangerous expedient of recruiting slaves for military service as well as in the American decision for independence.

Who Should Rule at Home?
The Revolution in the Carolina Backcountry

RACHEL N. KLEIN

Nearly a year before the colonies declared their independence from Great Britain, the South Carolina backcountry was already embroiled in a violent conflict between whigs and loyalists. Estimates of loyalist strength varied throughout the war, but several observers believed that the inhabitants of Ninety-Six District were about evenly divided and that tories may have outnumbered whigs in the fork between the

From "Frontier Planters and the American Revolution: The South Carolina Back-Country, 1775–1782," in Ronald Hoffman, Thad W. Tate, and Peter J. Albert, eds., *An Uncivil War: The Southern Backcountry During the American Revolution,* © 1985, pp. 37–55, 57–58, 61–69. Reprinted by permission of the University Press of Virginia.

Broad and Saluda rivers. As early as 1774 coastal radicals were concerned about inland allegiances and struggled, with only mixed success, to win frontier support. In September 1775 the British governor William Campbell could write with confidence that "the loyalty of those poor, honest, industrious people in the back part of this and neighboring provinces discontents them [the Charleston whigs] greatly." By November of that year the two sides had come to blows, and not until winter did whig forces finally gain a temporary ascendancy by rounding up the "most leading and active" tories whom they carried to jail in Charleston. Sporadic fighting persisted through the later 1770s, and in 1780, with the arrival of the British, the frontier exploded into a virtual civil war.

Historians have generally recognized a connection between frontier loyalism and sectional hostilities. On the eve of the Revolution the backcountry had only three seats allotted in the colonial assembly even though the region contained about three-fourths of the colony's white population. Before hundreds—perhaps thousands—of self-proclaimed Regulators drew attention to backcountry grievances, inland settlers had lacked local courts and jails. During the 1760s the growing colonial struggle had drawn legislative attention away from the backcountry, giving South Carolina frontiersmen added cause to resent coastal whigs. Finally, backcountry settlers, particularly those in the western piedmont, complained that lowcountry leaders had provided insufficient protection against the Indians. When the Revolution came, they had ample reason to resent requests for support from Charleston rebels.

This sectional interpretation of backcountry loyalism provides an insufficient explanation of frontier allegiances during the Revolution because it cannot account for the many frontier settlers who supported the Americans. Richard Maxwell Brown's discovery that only 6 of the 120 known Regulators actively supported the loyalists, while 55 joined the Americans, compounded the problem. Brown's research demonstrated that the most outspoken proponents of frontier demands for courts, schools, churches, and legislative representation tended to join the whig cause. Regulators resented the neglectful assembly, but their concern for the protection of property, their growing involvement in slavery, and their increasing interest in commercial agriculture tied them in fundamental ways to the wealthier planters and merchants of the coast. We can thus understand how Regulators managed to overcome their sectional animosity and join with lowcountry whigs, but the loyalty to the crown of many other inland settlers remains a mystery.

Nor is there evidence to suggest that ideology distinguished backcountry whigs from loyalists. Charles Woodmason, the Anglican minister who became the Regulators' leading spokesman, demonstrated how easily republican rhetoric could be turned against Charleston radicals. Woodmason was one of the few former Regulators who remained a staunch loyalist, and he admonished lowcountry rebels who made "such a noise about Liberty! Liberty! Freedom! Property! Rights! Privileges! and what not; And at the same time keep half their fellow subjects in a State of Slavery." Woodmason was not referring to black slaves but to the thousands of white frontiersmen who remained all but unrepresented in the South Carolina assembly. Inland and coastal leaders spoke the same political language, but on the frontier republican rhetoric could accommodate the loyalist as well as the whig position.

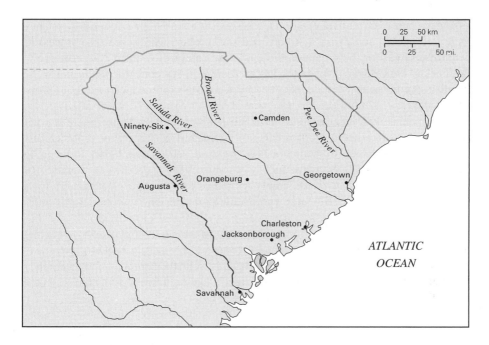

Finally, ethnic and simplistic economic interpretations can provide little additional help in distinguishing frontier whigs from tories. Wallace Brown, in his analysis of South Carolina's 320 loyalist claimants, found that foreign-born were more likely than native-born colonists to have sided with the loyalists, and contemporaries believed that the German origin of many settlers at the lower Broad and Saluda fork was largely responsible for loyalism in that region. But many Irish, English-born, and German South Carolinians joined the rebels. Similarly, Camden-area Quakers and New Light Baptists of latter-day Union County inclined to loyalism, and Regular Baptists of Charleston and Cheraw supported the Americans, but Presbyterians and Anglicans, who formed the majority of the inland population, were divided. Neither wealth nor occupation provides additional clues as to divisions on the frontier. Storekeepers, planters, slaveholders, and nonslaveholders were found in both rebel and loyalist camps.

If, however, the Revolutionary backcountry failed to divide along clearly defined class lines, the frontier struggle did have an important class dimension. Although ambitious planters and merchants chose one side or the other for a variety of reasons, the whigs more consistently represented the broad class interests of rising backcountry slaveholders. Those inland leaders who joined the whig side extended a process begun during the 1760s and gradually became the vanguard of an emerging planter class.

During the decade preceding the outbreak of the Revolution, South Carolina's backcountry had erupted into violence as Regulators struggled to suppress the bandit gangs that had been robbing and torturing frontier settlers and attracting slave runaways into their ranks. Leading Regulators were ambitious entrepreneurs. They were millowners, surveyors, distillers, and storekeepers who were in the process of acquiring slaves for the production of cash crops and were contributing to a growing backcountry demand for black labor. Their primary concern was to make the frontier safe for property holders, and they were especially concerned about property in slaves.

Regulators were also angered by those frontier hunters whose hunting practices, tendency to pilfer from planters, and inclination to support the more aggressive bandits ran counter to the interests of the more settled population. Referred to by their contemporaries as "white Indians," some of these hunters were squatters or even landowners, but they were simply unable or unwilling to plant enough for a subsistence. Regulators demanded various measures designed to restrict this hunting population.

Impelled to action by the immediate threat to their lives and property, Regulators took the opportunity to enumerate a series of smoldering backcountry grievances. In addition to calling for local courts, jails, schools, churches, and a vagrancy act, they expressed outrage that the backcountry had only two representatives in the assembly.

As the Regulator uprising progressed, a number of prosperous frontiersmen became alarmed by the violence of Regulator methods and urged the council to authorize an all-out offensive against the insurgents. They chose a man named Joseph Scoffel (also spelled "Scophol," "Scovil," or "Coffel") to lead the anti-Regulator forces. Apparently they saw Scoffel as a man who would attract precisely those people who had fallen victim to Regulator attacks. Scoffel himself was later convicted of hog stealing, and Gen. William Moultrie recalled him as "a man of some influence in the backcountry, but a stupid, ignorant blockhead."

Scoffel, assuming the title of "Colonel," succeeded very well in attracting followers who, not surprisingly, began to behave like bandits. According to one correspondent, Scoffel had "many returned horsethieves and banditti in his midst." Another insisted that Scoffel's party were impressing "provisions and horses" wherever they went, "leaving whole families destitute of both." These and other reports prompted the council to withdraw all support. Violence between the Regulators and Scoffel's people was narrowly averted.

With the passage of the South Carolina Circuit Court Act in 1769, the Regulators finally dispersed, but resentment persisted. Although Regulators had, by marching to places of election in 1768, elected six of their candidates to the assembly, the backcountry remained grossly underrepresented. Regulators had prompted coastal leaders to pass a law restricting hunters, but as the assembly became increasingly preoccupied by the broader colonial struggle, it failed to follow through on a proposed vagrancy act. The grievances and social divisions that had erupted in the Regulator uprising would influence the configuration and outcome of the longer struggle on the Revolutionary frontier.

As the Revolution approached, coastal whigs rightly feared that sectional animosities would incline South Carolina frontiersmen to support the loyalists. They sought to offset the loyalist threat not only by increasing backcountry legislative representation but by dispatching a three-man committee on a stump-speaking tour through loyalist strongholds. The committee, consisting of the Baptist minister

Oliver Hart, the Presbyterian minister William Tennent, and the Charleston radical William Henry Drayton, struggled to win the support of certain prominent "men of influence." They recognized that the primary divisions within the Carolina back-country were by neighborhoods or communities that tended to coalesce around such key individuals. The committee had only mixed success, but the record of their mission serves as a window onto the process by which backcountry settlers chose one side or the other during the first phase of the Revolution.

The committee concentrated its efforts on Thomas Fletchall, a militia colonel in the area between the Broad and Saluda rivers. Though he appears not to have joined the Regulation, Fletchall had publicly supported several Regulator demands. His defection to the loyalist side caused considerable alarm among lowcountry whigs. As one observer later wrote, Fletchall's position as colonel "of course gave him great influence in that part of the country." At a stump meeting held near Fletchall's home at Fairforest Creek, Oliver Hart observed "with Sorrow . . . that Col. Fletchall has all those people at his beck, and reigns amongst them like a little King." Not surprisingly, those areas in which Drayton, Tennent, and Hart enjoyed greatest success were neighborhoods in which militia captains were sympathetic to the whig cause.

There were other such loyalist men of influence who helped to make that region a persistent problem for South Carolina whigs. Among these were two former Regulators, Moses Kirkland and Robert Cunningham. The American militia general Andrew Pickens later testified to Cunningham's local prestige when he insisted that "there would not have been so virulent an opposition to our cause in this country" had Cunningham joined the rebels. Evan McLaurin, a prosperous storeowner at the lower Broad and Saluda fork, was also successful in attracting surrounding settlers to the loyalist cause. When Drayton visited the area in August 1775, he found that McLaurin was able to throw such "a damp on the people" that no one signed the Continental Association. McLaurin managed to put a stop to one meeting "only by his presence."

The very term *man of influence,* so frequently used by contemporaries, is revealing. In communities where settlers depended upon stores and mills for a variety of services, it is not surprising that merchants and millers, many of whom were also magistrates or militia officers, should have wielded extensive political influence. Drayton recognized the power of such men when, in the course of his journey, he declared that "no miller who was a subscriber [to the Continental Association] should grind wheat for a nonsubscriber." It is no coincidence that such prominent backcountry loyalists as Cunningham, McLaurin, and Kirkland were all involved in local trade and that Fletchall owned and operated large gristmills.

Influence could and apparently did work two ways. Thomas Fletchall lived on lands adjoining those of the pacifist and tory minister Philip Mulkey and presumably serviced the Mulkey community with his mills. One cannot help but wonder to what extent Mulkey and Mulkey's followers influenced Fletchall. Similarly, Evan McLaurin operated his store in the lower Broad and Saluda fork, where Germans predominated. According to contemporary reports, these "Dutch" settlers became tories because they feared that coastal rebels would retract all royal land grants. McLaurin's proximity to the German settlement may have encouraged him to remain loyal.

Whatever the interaction between various inland areas and their leading men, it worked to divide the Revolutionary backcountry by neighborhood. When persuasion failed, communities had ways of enforcing or trying to enforce unanimity. One loyalist refugee from the Camden area admitted to having taken the "Rebel Oath," but insisted that "the millers and blacksmiths would not work for any one who did not take the oath." That families and common ethnic groups often lived on adjoining lands only reinforced the tendency for clusters of population to act as whig or tory units. Following the British occupation, one loyalist officer could observe that "the whole province resembled a piece of patch work, the inhabitants of every settlement when united in sentiment being in arms for the side they liked best and making continual inroads into one another's settlements."

Not surprisingly, the storeowners, millers, magistrates, and officers most likely to wield local influence were also those most likely to entertain statewide political and military ambitions. For some, the decisive consideration in choosing sides was status. In January 1775 both Robert Cunningham and Moses Kirkland were, by all appearances, sympathetic to the American cause. Yet by the following summer, the two were among the staunchest opponents of the provincial government. Many years later Andrew Pickens offered what seems a plausible explanation. When the Council of Safety established a backcountry regiment, the candidates for colonel were Cunningham, Kirkland, and James Mayson—all former Regulators. The position went to Mayson which, according to Pickens, "so exasperated the others that they immediately took the other side of the Question." Pickens was not concerned with bad-mouthing tory leaders, for he also pointed out that he "never had any doubt but that . . . [Cunningham] . . . would have made the best officer." Henry Laurens, president of the Council of Safety, suspected that Thomas Fletchall had been motivated by similar concerns. "It has been said," wrote Laurens in a letter to Fletchall, "that you were in some measure disposed to unite with the friends of America, but that you were deterred partly . . . by the dread of losing your commission of Colonel and your rank of Justice of the Peace."

Recognizing both the ambition and the local authority of backcountry men of influence, lowcountry whigs sought to win support by offering access to political and military positions. In July 1775 Henry Laurens was eager to prevent the defection of a Captain Whitfield to the loyalists. It occurred to Laurens "that Captn. Whitfield however chearfully he may shew an inclination to serve the colony by resignation, may not be content with a subcommand," and he suggested that the captain petition the council for a higher rank. Also in 1775 the provincial congress established three regular regiments, one of which was to consist of backcountry mounted rangers. As the Revolutionary general William Moultrie later recalled, "It was thought not only useful, but political to raise them, because the most influential gentlemen in the backcountry were appointed officers which interested them in the cause."

As the Revolution progressed—as people lost friends and family in the fighting—the war assumed greater meaning for many of those involved. Some undoubtedly fought to preserve liberty as they conceived it. As one frontier officer wrote to his son from headquarters at Ninety-Six: "I feel myself distracted on both hands by this thought, that in my old age I should be obliged to take field in defense of my rights and liberties, and that of my children. God only knows that it is not by choice, but of necessity, and from the consideration that I had rather suffer anything than lose my birthright and that of my children." Experience on the frontier may well have made some such men particularly sensitive to colonial complaints about Parliament.

But during the early phase of the struggle most backcountry settlers were less concerned about Britain than their own local grievances and personal aspirations. Coastal whigs were able to win inland support precisely because they recognized and helped fulfill the political and military ambition of leading frontiersmen. In so doing, they extended the statewide political power of backcountry settlers and thereby furthered the political goals expressed by Regulators during the preceding decade. Following roughly the system of apportionment established for the provincial congress, the state constitution of 1776 allowed the backcountry 76 out of 202 seats in the assembly. Although the new constitution did not establish anything approximating proportional representation of the white population, it greatly increased the political influence of frontier settlers. For Moses Kirkland and Robert Cunningham, the whig offer was not good enough; but for others with similar ambitions, opportunities opened by the Revolution must have been very welcome.

Like their whig counterparts, many backcountry loyalists were ambitious slaveholders, storekeepers, millowners, and rising planters, but in their effort to attract followers they played on widespread resentments against the wealthier planters and merchants of the coast. Writing of his unsuccessful labors between the Broad and Saluda rivers, William Tennent complained that leading loyalists "blind the people and fill them with bitterness against the gentlemen as they are called." Settlers believed that "no man that comes from below, and that no paper printed there can speak the truth." At a meeting held near Fairforest Creek, Colonel Fletchall addressed the nonslaveholding population by intimating that "the people below wanted them to go down and assist them against the Negroes." Only a "Fool," suggested Fletchall, would agree to go. . . .

Although resentment against lowcountry planters proved a powerful weapon in the hands of backcountry loyalists, it also involved them in the first of a series of inconsistencies. Such prominent tories as Evan McLaurin, Moses Kirkland, and Robert Cunningham had various business connections with the coastal elite and, as slaveowners, had fundamental interests in common with them. They also had statewide political ambitions. By fueling antagonism toward the "gentlemen of fortune and ambition on the seacoast," loyalist leaders worked against the broad class interests of wealthy inland settlers who were seeking greater participation in statewide political and economic affairs. Although many backcountry whigs also felt personally suspicious of seacoast gentlemen, their participation in the American cause helped to accelerate a pre-Revolutionary trend toward growing political and economic association between the elites of both sections.

A far greater advantage for South Carolina whigs was their own inability to win support from the western Indians, a failure that actually strengthened the whig position among frontier settlers who lived in constant fear of Cherokee attack. As inland men of influence were drawing their local communities toward one side or the other during the first months of the Revolutionary conflict, many settlers were unwilling to become actively involved on either side. They were suspicious of coastal whigs, but apart from those areas in which loyalist men of influence held sway, they tended not to join the tories. Some of these previously uninvolved people—particularly those living in the western piedmont—became sympathetic to the American cause only after the broader colonial struggle became identified with a frontier war against the Indians.

During the summer and fall of 1775, many inland families had their attention focused not on the growing colonial crisis but on the growing threat from the western Indians. Both loyalists and whigs attempted to capitalize on the situation by accusing each other of trying to foment a Cherokee war. The accusations were probably groundless on both sides, but the ensuing rumors caused great alarm among western settlers, who had borne the brunt of the Indian conflicts of the 1760s. Writing from the backcountry in July 1775, the American officer Andrew Williamson told of "considerable confusion . . . on account of the expected danger from the Cherokees."

Although neither side wanted to instigate an Indian war, both whigs and tories were trying to win the allegiance of the Cherokee to prevent the Indians from joining the opposition. The British sent the deputy Indian agent, Alexander Cameron, to negotiate with the Cherokee, while the Council of Safety, in a last effort at conciliation, agreed to send a gift of ammunition. On November 3, 1775, a band of loyalists intercepted the shipment of powder and used it as evidence that the whigs were, in fact, attempting to provoke a conflict. Andrew Williamson's militiamen were able to retake the ammunition, but in late November two thousand loyalist troops laid siege to Fort Ninety-Six, where the powder was held. That Williamson had fewer than six hundred recruits for defense of the fort is itself testimony to the unpopularity of whig efforts at appeasement.

Recognizing the seriousness of the situation, the provincial congress tried to defend its actions by issuing a declaration claiming that "nothing could in the least degree satisfy them [the Cherokee] but a promise of some ammunition." Although the gift was "the only probable means of preserving the frontiers from the inroads of the Indians," it had been "by some nonassociators made an instrument for the most diabolical purposes." The whigs, by their very efforts to win the allegiance of the western Indians, were alienating backcountry settlers, particularly those in the vulnerable area of Ninety-Six District.

What finally decided the question of Cherokee allegiance and brought on an Indian war had little to do with whig or loyalist efforts. The Cherokee had good reason to be less suspicious of British officials than of the rebel government because the former had at least tried to restrict western migration onto Indian lands. By spring of 1776 the Cherokee were on the brink of war with South Carolina settlers over the familiar problem, and in April they attacked a community in latter-day York County.

With the Cherokee veering toward the British side, whig leaders abandoned their policy of conciliation and called for an all-out offensive against the Indians. This time Williamson had no problem in raising troops. By July 1776 he had approximately one thousand militiamen from Ninety-Six District who virtually burned their way through the Cherokee nation. William Henry Drayton, who had negotiated the gift of ammunition less than a year before, now called for the total destruction of the western Indians. "It is expected," wrote Drayton to a backcountry officer, "that you make smooth work as you go—that is, you cut up every Indian corn-field and burn every Indian town."

Though the whigs adopted an aggressive policy only after failing at conciliation, their new strategy was far more consistent with the experience and aspirations of backcountry settlers. Many, particularly in Ninety-Six District, had lost friends and relatives during the Cherokee War and other clashes of the 1760s. The threat of Indian attack had been a perpetual source of terror. By their all-out anti-Cherokee campaign, whig forces inevitably won some support from previously neutral settlers. That several active loyalists admitted to having served under Williamson during the summer of 1776 suggests the broad consensus that underlay the newly aggressive whig strategy.

Although greed for land was not an immediate motive behind Williamson's Cherokee campaign, the connection between land hunger and Indian war was obvious. Land hunger had been the source of the initial conflict. Even while Williamson was raising his troops, Drayton urged that the Cherokee nation "be extirpated, the lands become the property of the public." He promised never to support a treaty with the Indians "upon any other terms than their removal beyond the mountains." As it turned out, Drayton had his way. In the ensuing treaty, the Cherokee ceded the entire area of latter-day Pendleton County. From those lands South Carolina's militia and Continental soldiers would receive their bounty payments after the war.

Evan McLaurin, who eventually became a loyalist officer, inadvertently identified the tory dilemma. "The Indians," he wrote, "God knows they are good for Little." McLaurin believed that they could be used only as a "Bug Bear" to annoy whig settlements and interrupt communications. For that purpose he proposed the building of a frontier fort in order to protect the Indians' northern townships. But in return for a negligible military advantage, McLaurin found himself advocating a measure that could only have antagonized western settlers. All in all, the Indians did the Americans far more good as enemies than they could have done as allies. It was whigs, rather than loyalists, who found themselves in a position to continue the struggle for land and security begun during the preceding decade.

Loyalists attracted others as allies who, like the Indians, did them more harm than good. If, as seems to have been the case, the whigs had best success in winning allegiance from former Regulators, loyalists attracted the hunters and bandits who had inspired Regulator wrath. With the outbreak of Revolution, Joseph Scoffel, formerly the leader of anti-Regulator forces, reappeared in the backcountry, this time as a British supporter. The Council of Safety was alarmed in July 1775 by the appearance of "one Coffel" at Fort Charlotte, and Henry Laurens ordered that the fort be immediately taken. Later that year the council received information that "the Scoffel Lights were coming down from the backcountry in great force" to take public records and ammunition being held by whig forces at Dorchester. According to South Carolina's first historian, David Ramsay, "The names of scovilites and regulators were insensibly exchanged for the appellation of tories and whigs, or the friends of the old and new order of things." Many, he thought, had actually followed Scoffel, though the name "was applied to others as a term of reproach on the alleged similarity of their principles." . . .

By associating with well-known bandits, the British gave their opponents a moral advantage among backcountry settlers. In fighting the Revolution, whigs were also continuing the struggle against South Carolina's bandit and wandering population. They were better able than loyalists to present themselves as protectors of inland farmers. Thus William Thomson ordered another whig officer to "keep the inhabitants secure from the depredations of such unlawful banditty as may cross Savannah River . . . and protect those citizens who are well affected in their Persons and Properties." A whig militia colonel near Peedee requested aid for his regiment which was trying to protect neighboring settlements from "every murder, plundering, every cruelty, that could be perpetrated by a banditti of the most desperate villains and mulattoes, immediately bordering in our settlements." In characteristic fashion David Ramsay was able to pinpoint the British and loyalist dilemma. Referring to "horse thieves" and other "banditti" who attached themselves to parties of the British, he observed that "the necessity which their indiscriminate plundering imposed on all good men of defending themselves, did infinitely more damage to the royal cause than was compensated by all the advantages resulting from their friendship."

The British made matters worse by participating themselves in plundering raids, thereby failing to conciliate settlers who otherwise might have been willing to accept British protection. The British officer Banastre Tarleton, whose "Loyal Legion" moved into the backcountry during the spring of 1780, became infamous among back settlers for his pillaging raids. Writing to his cousin in 1782, a settler from Ninety-Six District described his personal experience of the British occupation in the following terms: "Our own true Colonels & head officers fled into the North State & a grat many of the young men went also. We being left like sheep among wolves, were obliged to give up to them our Arms & take purtection. But no sooner we had yielded to them but set to Rob us taking all our living things, horses, Cows, Sheep, Clothing, of all Sorts, money pewter, tins, knives, in fine Everything that sooted them. Untill we were Stript Naked.". . .

Despite complaints of plundered backcountrymen, the British general Cornwallis was less than sympathetic to the problems of frontier settlers. Writing from a backcountry post in November 1780, he observed that "if those who say they are our friends will not stir, I cannot defend every man's house from being plundered; and I must say that when I see a whole settlement running away from twenty or thirty robbers, I think they deserve to be robbed." By the following month Nathanael Greene could write that many tories were giving themselves up to the whigs, "being tired of such a wretched life & not finding the Support, Respect or attention which they expected from the British army."

Torn between policies of terrorizing and attracting the backcountry population, the British were never able to make the most of loyalist sympathies. They compounded their problems by issuing a series of orders that further alienated active whigs. Gen. Henry Clinton's proclamation of June 3, 1780, stated that all paroled prisoners, excepting those who had been in Charleston or Fort Moultrie at the time the city surrendered, were subject to British military service. In Camden the British Lord Rawdon attempted to enforce the order by imprisoning about 160 people, including John Chesnut and Joseph Kershaw, for refusing to join the royal militia. The result of this rigid policy was that many whig officers resumed active opposition to the invading army. To make matters worse, in August 1780 Lord Cornwallis ordered that the property of anyone refusing to take up arms with the British be confiscated. According to one prominent South Carolinian, it was "notorious that he [Cornwallis] has no abilities as a politician, or he would have endeavored to conciliate the affections of those he had subdued."

Plundering and banditry were not, of course, the exclusive province of British and loyalist forces. By the later years of the Revolution, South Carolina rebels and tories were, with considerable justification, accusing each other of behaving like bandits. Parties from both sides were plundering their opponents (and sometimes their allies) with impunity. Thomas Sumter, who solemnly urged the American general Francis Marion to "suppress every species of plundering," personally took the entire library of a wealthy backcountry loyalist. Officers who were genuinely concerned that at least whig settlements be protected still had considerable difficulty controlling their men. A chronic shortage of supplies exacerbated the problem. Through their repeated injunctions against plundering, Nathanael Greene, his generals, and even Gov. John Rutledge suggest that the practice was widespread.

But if whigs engaged in plunder along with their opponents, the behavior and policy of the two sides was far from identical. Whigs escaped the stigma of association with Scoffel's people, and their commanders were far more consistent in refusing to sanction plundering raids. General Greene understood what the British would never quite grasp: that the country would be "inevitably ruined" and the inhabitants "universally disgusted, if, instead of protection, they are exposed to the ravages of every party." Finally, it was whigs, rather than loyalists, who found themselves in a position to reestablish order. As rebel militiamen retook posts once held by the British, they, along with the government in Charleston, set about trying to suppress plundering parties. During the spring of 1781, Governor Rutledge issued a proclamation ordering an end to plunder and appointing magistrates in all parts of the state recovered from the British. In August 1782 Andrew Pickens requested twenty-five horsemen to suppress "such parties of men, as lost to every sense of justice or principle of honesty or humanity, make it their sole study to ruin and distress . . . every man who shews the least attachment to honesty, regular order and civil government." Also in 1782 the legislature passed a militia law establishing severe penalties for officers and men found guilty of plundering. It was whigs who, like the Regulators before them, became the champions of social order and defenders of private property.

The British attracted other allies, who, like Indians, hunters, and bandits, did them more harm than good. In June 1780 General Clinton issued a proclamation promising freedom to all rebel-owned slaves on the condition that they agree to serve the British throughout the war. Thousands of slaves followed Clinton's troops in the belief that the invading army was an army of liberation. many died in disease-ridden camps or were shipped to the West Indies for sale. But some made their way to East Florida and others became foragers, spies, workmen, or even soldiers for the British. Toward the close of the war, the whig major Henry Hampton attacked a black British regiment in the backcountry, and in 1782 British commanders created a black cavalry unit.

The problem for British and loyalist forces was obvious. By using slaves as soldiers with the promise of freedom in payment, they simultaneously threatened the slave system and evoked the specter of insurrection. In so doing, the British could only have alienated people from whose support they might have benefited. Writing to General Marion from a backcountry whig encampment, Sumter observed that "the Enemy oblige the negroes they have to make frequent sallies. This circumstance alone is sufficient to rouse and fix the resentment and detestation of every American who possesses common feeling."

Had the British been a true army of liberation for South Carolina's slave population, they might have gained considerable military advantage from their natural allies. The irony was that British leaders could not wholeheartedly embrace the notion of having large numbers of armed slave recruits. The prominent South Carolina loyalist William Bull was alarmed even by the formation of the small black cavalry unit that, he insisted, was committing the sort of "outrages" to which "their savage nature prompts them." In 1781 British commanders rejected or ignored proposals calling for the creation of two black regiments. Instead they followed a halfhearted policy. Clinton encouraged slaves to follow his armies, and he used some runaways as soldiers. But, ultimately, leading loyalists were as dependent on slavery as their whig opponents. They could not, without having threatened their own interests, exploit the potential military strength of the thousands of slaves who flocked to their camps.

By contrast, whig policies were consistent with the interests and attitudes of both actual and aspiring slave owners. Despite a serious problem in raising recruits, South Carolina's leadership continually resisted attempts to employ slaves as soldiers. In 1779 the legislature decisively rejected a proposal by Congress to recruit slave troops. According to David Ramsay, the plan was "received with horror by the planters [in the House], who figured to themselves terrible consequences." Subsequent efforts by Nathanael Greene and others to use slaves as soldiers fared no better in the legislature. Instead, the whig government chose to deal with the recruitment problem by appealing to the burgeoning backcountry demand for slaves.

That greed for slaves could become a motive for Revolutionary service was apparent as early as 1776 when Andrew Williamson asked the legislature whether he might tell his men that "such of those Indians as should be taken Prisoners would become slaves and the Property of the Captors." According to Governor Rutledge, that expectation already "prevailed in his [Williamson's] Camp insomuch that an Indian woman who had been taken prisoner was sold as a slave." William Drayton probably helped to encourage the notion by suggesting that "every Indian taken shall be the slave and property of the taker." The assembly refused to grant Williamson's request, insisting that Indians should be regarded as prisoners of war because enslavement might "give the Indians a precedent which may be fatal to our own people who may unfortunately fall into their Hands." Williamson's troops had to settle for indents issued in return for Indian scalps.

When it came to black slaves, South Carolina's legislature had no such reservations. Members sanctioned efforts by militia generals to raise recruits by providing a bounty payment not only in land, but in slaves taken from tory estates. Thomas Sumter set a precedent for other generals when, in April 1781, he sought to raise six regiments by offering a slave bonus to each militiaman who would serve for ten months. Even privates were to receive "one grown negro," and the numbers increased with rank. Sumter promised each lieutenant colonel "three large and one small negro." Other militia generals followed suit, with slight variations in their pay scales. The legislature also established a slave bonus for Continental troops.

So great was the demand for slaves among backcountry troops that Greene and others had considerable difficulty preventing soldiers and officers from taking slaves, without discrimination, from whigs and loyalists alike. After the war, numerous petitions requested that slaves taken by Sumter's troops be returned or that compensation be provided by the state.

Once again the British managed to act in opposition to the broad class interest of South Carolina's planters without incurring to themselves any significant military advantage. By serving as a magnet for runaway slaves, and by using such slaves as armed fighters, the British could hardly have endeared themselves to South Carolina's slave-owning population. Meanwhile, whigs not only avoided the contradictions of British policy, they also exploited and encouraged a growing backcountry demand for slaves.

The Revolution in South Carolina's backcountry cannot be called a class struggle in any simple sense. Rather than wealth or occupation, it was neighborhood affiliation reinforced by ethnic, religious, and familial ties that influenced the initial division between whigs and loyalists. Considerations of status more than ideological disagreements moved many leading men to choose one side or the other during the early phase of Revolutionary conflict. But if whig and loyalist forces failed to divide along clear-cut class lines, the British did attract groups that had fundamental grievances against the elites of both sections. The Cherokee, hunters, bandits, and slaves all gravitated to the British in opposition to an emerging social order more clearly represented by the whigs. Had the British been able fully to accept their "disaffected" allies, those groups might have done them considerable military service. As it was, leading loyalists were involved in a series of contradictions. By their various associations they alienated potential supporters and sealed the fate of the British war effort in the South.

It was finally the whigs who were best able to represent the interests and aspirations of those rising planters and merchants previously represented in the Regulator movement. The Revolution had forced lowcountry whigs to make political concessions to their inland counterparts. By joining the whig cause, leading frontiersmen could pursue their struggle for greater access into statewide political affairs. In fighting the war, whigs were also continuing a pre-Revolutionary struggle for Indian lands and security from Indian attack. By opposing backcountry loyalists, they were simultaneously working to suppress the bandits and "low" population previously opposed by the Regulators. And while South Carolina whigs may not have fought for anything so abstract as American slavery in general, many did, particularly in the backcountry, fight the Revolution for slaves.

人 *F U R T H E R   R E A D I N G*

John Richard Alden, *The South in the Revolution, 1763–1789* (1957)
Bernard Bailyn, *The Ideological Origins of the American Revolution* (1967)
Richard R. Beeman, *Patrick Henry: A Biography* (1974)

Ira Berlin and Ronald Hoffman, eds., *Slavery and Freedom in the Age of the American Revolution* (1983)

Irving Brant, *James Madison: The Virginia Revolutionist* (1941)

Richard Maxwell Brown, *The South Carolina Regulators* (1963)

Edward J. Cashin and Heard Robertson, *Augusta and the American Revolution: Events in the Georgia Back Country, 1773–1783* (1975)

Jeffrey J. Crow and Larry E. Tise, *The Southern Experience in the American Revolution* (1978)

David Brion Davis, *The Problem of Slavery in the Age of Revolution* (1975)

Sylvia R. Frey, *Water from the Rock: Black Resistance in a Revolutionary Age* (1991)

Jack P. Greene, "Slavery or Independence: Some Reflections on the Relationship Among Liberty, Black Bondage, and Equality in Revolutionary South Carolina," *South Carolina Historical Magazine* 80 (1979), 193–214

Don Higginbotham, *War and Society in Revolutionary America: The Wider Dimensions of Conflict* (1988)

W. Robert Higgins, ed., *The Revolutionary War in the South* (1979)

Ronald Hoffman, et al., eds, *The Economy of Early America: The Revolutionary Period, 1763–1790* (1988)

Ronald Hoffman, Thad W. Tate, and Peter J. Albert, eds., *An Uncivil War: The Southern Backcountry During the American Revolution* (1985)

Jean B. Lee, *The Price of Nationhood: The American Revolution in Charles County* (1994)

Dumas Malone, *Jefferson the Virginian* (1948)

Robert D. Mitchell, *Commercialism and Frontier: Perspectives on the Early Shenandoah Valley* (1977)

Jerome Nadelhaft, *The Disorders of War: The Revolution in South Carolina* (1981)

Mary Beth Norton, *Liberty's Daughters: The Revolutionary Experience of American Women, 1750–1800* (1980)

James H. O'Donnell III, *Southern Indians in the American Revolution* (1961)

Benjamin Quarles, *The Negro in the American Revolution* (1961)

John E. Selby, *The Revolution in Virginia, 1775–1783* (1988)

J. Russell Snapp, *John Stuart and the Struggle for Empire on the Southern Frontier* (1996)

Russell Frank Weigley, *The Partisan War: The South Carolina Campaign of 1780–1782* (1970)

Gordon S. Wood, *The Creation of the American Republic* (1969)

CHAPTER
5

The Emergence of

Southern Nationalism

*Despite the presence of slavery and the separate course of development on which the
South began to embark, little national consciousness of regional distinction existed
before the Revolution. Few colonists thought about a "South" or a "North," and
southerners had not developed a strong sense of their region as different or separate
from other American colonies.*

*With the Revolution and the founding of the United States, however, the first
signs of regional consciousness and self-consciousness appeared. The South continued to grow and develop in the decades after independence and did so in distinctively southern ways. The population rose, the area of settlement advanced, and
slavery expanded, especially in Georgia and South Carolina, becoming more deeply
entrenched throughout the entire region. Moreover, as time passed, slavery's influence spread throughout upcountry society (the settlements in Piedmont or hilly regions farther inland) as well as in coastal plantation districts.*

*Historians continue to examine why and when southerners began to regard
their region as a separate entity with distinct interests. Certain events caused southerners to consider themselves different, but how widespread this feeling was remains
in question. Slavery was at the heart of these differences, but the majority of southerners did not own slaves. Nevertheless, southerners began to think of themselves as
separate and apart, and historians continue to debate why such sentiments began to
emerge.*

 D O C U M E N T S

In the late eighteenth century, the passage of the Alien and Sedition Acts provoked a
protest that reflected sectional feelings; the legislatures of Virginia and Kentucky advanced constitutional theories (written by James Madison and Thomas Jefferson),
reprinted in part in Document 1, that would later support a states' rights sectional defiance
of federal dictates over slavery. Document 2, from a Richmond newspaper, indicates
the desire of whites to control the black population in their midst. The Missouri controversy, which is the focus of Document 3, awakened new anxieties in white southerners.

The battle over whether to admit Missouri as a free state or a slave state and where to allow slavery to exist revealed the divisiveness of the slavery issue; a major compromise was required to settle these issues. Margaret McCue's letter to her brother, Document 4, reminds us that political issues affected southern women as well as men. Another concern, the focus of Document 5, is the controversy over the removal of the Cherokee Indians from Georgia, a situation that exacerbated conflict among Native American rights to their land, a state's right to "seize that land, and the limited jurisdiction of the Supreme Court." Here, the Supreme Court opposes removal of the Indians. Later, however, Andrew Jackson defied the Supreme Court and ordered Cherokees off their land. Document 6 covers the nullification crisis in South Carolina in 1832. It is nearly universally accepted that the long, deepening confrontation between the federal government and the South began no later than this point, when South Carolina declared a congressional tariff act null and void. The ordinance states South Carolina's grievances against the federal government. John C. Calhoun, who developed the theoretical justification for nullification, was vice president of the United States until his resignation in 1833, at which time the South Carolina legislature sent him to the U.S. Senate. In Document 7 he defends slavery, calling it "a positive good."

1. The Virginia and Kentucky Resolutions, 1798, 1799

Virginia Resolutions

Resolved, That the General Assembly of Virginia doth unequivocally express a firm resolution to maintain and defend the Constitution of the United States, and the Constitution of this state, against every aggression either foreign or domestic; and that they will support the Government of the United States in all measures warranted by the former.

That this Assembly most solemnly declares a warm attachment to the union of the states, to maintain which it pledges all its powers; and that, for this end, it is their duty to watch over and oppose every infraction of those principles which constitute the only basis of that Union, because a faithful observance of them can alone secure its existence and the public happiness.

That this Assembly doth explicitly and peremptorily declare that it views the powers of the Federal Government as resulting from the compact to which the states are parties, as limited by the plain sense and intention of the instrument constituting that compact; as no further valid than they are authorized by the grants enumerated in that compact; and that, in case of a deliberate, palpable, and dangerous exercise of other powers not granted by the said compact, the states, who are parties thereto, have the right and are in duty bound to interpose for arresting the progress of the evil, and for maintaining within their respective limits the authorities, rights, and liberties appertaining to them.

That the General Assembly doth also express its deep regret, that a spirit has in sundry instances been manifested by the Federal Government to enlarge its powers by forced constructions of the constitutional charter which defines them; and that indications have appeared of a design to expound certain general phrases (which, having

Copies of these documents can be found in Henry Steele Commager, ed., *Documents of American History,* vol. 1, Appleton-Century-Crofts, Inc., © 1948, pp. 182–184.

been copied from the very limited grant of powers in the former Articles of Confederation, were the less liable to be misconstrued) so as to destroy the meaning and effect of the particular enumeration which necessarily explains and limits the general phrases; and so as to consolidate the states, by degrees, into one sovereignty, the obvious tendency and inevitable consequence of which would be to transform the present republican system of the United States into an absolute, or, at best, a mixed monarchy.

That the General Assembly doth particularly PROTEST against the palpable and alarming infractions of the Constitution in the two late cases of the "Alien and Sedition Acts," passed at the last session of Congress; the first of which exercises a power nowhere delegated to the Federal Government, and which, by uniting legislative and judicial powers to those of [the]executive, subverts the general principles of free government, as well as the particular organization and positive provisions of the Federal Constitution: and the other of which acts exercises, in like manner, a power not delegated by the Constitution, but, on the contrary, expressly and positively forbidden by one of the amendments thereto—a power which, more than any other, ought to produce universal alarm, because it is levelled against the right of freely examining public characters and measures, and of free communication among the people thereon, which has ever been justly deemed the only effectual guardian of every other right.

That this state having, by its Convention which ratified the Federal Constitution, expressly declared that, among other essential rights, "the liberty of conscience and of the press cannot be cancelled, abridged, restrained or modified by any authority of the United States," and from its extreme anxiety to guard these rights from every possible attack of sophistry or ambition, having, with other states, recommended an amendment for that purpose, which amendment was in due time annexed to the Constitution,—it would mark a reproachful inconsistency and criminal degeneracy, if an indifference were now shown to the palpable violation of one of the rights thus declared and secured, and to the establishment of a precedent which may be fatal to the other.

That the good people of this commonwealth, having ever felt and continuing to feel the most sincere affection for their brethren of the other states, the truest anxiety for establishing and perpetuating the union of all and the most scrupulous fidelity to that Constitution, which is the pledge of mutual friendship, and the instrument of mutual happiness, the General Assembly doth solemnly appeal to the like dispositions of the other states, in confidence that they will concur with this Commonwealth in declaring, as it does hereby declare, that the acts aforesaid are unconstitutional; and that the necessary and proper measures will be taken by each for cooperating with this state, in maintaining unimpaired the authorities, rights, and liberties reserved to the states respectively, or to the people.

The Kentucky Resolutions of 1799

Resolved, That this commonwealth considers the federal Union, upon the terms and for the purposes specified in the late compact, conducive to the liberty and happiness of the several states: That it does now unequivocally declare its attachment to the Union, and to that compact, agreeably to its obvious and real intention, and will be among the last to seek its dissolution: That if those who administer the general government be permitted to transgress the limits fixed by that compact, by a total disregard to the special delegations of power therein contained, an annihilation of the state governments, and the creation upon their ruins of a general consolidated government, will be the inevitable consequence: That the principle and construction contended for by sundry of state legislatures, that the general government is the exclusive judge of the the extent of the powers delegated to it, stop not short of *despotism*— since the discretion of those who administer the government, and not the *Constitution,* would be the measure of their powers: That the several states who formed that instrument being sovereign and independent, have the unquestionable right to judge of the infraction; and, *That a nullification of those sovereignties, of all unauthorized acts done under color of that instrument is the rightful remedy:* That this commonwealth does, under the most deliberate reconsideration, declare, that the said Alien and Sedition Laws are, in their opinion, palpable violations of the said Constitution; and, however cheerfully it may be disposed to surrender its opinion to a majority of its sister states, in matters of ordinary or doubtful policy, yet, in momentous regulations like the present, which so vitally wound the best rights of the citizen, it would consider a silent acquiescence as highly criminal: That although this commonwealth, as a party to the federal compact, will bow to the laws of the Union, yet, it does, at the same time declare, that it will not now, or ever hereafter, cease to oppose in a constitutional manner, every attempt at what quarter soever offered, to violate that compact. And, finally, in order that no pretext or arguments may be drawn from a supposed acquiescence, on the part of this commonwealth in the constitutionality of those laws, and be thereby used as precedents for similar future violations of the federal compact—this commonwealth does now enter against them its solemn PROTEST.

2. The *Richmond Virginian* Calls for Tighter Control of Blacks, 1808

The benefits to be derived from the establishment of a military corps cannot be denied: nor can it be pretended, that under the actual state of society, some provision of that sort is not absolutely necessary.

And why absolutely necessary? It is because the state of slavery which exists, added to recent events, impresses it on the mind of every man of reflection, that some effectual and permanent means ought to be employed to guard against actual danger, as well as to ensure public tranquility.

If this be so; if the necessity of incurring a heavy public expence, proceeds altogether from the situation of society as relates to the slaves—then nothing can be more reasonable, than that the whole expense ought to be borne by the holders of that particular species of property.

It is foreseen that this will be immediately opposed upon the allegation of partiality and inequality—It will be alledged [*sic*] that all the expenses of government ought to be mutually borne by all descriptions of people, and that every tax calculated to serve one portion of society, from the burthens which are imposed on others, is not only in itself unjust and oppressive, but will trench upon the established

---

This article appeared in the *Richmond Virginian,* January 1, 1808.

principles of a free government. All that can be now said in relation to this objection, is to deny it. The design of the writer is merely to bring into notice those opinions which prevail in his own mind. He believes that a public guard is absolutely necessary; that the system which he has recommended is far superior to that which exists; and that a tax on slaves is not only just and reasonable in itself, but by no means inconsistent with the equal principles of our constitution, and he would willingly afford aids to widows, orphans, and other cases of extreme hardship.

With respect to the slaves, it is likely that a general change of policy would be productive of greater benefits, than could have been expected from the public guard—In order to invite the attention of the public to the subject, the following remarks are submitted to notice.

Two opposing opinions now distract the state. One set of men, with honest, generous, but imprudent zeal, aim at a general and unconditional emancipation—Others influenced by motives equally pure, not only thwart and oppose these humane innovators, but seem to take delight in oppressing and embittering the fate of the unfortunates. In both of these cases perhaps true policy is neglected. The general weight and influence of public harmony is lost; the energies of the state are paralyzed; and men of equal respectability, of equal claims to public favour are arrayed against each other. Another course ought then to be adopted, promising not only to guard against general emancipation, but an amelioration of the condition of slaves.

Every slave ought to have some means of protection against the cruelty, injustice, and systematical oppressions of inhuman and flinty hearted masters; this may be done by competent tribunals, and upon terms dictated by justice and benevolence.

Indiscriminate and general emancipation at this time ought not to be countenanced, so far from it, the privilege ought to be extended, with care and caution, only to such as deserve so great a boon, by eminent service, or by a general course of a meritorious deportment.

Slaves ought to be solely employed in agricultural or other occupations of plain labour. It is also worthy of enquiry whether mechanics, house servants, waiters, waggoners, draymen, and water-men ought not to pay a higher tax, than those who are employed in agriculture, and whether in future, and by degrees the blacks should not be excluded from mechanical employments, and from being public carriers.

Innovations of this sort, would be at first attended with some inconvenience, but as soon as the regulations were known to be firmly settled and established, the labourers and industrious poor would very readily embrace those occupations, which are now, for the most part discharged by slaves—By this change alone, society would receive a much greater security than can result from the establishment of guards, even though their numbers and organization, should be equal to those ideas which have been partially unfolded. The dangers to be apprehended from slaves depend upon several causes; one is, they are the common carriers of the lower country—they have under their immediate care all the horses and accoutrements for horses—they are almost without exception good riders, and drivers, and among them may be found almost every kind of artist; Smiths and Carpenters without number. From these causes they have the means, without much exertion[,] of doing a great deal of mischief.

Now as the object of writing these sentences, is not to render the condition of the good and virtuous slave worse than heretofore, but to prevent the wicked from forming plots and conspiracies, the benevolent reader must not condemn what has been, or what may be said, before he looks through the vista of futurity, and impartially considers the different prospects which may be afforded. Peace, quiet industry on one hand—robbery, scourging, hanging, alarms and insurrections on the other.

If these or similar innovations are adopted, all the various duties now performed by slaves as carriers, artists, &c. will be performed by whites. The military strength of the city of Richmond alone, will be immediately doubled, and instead of danger from the black population, requiring a constant guard and patrol, there would be no other danger than that which is to be apprehended from the general depravity of mankind. The number of cultivators would be accordingly increased, and the general improvement of the country of course would be promoted.

3. Southern Congressmen Defend Slavery in Missouri, 1820

Speech of Benjamin Hardin of Kentucky to the House of Representatives, February 4, 1820

Sir, the manner in which this nation seems divided upon this subject [the admission of Missouri] convinces me of one thing that I have long suspected to be true, that our opinions, upon all that variety of subjects upon which we in the course of our lives are called upon to decide, are the result of affections and passions, and that judgment has no concern therein. Upon this occasion, we see this opinion fully illustrated; because men, distinguished both for integrity and talents, are to be found on each side; and the line that divides the parties is a local one. But, sir, the unwillingness manifested by the opposite side of the house to adjust and settle this dispute, and prevent an explosion that must shake the American world to its centre, induces me to believe that their judgments are warped by a passion, in this case, which may be denominated an unsatiable thirst after power, an unwarrantable lust of domination.

We now, Mr. Chairman, come to the last question I proposed to discuss. It is this: If there be no impediment to the powers of Congress from the constitution, and the national faith will not be violated by adopting the present amendment [providing for the emancipation of future descendants of slaves presently in Missouri], does policy dictate the measure? I do verily believe, that, instead of its being expedient to impose the proposed restriction upon the people of Missouri, that it would be unwise and impolitic, as it respects the nation; it would be unjust as it relates to the slave holding states; it would be iniquitous towards those who have been invited to settle there, and purchase our land at a high price; and a most aggravated and flagrant breach of public and national faith to those who lived there at the time of the ratification of the treaty between the United States and France. . . .

. . . This dispute is like no other that ever came into this house, that was ever before the legislative body of this nation. Party spirit, I know, has at times run high, but the great danger from this question as it relates to the safety and integrity of the

---

A copy of these documents can be found in the Annals of the Congress of the United States, Sixteenth Congress, First Session, Column Numbers 1084, 1090–91 (Hardin) and Column Numbers 225–25, 230, and 231–32 (Macon).

Union, is this, that it is not the same state divided into parties; it is not the states in the same section of the Union divided against each other. It is the north and east against the south and west. It is a great geographical line that separates the contending parties. And those parties, when so equally divided, shake mighty empires to their centre, and break up the foundations of the great deep, that sooner or later, if not settled, will rend in twain this temple of liberty, from the top to the bottom. My friends reply to me, and say, how can you compromise? how can you surrender principle?

It strikes me, Sir, that this matter can be settled with great facility, if each party be so disposed, and neither give up any point in this question which may be called principle. Can it not be done by permitting Missouri to go into the Union without the restriction, and then draw a line from the western boundary of the proposed state of Missouri, due west, to the Pacific? North of the line prohibit slavery, and south admit it?

The principle we contend for is, first, that Congress cannot demand a surrender of any sovereignty from a new state which is retained by the old states. In the proposed compromise this principle will not be violated. Next, we say that the faith of the nation is pledged to the people of that territory. Neither will this principle be given up, for the territory upon which the compromise, as contemplated, is intended to operate, is a wilderness, no inhabitants, citizens of the United States, living thereon. As it respects the gentlemen who are in favor of the present proposed restriction, it is no sacrifice of principle if they, finding that they cannot gain all they contend for, are content with partial success. I beg them to beware of one thing, as they love and revere this Union, not to push matters to extremities; for, although they may have a majority on this floor, we will never submit at discretion. I call on them to recollect the old proverb, "beware of the desperation of a peaceable man." No, Mr. Chairman, sooner than be delivered over, not to our brethren, either in politics or affection, but a federal party in the north, bound hand and foot, and to have no voice, no lot, no part, in this Union, we will burst all the ties and bonds that unite us together, and stand erect in our own majesty, as did that mighty man of old, when Delilah said, "the Philistines be upon thee, Sampson."

Speech of Nathaniel Macon of North Carolina to the Senate, January 20, 1820

The character of the present excitement is such, that no man can foresee what consequences may grow out of it.

But why depart from the good old way, which has kept us in quiet, peace, and harmony—every one living under his own vine and fig tree, and none to make him afraid? Why leave the road of experience, which has satisfied all, and made all happy, to take this new way, of which we have no experience? The way leads to universal emancipation, of which we have no experience. The eastern and middle states furnish none. For years before they emancipated they had but few, and of these a part were sold to the south, before they emancipated. We have not more experience or book learning on this subject than the French Convention had which turned the slaves of St. Domingo loose. Nor can we foresee the consequences which may result from this motion, more than the Convention did their decree. A clause in the Declaration of Independence has been read, declaring "that all men are created equal:" follow that sentiment, and does it not lead to universal emancipation? If it will justify putting an end to slavery in Missouri, will it not justify it in the old states? Suppose the plan followed, and all the slaves turned loose, and the Union to continue, is it certain that the present constitution would last long? Because the rich would, in such circumstances, want titles and hereditary distinctions; the negro food and raiment, and they would be as much, or more degraded, than in their present condition. The rich might hire these wretched people, and with them attempt to change the government, by trampling on the rights of those who have only property enough to live comfortably. . . .

. . . Can it be thought that the Convention which framed the constitution would have given the power to emancipate in so indirect a way that it was never discovered till the last session, when they were so particular as even to prohibit an interference with the slave trade until 1808? The following words in the constitution are chiefly relied on for the authority: "Congress shall have power to dispose of, and make all needful rules and regulations respecting the territory and other property belonging to the United States." The fair and only meaning of these words is, that Congress may sell and manage their own property, but not the property of the people. The power over the territories is very different from that over the District of Columbia, where exclusive legislation is granted. "New states may be admitted by the Congress into this Union." Under these words, a power is claimed to declare what shall be property in a new state. As well might a power be claimed to fix the age when people shall marry in the state. The ordinance so often referred to declares, that the new states shall be admitted on an equal footing with the original states. And so all the new states have been. It seems to be authority for every one but Missouri. . . .

It is to be regretted, that, notwithstanding the compromise made in the constitution about slaves, gentlemen had thought proper, at almost every session, to bring the subject before Congress, in some shape or other, and that they regularly, in their arguments, claim new power over them. What have the people of the southern states done, that such a strong desire should be manifested to pen them up? It cannot be because their representatives have uniformly opposed the African slave trade, or because they as uniformly opposed the impressment of American sailors by British officers; or because their banks are drained of specie to supply other places. . . .

If the decision be in favor of the amendment, it may ruin us and our children after us; if against it, no injury will result to any part of the United States.

4. Margaret Trimble McCue Wants to Live in a Free State, 1820

[February 25, 1820, from Staunton, Virginia]
My Dear Brother,

I Received our letter too weeks after Date. I was verry glad to find you had not forgotten me although you Did not write. I thought when Reading your letter I

Joan Cashin, ed., *Our Common Affairs: Texts from Women in the Old South.* Copyright © 1996 Johns Hopkins University Press. Reprinted by permission of the publisher.

would answer it immediately but its such a task for me to write it takes a week to get at it, but you will thats for want of Practice. I admits its so but my Domestic concerns Prevents my Practiseing much, & you must not neglect writing because I do not answer all your letters, but enough on this subject.

the friends are together with our own family well. we have Recieved no account from Brother W. since I wrote Mother. I suppose his whole time is taken up with this greate Missouri question which was not Desided the last account. we hope it will be decided favourably On the side of humanity. Received a letter a few days since from Brother Allen informing us that a Bill had passed for opening a Canal from Lake Erie to the Ohio River. This cirtianly will be of greate importance to the People of Ohio, & ought certainly to Be a greate inducement among many others to emigration.

I suppose it would surpris you all verry much to hear that Mr. Barry & myself have Been trying to Persuade our familys to move to Ohio, from Consciencious motives, but I fear the Difficultys are so great that I we will hardly Succeed. But there's nothing like Perseverance In a good Cause. the Difficulty of Disposeing of Property is verry great at this Time & the thoughts of moving scares Polly & James, Particularly when they Cannot see & feel the importance advantage to Soul and Body, the Deliverance from the Perplexing trials which we must ever expect while holding these unhapy affricans in Bondage. But we will try to Convince them that the Remove would be to our temporal interest. Mr. Barrys arguments are so Strong & so Plain, there is no getting over them. I think he says if his incumberance was not greater than Mr. McCues and the advantage of a home to go to he would be in Ohio before fall. But I meets waite with Patience untill the way is opened. Tell Mother she must pray for us Perhaps it is in answer to her prayers that our eyes have thus far been opened and if so they will be heard and the way opened.

you mentioned in your letter it was gratifying to see our Brothers thought worthy to fill the posts of honour to which the[y] have been Called By their fellow sitizens to which I agree. But O if we were all Members of the Church & House of God How much more Honerable, & that Crown of Glory which fadeth Not away than that of Princes. O My Dear Brother Seek the Lord in the Days of your youth Before the evil Days come.

write me often Give my Love to Mother—Brothers, & Sisters While I Remain your affectionet Sister, Margaret McCue.

5. The Supreme Court Addresses Removal of Indians from Georgia, 1831

MARSHALL, C. J. This bill is brought by the Cherokee nation, praying an injunction to restrain the state of Georgia from the execution of certain laws of that state, which, as is alleged, go directly to annihilate the Cherokee as a political society, and to seize for the use of Georgia, the lands of the nation which have been assured to them by the United States, in solemn treaties repeatedly made and still in force.

This document can be found in Henry Steele Commager, ed., *Documents of American History,* 5th ed. (New York: Appleton-Century-Crofts, 1949).

If courts were permitted to indulge their sympathies, a case better calculated to excite them can scarcely be imagined. A people, once numerous, powerful, and truly independent, found by our ancestors in the quiet and uncontrolled possession of an ample domain, gradually sinking beneath our superior policy, our arts and our arms, have yielded their lands, by successive treaties, each of which contains a solemn guarantee of the residue, until they retain no more of their formerly extensive territory than is deemed necessary to their comfortable subsistence. To preserve this remnant, the present application is made.

Before we can look into the merits of the case, a preliminary inquiry presents itself. Has this court jurisdiction of the cause? The third article of the constitution describes the extent of the judicial power. The second section closes an enumeration of the cases to which it is extended, with "controversies between a state or citizens thereof, and foreign states, citizens or subjects." A subsequent clause of the same section gives the supreme court original jurisdiction, in all cases in which a state shall be a party. The party defendant may then unquestionably be sued in this court. May the plaintiff sue in it? Is the Cherokee nation a foreign state, in the sense in which that term is used in the constitution? The counsel for the plaintiffs have maintained the affirmative of this proposition with great earnestness and ability. So much of the argument as was intended to prove the character of the Cherokees as a state, as a distinct political society, separated from others, capable of managing its own affairs and governing itself, has in the opinion of a majority of the judges, been completely successful. They have been uniformly treated as a state, from the settlement of our country. The numerous treaties made with them by the United States, recognise them as a people capable of maintaining the relations of peace and war, of being responsible in their political character for any violation of their engagements, or for any aggression committed on the citizens of the United States, by any individual of their community. Laws have been enacted in the spirit of these treaties. The acts of our government plainly recognise the Cherokee nation as a state, and the courts are bound by those acts.

A question of much more difficulty remains. Do the Cherokees constitute a foreign state in the sense of the constitution? The counsel have shown conclusively, that they are not a state of the Union, and have insisted that, individually, they are aliens, not owing allegiance to the United States. An aggregate of aliens composing a state must, they say, be a foreign state; each individual being foreign, the whole must be foreign.

This argument is imposing, but we must examine it more closely, before we yield to it. The condition of the Indians in relation to the United States is, perhaps, unlike that of any other two people in existence. In general, nations not owning a common allegiance, are foreign to each other. The term foreign nation is, with strict propriety, applicable by either to the other. But the relation of the Indians to the United States is marked by peculiar and cardinal distinctions which exist nowhere else. The Indian territory is admitted to compose a part of the United States. In all our maps, geographical treaties, histories and laws, it is so considered. In all our intercourse with foreign nations, in our commercial regulations, in any attempt at intercourse between Indians and foreign nations, they are considered as within the jurisdictional limits of the United States, subject to many of those restraints which are imposed upon our own citizens. They acknowledge themselves, in their treaties, to be under the protection of the United States; they admit, that the United States shall have the sole and exclusive right of regulating the trade with them, and managing all their affairs as they think proper; and the Cherokees in particular were allowed by the treaty of Hopewell, which preceded the constitution, "to send a deputy of their choice, whenever they think fit, to congress." Treaties were made with some tribes, by the state of New York, under a then unsettled construction of the confederation, by which they ceded all their lands to that state, taking back a limited grant to themselves, in which they admit their dependence. Though the Indians are acknowledged to have an unquestionable, and heretofore unquestioned, right to the lands they occupy, until that right shall be extinguished by a voluntary cession to our government; yet it may well be doubted, whether those tribes which reside within the acknowledged boundaries of the United States can, with accuracy, be denominated foreign nations. They may, more correctly, perhaps, be denominated domestic dependent nations. They occupy a territory to which we assert a title independent of their will, which must take effect in point of possession, when their right of possession ceases. Meanwhile, they are in a state of pupilage; their relation to the United States resembles that of a ward to his guardian. They took to our government for protection; rely upon its kindness and its power; appeal to it for relief to their wants; and address the president as their great father. They and their country are considered by foreign nations, as well as by ourselves, as being so completely under the sovereignty and dominion of the United States, that any attempt to acquire their lands, or to form a political connection with them would be considered by all as an invasion of our territory and an act of hostility. These considerations go far to support the opinion, that the framers of our constitution had not the Indian tribes in view, when they opened the courts of the Union to controversies between a state or the citizens thereof and foreign states.

In considering this subject, the habits and usages of the Indians, in their intercourse with their white neighbors, ought not to be entirely disregarded. At the time the constitution was framed, the idea of appealing to an American court of justice for an assertion of right or a redress of wrong, had perhaps never entered the mind of an Indian or of his tribe. Their appeal was to the tomahawk, or to the government. This was well understood by the statesmen who framed the constitution of the United States, and might furnish some reason for omitting to enumerate them among the parties who might sue in the courts of the Union. Be this as it may, the peculiar relations between the United States and the Indians occupying our territory are such, that we should feel much difficulty in considering them as designated by the term foreign state, were there no other part of the constitution which might shed light on the meaning of these words. But we think that in construing them, considerable aid is furnished by that clause in the eighth section of the third article, which empowers congress to "regulate commerce with foreign nations, and among the several states, and with the Indian tribes." In this clause, they are as clearly contradistinguished, by a name appropriate to themselves, from foreign nations, as from the several states composing the Union. They are designated by a distinct appellation; and as this appellation can be applied to neither of the others, neither can the application distinguishing either of the others be, in fair construction, applied to them. The objects to which the power of regulating commerce might be directed, are divided into three distinct classes—foreign nations, the several states, and

Indian tribes. When forming this article, the convention considered them as entirely distinct. We cannot assume that the distinction was lost, in framing a subsequent article, unless there be something in its language to authorize the assumption. . . .

A serious additional objection exists to the jurisdiction of the court. Is the matter of the bill the proper subject for judicial inquiry and decision? It seeks to restrain a state from the forcible exercise of legislative power over a neighboring people, asserting their independence; their right to which the state denies. On several of the matters alleged in the bill, for example, on the laws making it criminal to exercise the usual powers of self-government in their own country, by the Cherokee nation, this court cannot interpose; at least, in the form in which those matters are presented.

That part of the bill which respects the land occupied by the Indians, and prays the aid of the court to protect their possession, may be more doubtful. The mere question of right might, perhaps, be decided by this court, in a proper case, with proper parties. But the court is asked to do more than decide on the title. The bill requires us to control the legislature of Georgia, and to restrain the exertion of its physical force. The propriety of such an interposition by the court may be well questioned; it savors too much of the exercise of political power, to be within the proper province of the judicial department. But the opinion on the point respecting parties makes it unnecessary to decide this question.

If it be true, that the Cherokee nation have rights, this is not the tribunal in which those rights are to be asserted. If it be true, that wrongs have been inflicted, and that still greater are to be apprehended, this is not the tribunal which can redress the past or prevent the future. The motion for an injunction is denied. STORY, J. and THOMPSON, J. dissenting.

6. The Nullification Crisis in South Carolina, 1832

South Carolina Nullifies the Tariff, 1832

An Ordinance to Nullify certain acts of the Congress of the United States, purporting to be laws laying duties and imposts on the importation of foreign commodities.

Whereas the Congress of the United States, by various acts, purporting to be acts laying duties and imposts on foreign imports, but in reality intended for the protection of domestic manufacturers, and the giving of bounties to classes and individuals engaged in particular employments, at the expense and to the injury and oppression of other classes and individuals, and by wholly exempting from taxation certain foreign commodities, such as are not produced or manufactured in the United States, to afford a pretext for imposing higher and excessive duties on articles similar to those intended to be protected, hath exceeded its just powers under the Constitution, which confers on it no authority to afford such protection, and hath violated the true meaning and intent of the Constitution, which provides for equality in imposing the burthens of taxation upon the several States and portions of the Confederacy: *And whereas* the said Congress, exceeding its just power to impose taxes and collect revenue for the

This document can be found in Henry Steele Commager, ed., *Documents of American History,* Fourth edition (New York: Appleton-Century-Crofts, Inc., 1948), Vol. I, pp. 261–262. This document was originally taken from *Statutes at Large of South Carolina,* Vol. I, p. 329ff.

purpose of effecting and accomplishing the specific objects and purposes which the Constitution of the United States authorizes it to effect and accomplish, hath raised and collected unnecessary revenue for objects unauthorized by the Constitution:—

We, therefore, the people of the State of South Carolina in Convention assembled, do declare and ordain, . . . That the several acts and parts of acts of the Congress of the United States, purporting to be laws for the imposing of duties and imposts on the importation of foreign commodities, . . . and, more especially . . . [the tariff acts of 1828 and 1832] . . . , are unauthorized by the Constitution of the United States, and violate the true meaning and intent thereof, and are null, void, and no law, nor binding upon this State, its officers or citizens; and all promises, contracts, and obligations, made or entered into, or to be made or entered into, with purpose to secure the duties imposed by the said acts, and all judicial proceedings which shall be hereafter had in affirmance thereof, are and shall be held utterly null and void.

And it is further Ordained, That it shall not be lawful for any of the constituted authorities, whether of this State or of the United States, to enforce the payment of duties imposed by the said acts within the limits of this State; but it shall be the duty of the Legislature to adopt such measures and pass such acts as may be necessary to give full effect to this Ordinance, and to prevent the enforcement and arrest the operation of the said acts and parts of acts of the Congress of the United States within the limits of this State, from and after the 1st day of February next, . . .

And it is further Ordained, That in no case of law or equity, decided in the courts of this State, wherein shall be drawn in question the authority of this ordinance, or the validity of such act or acts of the Legislature as may be passed for the purpose of giving effect thereto, or the validity of the aforesaid acts of Congress, imposing duties, shall any appeal be taken or allowed to the Supreme Court of the United States, nor shall any copy of the record be printed or allowed for that purpose; and if any such appeal shall be attempted to be taken, the courts of this State shall proceed to execute and enforce their judgments, according to the laws and usages of the State, without reference to such attempted appeal, and the person or persons attempting to take such appeal may be dealt with as for a contempt of the court.

And it is further Ordained, That all persons now holding any office of honor, profit, or trust, civil or military, under this State, (members of the Legislature excepted), shall, within such time, and in such manner as the Legislature shall prescribe, take an oath well and truly to obey, execute, and enforce, this Ordinance, and such act or acts of the Legislature as may be passed in pursuance thereof, according to the true intent and meaning of the same; and on the neglect or omission of any such person or persons so to do, his or their office or offices shall be forthwith vacated, . . . and no person hereafter elected to any office of honor, profit, or trust, civil or military, (members of the Legislature excepted), shall, until the Legislature shall otherwise provide and direct, enter on the execution of his office, . . . until he shall, in like manner, have taken a similar oath; and no juror shall be empannelled in any of the courts of this State, in any cause in which shall be in question this Ordinance, or any act of the Legislature passed in pursuance thereof, unless he shall first, in addition to the usual oath, have taken an oath that he will well and truly obey, execute, and enforce this Ordinance, and such act or acts of the Legislature as may be passed to carry the same into operation and effect, according to the true intent and meaning thereof.

And we, the People of South Carolina, to the end that it may be fully under-stood by the Government of the United States, and the people of the co-States, that we are determined to maintain this, our Ordinance and Declaration, at every hazard, *Do further Declare* that we will not submit to the application of force, on the part of the Federal Government, to reduce this State to obedience; but that we will consider the passage, by Congress, of any act . . . to coerce the State, shut up her ports, de-stroy or harass her commerce, or to enforce the acts hereby declared to be null and void, otherwise than through the civil tribunals of the country, as inconsistent with the longer continuance of South Carolina in the Union; and that the people of this State will thenceforth hold themselves absolved from all further obligation to main-tain or preserve their political connexion with the people of the other States, and will forthwhile proceed to organize a separate Government, and do all other acts and things which sovereign and independent States may of right to do.

President Andrew Jackson's Proclamation to the People of South Carolina, 1832

. . . I, Andrew Jackson, President of the United States, have thought proper to issue this my proclamation, stating my views of the Constitution and laws applicable to the measures adopted by the convention of South Carolina. . . .

The ordinance is founded, not on the indefeasible right of resisting acts which are plainly unconstitutional and too oppressive to be endured, but on the strange po-sition that any one State may not only declare an act of Congress void, but prohibit its execution; that they may do this consistently with the Constitution; that the true construction of that instrument permits a State to retain its place in the Union and yet be bound by no other of its laws than those it may choose to consider as consti-tutional. It is true, they add, that to justify this abrogation of a law it must be palpa-bly contrary to the Constitution; but it is evident that to give the right of resisting laws of that description, coupled with the uncontrolled right to decide what laws de-serve that character, is to give the power of resisting all laws; for as by the theory there is no appeal, the reasons alleged by the State, good or bad, must prevail. If it should be said that public opinion is a sufficient check against the abuse of this power, it may be asked why it is not deemed a sufficient guard against the passage of an unconstitutional act by Congress? . . . If South Carolina considers the revenue laws unconstitutional and has a right to prevent their execution in the port of Charleston, there would be a clear constitutional objection to their collection in every other port; and no revenue could be collected anywhere, for all imposts must be equal. It is no answer to repeat that an unconstitutional law is no law so long as the question of its legality is to be decided by the State itself, for every law operat-ing injuriously upon any local interest will be perhaps thought, and certainly repre-sented, as unconstitutional, and, as has been shown, there is no appeal. . . .

Our present Constitution was formed . . . in vain if this fatal doctrine prevails. It was formed for important objects that are announced in the preamble, made in the name and by the authority of the people of the United States, whose delegates

This document can be found in Henry Steele Commager, ed., *Documents of American History,* 5th ed. (New York: Appleton-Century-Crofts, 1949).

framed and whose conventions approved it. The most important among these objects—that which is placed first in rank, on which all the others rest—is "*to form a more perfect union.*" Now, is it possible that even if there were no express provision giving supremacy to the Constitution and laws of the United States over those of the States, can it be conceived that an instrument made for the purpose of "*forming a more perfect union*" than that of the Confederation could be so constructed by the assembled wisdom of our country as to substitute for that Confederation a form of government dependent for its existence on the local interest, the party spirit, of a State, or of a prevailing faction in a State? . . .

I consider, then, the power to annul a law of the United States, assumed by one State, *incompatible with the existence of the Union, contradicted expressly by the letter of the Constitution, unauthorized by its spirit, inconsistent with every principle on which it was founded, and destructive of the great object for which it was formed.* . . .

This right to secede is deduced from the nature of the Constitution, which, they say, is a compact between sovereign States who have preserved their whole sovereignty and therefore are subject to no superior; that because they made the compact they can break it when in their opinion it has been departed from by the other States. Fallacious as this course of reasoning is, it enlists State pride and finds advocates in the honest prejudices of those who have not studied the nature of our Government sufficiently to see the radical error on which it rests. . . .

The Constitution of the United States, then, forms a *government,* not a league; and whether it be formed by compact between the States or in any other manner, its character is the same. It is a Government in which all the people are represented, which operates directly on the people individually, not upon the States; they retained all the power they did not grant. But each State, having expressly parted with so many powers as to constitute, jointly with the other States, a single nation, can not, from that period, possess any right to secede, because such secession does not break a league, but destroys the unity of a nation; and any injury to that unity is not only a breach which would result from the contravention of a compact, but it is an offense against the whole Union. To say that any State may at pleasure secede from the Union is to say that the United States are not a nation. . . .

Because the Union was formed by a compact, it is said the parties to that compact may, when they feel themselves aggrieved, depart from it; but it is precisely because it is a compact that they can not. A compact is an agreement or binding obligation. It may by its terms have a sanction or penalty for its breach, or it may not. If it contains no sanction, it may be broken with no other consequence than moral guilt; if it have a sanction, then the breach incurs the designated or implied penalty. A league between independent nations generally has no sanction other than a moral one; or if it should contain a penalty, as there is no common superior it can not be enforced. A government, on the contrary, always has a sanction, express or implied; and in our case it is both necessarily implied and expressly given. An attempt, by force of arms, to destroy a government is an offense, by whatever means the constitutional compact may have been formed; and such government has the right by the law of self-defense to pass acts for punishing the offender, unless that right is modified, restrained, or resumed by the constitutional act. . . .

This, then, is the position in which we stand: A small majority of the citizens of one State in the Union have elected delegates to a State convention; that convention has ordained that all the revenue laws of the United States must be repealed, or that they are no longer a member of the Union. The governor of that State has recommended to the legislature the raising of an army to carry the secession into effect, and that be may be empowered to give clearances to vessels in the name of the State. No act of violent opposition to the laws has yet been committed, but such a state of things is hourly apprehended. And it is the intent of this instrument to *proclaim,* not only that the duty imposed on me by the Constitution "to take care that the laws be faithfully executed" shall be performed to the extent of the powers already vested in me by law, or of such others as the wisdom of Congress shall devise and intrust to me for that purpose, but to warn the citizens of South Carolina who have been deluded into an opposition to the laws of the danger they will incur by obedience to the illegal and disorganizing ordinance of the convention; to exhort those who have refused to support it to persevere in their determination to uphold the Constitution and laws of their country; and to point out to all the perilous situation into which the good people of that State have been led, and that the course they are urged to pursue is one of ruin and disgrace to the very State whose rights they affect to support. . . .

If your leaders could succeed in establishing a separation, what would be your situation? Are you united at home? Are you free from the apprehension of civil discord, with all its fearful consequences? Do our neighboring republics, every day suffering some new revolution or contending with some new insurrection, do they excite your envy? . . .

. . . Having the fullest confidence in the justness of the legal and constitutional opinion of my duties which has been expressed, I rely with equal confidence on your undivided support in my determination to execute the laws, to preserve the Union by all constitutional means, to arrest, if possible, by moderate and firm measures the necessity of a recourse to force; and if it be the will of Heaven that the recurrence of its primeval curse on man for the shedding of a brother's blood should fall upon our land, that it be not called down by any offensive act on the part of the United States. . . .

ANDREW JACKSON.

7. John C. Calhoun Defends Slavery, 1837

Speech on the Reception of Abolition Petitions

However sound the great body of the non-slaveholding States are at present, in the course of a few years they will be succeeded by those who will have been taught to hate the people and institutions of nearly one-half of this Union, with a hatred more deadly than one hostile nation ever entertained towards another. It is easy to see the end. By the necessary course of events, if left to themselves, we must become, finally, two people. It is impossible under the deadly hatred which must spring up between the two great sections, if the present causes are permitted to operate

---

This document can be found in Robert L. Meriwether, *The Papers of John C. Calhoun* (Columbia: University of South Carolina Press, 1959), vol. I, pp. 331–333, 341–342, 347–353, 354–355.

unchecked, that we should continue under the same political system. The conflicting elements would burst the Union asunder, powerful as are the links which hold it together. Abolition and the Union cannot co-exist. As the friend of the Union I openly proclaim it,—and the sooner it is known the better. The former may now be controlled, but in a short time it will be beyond the power of man to arrest the course of events. We of the South will not, cannot surrender our institutions. To maintain the existing relations between the two races, inhabiting that section of the Union, is indispensable to the peace and happiness of both. It cannot be subverted without drenching the country in blood, and extirpating one or the other of the races. Be it good or bad, it has grown up with our society and institutions, and is so interwoven with them, that to destroy it would be to destroy us as a people. But let me not be understood as admitting, even by implication, that the existing relations between the two races in the slaveholding States is an evil:—far otherwise; I hold it to be a good, as it has thus far proved itself to be to both, and will continue to prove so if not disturbed by the fell spirit of abolition. I appeal to facts. Never before has the black race of Central Africa, from the dawn of history to the present day, attained a condition so civilized and so improved, not only physically, but morally and intellectually. It came among us in a low, degraded, and savage condition, and in the course of a few generations it has grown up under the fostering care of our institutions, reviled as they have been, to its present comparatively civilized condition. This, with the rapid increase of numbers, is conclusive proof of the general happiness of the race, in spite of all the exaggerated tales to the contrary.

In the mean time, the white or European race has not degenerated. It has kept pace with its brethren in other sections of the Union where slavery does not exist. It is odious to make comparison; but I appeal to all sides whether the South is not equal in virtue, intelligence, patriotism, courage, disinterestedness, and all the high qualities which adorn our nature. I ask whether we have not contributed our full share of talents and political wisdom in forming and sustaining this political fabric; and whether we have not constantly inclined most strongly to the side of liberty, and been the first to see and first to resist the encroachments of power. In one thing only are we inferior—the arts of gain; we acknowledge that we are less wealthy than the Northern section of this Union, but I trace this mainly to the fiscal action of this Government, which has extracted much from, and spent little among us. Had it been the reverse,—if the exaction had been from the other section, and the expenditure with us, this point of superiority would not be against us now, as it was not at the formation of this Government.

But I take higher ground. I hold that in the present state of civilization, where two races of different origin, and distinguished by color, and other physical differences, as well as intellectual, are brought together, the relation now existing in the slaveholding States between the two, is, instead of an evil, a good—a positive good. I feel myself called upon to speak freely upon the subject where the honor and interests of those I represent are involved. I hold then, that there never has yet existed a wealthy and civilized society in which one portion of the community did not, in point of fact, live on the labor of the other. . . . But I will not dwell on this aspect of the question; I turn to the political; and here I fearlessly assert that the existing relation between the two races in the South, against which these blind fanatics are waging war, forms the most solid and durable foundation on which to rear free and stable political institutions. It is useless to disguise the fact. There is and always has been in an advanced stage of wealth and civ-ilization, a conflict between labor and capital. The condition of society in the South ex-empts us from the disorders and dangers resulting from this conflict; and which explains why it is that the political condition of the slaveholding States has been so much more stable and quiet than that of the North. The advantages of the former, in this respect, will become more and more manifest if left undisturbed by interference from without, as the country advances in wealth and numbers. We have, in fact, but just en-tered that condition of society where the strength and durability of our political institu-tions are to be tested; and I venture nothing in predicting that the experience of the next generation will fully test how vastly more favorable our condition of society is to that of other sections for free and stable institutions, provided we are not disturbed by the interference of others, or shall have sufficient intelligence and spirit to resist promptly and successfully such interference. It rests with ourselves to meet and repel them. I look not for aid to this Government, or to the other States; not but there are kind feel-ings towards us on the part of the great body of the non-slaveholding States; but as kind as their feelings may be, we may rest assured that no political party in these States will risk their ascendency for our safety. If we do not defend ourselves none will defend us; if we yield we will be more and more pressed as we recede; and if we submit we will be trampled under foot. Be assured that emancipation itself would not satisfy these fa-natics:—that gained, the next step would be to raise the negroes to a social and political equality with the whites; and that being effected, we would soon find the present con-dition of the two races reversed. They and their northern allies would be the masters, and we the slaves; the condition of the white race in the British West India Islands, bad as it is, would be happiness to ours. There the mother country is interested in sustaining the supremacy of the European race. It is true that the authority of the former master is destroyed, but the African will there still be a slave, not to individuals but to the com-munity,—forced to labor, not by the authority of the overseer, but by the bayonet of the soldiery and the rod of the civil magistrate.

Surrounded as the slaveholding States are with such imminent perils, I rejoice to think that our means of defence are ample, if we shall prove to have the intelli-gence and spirit to see and apply them before it is too late. All we want is concert, to lay aside all party differences, and unite with zeal and energy in repelling approach-ing dangers. Let there be concert of action, and we shall find ample means of secu-rity without resorting to secession or disunion. I speak with full knowledge and a thorough examination of the subject, and for one, see my way clearly. One thing alarms me—the eager pursuit of gain which overspreads the land, and which ab-sorbs every faculty of the mind and every feeling of the heart. Of all passions avarice is the most blind and compromising—the last to see and the first to yield to danger. I dare not hope that any thing I can say will arouse the South to a due sense of danger; I fear it is beyond the power of mortal voice to awaken it in time from the fatal security into which it has fallen.

✗ E S S A Y S

Among the most important political crises that reflected the developing tension be-tween the South, on the one hand, and the North and the federal government, on the other, were the Missouri controversy of 1819–1821 and the nullification crisis of 1832. These two essays offer greater insight into both events. Don E. Fehrenbacher sees the Missouri controversy as a critical moment in the emerging crisis over slavery. He describes the political arguments and the South's commitment to ensuring the permanence of slavery as it spread westward. Pauline Maier, professor of history at MIT, explores the meaning of the nullification crisis, especially the thinking of John C. Calhoun and his central role in justifying the theory of nullification. Maier argues that South Carolina harked back to revolutionary precedents to insist on a constitutional protection of minority interests against the strength of the majority.

The Missouri Controversy: A Critical Moment in Southern Sectionalism

DON E. FEHRENBACHER

Historians generally agree that the Missouri controversy of 1819–1821 was a turning point in the history of the sectional conflict, but they differ about what phase it constituted in the development of southern distinctiveness and self-awareness. James A. Woodburn called the struggle "the first clear demarcation between the sections." Clement Eaton said that in political terms, the South "did not begin until 1820." Charles S. Sydnor suggested that it might be anachronistic to use the word "southerners" for the time before 1819; for, as he put it, "regional differences had not borne the evil fruit of sectional bitterness." On the other hand, Jesse T. Carpenter dated his study of *The South as a Conscious Minority* from the year 1789 and insisted, indeed, that "the inhabitants of those states below the Mason and Dixon line always considered themselves a separate and distinct people." Also, John R. Alden in his Fleming Lectures undertook to demonstrate the historical reality of what he called the First South. "It appeared," he said, "with the American nation; it was christened as early as 1778; and it clashed ever more sharply with a First North during and immediately after the War of Independence."

The disagreement between these scholars is partly one of their criteria and emphases, but it also reflects a cyclical pattern in the awakening of the South. That is, to some historians the Missouri Compromise looks like the beginning of southern sectionalism because in certain respects it was a *new* beginning of that phenomenon.

The underlying social and economic differences between the northern and southern colonies inspired open political rivalry from the formation of the Republic; and political rivalry, in turn, was the principal stimulant of sectional consciousness. In 1776, during early stages of work on the Articles of Confederation, members of the Continental Congress engaged in a sharp debate on the question of whether slaves should be counted in the apportionment of taxes. The division was almost totally along sectional lines. The same issue, tied to the problem of representation in Congress, troubled the deliberations of the Constitutional Convention in 1787, until the matter was at last settled by adoption of the three-fifths compromise. Yet slavery, though defended vehemently at times, especially by representatives of

South Carolina and Georgia, was not the primary subject of contention between North and South during the first quarter century of independence.

More serious were the sectional quarrels over navigation of the Mississippi River, over Alexander Hamilton's financial program for the new nation, and over Jay's treaty with Great Britain, negotiated in 1794. Mounting southern opposition to the Federalist regime stemmed primarily from the conviction that national policies were favoring northern commercial enterprise at the expense of southern agriculture. "We are completely under the saddle of Massachusetts and Connecticut," said Thomas Jefferson in 1798. "They ride us very hard, cruelly insulting our feelings as well as exhausting our strength and subsistence." The emergence of the Jeffersonian Republican opposition as an organized political party was to no small degree a sectional event. In the presidential election of 1796, Jefferson won fifty out of fifty-two electoral votes in the states south of Maryland; John Adams won all fifty-one electoral votes in the states north of Pennsylvania; and the thirty-six votes of New Jersey, Pennsylvania, Delaware, and Maryland were divided equally between them.

One way that the sectionalism of the 1790s foreshadowed the sectionalism of the 1850s was in the widespread fear of conspiracy on both sides. The Alien and Sedition acts confirmed many Republicans in their suspicion of a Federalist design to crush freedom of dissent and establish a monarchy. Jefferson predicted that the next step would be an attempt to make Adams president for life. On the other hand, the famous resolutions of Virginia and Kentucky attacking the Alien and Sedition acts only strengthened the conviction of many Federalists that Republican leaders were engaged in a treasonable plot to overthrow the Constitution and turn the United States into an appendage of Revolutionary France.

Within this context of intense partisan conflict, southerners in the 1790s did indeed have a growing sense of being mistreated as a section (though not on account of slavery), and their protests sometimes had the ring of prophecy. The Virginia and Kentucky Resolutions laid out the doctrines of strict construction, state sovereignty, and nullification. And among some Virginians there was apparently talk of secession and even of armed resistance to federal power. But the resolutions were not intended as blueprints for any organized southern action, except action at the polls. They were, in practical terms, campaign literature. Jefferson's goal was not a united South but control of the federal government. When that was achieved in 1800, much of the reason for southern sectionalism disappeared, and New England became the nation's conscious minority, ridden hard under a Virginia saddle.

With southern political power ascendant, the Jeffersonian era was a period without parallel in the territorial expansion of slavery. Jefferson himself did little to prevent it, and, in fact, he came to embrace the popular southern argument that a wide diffusion of slavery would benefit the slave population and the nation as a whole. In 1784, he had proposed that the institution be prohibited in the entire trans-Appalachian West, but as president he made no effort to secure the exclusion of slavery from the Louisiana Purchase. On the contrary, the plan for the government of Louisiana that he sent to Congress in November 1803 included a rigorous slave code.

Like a good many other enlightened Virginians of the Revolutionary generation, Jefferson had long since gone inactive in his opposition to slavery. Racial preconceptions and fears, as well as political considerations, had blunted his lifelong hatred of the institution and driven him to the conviction that the problem could be solved only by the slow working of time. He headed a political party of predominantly southern interest, but one that needed northern allies to control the presidency and Congress. The Jeffersonian Republicans, like their successors the Jacksonian Democrats, accordingly had good reason to muffle the issue of slavery, and northern members of the party were under strong though usually tacit pressure to restrain whatever antislavery feelings they may have had.

The Jeffersonian silence on domestic slavery was not sectionally neutral in its effect on westward expansion; for previous legislation dating back to 1790 had established the rule that slaveholding could be practiced anywhere in federal territory if it was not positively forbidden by federal law. This was doubly true of Louisiana, where slavery had been legal under both French and Spanish dominion. The Jeffersonians were consequently able to legitimate slaveholding throughout the whole of Louisiana simply by passing territorial organic acts that contained no provisions excluding it.

The strongest antislavery resistance arose in 1804. A proposal to limit (but not to abolish) slavery in Orleans Territory was defeated in the Senate by a vote of seventeen to eleven, with northern Federalists and northern Republicans both fairly evenly divided, while southerners provided the margin of defeat. During the next fifteen years, slavery continued to expand across the Mississippi as far north as St. Louis, without provoking sectional controversy.

Furthermore, slavery in several other respects seemed securely linked to the nation's destiny. The vitality of the institution was indicated by its continued existence in Illinois and Indiana more than thirty years after it had been officially prohibited there. Southerners could take their household slaves with them into free states for extended visits—up to nine months by law in New York, for example. The national capital was a slaveholding community, with a slave code enforced by federal authority, and the United States, in its relations with foreign powers, conducted itself as a slaveholding nation. The very power and respectability of the slavery interest, which had not been seriously challenged for more than a decade, made the shock of the Missouri crisis all the greater for southerners when it came.

Just why northern members of Congress, after so many years of passivity, chose to take a stand in 1819 is still an open question among historians. As late as April 1818, a proposal to forbid slavery in all states thereafter admitted was quickly smothered in the House of Representatives. Yet, within ten months, antislavery sentiment had swept into control of the chamber and precipitated the first sectional crisis over slavery. It did make a difference, of course, to have the War of 1812 ended and Europe generally at peace after a quarter century of upheaval and conflict. With American interest turning inward after 1815, a renewal of national self-scrutiny was bound to include consideration of the paradox of slavery in a nation formally dedicated to the principle that all men are created equal. Many northern congressmen seem to have awakened more or less suddenly to a realization that slavery had come to be fearfully predominant in the design of the nation's future. For confirmation they needed only to look at the boundaries proposed for the new state of Missouri, which would carry the institution northward two hundred miles above the mouth of the Ohio River.

To be sure, political motives also played their part. Jefferson's overwrought suspicion, shared by Madison and Monroe, that the Missouri controversy sprang from Federalist ambition to regain power, was not entirely groundless. Yet a Federalist effort alone could not have produced a crisis. It was the antislavery solidarity of so many northern Republicans that dismayed the South and inspired a new surge in the development of southern consciousness. The weakness of Federalism as a national party had slackened the need for loyalty and discipline within the Republican organization, thus making members of Congress more amenable to sectional pressures. It was not just accident that the Missouri crisis coincided with the demise of the first American party system.

In spite of Jefferson's famous comparison of the crisis to "a fire bell in the night," there were some intimations in 1818 of what was soon to come. An attempt to pass a more stringent fugitive-slave law ended in failure, but not before it had provoked a good deal of sectional feeling. Later in the year, Congressman James Tallmadge, Jr., spoke out against a bill admitting Illinois to statehood. He argued that slavery was not "sufficiently prohibited" in the Illinois constitution, and about one-third of the northern congressmen joined him in voting against admission.

It was this same James Tallmadge, a New York Republican of the disaffected Clintonian faction, who set off the Missouri struggle in February 1819. To a proposed enabling act for Missouri, he offered an amendment prohibiting the further introduction of slavery and providing that slave children born after the date of admission should be free at the age of twenty-five. Note that Tallmadge was not proposing emancipation of the ten thousand slaves already held in Missouri. His amendment amounted to a program of gradual abolition that would have extended over more than half a century.

With southern members almost unanimous in their opposition, the House of Representatives approved both parts of the Tallmadge proviso. What followed is a familiar chapter in American history. The Senate struck the proviso from the bill. The House refused to concur. The Senate insisted, and again the House refused to concur. Congress adjourned in March with the issue unsettled and the angry debate resounding across the country. A new Congress convened in December 1819, but the two houses quickly discovered that they were no nearer agreement on the Missouri question. After more than two months of further debate, a compromise package was put together and approved in the Senate, then accepted piecemeal by the House. It comprised the admission of Maine as a free state and an enabling act for Missouri without restriction on slavery, together with the provision that in the remaining federal territory acquired from France, slavery should be "forever prohibited" north of latitude 36° 30'.

The crisis accordingly appeared to be at an end, but it was furiously renewed a year later when Missouri applied for admission with a constitution that forbade free Negroes to enter the state. Again, heated debate extended over several months. Maine having already been admitted to statehood, southerners accused northerners of bad faith in setting up an additional barrier to the admission of Missouri. At last both houses of Congress accepted the terms of a second Missouri Compromise, which ambiguously guaranteed citizens the right to enter Missouri without saying whether free blacks were citizens.

In many obvious ways, the two-year struggle anticipated the sectional argument and the sectional anger of the late antebellum period, but it is important to note differences as well as similarities. The first Missouri controversy, in 1819–1820, was primarily over the power of Congress to set conditions on the admission of a state. The second, in 1821, was over the rights of free Negroes. As for the issue that would later preoccupy so much public discussion—namely, the power of Congress over slavery in the territories—it never assumed critical importance and rose when it did chiefly in connection with Arkansas, rather than in the Missouri debates. Legislation for the organization of Arkansas Territory, made necessary by the prospective admission of Missouri, proceeded through Congress virtually in tandem with the ill-fated Missouri bill of 1819. Discussion of the two measures became somewhat intermixed because antislavery leaders tried several times without success to fasten the Tallmadge restrictions on Arkansas.

Now, the Missouri debate tended to be heavily constitutional, involving several fundamental questions about the relationship between federal power and state sovereignty. And to some extent this tendency spilled over into the debate on Arkansas. Previously, the constitutional authority of Congress over slavery in the territories (which rested, after all, on a body of legislative precedent dating back to the Northwest Ordinance) had never been significantly challenged. During the Arkansas debate and even at some points in the Missouri controversy, a number of southerners did question that authority, and a few, like the future president John Tyler, emphatically denied it. These were but random beginnings, however, of the great constitutional debate that would convulse the nation by mid-century. In 1819, southern congressmen relied more on other arguments, such as economic necessity and sectional equity, to justify slaveholding in Arkansas. Probably a majority of them still had little doubt of congressional power to exclude slavery from the territories, and, indeed, many of them implicitly acknowledged the power by voting for the 36° 30′ restriction.

The efforts in the House of Representatives to impose antislavery restrictions on Arkansas Territory failed by very narrow margins. The House passed the territorial organization bill and sent it on to the Senate just three days after having passed and sent on the Missouri enabling bill with the Tallmadge amendment attached. By making no attempt to unite the two measures, antislavery leaders in the House neglected an opportunity to use slavery in Arkansas as leverage against slavery in Missouri. The Senate simply passed the Arkansas bill (which was then signed into law by President James Monroe) while refusing to accept the Missouri bill unless the Tallmadge amendment were deleted. When a similar opportunity presented itself to the Senate a year later, there was no hesitation about using the admission of Maine as leverage against slavery restrictions on Missouri. More often than not in later times of sectional crisis, the power advantage of an antislavery majority in the House of Representatives would be neutralized by the superior parliamentary skills of its adversaries.

For that matter, the Missouri Compromise in 1820 was, in behavioral terms, no compromise at all but essentially a caving-in of the House's slender antislavery majority that had managed to block passage of the Missouri bill for more than a year. Southerners, in contrast, never failed to present a solid front where Missouri was concerned. On the crucial proposal to strike out the slavery restriction (which finally passed the House with just one vote to spare), combined voting of both houses, broken down by sections, was: northern members, 19 in favor and 102 against; southern members, 98 in favor and *none* against.

In a sense, then, the only real compromisers were those nineteen northern members of Congress—and more particularly, the fourteen in the House—who forced their section to yield on the critical issue. But assignment of responsibility for the Missouri Compromise is not so easily accomplished. To begin with, there is a problem of terminology. The admission of Maine in 1820 and Missouri in 1821, being irrevocable acts of Congress, quickly faded from public controversy and became matters of settled history instead. In later years, accordingly, the phrase "Missouri Compromise" was often used to designate only that part of the settlement of 1820 that remained operative—namely, the 36° 30′ restriction by itself. Historians have generally followed the same practice. For instance, the Kansas-Nebraska Act of 1854 is commonly spoken of as having repealed the Missouri Compromise, whereas it actually repealed only the 36° 30′ restriction. This confusion of terms has led some scholars to the mistaken belief that congressmen from the free states were the principal authors of compromise, for the sectional voting on the 36° 30′ restriction in both houses combined was northern members, 115 in favor and 7 opposed; southern members, 53 in favor and 45 opposed. But the 36° 30′ restriction was actually just one-half of one side of the compromise. A grossly uneven division of the remaining federal territory, it had been proposed originally during the Arkansas debates by John W. Taylor, an antislavery Republican from New York. Later, however, it was brought forward by proslavery strategists as a concession to the North—as part of the price to be paid for the admission of Missouri as a slaveholding state.

Of course the real compromise, if there really *was* a compromise, consisted of the Missouri bill, the Maine bill, and the 36° 30′ restriction. Sectional attitudes are especially clear in the proceedings of the Senate, where the three measures were at one point voted on as a single package. Southerners supported the package, 20 to 2; northerners opposed it, 18 to 4. "The vote," says Glover Moore, "leaves no doubt about which section of the country favored and which did not favor the compromise of 1820." But the vote does *not* mean that southern members of Congress were generally more reasonable and flexible than their northern colleagues. It means only that in this *particular* compromise plan, formulated by proslavery leaders, the South got what it wanted most and the North did not. The contest from the beginning was for the future of Missouri, with the 36° 30′ restriction added as a consolation prize.

In retrospect, southern willingness to surrender the vast area north of 36° 30′ is somewhat surprising. No doubt it reflected a low estimate of the region's potential value, especially for plantation agriculture. But in addition, most southerners and northerners alike seem to have been convinced that the Missouri bird in the hand was worth more than several birds in the territorial bush.

In the House of Representatives, where no vote was ever taken on the Compromise as a whole, the vote on the 36° 30′ restriction provides the best measure, though an imprecise one, of various attitudes within the southern delegation. Southern representatives supported the restriction by the narrow margin of 39 to 37. The three border states (Delaware, Maryland, and Kentucky) voted 16 to 2 in favor; Virginia, 18 to 4 against; and the rest of the South, 19 to 17 in favor, with South Carolina contributing five affirmative votes and four negative ones.

Thus the center of proslavery extremism in 1820 was not the Lower South but Virginia, aptly described by Glover Moore as "a nation within a nation, eager to maintain its prestige and prerogatives." Thomas Ritchie's Richmond *Enquirer* led the newspaper attack on the Compromise, insisting that the South must not allow it-self to be browbeaten by the antislavery forces into ransoming Missouri by consent-ing to the 36° 30′ restriction. "Shall we," the *Enquirer* asked, "surrender so much of this region, that was nobly won by the councils of a Jefferson, and paid for out of a common treasury?" Warning that the precedent set would invite further sectional aggression, it added: "If we yield now, beware.—they will ride us forever." The *Enquirer* greeted passage of the Compromise in March 1820 with the words, "We scarcely ever recollect to have tasted of a bitterer cup. . . . The door is henceforth slammed in our faces. . . . What is a *territorial* restriction to-day becomes a *state* re-striction to-morrow."

The 36° 30′ restriction, though opposed by many southerners, provoked very little debate in either house. The restriction was not needed to get the Missouri bill through the Senate, and there is no clear evidence that it changed a single northern vote in the House of Representatives. As a generous concession to antislavery senti-ment, it made things much easier for history's original "doughfaces"—the northern-ers who voted with the South—but they were motivated by other considerations. Senators Ninian Edwards and Jesse B. Thomas of Illinois, for example, voted with the South because they were themselves southerners and slaveholders. Henry Bald-win of Pennsylvania voted with the South in the hope of softening southern opposi-tion to a higher tariff. Apparently several doughfaces agreed with the southern argument that imposing slavery restrictions on an incoming state would be uncon-stitutional. And apparently some northern Republicans were governed, like Jeffer-son, by deep suspicion of Federalist motives.

But what "perhaps did more than anything else to undermine Northern soli-darity," says Glover Moore, was the fear of disunion. Charles Kinsey of New Jer-sey, one of the handful of antislavery congressmen who determined the outcome of the struggle by switching to the southern side, gave eloquent expression to that fear in a speech delivered just before the decisive vote in the House. "On the next step we take depends the fate of unborn millions," he warned. Disunion, he said, pre-sented itself "in all the horrid, gloomy features of reality," and a northern victory in the confrontation would be "an inglorious triumph, gained at the hazard of the Union."

Throughout the crisis there was certainly a good deal of southern talk about disunion and civil war, much of it in the form of flowery prediction rather than plain threat. Thus Senator Freeman Walker of Georgia envisioned "a brother's sword crimsoned with a brother's blood." And Thomas W. Cobb, another Georgian, de-clared that antislavery leaders had "kindled a fire which all the waters of the ocean" could not put out, and which only "seas of blood" could extinguish. Yet the Mis-souri crisis was not a secession crisis, though it might have become one in time. Even the Richmond *Enquirer,* in bitterly accepting passage of the Compromise, ac-knowledged that the Union had never been in serious danger. "If there had been a civil war in 1819–1821," says Moore, "It would have been between the members of Congress, with the rest of the country looking on in amazement." Moore goes on to suggest that "the Union would almost certainly have broken up at some time in the 1820's if . . . there had been an absolute refusal to compromise." Perhaps so, but such a refusal, as he himself concludes, was a "remote possibility." For the longer the crisis lasted, the harder it became to keep Missouri out of the Union; and a truly imminent danger of disunion would have put unbearable pressure for compromise on many northern Republicans. Southerners did nevertheless begin to learn in the Missouri crisis how effectively the threat of disunion could be used as a weapon of southern defense.

The Missouri crisis in fact had many meanings and lessons for the South—some readily understood and others only vaguely sensed but often becoming clearer in the light of later events. For instance, the sudden appearance of an antislavery majority in the House of Representatives dramatically confirmed the southern need to maintain sectional equality in the Senate, but only dimly at best did any southerners in 1820 perceive the advantages of reestablishing a bisectional two-party system in national politics. The complaint of some southern congressmen that public discussion of the "delicate" subject of slavery increased the danger of slave revolts took on new meaning in 1822 after exposure of the Denmark Vesey conspiracy. It was not until the middle decades of the century, however, that the Missouri struggle came to be regarded as the beginning of southern degradation at the hands of the North. Thus Eli S. Shorter of Alabama would look back in anger from the floor of the House of Representatives in 1858: "We remember the compromise of 1820. The brand of inferiority was then stamped deep on the brow of southern manhood and southern honor; and there it remained, a burning disgrace, till the Kansas-Nebraska bill wiped it out and restored us to our long lost rights."

In its constitutional aspects, the congressional debate on Missouri lent reinforcement to the old Republican preference for strict construction. The Tallmadge amendment, by proposing the gradual abolition of slavery in a prospective state *after* its admission to statehood, offered a much greater constitutional threat to the security of slavery than the Wilmot Proviso of later years. For, if antislavery spokesmen were right in asserting that any one of several clauses in the Constitution (such as the clause guaranteeing each state a republican form of government) could be construed as authorizing congressional regulation of slavery in a *new* state, what constitutional barrier remained to prevent the same kind of interference in the *oldest* of the slaveholding states? The Missouri struggle therefore connected antislavery sentiment more closely to broad construction and nationalism than it had ever been connected before. After 1820, it became increasingly difficult for a defender of slavery to support the expansion of federal power. John C. Calhoun managed to do so for just a few more years.

The Missouri debates also drew many a southerner unwillingly into discussion of the moral aspects of the slavery problem. Only a few militants like Senator William Smith of South Carolina defended the institution openly and absolutely, thus ushering in the "positive good" phase of proslavery ideology. For the most part, southern members of Congress were still willing to say that slavery was an evil—a curse, a cancer. Moore accordingly views the Missouri controversy as marking the end of an age in which southern thought had been dominated by the liberalism of the Enlightenment.

Yet, upon close scrutiny, southern acknowledgment of the wrongness of slavery was largely an empty gesture in 1820. It had no effect on the main line of southern argument, which held the institution to be indispensable and ineradicable. The conflict between southern rhetoric and southern conviction was strikingly revealed in a speech by Congressman Robert Reid of Georgia. Reid at one point declared that the day when black Americans were given equal rights as citizens would be "most glorious in its dawning." But then he immediately added that such a "dream of philanthropy" could never be fulfilled, and that any person who acted upon such "wild theories" would become a "destroyer of the human family."

The votes of southern congressmen in the Missouri struggle spoke more clearly than many of their speeches. Those votes indicated that the South had already made the most important decision in the whole history of the slavery controversy—and made it with virtual unanimity. That is, the Slaveholding South by 1820 had rejected the possibility of gradual emancipation, even in a new part of the country where it would have been neither impractical nor dangerous. It was this southern commitment to the *permanence* of slavery, and not the mere presence of slavery in the land, that made sectional conflict irrepressible and disunion increasingly probable as the nineteenth century advanced.

The Road Not Taken: Nullification, John C. Calhoun, and the Revolutionary Tradition in South Carolina

PAULINE MAIER

It is important here to begin with the Revolution itself, to note how its message and so the revolutionary tradition itself shifted, taking new forms and directions in the final years of the eighteenth century. As of 1760 the Americans' revolutionary tradition had emerged from the struggle of their English ancestors to protect liberty from the power of kings and magistrates. Power, according to Whig tradition, came from the people and was granted to rulers only on a limited, contractual basis. When the terms of that contract or trust were violated—when rulers exercised powers that had not been given them, and became oppressors of the people they were meant to serve—they automatically forfeited their authority, which reverted to the people from whom it had originally come. The people could reclaim the whole of governmental power in acts of revolution where the constitutional order had been totally undermined. But the people could also reclaim governmental power in part, through acts of resistance to isolated wrongful acts of authority. This right of resistance, though founded upon the same theoretical foundation as the right of revolution and therefore a constituent part of the Anglo-American revolutionary tradition, was understood as a critical element in containing power and so in preserving a stable constitutional order and preventing the need for revolution. The readiness of a people to resist deterred rulers from attempting acts that would provoke their subjects. Resistance therefore served as a check on power comparable to the institutional divisions of authority within England's "mixed constitution." It was with this understanding of resistance as a conservative force that the American colonists rose up against Parliamentary taxation in 1765: they blocked execution of the Stamp Act, which was, they argued, unwarranted by the constitution and therefore null and void, and thereby sought to protect the established constitutional order, to discourage further

Pauline Maier, "The Road Not Taken: Nullification, John C. Calhoun, and the Revolutionary Tradition in South Carolina," *South Carolina Historical Magazine* 82 (January 1981), 1–19.

violations of that order, and to prevent the establishment of grievances or precedents that might in time necessitate revolution.

Resistance could, of course, occasion a licentiousness that itself threatened the constitutional order. Therefore Americans of the late colonial period, drawing upon earlier British political thought, stressed the limits upon its just implementation: resistance, like revolution, could only be undertaken against serious threats to freedom and the constitution; force could be used only after all peaceful means of seeking redress had been exhausted, and then only to the extent necessary to prevent the execution of a dangerous exercise of power. Finally, resistance could not be the work of an elite. It had to draw upon the "body of the people." Legitimate acts of resistance were consequently rare, but nonetheless essential: a submissive and docile people would not long remain free, so insistent, it seemed, were the natural tendencies of power to expand until despotism replaced the liberty upon which was built a people's happiness and welfare. To keep resistance within the bounds of legitimacy—to restrain licentiousness while protecting freedom—was a challenge met by the American revolutionaries in ways that had far-reaching consequences for the United States. It led them to organize carefully the resistance movement, and in that organization lay the beginnings of American self-government. From the Sons of Liberty of the Stamp Act crisis through the nonimportation associations of 1767–70 and the committees and congresses of the mid-1770s—or the "town meeting" that emerged to promote nonimportation and continued to govern Charleston until the city's incorporation in 1783—the governmental institutions born of the revolution assumed ever more strength and scope. As American grievances multiplied and resistance gave way to revolution, the ad hoc institutions of the resistance era yielded to the first formal governments of the new nation which, like their immediate predecessors, took their authority not from hereditary title but from the "body of the people," which is to say they were "republican." And in founding a republic the Americans made their struggle for independence a revolutionary event of considerable importance in the history of the Western World.

By the late 1780s, some of the assumptions within the Anglo-American tradition had begun to shift. Experience with the powerful democratic legislatures of the late 1770s and early 1780s suggested that danger to liberty lay not only in kings and magistrates, but that the people themselves—the majority—was also prone to abuse its power at the cost of minorities. The institutions founded at the time of independence were therefore redesigned: senates and governors were revived as checks on popular legislatures, and the executive, judiciary, and legislative powers were separated to limit further the impact of simple majorities. Even the campaign to strengthen national government, Gordon Wood has argued, was part of this effort to contain the tyranny of the majority within the separate states. The Founding Fathers hoped at first that the new federal government would have a veto on state laws, but on further reflection thought better of the idea. The federal government, they came to understand, need not and should not act directly upon the states but could enforce its authority on the people who, through their constitutional conventions, had set up both state and national governments with distinct and separate responsibilities. And that division of tasks between the states and the nation was of course itself a limit on power and so a means of protecting liberty.

In this elaboration of republican institutions, it seemed to many that the right of resistance and of revolution had also become outmoded for Americans, at least in the forms they had taken in the past. Direct popular action could be no longer exercised legitimately by those who lived under a constitutional republic, and so could never exhaust the "peaceful means of redress." With the abolition of hereditary rule all persons in power became answerable, directly or indirectly, to the ballot box. And where the direct control of the electorate proved insufficient, office-holders remained subject to impeachment and to the surveillance of the courts. "No people can be more free [than] under a Constitution established by their own frequent suffrages," Governor Samuel Adams told the Massachusetts legislature in 1795. "What excuse then can there be for forcible opposition to the laws? If any law shall prove oppressive in its operation, the future deliberations of a freely elected Representative, will prove a constitutional remedy."

The followers of Daniel Shays, or the farmers of western Pennsylvania—whose Whiskey Rebellion prompted Adams' remarks—apparently disagreed, and followed instead older patterns of popular insurgency. In South Carolina, too, the people continued to "rise up" as they had in colonial days, and provoked denunciations much like those of spokesmen for the new order elsewhere in the nation. Even partisan politics seemed dangerously licentious to many who were anxious to regain the "enduring internal harmony" South Carolina had achieved in the mid-eighteenth century. Christopher Gadsden, who once helped mobilize Charleston's mechanics in the cause of their country, argued in the mid-1780s that all men should fall "cheerfully into the ranks again," acquiescing *peaceably without doors* in what the majority had *agreed* upon and *fairly* carried within." That was *"true genuine Republicanism"* for him and, it would seem, for those lowcountry planters whose "artistocratic" domination of South Carolina politics in the late eighteenth century was continued thereafter as the spread of cotton culture placed many inland districts under the power of a planting elite.

And yet it was members or representatives of that planting elite who in the late 1820s and 1830s evoked their revolutionary ancestors and revolutionary precedents in an empassioned campaign against federal "tyranny." As George C. Rogers has noted, a great revival of Carolinians' interest in the revolutionary past occurred in the 1820s, which saw, for example, the publication of Major Alexander Garden's *Anecdotes of the Revolutionary War* and a wave of name-changing as South Carolina families revived the surnames of their revolutionary ancestors. Robert Barnwell Smith (later Rhett), whose Colleton district became "the Faneuil Hall where the cradle of Southern sovereignty" was "constantly rocked," similarly stressed his political descent from earlier English and American revolutionaries—from "Samuel Adams, Patrick Henry, Jefferson, Rutledge," all of whom were, he claimed, "disunionists and traitors." And at the Jefferson Day dinner of April 1830, George McDuffie toasted "the memory of Patrick Henry: the first American statesman who had the soul to feel, and the courage to declare, in the face of armed tyranny, that there is no treason in resisting oppression.". . .

The purpose of these ritualistic invocations of 1776 was clear: they served to glorify intransigence and to legitimize the Carolinians' more extreme threats of disunion by linking that resort with the "secession" of colonists from the British Empire. Accordingly Andrew Jackson condemned nullification as an effort "to destroy the union," as tantamount to secession or treason, part of a scheme to "form a southern confederacy bounded, north, by the Patomac river," as an example of "wickedness, madness and folly" without parallel "in the history of the world." For him, as later for Lincoln, the Union was—in Daniel Webster's words of 1830— "now and forever, one and inseparable," a marriage without possibility of divorce.

In fact, however, the more conservative advocates of nullification—who developed that device as a way of containing the extremists in their midst—were nearer the cautious ways of their ancestors than firebrands like Rhett or McDuffie, and built more firmly upon American political and constitutional precedents while remaining truer to the nationalistic enthusiasms of their time than either Jackson or Webster were prepared to recognize. Nullification, or "state interposition" as it was more often called at the time, was not in the hands of John C. Calhoun a plea for revolution on the model of 1776; it was instead a revival of the old right of resistance, with all of its conservative connotations. Secession, Calhoun stressed, was an act of revolution which sought *"to free* the withdrawing member from the *obligation* of the association," and so, in effect, to dissolve the union. But in 1832, Calhoun argued, Carolinians were contending for "a very different and . . . far less revolutionary right; the right not of setting aside the provisions of the Constitution . . . , but the right to maintain and preserve them in their full force, by arresting all attempts on the part of the General Government to violate them." Nullification was therefore—like the Stamp Act resistance of 1765 and 1766—conservative in conception: South Carolina sought "reformation, and not revolution; a reformation essential to the preservation of the Union, the Constitution, and the liberty of the country." Nullification was of course capable of being abused; if unchecked, it could serve to "debilitate the Government." And so, like earlier British and American spokesmen of resistance, Calhoun emphasized that the states could not invoke their "high power of interposition" except where the constitution was clearly and dangerously violated, when "all reasonable hope of relief, from the ordinary action of the government" had failed, and when "if the right to interpose did not exist, the alternative would be submission and oppression on one side, or resistance by force on the other."

The South Carolina Convention of 1832 followed Calhoun's lead when it called for "prompt and efficient measures . . . to stay the hand of oppression, to restore the Constitution to its original principles, and thereby to perpetuate the Union." The Convention also implicitly recognized the limits upon resistance when it stressed the seriousness of the Congressional "usurpations" that it opposed—if submitted to they would "entirely change the character of the Government, reduce the Constitution to a dead letter, and on the ruins of our confederated republic, erect a consolidated despotism." Repeated protests from South Carolina and other Southern states brought only "repeated injuries and insults"—the tariffs of 1824, 1828, and 1832—such that "it would be idle to remonstrate, and degrading to protest further," and a "decisive course of action" had become the only alternative to submission. The proponents of nullification did, however, pay less honor than their revolutionary ancestors to the old Whig demand that resistance and revolution draw their power and legitimacy from the "body of the people." Not that the movement was without a concern for popular participation: the South Carolina Association, organized in 1823 to ensure the enforcement of Negro laws, was transformed by James Hamilton into a powerful organization that mobilized small slaveholders and even Charleston's mechanics for the cause of nullification; only yeoman farmers in mountain districts and East Bay merchants remained impervious to its appeal. But the Convention of 1832 was—like the state legislature—malaportioned, giving weight to property as well as persons; and when the Unionist Henry Middleton moved that the convention deem itself "incompetent . . . to wield the sovereign authority of the people it unequally represents" and so open the way for the legislature to call a new convention with a "full and equal representation of the people," the delegates simply refused to consider his proposal. Policy-making would remain the work of an elite, though the preservation of freedom demanded, for the proponents of nullification as for earlier participants in the Anglo-American revolutionary tradition, an aroused people "jealous" for their rights.

In other ways, too, nullification constituted something more than a simple revival of the old, pre-1776 right of resistance—of the people's right, that is, to judge their rulers and to block "unconstitutional" or unlawful acts of power. Resistance had traditionally served to limit the power of kings and magistrates, but nullification built instead upon the fears of majoritarian tyranny that emerged after Independence and shaped American constitutional development in the 1780s. "No government, based on the naked principle, that the majority ought to govern . . . ever preserved its liberty even for a single generation," Calhoun wrote; and he cited with approval the Fifty-first Federalist Paper where—as earlier in Federalist Number Ten—James Madison had addressed himself to the problem of securing minority rights under popular governments. Madison argued that the very multiplicity of interests within the United States made "an unjust combination of a majority of the whole very improbable," such that the extent and diversity of the country served to protect minority interests. But history did not bear him out: the nation had become divided into sections that differed "on the great and vital point, the industry of the country, which comprehends almost every interest." And there, Calhoun claimed, the South's opponents "act and feel . . . as sovereigns, as men invariably do, who impose burdens on others for their own benefit." That the South's industry was "controlled by many, instead of one, by a majority in Congress elected by a majority in the community, having an opposite interest, instead of hereditary rulers," served not to mitigate but to aggravate the evil. And so Calhoun turned again to that "diversity of interests" within the nation which was for Madison the salvation of popular government, but which for Calhoun—as for the spokesmen of traditional eighteenth-century political wisdom whom Madison had attacked—was a major obstacle to the formation of "free and just Governments" and "the door through which despotick power has . . . ever entered, and through which it must ever continue to do till some effectual barrier be provided." The barrier he advocated, state interposition, was for him, moreover, but another of a series of checks on power that characterized the American system of constitutional government.

Here again nullification modified resistance as practiced and understood by Americans before Independence, for Calhoun attempted in effect to reconcile resistance with the more recent demand that the people act only through regular, constitutional procedures and within established institutions. An effort to "institutionalize" an insurgent people may well characterize post-revolutionary eras: in eighteenth-century England the jurist William Blackstone denied that the people retained a Lockean right "to remove or alter the legislative, when they find the legislative act contrary to the trust reposed in them," because for him, as for other supporters of the British standing order, the people had yielded their right to Parliament, which after the Revolution of 1688 became "absolute and without control." In early nineteenth-century America, many argued that the people had similarly yielded to the Supreme Court their role as guardian of the constitution, as an agency empowered to declare null and void those acts of authority that contravened the constitution. Here Calhoun dissented. He was willing to grant the Court considerable authority in deciding constitutional issues, but not plenary power. It could not above all hold final authority over conflicts of constitutional jurisdiction between the states and the central government, he argued, because the Court was itself part of the central government and therefore a party to such conflicts. Because no impartial agency of government existed to decide such disputes they had to be resolved by the people themselves, acting through conventions—those extraordinary institutions by which the people of the several states had exercised sovereign power in establishing both state and national governments. But to say the people were to act in conventions was itself to institutionalize the popular uprisings that had played so important a role in constitutional crises of the Anglo-American past. Constitutional conventions were in fact so established a part of American constitutional processes by the 1820s, and their implementation to preserve as well as to write or ratify constitutional law seemed so logical an extreme of American constitutional procedures that Calhoun and the South Carolina Convention of 1832 insisted that nullification through state conventions was not a natural but a "constitutional" right.

Interposition was limited in effect because a state could nullify a federal law only within its own borders. And if three-quarters of the states so chose, they could, by the explicit provisions of the federal constitution, resolve the dispute by amending the constitution so as to grant the contested power to the federal government. Then, it seemed, a recalcitrant state could only withdraw from the Union; but the whole of Calhoun's procedures were designed to obviate that end, to reduce the danger of insurrection and disunion. The "great number" of persons necessarily involved, "the solemnity of the mode, a convention specially called for the purpose, and representing the State in her highest capacity, the delay, the deliberation" were all "calculated to allay excitement, to impress on the people a deep and solemn tone, highly favourable to calm investigation and decision." Nullification provided a means of correcting those constitutional "aberrations to which all political systems are liable, and which, if permitted to accumulate, without correction, must finally end in a general catastrophe." Acknowledgment of the states' right to interpose would, Calhoun argued, make the general government moderate in the exercise of doubtful powers, and so render the exercise of that right unnecessary. Establishment of the right of state interposition would also enhance the states' sense of security within the union, "put down jealousy, hatred and animosity, and . . . give scope to the natural attachment to our institutions, to expand and grow in the full maturity of patriotism." The doctrine of nullification was therefore "evidence of . . . high wisdom, . . . not of anarchy . . . , but of peace and safety," and suggests that Calhoun's development and support of interposition marked less an abandonment of his earlier nationalism, as historians have often assumed, than an adaptation of it to altered circumstances.

The extent of the nullifiers' commitment to minority rights may be questioned given their severe repression of their Unionist opponents, and the fact that nullification was designed in part to protect the institution of slavery. The military preparations that accompanied South Carolina's advocacy of interposition along with the forceful response of President Andrew Jackson and the United States Congress to the Nullification Ordinance made clear, moreover, that what was for Calhoun a safe and peaceful "constitutional" resort would in fact have resulted in bloodshed had his state persisted in its course. And yet the proposal had non-revolutionary precedents apart from the immediate circumstances of South Carolina in the 1820s and 1830s that confirm its significance in the development of American constitutionalism. Calhoun and his supporters looked back to the Virginia Resolutions of 1798, which asserted that "in case of a deliberate, palpable, and dangerous exercise" of powers not granted by the constitutional contract, "the States, who are parties thereto, have the right, and are in duty bound to interpose for arresting the progress of the evil, and for maintaining within their respective limits the authorities, rights, and liberties appertaining to them." And they recalled the Kentucky Resolutions of 1798, which denied that the Federal Government was "the exclusive or final judge of the powers delegated" under the federal constitution, asserted that in disputes "among parties having no common [J]udge," each party had "an equal right to judge for itself as well as of infractions as of the mode and measure of redress," and went on to declare the Alien and Sedition Acts "not law, but . . . altogether void and of no force."

The Carolinians might well also have cited the Hartford Convention of 1814, which argued again that it was the right and duty of a state to "interpose its authority" where the federal government was guilty of "deliberate, dangerous, and palpable infractions of the Constitution." The Hartford Convention shared fully the Carolinians' distrust of what the New Englanders called the "sudden and injudicious decisions of bare majorities." It sought government by what would later be called the "concurrent majority" because it feared New England's commercial interests would otherwise become those of an oppressed minority as southern states joined their "new confederates" in the west "to govern the east." But history took another course. By the 1830s Calhoun found the South "in a permanent and helpless minority" on the important issues of the day, and South Carolina took up the cause of state interposition. The defense of state prerogatives in constitutional disputes was not therefore—as Arthur Meier Schlesinger observed nearly sixty years ago—confined to any one section or, as he also noted, to any one political party. The doctrine's widespread appeal in the opening decades of the new nation confirms its cogency to a generation of Americans fully emersed in the revolutionary and constitutional traditions of the Anglo-American world, for whom power evoked not hope but fear, and who considered the division of authority between state and nation a critical safeguard of their freedom.

Yet nullification remains a constitutional road not taken. Members of the Hartford Convention, for the most part moderate men who proposed a series of amendments to the federal constitution "to strengthen, and if possible to perpetuate, the union of the states, by removing the grounds of existing jealousies" and to undercut the overt calls for disunion that preceded their meeting, were branded traitors; and South Carolina's call for state interposition evoked no more support than had the Virginia and Kentucky Resolutions over three decades earlier, which makes clear how anachronistic even so modified a version of popular resistance had become in the new republic. Southern states were no less vocal than those of the North in condemning the "Carolina doctrine" as "neither a peaceful, nor a constitutional remedy," as "tending to civil commotion and disunion," "rash and revolutionary;" and many stated that issues of constitutionality were the province not of states or of conventions, but of the Supreme Court. Americans did not, however, reject the *fact* of resistance to federal authority: as Charles Sydnor noted, Alabama continued to resist efforts on the part of the United States to enforce its treaty of March 1832 with the Creek Indians against squatters on Indian lands, much as New Englanders had resisted Jefferson's embargo, and South Carolina had continued to enforce its Negro Seamens Act despite the opposition of federal courts. Americans rejected, Sydnor suggested, only the possibility of resisting federal law through established civil processes. And with the failure of nullification—of Calhoun's intermediate step between submission and disunion—"it was the opinion of some of the wisest men of South Carolina" that the leading nullifiers "had turned into secessionists."

Calhoun's arguments for nullification, which constitute the fullest development of that doctrine, have a particular importance for those who would understand his place in the American past. They indicate that he was far more the last of the Founding Fathers, the last of a generation of creative constitutional statesmen, than an early Marxist. Certainly his roots were firmly based in the eighteenth century, in which he was born (in 1782), and in which his fundamental political assumptions were formed. It was from the eighteenth century that he first acquired his enduring conviction that power bred corruption and was a universal antagonist of liberty. His suspicions of class domination, as of unchecked majorities, followed logically from that assumption: unlimited power wherever found would lead to the abuse and impoverishment of those subject to it. But he considered class to be a European phenomenon, something that might emerge in America's manufacturing states, but which generally depended upon [artificial] distinctions between people that had been ended in the United States with the Revolution. The American republic therefore had interests rather than classes, interests which were for the most part economic in character and had unfortunately taken on geographical identities. But the conflict of those interests, and the victory of one over another played no inevitable part in his sense of history—which was a major difference between Calhoun and Marx, but linked him with his intellectual mentor, James Madison, who, like Calhoun, believed in the possibility of achieving both liberty and harmony through the design of political institutions.

In his search for institutional solutions to political problems Calhoun was again a son of the eighteenth century. Unlike many other Americans of the post-revolutionary era, he doubted that all the great advances in political engineering lay in the past. How could that be when the science of politics had yet to make its last discovery? "We have yet much to learn," he wrote in 1832, as to the "practical operation" of the American system of government, and even as to how the "entire scheme" could be kept from proving "abortive." His experience confirmed the critical importance of compromise to a free society, for compromise provided an alternative to the simple domination of majoritarian interests over those of minorities. The great compromises of his day were the work of politicians whose skill at that art would not be carried over into the next generation. But Calhoun, true to his eighteenth-century origins, was not content to depend upon the fortuitous appearance of such men in each generation; he wanted the imperative to compromise built into the nation's institutions. Nullification was therefore for him a constitutional means of forcing majorities to respect the minority interests represented by the various states, as was his later proposal for a sectional veto on national policy.

This insistence on claiming the authority of the Founding Fathers indicates again how much Calhoun was working within the American constitutional tradition. It is in fact striking how few authorities he cited. Calhoun might refer to antiquity, he might mention the English constitution, but he rarely cited political authorities from other countries or from before the American revolutionary era. Where his countrymen had once drawn upon Milton, Sidney, Locke, where they had cited the Scottish philosopher Frances Hutcheson and even Lord Bolingbroke, they now turned to the Philadelphia debates of 1787 or the writings of the Founding Fathers; where "Cato's Letters" by John Trenchard and Thomas Gordon, English political writers of the early eighteenth century, had once been their handbook, they now turned to the Federalist Papers. Once the federal constitution had been drafted and ratified, it seemed, all earlier authorities became anachronistic. "Our political system is admitted to be a new Creation—a real nondescript," Madison observed in March 1833. "Its character therefore must be sought within itself; not in precedents, because there are none, not in writers whose comments are guided by precedents." The constitution became, in a sense, its own and the only relevant precedent. And so a people who were once students of political theory became instead laborers in constitutional thought, as if all the liberal traditions of Britain and indeed of the West had been telescoped into the United States, whose government was their greatest achievement, and where alone further progress in the understanding and perfection of government might be realized for the good of mankind.

That the person most anxious to realize that progress, not just to honor but to add to the heroic accomplishments of the past, a man who was "probably the last American statesman to do any primary political thinking," came from South Carolina was, finally, appropriate and even necessary. The "remarkable intellectual leadership" of the American Revolution had been nurtured in a world where gentlemen ruled, where statesmen "believed that their speeches and writings" need influence only "the rational and enlightened part" of the population. A "decline in the intellectual quality of American political life and an eventual separation between ideas and power" was, according to Gordon Wood, the price paid for "what we have come to value most—our egalitarian culture and our democratic society." But the old ways had lived on in the elitist and deferential politics of South Carolina, whose economy allowed planters time both for politics and for study and whose political system encouraged "the felicitous debates of disinterested aristocrats" who had often first come to know each other at the South Carolina College in Columbia. In such a society, and perhaps only there, a man could rise in influence unhindered by the jealousies of a deTocquevillian democracy; there a man could, like Calhoun, still aspire to the approbation only of the "intelligent and disinterested." There, in short, in the increasingly anachronistic politics of South Carolina, ideas and power could remain united, as they had been in what was rapidly becoming for Americans elsewhere only the heroic days of a revolutionary past.

⼊ F U R T H E R   R E A D I N G

Thomas P. Abernethy, *The South in the New Nation, 1789–1819* (1961)
John Richard Alden, *The First South* (1961)
Richard R. Beeman, *The Evolution of the Southern Backcountry: A Case Study of Lunenburg County, Virginia, 1746–1832* (1984)
James Broussard, *The Southern Federalists, 1800–1816* (1978)
Margaret L. Coit, *John C. Calhoun, American Portrait* (1950)
George Dangerfield, *The Awakening of American Nationalism, 1815–1828* (1965)
Joseph J. Ellis, *American Sphinx: The Character of Thomas Jefferson* (1997)
William W. Freehling, *Prelude to Civil War: The Nullification Controversy in South Carolina, 1816–1836* (1966)
Rachel N. Klein, *Unification of a Slave State: The Rise of the Planter Class in the South Carolina Backcountry, 1760–1808* (1990)
Jan Lewis, *The Pursuit of Happiness: Family and Values in Jefferson's Virginia* (1983)
Robert McColley, *Slavery and Jeffersonian Virginia* (1964, 1973)
Richard P. McCormick, *The Second American Party System: Party Formation in the Jacksonian Era* (1966)
Drew McCoy, *The Last of the Fathers: James Madison and the Republican Legacy* (1989)
John Chester Miller, *The Wolf by the Ears: Thomas Jefferson and Slavery* (1977, 1991)
Glover Moore, *The Missouri Controversy, 1819–1821* (1953, 1966)
John Niven, *John C. Calhoun and the Price of Union* (1988)
Robert V. Remini, *Andrew Jackson and the Bank War* (1967)
——, *Henry Clay: Statesman for the Union* (1991)
Norman K. Risjord, *The Old Republicans: Southern Conservatism in the Age of Jefferson* (1965)
Marshall Smelser, *The Democratic Republic, 1801–1815* (1968)
Charles Sydnor, *The Development of Southern Sectionalism, 1819–1848* (1948)
——, *Gentlemen Freeholders: Political Practices in Washington's Virginia* (1952)

The Slaveholders' South

Though only a minority of southerners owned slaves during the antebellum period, we tend to think of the South as a land of white slaveholders and oppressed black slaves. Students of history have long been fascinated by the nature and character of this image of the Old (or antebellum) South—the period between the early national period and the Civil War. Compared to the colonial South, the slaveholders' South was a far larger, trans-Appalachian region that spread from Texas to coastal Florida, from southern Alabama into Kentucky and Maryland. The region relied on slave labor to grow its principal cash crops—cotton, sugar, tobacco, rice, and corn—and it profited from a sustained cotton boom fostered by demand from the British textile industry. As the most extensive slaveholding region in the Western Hemisphere and as the region that ultimately seceded from the Union, the slaveholders' South has generated much attention.

Historians have focused on several key issues to try to understand more about the slaveholders' South. Recent studies have revealed the variety of slave owners— Louisiana and Mississippi sugar nabobs, yeoman farmers, Cherokee Indians, women, and even a few free blacks. Not all were planters; urban dwellers depended on slaves for domestic help and day laborers, and factory owners rented or purchased slaves as laborers. One of the major issues historians debate is how capitalistic slave owners were: whether the slave labor system reflected a traditional approach to economic development or whether it reflected more modern, capitalistic values. In other words, was the southern planter all that different from his northern industrial counterpart? These issues have sparked lively debate among historians and created an abundance of research.

✴ D O C U M E N T S

Document 1 presents a map showing how cotton (and presumably slavery as well) spread as planters, their families, and their slaves moved westward and southward to rich, often inexpensive land. Like many others, Joseph G. Baldwin, a Virginian, moved in 1836 to what was then the Southwest and became a lawyer and writer. His sketches, published as *The Flush Times of Alabama and Mississippi,* some of which appear in Document 2, describe southwestern society in the late 1830s. Document 3 presents selections from Bennet Barrow's journal, a fine example of a cotton planter's diary. Barrow represented fairly new wealth, since whites primarily settled the rich lands around his Louisiana homestead between 1800 and 1830. His diary reveals much about his attitudes and values, as well as the daily routine and commercial problems of cotton planters. In Document 4, two architectural plans, the first of a Georgia rice plantation and the second of a plantation in Alabama, suggest the well-ordered life that wealthy white planters fashioned for themselves. Document 5 presents excerpts from the diary of William Johnson, a barber, property owner, and free black of Natchez, Mississippi. It is difficult to detect his status, for Johnson owned slaves, gambled, gossiped, and, at least in his telling, interacted comfortably with whites. But as one entry suggests, he and his wife faced problems when booking passage on a Mississippi steamer. Document 6 includes selections from Charles Manigault's Argyle Island plantation journal. Here we see slave lists from two plantations, correspondence to an overseer from an absentee owner traveling in Europe, and an overseer's contract.

1. The Cotton South

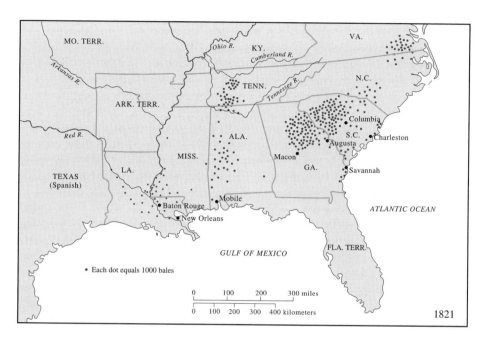

1821

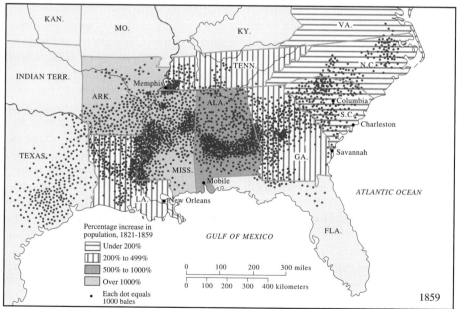

Percentage increase in population, 1821-1859

Under 200%

200% to 499%

500% to 1000%

Over 1000%

• Each dot equals 1000 bales

1859

From Mary Beth Norton et al., *A People and a Nation: A History of the United States,* © 1998, p. 254. Reprinted by permission of Houghton Mifflin Company.

2. Joseph Baldwin Examines Frontier
Law in Alabama and Mississippi, 1835–1837

In trying to arrive at the character of the South-Western bar, its opportunities and advantages for improvement are to be considered. It is not too much to say that, in the United States at least, no bar ever had such, or so many: it might be doubted if they were *ever* enjoyed to the same extent before. Consider that the South-West was the focus of an emigration greater than any portion of the country ever attracted, at least, until the golden magnet drew its thousands to the Pacific coast. But the character of emigrants was not the same. Most of the gold-seekers were mere gold-diggers—not bringing property, but coming to take it away. Most of those coming to the South-West brought property—many of them a great deal. Nearly every man was a speculator; at any rate, a trader. The treaties with the Indians had brought large portions of the States of Alabama, Mississippi and Louisiana into market; and these portions, comprising some of the most fertile lands in the world, were settled up in a hurry. The Indians claimed lands under these treaties—the laws granting preemption rights to settlers on the public lands, were to be construed, and the litigation growing out of them settled, the public lands afforded a field for unlimited speculation, and combinations of purchasers, partnerships, land companies, agencies, and the like, gave occasion to much difficult litigation in after times. Negroes were brought into the country in large numbers and sold mostly upon credit, and bills of exchange taken for the price; the negroes in many instances were unsound—some as to which there was no title; some falsely pretended to be unsound, and various questions as to the liability of parties on the warranties and the bills, furnished an important addition to the litigation: many land titles were defective; property was brought from other States clogged with trusts, limitations, and uses, to be construed according to the laws of the State from which it was brought: claims and contracts made elsewhere to be enforced here: universal indebtedness, which the hardness of the times succeeding made it impossible for many men to pay, and desirable for all to escape paying: hard and ruinous bargains, securityships, judicial sales; a general looseness, ignorance, and carelessness in the public officers in doing business; new statutes to be construed; official liabilities, especially those of sheriffs, to be enforced; banks, the laws governing their contracts, proceedings against them for forfeiture of charter; trials of right of property; an elegant assortment of frauds constructive and actual; and the whole system of chancery law, admiralty proceedings; in short, all the flood-gates of litigation were opened and the pent-up tide let loose upon the country. And such a criminal docket! What country could boast more largely of its crimes? What more splendid rôle of felonies! What more terrific murders! What more gorgeous bank robberies! What more magnificent operations in the land offices! Such . . . levies of black mail, individual and corporate! Such superb forays on the treasuries, State and National! Such expert transfers of balances to undiscovered bournes! Such august defalcations! Such flourishes of rhetoric on ledgers auspicious of gold which had departed for ever from the vault! And in INDIAN affairs!—the very mention is suggestive of the poetry of theft—the romance of a wild and weird larceny! What sublime conceptions of

This document can be found in Joseph G. Baldwin, *The Flush Times of Alabama and Mississippi* (New York: D. Appleton & Co., 1853), pp. 236–240.

super-Spartan roguery! Swindling Indians by the nation! (*Spirit of Falstaff, rap!*) Stealing their land by the township! (*Dick Turpin and Jonathan Wild! tip the table!*) Conducting the nation to the Mississippi river, stripping them to the flap, and bidding them God speed as they went howling into the Western wilderness to the friendly agency of some sheltering Suggs duly empowered to receive their coming annuities and back rations? What's Hounslow heath to this? Who Carvajal? Who Count Boulbon?

And all these merely forerunners, ushering in the Millennium of an accredited, official Repudiation; and IT but vaguely suggestive of what men could do when opportunity and capacity met—as shortly afterwards they did—under the Upas-shade of a perjury-breathing bankrupt law!—But we forbear. The contemplation of such hyperboles of mendacity stretches the imagination to a dangerous tension. There was no end to the amount and variety of lawsuits, and interests involved in every complication and of enormous value were to be adjudicated. The lawyers were compelled to work, and were forced to learn the rules that were involved in all this litigation.

Many members of the bar, of standing and character, from the other States, flocked in to put their sickles into this abundant harvest. Virginia, Kentucky, North Carolina and Tennessee contributed more of these than any other four States; but every State had its representatives.

Consider, too, that the country was not so new as the practice. Every State has its peculiar tone or physiognomy, so to speak, of jurisprudence imparted to it, more or less, by the character and temper of its bar. That had yet to be given. Many questions decided in older States, and differently decided in different States, were to be settled here; and a new state of things, peculiar in their nature, called for new rules or a modification of old ones. The members of the bar from different States had brought their various notions, impressions and knowledge of their own judicature along with them; and thus all the points, dicta, rulings, offshoots, quirks and quiddities of all the law, and lawing, and law-mooting of all the various judicatories and their satellites, were imported into the new country and tried on the new jurisprudence.

After the crash [a sharp recession] came in 1837—(there were some *premonitory fits* before, but *then* the *great convulsion* came on)—all the assets of the country were marshalled, and the suing material of all sorts, as fast as it could be got out, put into the hands of the workmen. Some idea of the business may be got from a fact or two: in the county of Sumpter, Alabama, in one year, some four or five thousand suits, in the common-law courts alone, were brought; but in some other counties the number was larger; while in the lower or river counties of Mississippi, the number was at least double. The United States Courts were equally well patronized in proportion—indeed, rather more so. The white *suable* population of Sumpter was then some 2,400 men. It was a merry time for us craftsmen; and we brightened up mightily, and shook our quills joyously, like goslings in the midst of a shower. We look back to that good time, "now past and gone," with the pious gratitude and serene satisfaction with which the wreckers near the Florida Keys contemplate the last fine storm.

It was a pleasant sight to professional eyes to see a whole people let go all holds and meaner business, and move off to court, like the Californians and Australians to the mines: the "pockets" were picked in both cases. As law and lawing soon got to be the staple productions of the country, the people, as a whole the most intelligent—in the wealthy counties—of the rural population of the United States, and, as a part, the *keenest* in all creation, got very well "up to trap" in law matters; indeed, they soon knew more about the delicate mysteries of the law, than it behooves an honest man to know.

3. Cotton Planter Bennet Barrow Describes Life in Louisiana, 1838, 1839, 1841

September 18 Cloudy damp morning—some rain at noon. picking cotten since Breakfast—went driving with james Leak   Dr Desmont and Sidney Flower. started two Fawns in my field, ran some time. dogs quit them.

19 Clear pleasant morning—62 Bales pressed last night—Cotten bend down verry much from wind on Sunday—between 90 & 100 Bales out in No—Went hunting in my field   started 3 Deer. Killed a fine young Buck—Several joined me afterwards—went driving on the swamp—started a Deer dogs ran off—in coming out of the drive started a Bear. only one dog—he became too much frightened to do any thing

20 Clear pleasant picking P. Rice bottom—hands pick well considering the storm—several sick

21 Verry Foggy morning—Com'enced hauling Cotten this morning—1st shipment—Bales will avreage 470 lbs   upwards of 100 out in No   100 & 15 of 400. this time last year had out 125—25 behind last year. owing to the season—cotten more backward in opening—at first picking—never had Cotten picked more trashy than yesterday. And to day by dinner—some few picked badly—5 sick & 2 children

22 Considerable rain before Breakfast, Appearance of a bad day—pressing—4 sick—Caught Darcas with dirt in cotton bag last night. weighed 15 pounds—Tom Beauf picked badly yesterday morning   Whiped him. few Cuts—left the field some time in the evening without his Cotten and have not seen him since—He is in the habit of doing so yearly. except last year Heavy rains during the day   women spinning—trashing Cotten   men & children—Tom B. showed himself—"sick"—Cotten picked since the storm looks verry badly—Cotten market opened this year at 13 & 13¾ cts—Bagging & *cordage* 20 & 24 and 8½ & 9 cts—Porke from $16 to $24 a Barrel—Never com'ence hauling Cotten that it did'ent rain— . . .

[October] 12 Clear verry cold morning—hands picked worse yesterday than they have done this year. lowest avreage 157—picked in the morning—in the bottom on L creek—rotten open long time—the same this morning—Whiped near half *the* hands to day for picking badly & trashy   Tom Beauf came up and put his Basket down at the scales and it is the last I've seen of him—will Whip him more than I ever Whip one, I think he deserves more—the second time he has done so this year—light Frost yesterday and to day . . .

27 Clear warm—picking Gns—Dennis ran off yesterday—& after I had Whiped him—hands picked verry light weight by dinner—complaint picking in Rank & Rotten Cotten—4 sick—have out 270 Bales or upward of 400. certain 250 or upwards out in No by 1st of November. Will [be] at least 30 Bales ahead of last year

28 Cloudy cool wind from the North. Misty—Ruffins overseer was over here this evening and informed me that his Home place hands avreaged 353   never heard any thing to Eaquel it—trashy as could be—my hands picked verry trashy yesterday evening. had a settlement with Mrs Joor & *Estate*—275 B. out of 400—232 pressed   in No 255 of 400 pressed

29 Clear cold—Mrs Joor returned to Woodvill—Mrs Joor owes me $13387.73. her notes payable in 5 years from Oct. 29, 1838

30 Clear.cool—Frost—hands picked badly and Trashy—yesterday

31 Clear pleasant. Mr Warfield my Cotten merchant or "Factor" came home with me last night. looking through the Country for buisness—Com'enced as comn merchant this Fall—as Finley & Co. Verry much pleased with him. . . .

1839

[August] 13 Morning cloudy—Bartley was not to be found last night 'till late, was not seen after 12. taken sick at Gns   found in the night—& never saw hands in better spirits. worked finely—Ginny Jerry has not been seen since Friday morning last—has been shirkin for some time   came to me Friday morning sick—suspecting him   Examined him   found nothing the matter complaining of pains &c. told him to go & work it off—he has concluded to woods it off—cotten in Lower part Gns place improved verry much new land still doing well old Land past recovery—owing I am certain to its having been broke up wet—both an injury to the land Horses & negros to work in the mud & wet

14 Cloudy—Com'enced working the road this morning from Wades to the river—verry bad—women & children picking cotten

15 Morning cloudy   sprinkle of rain this evening, started 5 scrapers old Land above

16 Cloudy morning—Finished the roade last night—well done—never finished as soon   part or most of it worse than usual—negroes . . . at the rascal in giving them Whiskey &c. 5 scrapers running—2 putting up scaffolds—all others picking cotten—was taken yesterday with violent pain in my right side in going to swamp—had to stop & get a blister at Ruffins &c. I Bennet H. Barrow do certify that I the said Bennet have got the meanest crop in this neighborhood & the meanest by far I ever had—been absent too often—would not care how mean it was if I was not in Debt—& last accounts from England verry unfavorable—two thirds of the people must be ruined—should the times continue beyond this season

17 Morning Clear   pleasant—wind from the East for some days past—cause some sickness—sprinkle of rain at 2. appearance of Heavy rain this evening—Hands do not appear as lively picking as I expected to see them

18 Cloudy warm morning—I have 20 Bales *out.* "last night"

20 Damp cloudy morning   started Gins at Home yesterday picking to day at Gns   avreaged yesterday 176—picking as clean cotten as I ever saw—Dr Desmont

an Englishman has left here. verry strangely   a villian no doubt—& left me to pay
between 10.000 & 16.000 for him—his uncommonly gentlemanly manners—modesty & chastity caused me to be discerned by him—I've allways been opposed to
Yankey speculators coming out here to seek their fortunes. by marrying or any thing
else that suits their purpose—particular the D———proffessional Preachers—
stragling foreigners, are no better—sister Eliza here to day

    21 Foggy morning—Hands picked well yesterday   highest 265   clean cotten

    22 Clear   verry warm—B S Joor came down yesterday. Went out last night
to have a Fox hunt. could'ent start—Son Bat threatened to be sick again—well dig-
ger repairing my well—more water &c.

    23 Clear   verry warm—hands picking well—Avreaged 201 day before yes-
terday—picked 3 days at Gns 15 Bales—most ever picked there in Augst—Want
rain very much—ground as dry as can be—cotten com'enced forming in the last 8
days verry fast. rain now & a late fall would make a verry fair crop—attempting to
Learn James & John their book—had rather drive a Team of Mules—James 8 years
old John 6—Johns looks one way & thinks another—more sickness for week past
than I've had this season, bowel complaints &c. . . .

    28 Clear cool morning—more sickness yesterday & to day than I've had this
season—avreaged two day 203—never saw a better crop than Turnbulls Home
crop—my crop injured as much "I think" from being too thick *as the drought*

    29 Cool wind from the North   two negros verry sick (*child & boy*) suffering
for rain verry much. Com'enced pressing 1st time

    30 Clear morning   verry cool. caught Ben with stollen cotten in his Basket
last night—My Lauderdale has the scratchers verry bad. running in corn field

    31 Nights & mornings verry cool—never saw as much cotten open in August
by 3 fourths—White every Where—dry as can be—picks verry trashy . . .

November 6 . . . Mrs Joor owes me from the 1st of this month $14727.23   not
paying me the interest yearly—& nothing 'till the End of 5 years—I will loose
$1500 thus—interest—Each year added to the principle for 5 yrs   will make
21559.30—upon the Amount she owes me dated 29 Oct. 1838 $13387.73, I wish all
young persons knew What I've learnt of this world in the last 3 years—one thing
marry a Daughter against the mothers will—hatred or dislike remains with her forever, & 99 out of a 100 think of nothing but self—corruption appears the order of
the day—a corrupt govement makes corrupt people—Gnl Jackson 1st destroying
the United S. Bank & then distributing the revenue among the State Bank inducing
them to over issue—& this creating a spirit of speculation—not with the people but
by the Banks themselves—through their agents buying up large bodies of Land &
he then issued his Specie circular—that nothing but Gold & Silver would be taken
for dues to the Government. caused a rush for Metals—Banks having over issued
people borrowed largely—everything rose to an enormous price—& altogether fic-
titious—the consequence was the Banks were forced to stop specie paying—curtail
money greatly depreciating—has caused the Whole country to be Bankrupt. We are
forced in buying any thing not to give What it is worth in Gold & Silver—or What
our money is worth here—but What it is worth to the trader in his country—an Excuse for them to add from 25 to 100 pr. ct above the usual rates   you cannot buy a

decent horse for less $200. 5 yr ago $200 bought the finest saddle horse &c. turning verry cold. . . .

1841

July 17 Clear verry warm Returned from Woodville this morning, Caroline B. Joor was Married on 15th to James Flower jur, Received a note from Ruffin stating that several of my negros were implicated in an intended insurection on the 1st of August next. It seems from What he writes me, it was to have taken place Last March—mine are O Fill O Ben Jack Dennis & Demps—will go up to Robert J. B to have them examined &c. six negros were found guilty in the first degree, it appears they were to meet at jno. Towles Gate and at Mr Turnbulls inheritance place, Leaders one of Robert J. Barrow one Bennet J. B. one of Towles one of C. Perceys one W. J. Forts & one of D. Turnbulls, none of mine were implicated farther than one of Robert J. B boys said he heard the names of the above mentioned &c. intend having an examination of the Whole plantation & the neighbourhood

   19 Clear Verry Hot—Examined Mrs Stirlings negros Courtneys & my own yesterday found none of them concerned in the Expected insurection, Went to Judge Wades this morning, found several of his men concerned it. Dave Bonner the most & he was the Leder, Sent to Jail for trial . . .

   August 13 Clear cool morning. all hands on the road. hard work

   14 Clear morn night quit cool—Son John & Clifford sick—several negros quit sick yesterday

   15 Clear pleasant morning. Finished working the road yesterday, our District Attorney, (W. D. Boyle) made a beggininng towards enforcing the Law, in removing free negros from the Parish, came to old Greys family, saw the Law in a different Light, no doubt Bribed

   16 Cloudy warm—Several of my negros in returning off of the road Saturday night came through Ruffins Quarter. he having the measles forbid their Returning that way. had them staked down all yesterday, several of them had killed a hog, found out the right ones. gave them all a severe Whipping, Ginney Jerry has been sherking about ever since Began to pick cotten. after Whipping him yesterday told him if ever he dodged about from me again would certainly shoot him. this morning at Breakfast time Charles came & told me that Jerry was about to run off. took my Gun found him in the Bayou behind the Quarter, shot him in his thigh—&c. raining all around

4. Two Plantation Site Plans in Georgia and Alabama

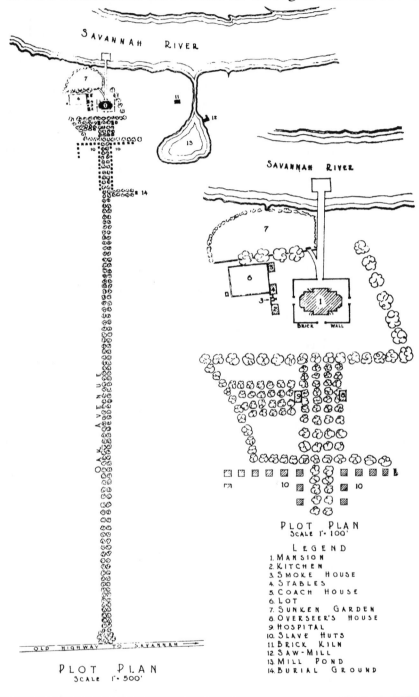

Site plans of the Hermitage. Drawn by William B. Harper, 1936.

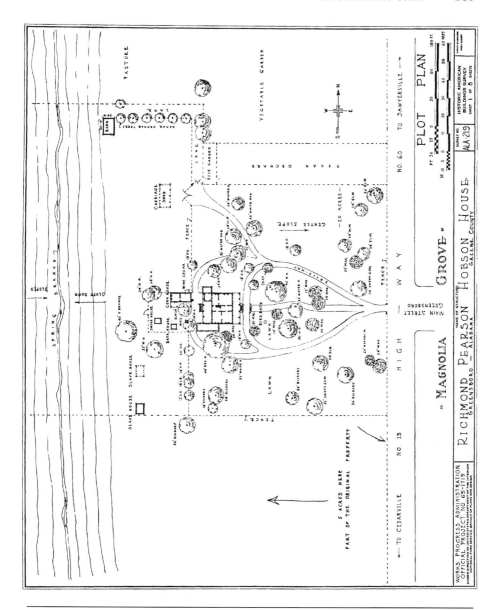

Site plan of Magnolia Grove, Hale County, Alabama. Drawn by Kirby Stringer, 1936.

5. Experiences of William Johnson, a Free Black, in Natchez, Mississippi, 1838–1842

1838

[March] 12   The town full of strangers to see the Races   To day I Took my acct to Mr Spielman which was, Interest included, $319.50   I took a saddle at 40 and a Briddle & martingale $7, which still Leaves him in my debt $272.50   Mr N Barlow pd me $20. He said that He owed me for two years shaving up to the 1st of Sept. Last. He still Owes me a Balance of $10 yet, up to the date, 12th of March, 1838

13   To day The Large Race between Linnet and Angorah Came off for ten thousand Dollars a side, It was a very pretty Race, for the first two miles and a Half, Angorah in the Lead and all at wonce the Boy fell off Directly after Linnet passed Her   She ran on out . . .

19   Buisness not very good. Steven got drunk Last night and went of[f] and remained all night and was not Here this morning to go to Market. I sent Bill Nix to the Jail to see if He was there and He was not there. I then sent Him out to Dr Ogdons and in going there He found Him and brought Him Down and Left Him in the gate and he Jumped over the Fence and went threw in Judge Montgomerys yard. Bill He ran around the Corner and found him and brought Him in, I Kept him [in] the shop a Little while and then sent him to Help Mrs Lieper to move from the old House Down to the House belonging to Bill Hazard   He ran off 4 times in about three hours and Bill Nix Caught Him Every time, so He Brought Him Home after a while and I went to the stable and gave him a pretty sefveere thrashing with the Cow hide—then he was perfectly Calm and Quite [sic] and could then do his work. Tis singular how much good it does some people to get whiped   Mr. Kenney paid me $40.00 for One months House rent due to day, the 19th inst   I then told him here after He could have the Room for $35 per month

20   I was up to auction to day and Mr Soria was selling off the Furniture of Dr James Denny—Sold on a credit of six months from Date

21   Mr S. S. Prentiss Dellivered a fine speech at the Court House in presence of a very Large Congregation—I was Out to day . . .

24   It is the Last day of the Jocky Clubb Races Here and it was the most Splendid days Raceing that I Ever saw on this tract I think

25   I remained Home all day—Nothing New to day that I know of Except there are a greate many persons that are now awaiting a Boat To go to The New Orleans Races.

26   A good many Citizens Left Here for New Orleans   Col Bingaman Left about 2 Oclock this morning On Bourd of the st Boat St. Louis—He took several other Horses down besides what he had already Down. William made in the shop this week about $30, This has been Quite a buisness day, good Deal of Hair Cutting this Evening, Bond opened his Dancing School To day at the City Hotell

---

27   Steven ran off Last night and God Only Knows where he has gone to, for I dont, tho if I should have the Good Luck to Get Him again I will be very apt to Hurt his Feelings—This is the second time he has ranaway in a week.

29   To day it was that I paid Mr W W. Wilkins a note that He held against me for thirty six Dollars due the Estate of Mr Perry. R McCary was the Indorser on it— To day I took one of the bigest Kind of a hunt for Steven But could not find the Rascal at all

31   I got on my Horse Early this morning and wrode Out to Washington in search of Steven but Could not find Him at all   I also went Out again in the afternoon to Becon Landing but could not hear of Him. During the time that I was in sea[r]ch of him He sent me word that if I would Only Let him off without whiping him that he would never runaway again Durring His Life . . .

1839

June 19   Coming from Supper to night I [saw] Bill & Charles with a Big Nig Standing at the front Door as is usual when I am away—Oh what Low minded wretches   Mr W Harris Left to Day for the North

20   Mr Lambdin Left to Day for the North

21   Buisness has been Dull—Mr S Davis paid me $5.50 to night which pays his acct. up to the 1st of July 1839

22   Buisness good for the Season   My third Son was Born to night near ten Oclock.

23   Nothing new that I Know of

24   Nothing new that I know of   Jud[g]e Dunlap paid me to day five Dollars on acct.

25   The New Store that I Built was Rented to Day by me to Col Waymoth at the Rate of One Thousand Dollars per anum, payable monthly—I Gave Him a Small instrument of writing to this Effect and wish it perfectly understood that I Rented it only for the One Year . . .

1841

[August] 11   I wrode down this Evening to Mr Barland To put my Horses to pasture and I Bot a Cow from Mr Winn for 17 Dollars and Brot up another to take if I Chose, I put my two Horeses in Mr Barlands Pasture this Evening To grass

12   Considerable Humbugery going on in town and some men are on the List that I Know is too much the Gentleman to have any thing to do with it, Mrs C C. Binghaman Died Last night   Was Sick for Several days

13   Nothing of much interest Occured to day. Mr Oblemis is Sick. I wrode Out to his House this morning and cut his Hair, He was Telling Mr McGraw about some of the Citizens of Arkensaw taking the Life of twenty three men who He herd had Commited Roberrys and Counterfeiting &c. He Said that they Drowned 11 of them and shot the rest. Mrs C C Bingaman was Buried this Morning Out at Fatherland, the old Home Plantation   It was a very Large Funeral indeed   The Largest Ever Known in the place

14   Nothing new To day worth the attention of any Bond payer—Several hits at the Different papers relative to the Bond Discussion in Vicksburgg &c.

16   The City is at this time perfectly Healthy and nothing new thats interesting

17   All Sorts of Tryals going on   The different Offices has been full all day and they Continue to arrest Still—The Lord Knows how those things will terminate for I have no Conception myself   Buisness is very dull indeed, nothing Lively in the way of my Profession at all . . .

27   To day has been a day of much interest to the Citizens of this place. The Veto of the Bank Bill reached this place to day and the Whigs are very much Disappointed whilst the Demmocrats are rejoiceing at the veto—The people have something to do to day in the way of Talking Politicks

28   Nothing new that I Know of—The Democrats Last night Set a Couple of Barrells of Tar on fire at the Bluff where the Log Cabbin stood—I believe that was all that was done on the Ocasion—The Sale of George Sniders Property Came off to day on a Credit of 6 months. He had a Large Quantity of things of One Kind or other—There were a great many Persons at the tract to day to Shoot Pigeons   They Shot at about Eigty of them and Killed 49 of them—Mr J Stockton and Mr Combay, both of them Killed a pigeon Every Shot   I paid Mr G. Weldon ten Dollars to day and did not take a Receipt for it

29   In the afternoon I took my Horse and wrode down into the Swamp as far as Maj Tom Winns Plantation   I went down to take Steven as I found him in town to day and 1/2 Drunk. I made him Lead down the Sorril Horse for young Winslow Winn to wride in place of his Horse that is Lame. I wrote a Letter to day and Took it down to the Baton Rogue and when I got down thare I Knew no One on the Boat so I did not send it . . .

September 12   Nothing new that I Know of—I understood this morning Early that Steven was in town and I Knew if he was in town that he must have runaway from Mr Gregory where I had hired [him] to haul wood in the swamp. It was after Breakfast and I got on my Horse and wrode up the street and I found him in the Back St. near P. Bakers—Gave him a tap or two with my wriding whip and then Brot him to my shop and in a few minutes after I got to the shop Mr Vernon Came to inform me that Steven had took a watch from one of his men and that he had been seen to have it and that he had taken it yesterday as he passed there. I Commenced a Search on his person and I found it in his Coat Pocket   I gave it to Mr Vernon and was Glad that he Came So Soon for it. I then made him get on a horse and go on down to Mr Vernons place and there I made his Driver Give him a good Floging with his Big whip. I then took him down as far as Mr Fords Lane and Left him with Mr Gregory and he took him down and Set him to work   I Borrowed a Gun from young Mr Barland and I Gave my Little Gun to Winston and we went into the Lake. I killed 5 Large Snipe and 2 Squirrells and he Killed 1 Sparrow hawk and 6 Snipes—Justices office were full all day   J Soria was tring to recover his money that he Lost. They were trying a Boy [of] Mr Fields. The Boy was Sentenced to be whiped but was not. His master [entered] an apeal I herd . . .

1842

July 9   I Spoke to A. L. Willson the other day to procure me a passage on the Steam Boat, Maid of Arkensaw, which he promised to do and to day when the Boat Came I went down to see about it and I saw him and He told me that he had spoke to the

Capt. and that he had Refused to Let a State Room, But that my wife Could have the whole of the Ladies Cabbin to Herself but it was a Rule on his Boat not to Let any Col persons have State Rooms on Her—I askd him to go with me on Bourd—He went on Board and showd me the Capt. and I asked him if could not spare a State Room and he told me that He Could not spare one that it was against the Rules of His Boat and that he had said it once and that was Enough and that he was a man of his word and Spoke of Prejudice of the Southern people, it was damd Foolish &c, and that he was a doing a Buisness for other people and was Compelld to adopt those Rules—I did not prevail by no means—He then said that I Could Have a State Room on Conditions which I told him would answer.

6. Excerpts from Charles Manigault's Plantation Journal and Letter, 1833–1853

Slave Lists

Negroes purchased at Gowrie (Savannah River) Jany. 1st 1833

			AGE	QUANTITY OF CLOTH	QUALITY	
same family	Harry	Driver	40		P (prime)	
	Bina ⎱ twins		42		P	
	Patty ⎰		42		$\frac{3}{4}$	P
	Bina		20		P	
	Matilda		18		P	
	Becky	child	5			
	Peggy	child	4			
	John	child				
	Ned		50		P	
	Stephen		28		P	
	Binah		25		P	
	Louisa	child	2			
	Nancy		16		P	
	Hector	Waiting Boy to Overseer	13			
same family	Mary		50		H (half)	
	Maria		32		P	
	Chloe		28		P	
	Susy		24		P	
	Charles	(2d Driver)	21		P	
	Ben	frost bitten hands & feet	30		H	
	Martha	child	4			
same family	Scotland		45		P	
	Hannah		25		P	
	Minty		24		P	
	Rinah	child	10			
	Paris	child	3			
	William	child	3			
	Molly	child	1			
	Abram		40		P	
	Rachel		50		$\frac{3}{4}$	
	Elick	Cooper	30		P	
	London	Miller	24		P	
	Jemimah		24		$\frac{3}{4}$	
	Jane	child	2			

From James M. Clifton, ed., *Life and Labor on Argyle Island,* Beehive Press, Savannah, GA, © 1978.

				AGE		QUALITY
Charity	Plantation Cook			50		$\frac{1}{2}$
Eleanor				70		
Billy	Miller & Carpenter			30		P
Catey				25		P
Martha	child			11		
Charles	Cooper, Gardener, & Wood Cutter			50		$\frac{1}{2}$
Nancy				35		P
Friday				26		P
Charlotte				16		P
Sampson	child			10		
Maria				23		P
Sandy	child			2		
Minda				26		P
Binkey				24		P
Toney	Carpenter			50		P
Betsey				27		P

Negroes Moved to Gowrie from Silk Hope 1st Jany. 1833

		AGE	YARDS OF CLOTH	QUALITY
Fortune		35	$5\frac{1}{4}$	P
Juna		18	5	P
Maria	child			
Julia		17	5	P
Joaney		15	5	$\frac{1}{2}$
March		23	$5\frac{3}{4}$	P
Moses	slow & complaining	30	$5\frac{1}{4}$	P
Jupiter		30	5	P
Jacob	smart & intelligent	21	$5\frac{1}{4}$	P
Sukey		45	$5\frac{1}{4}$	$\frac{1}{2}$
Bob	slow, honest, good	30	$5\frac{1}{2}$	P
Latrance	slow—wants pushing	22	$5\frac{1}{4}$	P
Plato	good & trusty	20	$5\frac{3}{4}$	P
Cushina	weakly	18	5	P
Charles	smart boy	14	$3\frac{1}{2}$	$\frac{1}{2}$
Molly		25	$5\frac{1}{4}$	P
Bolfour		30	$5\frac{1}{2}$	P
Jackey		20	5	P
Patty		19	5	P
Nanny		18	$4\frac{3}{4}$	P
Young John	lazy	20	$5\frac{1}{4}$	P
Simon		21	$5\frac{1}{2}$	P

Letter to Overseer

Charles Manigault to Jesse T. Cooper

Naples 10th January 1848

Dear Sir

I received a Letter from "Mr. Habersham" informing me of his having engaged you to attend to my planting affairs & interests. Your residence being on Mr. Barclay's plantation (near mine) and I now write you a few lines to give you some of my rules & regulations in relation to my Concerns now under your

Charge which have been always strictly attended to. My Negroes have the reputation of being orderly & well disposed—but like all Negroes, they are up to anything, if not watched & attended to. I expect the kindest treatment of them from you—for this has always been a principal thing with me. I never suffer them to work off the place—or to exchange work with any plantation. I never lend my flat, or anything from my plantation nor do I wish to borrow. I have suffered enough already from this lending to my neighbours. Anything you think my Place is in want of, just send to Mr. Habersham, & he will furnish you with it for my account. It has always been my plan to give out allowance to the Negroes on Sunday in preference to any other day, because this has much influence in keeping them at home that day whereas, if they received allowance on Saturday for instance, Some of them would be off with it that same evening to the shops to trade & perhaps would not get back until Monday morning. I allow no strange Negro to take a wife on my place, & none of mine to keep a boat & should there be one belonging to me at the landing I request you to have it locked, & keep the Key yourself. Cut up, or lock up in the mill any Negro Canoe found anywhere on my place, & particularly near the Mill—whether it be on my land or on "Mr. Potter's" as that gentleman requested me, to do so, if I found any near my Mill on his land. I allow no one to cut wood on my Island opposite "Mr. Legare's" place, & I request you to attend to this as far as lays in your power. You will get Cotton Oznaburgs in May, & give $5\frac{1}{2}$ yards to the women, & 6 to the men, & proportionally to the Children, with a Handkerchief to each female, who works. I wish you to engage as soon as possible 20,000 Staves, to be put away in the Cooper's Shop early in the summer, by which they will be well seasoned for making Barrels when you set the Coopers at work in midsummer. Put nothing under my dwelling House, you can help, & don't have a plank across the ditch anywhere near it. Make all pass thro the settlement, for I dislike a public way so near my dwelling & as there is no white person now residing on the place, I beg you to nail up the necessary door—it is not intended for Negroes. The garden is very productive, & if you have anyone who has nothing else to do (such as "Old Ned") who would attend to it it would add much to their health & comfort, & I wish you to keep up the fences around the garden, the Barn Yard, & my house, and have everything of the kind looking snug & in good repair, just as if I was living on the place. "Mr. Barclay" gives more meat than I do but my people besides being the best clothed in the Country have other advantages—for instance, I keep all the small Rice for them, unless on one or two occasions when they have done anything wrong, when I have sold the whole of it. The Dirty Rice amounting usually to 10 or 12 Barrels, is always kept for them at harvest when hard work don't give them time to grind Corn. But you will give them meat, now & then, when you think proper. The House in the High Land you will look to now & then, when convenient, & have it in repair for the little Children in May. You will sell the Rice Flour for me to the best advantage, or if you find it accumulating, & no demand for it, you will inform "Mr. Habersham," who will probably be able to sell it by the quantity to someone, who will send a boat for it. If you Keep it to March, or April, it will get heated, & turn sour. You take charge of my interests under high recommendations. I am therefore prepossessed in your favor. "Mr. Bagshaw" a distinguished Rice Planter, while living on an adjoining place, managed all my affairs for 7 years. I began with him at a salery of $150 per an. But I am quite satisfied to pay you what Mr. H[abersham] writes me, viz., $250 per an. for your services. If things go on well, it can be increased a little for another year. I request you to write me once a month. Just put my name on the letter. Mr. H[abersham] will add my address in Europe. I shall be home in October next.

Overseer Contract

Contract Between Charles Manigault and His Overseer, S. F. Clark, for the Year 1853, Chatham County, Georgia

The following agreement is hereby made and concluded between Charles Manigault and Stephen F. Clark for the year 1853.

I, Stephen F. Clark hereby undertake to manage to the best of my abilities the two Plantations on Argyle Island (which are now joined into one) comprising about 500 acres of Rice land, all of which is to be planted in Rice and I will devote all my experience and exertions to attend to all Mr. Manigault's interests and Plantation concerns according to his wishes and instructions and as most conducive to his interest and to the comfort and welfare of his Negroes. I will treat them all with kindness and consideration in sickness and in health. I will be at both settlements every day, and supervise all that is going on at each place, and attend personally to giving out allowance every Sunday morning and see to all other things myself. I will put the banks and lands etc., of his plantation in the best possible order so as to have every branch of it in such a secure and forward state as to give the best hopes of success, with a view of planting, bullwarking, harvesting, placing safely and securely in the Barn yard, threshing (by steam or otherwise) milling and sending away such a crop as his Plantation ought to produce under good management and my best personal attendance to all things. I will never work his Negroes off the Place, no lending and borrowing of hands being permitted by Mr. Manigault. I will keep the Flats and other things in good repair and will never lend out his flat or other boat or any thing belonging to his Plantation and never send either away unless there is absolute necessity for it. Mr. Manigault never borrows or lends if he can help it and hereby instructs Mr. Clark to write to Messrs. Habersham & Son for any thing which in his judgment Mr. Manigault's Plantation stands in need of. I will take special care to keep the Carpenters constantly employed in the most useful and necessary Plantation works, and when work is slack with them I will put them at the old and new Wharf, etc., or to caulking and repairing Flats Etc. I will attend to the Steam Thresher and Rice Mill as far as lays in my power and see that the measurements of rough rice and the delivery of it and of barrels of clean rice from Mill for market be all properly attended to and written down and I will have a close supervision, but at the same time be careful not to interfere too much with the beating and management of the Rice Mill in cases where I am unacquainted with such machinery and the working of it, as the Negroes in charge have much experience therein. In case of accident I will use all my energy to have it repaired in Savannah as soon as possible. There being no physician engaged on the place I will provide myself with a good book of Medical instruction and be careful to have at hand the few requisite Plantation Medicines and I will attend myself to mixing and instructing the nurses how to administer them. And in the event of any serious accident resulting in the fracture of a limb, I will place the patient on a door in the fastest boat I can command and immediately send him to Savannah to be conveyed on the door by the boat hands and placed in the care of Dr. Bullock or at his Hospital. I engage to keep neither Horse, Hog or Poultry of any kind on Mr. Manigault's Plantation. I am to be supplied (solely for myself and family) with Plantation provisions consisting only of Corn and small Rice, all other provision and supplies for myself I am to procure at my own expense. I am to have a woman exclusively devoted to washing and cooking for me, she being the only person belonging to the Plantation that I am to give any call or occupation to whatever for any of my household affairs, she never to be a field hand. I am also to be provided with a boy to wait on me and to go to the new Ground to cut wood from any logs or stumps for my fire wood. I will endeavour to prevent any one trespassing on Mr. Manigault's Island in wood opposite Mr. Legare's Plantation, by forbidding any one whatever cutting the wood or digging and flatting mud from it. Mr. Manigault's row boat being kept solely for his own use, with its oars &c. is always to be placed carefully in the Mill during his absence. I shall always prefer transacting any business I have with Savannah by letter sent by a boy in a canoe. Whenever a hard storm of rain sets in and does not clear off towards the afternoon, unless the people are at some very pressing and important work Mr. Manigault wishes me to call them in to their houses for the rest of the rainy stormy afternoon, and Mr. Manigault wishes the Driver to be told this, so that should the Overseer not be present with them the Driver can act accordingly and bring the people home, for Mr. Manigault's long experience is that always after a complete wetting particularly in cold rainy weather, in winter or spring one or more of them are made sick and lie up, and at times serious illness ensues. Mr. Manigault wishes Mr. Clark to sell for him all the Rice flour made in his Mill to any one in small or large quantities, always and to every one for cash and should Mr. Clark be induced on any occasion to give credit to any one it must be at his own risk, and my account with Mr. Clark must be credited with the amount.

To all of which terms I, Stephen F. Clark hereby agree and bind myself to conform to it in every respect, and on my fulfilling all that I hereby agree to in the above agreement then and in that case Mr. Charles Manigault hereby binds himself to pay me for my aforenamed services at and after the rate of Five Hundred Dollars pr. annum for this present year and at the same rate for any portion of the year that I may continue in his services.

S. F. Clark–Charles Manigault.

✗ E S S A Y S

These two essays address the important debate over the extent to which capitalism influenced southern slaveholders. Mark M. Smith of the University of South Carolina, author of *Mastered by the Clock,* argues that contrary to what one might expect, southerners by the 1830s had begun to adopt clock time as critical to plantation management. Planters became time-conscious, seeing clock time as important in order to regulate production, ensure ordered and timely output, and encourage higher plantation profits. By contrast, historian Eugene Genovese, from his book *The Political Economy of Slav-*

ery, questions whether the Old South was capitalist and argues that the dependence on slave labor suggests that planters were traditional landlords who were being forced to deal with markets in a modern, changing world order.

Plantation Management by the Clock

MARK M. SMITH

For a variety of reasons, but mainly because they have seldom considered the question of time consciousness, historians of the American slave South have suggested that antebellum masters and bondpeople, caught as they were in the webs of seasonal agriculture and non-wage economic and social relations, were necessarily peripheral to the emergence of clock time. But viewed and evaluated in comparative perspective, it seems that rather than constituting a place on the edge of modern time consciousness, the post-1830 slave South was very much in and of it. In fact, the Old South, though a society nurtured in nature's womb, was possibly more clock conscious than many nineteenth-century free wage labor industrial societies. This possibility has eluded not only historians of the Old South but also those committed to the historical study of time generally. With few exceptions, historical analyses of time consciousness have concentrated on the evolution of clock consciousness and time discipline in wage-labor, urban-industrial, conventionally capitalist societies. Even on those occasions when historians of slave societies have ventured to consider the relationship between clock consciousness and slavery, they have done so by borrowing a conceptual lens from historians who have examined the emergence of time discipline under industrial, free wage labor capitalism. . . .

. . . Because of their place in the Atlantic marketplace, eighteenth and nineteenth-century southern merchants appear to have developed a keen sense that time was money, that punctuality in business transactions was a virtue and necessity, not only from the requisites of their own trade but from their dealings with northern and European merchants. Yankee merchants throughout the colonial period, for example, coached their southern counterparts in the need for punctuality in business. As Boston merchant Jonathan Johnson advised Edward Telfair's Georgia mercantile firm in 1775, "let me however request of you to execute this order with the utmost punctuality & Expedition." By 1802, however, the situation was reversed. Charleston merchant Thomas Aiton complained to his firm's parent company, William Stanley and Company of New York: "Three mails have arrived since we received yours by Post informing us of your intention to Send us by next Mail 2,000 dollars. We have neither received money nor letter." Aiton then warned: "Such Conduct may be attended with very serious circumstances if repeated. You know as well as us that the most strict punctuality is necessary in money matters." Similarly, punctuality with credit payments became a point of pride, indeed, of virtue, for southern merchants. When Virginian George Carter failed to pay the credit on a note signed by Landon Carter in 1806, the latter complained that "you [have] done more injury to the respectability of my punctual habits in Fredericksburg than any I have ever had before." While no doubt influenced by the presence of public, church-based time, the

Taken from "Old South Time in Comparative Perspective." Originally appeared in *American Historical Review,* vol. 101, no. 5 (December 1996), pp. 1432–1469. Reprinted by permission of the *American Historical Review* and the author.

South's urban merchants, then, like their medieval forebears, developed their own partially secularized notion of time. Atlantic merchants, in short, bequeathed an important legacy to the antebellum South as, in fact, they had to the nineteenth-century Western world.

The most conspicuous source of this mercantile and civic time consciousness in the South was in its urban environs. Eighteenth and nineteenth-century southern towns constituted the physical space where secular and sacred time meshed. Although southern industry was woefully undeveloped in both centuries, its absence does not seem to have made the region's urban areas any less clock conscious. . . . Charleston's St. Michael's clock, installed in the 1760s, for example, was "a strong 30 Hour Clock, to show the Hour Four Ways, to strike the Hour on the largest Bell." In the antebellum period, civic authorities expanded the function of the church's time: "It will be noticed that it is 'to show the *Hour* Four Ways,' and this is all it showed till 1840, when, with the consent of the vestry, the City Council added minute hands." One should not underestimate the aural and temporal power of these and similar church bells. . . .

Added to the mercantile and urban forces promoting a clock consciousness in the South was an increasing disposition on the part of white southerners, both rural and urban, slaveholding and non, to own timepieces, especially in the nineteenth century. . . . The increasing availability of clocks and watches, combined with a reduction in their relative costs in the early antebellum period, had an impact on southern rural and urban areas just as it did on northern ones. And the basic reasons for increased watch and clock ownership in the South were the same as elsewhere. . . . By 1851, three entries in one southerner's diary could speak for the South generally: "Am to send for my carriage today at 5 PM . . . Mitchell & Allen family arrive from Glenroy a little before 2 PM . . . Am to call Board of Medical College to meet on Saturday 1 PM at Courthouse."

Similarly, if the railroads were primarily responsible for the diffusion of the North's urban time consciousness, the same process is in operation in the antebellum South. In 1834, for example, the Charleston & Hamburg railroad in South Carolina, at the time the world's longest railway under single management, achieved "the greatest possible regularity in the time of running Passenger Engines" by placing clocks at six of its stations. The chief engineer stipulated fines for unpunctual drivers: "regulations have been established fixing the hour of departure, . . . as well as that of the earliest time, at which they are permitted under a penalty of five dollars, to arrive at the following [station]."

The antebellum South, however, was not like everywhere else in one important respect: the peculiar institution. But rather than a fetter on clock consciousness and time-thrift, slavery proved to be a powerful stimulant in pushing southern planters toward the clock. The South's shift to clock time in the last thirty or so years of the antebellum period was undoubtedly due to railroads, urban time, mercantile time, and . . . other forces. . . . But there were also forces created by late antebellum slavery that helped master and slave adopt the clock. Whereas early experiments with the timing of hired labor in the rural North and the emergence of free wage industrial-urban labor elsewhere promoted clock consciousness, southern slaveowners' bid for slave-based modernity provided a similar catalyst. The notion of premodern impulses in southern slavery is, thanks to the pioneering work of Eugene D.

Genovese, well known and probably true. But when it comes to conceptions of time, it appears that different impulses applied, impulses from both inside and outside the South's putatively non-capitalist slave regime. . . .

. . . The fundamental push toward time discipline among the South's master class came in the 1830s. With their time consciousness heightened by railroads and the postal service, and drawing on a long familiarity with the imperatives of mercantile and urban time, slaveholders of the 1830s began to push for more efficient agriculture and a better ordering of their slave work force. Surrounded by a world moving toward free wage labor capitalism, slaveholders were at once repulsed by the dangerous rise of a landless and politically volatile proletariat and eager to garb themselves in modern clothes. The answer to this dilemma, or at least one part of it, was in the use of clock time. The nineteenth century's most obvious icon of modernity, the clock and the time it kept, was simultaneously modern but controlling, at once an engine for economic efficiency and a tool of social discipline. In the context of the late antebellum period, when slaveowners aimed to modernize slavery without threatening its fundamentally conservative social relations, the clock proved particularly attractive. Not only could clock time be spliced with more traditional forms of social control like the whip and the old, even revered, urban practice of sounding time, not only was clock time perceived to be in harmony with that arbiter of southern agriculture, nature, but the clock could be recruited to help create a modern, efficient, and disciplined slaveholders' regime. It would, ideally, be a regime that borrowed the discipline of the factory—a free wage labor clock without importing wage labor's associated, essentially mobocratic, tendencies. In a society that coveted profit and enslavement, efficiency and order, clock time—owned and controlled exclusively by masters—proved irresistibly alluring.

As Bertram Wyatt-Brown has pointed out, in their efforts to "modernize, to improve the 'home system,' so that its foundations were no less secure, no less progressive than those on which free labor rested," masters looked, of all places, to the free but materialist North. Specifically, they turned to northern agricultural societies and scientific journals, they noted Benjamin Franklin's counsel that time is money, and they reinterpreted this advice in the context of their slave society. A reprint from the *Boston Cultivator* in the *Southern Planter* for January 1850, for example, suggested that all agriculturalists, southern ones included, should allow "twelve working hours to a day," for "he who by rising at eight instead of five O'clock in the morning, thereby loses three hours daily, parts with one-fourth of his means of supporting himself and family: ten years' labor lost on the course of forty years!" The careful harvesting of this time was essential for profit, and the responsibility rested, in the first instance, with the planter. Moreover, efforts to inculcate an internal time discipline among some planters appear to have succeeded. "My plan for working," revealed one small slaveholder in 1836, "was formed by necessity." Owning few slaves, he was obliged to organize his own time efficiently: "As soon as it was light enough to see, I hitched up and drove briskly until breakfast time—took out and fed while I ate, and for which I only allowed forty-five minutes—worked till one o'clock—rested an hour and a half when cool, two hours when warm." . . .

. . . In some instances, planters bought time-saving machinery, especially cotton gins, which promised to clean five hundred pounds "in 31 minutes." Equally, planters tried to import factory methods directly to the plantation. Again, the aping of the North was obvious. Lowell mills, for instance, become models of efficiency, and planters were encouraged to emulate the factory's use of clock-regulated labor. The *Southern Agriculturalist,* for example, published one southerner's account of a visit to Lowell in 1845 and advised "all those who are politically or otherwise unfriendly to the factory system, to read the following article." The visitor, from Kentucky, was impressed by the fact that "[t]he very few persons that were occasionally seen at all, hurried to and fro, as if their time was precious," enthused over "the most perfect order, system, and regularity . . . everywhere exhibited," and praised the factory's use of aural time control: "At 12 o'clock, M., the factory bells chimed merrily, and the whirl of the spindles, the clatter of the looms, and the hum of the drums and wheels all ceased." In their efforts, then, to realize the ideal of time discipline and precise temporal coordination on their plantations, masters turned to the watch and the clock. Plantation clock time often mimicked the southern urban and northern factory form: it was communicated through sound. Bells and bugles, for instance, were rung or blown "at 9 o'clock, P.M.," when "every servant is required to return to his own cabin."

Sometimes, to be sure, nature intruded, but not as much as might be expected. Natural time and clock time did, of course, coexist on plantations; slaveowners' journals are eloquent on this point. Virginia planter George Llewellyn Nicolson, for example, took his temperature readings by the sun in one journal entry ("Thermometer 18 [degrees] at Sunrise") but also measured work done by the clock: "Filled ice House by 11 Oclock." Certainly, nature could be cruel and rush frazzled planters. William Fanning Wickham of Virginia could on one day in June 1828 congratulate himself that "[t]he corn is I think forward for the time of year," and four days later complain: "Finished the harvest early this morning—We should have been done some days sooner, but the weather this week has been so intensely hot that the reapers could make little progress." Nature proved difficult the next year, too. In January 1829, Wickham lamented, "The wheat in general is very backward." In March, he moaned, "nearly a weeks work has been entirely lost by rain & bad weather." Yet Wickham did his best to minimize the impact of nature's unkind vagaries, and he often recruited the clock to regulate the work and time that he could control. In July 1830, he used clock time to describe his agricultural operations: "Began yesterday at eleven OClock to thresh wheat." On other occasions, lost time to nature was minimized by forward planning and time harvesting: "We are later to sow wheat this year than I have ever been before—but by continuing to plough in the cornfield we shall be forward in our preparation—& no time shall be lost." . . . When nature could cost time, when it could expand and contract it, planters believed that agricultural operations were more likely to be completed in time if they paid close attention to time, its passage, and the clock.

In some respects, in fact, the vagaries of nature and the strictures they placed on planters' time were important for heightening masters' desire to make the most of time. Planters respected nature and its merciless control of time and, rather than trying to control it, looked instead to natural rhythms for inspiration. Even the most ardent scientific reformers of the 1830s agreed and counseled that "if we would catch the true spirit of improvement, we must bow at nature's shrine, and consult her oracles." The seasons still, as they always would, dictated planting and harvesting cycles, and planters deemed this proper and correct. But within these larger rhythms, the clock could be recruited, not to supplant nature but rather to complement and exploit its sometimes frenetic rhythms.

For some planters, the rhythm of the agricultural year, with its slack times, harried periods, and seasonal variations, did require a work schedule that was more flexible than that provided by a clock-defined, standard working day. But significantly, when planters most needed efficiency in slaves' labor, they invoked the clock and rendered all time into masters' time. Among the rules and "Priveleges" on Richard Eppes's Hopewell, Virginia, plantation, for example, was the following fiat issued to his bondpeople in 1857: "You will work from sunrise until sunset but when a press longer. Three quarters of an hour will be allowed you to breakfast and one hour and a quarter to dine from the month of October until April. One hour to breakfast and one hour and three quarters to dine from April until October." In other words, during the busiest but hottest seasons, when Eppes needed intensive and efficient labor the most, he seemed to give his slaves more time off, measured to within fifteen minutes. Yet these "apparently long breaks for meals and rest, especially during the summer," ought not, as one econometrician has recently contended, "be attributed to the philanthropic instincts of the planters." The effect of giving longer, clock-regulated recuperative breaks in the South's sweltering months actually increased slaves' efficiency at precisely the time when masters needed their people to labor most intensively. Moreover, that Eppes awarded his slaves an additional forty-five minutes to eat in the summer is hardly testimony to paternal magnanimity when we bear in mind that southern summer days were, on average, over three hours longer than winter ones. Eppes, in short, could afford to allow his hands more time to breakfast and lunch in the summer not only because it made economic sense but simply because there was more daytime to bestow. Plainly, then, all hands were primed for efficiency at all times, literally. . . .

The time spent cultivating some crops had to be more carefully monitored than with growing other staples. Tobacco, for instance, "requires a great deal of labor and attention to produce it of a fine quality." And quality tools were essential in the tobacco planter's fight against losing time:

> how much labor is often lost by giving a hand an indifferent axe or worn out hoe, . . . How much time is often lost in sending to a neighbor's to borrow a spade, or to grind axes for want of a grindstone at home. Half the time lost in this way in the course of a year would if employed in some useful labor more than purchase a spade and grindstone.

But whatever the crop, time lost was a pressing worry for masters. While individual planters were certainly free to impose their own temporal parameters and devise their own work regimes to suit their crop and labor force, all shared in an appeal to the clock as an arbiter of plantation order. In other words, while certain crops demanded particular work hours at particular points in the year, all crops, because they were cultivated by slaves, were clock regulated to some extent. It was more the labor and to a lesser extent the crop that was being timed and regulated.

If crop cycles could be coordinated by the clock, so could the specific stages and components of agricultural production. Amelia County, Virginia, planter James Powell Cocke, for example, commenced threshing wheat "at 10 OCk" in August

1854, "[f]inished sowing [the winter] wheat about 12 OCl" in November 1854, and in July of 1856 "[b]egan my wheat Harvest at 10 OcK A.M." So, too, with the human cogs of the plantation machine. In published plantation journals, owners reveal how they attempted to cultivate among overseers the habit of making precise, clock-oriented daily journal entries and provided advice on how long slaves should reasonably spend on particular aspects of plantation agriculture. Before the running of the plantation could be rendered orderly, the overseers themselves had to acquire the habit of time discipline: "The operations, events and remarks of each day should be recorded in the evening of the same day, and not put off until forgot, or until necessarily omitted for want of time. Attention to keeping up the Journal will soon become a habit." Once the overseers had acquired this discipline, then so could the laborers, and managers were urged to regulate rising, work times, and breaks by the clock. Time for kindnesses could then be found or created within the clock-defined working day, regardless of crop:

> Notice them, encourage and reward such as best perform their duties. Even a word of kindness, if judiciously used, will effect much. At other times respite from labor for a few hours of any day, or at the end of the week, may be granted, and when such loss of time will not materially affect the plantation operations. . . .

The introduction of the clock to the plantation field made temporal coordination and regulation under southern slavery very similar to that being enforced in free wage labor, industrializing societies. Clock-regulated bells and bugles especially were one way to regulate the work times of laborers slave and free. Compare, for example, the following two statements, the first by a southern slaveowner in 1860, the second depicting the regulation of work time in English factories in 1833. The southern slave, apparently, was "not overworked; . . . He goes out when it is light enough to work, at 8 o'clock takes his breakfast, at 12 o'clock his dinner, at 2 o'clock goes to work again, . . . [at] 9 or 10 o'clock goes to bed." Similarly, child laborers in Leeds "commenced at six o'clock; at nine, half an hour for breakfast; from half past nine till twelve, work. Dinner, one hour; from five till eight, work; rest for half an hour. From half past eight till twelve, (midnight,) work; an hour's rest."

If aural clock time was one weapon in the masters' arsenal to fight for progress, regulated slave behavior, and increased productivity, the watch was another. It was especially suited to gauging the economic productivity of labor. Because antebellum "laborlords," as Gavin Wright has called Old South planters, sought to maximize output per hand rather than yield per acre, the saving and manipulation of slaves' labor time was of great importance. Although, as John F. Olson has pointed out, slaves worked fewer clock-time hours per year than free laborers, North and South, slaves nevertheless "worked more intensively per hour" because their masters were able to regulate their productivity with the watch backed by the whip. According to Olson, "slaves on plantations using the gang system worked 94 per cent more (harder) each hour than did free men." This level of intensity was achieved because slaveholders, like nineteenth-century managers elsewhere, came to recognize that work and leisure regulated by clock time was a means to increase and maintain the productivity of labor. Of course, if slaves did work so much harder per hour than free workers who were similarly regulated by the clock, one must assume that the whip *coupled* with the clock or watch was a better regulator of productivity than the watch and wage incentive. But planters, while undoubtedly linking the two in their discourse, tended to emphasize the role of the clock alone in maintaining productivity. Georgia planter James Thomas, for example, described how he gave his bondpeople a five-minute break every thirty minutes because he found that such respites from labor increased the amount of work performed by his slaves 15 percent. Other planters also devised procedures to "ascertain the actual cost of any specific work," when "the time it occupies being known." Examples were disseminated in southern agricultural journals. "The *daily labor of a team,*" reported the *Farmers' Register* in 1834, "must necessarily be regulated by the manner in which it is employed, as well as by its strength." "In some southern and midland counties," the writer explained, "the carters who generally sleep in the house, rise at four in the morning, feed, clean, and harness the horses, get breakfast, and are ready to go a-field at six-'clock, or after seven in the winter, when they work till two, thus making at the utmost a yoking of eight hours." Some antebellum plantation journals had sections like "Work Timed by Watch" and entries detailing that "[i]t takes exactly five minutes to run a furrow," as well as notations documenting that a particular piece of plantation work "took Josey & Adam about 1/2 hour." The avowed ideal that clock-regulated plantations would render the coordination of plantation labor "like clock-work" was more often than not realized.

We need not rely solely on planters' records to verify that clock time was an important arbiter of work and life on antebellum southern plantations. Slaves remembered the clock and watch and testified that they had come to accept, albeit grudgingly, timed agricultural labor under slavery. Although they originally came from societies where natural time was predominant and that same reliance on natural time remained important to them, southern slaves, like nineteenth-century urban-industrial workers, found their reliance on sun and stars as exclusive arbiters of time attacked and, ultimately, undermined. . . . American slaves appear to have succumbed . . . to their masters' admonitions concerning clock-regulated plantation labor. On the one hand, this is surprising because, some black slave drivers excepted, very few slaves actually owned a mechanical timepiece, something E. P. Thompson and others believe to have been important for the inculcation of clock consciousness among workers. But, on the other, it is of little surprise, especially when one considers how masters enforced slaves' obedience to the clock and how potent the aural power of time had proven in all societies, the South's included. Masters' two-pronged method to foist time obedience on their bondpeople, aurally communicated clock time backed up by the discipline of the whip, suggests that wage incentives, fines for lateness, and industrialization were not always necessary for the successful inculcation of clock time.

As has been noted, not all plantations at all times could establish a work regime committed wholly to regular clock hours. Different crops required different types of work at different times of the year, resulting in slack times and intense periods of work. But, as we have seen, slaveowners diversified their crops so that labor was always employed in some capacity. Whatever the crop or season, clock time, though of varying length, was still an important monitor of plantation labor. The importance planters attached to clock time, even within the undulating seasonal and working rhythm of the southern plantation, was not lost on slaves. As former Virginia slave Clara Robinson put it: "We raise terbaccer, corn, an' wheat. We raise our own meat too. When I wuked in de fiel, I digged crops." This variety notwithstanding, she still recalled a clock-defined aspect to her plantation work: "Go to work 'round five er six an' git off after dark."

Because of the ubiquity of the clock in plantation affairs, slaves of the antebellum period as well as former slaves interviewed in the 1930s recalled clearly that clocks and watches were used to regulate their labor. Slaves who were timed in the field by their master's watch, for example, remembered the time pressure of work. A fugitive slave of the 1850s, Moses Grandy, acknowledged that on his North Carolina plantation, work and work breaks were watch regulated: "The overseer stood with his watch in hand, to give us just an hour; when he said, 'Rise,' we had to rise and go to work again." Moreover, being hectored by the timepiece in this way seems to have made slaves punctual. If other masters were anything like Lue Bradford's Texas owner, slaves' compulsion was understandable. "They would have to work until the horn sounded before they could stop for noon. In the morning the field boss would have the record book and each person was supposed to report before starting for work and all were punished who were late." The rationale for such a practice was clear to her: "This encouraged punctuality." Others, like John Washington of Virginia, recalled that during the 1850s if he "had any desire to go out again in a reasonable time," the time specified by his master on his "permission" slip enabling him to leave the plantation "must be punctually obeyed." According to Lu Lee of Texas, the slave knew when to return: "[T]he nigger would get a pass and come over and stay with he gal and then he would say, 'I am sorry but it is that certain time and I got to go.'"

Born of their own experience with public, urban time, planters realized the power of communicating time through sound and so regulated plantation operations with clock-governed bells and horns. Cole Thomas of Texas explained at some length the system of rising by bugle on his plantation and the method his master used to ensure that it would be heard:

> We has ter git up early every day in de year, rain or shine. De slaves was woke up every mornin at four thirty by a slave blowin a horn it was his job ter gits up and blow a bugle and den he would go ter work in de fiels wid de rest of de slaves. Dar was no danger of you not waking up when de bugle blowed cause he blows it long and loud. He allus gits up of a mornin and gits his bugle down and comes out and climbs up on a platform wintah and summah and blows his bugle. Dis platform was about eight or ten feet tall.

"All the stock men worked in the field also—so many hours," remembered Cora Carroll of Mississippi. She explained: "They had a bell for them to go to work in the morning, a bell for them to get up by, and another one for noon, and another in the evening when they would knock off for dark." And it was through the constant reinforcement of time through sound that planters developed in their slaves a keen understanding of the precise time at which plantation affairs occurred: "[At] half-past eleven they would send the older children with food to the workers in the field," recalled one South Carolina ex-slave.

Slaves' obedience to the sound of plantation time was a product not simply of the imperious quality of the bell; it had just as much to do with the way masters ensured obedience to their sounding of the times. Former slave Bill Colins felt that the "large plantation bell which rang every morning at four o'clock" had a despotic quality, because "[t]he bell called and said, get up I'm coming to get you," and he understood that if slaves "did not answer the call the overseer would whip them." Controlling both the tools of time and of violence, planters ensured bondpeople's obedience to the sound of time with the whip. Jerry Boykins of Texas hinted at such a connection. "A big ole brass bell rang every mornin' at four o'clock on the plantashun," recalled Boykins, adding, "an' when that bell begin its racket, every darky roll out his bed, don't you forget!" John Barker was more explicit: "Maybe dey puts you on a task dis mawnin' and dat dere task got to be finished by seben o'clock dis evenin' an' if it ain't, dey whip you." Indeed, William Brown's 1847 testimony accords with later recollections by ex-slaves. On his tobacco and hemp Missouri plantation, field hands "were summoned to their unrequited toil every morning at four o'clock, by the ringing of a bell, hung on a post near the house of the overseer. They were allowed half an hour to eat their breakfast, and get to the field." Once there, aural plantation time, like the factory bell, signaled the beginning of work. The whip substituted for the free wage labor fine for those who were dilatory: "At half past four, a horn was blown by the overseer, which was the signal to commence work; and every one that was not on the spot at the time, had to receive ten lashes from the negro-whip, with which the overseer always went armed." Lateness was measured in minutes. "My mother was a field hand," explained Brown, "and one morning was ten or fifteen minutes behind the others in getting to the field." The punishment was as predictable to Brown as wage docking was to tardy industrial workers: "As soon as she reached the spot where they were at work, the overseer commenced whipping her." Plantation clock time and physical violence, then, went together.

What differentiated slaves from . . . industrial laborers was that bondpeople succumbed more readily to the dictates of clock time. Unlike free laborers, slaves could not engage fully in a debate over the worth and sanctity of their time. Certainly, they resisted masters' efforts to regulate their work by clock and watch. Some ran away, thus depriving masters of their labor time; others, most notably house hands, feigned ignorance of clock time altogether; and many attempted to carve out their own niches of free time. At most, some slaves negotiated with their masters over how much time was theirs to have. . . . Most slaves' efforts to resist plantation clock time were unsuccessful because the master could always resort to the whip to enforce punctuality to the clock. The slaves' inability to enter the protracted battle over the legitimacy of the clock as an arbiter of work and rest is revealed most graphically in their almost frenetic responses to the sound of the plantation clock. . . .

. . . The slave South was evidently one of the few rural regions in the nineteenth-century world to be affected by a modern clock consciousness. The reasons for this are twofold. First, the slave South either shared or imported most of the forces that had promoted time discipline in other nineteenth-century societies. Second, what it refused to import, free wage labor in factory or agricultural form, mattered less than we have sometimes been led to believe. The slaveholders' drive for a qualified, clock-defined modernity was sufficient to impel both masters and their chattel toward a clock consciousness that was little different from, and in some ways more advanced than, the northern or British form. The whip coupled with the sound of clock time proved as effective in the South as the Protestant work ethic/free wage labor/industrial combination had in the North.

The Shaping of a Unique Society

EUGENE D. GENOVESE

The uniqueness of the antebellum South continues to challenge the imagination of Americans, who, despite persistent attempts, cannot divert their attention from slavery. Nor should they, for slavery provided the foundation on which the South rose and grew. The master-slave relationship permeated Southern life and influenced relationships among free men. A full history would have to treat the impact of the Negro slave and of slaveless as well as slaveholding whites, but a first approximation, necessarily concerned with essentials, must focus on the slaveholders, who most directly exercised power over men and events. The hegemony of the slaveholders, presupposing the social and economic preponderance of great slave plantations, determined the character of the South. These men rose to power in a region embedded in a capitalist country, and their social system emerged as part of a capitalist world. Yet, a nonslaveholding European past and a shared experience in a new republic notwithstanding, they imparted to Southern life a special social, economic, political, ideological, and psychological content.

To dissolve that special content into an ill-defined agrarianism or an elusive planter capitalism would mean to sacrifice concern with the essential for concern with the transitional and peripheral. Neither of the two leading interpretations, which for many years have contended in a hazy and unreal battle, offers consistent and plausible answers to recurring questions, especially those bearing on the origins of the War for Southern Independence. The first of these interpretations considers the antebellum South an agrarian society fighting against the encroachments of industrial capitalism; the second considers the slave plantation merely a form of capitalist enterprise and suggests that the material differences between Northern and Southern capitalism were more apparent than real. These two views, which one would think contradictory, sometimes combine in the thesis that the agrarian nature of planter capitalism, for some reason, made coexistence with industrial capitalism difficult.

The first view cannot explain why some agrarian societies give rise to industrialization and some do not. A prosperous agricultural hinterland has generally served as a basis for industrial development by providing a home market for manufactures and a source of capital accumulation, and the prosperity of farmers has largely depended on the growth of industrial centers as markets for foodstuffs. In a capitalist society agriculture is one industry, or one set of industries, among many, and its conflict with manufacturing is one of many competitive rivalries. There must have been something unusual about an agriculture that generated violent opposition to the agrarian West as well as the industrial Northeast.

From *The Political Economy of Slavery* by Eugene D. Genovese. Copyright © 1961, 1963 by Eugene Genovese. Reprinted by permission of Pantheon Books, a division of Random House, Inc.

The second view, which is the more widely held, emphasizes that the plantation system produced for a distant market, responded to supply and demand, invested capital in land and slaves, and operated with funds borrowed from banks and factors. This, the more sophisticated of the two interpretations, cannot begin to explain the origins of the conflict with the North and does violence to elementary facts of antebellum Southern history. . . .

Capitalist and Pseudo-Capitalist Features of the Slave Economy

The slave economy developed within, and was in a sense exploited by, the capitalist world market; consequently, slavery developed many ostensibly capitalist features, such as banking, commerce, and credit. These played a fundamentally different role in the South than in the North. Capitalism has absorbed and even encouraged many kinds of precapitalist social systems: serfdom, slavery, Oriental state enterprises, and others. It has introduced credit, finance, banking, and similar institutions where they did not previously exist. It is pointless to suggest that therefore nineteenth-century India and twentieth-century Saudi Arabia should be classified as capitalist countries. We need to analyze a few of the more important capitalist and pseudo-capitalist features of Southern slavery and especially to review the barriers to industrialization in order to appreciate the peculiar qualities of this remarkable and anachronistic society.

The defenders of the "planter-capitalism" thesis have noted the extensive commercial links between the plantation and the world market and the modest commercial bourgeoisie in the South and have concluded that there is no reason to predicate an antagonism between cotton producers and cotton merchants. However valid as a reply to the naive arguments of the proponents of the agrarianism-versus-industrialism thesis, this criticism has unjustifiably been twisted to suggest that the presence of commercial activity proves the predominance of capitalism in the South. Many precapitalist economic systems have had well-developed commercial relations, but if every commercial society is to be considered capitalist, the word loses all meaning. In general, commercial classes have supported the existing system of production. As Maurice Dobb observes, their fortunes are bound up with those of the dominant producers, and merchants are more likely to seek an extension of their middlemen's profits than to try to reshape the economic order.

We must concern ourselves primarily with capitalism as a social system, not merely with evidence of typically capitalistic economic practices. In the South extensive and complicated commercial relations with the world market permitted the growth of a small commercial bourgeoisie. The resultant fortunes flowed into slaveholding, which offered prestige and economic and social security in a planter-dominated society. Independent merchants found their businesses dependent on the patronage of the slaveholders. The merchants either became planters themselves or assumed a servile attitude toward the planters. The commercial bourgeoisie, such as it was, remained tied to the slaveholding interest, had little desire or opportunity to invest capital in industrial expansion, and adopted the prevailing aristocratic attitudes.

The Southern industrialists were in an analogous position, although one that was potentially subversive of the political power and ideological unity of the planters. The preponderance of planters and slaves on the countryside retarded the home market. The Southern yeomanry, unlike the Western, lacked the purchasing power to sustain rapid industrial development. The planters spent much of their money abroad for luxuries. The plantation market consisted primarily of the demand for cheap slave clothing and cheap agricultural implements for use or misuse by the slaves. Southern industrialism needed a sweeping agrarian revolution to provide it with cheap labor and a substantial rural market, but the Southern industrialists depended on the existing, limited, plantation market. Leading industrialists like William Gregg and Daniel Pratt were plantation-oriented and proslavery. They could hardly have been other.

The banking system of the South serves as an excellent illustration of an ostensibly capitalist institution that worked to augment the power of the planters and retard the development of the bourgeoisie. Southern banks functioned much as did those which the British introduced into Latin America, India, and Egypt during the nineteenth century. Although the British banks fostered dependence on British capital, they did not directly and willingly generate internal capitalist development. They were not sources of industrial capital but "large-scale clearing houses of mercantile finance vying in their interest charges with the local usurers."

The difference between the banking practices of the South and those of the West reflects the difference between slavery and agrarian capitalism. In the West, as in the Northeast, banks and credit facilities promoted a vigorous economic expansion. During the period of loose Western banking (1830–1844) credit flowed liberally into industrial development as well as into land purchases and internal improvements. Manufacturers and merchants dominated the boards of directors of Western banks, and landowners played a minor role. Undoubtedly, many urban businessmen speculated in land and had special interests in underwriting agricultural exports, but they gave attention to building up agricultural processing industries and urban enterprises, which guaranteed the region a many-sided economy.

The slave states paid considerable attention to the development of a conservative, stable banking system, which could guarantee the movement of staple crops and the extension of credit to the planters. Southern banks were primarily designed to lend the planters money for outlays that were economically feasible and socially acceptable in a slave society: the movement of crops, the purchase of land and slaves, and little else.

Whenever Southerners pursued easy-credit policies, the damage done outweighed the advantages of increased production. This imbalance probably did not occur in the West, for easy credit made possible agricultural and industrial expansion of a diverse nature and, despite acute crises, established a firm basis for long-range prosperity. Easy credit in the South led to expansion of cotton production with concomitant overproduction and low prices; simultaneously, it increased the price of slaves.

Planters wanted their banks only to facilitate cotton shipments and maintain sound money. They purchased large quantities of foodstuffs from the West and, since they shipped little in return, had to pay in bank notes. For five years following the bank failures of 1837 the bank notes of New Orleans moved at a discount of from 10 to 25 per cent. This disaster could not be allowed to recur. Sound money and sound banking became the cries of the slaveholders as a class.

Southern banking tied the planters to the banks, but more important, tied the bankers to the plantations. The banks often found it necessary to add prominent planters to their boards of directors and were closely supervised by the planter-dominated state legislatures. In this relationship the bankers could not emerge as a middle-class counterweight to the planters but could merely serve as their auxiliaries.

The bankers of the free states also allied themselves closely with the dominant producers, but society and economy took on a bourgeois quality provided by the rising industrialists, the urban middle classes, and the farmers who increasingly depended on urban markets. The expansion of credit, which in the West financed manufacturing, mining, transportation, agricultural diversification, and the numerous branches of a capitalist economy, in the South bolstered the economic position of the planters, inhibited the rise of alternative industries, and guaranteed the extension and consolidation of the plantation system.

If for a moment we accept the designation of the planters as capitalists and the slave system as a form of capitalism, we are then confronted by a capitalist society that impeded the development of every normal feature of capitalism. The planters were not mere capitalists; they were precapitalist, quasi-aristocratic landowners who had to adjust their economy and ways of thinking to a capitalist world market. Their society, in its spirit and fundamental direction, represented the antithesis of capitalism, however many compromises it had to make. The fact of slave ownership is central to our problem. This seemingly formal question of whether the owners of the means of production command labor or purchase the labor power of free workers contains in itself the content of Southern life. The essential features of Southern particularity, as well as of Southern backwardness, can be traced to the relationship of master to slave.

The Barriers to Industrialization

If the planters were losing their economic and political cold war with Northern capitalism, the failure of the South to develop sufficient industry provided the most striking immediate cause. Its inability to develop adequate manufactures is usually attributed to the inefficiency of its labor force. No doubt slaves did not easily adjust to industrial employment, and the indirect effects of the slave system impeded the employment of whites. Slaves did work effectively in hemp, tobacco, iron, and cotton factories but only under socially dangerous conditions. They received a wide variety of privileges and approached an elite status. Planters generally appreciated the potentially subversive quality of these arrangements and looked askance at their extension.

Slavery concentrated economic and political power in the hands of a slaveholding class hostile to industrialism. The slaveholders feared a strong urban bourgeoisie, which might make common cause with its Northern counterpart. They feared a white urban working class of unpredictable social tendencies. In general, they distrusted the city and saw in it something incongruous with their local power and status arrangements. The small slaveholders, as well as the planters, resisted the assumption of a heavy tax burden to assist manufacturers, and as the South fell further behind the North in industrial development more state aid was required to help industry offset the Northern advantages of scale, efficiency, credit relations, and business reputation.

Slavery led to the rapid concentration of land and wealth and prevented the expansion of a Southern home market. Instead of providing a basis for industrial growth, the Southern countryside, economically dominated by a few large estates, provided only a limited market for industry. . . .

The Ideology of the Master Class

The planters commanded Southern politics and set the tone of social life. Theirs was an aristocratic, antibourgeois spirit with values and mores emphasizing family and status, a strong code of honor, and aspirations to luxury, ease, and accomplishment. In the planters' community, paternalism provided the standard of human relationships, and politics and statecraft were the duties and responsibilities of gentlemen. The gentleman lived for politics, not, like the bourgeois politician, off politics.

The planter typically recoiled at the notions that profit should be the goal of life; that the approach to production and exchange should be internally rational and uncomplicated by social values; that thrift and hard work should be the great virtues; and that the test of the wholesomeness of a community should be the vigor with which its citizens expand the economy. The planter was no less acquisitive than the bourgeois, but an acquisitive spirit is compatible with values antithetical to capitalism. The aristrocratic spirit of the planters absorbed acquisitiveness and directed it into channels that were socially desirable to a slave society: the accumulation of slaves and land and the achievement of military and political honors. Whereas in the North people followed the lure of business and money for their own sake, in the South specific forms of property carried the badges of honor, prestige, and power. Even the rough parvenu planters of the Southwestern frontier—the "Southern Yankees"—strove to accumulate wealth in the modes acceptable to plantation society. Only in their crudeness and naked avarice did they differ from the Virginia gentlemen. They were a generation removed from the refinement that follows accumulation.

Slavery established the basis of the planter's position and power. It measured his affluence, marked his status, and supplied leisure for social graces and aristocratic duties. The older bourgeoisie of New England in its own way struck an aristocratic pose, but its wealth was rooted in commercial and industrial enterprises that were being pushed into the background by the newer heavy industries arising in the West, where upstarts took advantage of the more lucrative ventures like the iron industry. In the South few such opportunities were opening. The parvenu differed from the established planter only in being cruder and perhaps sharper in his business dealings. The road to power lay through the plantation. The older aristocracy kept its leadership or made room for men following the same road. An aristocratic stance was no mere compensation for a decline in power; it was the soul and content of a rising power.

Many travelers commented on the difference in material conditions from one side of the Ohio River to the other, but the difference in sentiment was seen most clearly by Tocqueville. Writing before the slavery issue had inflamed the nation, he remarked that slavery was attacking the Union "indirectly in its manners." The Ohioan "was tormented by wealth," and would turn to any kind of enterprise or endeavor to make a fortune. The Kentuckian coveted wealth "much less than pleasure or excitement," and money had "lost a portion of its value in his eyes."

Achille Murat joined Tocqueville in admiration for Southern ways. Compared with Northerners, Southerners were frank, clever, charming, generous, and liberal. They paid a price for these advantages. As one Southerner put it, the North led the South in almost everything because the Yankees had quiet perseverance over the long haul, whereas the Southerners had talent and brilliance but no taste for sustained labor. Southern projects came with a flash and died just as suddenly. Despite such criticisms from with the ranks, the leaders of the South clung to their ideals, their faults, and their conviction of superiority. Farmers, said Edmund Ruffin, could not expect to achieve a cultural level above that of the "boors who reap rich harvests from the fat soil of Belgium." In the Northern states, he added with some justification, a farmer could rarely achieve the ease, culture, intellect, and refinement that slavery made possible. The prevailing attitude of the aristocratic South toward itself and its Northern rival was ably summed up by William Henry Holcombe of Natchez: "The Northerner loves to make money, the Southerner to spend it."

At their best, Southern ideals constituted a rejection of the crass, vulgar, inhumane elements of capitalist society. The slaveholders simply could not accept the idea that the cash nexus offered a permissible basis for human relations. Even the vulgar parvenu of the Southwest embraced the plantation myth and refused to make a virtue of necessity by glorifying the competitive side of slavery as civilization's highest achievement. The slaveholders generally, and the planters in particular, did identify their own ideals with the essence of civilization and, given their sense of honor, were prepared to defend them at any cost.

This civilization and its ideals were antinational in a double sense. The plantation offered virtually the only market for the small nonstaple-producing farmers and provided the center of necessary services for the small cotton growers. Thus, the paternalism of the planters toward their slaves was reinforced by the semipaternal relationship between the planters and their neighbors. The planters, in truth, grew into the closest thing to feudal lords imaginable in a nineteenth-century bourgeois republic. The planters' protestations of love for the Union were not so much a desire to use the Union to protect slavery as a strong commitment to localism as the highest form of liberty. They genuinely loved the Union so long as it alone among the great states of the world recognized that localism had a wide variety of rights. The Southerners' source of pride was not the Union, nor the nonexistent Southern nation; it was the plantation, which they raised to a political principle.

<h1>⅄ F U R T H E R   R E A D I N G</h1>

Edward L. Ayers, *Vengeance and Justice: Crime and Punishment in the Nineteenth-Century American South* (1984)

Peter W. Bardaglio, *Reconstructing the Household: Families, Sex, and the Law in the Nineteenth-Century South* (1995)

John B. Boles, ed., *Masters and Slaves in the House of the Lord, 1740–1870* (1988)

Dickson D. Bruce, Jr., *Violence and Culture in the Antebellum South* (1979)

Orville Vernon Burton and Robert C. McMath, Jr., eds., *Class, Conflict, and Consensus: Antebellum Southern Community Studies* (1982)

Randolph B. Campbell, *An Empire for Slavery: The Peculiar Institution in Texas, 1821–1865* (1989)

Joan E. Cashin, *A Family Venture: Men and Women on the Southern Frontier* (1991)

Bruce Collins, *White Society in the Antebellum South* (1985)

Daniel S. Dupre, *Transforming the Cotton Kingdom* (1977)

Clement Eaton, *The Growth of Southern Civilization, 1790–1860* (1961)

Eugene D. Genovese, *The Political Economy of Slavery* (1965)

J. William Harris, *Plain Folk and Gentry in a Slave Society: White Liberty and Black Slavery in Augusta's Hinterlands* (1985)

William M. Mathew, *Edmund Ruffin and the Crisis of Slavery in the Old South* (1988)

Donald G. Mathews, *Religion in the Old South* (1977)

John Hebron Moore, *The Emergence of the Cotton Kingdom in the Old Southwest: Mississippi, 1770–1860* (1988)

James Oakes, *The Ruling Race: A History of American Slaveholders* (1982)

———, *Slavery and Freedom: An Interpretation of the Old South* (1990)

Laurence Shore, *Southern Capitalists: The Ideological Leadership of an Elite, 1832–1885* (1986)

Mark M. Smith, *Mastered by the Clock: Time, Slavery, and Freedom in the American South* (1997)

Randy J. Sparks, *On Jordan's Stormy Banks: Evangelicalism in Mississippi, 1773–1876* (1994)

Kenneth Moore Startup, *The Root of All Evil: The Protestant Clergy and the Economic Mind of the Old South* (1997)

Steven M. Stowe, *Intimacy and Power in the Old South: Ritual in the Lives of Planters* (1987)

Michael Tadman, *Speculators and Slaves* (1989)

Larry E. Tise, *Proslavery: A History of the Defense of Slavery in America, 1701–1840* (1987)

John Michael Vlach, *Back of the Big House: The Architecture of Plantation Society* (1993)

Bertram Wyatt-Brown, *Southern Honor: Ethics and Behavior in the Old South* (1982)

Anne E. Yentsche, *A Chesapeake Family and Their Slaves* (1994)

The Slave and Free
Black Experience

Modern scholars have focused a great deal of attention on slaves and free blacks in the South, probing their daily experiences, the amount of oppression they endured, their ability to carve out an existence, the importance of family and community, the role of women, health concerns, economic contributions to the region, and numerous other topics. The outpouring of works makes these exciting fields. At the core of the debate is an effort to try to understand what it was like to be a slave or free black in the South. Scholars have examined the relationship of slaves and free blacks to owners and to other whites, seeking to understand the motives and dynamics in these complex relationships. Comparative studies and the diversity of the black experience over the past 250 years offer new, exciting perspectives.

Various viewpoints have emerged. Historians agree that slaves were not psychologically helpless before their masters; they had a culture and developed a support system within their family and community on which they could draw for strength. But within that system, whites exerted a degree of control that varied with individual circumstances. The situation of free blacks suggests that many were anything but free, for whites regarded them as a visible threat to the social order. Yet many carved out meaningful lives and would play a significant role in the African American community after the Civil War.

🗡 D O C U M E N T S

Opportunities to acquire testimony by slaves about their bondage were rare, but one opportunity arose during the Civil War. The American Freedmen's Inquiry Commission, established in 1863, gathered information and reported to the secretary of war with recommendations on the future of slaves. The frank account that Harry McMillan gave the commission about his experiences during bondage appears in Document 1. Many decades later, in the 1930s, individuals hired by the Federal Writers' Project interviewed former slaves. The recollections of the men and women interviewed, who were then quite elderly, provide valuable insights into the slave experience. One account from a female slave appears in Document 2. A few slaves managed to escape bondage. One of the best known fugitives was Harriet Jacobs, who, in Document 3, describes some of the trials she endured. Talented and trusted slaves sometimes managed their owner's plantation in his or her absence, as Document 4 shows. The slave George Skipwith did so on the Alabama plantation of John Hartwell Cocke, an absentee landlord. Letters to Cocke from Lucy Skipwith, George's daughter, reveal her religious nature, which developed during adulthood. Successful free blacks in Charleston, South Carolina, did not have to deal with overseers and owners but faced a different threat. Affluent and frequently well known to a few elite whites, these free people suddenly were confronted by the demand that free blacks be reenslaved unless they could furnish legal proof of their free status. James M. Johnson, a tailor, describes these frightening developments to his brother-in-law Henry Ellison in Document 5. Finally, Document 6 presents a photograph from the Library of Congress of five generations of a South Carolina slave family, suggesting the importance of family ties to those in bondage.

1. Harry McMillan, a Freedman, Describes His Bondage, 1863

I am about 40 years of age, and was born in Georgia but came to Beaufort when a small boy. I was owned by General Eustis and lived upon his plantation.

Q. Tell me about the tasks colored men had to do?

A. In old secesh times each man had to do two tasks, which are 42 rows or half an acre, in "breaking" the land, and in "listing" each person had to do a task and a half. In planting every hand had to do an acre a day; in hoeing your first hoeing where you hoe flat was two tasks, and your second hoeing, which is done across the beds, was also two tasks. After going through those two operations you had a third which was two and a half tasks, when you had to go over the cotton to thin out the plants leaving two in each hill.

Q. How many hours a day did you work?

A. Under the old secesh times every morning till night—beginning at daylight and continuing till 5 or 6 at night.

Q. But you stopped for your meals?

A. You had to get your victuals standing at your hoe; you cooked it over night yourself or else an old woman was assigned to cook for all the hands, and she or your children brought the food to the field.

Q. You never sat down and took your food together as families?

A. No, sir; never had time for it.

Q. The women had the same day's work as the men; but suppose a woman was in the family way was her task less?

A. No, sir; most of times she had to do the same work. Sometimes the wife of the planter learned the condition of the woman and said to her husband you must cut down her day's work. Sometimes the women had their children in the field.

Q. Had the women any doctor?

Harry McMillan testified before the American Freedmen's Inquiry Commission in 1863. A copy of his testimony can be found in John Blassingame's *Slave Testimony* (Baton Rouge: Louisiana State University Press, 1977), pp. 379–384.

A. No, sir; There is a nurse on the plantation sometimes—an old midwife who attended them. If a woman was taken in labor in the field some of her sisters would help her home and then come back to the field.

Q. Did they nurse their children?

A. Yes, sir; the best masters gave three months for that purpose.

Q. If a man did not do his task what happened?

A. He was stripped off, tied up and whipped.

Q. What other punishments were used?

A. The punishments were whipping, putting you in the stocks and making you wear irons and a chain at work. Then they had a collar to put round your neck with two horns, like cows' horns, so that you could not lie down on your back or belly. This also kept you from running away for the horns would catch in the bushes. Sometimes they dug a hole like a well with a door on top. This they called a dungeon keeping you in it two or three weeks or a month, and sometimes till you died in there. This hole was just big enough to receive the body; the hands down by the sides. I have seen this thing in Georgia but never here. I know how they whip in the Prisons. They stretch out your arms and legs as far as they can to ring bolts in the floor and lash you till they open the skin and the blood trickles down. . . .

Q. Suppose a son of the Master wanted to have intercourse with the colored women was he at liberty?

A. No, not at liberty, because it was considered a stain on the family, but the young men did it. There was a good deal of it. They often kept one girl steady and sometimes two on different places; men who had wives did it too sometimes, if they could get it on their own place it was easier but they would go wherever they could get it.

Q. Do the colored people like to go to Church?

A. Yes, Sir; They are fond of that; they sing psalms, put up prayers, and sing their religious songs.

Q. Did your Masters ever see you learning to read?

A. No, Sir; You could not let your Masters see you read; but now the colored people are fond of sending their children to school.

Q. What is the reason of that?

A. Because the children in after years will be able to tell us ignorant ones how to do for ourselves.

Q. How many children have you known one woman to have?

A. I know one woman who had 20 children. I know too a woman named Jenny, the wife of Dagos, a slave of John Pope, who has had 23 children. In general the women have a great many children[;] they often have a child once a year.

Q. Are the children usually obedient?

A. There are some good and some bad, but in general the children love their parents and are obedient. They like their parents most but they stand up for all their relations.

Q. Suppose a boy is struck by another boy what does he do?

A. If he is injured bad the relations come in and give the boy who injured him the same hurt. I would tell my boy to strike back and defend himself.

Q. How about bearing pain—do you teach your children to bear pain?

A. Yes, sir.

Q. When a colored man was whipped did he cry out?

A. He would halloa out and beg, but not cry for pain but for vexation.

Q. Did they try to conceal their whippings and think it a disgrace?

A. Yes, sir; they tried to conceal it; a great many are marked all over and have not a piece of skin they were born with.

2. Nancy Boudry, an Ex-Slave, Recalls Slavery, 1936

"If I ain't a hunnerd," said Nancy, nodding her white-turbaned head, "I sho' is close to it, 'cause I got a grandson 50 years old."

Nancy's silky white hair showed long and wavy under her headband. Her gingham dress was clean, and her wrinkled skin was a reddish-yellow color, showing a large proportion of Indian and white blood. Her eyes were a faded blue.

"I speck I is mos' white," acknowledged Nancy, "but I ain't never knowed who my father was. My mother was a dark color."

The cottage faced the pine grove behind an old church. Pink ramblers grew everywhere, and the sandy yard was neatly kept. Nancy's paralyzed granddaughter-in-law hovered in the doorway, her long smooth braids hanging over Indian-brown shoulders, a loose wrapper of dark blue denim flowing around her tall unsteady figure. She was eager to take part in the conversation but hampered by a thick tongue induced, as Nancy put it, "by a bad sore throat she ain't got over."

Nancy's recollections of plantation days were colored to a somber hue by overwork, childbearing, poor food and long working hours.

"Master was a hard taskmaster," said Nancy. "My husband didn' live on de same plantation where I was, de Jerrell place in Columbia County. He never did have nuthin' to give me 'cause he never got nuthin'. He had to come and ask my white folks for me. Dey had to carry passes everywhar dey went, if dey didn't, dey'd git in trouble.

"I had to work hard, plow and go and split wood jus' like a man. Sometimes dey whup me. Dey whup me bad, pull de cloes off down to de wais'—my master did it, our folks didn' have overseer.

"We had to ask 'em to let us go to church. Went to white folks church, 'tell de black folks got one of dere own. No'm, I dunno how to read. Never had no schools at all, didn't 'low us to pick up a piece of paper and look at it."

"Nancy, wasn't your mistress kind to you?"

"Mistis was sorta kin' to me, sometimes. But dey only give me meat and bread, didn' give me nothin' good—I ain' gwine tell no story. I had a heap to undergo wid. I had to scour at night at de Big House—two planks one night, two more de nex'. De women peoples spun at night and reeled, so many outs a night. Us had to git up befo' daybreak be ready to go to de fiel's.

"My master didn' have but three cullud people, dis yuh man what I stayed wid, my young master, had not been long married and dus' de han's dey give him when he marry was all he had.

This document can be found in George Rawick's *The American Slave: A Composite Autobiography* (Westport, CT.: Greenwood Publishing Company, 1972), vol. XII, pp. 113–117.

"Didn' have no such house as dis," Nancy looked into the open door of the comfortable cottage, "sometimes dey have a house built, it would be daubed. Dus' one family, didn' no two families double up."

"But the children had a good time, didn't they? They played games?"

"Maybe dey did play ring games, I never had no time to see what games my chillun play, I work so hard. Heap o' little chillun slep' on de flo'. Never had no frolics neither, no ma'm, and didn' go to none. We would have prayer meetings on Saturday nights, and one night in de week us had a chairback preacher, and sometimes a regular preacher would come in."

Nancy did not remember ever having seen the Patterollers [patrollers].

"I hearn talk of 'em you know, heap o' times dey come out and make out like dey gwine shoot you at night, dey mus' been Patterollers, dey was gettin' hold of a heap of 'em."

"What did you do about funerals, Nancy?"

"Dey let us knock off for funerals, I tell de truth. Us stay up all night, singin' and prayin'. Dey make de coffin outter pine boards."

"Did you suffer during the war?"

"We done de bes' we could, we et what we could get, sometimes didn' have nothin' to eat but piece of cornbread, but de white folks allus had chicken."

"But you had clothes to wear?"

"Us had clothes 'cause we spun de thread and weaved 'em. Dey bought dem dere great big ole brogans where you couldn' hardly walk in 'em. Not like dese shoes I got on." Nancy thrust out her foot, easy in "Old Ladies' Comforts."

"When they told you were free, Nancy, did the master appear to be angry?"

"No'm, white folks didn' 'pear to be mad. My master dus' tole us we was free. Us moved right off, but not so far I couldn' go backwards and forwards to see 'um." (So it was evident that even if Nancy's life had been hard, there was a bond between her and her former owners.) "I didn' do no mo' work for 'um, I work for somebody else. Us rented land and made what we could, so we could have little somethin' to eat. I scoured and waited on white people in town, got little piece of money, and was dus' as proud!"

Nancy savored the recollection of her first earned money a moment, thinking back to the old days.

"I had a preacher for my second marriage," she continued. "Fo' chillun died on me—one girl, de yuthers was babies. White doctor tended me."

Asked about midwifery, Nancy smiled.

"I was a midwife myself, to black and white, after freedom. De Thomson doctors all liked me and tole people to 'git Nancy.' I used 'tansy tea'—heap o' little root—made black pepper tea, fotch de pains on 'em. When I would git to de place where I had a hard case, I would send for de doctor, and he would help me out, yes, doctor holp me out of all of 'em."

Asked about signs and superstitions, Nancy nodded.

"I have seed things. Dey look dus' like a person, walkin' in de woods. I would look off and look back to see it again and it be gone." Nancy lowered her voice mysteriously, and looked back into the little room where Vanna's [her paralyzed granddaughter-in-law] unsteady figure moved from bed to chair. "I seed a coffin floatin' in de air in dat room . . ." she shivered, "and I heard a heap o' knockings. I dunno what it bees—but de sounds come in de house. I runs ev'y squeech owl away what comes close, too." Nancy clasped her hands, right thumb over left thumb, "does dat—and it goes on away—dey quite hollerin', you chokin' 'em when you does dat."

"Do you plant by the moon, Nancy?"

"Plant when de moon change, my garden, corn, beans. I planted some beans once on de wrong time of de moon and dey didn' bear nothin'—I hated it so bad, I didn' know what to do, so I been mindful ever since when I plant. Women peoples come down on de moon, too. I ain't know no signs to raise chillun. I whup mine when dey didn' do right, I sho' did. I didn' 'low my chillun to take nothin'—no aigs and nothin' 'tall and bring 'em to my house. I say 'put dem right whar you git 'em.' "

"Did you sing spirituals, Nancy?"

"I sang regular meetin' songs," she said, "like 'lay dis body down' and 'let yo' joys be known'—but I can't sing now, not any mo'."

Nancy was proud of her quilt-making ability.

"Git 'um, Vanna, let de ladies see 'um," she said; and when Vanna brought the gay pieces made up in a "double-burst" (sunburst) pattern, Nancy fingered the squares with loving fingers. "Hit's pooty, ain't it?" she asked wistfully, "I made one for a white lady two years ago, but dey hurts my fingers now—makes 'em stiff."

3. Harriet Jacobs Laments Her Trials as a Slave Girl (1828), 1861

During the first years of my service in Dr. Flint's family, I was accustomed to share some indulgences with the children of my mistress. Though this seemed to me no more than right, I was grateful for it, and tried to merit the kindness by the faithful discharge of my duties. But I now entered on my fifteenth year—a sad epoch in the life of a slave girl. My master began to whisper foul words in my ear. Young as I was, I could not remain ignorant of their import. I tried to treat them with indifference or contempt. The master's age, my extreme youth, and the fear that his conduct would be reported to my grandmother, made him bear this treatment for many months. He was a crafty man, and resorted to many means to accomplish his purposes. Sometimes he had stormy, terrific ways, that made his victims tremble; sometimes he assumed a gentleness that he thought must surely subdue. Of the two, I preferred his stormy moods, although they left me trembling. He tried his utmost to corrupt the pure principles my grandmother had instilled. He peopled my young mind with unclean images, such as only a vile monster could think of. I turned from him with disgust and hatred. But he was my master. I was compelled to live under the same roof with him—where I saw a man forty years my senior daily violating the most sacred commandments of nature. He told me I was his property; that I must be subject to his will in all things. My soul revolted against the mean tyranny. But where could I turn for protection? No matter whether the slave girl be as black

This reading also appears in Harriet A. Jacobs, *Incidents in the Life of a Slave Girl,* Jean Fagan Yellin, ed., Harvard University Press, © 1987, pp. 27–29.

as ebony or as fair as her mistress. In either case, there is no shadow of law to protect her from insult, from violence, or even from death; all these are inflicted by fiends who bear the shape of men. The mistress, who ought to protect the helpless victim, has no other feelings towards her but those of jealousy and rage. The degradation, the wrongs, the vices, that grow out of slavery, are more than I can describe. They are greater than you would willingly believe. Surely, if you credited one half the truths that are told you concerning the helpless millions suffering in this cruel bondage, you at the north would not help to tighten the yoke. You surely would refuse to do for the master, on your own soil, the mean and cruel work which trained bloodhounds and the lowest class of whites do for him at the south.

Every where the years bring to all enough of sin and sorrow; but in slavery the very dawn of life is darkened by these shadows. Even the little child, who is accustomed to wait on her mistress and her children, will learn, before she is twelve years old, why it is that her mistress hates such and such a one among the slaves. Perhaps the child's own mother is among those hated ones. She listens to violent outbreaks of jealous passion, and cannot help understanding what is the cause. She will become prematurely knowing in evil things. Soon she will learn to tremble when she hears her master's footfall. She will be compelled to realize that she is no longer a child. If God has bestowed beauty upon her, it will prove her greatest curse. That which commands admiration in the white woman only hastens the degradation of the female slave. I know that some are too much brutalized by slavery to feel the humiliation of their position; but many slaves feel it most acutely, and shrink from the memory of it. I cannot tell how much I suffered in the presence of these wrongs, nor how I am still pained by the retrospect. My master met me at every turn, reminding me that I belonged to him, and swearing by heaven and earth that he would compel me to submit to him. If I went out for a breath of fresh air, after a day of unwearied toil, his footsteps dogged me. If I knelt by my mother's grave, his dark shadow fell on me even there. The light heart which nature had given me became heavy with sad forebodings. The other slaves in my master's house noticed the change. Many of them pitied me; but none dared to ask the cause. They had no need to inquire. They knew too well the guilty practices under that roof; and they were aware that to speak of them was an offence that never went unpunished.

I longed for some one to confide in. I would have given the world to have laid my head on my grandmother's faithful bosom, and told her all my troubles. But Dr. Flint swore he would kill me, if I was not as silent as the grave. Then, although my grandmother was all in all to me, I feared her as well as loved her. I had been accustomed to look up to her with a respect bordering upon awe. I was very young, and felt shamefaced about telling her such impure things, especially as I knew her to be very strict on such subjects. Moreover, she was a woman of a high spirit. She was usually very quiet in her demeanor; but if her indignation was once roused, it was not very easily quelled. I had been told that she once chased a white gentleman with a loaded pistol, because he insulted one of her daughters. I dreaded the consequences of a violent outbreak; and both pride and fear kept me silent. But though I did not confide in my grandmother, and even evaded her vigilant watchfulness and inquiry, her presence in the neighborhood was some protection to me. Though she had been a slave, Dr. Flint was afraid of her. He dreaded her scorching rebukes. Moreover, she was known and patronized by many people; and he did not wish to have his villainy made public. It was lucky for me that I did not live on a distant plantation, but in a town not so large that the inhabitants were ignorant of each other's affairs. Bad as are the laws and customs in a slaveholding community, the doctor, as a professional man, deemed it prudent to keep up some outward show of decency.

O, what days and nights of fear and sorrow that man caused me! Reader, it is not to awaken sympathy for myself that I am telling you truthfully what I suffered in slavery. I do it to kindle a flame of compassion in your hearts for my sisters who are still in bondage, suffering as I once suffered.

I once saw two beautiful children playing together. One was a fair white child; the other was her slave, and also her sister. When I saw them embracing each other, and heard their joyous laughter, I turned sadly away from the lovely sight. I foresaw the inevitable blight that would fall on the little slave's heart. I knew how soon her laughter would be changed to sighs. The fair child grew up to be a still fairer woman. From childhood to womanhood her pathway was blooming with flowers, and overarched by a sunny sky. Scarcely one day of her life had been clouded when the sun rose on her happy bridal morning.

How had those years dealt with her slave sister, the little playmate of her child-hood? She, also, was very beautiful; but the flowers and sunshine of love were not for her. She drank the cup of sin, and shame, and misery, whereof her persecuted race are compelled to drink.

4. George and Lucy Skipwith Write Their Master, 1847, 1857, 1859

may the 11 [1847] green County Ala

Sir

I imbrace this oppertunity to write you a few lines. I Reseved your letter and should have anserd it before now but master John was from home on busness and I could not write untel he returned wich was last Sunday. You told me in your letter that you was glad that I had the management of the farm my self, and you said that you noed that I was able to do as you and master John wish providing that I would not make use of ardent spirits, but I am convinced that it has been my greatest en-emy and I shall consider it so as long as I live. We have not been able to do any thing towards marling our land our team could not be spared from farming except wet spells and it would be too wet for hauling, and master John thougt we could do as good busines by toating leaves to put on the poorest partes of the land by the spare hands and we put down two thousand and five hndred baskets full weighing from thirty five to forty, and thirty cart load out of the farm pen, and ninety out of the horse lot. We have a very good stand of cotton, but it has been so cold that it does not grow but our corn cannot be beaten and about three days from now we will finish plowing our corn the second time and our peas. we will be then reddy to com-

Cocke Family Papers (#2433-b, #5685, #1480), Special Collections Department, University of Virginia Library.

mence plowing our cotton the second time. it has been about a week since the hoes started over the second time. our oats crop hav been somwhat backward but we had a very fine rane and I am in hopes they will start to growing again. Lee and archa hav been working with us for sum time building a screw whiat looks very fine   I have not herd any thing from brother peyton sence you was out here   I should be very glad to hear when you herd from him   We are all well and hav had no call for a docter this year and I hope that you will reseve this letter in good helth   my self and master John gets on very smooth together   he have not given me a cross worde this year. give my love to every boddy boath white and black and beleave me to be your umble servant

George Skipwith

hopewell   July the 8 1847

Sir

on the forth day of July I reseved your letter dated may the 25. I wrote to yo the 15 of June the second time giveing you a true statement of the crops, horses, hogs, and chickeins but I am sorry that I shall have to write yo princerble about other matters. I hav a good crop on hand for you, boath of cotten and corn. this you knoe could not be don without hard worke. I have worked the people but not out of reason, and I have whiped none without a caus   the persons whome I have correct I will tell you thir name and thir faults.

Suky who I put to plant som corn and after she had been there long anuf to hav been done I went there and she had hardly began it   I gave her som four or five licks over her clothes   I gave isham too licks over his clothes for covering up cotton with the plow.

I put frank, isham, violly, Dinah Jinny evealine and Charlott to Sweeping cotten going twice in a roe, and at a Reasonable days worke they aught to hav plowed seven accers a peice, and they had been at it a half of a day, and they had not done more than one accer and a half and I gave them ten licks a peace upon thir skins   I gave Julyann eight or ten licks for misplacing her hoe. that was all the whiping I hav done from the time that I pitched the crop untell we comenced cutting oats.

Hopewell   Aug the 31st 1857

my Dear Master

I would have writen to you before this but for eight or ten days I have been sick. I feels better at this time tho not well. Maria also has been very sick but is up again. mrs Carters Baby also has been very sick but it is now a little better. it has fallen off a great deal. mrs Carters health is not very good. the Children all seem to be suffering with very bad Colds. the old ones seem to stand very well. we have two very fine young Babies. one is Jinneys, and the other Bettias. Matilda also had one but it died. I do not think that our sweet potatoe patch will make us many potatoes. they were planted so late I think that the frost will catch them. the Cotton seem to be opening very fast they will start to picking it out before very long. the Carpenters are still workeing at the low place mr Powell told Archa to try to get the Buildeings done by the first of November any how. mr Powell left this place on the 27th. he wrote to you from this place. you have heard I supose of his wifes sickness   he expects to be here again the middle of November   Mr Bendon visited him while he was here. mrs Avery and miss mary was here a few days ago   they were well. miss Fanny has not yet returned from North Carolina. mr Ben Carter is still liveing with them, and expect to live there next year. the Topp mare has a very fine horse colt. it is a very pretty Male. I am in hopes that you will soon be makeing ready to start out here and spend a longer time than ever with us, and should any thing pervent you comeing I hope that master Charles will come. I send you [some] verses which I have taken from the 10 Commandments. I wish you would have them printed for me in a small track. I will now bring my letter to a close   hopeing soon to hear from you I remane your servant

Lucy Skipwith

Hopewell   June the 9th 1859

my Dear Master

I received your message by mr Powell, also the one by mr Lawrence about not writeing to you, and I am sorry that you had to remind me of it. I would have writen to you before this but I have been waiteing to hear of your safe arival at home. as we had not heard a word from you we did not know but what you was sick on the road. we are much releaved by hearing from you and will try to let you hear from us as often as necessary, and keep you informed of our movements here.

I knoe that you will be mortified to hear of the troble that my little girl Betsey has got into at mr Joe Bordens by being perswaded by one of their servants to steal money for him, and I lear[ne]d that this is the second time that he has made her do it. she says that she had no thought of it being so much monney   neither did he. he saw that she did not dress up like the other girls did and he tempted her with such things as he knew she wanted. I do not know what master Joe will do with the man. he belongs to mr Ben Borden but he lives with master Joe. he has a wife and four Children at master Joes. he also has Brothers and Sisters there, and I heard mas Joe say to day that they were good hands to work, but they would steal, and that girl is growing up among them and if she continue there they will bring her to everlasting destruction. her mistress has taken very little pains to bring her up right. the girl has had the raising of her self up. she has been left down there among those people four and six weeks at a time with not as much as a little sewing to do, and now they complains of her being so lazy. It seems to be almost Imposeing upon you to ask the faver of you to let the Child come home, but I would thank you a thousand time If you would do so. I want to give her religious instructions and try to be the means of saving her soul from death. master Joe says he rather that she would come home. mr Powell says he thinks she had better come home and work in Williams place and let him work out. I hope that you will not sell her if you can posuble do any thing else with her. if you do sell her, have you any objection of my trying to get mr Powell to bye her, providing he is willing to do so, as I think that he could make a woman of her. let me hear from you on the Subject by the first of July. if it was not for the grace of god I would sink beneath such a load as this, but I have a preasant help in the time of troble. I have not seen the girl but once in twelve months. We are all geting along very well at this time. the people are all well, and in good Spirits, and I hope that we may continue to do well. mr Lawrence still holds family Prayers with us every Sunday morning, and explains the scriptures to us. we have had preaching at the Chapple three times this year. we have mr Duboise and Dr Mears the school teacher from greensboro. they will preach every second and fourth sunday in the month. we have Just received a letter from mr Crains sister. she wants his things to be sent to her by mr Powells wagon when it comes down after his goats next monts. we have seven beautiful little kids since you went away, and two very pretty Coalts. we have a very nice garden but every thing is suffering very much for rain.

I have seen nothing of the Japan plum seed in the flower pots nor the garden. only one of the Chessnuts have come up. I will write to you again soon. the people Joines me in love to you. nothing more at preasant from your servant

Lucy Skipwith

To Gen John H Cocke

5. Charleston's Free Blacks Fear Reenslavement, 1859–1860

Charleston, Decr 23d/59

Dear Henry,

I hope this will find you relieved from your cold. I am annoyed with one. The wedding came off in style. Nat Fuller was the caterer. He had oysters served for E Ann at 9 o'clock. We left soon after. We had two bottles of champagne broached before leaving & did not even eat a piece of cake. The crowd was a large & respectable one. Mr Gadsden performed the ceremony, Dr Hanckel being sick. There were 10 attending of each sex. Some of the bridesmaids left before we did for Savannah. Beard went down with them but took care to get back before supper. The bride & groom are gone on a Tour in the country.

Matilda was at Home today for the first time. She is well. Mrs Bonneau is quite feeble. R Kinloch gets married shortly, also Miss Gourdin, an apprentice of Mrs. Lee.

Do tender my congratulations to your Father on the adjournment of the Legislature. He ought to read Col Memminger's speech against Moore's bill. It is in the Courier of 16th. I prophesied from the onset that nothing would be done affecting our position.

We have sent some little nick nacks for the children, not having room for the grown folks. You must come down & follow the fashion. I heard a few days ago my cotton was sold, but did not learn the rates. I will be able to settle up with your Father for Bagging, Rope, &c. Do see that Sarah behaves herself & salts the creatures regularly. We have not heard from Charley for some days. Father, Mother, Gabriella, & E Ann unite with me in wishing you & all at Wisdom Hall a Merry Christmas. As ever, I am yrs truly

J M J

From *No Chariot Let Down: Charleston's Free People on the Eve of the Civil War,* edited by Michael P. Johnson and James L. Roark. Copyright © 1984 by the University of North Carolina Press. Used by permission of the publisher.

Charleston Aug 28th 1860

Dear Henry,

Yours is recd. I am sorry to hear of Wm & Charlotte's indisposition. We are not very well. The heat is oppressive.

The stir has subsided, but arrests are still made & the people are leaving. It is vain for us to hope that if it is not the *will* of God he will not permit it. The bible tells us He is not the minister of Sin, & again the wicked shall flourish &c. In that model prayer we are taught to pray that His will may be done on earth as it is in heaven, & yet as free agents we are free to obey or reject. Hence it is that on earth wicked rule prevails, while in Heaven His will is done by the Just. I have implicit Faith in Providence & recognize its doing in directing those who seek His guidance, by overruling what is a present calamity to the future good of the virtuous. But I very much doubt that He wills or sanctions unrighteous acts, although in answer to prayer He often overthrows them & converts them into an engine of good provided we will act in accordance with His will as suggested by His Spirit & not supinely wait for the working of a miracle by having a Chariot let down to convey us away.

The magistrates boast of the good it has done them & Trusted that they did not know they were so rich. Slaves have come by magic. It is evident that the movement is intended for their emolument. On the other hand it must prove the Death of many & the loss of earthly goods, the hard earnings of a life time, to others. And yet those who put their trust in God may derive benefits spiritually & temporally.

Our Friends sympathise & express indignation which has checked it, but they are not in power & cant put down the majority. Nothing more is heard of the suits. Fordham had to comply with the Law. Gen. Schnierlie placed himself in the stead of a Man he holds & defied them to touch him. He would beat the one to Death who did. And Col. Whaley says he will stand a lawsuit before complying, but the majority has succumbed. The money has to come out of the purses of those held in Trust.

Hicks had his watch & chain taken from him in a Mob raised in Market St.

Col. Seymour stood in front of our House speaking to an Irish carter on the subject & pointed to No 7 & 9 as being for sale. And you can see Hand bills on property held by cold. people in every quarter, which will have the effect of depreciation. The action of the people has taken them by surprise & the originators blame the Mayor for being so rash. They say All must leave but they did not want them ran off thus.

As it regards the Miss D's I expected you to select for yourself first, which would be a good recommendation. They wont leave before their Father except entrusted to better hands. He is not disposed to move quick enough for them.

Father has been to Niagara Falls with Charley & to Love Feast & class meetings with Marshall & R. Clark & to pic nics with Gabriella & Charlotte & is enjoying the sights with a zest. Charley begs to join with Father in Love to you & to assure you that you have never been forgotten.

Jas Glover was taken to the Guard House at the instance of Dr Dessausure for standing in a Drug store with his Hat on. I have not heard the sentence. Beard has closed his school & is about to leave before he is pounced upon.

Dr. Dereef is flourishing in Washington yet. He has written about 30 Letters home since he left. They come daily. If the one I saw is a sample he must have more constant employment than the Secry of State.

I cant write your Father for the present. I suppose the H & G affair has attained the result. I fancy I see them in a Fond embrace.

W. P. Dacoster appears to be circumspect. De Large has got back to fret a few. Sasportas has Returned from Aiken with his daughter. They tried to prevail on him to make his abode there. The Family joins me in Love.

Yours,

J M J

6. Five Generations of a South Carolina Slave Family

This photograph is from the Library of Congress.

⚔ *E S S A Y S*

One of the most contested areas in scholars' studies of the slave experience is the degree of freedom that slaves carved out for themselves and the extent to which whites controlled their lives. In the first essay that follows, Brenda Stevenson, a professor at UCLA, examines slave families on several Virginia plantations. Though she points out the importance of family and shared duties, and the sense of community that existed, she also argues that slaves often had little control over their destiny. A master's right to sell his slaves created enormous distress in slave families. And the tension, strain, and sorrows of their daily existence often fostered real tension in the family and slave community. Peter Kolchin, a historian at the University of Delaware, presents a balanced view of the slave experience in the second essay. Here he explains the evolution of slave religion that gradually combined Christian and African elements. He examines the complexity of slave identification as slaves tried to carve out a semi-autonomous life within their family and community but a life always under control of their masters.

Distress and Discord in Slave Families

BRENDA STEVENSON

The family was an institution that was by all measures vitally important to every faction of the population of antebellum Virginia, white and black, slave and free. Moreover, the family was important to these various groups of Southerners for quite similar reasons. They believed that a positive family life was necessary to both individual and group survival—emotional, physical, cultural, economic, and social. For many, its existence implied an assurance of comfort in a world that more often than not proved to be harsh, unpredictable, and violent. Regardless of one's racial or cultural identity, political status, social class, or religious beliefs, "family" was an ideal and a reality that antebellum Southerners prodigiously sought and fought to protect. Family was for them the most natural of institutions, and within its confines the most fundamental human events—birth, life, marriage, and death— took on a legitimacy that guaranteed one's humanity and immortality. The family institutions that antebellum Southerners erected provided organization and structure to their lives and resources.

Yet, for many residents of pre–Civil War Virginia, the opportunity to live, act, and take comfort within the physical and emotional boundaries of one's family were privileges that were often elusive, if not impossible to obtain. No group of early nineteenth-century Virginians found it more difficult to create and maintain stable marriages and families than did slaves. This essay is an examination of Virginia slave families during the latter half of the antebellum era. Of primary concern are the problems that adult slaves encountered within their families, particularly as marital partners and parents.

Blacks suffered greatly from the constant pressures attendant to living and working within a slave society. Ideologies of race differences and hierarchy were so popular that few whites, even those who did not benefit directly from the slave system, could conceive of any roles for blacks in their communities other than as exploited, dehumanized workers—and producers of workers. As members of a numerical minority defined by racial difference, they were the targets of profound sociocultural, political, and economic oppression that was meant to create and maintain the financial success and social prestige of elite whites in antebellum society. Moreover, white Virginians tried to impose their authority on every aspect of slave life, including the family in order to fulfill their need to control the labor of their human chattel. It was not unusual for slave masters to choose their slaves' marital partners, to separate those couples they had united, to force extramarital sexual partners on them, and even to sell off their children when it became economically advantageous, promoted discipline in the quarters, or helped to secure their own authority.

The negative implications of such actions for slaves who were trying to maintain functional family groups were, of course, substantial. An acutely detrimental phenomenon was the forced outmigration of slaves from Virginia in the antebellum period to other parts of the South as part of the lucrative domestic slave trade. This mandatory and often indiscriminate exodus which separated husband from wife, and mother from child, stripped many slaves of the kin- and community-based networks that they had managed to construct over generations of residence in Virginia. Slave owners sold and shipped literally hundreds of thousands of slave men, women, and children representing all age groups with various family and marriage commitments out of the state. Richard Sutch conservatively estimates that during the decade from 1850 to 1860 alone, slaveholders and traders exported almost sixty-eight thousand Virginia slaves to the lower South and Southwest. More often than not, masters sold their slaves without regard to family groups or marital status. Even those slaveholders who wanted to keep slave families united had little control over their future unity once the slave family was purchased by someone else. Donald Sweig's survey of the marital histories of slaves in northern Virginia, for example, indicates that as many as 74 percent of those exported left the state without accompanying family members. Moreover, one can reasonably surmise that since most of the slaves exported were between twenty and forty-nine years old, many of them were spouses and parents at the time of their departure. Regional studies substantiate this generalization. When Jo Ann Manfra and Robert Dykstra reviewed a survey of late antebellum slave marriages in southern Virginia, for example, they found that at least one-third of those couples who separated did so as a result of slaveholder demands. Manfra and Dykstra's analysis also documents that mandatory division was the predominant reason young married slave couples separated. Separated slave couples and the breakup of families also produced orphans. The disruption of family ties and its consequences (such as orphaned children) were especially serious problems for Virginia bondsmen and women during the latter half of the antebellum period. . . .

Slave kin groups and communities on large holdings ideally provided alternate means for slaves to exchange and share emotional and economic support with loved ones in spite of the potentially destructive power of the owners to separate slave families. Regardless of the many Virginia slave family groups that had some characteristics of a nuclear structure, extended and stepfamilies persisted in slave communities as innovative sources of socialization, social intercourse, material aid, and cultural expression.

Within the arena of the slave community, child rearing was a shared responsibility. In the absence of a parent, other nuclear and extended family members and sometimes fictive kin took on the major responsibility of rearing children. Adult female siblings or maternal female kin were the first choices as surrogate primary care-givers. When Robert Bruce constructed a list of slaves located on his plantation in Charlotte County, Virginia, during the late 1830s, he noted that three maternal grandmothers served as the primary care-givers of small children whose mothers were either dead or had been sold away. Hannah Valentine, a domestic servant to Governor David Campbell of Abingdon, Virginia, took on the care and rearing of her grandchildren when her daughter, Eliza, accompanied the governor's family to Richmond. Writing to her in 1838, the surrogate mother noted reassuringly: "Your Children are all . . . doing very well and have never suffered from sickness one moment since you Left here. [T]hey talk some Little about you but do not appear to miss you a great deal." . . .

Slave masters insisted on the importance of the slave mother in the slave family, particularly in regard to child rearing. In so doing, they helped to sustain both African and European cultural traditions that slaves drew upon when deciding how to order their social world. Accordingly, slave mothers took on the most significant long-term obligations of child care. Virginia slave owners promoted matrifocal and matrilocal families among their slaves in several ways. First, a Virginia law dated 1662 stipulated that black children take the status of their mothers. This legal association between slave mother and child reinforced, within the slaveholder's perception of an ordered domestic world, the cultural dictates of their society concerning gender differentiated responsibility. Masters believed that slave mothers, like white women, had a natural bond with their children and that therefore it was their responsibility—more so than that of slave fathers—to care for their offspring. Consequently, young slave children routinely lived with their mothers or female maternal kin, thus establishing the matrilocality of slave families. Moreover, masters compiling lists of their human property routinely identified the female parent of slave children but only sometimes indicated paternity. Also, when prompted to sell a group of slaves which might include parents and their children, owners sometimes tried to sell a mother with her small children as a single unit but rarely afforded slave fathers this same consideration.

At the same time that slaveholders promoted a strong bond between slave mothers and their children, they denied to slave fathers their paternal rights of ownership and authority, as well as denying them their right to contribute to the material support of their offspring. Undoubtedly, slave masters felt that if it became necessary for them to challenge the power that slave parents had in the lives of their children, it would be much easier to do so if the parent with whom the child most readily identified as an authority figure was a female rather than a male. Slaveholders' insistence on the importance of the slave mother by identifying her as the head of the slave family and primary care-giver of the children, along with the derivation of the slave child's status from that of the mother, firmly established the matrifocality of most slave families. Thus, while slave fathers had a significant presence in the consciousness of their children, mothers obviously were much more physically and psychologically present in the children's lives. . . .

The absence of slave fathers was not a problem which was restricted to the latter part of the antebellum period. Since the colonial period, young male slaves were the primary targets of intrastate and interstate trading in Virginia. As such, their arbitrary removal from wives and children always was a source of difficulty plaguing slave families. Of course, the numbers of young male slaves exported increased over time. Their continual decline on some farms and plantations in Virginia meant a decrease in the number of slave families with both parents present. (Significantly, only 42 percent of the ex-slaves interviewed as part of the Virginia Federal Writers' Project suggested in their autobiographical accounts that they had close physical contact with both of their parents.) Moreover, the removal of adult male slaves from their Virginia kin networks robbed even slave families that were matrifocal, since they, too, had benefited significantly from material and emotional resources that fathers, husbands, and other male relatives who lived close by routinely provided. Many Virginia slave children born in the last decades before the Civil War, therefore, grew up without fathers or black male role models and nurturers, while women bore and reared children without the comfort and support of their husbands or other male kin. . . .

Although many of the ex-slaves interviewed obviously knew and lived with their mothers, some slaves also grew up without their mothers. This was particularly so for the last generations of Virginia slaves who were born and reared between 1830 and 1860 when masters increasingly were selling women to traders who took them out of the state. Information descriptive of the slave exports from the state documents this activity. Richard Sutch estimates that by 1850, slaveholders were selling equal numbers of adult women and men and actually more adolescent and young adult females than males within those broad age cohorts. Because the average age at first birth for Virginia slave women was between nineteen and twenty years, large numbers exported were probably young mothers, many of whom were forced to leave without their young. Liza McCoy recalled that her Aunt Charlotte, a slave who lived in Matthews County, "was sold to Georgia away from her baby when de chile wont no more three months." . . .

Unfortunately, the socialization of slave youth was a difficult task for slaves regardless of the composition of their individual families. Slave child rearers faced obstacles to success that most whites did not. The most important deterrent was a legal one which had negative implications for all aspects of the relationship between rearer and child. Simply, slave parents were not the legal guardians of their children—white owners were. Moreover, since slaveholders were quite willing to share their authority with persons other than slave kin, particularly nurses, overseers, drivers, and other whites residing on their property, slave family members had many threats to their influence over the lives of their youngsters. Slave children were confronted with a variety of authority figures, white and black, each with his or her own priorities, demands, and contributions to their upbringing. These youths had to learn to assess the power and value of each of these adults as well as to appease their demands, often simultaneously.

Slave kin and white owners held the most important positions of power in the lives of slave children. Yet, as the balance of power was both a delicate and complex phenomenon that could shift quite suddenly, slave kin had to work diligently to retain some control in the face of unsolicited interference from others. White owners balked at attempts by slave kin to gain control over the lives or allegiances of black children in opposition to their authority as masters. They understood that such challenges to their authority showed that their slaves did not accept their assigned inferior status and were teaching their slave children to resist as well. Masters met such trials with extreme hostility and often open brutality. Also, since most antebellum Virginia slaveholders were white and male and most slave child care-givers were bondswomen; masters, especially, were incensed at the notion that their authority and power might be questioned by someone they viewed as three times their inferior—that is, black, female, and slave. A slave mother's successful defiance of an owner's authority would have meant a weakening of the control that the slaveholder hoped to exert over his other slaves—a situation few Virginia masters would tolerate. . . .

One can expect that with the decline of the viability of the extended slave family and the nonrelated surrogate kin network in the wake of increased exportation of slaves, the overall socialization of many slave youth suffered. One must also concede, however, that even under optimum conditions for success, slave kin rarely were able to rear children that were not affected to some degree by the actions and ideologies of whites who held so much power over their physical, psychological, and intellectual developments. Obviously, slaves sometimes internalized prevalent racist views which created tension within their families and communities. Color stratification was a problem which posed particularly negative consequences for those slaves touched by it, because of the explosive issues of force, sex, female purity, and marital sanctity that it evoked. Color consciousness and stratification among blacks resulted from a combination of factors, such as a consistently high rate of miscegenation and, relatedly, a large biracial population among slaves and free blacks, as well as the popularity of racist ideologies concerning race difference and hierarchy and their practical application in antebellum Virginia society.

Much of the interracial sexual activity that resulted in the state's biracial population involved white-male coercion and rape of black females. Consequently, the children born of these assaults were potent symbols of the immense power that whites held over the most intimate spheres of black life. They were a constant reminder to their mothers and her kin of their powerlessness in the face of white male domination and violence. "My mama said that in dem times a nigger 'oman couldn't help herself," May Satterfield recalled, "fo she had to do what de marster say. . . . she had to go." Consequently, the presence of racially mixed children in homes of slaves sometimes engendered feelings of shame, humiliation, and anger.

Slave families and communities usually attached an even deeper stigma to those children conceived as a result of the voluntary sexual relations between black women and white men. Although slaves were very empathetic to those women who were the victims of coercion, they often ostracized slave women who openly consorted with white men. Many bondswomen and men viewed these concubines as promiscuous and disloyal. Their children shared, to a certain extent, the dishonor of their mothers. . . .

Of course, other problems related to the flaws in the antebellum South also haunted the families of bondsmen and women. Reared in a society that was extremely violent, even by standards of the nineteenth century, slaves sometimes also chose brutal force as a means of control of their families and among their peers. . . . Privy to some of these events, whites from the South and North did not hesitate to comment on what they perceived as violent behavior that some slave child rearers exhibited when they punished their children.

Indeed, the stories regarding widespread violence of slaves toward each other were prevalent enough to warrant discussions of this issue in nineteenth-century guides outlining appropriate measures of treatment and control of slave property. Authors writing on the subject of slave management, on the one hand, routinely advised masters to carefully scrutinize the domestic relations of their slaves in order to prevent physical abuse within the quarters. Slaves, on the other hand, drew on both West African and European cultural dictates concerning the issue of corporal punishment. Most believed that, "a few licks now and then, does em good," and whippings in response to numerous offenses were an important part of their children's socialization.

The violence and brutality that whites imposed on their slaves undoubtedly influenced the ways in which bondsmen and bondswomen treated their own children and other dependents. The ability to beat someone, to hold that kind of physical control over another human, was a sadistic expression of power that blacks learned repeatedly from their interaction with and observation of white authority figures. This expression of control was meant to impress children with their parents' ability to command some power over their offspring's behavior. Also, adult slave kin wanted to demonstrate to whites, who often tried to usurp or demean slave parental authority, that they claimed a right to control and chastise their own children regardless of the legal guardianship that white owners possessed. Perhaps it was this demonstration of black slave power within their own domestic sphere rather than the concern for the actual physical pain the children endured that really offended whites. . . .

Abuse in slave families was not limited to children alone. Spousal ill-treatment was another serious problem. Relationships between husbands and wives suffered from slaveholders' usurpation of control in slave marriages even more profoundly than those relationships between parents and children. Verbal and physical abuse among married partners were sometimes responses to complex issues of discord within slave marriages. This prevalence of mistreatment among some antebellum blacks toward their spouses prompted one ex-slave to comment that "some good masters would punish slaves who mistreated womenfolk and some didn't."

Unfounded in Virginia law, slave marriages were tenuous relationships in which couples struggled to survive among the immense and divisive pressures of slave life. Slaveholders had the final say as to which slaves would marry and whom they could marry and when and, therefore, exercised immense dominion over this most intimate of decisions affecting adult slaves. Because they controlled vital aspects of slave marriage, owners' actions often meant the success or failure of these relationships.

Concerned with economic and logistic issues that slaves were not privy to, masters sometimes imposed marriage partners on slaves whom the individual bondswoman or man might not have chosen if given the opportunity to decide otherwise. Charles Grandy, an ex-slave from Norfolk recalled that on the farm where he resided:

> Marsa used to sometimes pick our wives fo' us. If he didn't have on his place enough women for the men, he would wait on de side of de road till a big wagon loaded with

slaves come by. Den Marsa would stop de ole nigger-trader and buy you a woman. Wasn't no use tryin' to pick one, cause Marsa wasn't gonna pay but so much for her. All he wanted was a young healthy one who looked like she could have children, whether she was purty or ugly as sin.

Although Grandy spoke specifically of the lack of choice male slaves had in acquiring wives, it is evident from his description of the process that the women involved—young women recently sold away from families and perhaps husbands—had absolutely no choice in the matter whatsoever. Apparently, the sexist perspectives of many male owners persuaded them to be more solicitous of the desires of male slaves in the matter than those of female slaves. Ex-slave Katie Blackwell Johnson explained that the slave women she knew "had no choice in the matter as to whom they would marry. If a man saw a girl he liked he would ask his master's permission to ask the master of the girl for her. If his master consented and her master consented, then they came together." The emotional and sexual exploitation of some women slaves forced to marry men whom they did not love undoubtedly increased their resentment toward their masters and their husbands, which then sparked marital discord. Likewise, those males forced to marry women they did not know or even think physically appealing hindered the development of a loving, respectful marital relationship. . . .

Clearly, the marital forms and relationships of slaves were related in part to their owners' desires to increase their slave holdings. Many antebellum Virginia slaveholders insisted that their slaves exercise their procreative powers to the fullest extent and encouraged various forms of marriage or sociosexual bonding between male and female slaves to insure high rates of birth. Slave breeding in Virginia is well documented through child-to-woman ratios, the personal papers of owners, and the testimonies of slaves. As one ex-slave noted: "The masters were very careful about a good breedin' woman. If she had five or six children she was rarely sold." A comparison of white and slave child-to-woman ratios from the period 1820 to 1860 as an indicator of fertility, for example, documents that slave women began having children at an earlier age than white females, although Anglo-American women eventually did bear more children than black slave women. An analysis of several slave lists from Virginia, which include information descriptive of the age at first birth of slave mothers, further substantiates these findings. The average age at first birth for Virginia slaves was approximately twenty years. White women, on the other hand, began to have children later, at about twenty-two. Moreover, while white child-to-woman ratios for both the considered age cohorts 0–14 years (child):15–49 years (mother) and 0–9 years:10–49 years declined over the antebellum era, child-to-woman ratios for slave women considered in the cohorts 0–14 years (child):15–49 years (mother) increased noticeably during the same time period. This evidence along with a review of the changes in demographic patterns among slaves over time documents that slave breeding was, in some cases, an important priority among Virginia slaveowners. . . .

While the information is less conclusive regarding the change in the average number of live children these women bore, it is clear that women in the last years of the antebellum era were having more children than those in the earlier decades. Within the ten-year period from 1850 to 1860 alone, the slave mothers on the Bolling plantations bore an average of four live children. Significantly, this figure conservatively represents only one-half of the childbearing years of these mothers. When one analyzes the numbers of children that Bolling slave women had during the period 1820 to 1850 (which represents a more complete childbearing cycle), an average of five live births is calculated. Clearly, those slave women who were beginning to bear children at the end of the antebellum era demonstrated a greater potential for natural increase than those of earlier generations. That this demographic change came at a time when slave marriages and families were so threatened by substantial exportations of adult slaves of childbearing age speaks to the resolve of owners to encourage procreation among their slaves. In order to promote the rapid birth of slave children, slave masters not only offered material incentives and may have threatened those slaves who refused to cooperate, but they also usurped the slaves' decision as to whether or not to participate in monogamous marital relationships. Thus, some slaveholders forced slave women and men to have several sexual partners outside of their marriage. Elige Davisson of Richmond, for example, stated that he was married once before he became free, but his owner still brought "some more women to see" him. Davisson insisted that his master would not let him have "just one woman" but mandated that the young male slave have sexual relations with several other female slaves so that they would bear children. Such demands to participate in their owner's breeding schemes brought a great deal of pain and anger to the individual slaves and to the couples involved.

Undoubtedly, slave marriages varied in terms of quality, length, and ideals even in the most supportive environment. Most slaves wanted long-standing, loving, affectionate, monogamous relationships with their spouses. Yet, they could not expect that their partners would be able to protect them from some of the most violent and abusive aspects of slave life. Most could only hope that their spouses would understand the lack of choices they had with regard to labor, attention to domestic responsibilities, and to their relationships with whites. The inability of slave wives and husbands to actualize their ideals of gender differentiated behavior, even those which were obviously unrealistic given their positions as slaves, often was the source of marital discord.

Slave women with "abroad marriages" usually had no alternative but to take on the role of the central authority figure within their immediate families, especially as child rearers, while their husbands lived on separate plantations. In doing so, however, they challenged Western tradition concerning gender specific behavior and power in nineteenth-century households that slaves often respected. Consequently, matrifocal families were common among late antebellum Virginia slaves but were not always acceptable to the couples who comprised them. Since many slave women and men hoped to function in their families according to the proposed ideal of the larger Southern society, their inability to do so engendered resentment, frustration, and anger. . . .

The instances of white male sexual aggression toward married slave women created a great deal of tension and discord in the marital relationships of slaves. Although slave husbands theoretically understood the inability of their wives to protect themselves against the sexual overtures and attacks of white men, they resented and were angered by such occurrences. Their reactions were in response equally to their own sense of powerlessness to defend their wives and to a recognition of the physical and psychological pain their spouses experienced. When slave husbands did intervene, they suffered harsh retaliation—severe beatings, sometimes permanent separation from their family, or even murder. Many probably felt, as did Charles Grandy, who spoke of the murder of a male slave who tried to protect his wife from the advances of their overseer, that a "Nigger ain't got no chance."

Consequently, some slave husbands targeted their helpless wives to be the recipients of their frustration, pain, guilt, and rage rather than the white men who attacked them. Regardless of whom the slaves struck out at, however, their responses had little effect on modifying the behavior of those white men who raped female slaves. "Marsters an' overseers use to make slaves dat wuz wid deir husbands git up, [and] do as they say," Israel Massie noted. "Send husbands out on de farm, milkin' cows or cuttin' wood. Den he gits in bed wid slave himself. Some women would fight an tussel. Others would be 'umble—feared of dat beatin.' What we saw, couldn't do nothing 'bout it. . . . My blood is bilin' now [at the] thoughts of dem times. Ef dey told dey husbands he wuz powerless."

Many slave women were ashamed that they had been victimized by their white masters and were afraid of the consequences for themselves, their families, and the children they might have conceived. They tried to conceal the sexual assault from their husbands. "When babies came," Massie went on to explain, "dey [white fathers] ain't exknowledge 'em. Treat dat baby like 'tothers—nuthing to him. Mother feard to tell 'cause she know'd what she'd git. Dat wuz de concealed part." Some slave wives went to great lengths to keep the truth from their husbands, claiming that mulatto children actually belonged to their spouses. "Ole man, . . . stop stedin' [studying] so much foolishness," responded one frightened slave wife when her husband noted that their youngest child was very physically distinct from their other children. She was able to end her husband's open suspicions by constructing a story, but few could hide the obvious.

Faced with such overwhelming problems, some slave couples responded in ways that further augmented the destruction of their marriages and families. Alcoholism, domestic violence, jealousy, and adultery were internal problems which sometimes plagued these relationships. More than a few slave couples voluntarily separated. Manfra and Dykstra's review of a survey of late antebellum slave couples who resided in the south of Virginia, for example, indicates that of those marriages terminated before general emancipation, 10.1 percent ended as a result of mutual consent and another 10.8 percent because of the desertion of a spouse. . . .

The forced separation of slave couples, of course, had the most devastating impact on slave marriages. Large numbers of loving commitments ended in this manner. When slaveholders separated husbands and wives by long distances, it was almost impossible for these couples to retain close ties to one another. The difficulty was a result of the emotional and sociosexual needs of adult slaves as well as of the insistence of their owners that they remain sexually active and thus naturally reproductive. Some masters expected these separated couples to form new relationships as soon as possible. Many did eventually remarry, but the pain and sense of loss that they felt must have been a source of continual anguish for them and their children, who had to adjust to the authority of stepparents and to their inclusion in stepfamilies.

When one Virginia "contraband" woman found her first husband in a refugee camp in 1864, she testified that the two, "threw [them]selves into each others arms and cried." The husband as well as the woman, however, had remarried since their forced separation. While his new wife looked on the touching scene of reunion with obvious jealousy, the older wife was disturbed for other reasons. Although she described her present husband as "very kind" and she was determined not to leave him, she had to admit that she could not be happy after seeing her first husband. The thought of the source of their permanent separation still angered and frustrated her, even though she claimed she was pleased with her present spouse. "White folk's got a heap to answer for the way they've done to colored folks! So much they wont never *pray* it away!" she concluded in disgust.

The voice of this one ex-slave in condemning of those slaveholders who purposefully destroyed slave marriages and families is no doubt representative of the voices of many who were similarly hurt. Their personal testimonies as well as the plantation records of their owners document the destruction that came to many Virginia slave families during the last decades of the antebellum era. Involuntary separation and the dispersal of husbands and wives from the rest of their families, sexual abuse, material deprivation, and forced marriages were some of the tremendous problems faced by slave families. Domestic violence, color stratification, spousal abandonment, and adultery were some of the manifestations of the internal strife within black slave families and marriages which were caused in large measure by their oppressive living conditions.

Late antebellum Southern society was indeed a harsh environment within which slaves tried to establish and maintain successful marriages and families. Many were able to do so, yet others failed in their efforts to sustain viable slave marriages and kin networks. The lives of Virginia slaves were too precarious to guarantee the complete and the constant success of any social institution, including marriage and the family. Consequently, the slave family emerged in the postbellum South as a viable but battered institution, threatened by new forms of economic and social oppression as well as the internal strife inherited from the previous era.

Antebellum Slavery: Slave Religion and Community

PETER KOLCHIN

. . . Slave religion exhibited fragile autonomy and evolution over time. During most of the colonial period, white efforts to proselytize among blacks were sporadic, and first- or second-generation African-Americans were at best indifferent to the Christian message; the second half of the eighteenth century saw widespread conversion of blacks to Christianity, a process that accelerated in the religious revivals of the early nineteenth century; by the late antebellum period, evangelical Christianity had emerged throughout the South as a central feature of slave life. The slaves' exposure to Christianity was uneven: some lived in isolated areas without ready access to religious services, and others were subject to the arbitrary whim of masters who prevented them from attending church. But antebellum slaves increasingly experienced a number of overlapping—sometimes competing—religious influences, from paternalistic masters who prayed and read the Bible with their "people," from white religious denominations that mounted a "mission to the slaves," and from the "invisible church" that operated quasi-secretly among the slaves themselves. Most mid-nineteenth-century slaves, unlike their ancestors a century earlier, were devoutly Christian.

The "invisible church" possessed a number of distinctive features that reveal how blacks adapted white forms to their own needs. Slaves who assembled in the quarters, in open-air "hush arbors," and in space sometimes provided by white churches spurned the lectures they received elsewhere on obedience to authority as a central tenet of Christianity in favor of a religion of the oppressed that promised them deliverance from their earthly troubles. White ministers from staid denominations that appealed primarily to upper-class parishioners had special difficulty in attracting slaves: Presbyterian minister Charles C. Jones noted that when he lectured a group of slaves in Liberty County, Georgia, on the Christian virtue of obedience, "one half of my audience deliberately rose up and walked off with themselves, and those that remained looked anything but satisfied." Similarly, Harriet Jacobs recalled how when an Episcopal clergyman began holding separate services for blacks in Edenton, North Carolina, "his colored members were very few, and also very respectable"; soon after, displeased with the injunction that "if you disobey your earthly master, you offend your heavenly Master," "the slaves left, and went to enjoy a Methodist shout." White Methodists and Baptists had far more success with the slaves than did Presbyterians and Episcopalians, but they, too, often found blacks leery of what they heard. "Dat ole white preacher jest was telling us slaves to be good to our marsters," recalled former slave Cornelius Garner. "We ain't keer'd a bit 'bout dat stuff he was telling us 'cause we wanted to sing, pray, and serve God in our own way."

The religious services of the slaves differed appreciably from those provided for them by whites. Accounts of Moses leading his people out of bondage replaced injunctions to obey authority. Although self-called black preachers, often illiterate and almost always ignorant of the fine points of theology, stressed the importance of virtuous behavior, they ignored the traditional Protestant emphasis on human depravity; the slaves' Christianity was a religion of the heart in which they could lose themselves in ecstatic joy, their God a redeemer and friend with whom they could communicate on a personal basis. A high level of emotional fervor characterized Southern evangelical Protestantism, whether white or black, but black Baptists and Methodists took this "enthusiasm" to a level that often shocked white observers—especially those of "genteel" backgrounds, whose religious behavior was likely to be more restrained—and derided white Christianity as stuffy and bloodless. Presbyterian minister R. Q. Mallard opined that a black revival meeting he witnessed in 1859 lacked any true religion, for it consisted of "one loud monotonous strain, interrupted by . . . groans and screams and clapping of hands," but many slaves believed their *masters* lacked true religious feeling: "You see," one explained later, " 'legion needs a little motion—specially if you gwine feel de spirret."

Despite the distinctive features of the black Christianity that emerged in the slave quarters, that Christianity was marked by pervasive white influence and indeed was itself a sign of the degree to which the masters impinged on the lives of their slaves. Differences between black and white religious practices were significant because those differences reveal the slaves as subjects whose behavior helped shape their own lives rather than merely as passive victims of white action, but from a broad view those differences must be regarded as relatively minor. Not only did the slaves adopt the general religion of their masters—Christianity—but they also adhered to the same specific (usually Protestant) denominations. Antebellum Southern blacks were, like antebellum Southern whites, most often Baptists and Methodists, with much smaller numbers of Presbyterians, Episcopalians, Catholics, and members of other sects. There were differences between black and white Baptists and between black and white Methodists, but there were also differences between black Baptists and black Methodists, or for that matter between white Baptists and white Presbyterians. American Christianity constituted an amorphous and highly heterogeneous religion, within which slaves found it easy to develop their own variants while remaining part of the mainstream.

Equally important, the shared religious heritage of white and black Southerners provided important bases of contact between them. Much of this contact occurred within the confines of slave-owner paternalism, as masters increasingly embraced the "mission to the slaves." Much of it, however, transcended the master–slave relationship and thrust blacks and whites together as believers in an environment that at least temporarily subverted consciousness of class and race. If the religious exposure of some slaves consisted primarily of slave owners reading the Bible to them, praying with them, and arranging for special services where they heard of Christian duty to obey their masters, that of others included attending interracial revival meetings as well as services that exhibited a high level of Christian fellowship. Several recent historians have emphasized the degree to which many white and black Southerners shared not just similar religious views but common religious experiences. "[T]he normative worship experience of blacks in the antebellum South was in a biracial church," suggested John B. Boles: although slaves usually sat in segregated slave galleries, "black and white co-worshipers heard the same sermons, were baptized and took communion together, and upon death were buried in the same cemeteries."

Whether slaves worshipped separately or with whites, historians have recently been so impressed by the force of slave religion that they have may well have exaggerated its universality and slighted some of its contradictory implications. Many slaves lacked access to regular religious services, either because they lived in remote areas or because they had owners who regarded their religious aspirations with distaste. Bennet H. Barrow's plantation diary (1836–46), for example, is filled with expressions of disgust at the religious enthusiasm of both whites and blacks; he frequently forbade his slaves to attend nearby religious meetings, and when sixteen slaves temporarily ran away from a neighboring plantation he blamed the flight on their owner's "having them preached to for 4 or 5 years past," an action that constituted the "greatest piece of foolishness any one [was] ever guilty of." Other slaves were simply uninterested in religion, and, in the words of slave autobiographer Henry Bibb, "resort[ed] to the woods in large numbers on [Sundays] to gamble, fight, get drunk, and break the Sabbath." Although Bibb expressed typical nineteenth-century outrage at such desecration of the Sabbath, many slaves eagerly looked forward to their day "off" as a time to work on their garden plots, spend time with their families, and simply relax.

Christianity had to compete for the slaves' time and attention not only with secular concerns but also with a host of pre-Christian beliefs and practices that persisted even among ardent Baptists and Methodists. Slaves commonly resorted to potions, concoctions, charms, and rituals to ward off evil, cure sickness, harm enemies, and produce amorous behavior. Dellie Lewis, interviewed in the 1930s for the Federal Writers' Project, described some of the magic tricks she had learned from her midwife grandmother, tricks that included both folk remedies such as prescribing cloves and whiskey to ease the pain of childbirth and magic rituals such as putting a fresh egg at the door of a sick person to prevent anyone from entering the room. "If you is anxious fo' yo' sweetheart to come back f'um a trip," she added, "put a pin in de groun' wid de point up an' den put a aig on de point. When all de insides runs outen de aig yo' sweetheart will return."

Although educated whites derided such "superstition" and slave autobiographers seeking to appeal to "enlightened" nineteenth-century sensibilities wrote of it with extreme embarrassment, magic, conjuring, and folk medicine continued to exercise a powerful hold over most antebellum slaves—at the same time that those slaves also considered themselves practicing Christians. Indeed, it was not uncommon for slaves to develop practices that fused Christian and non-Christian elements, as in the method described by autobiographer Jacob Stroyer of watching how a Bible turned when hung by a string to determine whether an accused person was guilty of stealing. One reason slaves were so easily able to combine belief in Christianity with belief in conjurers, witches, and spirits is that many apparently saw little difference between the two; noting that his father was a root doctor who could cure the sick, George White explained that he, too, knew "all de roots" and could "cure most anything," but he added that "you have got to talk wid God an' ask him to help out."

The particular combination of Christian and pre-Christian religion that coexisted in the slave quarters originated, of course, in the contact and interaction of African and European cultures and was one component of the new, African-American culture that resulted from the enslavement of blacks in America. This combination bore striking resemblance, however, to the mixture of Christian and pre-Christian beliefs embraced by many of the European immigrants to America in the seventeenth and eighteenth centuries, when, as historians such as Jon Butler have recently stressed, adherence to Christian theology constituted a thin veneer beneath which flourished widespread belief in magic and the occult. The similarity between the pre-modern worldviews held by whites and blacks in the South facilitated the continuing interaction between them in the antebellum period, in both Christian and non-Christian manifestations. It was by no means unknown for lower-class whites to consult black conjurers.

Slave magic and slave Christianity coexisted, but appropriated different spheres. Magic was most often directed at a concrete and immediate goal: to cure an illness, punish a rival suitor, prevent an overseer from applying the lash. Christianity was inevitably more abstract, more long-term in orientation: the rewards it promised were not in this world but in the next. As such, it exercised diverse and contradictory influences. It provided enormous comfort to an oppressed people, but in doing so it offered them an escape that could temper their real-world response to oppression. Why struggle to improve conditions in this world when the virtuous would receive everlasting happiness in the next?

Although slave owners had long disagreed over the likely impact of Christianity on their slaves, by the late antebellum years the vast majority had concluded that religion would make them more docile and obedient rather than more troublesome. Although the evidence is mixed, they may well have been correct. At times, Christianity could produce the fervor of a Nat Turner determined to wreak vengeance on the wicked. It could also create a culture of collaboration, one that emphasized rendering unto Caesar what was Caesar's. More often than either of these, however, it appears to have fostered in the slaves both a sense of short-term resignation and fatalism and a belief in eventual freedom. Under existing conditions, deliverance was something to be prayed for and awaited, not worked for and created. Under different conditions, however, that deliverance could certainly be helped along.

The slave community has become one of the central—albeit least well defined—concerns of recent historians of slavery. Eager to rebut images of slave passivity and docility, many of these historians have elevated the slave community to an all-embracing agency that gave order to the slaves' lives, expressed their deepest aspirations, and prevented their complete victimization. In the process, they have offered a real corrective to previous, one-sided interpretations that treated slaves largely as objects of white action rather than as subjects in their own right. At the same time, however, they have often reified "slave community," a slippery and emotionally laden term unused in antebellum years and used with varying (often unspecified) meanings today; "as the word is currently used, . . ." Clarence E. Walker has recently suggested, "[*community*] is a romantic construct that obscures more than it reveals." They have also come dangerously close to replacing a mythical world in which slaves were objects of total control with an equally mythical world in which slaves were hardly slaves at all.

Any evaluation of the problem of "community" must come to grips with two partially distinct but interrelated questions, those of autonomy and communality. The first of these involves the degree to which the slaves were able to secure control of their own lives, while the second involves the degree to which, in doing so, they acted on the basis of mutuality and collective interests. Resolving these questions is difficult, because levels of slave autonomy and communality were by no means synonymous (substantial autonomy did not necessarily imply substantial communality), because neither was constant over time or space, and because behavior, sharply limited by physical constraints, was closely linked to but never entirely a function of thought. The historian needs to distinguish between the elusive bundle of mental processes that represented the way slaves thought—"consciousness," "worldview," "ideology," "mentality"—and the behavioral patterns that represented the way they acted.

As the existence of slave families and slave religion indicates, large numbers of slaves throughout the antebellum South were able to forge ties other than the master–slave relationship that was central to slavery, in the process creating social and cultural formations that were essentially peripheral to that relationship even though they operated within its overall context. For the majority of slaves who lived on or near plantations, it was the slave quarters that provided the setting and the opportunity for leading lives partially free from white supervision. Composed of cabins grouped together to form a slave "village," the quarters was typically set a considerable distance from the master's "big house," to shield planter families from the intrusive presence of a large slave population. This isolation of the quarters, although primarily for the convenience of the masters, provided an important measure of privacy to the slaves, affording them a real if insecure refuge from the outside world.

Within the quarters, slaves engaged in a myriad of "leisure" activities that belied their condition as human property. When the master's work was done, they ate, sang, prayed, played, talked, quarreled, made love, hunted, fished, named babies, cleaned house, tended their garden plots, and rested. They strove to fill their lives with pleasurable activities that would enable them to transcend their status as slaves. "Whooppee, didn' us have good Sa'dd'y night frolics and jubilees," remarked ex-slave Abraham Chambers in a typical recollection. "Some clap and some play de fiddle, and, man, dey danced most all night." Christmas, harvesttime, corn shucking, and hog killing provided occasions for celebrations that slaves eagerly anticipated and long remembered.

Away from the immediate control of white authorities, slaves developed their own traditions and customs that reflected shared values. Forged out of varying combinations of African and European cultural practices, these customs differed over time and space. In southern Louisiana, voodoo, a syncretic, highly ritualized religion based on African beliefs fused with elements of French Catholicism, flourished, but it was unknown in most of the South; in the low country of South Carolina and Georgia, Gullah, reinforced by geographic isolation and a huge slave majority, fostered a distinctive slave culture, for, as historian Charles Joyner has pointed out, "speech communities, to an even greater extent than political communities, imply a shared culture and world view."

Nevertheless, common experiences—and the domestic slave trade—shaped a shared cultural mainstream in much of the slave South. Slaves dressed up for church on Sundays, favoring bright colors to distinguish their appearance from the normal workaday attire. They sang spirituals and work songs, often using an antiphonal, call-and-response pattern of African origin. They told stories that, like folktales elsewhere, were filled with ghosts, spirits, talking animals, and didactic lessons for the young. They put great emphasis on proper wedding and funeral ceremonies, which, as in traditional peasant cultures, provided occasions for marking key points of transition in the human experience and assumed enormous symbolic importance. In many of these ways, the slaves approached a kind of peasant autonomy, developing their own folkways even while under conditions of severe economic and political dependence.

It is important, however, to keep in mind the limitations to this slave autonomy. What is at issue is not whether slaves developed their own customs and cultural activities but the nature of those customs and activities: the degree to which they were able to operate free from white influence and the degree to which they indicated communal values and behavior. Because historians for many years paid little attention to the slaves' internal lives, accentuating the strength of the "slave community" served as a much needed historical corrective in the 1970s and 1980s. In their efforts to dispel the stereotype of slave passivity, however, many scholars lurched to the other extreme, lacing their writings with an evocative language of celebration in which terms like "community," "culture," "kinship ties," "solidarity," and "human dignity" replaced those suggesting victimization, and presenting such a felicitous portrait of life in the quarters that slavery itself seemed to fade into the background. "To understand the nature of education in the slave quarter community is to come to grips with the paradox of the 'free slave,' . . ." wrote historian Thomas L. Webber in 1978. "By passing their unique set of cultural themes from generation to generation, the members of the quarter community were able to resist most of white teaching, set themselves apart from white society, and mold their own cultural norms and group identity. While still legally slaves, the black men, women, and children of the quarter community successfully protected their psychological freedom and celebrated their human dignity." I believe that an even-handed appraisal must not only incorporate the important revisionist work of the past two decades but also come to grips with the insecurity of slave life, the limits to slave autonomy, and the particular character that "community" assumed among the slaves. These stemmed both from the inherent realities of slavery in general and from the specific characteristics of Southern slavery in particular.

The nature of slave life in the South changed significantly over two and a half centuries. Some of the most emphasized communal features of that life—for example, the central role of slave Christianity—developed relatively late and were dominant characteristics only during the last years of the slave regime. Others—most notably African cultural influences—were strongest early, when the arrival of new slaves from Africa perpetuated knowledge of traditional ways, but gradually weakened in most of the South among slaves who were second-, third-, and fourth-generation Americans. By ignoring these changes over time, telescoping the slave past can distort the reality of slave life at any specific moment and suggest the existence of a generalized communal culture whose constituent parts did not always coexist.

A comparative perspective makes clear some of the particular limitations to both slave autonomy and slave communality in the antebellum South. Some of these limitations were demographic. The relatively small size of most Southern holdings, together with the high population ratio of whites to blacks, meant that most Southern slaves came in contact with whites far more often than did those in Jamaica or Saint Domingue. Reinforcing these demographic realities was the paternalistic meddling of resident masters who, as we have seen, strove to order virtually every element of their slaves' lives. Southern slaves persistently endeavored to augment their social autonomy, taking advantage of every opportunity provided them to manage their own affairs in their own ways, but in their efforts to maximize their day-to-day independence they faced unusually severe limitations, even for slaves. Slaves in Saint Domingue and Jamaica lived in a world that was overwhelmingly black, a world in which European planters felt intensely uncomfortable and from which they frequently retreated; serfs in Russia lived in a world that was even more overwhelmingly peasant, one alien to and usually avoided by their noble masters. Southern slaves, by contrast, lived in, and had to adjust to, the world of their masters.

The slaves' status as societal outsiders impeded their ability to carve for themselves the kind of autonomy typically enjoyed by dependent peasants. Even where the dependence of such peasants was most extreme—as in Russia, where serfs were in many ways indistinguishable from slaves—peasants were typically regarded as constituting the lowest element of society, and enjoyed certain clearly delineated rights (either by law or custom), including the right to marry, hold land, and form communal organizations. Students of peasant life in diverse areas of the world have recently emphasized "community" as an organizing principle of rural life. Communities had geographic, economic, and political bases; they were marked by intense attachment to place, a corresponding distrust of outsiders, a sense of collective interests (often centered on property rights), and the formation of institutions designed to protect those interests. Above all, a village community was composed geographically, by people living in one locality and having a sense of a shared past and mutual responsibility. "To belong to a rural community," sociologist Victor V. Magagna has stated, "was to belong to a specific place with a particular history."

Slaves, by contrast, generally lacked the economic and institutional bases for "community," as well as the local attachments that accompanied them. They did not constitute the bottom level of society so much as outsiders to it; that society provided no formal recognition of what tradition sanctified as theirs by right. It is for this reason that historian James Oakes insists that slavery was "a qualitatively distinct form of subordination" that left its victims far less control over their lives than other forms of unfree and quasi-free labor. In short, slaves did not really form communities in the sense that peasants did. As I will suggest in section VII, however, they did develop a common identification that substituted for—and has often been confused with—a sense of community.

If slaves in general were unable to achieve the kind of folk autonomy typically enjoyed by dependent peasants, *American* slaves faced obstacles that in important respects made their struggle for independence especially difficult. In much of the Caribbean, and to a lesser extent in Brazil, slaves approached a "proto-peasant" status based on a substantial degree of economic independence. Assigned "provision grounds" in much the same way that Russian serfs were allotted land, slaves cultivated their "own" land, providing their own sustenance and selling the surplus in flourishing local markets; in the process, they acquired their "own" property as well as a strong sense of their rights and privileges. Southern slave owners, however, rarely allowed their slaves this kind of economic independence. Historians such as Ira Berlin and Philip D. Morgan have recently explored the development of an internal slave economy in the South, noting the widespread existence of garden plots—which slaves came to regard as theirs by right—as well as the buying, selling, and bartering by slaves that ensued. But the internal economy faced severe limitations in the antebellum South, where, as we have seen, slave owners assiduously strove to keep their people in a state of complete dependence. Commercial activity on the part of slaves was most highly developed in the low country of South Carolina and Georgia, where the task system and widespread owner absenteeism created particularly favorable conditions, but even there it was on a modest scale by Caribbean standards. In most of the South, although masters often allowed their slaves to have garden plots, those masters usually kept control of slave provision, took pains to limit garden plots to at best a supplementary role, and imposed severe restrictions on any commercial activity on the part of the slaves.

Economic dependence did not, of course, totally preclude the development of social and cultural autonomy among the slaves; even under the most adverse of circumstances, slaves strove in countless small ways to wrest as much control of their lives from their masters as they could. The conditions under which they lived, however, subjected them to unusually pervasive outside influence as paternalistic masters strove to control their every action. Those conditions also impeded collective action on their part and fostered an ethos in which individuals struggled to find their niche and make the best of a bad situation.

Slave folktales offer suggestive if sometimes elusive clues to the consciousness of the quarters. Through stories of talking animals, ghosts, and magic as well as those offering semi-realistic depictions of plantation relations, slaves entertained one another, expressed fears and longings, and presented their children with didactic lessons on how to get along in a dog-eat-dog world. A number of scholarly debates have swirled over the origins, transcription, and interpretation of these tales, but researchers have properly seen their very existence as strong evidence of autonomous slave behavior and consciousness. Animal trickster tales, in which small but smart animals typically outsmart those that are large and dumb, as well as stories centered on persistent rivalry between "Old Master" and his slave John or Jack, provided only thinly disguised reference to surrounding social relations and enabled the slaves to poke vicarious fun at their masters, themselves, and the world in which they lived.

But in addition to pointing to slave autonomy, those tales also offer revealing hints concerning the slaves' mentality and suggest the limits to their communal consciousness. Notably absent from Southern slave folklore are stories depicting heroic behavior—stories of dragon slayers, popular liberators, or people who sacrificed themselves for the good of the whole. Rather, the dominant themes are trickery, subterfuge, and securing as much as possible of a desired item (often food) for oneself. Justice, fair play, and compassion for one's rivals rarely emerge as desirable characteristics. In short, surviving in a heartless world assumes overriding importance; as historian Michael Flusche perceptively argued, "The recurring themes of these stories suggest that slavery tended to engender an atomistic, individualistic world view among the slaves and that the slaves' sense of community was more complicated than simple unity in the face of white oppression."

The existence of antisocial behavior in slave folktales should not be surprising; such behavior is present in the folktales of many peoples and does not necessarily indicate an acceptance of antisocial values. (The slaves' Christianity did emphasize idealism and heroic figures such as Moses.) The highly competitive and aggressive behavior featured in so many slave stories, however, should serve to alert us to a notable fact: the grubby reality of day-to-day social relations in the quarters—with all the conflicts and jealousies that inevitably exist in human relations even under the best of circumstances—has been almost totally unexplored by historians interested in demonstrating the vitality of the slave community. Slaves struggled against overwhelming odds to build decent lives for themselves and took pleasure when they could in their friends and families. They were also human beings, however, and exhibited the full panoply of human failings, including their share of theft, violence, jealousy, deceit, wife beating, and child abuse. Slaves successfully resisted being turned into docile, obedient creatures of their masters' will; they did not turn the "slave community" into atopia.

An examination of the ways in which Southern slaves resisted their thralldom and struggled to improve their condition helps clarify the nature of their social outlook as well as their social relations. Conducting such an examination is tricky, because it must rely heavily on behavior—frequently reconstructed on the basis of fragmentary evidence—to explore thought, while at the same time avoiding the tendency to inflate every minor expression of pique into a sign of covert revolutionary activity. Perhaps in part for this reason, there has been remarkably little good historical work done on the resistance of Southern slaves. Nevertheless, because the very act of resisting authority involved expressing sentiments that were normally unvoiced, that resistance—its forms and frequency as well as its character and consequences—can provide revealing insights into the worldview of the slaves.

Concrete political realities (that is, power relationships) shaped the specific patterns of resistance in the slave South. The high ratio of whites to blacks, the relatively small size and dispersed nature of slaveholdings, the presence of well-armed resident masters who took an active interest in local affairs, and—with the important exceptions of the War for Independence and the Civil War—the region's political stability combined to create conditions that were extremely unfavorable for armed rebellion. It is hardly surprising, then, that American slaves engaged in few such rebellions, and that those few were by international standards small and easily suppressed. Some of the most noted "conspiracies," including those led by Gabriel Prosser in Virginia in 1800 and by Denmark Vesey in South Carolina in 1822, were nipped in the bud before any outbreak of violence by a combination of white vigilance and black informers; others, such as that in New York City in 1741, may have existed only in the minds of panicked whites.

The handful of insurrections that actually came off were invariably local outbreaks that were quickly crushed with a minimum of armed force; none lasted more than a couple of days, threatened more than local havoc, or overcame the repressive efforts of local authorities. These revolts included the Stono rebellion of 1739, in which several dozen slaves near Charleston killed a number of whites but were routed the same day by armed planters; a larger but more obscure effort in 1811 in which some two hundred slaves tried to march on New Orleans before meeting the same fate; and, most famous of all, the Turner insurrection of 1831, which for two days produced panic—and fifty-nine deaths—among whites of Southampton County, Virginia, before local residents succeeded in capturing or killing most of the seventy-odd rebels. (Their charismatic leader, Nat Turner, managed to hide out in the woods eluding his pursuers for more than two months before being seized, tried, and hanged.)

Although these and other outbreaks sowed fear in the hearts of slaveholders and served as sources of inspiration for slaves (and generations of their descendants), they never came close to threatening the security of the slave regime. Nothing in the South remotely resembled the Haitian insurrection in which the slaves took advantage of the French Revolution to wage a triumphant revolutionary war of their own, or the massive "peasant wars" of the seventeenth and eighteenth centuries in which hundreds of thousands of Russian serfs joined other downtrodden peasants, cossacks, and town dwellers in protracted although ultimately unsuccessful assaults on established authority. In contrast to Russia and Haiti (and, to a lesser extent, much of the Caribbean and Brazil), the South had a balance of forces that was profoundly inhospitable to massive collective resistance. The waves of repression that followed each insurrection, conspiracy, and rumored conspiracy simply reinforced what was obvious to most slaves: under existing conditions, armed revolt was folly.

Absence of massive rebellion, however, hardly indicated passive acceptance of slavery. In a wide variety of ways, slaves expressed their dissatisfaction with the conditions they were forced to endure. Most common, but also most difficult to isolate, was a collection of acts that historians have labeled "silent sabotage" or "day-to-day resistance," acts through which slaves, without threatening the security of the slave regime, caused considerable aggravation to individual slave owners. Throughout the South, slaves dragged their feet, pretended to misunderstand orders, feigned illness, "accidentally" broke agricultural implements, and stole coveted items (especially food) from their owners, viewing such appropriation as "taking" what rightfully belonged to them. In noting that the slaves commonly adhered to "the agrarian notion . . . that the result of labour belongs of right to the labourer," Frederick Law Olmsted drew attention to a fact widely recognized by slaves and slave owners alike; as former slave Charles Ball put it, "I was never acquainted with a slave who believed, that he violated any rule of morality by appropriating to himself any thing that belonged to his master, if it was necessary to his comfort."

Silent sabotage had ambiguous implications. It provided an accessible outlet through which slaves could express their frustrations with relatively little risk, but it also served to foster patterns of behavior that accentuated dissembling and shirking, and to reinforce among whites the notion that blacks were by nature lazy, foolish, and thieving. A pervasive irritant to masters, it represented a borderline form of resistance that did not directly challenge authority and that merged imperceptibly with the impulse common among slaves and non-slaves alike to get away with something.

Far more clear-cut were two intermediate forms of resistance that, unlike rebellion, occurred with great frequency and, unlike silent sabotage, represented direct challenges to slave owners and their employees. Of these, running away was by far the most common. In the antebellum period, unlike the colonial, the existence of free states to the north served as a powerful magnet to those who dreamed of escaping bondage. Reaching the North could be a task of almost herculean proportions requiring endurance, evasion of slave catchers, and deception of suspicious whites. Fugitives resorted to a variety of imaginative devices to achieve their goals. Frederick Douglass borrowed the identification papers of a free black sailor and took a train from Baltimore to Wilmington, Delaware, and then a boat to Philadelphia, all the time worrying that the considerable contrast between his friend's description and his own appearance would lead to his detection; Henry Box Brown had himself shipped in a crate from Richmond to Philadelphia. Some runaways received food and shelter from sympathetic blacks and whites—the fabled "Underground Railroad"—on their trek to freedom, and others were fortunate enough to have the guidance of a "conductor" such as Harriet Tubman, who, following her own escape from bondage, returned repeatedly to Maryland's Eastern Shore to shepherd others to freedom.

Most fugitives to the North, however, made the journey alone, on foot, traveling by night and resting by day and taking care to avoid blacks as well as whites because, as William Wells Brown later put it, "twenty-one years in slavery had taught me that there were traitors even among colored people." Perhaps one thousand runaways per year managed to reach the North during the late antebellum years, the great majority young males from the upper-South states of Maryland, Virginia, Kentucky, and Missouri; many more attempted the feat but suffered capture (and return home) in the process. Despite conditions that rendered escape to the North extraordinarily difficult, tens of thousands of slaves showed their hatred of slavery by "voting with their feet" for freedom.

An even larger number of fugitives remained in the South. As in the colonial period, most runaway slaves hid out within a few miles of their homes. A few managed to elude capture for prolonged periods, either on their own—by holing up in caves and other rural retreats or by making their way to cities and merging with the free black population—or in groups of escaped slaves known as maroons that found refuge on the frontier and in unsettled internal areas such as the Great Dismal Swamp along the border between Virginia and North Carolina. But long-term survival on the loose was relatively rare in the antebellum South: the increasing density of settlement, improved communication, and the local hegemony of resident masters facilitated the capture of fugitives, and maroon colonies in the South never rivaled those in Brazil, Surinam, or Jamaica in numbers, size, or durability.

The vast majority of fugitives were temporary runaways. Most large plantations and many smaller holdings as well suffered from persistent truancy, as dissatisfied slaves "took off," lurking in the woods, visiting friends and relatives, or sometimes concealing themselves in outbuildings on their owners' plantations. Some such vagrants returned home on their own, tired and hungry, after a few days of uneasy freedom; others were eventually tracked down by irritated masters and overseers or turned in by loyal slaves hoping for a reward; still others proved more elusive. "I am sorry to hear of your having so many runaways from the plantation," wrote a member of a prominent South Carolina planting family to his brother, describing his own unsuccessful attempt, accompanied by "a parcel of overseers and professional negro hunters with nine dogs," to find fugitives who were hiding out in an area "known to be a safe and unmolested refuge for runaways." Advising his brother to use dogs to track down his truants, the letter writer warned that "the utmost secrecy and caution should be observed, as it is *extremely* difficult to prevent the runaways from being informed of a search after them being in preparation."

Slave owners complained vociferously about the "thoughtlessness" and "ingratitude" of truants, but many masters and overseers took temporary flight as a virtual given, a routine annoyance that went with the job of slave manager and underlined the need for constant vigilance. Slave owners rarely bothered to advertise for slaves thought to be in the vicinity (the way they did for those headed North), or to hire slave catchers to track them down. Although slaves who repeatedly absconded and those whose prolonged absence caused their masters unusual aggravation and expense could expect to be severely punished, runaways who returned home quickly on their own sometimes received little more than verbal harangues or "light" whippings.

More threatening, although less common, was a second form of intermediate resistance, through which slaves directly confronted masters and their assistants by force. Slave owners, embarrassed by such blatant challenge to their authority, rarely described these confrontations in detail, and their precise frequency is impossible to gauge. Nevertheless, ex-slave interviews and autobiographies, as well as judicial records and oblique references in planter journals, point to a surprisingly wide-spread pattern of small-scale confrontations in which slaves offered physical resistance to owners, overseers, and hirers. At times, such resistance resulted in the death of the assaulted white authority, but murder was rarely the goal of these slaves who assaulted white authorities; slaves occasionally conspired, either individually or with comrades, to do away with hated whites—poison, arson, and "accidents" were the preferred methods—but the far more numerous direct confrontations were usually opportunistic encounters involving less planning than impulsive response to intolerable provocation. Confrontations were often followed by flight as resisters, pondering the likely consequences of their actions, opted to give their enraged targets a chance to cool off.

Although slave confrontations had numerous scenarios, they typically occurred when bondsmen, and less often bondswomen, felt that they were being pushed too far and determined to resist. In Alabama, a slave named Abram claimed to be sick and "moved off slowly" when ordered to work by the overseer, who for good measure gave him a lash with his whip; the enraged Abram grabbed the whip and a gun from the overseer, knocked him to the ground, bit off a piece of his ear, and in turn received a knife wound as they struggled. Virginian William Lee got tired of the beatings he suffered from his mistress, who would hold his head between her knees and "whack away" on his back, so he grabbed her legs and "bodily carried ole missus out an' thro her on de ground jes' as hard as I could." Frederick Douglass, hired for a year to an abusive "slave breaker" named Edward Covey, suffered mistreatment in silence for six months before finally refusing to submit to more and resisting when Covey attempted to whip him; the two men struggled with each other for a prolonged period before Douglass's adversary "gave up the contest." Although Covey chided the recalcitrant slave, proclaiming, "I would not have whipped you half so much as I have had you not resisted," Douglass noted in his autobiography that "the fact was, *he had not whipped me at all.*"

If it is impossible to determine exactly how often slaves took part in the kind of confrontation with which Douglass challenged Covey, it is clear that such action, together with the flight in which Douglass also engaged, represented by far the most characteristic, and significant, forms of direct slave protest. Indeed, these two forms of resistance occurred so often, and with such consistency, that they may be regarded as pervasive features of antebellum slavery, features that clearly give the lie to assertions of general slave contentment. They also provide significant clues to understanding the worldview as well as the world of the bondspeople.

Like slave folklore, slave resistance can tell us much about autonomy and communality in the antebellum South. One of the most striking characteristics of that resistance—aside from its very existence—is that it was largely the work of individuals. If collective forms of resistance such as rebellion and marronage were minor features of Southern society, the types of resistance that *were* widespread featured slaves who acted alone or in very small groups rather than as communal representatives. Slaves learned by experience that such individual resistance—although by no means risk-free—had the greatest chance of success.

This was true of both confrontations and flight. Physical confrontation initiated by a large group of slaves was indistinguishable from revolt in the eyes of most slave owners, and invariably called forth swift and merciless response. Slaves who challenged a group of whites also faced almost certain repression, because the nature of the conflict transformed it from a struggle between two individuals into an affront to the honor of those challenged; however they might respond in private, masters could not tolerate public assaults on their authority. Slaves who ran away found that they could travel most safely in a white-dominated world either alone or in pairs; larger groups of fugitives inevitably risked attracting attention and lost mobility. In short, the particular conditions under which Southern slaves lived permitted a significant degree of individual resistance but severely discouraged collective protest.

This should not be taken to imply an absence of cooperation among slaves resisting authority. Slaves joined together to pilfer their masters' larders, as well as, less often, to burn their barns and poison their food. Despite the existence of slave informers, many bondspeople protected those accused of criminal behavior if that behavior was directed at whites rather than at other slaves, and slave owners trying to identify the perpetrators of vandalism or theft often ran into a wall of silence when they questioned their people. Fugitives rightly feared being betrayed by slaves seeking to curry favor with authorities, but some runaways received food, shelter, and guidance from sympathetic blacks, both slave and free; Harriet Jacobs hid for seven years in the attic of her grandmother, a respected free black woman who kept her secret and eventually helped her escape to the North.

But although there was extensive cooperation among slaves resisting authority, this cooperation was almost always that of individuals. Slaves lacked any kind of institutional body like the Russian peasant commune, which represented a whole village or estate and made decisions on behalf of all peasants. Decisions to flee or confront authorities were not reached communally, through collective deliberation, but individually, through private deliberation; indeed, slaves planning to escape usually took care *not* to inform others and thus risk their chance at freedom. Although occasionally a large group of slaves, unexpectedly caught by a slave patrol in a forbidden nighttime revelry, might put up spirited if futile resistance, virtually never in the antebellum South did all the slaves on a plantation decide collectively to go on strike or run away, as serfs often did in Russia. The pattern of slave resistance in the antebellum South thus points to a complex environment that permitted extensive cooperation among slaves but at the same time severely limited the kinds of communal behavior that were possible.

Examining when and why slaves resisted yields equally significant observations. The trigger for slave flight and confrontations almost always consisted of a violation by white authorities of commonly accepted standards of behavior. No matter how much they detested slavery, the balance of forces—and the need to get on with their lives, even under harsh conditions—prevented slaves from engaging in constant struggle against it; resistance was by no means random, or constant across time and space. Certain actions by slave owners and their agents, however, were clearly intolerable. These included most notably excessive or unjustified punishment—that is, punishment that exceeded "normal" parameters or that was meted out for misdeeds not actually committed—but also a host of other breaches of civilized treatment, including separation of family members, sexual assaults, and arbitrary or erratic management. The death of an owner was also a particularly stressful time for slaves, because no one could be sure what would follow; estates were often broken up to pay off debts or satisfy claims of heirs, and at the very least the slaves would have to adjust to a new owner, who would want to establish his or her own authority and would be likely to have new ideas of how things should be done. It is not surprising, then, that such death occasioned heightened concern on the part of slaves, concern that could manifest itself in real (if ambivalent) grief as well as flight and resistance to new rules and regulations.

Although there were variations in the circumstances surrounding decisions to run away or confront whites—confrontations and temporary flight were frequently impulsive acts, immediate responses to unacceptable behavior, whereas flight to the North more often came after considerable thought and even preparation—these decisions almost always rested on specific grievances that triggered the determination to act. In their autobiographies, fugitive slaves typically combined assertion of what Henry Bibb called "a longing desire to be free" with reference to some catalyst, most often involving punishment, that caused them to act on that desire; Bibb decided to flee in 1835, when his Kentucky mistress began abusing him physically, "every day flogging me, boxing, pulling my ears, and scolding." As this example suggests, abuse of a slave accustomed to relatively lenient treatment was especially likely to provoke resistance. Frederick Douglass found hirer Covey's abuse especially hard to take because he had been used to the privileged life of a house servant in Baltimore; Isaac Throgmorton, sold to Louisiana after enjoying considerable freedom as a barber in Kentucky, found "all the privileges were taken from me" and decided to escape to the North. But virtually any substantial change was unsettling and therefore conducive to resistance, both because it threatened established procedures and because it reminded slaves that those procedures were by no means immutable.

In short, although a general hatred of slavery and yearning for freedom underlay slave resistance, particular circumstances provoked individual decisions to resist. Despite their bitter detestation of bondage, on a day-to-day level most slaves came to terms with their conditions—because they had little choice—striving all the while to maximize their autonomy and preserve as "rights" the little privileges they were allowed to enjoy. When those rights were violated, however, slaves were likely to respond. Their resistance thus points both to a shared if never precisely defined understanding of what was acceptable and what was unacceptable within the general framework of a hated system, and to a conservative mentality under which slaves for the most part grudgingly made their peace with an oppressive reality but, when pushed too far, resisted behavior that violated that understanding.

If most slave resistance represented specific responses by individuals to intolerable situations rather than revolutionary efforts to overthrow the system, the consequences were nevertheless often far-reaching. Unlike armed revolt, which invariably called forth severe repression, flight and confrontation produced highly variable—indeed, unpredictable—results. Slaves who struck whites or ran away too often could find themselves brutally whipped, sold down the river, or even killed, and most could expect to receive at least some physical punishment for their insolence. Many, however, were decidedly more fortunate. Some fugitives reached the North, and others remained on the loose for protracted periods in the South. Still others, together with slaves who confronted white authorities, gained ameliorated treatment for themselves even under slavery. Every slave owner, overseer, and hirer had to consider, on a daily basis, how individual slaves would respond to specific treatment and whether a particular action—a whipping or a new rule—was worth the risk of the response it might provoke. Slaves who gained a reputation for standing up to authority often gained a measure of respect and tolerance from white authorities and secured for themselves greater freedom of action.

This was true both of "ungovernable" slaves—the proverbial "bad niggers" who made it clear that they would not let anyone touch them without trouble—and of those who lashed out at or ran away from tormentors after meekly submitting to their oppression. It was common knowledge among both whites and blacks that there were a few slaves who were so "mean" that it was not worth messing with them; although whites sometimes made special efforts to "tame" such recalcitrants, many masters and overseers decided that discretion was the better part of valor and gave free rein to those who did not make too much trouble. But as Frederick Douglass and numerous other slaves showed, under the right circumstances previously tractable slaves could also prove remarkably resistant; what is more, their resistance could have equally beneficial results. During the six months that Douglass remained with Covey after their fight, Covey never again tried to whip him. Douglass drew the appropriate lesson, generalizing that "he is whipped oftenest, who is whipped easiest."

By standing up to and running away from their masters, then, individual slaves helped set limits to their own oppression. They also helped set limits to the oppression of their fellow slaves, for no slave owner or overseer could ever be entirely sure in which apparently compliant soul there secretly lurked the heart of a "bad nigger" and rather than find out the hard way, it did not hurt to give slaves an occasional benefit of the doubt. Slave resistance never seriously threatened the security of the regime, but such resistance constituted an important part of the slaves' efforts to shape their own lives.

Patterns of slave resistance, like slave folklore and recollections, thus point to the complex, even contradictory, nature of the consciousness that developed in the quarters as the slaves managed to carve for themselves a partially autonomous world even while subject to extensive white controls. Intense individualism coexisted with widespread cooperation among individuals. Associative behavior was pervasive as slaves interracted with one another in their families and churches, as well as through friendships and self-help networks. At the same time those slaves lacked the communal institutions—and loyalties—that typically united peasant villagers throughout much of the world.

Of course, antebellum Southern slaves, like people everywhere, felt diverse, overlapping attachments: to self, family, friends, locality, class, and ethnicity. But evidence suggests that they usually identified most strongly at the two extremes, as individual and family members on the one side and as slaves—or even blacks—on the other, with relatively weak intermediate ties to local "communities." Plantation residents lacked, for example, the intense sense of oneness with each other that Russian serf villagers exhibited, a sense of oneness that often produced equally intense suspicion of and even hostility to all outsiders, including serfs from neighboring villages.

Except in isolated areas, the slaves' geographic mobility combined with their lack of institutional autonomy to reduce local distinctions and attachments and create instead a common slave culture with which residents of widely scattered farms and plantations could identify. Just as the slaves' attenuated occupational differentiation reduced status conflict on given holdings, so, too, did the absence of sharp geographic-based differences make it easier for slaves to see themselves as one with other slaves, and indeed with other blacks in general, whether slave or free.

Racial identification among slaves drew strength from several sources. Because slaves constituted an overwhelming majority of the black population in most of the South, the line separating white from black approximated that separating free from slave, and it was easy for slaves, and their masters, to confuse race with class. Slaves and slave owners alike commonly used racial terminology: if a master spoke of "my negroes" (or "my niggers") to refer to his or her slaves, those slaves also called each other "niggers" or "colored folk" and looked upon whites in general as their oppressors. "White folks jes' naturally different from darkies," explained one ex-slave. "We's different in color, in talk and in 'ligion and beliefs. We's different in every way and can never be spected to think or live alike." Such views drew support from the virulent white racism of many non-slaveholding whites, as well as from the close ties—including, at times, those of kinship—that existed in much of the South between slaves and free blacks.

Substituting for a communal identification with one's local group, then, was a generalized racial consciousness that at times approached but never quite merged into class consciousness. The use of "brother," "sister," "aunt," and "uncle" as terms of endearment commonly applied to blacks whether physically related or not suggests an outlook that incorporated all blacks as members of a kind of giant extended family, or community of the whole. So, too, do the patterns of slave resistance, which, despite their individual manifestation, showed such consistency in form and origin that they clearly reflected shared values that existed among blacks across the South.

The complexity of slave identification in the antebellum South reflected a world full of contradictions and ambiguities. In describing this world, historians have largely swung away from a model of victimization to one of autonomy, from a view of slaves as objects acted upon to one of independent beings defying the theory of slavery by leading their own lives. A balanced appraisal must recognize the validity as well as the exaggeration of both these models: slaves were subjects who strove with considerable success to carve for themselves areas of partial autonomy within a system designed to exploit their labor, but they were also victims of that system and the power relations that went with it. If the slaves helped make their own world, they nevertheless remained slaves, and the "internal" lives they forged in the quarters operated within the confines of the political, economic, and social hegemony of white slave owners who interfered in the daily lives of their "people" far more intrusively than most masters did elsewhere.

The complexity of this world and of the social relations it engendered is suggested not just in the self-identity of the slaves but also in their judgments—as expressed in subsequent autobiographies and oral interviews—of their owners. Slavery itself they remembered as a barbaric institution, and most had bitter memories of particular injustices they had endured. "I kin tell you things about slavery times dat would make yo' blood bile, but dey's too terrible. I jus' tries to forgit," Amy Chapman told an interviewer. After describing a series of tortures, she abruptly stopped, declaring, "I ain't never tol' nobody all dis an' ain't gwine tell you no mo'." Delia Garlic's memories were equally painful: "Dem days was hell," she recalled bluntly.

But many former slaves tempered their overall condemnation of slavery with fond recollections of particular experiences and sympathetic portrayals of particular owners, and testified to the pervasive nature of slave-owner paternalism. "Slavery did its best to make me wretched," wrote Josiah Henson, "but, along with memories of miry cabins, frosted feet, weary toil under the blazing sun, curses and blows, there flock in others, of jolly Christmas times, dances before old massa's door for the first drink of egg-nog, extra meat at holiday times, midnight-visits to apple-orchards, broiling stray chickens, and first-rate tricks to dodge work." Like numerous other autobiographers, Charles Ball distinguished sharply among his various owners, terming one of three masters he had in Maryland "an unfeeling man" but praising the other two and declaring that "my mistresses, in Maryland, were all good women"; although his Georgia master once gave him a brutal whipping—for no reason except that he had not received one since childhood—Ball recalled that he "really loved" that master; and when he died "I felt that I had lost the only friend I had in the world."

A remarkably common pattern in the recollections of former slaves juxtaposed benign judgments of their *own* masters with harsh denunciations of the cruelties of neighboring slave owners and of slavery in general. Mandy McCullough Cosby of Alabama was typical of many ex-slaves in contrasting her owner, who was "good to his black folks" and rarely resorted to the lash, with other masters: "on some places close to us," she remembered, "they whipped until blood ran down." Lillian Clarke of Virginia told a similar story: although her parents received kind treatment from their owners, the master on the adjoining plantation was "mighty mean to his slaves." The pattern was by no means universal: some ex-slaves had nothing good to say of their masters, and others presented at best mixed portraits. It was widespread enough, however, to be highly significant, as well as to be recognized by a number of ex-slaves themselves, who commented, frequently with some embarrassment, on the vicarious pride that many bondsmen took in the wealth, power, and benevolence of their masters. As Frederick Douglass noted, it was common for slaves to fight over who had the best owner, for "they seemed to think that the greatness of their masters was transferable to themselves."

This juxtaposition of general condemnation of slavery with expressions of affection for particular slaveholders is subject to a variety of interpretations, most of which cannot be explored here. In some cases, blacks who sang the praises of their owners were no doubt protecting themselves against possible trouble: one could never be sure when criticism of a white might be considered rude or uppity, and prudent discretion dictated extreme caution when discussing slavery and slave owners in front of whites. But the pattern is evident in such a broad array of ex-slave testimony, encompassing such a variety of genres—antebellum autobiographies left by fugitives who escaped to the North as well as those written after the Civil War by blacks who remained in the South, narratives dating from the 1860s and those dating from the 1930s, interviews conducted by whites and those conducted by blacks—that it is impossible to attribute it exclusively to dissembling.

Slavery as a system was intrinsically exploitative, brutal, and unjust, and on a general level virtually all slaves detested it and longed for the day when they would be free. On an individual, personal, and day-to-day level, however, many slaves experienced pleasure as well as pain, and had contacts with whites that extended far beyond the exploitation of labor. The American version of this exploitative, brutal, and unjust system developed under conditions that at the same time left the slaves room to develop their own vital but fragile subculture and produced particularly intense, and contradictory, relations between masters and slaves, relations that were marked by affection and intimacy as well as by fear, brute force, and calculation of self-interest.

人 *F U R T H E R   R E A D I N G*

Roger D. Abrahams, *Singing the Master* (1992)

Herbert Aptheker, *American Negro Slave Revolts* (1943)

Ira Berlin, *Slaves Without Masters* (1974)

———, *Many Thousands Gone: The First Two Centuries of Slavery in North America* (1998)

John W. Blassingame, *The Slave Community,* 2nd ed. (1979)

John B. Boles, *Black Southerners, 1619–1869* (1983)

Dickson D. Bruce, Jr., *And They All Sang Hallelujah: Plain-Folk Camp-Meeting Religion, 1800–1845* (1974)

Edward D. C. Campbell, ed., *Before Freedom Came: African-American Life in the Antebellum South* (1991)

Judith Wragg Chase, *Afro-American Art and Craft* (1971)

Janet Cornelius, *"When I Can Read My Title Clear": Literacy, Slavery, and Religion in the Antebellum South* (1991)

Douglas R. Egerton, *Gabriel's Rebellion* (1993)

Dena J. Epstein, *Sinful Tunes and Spirituals* (1977)

Paul D. Escott, *Slavery Remembered: A Record of Twentieth-Century Slave Narratives* (1979)

Robert William Fogel, *Without Consent or Contract: The Rise and Fall of American Slavery* (1989)

Eric Foner, ed., *Nat Turner* (1971)

Eugene D. Genovese, *Roll, Jordon, Roll: The World the Slaves Made* (1974)

Herbert Gutman, *The Black Family in Slavery and Freedom, 1750–1925* (1976)

Michael P. Johnson and James L. Roark, *Black Masters: A Free Family of Color in the Old South* (1984)

Charles Joyner, *Down by the Riverside* (1984)

Peter Kolchin, *American Slavery, 1619–1877* (1993)

Lawrence W. Levine, *Black Culture and Black Consciousness* (1977)

Ann Patton Malone, *Sweet Chariot: Slave Family and Household Structure in Nineteenth Century Louisiana* (1992)

Melton A. McLaurin, *Celia, a Slave* (1991)

Patricia Morton, ed., *Discovering the Women in Slavery: Emancipating Perspectives on the American Past* (1996)

Leslie Howard Owens, *This Species of Property: Slave Life and Culture in the Old South* (1976)

Dylan C. Penningroth, "Slavery, Freedom and Social Claims to Property Among African Americans in Liberty County, Georgia, 1850–1880," *Journal of American History* 84 (1997), 405–435

Albert J. Raboteau, *Slave Religion: The "Invisible Institution" in the Antebellum South* (1978)

George P. Rawick, *From Sundown to Sunup: The Making of the Black Community* (1972)

Todd L. Savitt, *Medicine and Slavery: The Diseases and Health Care of Blacks in Antebellum Virginia* (1978)

Leslie Ann Schwalm, *A Hard Fight for We: Women's Transition from Slavery to Freedom in South Carolina* (1997)

Jon F. Sensbach, *A Separate Canaan: The Making of an Afro-Moravian World in North Carolina, 1763–1840* (1998)

James Sidbury, *Ploughshares into Swords: Race, Rebellion and Identity in Gabriel's Virginia, 1730–1810* (1997)

Julia Floyd Smith, *Slavery and Rice Culture in Lowcountry Georgia, 1750–1860* (1985)

Kenneth M. Stampp, *The Peculiar Institution: Slavery in the Ante-bellum South* (1956)

Robert S. Starobin, *Industrial Slavery in the Old South* (1970)

Brenda Stevenson, *Life in Black and White: Family and Community in the Slave South* (1996)

Sterling Stuckey, *Slave Culture* (1987)

Deborah Gray White, *Ar'n't I a Woman?* (1985)

Betty Wood, *Women's Work, Men's Work: The Informal Slave Economies of Lowcountry Georgia* (1995)

Nonslaveholding Whites

*Although wealthy planters and black slaves figure most prominently in popular im-
ages of the South, nonslaveholding whites formed a larger group than either. In
terms of numbers, they might be considered "typical" southerners in the antebellum
period, since three-quarters of all southern whites in 1860 did not own a single
slave. Their experiences as small farmers and laborers were familiar to almost all
free families in the agrarian South. Historians are endeavoring to learn more about
this large, important group, despite the comparative lack of surviving letters, diaries,
wills, and other manuscript sources of the kind that provide insight into the lives of
wealthier southerners.*

*More than a generation ago, the late historian Frank Lawrence Owsley called
attention to the "plain folk" and pointed out that most of them were land-owning
agriculturalists, often called yeoman farmers. Following his lead, other historians
continue to discover more about their values, culture, goals, attitudes, way of life, and
relationship to both slaves and slaveholding whites. Recent studies explore social and
economic differences within this large group of nonslaveholders. Another important
issue is whether nonslaveholders were subject to planter class dominance or whether
they carved out their own identity and developed distinctive ideas and culture, and to
what extent they influenced political and economic issues in the region.*

D O C U M E N T S

Ferdinand L. Steel was a literate southern yeoman who kept a diary that has survived. The entries in Document 1 describe his daily routine as a small farmer in
Mississippi in the 1830s and 1840s. He worked the land with the help of his brother
Samuel and was deeply religious. The minutes of North Carolina's Mount Zion Baptist Church, which appear in Document 2, illustrate the importance of churches to
the community life of small farmers, white and black. This congregation adjudicated
disputes among its members, punished wrongdoers, and received blacks into its
membership. In Document 3, Hinton Helper expresses his reactions to the elite. Although some southern writers discounted the likelihood of collisions between slaveholders and nonslaveholders, Helper demonstrates the possibility of overt class
conflict. The census record of 1850 from Guilford County, North Carolina,

Document 4, suggests how important population records can be for information on nonslaveholding yeoman farmers. Document 5 is an excerpt from D. R. Hundley's descriptions of yeomen and their attitudes from his 1860 book, *Social Relations in Our Southern States*. Northerners and Europeans found the antebellum South a fascinating area to visit and then describe to readers at home. In Document 6, the first writer describes his travels through Georgia and the rural scenes and accommodations he encountered. The second individual, perhaps the best-known traveler to the region and certainly a keen observer of its people, was Frederick Law Olmsted (who later designed Central Park in New York City).

1. Ferdinand L. Steel's Diary of a Yeoman, 1838–1841

Sunday, June 3d, 1838

Went to Meeting Mr. Fitzgerald preach a fine sermon.

Monday, June 4th, 1838

We run around cotton with both ploughs.

Tuesday, June 5th, 1838

finished running around cotton and commenced to work in corn. Sam'l chopped through cotton. We have been something like a month almost exclusively [in] the cotton. And I find it has hurt our corn very much. I do not think that it is a good plan to depend so much on cotton; it takes up all our time; we can find no time scarcly to do the smallest business. I at this time think that we had better raise corn and let cotton alone. We are to[o] weak handed; we had better raise small grain and corn and let cotton alone; raise corn and keep out of debt and we will have no necessity of raising cotton. Another thing it makes us work to excess as well as do many other things to excess. Look at this by and by.

Monday, September 17, 1838

We went to work on the road; rained very hard. I got very wet. This day is my birthday; this day closes my 25th year. My life is thus prolonged. Bless the Lord, may I set out afresh this coming year to love & serve the Lord more faithfully.

Monday, September 24, 1838

I picked out 107 lbs. Cotton. Sam'l went to mill, returned and picked out some cotton.

Tuesday, September 25, 1838

I picked out 103 lbs. of Cotton. Sam'l picked out 100 lbs. Fine weather.

Wednesday, September 26, 1838

I picked out 105 lbs. of cotton; Sam'l 105.

Thursday, September 27, 1838

We picked out cotton; 106 lbs. each

Excerpts from Ferdinand L. Steel Diary, in the Steel Family Papers, #4504. These documents can be found in the Southern Historical Collection, Wilson Library, The University of North Carolina at Chapel Hill. Reprinted by permission.

Friday, September 28, 1838

    We picked out cotton. S 122 lbs., F. 110.

Saturday, September 29, 1838

    We gathered some corn, about 20 bushels; hauled wood. I went to Grenada & bought 2 pr. of fine shoes. One pair for Mar & the other for myself. Bought also 2 dols worth coffee, $1 worth nails.

Sunday, September 30, 1838

    We had Sunday school & class meeting.

Friday, March 22, 1839

    A few Remarks on my Present manner of life, which will do for me to look at in after days. I arise regularly at 5 o'clock in the morning. After the rest of the family have arisen we have Prayers. I then feed 2 horses and with the assitance of m[y] Brother milk 3 cows. From then to Breakfast I jenerally do some little job about the house. After breakfast I go to my regular work which is cultivating the soil, and work untill 12 o'clock at which time I come into dinner. Rest jennerally 2 hours, during which time I dine, then Pray to God and endeavor to improve my mind by some useful study. At 2 o'clock I again repair to work, and work untill sun down. I then come in, feed horses, milk Cows, and the days work is done. I sup and then I have a few hours for study. At 9 o'clock we have Prayers, and then we all retire to Rest. This is the manner in which my time is spent. My life is one of toil, but blessed be God that it is as well with me as it is. I confess with shame, that when I look ahead, I am prone to give way to anxiety. But I truly desire and humbly Pray that I may be anxious for nothing. I cannot add one cubit to my statu[r]e by taking thought. When I look back on my past life I can see great cause of Gratitude to my heavenly father. He hath hitherto helped me, and I will endeavor hearafter to trust in him.

Wednesday, July 28, 1841

    It is, undoubtedly, the Dryest time of any I have ever seen, Cotton suffering greatly for the want of rain, Corn crops will be cut short, in this neighborhood. What would now be my case, if I had no other Comfort, but that which is derived from the acquisition of Temporal good? It would be a pitiful case. But blessed be God, I am enabled to believe, that he does all things Well, and although I suffer loss in temporal things; I believe my soul prospers, & grows in the love of God.

Wednesday, August 4, 1841

    Our Camp Meeting Commenced, and continued until Tuesday 10th. We had a Blessed Time from the presence of the Lord. The Merciful Giver of all Good, not only blessed us spiritually, But he also Blessed us temporily. During the time, the long needed showers of Rain, were poured out on our thirsty land. A goodly number of Persons proffessed Religion, among which was one Sullivan who was reported to have been the most ungodly man in Yalobusha County. He had (contrary to the Rules of the meeting), brought two bottles of ardent Spirits. After he obtained Religion, on Some of his Companions saying, now he had got Religion [he] give them the liquor. He declared (It is said) I will never touch it again.

2. A Baptist Church Meets in Conference, 1859

The [Baptist] Church of Mt. Zion [in Alamance County, North Carolina] met in Conference on Saturday before the 2nd Sunday in January 1859 and the way opened for Complaints. There being a Difficulty existing betwixt some of the Brethren of this church, on motion the church agreed to apoint a Committee to investigate the Difficulty, the Committee to wit Brother H. Kevitt, Brother Teague, Brother Brothers, and Brother Foster & Brother Burgess to act and make Report at next meeting at this place; the Difficulty between Semour Alred and Enoch Crutchfield about some unmarked hogs which Alred Claims as his which hogs Crutchfield also claims.

The Church of Mt. Zion met in Conference on Saturday before the 2nd Sabath in February. . . . The Committee was Call on to report and the report Rec'd. Brother Crutchfield made satisfactory acknowledgements for what he said on that occation & Brother Alred was laid under Censure of the church until next Church meeting for not Confessing that he had Charged Crutchfield wrongfully.

Committee Report Whereas a serious difficulty exists between Brother Elder Enoch Crutchfield and Semour Alred in regard to some unmarked hogs which the said Crutchfield has in his possession, the said Alred Claiming the same, & We the Committee appointed by the Church By the Request of the parties at the last meeting to [inqu]ire into & investigate the above named Difficulty Proceeded immediately to hear the Claims and examine witnesses for each; & after mature deliberation we the committee unanimously decided that the hogs in Dispute were the property of Enoch Crutchfield and he is inocent of the Charge Confered against him by the said Alred & as the Charge against Brother Enoch Crutchfield has Bin Circulated greatly to his injury as a man & as a Cristian & more particularly a minister of the gospel

We suggest that the church Require Brother Alred to take back the charge against Elder Crutchfield and repent of the wrong done him & repair the injury as much as in his power hath & that the said Crutchfield render unto the Church all nessessary acknowledgements for any thing he has said or done inconsistant with the Christian Character.

The Church of Mt. Zion met in Conference on Saturday before the 2nd Sabath in March. . . . On motion the case of Brother Alred Continued until next church meeting. . . . On motion the church agreed to set apart a Day for the particular Benefit of the Coloured people to be on to morrow. . . . Also the same priviledge for the Coloured people to be Continued indeffinately.

Reprinted by permission of the State of North Carolina Department of Cultural Resources.

The Church of Mt. Zion met in Conference on Saturday before the 2nd Sabath in April. . . . On motion the case of Brother Alred taken up & on motion at his request Continued until next Saturday at Mount Pleasant. . . .

The Church of Mount Zion met at Mount Pleasant on Saturday night before the 3d Sunday in April acording to Previous appointment and on motion the Case of Brother Alred taken up, he being absent, and after some deliberation [he] was Excluded from the fellowship of this Church, for not makeing acknowledgements that he had charged Crutchfield wrongfully, until he gives satisfaction.

The Church of Mt. Zion met in Conference on Saturday before the 2nd Sabath in May. . . . On Sunday after preaching an invitation was given to the Coloured people & Samuel a man of Colour formerly belonged to Enoch Crutchfield Came forward and was Rec'd by Experience & baptised. Also Nathan a man of Colour belonging to Robt Letha Rec'd at a former meeting was baptised as members of our body.

The Church of Mt. Zion met in Conference on Saturday before the 2nd Sunday in June. . . . On Sunday the door of the church was opened for the Reception of Colloured members and James a man of Colour belonging to Dr. B. A. Sellars came forward and Related his Experience and was Rec'd as a Candidate for Baptism to be baptised at next meeting in Course on Sunday at 2 o'clock.

The Church of Mt. Zion met in Conference on Saturday before the 2nd Sunday in July. . . . The Door of the church was opened for the Reception of Member[s] and Sam a man of Coluor Belonging to Wm Patterson Came forward and Related a very good Experience & was Rec'd as a Candidate for baptism to be baptised to morow at 9 o'clock.

3. Hinton Rowan Helper Attacks Slavery, 1857

The causes which have impeded the progress and prosperity of the South, which have dwindled our commerce, and other similar pursuits, into the most contemptible insignificance; sunk a large majority of our people in galling poverty and ignorance, rendered a small minority conceited and tyrannical, and driven the rest away from their homes; entailed upon us a humiliating dependence on the Free States; disgraced us in the recesses of our own souls, and brought us under reproach in the eyes of all civilized and enlightened nations—may all be traced to one common source, and there find solution in the most hateful and horrible word, that was ever incorporated into the vocabulary of human economy—*Slavery!* . . .

The first and most sacred duty of every Southerner, who has the honor and the interest of his country at heart, is to declare himself an unqualified and uncompromising abolitionist. No conditional or half-way declaration will avail; no mere threatening demonstration will succeed. With those who desire to be instrumental

This document can be found in Hinton Rowan Helper, *The Impending Crisis of the South,* (New York: A.A. Burdick, 1860), pp. 25–28, 31–34, and 39–45.

in bringing about the triumph of liberty over slavery, there should be neither evasion vacillation, nor equivocation. We should listen to no modifying terms or compromises that may be proposed by the proprietors of the unprofitable and ungodly
institution. Nothing short of the complete abolition of slavery can save the South
from falling into the vortex of utter ruin. Too long have we yielded a submissive
obedience to the tyrannical domination of an inflated oligarchy; too long have we
tolerated their arrogance and self-conceit; too long have we submitted to their unjust and savage exactions. Let us now wrest from them the sceptre of power, establish liberty and equal rights throughout the land, and henceforth and forever guard
our legislative halls from the pollutions and usurpations of proslavery demagogues. . . .

    . . . It is not so much in its moral and religious aspects that we propose to
discuss the question of slavery, as in its social and political character and influences. To say nothing of the sin and the shame of slavery, we believe it is a most
expensive and unprofitable institution; and if our brethren of the South will but
throw aside their unfounded prejudices and preconceived opinions, and give us a
fair and patient hearing, we feel confident that we can bring them to the same
conclusion. . . .

    . . . Agriculture, it is well known, is the sole boast of the South; and, strange to
say, many pro-slavery Southerners, who, in our latitude, pass for intelligent men,
are so puffed up with the idea of our importance in this respect, that they speak of
the North as a sterile region, unfit for cultivation, and quite dependent on the South
for the necessaries of life! Such rampant ignorance ought to be knocked in the
head? We can prove that the North produces greater quantities of bread-stuffs than
the South! Figures shall show the facts. Properly, the South has nothing left to boast
of; the North has surpassed her in everything, and is going farther and farther ahead
of her every day. . . .

    . . . In the South, unfortunately, no kind of labor is either free or respectable.
Every white man who is under the necessity of earning his bread, by the sweat of
his brow, or by manual labor, in any capacity, no matter how unassuming in deportment, or exemplary in morals, is treated as if he was a loathsome beast, and shunned
with the utmost disdain. His soul may be the very seat of honor and integrity, yet
without slaves—himself a slave—he is accounted as nobody, and would be deemed
intolerably presumptuous, if he dared to open his mouth, even so wide as to give
faint utterance to a three-lettered monosyllable, like yea or nay, in the presence of
an august knight of the whip and the lash. . . .

    . . . Notwithstanding the fact that the white non-slaveholders of the South, are
in the majority, as five to one, they have never yet had any part or lot in framing the
laws under which they live. There is no legislation except for the benefit of slavery,
and slaveholders. As a general rule, poor white persons are regarded with less esteem and attention than negroes, and though the condition of the latter is wretched
beyond description, vast numbers of the former are infinitely worse off. A cunningly devised mockery of freedom is guarantied to them, and that is all. To all in-
tents and purposes they are disfranchised, and outlawed, and the only privilege
extended to them, is a shallow and circumscribed participation in the political
movements that usher slaveholders into office.

We have not breathed away seven and twenty years in the South, without be-coming acquainted with the demagogical manœuverings of the oligarchy. Their intrigues and tricks of legerdemain are as familiar to us as household words; in vain might the world be ransacked for a more precious junto of flatterers and ca-jolers. It is amusing to ignorance, amazing to credulity, and insulting to intelli-gence, to hear them in their blattering efforts to mystify and pervert the sacred principles of liberty, and turn the curse of slavery into a blessing. To the illiterate poor whites—made poor and ignorant by the system of slavery—they hold out the idea that slavery is the very bulwark of our liberties, and the foundation of American independence! For hours at a time, day after day, will they expatiate upon the inexpressible beauties and excellencies of this great, *free* and *independ-ent* nation; and finally, with the most extravagant gesticulations and rhetorical flourishes, conclude their nonsensical ravings, by attributing all the glory and prosperity of the country, from Maine to Texas, and from Georgia to California, to the "invaluable institutions of the South!" With what patience we could com-mand, we have frequently listened to the incoherent and truth-murdering decla-mations of these champions of slavery, and, in the absence of a more politic method of giving vent to our disgust and indignation, have involuntarily bit our lips into blisters.

The lords of the lash are not only absolute masters of the blacks, who are bought and sold, and driven about like so many cattle, but they are also the oracles and arbiters of all non-slaveholding whites, whose freedom is merely nominal, and whose unparalleled illiteracy and degradation is purposely and fiendishly perpetu-ated. How little the "poor white trash," the great majority of the Southern people, know of the real condition of the country is, indeed, sadly astonishing. The truth is, they know nothing of public measures, and little of private affairs, except what their imperious masters, the slave-drivers, condescend to tell, and that is but pre-cious little. . . .

It is expected that the stupid and sequacious masses, the white victims of slavery, will believe, and, as a general thing, they do believe, whatever the slave-holders tell them; and thus it is that they are cajoled into the notion that they are the freest, happiest, and most intelligent people in the world, and are taught to look with prejudice and disapprobation upon every new principle or progressive movement. Thus it is that the South, woefully inert and inventionless, has lagged behind the North, and is now weltering in the cesspool of ignorance and degra-dation.

4. Census Record of Guilford County, North Carolina, 1850

Schedule 1.   Free Inhabitants in *Northern Division* in the County of *Guilford* State of *North Car* enumerated by me, on the *3rd day of Sept 1850*. *Arch Wilson Ass't Marshal.*

1	2	3	DESCRIPTION			7	8	9	10	11	12	13	
DWELLING-HOUSES NUMBERED IN THE ORDER OF VISITATION.	FAMILIES NUMBERED IN THE ORDER OF VISITATION	THE NAME OF EVERY PERSON WHOSE USUAL PLACE OF ABODE ON THE FIRST DAY OF JUNE, 1850, WAS IN THIS FAMILY.	AGE.	SEX.	COLOR (WHITE, BLACK, OR MULATTO).	PROFESSION, OCCUPATION, OR TRADE OF EACH MALE PERSON OVER 15 YEARS OF AGE.	VALUE OF REAL ESTATE OWNED.	PLACE OF BIRTH NAMING THE STATE, TERRITORY, OR COUNTRY.	MARRIED WITHIN THE YEAR.	ATTENDED SCHOOL WITHIN THE YEAR.	PERSONS OVER 20 Y'RS OF AGE WHO CANNOT READ & WRITE.	WHETHER DEAF AND DUMB, BLIND, INSANE, IDIOTIC, PAUPER, OR CONVICT.	
			4	5	6								
728	728	Thomas McMichal	34	M		Blacksmith	100	Guilford NC					1
		Margaret McMichal	22	F				do* NC					2
		James M McMichal	8	M				do NC		✓			3
		William L McMichal	7	M				do NC		✓			4
		Mary J McMichal	4	F				do NC					5
		Sarah McMichal	5/12	F				do NC					6
		George Colman	19	M		B. Smith		do NC					7
		Sarah Colman	21	F				do NC					8
		Adison Smith	15	M				do NC					9
729	729	Vincent P Russum	31	M		Farmer	425	Guilford NC					10
		Margaret Russum	37	F				do NC					11
		Morandy Russum	9	M				Rockingham NC		✓			12

[Continued on next page]

[Continued from previous page]

No.			Name	Age	Sex		Occupation	Value	Birthplace
13			Vincent E Russum	6	M				do NC
14			Wellise Abigal	3	F				do NC
15		730	John T Russum	1	M				Guilford NC
16	730		Branch Gorden	63	M		Farmer	700	Virginia
17			Martha Gorden	24	F				Guilford NC
18			Eunice Gorden	3	F				do NC
19	731	731	Thomas Case	28	M		Farmer	300	Guilford NC
20			Armisted Ellington	21	M				do NC
21	732	732	William Donnell	27	M		Farmer	550	Guilford NC
22			Mary Donnell	25	F				Washington NC
23			Milton Ross	21	M	M	Carpenter		Guilford NC
24	733	733	James Hobbs	50	M		Farmer	300	Guilford NC
25			Anna F Hobbs	44	F				do NC
26			Alfred F Hobbs	27	M				do NC
27			Amanda C Hobbs	19	F				do NC
28			M V Hobbs	21	M		Farming		do NC
29			Olivir T Hobbs	17	M				do NC
30			William T Hobbs	14	M				do NC
31			John W Hobbs	11	M				do NC
32			Emma V. Hobbs	7	F				do NC
33			Edward Hobbs	5	M				do NC
34			Thomas Hobbs	3	M				do NC
35	734	734	Thomas S. Holt	49	M		Black Smith		Orange NC
36			Elizabeth Holt	46	F				Guilford NC
37			Letha M Holt	22	F				do NC
38			Eliza Holt	19	F				do NC
39			Henry Holt	16	M				do NC
40			Sarah Holt	7	F				do NC
41			Thomas Holt	4	M				do NC
42			James Long	16	M		Hireling		do NC

*Ditto.

Source: This document can be found in the U.S. Census of Population, Free Inhabitants, Manuscript Schedules.

5. D. R. Hundley Defends Nonslaveholders, 1860

Of all the hardy sons of toil, in all free lands the Yeomen are most deserving of our esteem. With hearts of oak and thews of steel, crouching to no man and fearing no danger, these are equally bold to handle a musket on the field of battle or to swing their reapers in times of peace among the waving stalks of yellow grain. For, in the language of the poet:

> ———Each boasts his hearth
> And field as free as the best lord his barony,
> Owing subjection to no human vassalage
> Save to their king and law. Hence are they resolute,
> Leading the van on every day of battle,
> As men who know the blessings they defend.
> Hence are they frank and generous in peace,
> As men who have their portion in its plenty.

But you have no Yeomen in the South, my dear Sir? Beg your pardon, our dear Sir, but we have—hosts of them. *I thought you had only poor White Trash?* Yes, we dare say as much—and that the moon is made of green cheese! You have fully as much right or reason to think the one thing as the other. *Do tell, now; want to know?* Is that so, our good friend? do you really desire to learn the truth about this matter? If so, to the extent of our poor ability, we shall endeavor to enlighten you upon a subject, which not one Yankee in ten thousand in the least understands.

Know, then, that the Poor Whites of the South constitute a separate class to themselves; the Southern Yeomen are as distinct from them as the Southern Gentleman is from the Cotton Snob. Certainly the Southern Yeomen are nearly always poor, at least so far as this world's goods are to be taken into the account. As a general thing they own no slaves; and even in case they do, the wealthiest of them rarely possess more than from ten to fifteen. But even when they are slaveholders, they seem to exercise but few of the rights of ownership over their human chattels, making so little distinction between master and man, that their negroes invariably become spoiled, like so many rude children who have been unwisely spared the rod by their foolish guardians. . . .

The Southern Yeoman much resembles in his speech, religious opinions, household arrangements, indoor sports, and family traditions, the middle class farmers of the Northern States. He is fully as intelligent as the latter, and is on the whole much better versed in the lore of politics and the provisions of our Federal and State Constitutions. This is chiefly owing to the public barbecues, court-house-day gatherings, and other holiday occasions, which are more numerous in the South than in the North, and in the former are nearly always devoted in part to political discussions of one kind or another. Heard from the lips of their neighbors and friends, and having the matter impressed upon their minds by the presentation of both sides of every disputed question at the same time, it is not strange that poor men in the South should possess a more comprehensive knowledge of the

This document can be found in D. R. Hundley, *Social Relations in Our Southern States* (New York: Henry B. Price, 1860), pp. 192–194, 198–202, 216–221.

fundamental principles of our artificial and complex system of government, or should retain a clearer perception of the respective merits of every leading political issue, than if they derived their information solely from books or newspapers; which always furnish but one view of the matter in dispute, and which they must painfully peruse after a long day of toil, being more exercised meanwhile (aside from the drawback of physical weariness) in laboring to interpret the meaning of the "dictionary words," than in attempting to follow the facts or the argument of the writer, be he never so lucid and perspicuous. . . .

Besides being given to hospitality, although in a very primitive way, . . . the Yeomen of the South are also quite social and gregarious in their instincts, and delight much in having all kinds of frolics and family gatherings during the long winter evenings. On all such occasions, nearly, something serviceable is the ostensible cause of their assembling, though the time is devoted almost wholly to social pleasures: sometimes, 'tis true, there is a wedding, or a birth-day party, or a candy-pulling; but much more frequently it is a corn-husking, or the everlasting quilting—this last being the most frequent and most in favor of all the merrymakings which call the young people together. There is, indeed, nothing to compare to a country quilting for the simple and unaffected happiness which it affords all parties. The old women and old men sit demurely beside the blazing kitchen fire, and frighten one another with long-winded ghost stories; thus leaving the young folks all to themselves in the "big room," wherein is also the quilt-frame, which is either suspended at the corners by ropes attached to the ceiling, or else rests on the tops of four chairs. Around this assemble the young men and the young maidens, robust with honest toil and honesty ruby-cheeked with genuine good health. . . .

In their religious convictions and practices, the Southern Yeomen very much resemble the Middle Classes; are prone to shout at camp-meetings, and to see visions and dream dreams. Although generally moral in their conduct and punctilious in all religious observances, they do yet often entertain many very absurd ideas in regard to Christianity, ideas wholly at variance with any rational interpretation of the Sacred Scriptures; and hence they are led not infrequently, to mistake animal excitement for holy ecstasy, and seem to think, indeed, with the old-time priests of Baal, that God is not to be entreated save with *loud* prayers, and much beating of the breasts, and clapping of the hands, accompanied with audible groans and sighs. For all which, however, their officiating clergy are more to blame than themselves; for they are often ignorant men of the Whang Doodle description, illiterate and dogmatic, and blessed with a nasal twang which would do no discredit to New-England. . . .

As to the Vital Question of the Day, to make use of the cant phrase so greatly in vogue at the present writing, although not as a class pecuniarily interested in slave property, the Southern Yeomanry are almost unanimously pro-slavery in sentiment. Nor do we see how any honest, thoughtful person can reasonably find fault with them on this account. Only consider their circumstances, negrophilist of the North, and answer truthfully; were you so situated would you dare to advocate emancipation? Were you situated as the Southern Yeomen are—humble in worldly position, patient delvers in the soil, daily earning your bread by the toilsome sweat of your own brows—would you be pleased to see four millions of inferior blacks suddenly raised from a position of vassalage, and placed upon an equality with yourselves?

made the sharers of your toil, the equals and associates of your wives and children? You know you would not. Despite your maudlin affectation of sympathy in behalf of the Negro, you are yet inwardly conscious that you heartily despise the sooty African, and that you deny to even the few living in your own midst an equality of rights and immunities with yourselves. You well know that you entertain a natural repugnance to coming in contact with Sambo—a repugnance so great that you slam your church doors in his face, shut him out of the theatres, refuse him a seat in your public conveyances, and, so fearful are you of the contamination of a black man's presence any where, in nine tenths of your States drive him away from the ballot-box, thus making your statute-books even belie your professions of philanthropy. And yet you seek to turn loose upon your white brethren of the South *four millions of these same despised Africans,* congratulating yourselves meanwhile that you would be doing a most disinterested act of benevolence! Shame on your consistency, gentlemen. Judged by your own acts, were you situated as the Southern people are to-day, stronger pro-slavery men than yourselves would not be found in the world. Hence we ask you again, did you occupy the position of the Southern Yeomanry in particular, is there a man in your midst who would favor emancipation? You know there is not. By the love you owe your race—by all the sacred ties of family and home—by every instinct of a superior nature—you would be restrained from perpetrating so iniquitous an act; an act which would sweep away in one overwhelming flood of anarchy and barbarism every trace of civilization, as well as every semblance of law and order. And do you suppose the Yeomen or our Southern States are not rational and reflecting beings like yourselves? Although not so learned as some others, they yet possess the hearts of men, of fathers and husbands, and they know as well as any political economist of you all, that their own class, in the event of emancipation, would suffer the most of all classes in the South, unless we except the negroes themselves. For the Southern Gentleman would soon convert his property into cash, as did the wealthier planters of Jamaica, and immediately retire to some more congenial soil to enjoy his *otium cum dignitate.* So, too, the thrifty Middle Classes would retire to the present Free States, and begin business in a different line; but the Yeomen would be forced to remain and single-handed do battle with Cuffee, who, no longer forced to labor, and resorting again to toad-eating and cannibalism for the food necessary to sustain life, would in a few years reproduce on the shores of the New World a second Africa, all except the lions and elephants, the sandy deserts, and the anacondas.

6. Travelers' Accounts of Yeoman Life, 1849, 1855

A Southern Traveler Describes Life in the Georgia Mountains, 1849

Mounted on horseback, with coarse leggings and a heavy blanket to protect me from the weather, saddle-bags filled with clothing and provisions, and armed (as is the custom of those who travel in this section of the country) with pistol and bowie-knife, I set off alone to wander for a few days among the mountains of Georgia, filled with high anticipations of a pleasant and novel excursion.

The first day of my journey was mild and pleasant; unusually so, for January. My road lay along a bold ridge, which sloped in some places gently, now abruptly off on either side, leaving me a commanding view of the surrounding country, dull and uninteresting though it was, seeming like an almost interminable forest. Here and there in the distance might be seen the light blue smoke curling gracefully upward from some "settler's cabin," or a denser, gloomier mass, rising from the black and charred trunks of an hundred trees: still farther in the distance, bordering on the horizon's edge and rising in bold relief against the sky, the lofty snow-capped summits of the "Blue Ridge" appear. . . .

Toward evening I overtook a man, who from his dress, a homespun suit, mud-color, and a broad-brimmed wool hat, I took to be a "native." We jogged along together, and in half an hour I knew him well: with the frankness and confidence of a southerner, he had, unasked, told me his whole history. He frankly acknowledged that he could neither read nor write; which by the way is no uncommon thing in Georgia, even among people of considerable wealth. And his greatest pride seemed to be his "faculty for a horse swap": in this he considered himself *par excellence,* to use his own expression, "right smart." Yes, and he strode a "right smart chance of a critter," that couldn't be beat in "them diggins," if you'd believe him.

Having ridden ninety miles, over an exceedingly rough road, and through a monotonous country, stopping the first night in Gainsville, the second in Clarksville, I arrived on the morning of the third day at Toccoa Falls, twelve miles from Clarksville.

I lingered here long after the sun had departed, till the mountains were obscured by the thickening shades of evening, and then hastened on to find lodgings for the night. A ride of a mile brought me to a log-cabin, the only house near the falls. . . .

After partaking heartily of a venison supper (which no one can cook superior to Mrs. Beale), and drinking a gourd of water, feeling fatigued by the day's exposure, I asked where I was to sleep. They led me into an unoccupied part of the house, and up into the second loft, reached only by a ladder. I did not like its open-work looks, for the night was bitter cold, but as my only alternative was this or nothing, I wrapped myself up in my blanket, piled the bed-clothes over me a foot high, and tried to find the soft side of a corn-shuck mattress.

Lulled by the roar of the distant cataract, I strove to sleep, but strove in vain. I tried to forget my woes by counting the stars which glistened through the many cracks in the roof; but through those same cracks the wind, cold and chilling, came whistling through two holes, cut to let in the light, in which there was no sign of glass. Shivering, shaking, was my song during the whole long night, and happy was I when morning dawned.

It was morning when I left Tallula, and before nightfall I had ridden thirty miles. No pleasant villages, with neat white cottages and ornamented gardens, so many of which one sees in a day's ride through New-England, greeted my vision; but the log-cabins of the "squatters" scattered here and there, with an occasional frame-house of the rudest construction, were seen.

I met no one walking: all ride, however poor. Sometimes two are seen on the same animal; a man and woman, perhaps, on one poor doleful-looking mule, or on some antiquated horse, more cadaverous looking than themselves. I met also large wagons, canvass covered, drawn by four or six mules, and driven by negroes. As night approached, I saw the camp-fires of these drivers, they sitting about the fire, on the ground, cooking "hog and hominy," cracking rude jokes, singing "corn songs" and laughing their loud "Yah! yah!" as the whiskey-bottle passed among them.

Being anxious to see how the poorest class of people lived in the interior, at night I stopped at the door-way of a very small and rudely-constructed hut, and inquired if I could "get stay" for the night. At first I was refused; but upon representing myself a stranger in the country, and fearing to go farther, as there were "forks in the road" and "creeks to cross" before reaching another house, they finally consented to my staying.

The cabin contained but one room, with no windows; the chimney, built of mud and stones, was, as is usual in the South, outside the house. The furniture of the house was scanty in the extreme; a roughly-constructed frame, on which was laid a corn-shuck mattress, a pine table, and a few shuck-bottomed "cha'rs."

I had not been long in this place, before preparations for supper commenced. An iron vessel—a "spider," so called—was brought and set over the fire; in this dish was roasted some coffee; afterward, in the same dish, a "corn cake" was baked, and still again some rank old ham was fried, and the corn-cake laid in the ashes to have it "piping hot." This constituted our supper, which, being placed on the table, three of us sat down to partake, of, while Cynthia, the youngest daughter, held a blazing light-wood knot for us to see by, and the "gude woman" sat in the corner "rubbing snuff," or "dipping," with her infant in her arms. A pet deer stalked in through the open door-way, and helped himself from the table without molestation.

Bed-time coming, one by one the family retired to the corner, and all lay together on the corn-shucks, sleeping as soundly as on "downy couch." Taking my saddle-bags for a pillow, and wrapping my blanket around me, I laid down before the fast dying embers, and was soon in the embrace of "tired nature's sweet restorer." Morning came, and as I was to leave early, all were up "by sun." I asked the hostess for a wash, and the vessel which had served for roasting, baking and frying in the evening previous was now brought; and, "'tis true, 'tis pity, and pity 'tis 'tis true," I washed myself in the dish out of which twelve hours before I had eaten a hearty supper. I paid them well, and thanked them kindly, for they had given me the best they had. Destitute as they were, they seemed contented and happy: "Where ignorance is bliss, 'tis folly to be wise."

Frederick Law Olmsted Observes Life in the Cotton Kingdom, 1855

Fayetteville.—The negroes employed in the turpentine business, to which during the last week I have been giving some examination, seem to me to be unusually intelligent and cheerful, decidedly more so than most of the white people inhabiting

From *The Cotton Kingdom* by Frederick Law Olmsted, edited by Arthur M. Schlesinger, Sr. (New York: Modern Library, 1984).

the turpentine forest. Among the latter there is a large number, I should think a majority, of entirely uneducated, poverty-stricken vagabonds. I mean by vagabonds, simply, people without habitual, definite occupation or reliable means of livelihood. They are poor, having almost no property but their own bodies; and the use of these, that is, their labour, they are not accustomed to hire out statedly and regularly, so as to obtain capital by wages, but only occasionally by the day or job, when driven to it by necessity. A family of these people will commonly hire, or "squat" and build, a little log cabin, so made that it is only a shelter from rain, the sides not being chinked, and having no more furniture or pretension to comfort than is commonly provided a criminal in the cell of a prison. They will cultivate a little corn, and possibly a few roods of potatoes, cow-peas, and coleworts. They will own a few swine, that find their living in the forest; and pretty certainly, also, a rifle and dogs; and the men, ostensibly, occupy most of their time in hunting. I am, mainly, repeating the statements of one of the turpentine distillers, but it was confirmed by others, and by my own observation, so far as it went.

A gentleman of Fayetteville told me that he had, several times, appraised, under oath, the whole household property of families of this class at less than $20. If they have need of money to purchase clothing, etc., they obtain it by selling their game or meal. If they have none of this to spare, or an insufficiency, they will work for a neighbouring farmer for a few days, and they usually get for their labour fifty cents a day, *finding themselves*. The farmers and distillers say, that that they do not like to employ them, because they cannot be relied upon to finish what they undertake, or to work according to directions; and because, being white men, they cannot "drive" them. That is to say, their labour is even more inefficient and unmanageable than that of slaves. . . .

At Columbus, I spent several days. It is the largest manufacturing town, south of Richmond, in the Slave States. It is situated at the Falls, and the head of steamboat navigation of the Chattahoochee, the western boundary of Georgia. The water-power is sufficient to drive two hundred thousand spindles, with a proportionate number of looms. There are, probably, at present from fifteen to twenty thousand spindles running. The operatives in the cotton-mills are said to be mainly "Cracker girls" (poor whites from the country), who earn, in good times, by piece-work, from $8 to $12 a month. There are, besides the cotton-mills, one woollen-mill, one paper-mill, a foundry, a cotton-gin factory, a machine-shop, etc. The labourers in all these are mainly whites, and they are in such a condition that, if temporarily thrown out of employment, great numbers of them are at once reduced to a state of destitution, and are dependent upon credit or charity for their daily food. Public entertainments were being held at the time of my visit, the profits to be applied to the relief of operatives in mills which had been stopped by the effects of a late flood of the river. Yet Slavery is constantly boasted to be a perfect safeguard against such distress. . . .

. . . The next house at which I arrived was one of the commonest sort of cabins. I had passed twenty like it during the day, and I thought I would take the opportunity to get an interior knowledge of them. The fact that a horse and waggon were kept, and that a considerable area of land in the rear of the cabin was planted with cotton, showed that the family were by no means of the lowest class, yet, as they were not able even to hire a slave, they may be considered to represent very favourably, I believe, the condition of the poor whites of the plantation districts. The whites of the country, I observe, by the census, are three to one of the slaves; in the nearest adjoining county, the proportion is reversed; and within a few miles the soil was richer, and large plantations occurred. . . .

The house was all comprised in a single room, twenty-eight by twenty-five feet in area, and open to the roof above. There was a large fireplace at one end and a door on each side—no windows at all. Two bedsteads, a spinning-wheel, a packing-case, which served as a bureau, a cupboard, made of rough hewn slabs, two or three deer-skin seated chairs, a Connecticut clock, and a large poster of Jayne's patent medicines, constituted all the visible furniture, either useful or ornamental in purpose. A little girl, immediately, without having had any directions to do so, got a frying-pan and a chunk of bacon from the cupboard, and cutting slices from the latter, set it frying for my supper. The woman of the house sat sulkily in a chair tilted back and leaning against the logs, spitting occasionally at the fire, but took no notice of me, barely nodding when I saluted her. A baby lay crying on the floor. I quieted it and amused it with my watch till the little girl, having made "coffee" and put a piece of corn-bread on the table with the bacon, took charge of it.

I hoped the woman was not very ill.

"Got the headache right bad," she answered. "Have the headache a heap, I do. Knew I should have it to-night. Been cuttin' brush in the cotton this arternoon. Knew't would bring on my headache. Told him so when I begun."

As soon as I had finished my supper and fed Jude, the little girl put the fragments and the dishes in the cupboard, shoved the table into a corner, and dragged a quantity of quilts from one of the bedsteads, which she spread upon the floor, and presently crawled among them out of sight for the night. The woman picked up the child—which, though still a suckling, she said was twenty-two months old—and nursed it, retaking her old position. The man sat with me by the fire, his back towards her. The baby having fallen asleep was laid away somewhere, and the woman dragged off another lot of quilts from the beds, spreading them upon the floor. Then taking a deep tin pan, she filled it with alternate layers of corn-cobs and hot embers from the fire. This she placed upon a large block, which was evidently used habitually for the purpose, in the centre of the cabin. A furious smoke arose from it, and we soon began to cough. "Most *too* much smoke," observed the man. "Hope 'twill drive out all the gnats, then," replied the woman. (There is a very minute flying insect here, the bite of which is excessively sharp.)

The woman suddenly dropped off her outer garment and stepped from the midst of its folds, in her petticoat; then, taking the baby from the place where she had deposited it, lay down and covered herself with the quilts upon the floor. The man told me that I could take the bed which remained on one of the bedsteads, and kicking off his shoes only, rolled himself into a blanket by the side of his wife. I ventured to take off my cravat and stockings, as well as my boots, but almost immediately put my stockings on again, drawing their tops over my pantaloons. The advantage of this arrangement was that, although my face, eyes, ears, neck, and hands, were immediately attacked, the vermin did not reach my legs for two or three hours. Just after the clock struck two, I distinctly heard the man and the woman, and the girl and the dog scratching, and the horse out in the shed stamping and gnawing himself. Soon afterward the man exclaimed, "Good God Almighty—mighty! mighty! mighty!" and jumping up pulled off one of his stockings, shook it, scratched his foot vehemently, put on the stocking, and lay down again with a groan. The two doors were open, and through the logs and the openings in the roof, I saw the clouds divide and the moon and stars reveal themselves. The woman, after having been nearly smothered by the smoke from the pan which she had originally placed close to her own pillow, rose and placed it on the sill of the windward door, where it burned feebly and smoked lustily, like an altar to the Lares, all night. Fortunately the cabin was so open that it gave us little annoyance, while it seemed to answer the purpose of keeping all flying insects at a distance. . . .

June 17th.—The country continues hilly, and is well populated by farmers, living in log huts, while every mile or two, on the more level and fertile land, there is a larger farm, with ten or twenty negroes at work. A few whites are usually working near them, in the same field, generally ploughing while the negroes hoe.

About noon, my attention was attracted towards a person upon a ledge, a little above the road, who was throwing up earth and stone with a shovel. I stopped to see what the purpose of this work might be, and perceived that the shoveller was a woman, who, presently discovering me, stopped and called to others behind her, and immediately a stout girl and two younger children, with a man, came to the edge and looked at me. The woman was bareheaded, and otherwise half-naked, as perhaps needed to be, for her work would have been thought hard by our stoutest labourers, and it was the hottest weather of the summer, in the latitude of Charleston, and on a hill-side in the full face of the noon sun. I pushed my horse up the hill until I reached them, when another man appeared, and in answer to my inquiries told me that they were getting out iron ore. One was picking in a vein, having excavated a short adit; the other man picked looser ore exterior to the vein. The women and children shovelled out the ore and piled it on kilns of timber, where they roasted it to make it crumble. It was then carted to a forge, and they were paid for it by the load. They were all clothed very meanly and scantily. The women worked, so far as I could see, as hard as the men. The children, too, even to the youngest—a boy of eight or ten—were carrying large lumps of ore, and heaving them into the kiln, and shovelling the finer into a screen to separate the earth from it.

✝ E S S A Y S

Both essays focus on the North Carolina Piedmont and its large population of nonslave-holding whites. Charles Bolton, a historian at the University of Southern Mississippi, in a selection from his book *Poor Whites in the Antebellum South,* focuses on landless whites, distinguishing them from yeomen farmers. He describes their difficult existence and the prevalence of tenancy in antebellum North Carolina, a labor situation that scholars often wrongly associate solely with the postbellum South. Acquiring land was usually beyond the means of poor whites, even as more prosperous yeomen farmers began to expand production and take advantage of commercial markets. Victoria Bynum, a professor of history at Southwest Texas State University, in her book *Unruly Women,* explores the lives of poor white women, especially those who were defiant or sexually deviant, or who lived on the margins of society. Because they ignored sexual and social taboos (occasionally crossing racial lines) and were often neither wives nor slaves, courts intervened to apprentice their children, using the system to ensure that youngsters lived productive lives and were not dependent on the state. While most poor women in the South were neither deviant nor unruly, they struggled to survive and existed under a system that generally punished their sexual transgressions more harshly than those of white men.

Edward Isham and the World of Poor Whites

CHARLES BOLTON

Poor whites of the antebellum South are generally invisible beyond the kind of records that consist essentially of numbers—census and tax records. Very little evidence survives, in other words, from which to build a portrait of human beings. Many of the clues we do have are encased in what is essentially a negative context—court records, ejectment proceedings, and records of insolvent debtors. But by searching through such material, we can begin to peer into this unchartered world and gain certain substantive insights into the kinds of daily lives that hundreds of thousands of southern whites lived in the days before the Civil War.

For example, a poor white man named Edward Isham became historically visible because he was hotheaded, sexually promiscuous, and frequently ran afoul of the law. After Isham was charged with murder in Catawba County, North Carolina, in 1859, the court appointed a young lawyer named David Schenck as Isham's defense counsel. Sometime before Isham was executed in May 1860, Schenck recorded the life story of Edward Isham in lengthy detail. The Schenck biography allows us to glimpse, despite the often atypical behavior of its protagonist, the social relations of the southern poor.

Edward "Hardaway Bone" Isham was born in the late 1820s in Jackson County, Georgia. During the 1830s his father lost the small tract of land he owned and moved the family to Pinetown in Carroll County, Georgia. There, his father labored primarily as a landless miner. During Isham's childhood, his parents separated, and he grew up in a house with his father and his father's common-law wife. Limited educational opportunities existed in the Pinetown area, and Isham attended school for a total of five days. Religion did not flourish in his hometown either. He recalled that during his childhood "no preacher could ever live or preach in Pine town, one lived there once and they tore down his fences and run him off."

Throughout his life, Edward Isham moved frequently because of a need to search for work and also to avoid punishment for a series of petty escapades, almost invariably concerning fighting. His initial scrape with the law came in Carroll County in the mid-1840s when he apparently attacked a man in front of a justice of the peace as the victim sought a warrant for an earlier assault perpetrated by Isham. The justice arrested Isham, but he escaped jail and fled to his uncle's house in De Kalb County, Georgia. There, he joined the Methodist church, but the congregation soon dismissed him for fighting with a slave member. Isham then moved to Forsyth County, Georgia, to labor in that county's gold mines. While he was working on the public roads there, the local authorities charged him with stealing some milk and then assaulting his accuser. To avoid prosecution, Isham fled the county.

Occasionally, Isham traveled to Macon County, Alabama, to visit one of his brothers. During one of these trips, he became romantically involved with a married woman, and she eventually returned to Pinetown with him, where the two of them soon married. Shortly after the wedding, Isham left his new wife in Carroll County with his mother while he went off to look for work. He journeyed to Walker County, Georgia, where he worked splitting rails and farming as a tenant, but he had to forfeit his crop because of legal troubles resulting from a fight. From there, Isham proceeded to Chattanooga, where he worked on the railroad, but he soon "got into a difficulty with some Irishmen boat hands about some lewd woman" and had to leave that job. Finally, before returning to Georgia, Isham labored for a time as a fireman on a boat on the Tennessee River. When he returned to Walker County, he found that his wife had not successfully endured his long absence alone, and he promptly became embroiled in a fight with his wife's lover. With several outstanding arrest warrants issued against him, Isham continued to roam around the up-country and mountains of Georgia working at various jobs, although he periodically returned for short stays in the Pinetown neighborhood.

In late 1850 Isham took a job driving a herd of cattle from Pinetown to Montgomery, Alabama. After completing this task, he went to Macon County, Alabama, where, together with his brother, he "built a little shantie on the river and rafted lightwood to Montgomery." This little foothold, however, soon vanished. Isham became enmeshed in a love affair with his sister-in-law and found it expedient to leave town. He ended up back in Pinetown, where he married another woman, apparently without formally divorcing his previous wife. After he worked for several months in the Carroll County mines and made some money, Isham's troubles began again when he became romantically involved with a free black woman. This relationship and more fighting led to the issuance of additional warrants for his arrest. A group of men eventually captured him, but he broke out of jail and escaped to his mother's house in Chattanooga, where she had recently moved and "sold cakes and whiskey and boarded work hands for a living."

In Chattanooga, Isham met a woman of some means, and the pair traveled to Atlanta by train. After stealing money from this woman, Isham returned once again to his second wife in Carroll County. He worked steadily for about six months in the mines and on the railroad, but he eventually quit and started gambling with another man along the railroad line. The two men and their wives soon decided to go west. Settling in Johnson County, Arkansas, but unable to purchase land, Isham worked at splitting rails, hunting deer, and collecting bees.

Before long, Isham became involved in another fight that attracted the attention of the law, and he decided to leave Arkansas and his second wife and return to Macon County, Alabama. During this stay in Macon County, he and two of his brothers cut timber and formed "a company to fish and gamble." The enterprise, however, was soon dissolved because of frequent disputes. After this setback, Isham wandered through north Alabama, northwest Georgia, east Tennessee, and western

North Carolina, working at a number of different tasks for various individuals, including one stint for a free black farmer in Tennessee.

In the late 1850s, Isham married for a third time. His new wife was the daughter of a man who had hired Isham to dig a well near the town of Statesville in Iredell County, North Carolina. Perhaps with help from his new father-in-law, Isham bought his first piece of land—a plot of ten acres. He promptly and successfully set about making a crop, but an Iredell County grand jury soon indicted him for fighting at the election, and Isham fled the area, leaving behind his new bride, his land, and his growing crop.

Isham spent the last months of his life performing odd jobs around the foothills of North Carolina, occasionally taking time out for socializing. For instance, he spent a week or more "gambling with some white men and free negroes" near Taylorsville, North Carolina. He performed his last job in Catawba County, North Carolina, where he stopped to dig some ditches for James Cornelius, a slaveowner. When Cornelius failed to pay Isham for the job, he filed suit, seeking $7, but the jury only awarded him $5. Unfortunately, this did not end the affair. Cornelius had the judgment stayed, and a few days later, he was murdered. The evidence overwhelmingly pointed toward Isham as the murderer, and a jury eventually convicted him of the crime. On May 25, 1860, Edward Isham died on the gallows.

Ten years earlier, in the summer of 1850, a federal census enumerator had listed Edward Isham—the head of household number 1137 in Carroll County, Georgia—as a twenty-three-year-old, illiterate, landless miner. Most of Isham's immediate neighbors shared the poverty of the Isham household. Of the thirty surrounding households, only four owned any real property. Landless farmers, laborers, and miners headed most of the nearby households, and almost 60 percent of the men and women who headed these households could not read or write.

Applying the descriptive appellation "poor white" to Edward Isham and his landless Pinetown neighbors is problematic. Over the years, the term has acquired a discernible amount of negative baggage. In current southern usage, the phrase "poor white" means a person with little or no property who also has low social standing because of certain negative attributes: laziness, shiftlessness, and irresponsibility. By this definition, Isham might fall into the category of poor whites, but without further evidence, the label probably would be inappropriate to describe his landless neighbors.

The practice of making distinctions between different kinds of impoverished white southerners has deep roots. During the antebellum period, southerners differentiated between whites who were poor and "poor whites" or, even more descriptively, "poor white trash." Antebellum southerners seem to have separated the two groups on the basis of geography and culture. D. R. Hundley, a southern slaveholder writing about southern social classes in 1860, claimed that poor whites were those who lived in distinct, isolated settlements in the mountains, hills, pine barrens, and sandhills but not in his own plantation district. According to Hundley, poor whites did little farming; they survived primarily by hunting and fishing. Hundley described "the poor whites" as illiterate, superstitious, and, above all, lazy and perpetually drunk. According to Hundley's depiction of southern social groups, the only "degraded" or "poor white" southerners were those who chose to go off and live by themselves because they did not want to work and because they had habits at odds with respectable southern society, which they could more freely practice in isolation. For Hundley, the white property that existed in the antebellum South resulted from voluntary choices made by people already beyond the pale of respectable southern society.

While even some contemporary observers may have considered Hundley's portrait overdrawn, it served as a useful description to southerners at the time because it maintained that the slave system of the South had not impoverished whites. In part, Hundley's analysis of southern social classes was in response to assertions by northern travelers and abolitionists that an economy dependent on black slavery reduced all nonslaveholders to a position of permanent poverty and to subjugation by a class of aristocratic slaveowners.

Clearly, the question of poverty in the South, as in the nation at large, was often approached in a partisan manner that obscured more than it revealed. Twentieth-century historians have labored with some success to shed new light on the subject. Beginning with Frank Lawrence Owsley, historians of the antebellum South have shown that slavery did not impoverish all white nonslaveholders and that nonslaveholding yeomen who owned their own farms comprised the largest group of white people living and working in the antebellum South. Among others, Steven Hahn, J. William Harris, and Lacy K. Ford had recently expanded and enriched Owsley's conclusion that the nonslaveholding yeomanry of the antebellum South played an important role in the region. . . .

"A Third Class of White People": Poor Whites in North Carolina's Central Piedmont

For the poor whites of antebellum North Carolina's central Piedmont, economic success, especially the acquisition of land, remained elusive. The existence of black slavery, the increasing commercialization of agriculture, and the often harsh operations of a credit-based economy all worked to limit the economic opportunities of the region's landless white population. Even so, central Piedmont poor whites carved out their own viable niche in the area economy. They worked as a casual labor force in a wide variety of jobs and farmed as tenants on the surplus land of their neighbors. By relying on assistance from their families and by utilizing the common rights of property, poor whites managed to survive despite their generally bleak economic prospects.

On the eve of the Civil War, the central Piedmont region of North Carolina was a white-majority district. None of the fourteen counties in the area had a black slave population that exceeded one-third of the total population; six of the counties had slave populations of less than 20 percent (see figure 1). Few whites owned slaves, some 15 to 20 percent of the region's white farmers falling into this category. Among the remaining population of nonslaveholders, most were yeoman farmers. These agriculturalists worked their own land and relied on family labor and primarily local networks of exchange to maintain and reproduce largely self-sufficient households. While the numerous nonslaveholding yeoman farms in the area could not match the wealth generated by the scattered slaveholding plantations, landownership and the practice of semisubsistence agriculture guaranteed a large measure of security and independence for the leaders of the central Piedmont's yeoman households (see table 1).

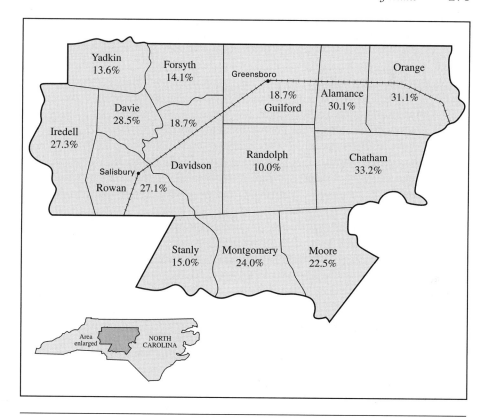

Figure 1.   Slave population of North Carolina's central Piedmont, 1860.

Table 1.   Free Households in the Agricultural Population of the Central Piedmont, North Carolina, 1850 and 1860

	DAVIDSON CO.		RANDOLPH CO.	
	1850	1860	1850	1860
Landless:				
Landless farmers without slaves	15%	13%	26%	13%
Landless farmers with slaves	3	1	2	0
Laborers	11	12	16	16
Overseers	2	0	0	1
Total	31	26	44	30
Yeomen without slaves	51	53	45	56
Yeomen with slaves	18	19	10	13
Wealthy farmers	1	2	1	2
% of population engaged in agriculture	79	82	86	79

Source: Samples from the 1850 and 1860 Federal Censuses for Davidson and Randolph counties, Schedules I (Population), II (Slave), and IV (Agriculture).
Note: Free blacks headed approximately 5 percent of the free households in these two counties during the 1850s. Numbers in this and subsequent tables have been rounded off.

In addition to slaveholders and yeomen, the central Piedmont was also home to a sizable number of poor whites, remembered by the son of an Iredell County slaveowner as "a third class of white people, such as depended on there [*sic*] day labour." In 1860, landless farmers and laborers headed from 26 to 30 percent of the area's agricultural households (see table 1). In addition, over 60 percent of the small group of nonagricultural households in the region—primarily headed by women and artisans—did not own land. All told, landless whites headed from 30 to 40 percent of the free households in the central Piedmont in 1860.

Although no formal, rigid social barriers separated slaveholders from non-slaveholders or the landless from the landed, few of the landless tenants, landless laborers, and other poor whites living in the central Piedmont during the 1850s stood on the verge of prosperity or even landownership. While many poor white families left the area every year between 1840 and 1860, looking for economic success at various locales further west, many of those who stayed remained permanently mired in poverty. Upward economic mobility for the landless whites of the central Piedmont sometimes proved difficult during the 1840s, but the situation apparently worsened during the next decade. By the 1850s, even greater numbers of poor whites were leaving the area. But those householders without land who stayed in the central Piedmont during the decade before the Civil War faced a significantly greater chance of remaining landless than of acquiring real property. . . .

By the 1850s, tenancy in the central Piedmont was not merely a temporary stage for younger sons or a stepping stone to landownership; rather, renting was a permanent way of life for many area farmers. . . .

Several factors coalesced to create this permanently impoverished white class in the central Piedmont. The existence of black slavery played a major role in perpetuating white poverty by limiting the development of industrial wage jobs and curbing the need for white farm labor—typical avenues of employment and advancement for landless whites in the antebellum North and Midwest. The presence of a permanent poor white class in the region also sprang from early manifestations of two developments that would lead to the impoverishment of millions of southerners in the postbellum countryside: the commercialization of agriculture and an oppressive credit system. In the central Piedmont during the 1850s, agricultural production moved toward more marketable crops, and for increasing numbers of landless people this change helped foreclose the possibility of a life of yeoman independence. At the same time, the vicious cycles of debt and credit that ensnared millions of postbellum whites and blacks in poverty also limited the chances of the antebellum poor to improve their lives.

Although the institution of slavery in the antebellum South reduced the number of employment opportunities for poor whites, they were not excluded from either the economy of the central Piedmont in particular or white-majority areas of the South in general. They essentially served as a mobile work force that filled the temporary labor needs of prosperous yeomen and slaveowners. In short, poor whites in the central Piedmont found a number of both agricultural and nonagricultural wage positions available on a sporadic basis.

During the busy planting and harvesting seasons, slaveholders, though relatively few in number in the central Piedmont, often hired white farm labor to augment slave work forces. At such times, poor white laborers worked side by side with black slaves in the fields of area farms. Elias Thomas, a former slave from Chatham County, recalled that his master, who owned more than ten slaves, "hired both men and women of the poor white class to work on the plantation. We all worked together. We had a good time. We worked and sang together and everybody seemed happy. In harvest time, a lot of help was hired."

In ways that pointed to intriguing social and economic dynamics between the races, slaveholders might also hire white farm labor to replace slave labor that could be employed more profitably elsewhere. For example, Calvin Wooley of Montgomery County, who owned one slave named Dick, hired two white farm laborers in 1840 to help him make his crop of corn, cotton, and wheat so that Dick could work in a blacksmith shop where "he can make much more than the wages I have to give for a hand.". . .

Like slaveholding farmers, nonslaveholding yeomen with large farms sometimes needed and could afford the expense of hired white farm labor. For example, in western Randolph County in 1860, twenty-three households headed by landless farm laborers clustered around five large farms where only one slave worked. Each establishment had improved land of 100 acres or more. The large enclave of landless white laborers surrounding these farms probably provided the additional labor needed to work such sizable yeoman operations. Another indication of who employed white farm laborers is the fact that among the farm laborers boarding with their employers in the central Piedmont, more than 75 percent lived either with slaveholders or yeomen owning more than fifty improved acres.

Some nonagricultural wage opportunities for white labor also existed in the central Piedmont. An Orange County promoter claimed in 1853 that there was no place "where there is a better chance for the poor man than here." He listed numerous possible places of employment for poor whites: gold, copper, and lead mines; the railroad; plank roads; river navigation; and the turpentine and lumber business. Much like white farm laborers, however, white workers performing nonfarm work faced continual competition from slave labor. For instance, the owners of the Silver Hill mine in Davidson County replaced white miners with slave labor in the late 1850s. In 1857 the mine owners apparently stopped employing white labor while, at the same time, they began to spend large sums of money to hire black slaves. In its report of 1860, the company noted the new addition of "negro quarters," an indication of their desire to rely regularly on rented slave labor. Likewise, future governor Jonathan Worth of Randolph County, citing the need to reduce costs, replaced part of the white labor force at his Cumberland County turpentine operation with slave labor in 1855. . . .

. . . Changes in agricultural production during the 1850s in the central Piedmont did not represent a wholesale embrace of market agriculture by the area's landed farmers. Rather, the region's yeomanry took halting and uneven steps to benefit from the improved transportation links established in the 1850s. More yeomen began to grow wheat, selling the surplus to distant markets; some even ventured into the world of cash-crop agriculture. Yeoman farmers tested the new opportunities available for selling market surpluses while maintaining their strong commitment of a farming policy that focused on raising food for household consumption first. . . .

Although generally associated with the postbellum South, tenancy had a long pre-war history. Underlying this circumstance was the remarkable fact that widespread tenancy coexisted with the availability of "free" land. Although tracts of govern-ment land in the central Piedmont remained unclaimed throughout the antebellum period, by the 1830s most of the acreage taken up by state grant consisted of small tracts acquired by landowners to increase their existing holdings. Few landless peo-ple got land through state grants. Between 1832 and 1835, only 18 percent of the land grants issued to people in the central Piedmont went to landless men and women; between 1850 and 1852, landless people in the central Piedmont claimed only 27 percent of the grants.

Either a lack of funds—North Carolina charged 10 cents per acre for state-granted land—or the inability to fulfill the formal requirements for legal entries prevented landless whites from obtaining title to the available state land. A Ten-nessee man explained that a poor man could not get land there "unless it was handed to him by His ancester. [State] land at that time had to be entered and The poor young men could not get the money." Or in the words of another landless Tennessean: "They could have entered land but they had to go to Nashville to pay entry fees and for this reason poor people took leases and never did have anything a head." As in Tennessee, even minor obstacles, such as small fees and other mod-est legal requirements, barred many poor whites from acquiring state land in North Carolina.

Some landless farmers tried squatting on unclaimed or unoccupied land, but by the early nineteenth century the central Piedmont had become a settled region, and squatting became difficult except in the most remote areas. Besides, squatting always offered a precarious alternative to landownership since the appearance of a legal owner meant ejection. An absentee owner of Moore County lands in-structed his agent in 1831 to tell John McKennel "that I intend to make him pay one dollar pr day for every day he stays on the land for trespass or damages unless he pays legal rent to you." In 1853, when John McDuffie entered a state land grant in Moore County, he found a man living there working turpentine from the pine forest. McDuffie quickly sought a surveyor to make the grant legal, thus al-lowing him to remove the squatter. In 1850 on surveying his new lands in Ran-dolph County Samuel Means discovered that John Elder had long been a squatter, "having a field of some 10 acres . . . which he has been cultivating for several years." Elder, aged forty-three and landless, faced the prospect of either being sued for trespass or reaching an agreement with Means on future tenancy arrange-ments.

By the 1850s, most landless farmers in the central Piedmont lived and worked at tenants, not squatters. No accurate information exists about the extent of tenancy in the region before 1850, but the manuscript censuses for 1850 and 1860 provide an estimate for the decade before the Civil War. Data from this source suggest that as many as 25 percent of farmers in the central Piedmont worked as tenants during the 1850s (see table 1).

While some individuals paid cash rent for farms, most tenants in the area farmed under share-tenancy agreements. Under this arrangement, lessees paid a share of the crop as their rent, the proportion usually ranging from one-fourth to one-third of the amount produced. When Ephraim Brattain of Davidson County rented a farm in 1854, he agreed "to pay 1/3 of the crops." Likewise, forty-five-year-old John Redding, Jr., of Randolph County had a share-rental agreement on a forty-acre farm in 1859, twenty acres in wheat and twenty acres in oats. Redding paid rent in the amount of one-third of each crop. Given the lack of cash in the southern economy, share renting probably represented the most common form of tenancy arrangement throughout the region. For instance, the 1850 census enumerator for Smith County, Mississippi, identified two types of tenants in his county, but he claimed the larger of the two groups were "cultivators on shares not renters.". . .

Nevertheless, antebellum tenancy, like its postbellum counterpart, cannot be said to have provided either the security or the independence that yeomen enjoyed. For one thing, antebellum tenants lived on impoverished homesteads; they possessed few farm implements and only a small number of farm animals. In fact, rented farms in Davidson and Randolph counties in 1850 controlled less than half as much equipment and livestock as the nonslaveholding yeoman farms in those counties. . . . Such disparities necessarily handicapped tenants' attempts to secure an independent existence.

In addition to controlling limited quantities of the basic resources necessary for successful farming, tenants could be summarily removed from the land they farmed. For example, James Miles rented a farm in Orange County for ten years; one of the terms of his tenancy agreement stipulated that he could be removed "at any time" his landlord demanded, with his labor for the year converted to an unspecified wage. Similarly, in 1856, William Murdock of Davidson County had already begun ejection proceedings against his tenant, Selina Kepley, when he sold the property to Meshack Pinkerton. After the sale, Pinkerton gave Kepley two months to get off the land, and when she did not leave in time, the sheriff was called in to remove her. Such examples illustrate a general reality: tenancy agreements usually covered only a period of one year, leaving tenants with little long-term security about their prospects for farming a particular piece of land. Among other disadvantages, this meant that most renters failed to gain from any improvements they made to their landlords' properties. . . .

Since tenants farmed at the whim of individual landlords, making a crop could be a precarious undertaking for those tenants who rented from unscrupulous individuals. For example, in 1839 Thomas Varner of Davidson County rented a field of seven acres from Lewis Newsome. Varner planted corn on the land, but Newsome, apparently convinced that Varner did an inadequate job working the plot, refused to allow his tenant to harvest the crop. Newsome physically attacked Varner to keep him out of the field, and Varner received nothing for his farming efforts.

Much like postbellum tenants, antebellum tenants in debt faced little chance of benefiting from their agricultural toil. North Carolina law did not protect the crops of tenants from execution under debt. A member of the state legislature explained the plight of indebted tenants to the North Carolina General Assembly during the 1840s: "As soon as the tenant [in debt] pitches his crop and prepares his land, a constable comes and levies upon the growing crop." Realizing that this system actually encouraged indebted tenants to flee the land in the middle of the crop season, the General Assembly altered the law in the 1840s in ways that benefited creditors and landlords. The new law protected growing crops until they had matured, apparently in an effort to insure that creditors would have something to collect. The legislators also exempted from execution for debt the share of a tenant's crop due the landlord for rent. In effect, a form of the crop lien system existed in North Carolina twenty years before the end of the Civil War. . . .

To survive in a world of limited and often sporadic economic opportunities, poor whites, and especially nontenants, became adept at performing a wide variety of jobs. While census records list single occupations for landless white men, most moved readily among a number of jobs. We can gain a sense of this world by following some of its occupants. For example, Sampson Glenn of Randolph County worked as a carpenter in 1842, but in that year he also worked as a farmhand on the homestead of a female farmer in the neighborhood, receiving one-fourth of the corn, oats, and wheat produced on the farm in exchange for his efforts. Between 1843 and 1860, Ephraim Brattain of Davidson County failed to acquire real property of his own; however, he worked at various jobs during these years, including stints as a blacksmith in various shops, as a hauler for several farmers, and as a tenant. In the 1850s John Moon, a landless man of Randolph County, occasionally found work that utilized his skills as a cooper, but he also clerked at a store and worked at a sawmill. In addition, he boarded poor women who worked at a nearby cotton factory. Isham Sheffield worked at the same Randolph County sawmill for the first three months of 1860; that summer he farmed as a tenant in neighboring Moore County.

    Given the fleeting nature of most work opportunities for white laborers and tenants, many poor whites moved frequently, working short periods at various locations. The work record of a laborer from Chatham County illustrates this pattern. From 1844 to 1850, Moses E. D. Pike recorded his work history at fourteen different places, including farms, cotton factories, a furnace, a flour mill, and a sawmill. His work week ranged from one to six days. His longest stint during this period was 122 ½ days at the flour mill. At the time of the 1850 census, Pike did not own land and lived with nine other landless men (one had a family) and two landless women. Between December 1853 and August 1856, Pike worked 158 days at Ruffin's Mill; 133 days for Thomas Sellars, a very wealthy farmer in Alamance County; and 220 days divided between two other employers. Pike's unique persistence in record-keeping helps make more visible an enormous class of southerners who remain, for the most part, invisible.

    Some poor whites moved so frequently in search of work that antebellum census enumerators counted them more than once during their decennial treks through the central Piedmont. For example, on July 19, 1860, the census enumerator for the southern half of Guilford County listed Gethro Yates as a thirty-seven-year-old laborer with no real or personal property and with a wife and three children. Exactly two months later, the same enumerator listed the same Gethro Yates again, this time in another part of the county. Ten years earlier, an enumerator for Randolph County counted the landless laborer Alson Robbins as living in two separate households on consecutive days.

The fact that central Piedmont poor whites owned little in the way of material possessions facilitated their frequent moves around the countryside. On the eve of the Civil War, nonslaveholding yeomen in the region owned, on average, four to five times more personal property than their poor white neighbors (see table 2). Scattered evidence from debtors' records suggests that the most common items of personal property held by area poor whites were farming tools, hogs, furniture, and kitchen utensils. . . .

Work in one of the emerging corporately controlled enterprises of the central Piedmont, such as ore mines, also offered poor whites an alternative to the nomadic life often dictated by sporadic work opportunities. Mining operations in the central Piedmont had originally been conducted by independent groups of men. After Tobias Barringer discovered gold on his farm in Stanly County in the 1820s, men all over the Piedmont of North Carolina began to search for valuable ores. Periodic discoveries of minerals in a particular area would lead many local men to stop farming and begin searching for minerals. After the discovery of a large copper deposit in Guilford County, a local observer noted that "the mining feavour is so High that a grat menney is neglection thar crops and Turnd thar attention to Hunting copper." All classes of white men engaged in these quests. After a discovery, local landowners might lease land in potentially mineral-rich areas to individuals or groups of men. The miners would then work the land and keep most of the profit for themselves.

Increasingly, however, large companies (often financed by New York capital) searched for and acquired land containing the major deposits. For example, the Gold Hill region in Rowan County, which became a center of the mining industry in the state, had eight different firms working fifteen mines in 1848. This cluster of enterprises employed several hundred white men and boys and about fifty teenage and adult slaves. Other smaller corporately controlled mines arose throughout the central Piedmont, such as the operation at Silver Hill, ten miles southeast of Lexington

---

Table 2.   Average Value of Personal Property Owned by Nonslaveholding Households in Davidson and Randolph Counties, 1860

	DAVIDSON CO.	RANDOLPH CO.
Tenants and laborers	$143	$175
Yeomen	755	747

Source: Samples from the 1860 Federal Census for Davidson and Randolph counties, Schedule 1.

in Davidson County, which produced gold, silver, lead, and zinc. Owned by a shift-ing group of New York investors, the mine (called the Washington Mining Com-pany and later the Silver Hill Mining Company) employed anywhere from 30 to 100 men and boys at the task of crushing, separating, and smelting various ores dur-ing the 1840s and 1850s. The men made from 55 cents to $1.50 a day, depending on the job; the boys received 25 cents a day. Many of the men also participated in the actual mining, receiving pay of 3 cents a ton. Judging by the company's account book, most of the mine workers at Silver Hill could count on at least twenty days of work a month.

The trade-off for steady employment at this mine, however, proved to be a loss of personal freedom. Most of the wage miners working the Silver Hill mine during the 1840s and 1850s lived in a world in which the company completely owned the neighborhood: the houses, the school, the stables, the blacksmith shop, and the store. The company maintained strict discipline over its workers, and those who would not submit to the regimen found themselves unwelcome at the mine. In 1845 the company managers "expelled several dissipated and unruly characters from our neighborhood," most likely for violating the company's policy of "industry and so-briety" among its workers. . . .

Other emerging companies besides mines provided steady employment oppor-tunities for landless whites. For instance, many landless white men and boys from Davidson County skilled at shoe making found regular work at the Lines Shoe Fac-tory after its construction in the late 1850s, reportedly the largest shoe factory in the South at the time of the Civil War.

Working as a sharecropper offered another way for white laborers to secure rel-atively steady work. Antebellum sharecropping apparently evolved as an alternative to short-term farm labor stints; sharecropping agreements offered a way for em-ployers to formalize casual labor arrangements with white laborers. Essentially, poor white sharecroppers were laborers who worked on a specific farm for an entire year. They accepted a share of the crops produced, rather than a monthly wage, in exchange for their labor. For example, a Montgomery County farmer noted in 1839, "I have employed old Mr. Davis to live with me another year. I am to give him one fourth part of the Crop." When John Lowdermilk, a Randolph County farmer with three slaves, needed additional help around his farm in 1841, he signed the son of a nearby landless farmer to a sharecropping agreement, an arrangement apparently cheaper than hiring or buying additional slave labor. Lowdermilk agreed to pay two-thirds of the young man's expenses and to give him one-third of all the corn, wheat, and oats produced. . . .

In addition to exploiting the various economic niches available to them through the development and utilization of diverse skills, poor whites managed to make ends meet by employing all available family members in optimal ways. To insure survival, labor outside the home was often required of all members of poor white families. The wives of poor white men, like the wives of the yeomanry, jug-gled a wide variety of tasks necessary for the maintenance of their households: raising children, cleaning house, making clothes, preparing meals, caring for live-stock, tending gardens, and, in many cases, helping to plant and harvest crops. Un-like yeoman wives, however, the wives of poor white men often contributed to the income of their households by laboring outside the home. Economic necessity required that many poor white families extend the labor of women beyond the confines of the household. For example, in 1848 Nancy Burgess, the wife of a laborer in the northern part of Randolph County, worked for wages for a landless farmer across the county line in southern Guilford County. She made more than $7 for performing a variety of jobs: weaving, washing, scouring, and binding wheat and oats.

Wage labor by poor white women in the area was not unusual. In fact, women who headed landless households in the central Piedmont regularly worked for wages outside the home to support themselves and their families. Census records often list unmarried, landless women who headed households as having no occupation, but most of these poor white women did work in a variety of occupations—as farm laborers, as seamstresses, and, perhaps most often, as domestics in the houses of neighbors. After her tenant husband died in 1842, Ellen Chambers of Iredell County "hired out for domestic work" for two years, until the time she married a prosperous widower. In 1854 Elizabeth Millikan, the daughter of a landless laborer of Randolph County, was abandoned by her husband, who left her little in the way of property. She promptly went to work at the home of a prosperous free black artisan whose wife was "sick & unable to work." After working there for eight weeks, she moved to Asheboro "to wait upon the family of Rueben H. Brown," a local lawyer. For the next several years, she traveled around Randolph County, "living at different places upon wages."

Child labor outside the home played an equally important role in providing supplemental income for poor white households. The son of a renter in east Tennessee remembered that he "choped grubed split railes made hand plowing from the time I was nine yeares of age every year until the war as a hired hand on other men's farmes." When John Bryant, a landless man from Davidson County, purchased three bushels of corn from a neighboring yeoman in 1848, Bryant had his son Felix work on the yeoman's farm for eight days to pay for the food, at the rate of 12 1/2 cents a day. Tabitha Amick, the oldest daughter of a landless farmer from Guilford County, periodically worked for local yeomen during the late 1840s, harvesting crops, cleaning house, and sewing clothes.

The advent of cotton mills in the central Piedmont provided poor whites with an additional source of work for themselves and their children. The first cotton mills in Davidson and Randolph counties opened in the late 1830s. A large Davidson mill, the Lexington Steam Cotton Factory, employed ninety-six hands in 1840, who were housed in tenant buildings surrounding the mill. This early textile mill village disappeared, however, when the factory burned during the winter of 1844–45. No one stepped forward to rebuild the Lexington cotton mill, and industrial activity of his kind did not reemerge in the county until after the Civil War. In contrast, industrialists built eight cotton mills on the Deep River of Randolph County between 1836 and 1860. . . .

Slavery blocked the development of regular wage positions for white laborers; consequently, they moved frequently between a wide variety of jobs, a life-style that allowed them to avoid starvation but offered few chances for economic advancement and independence. Likewise, white tenants could certainly make a living on their rented farms, but tenancy provided little of the autonomy and security enjoyed by most yeomen. Many central Piedmont poor whites escaped poverty by acquiring land or by leaving the region for the West. But both the increasing commercialization of the central Piedmont's agricultural economy during the 1850s and the workings of an oppressive credit-based system of exchange played major roles in keeping a significant number of area poor whites down and out. Nevertheless, the white tenants and laborers of the central Piedmont who stayed in the area managed to subsist by working on the margins of the area economy, with help from their families and the bounty of the countryside.

Punishing Deviant Women: The State as Patriarch

VICTORIA BYNUM

On April 8, 1861, Susan Williford pleaded with the magistrates of the Granville County court to allow her to maintain custody of her two youngest children—Nancy, aged eight, and Louisa, aged six. Williford charged two planters of the county with forcibly removing the girls from her home despite her objections. In defending the right to raise her own daughters, Williford declared in an affidavit that although she was poor, through "industry and frugality" she had always supported Nancy and Louisa comfortably and, further, that she was an "honest and hardworking woman . . . much distressed at being separated from her children of such tender years." The court ordered an investigation but apparently did not rescind the apprenticeships.

Susan Williford's predicament was not unique. Courts in the antebellum South often apprenticed children judged to be indigent, ill-raised, illegitimate, orphaned, or of free black parentage. The apprenticeship of illegitimate or free black children removed them from the homes of their parents (usually single women) to those of court-appointed masters (usually white men) for whom they were bound by contract to labor in return for their livelihood. Rarely did the contracts specify that a skill be taught the children other than farming for boys and spinning for girls. Though Williford, a white woman, might truthfully argue that she loved and took good care of her children, the fact that they were the illegitimate offspring of a racially mixed union branded her a social deviant incapable of raising them properly. Committing the crime of miscegenation condemned her to a legal rung just above slavery—a rung usually reserved for free black women.

Williford's life from childhood to middle age demonstrated how courts punished women who defied the sexual and racial constructs of southern society. How and why did she become an outcast, even an outlaw? Although she suffered from poverty and the stigma of deviancy throughout most of her adult life, her family roots probably originated among the yeomanry of Granville County. The economic and sexual vulnerability of women, however, had reduced her mother, Elizabeth Williford, to the ranks of poor whites. Elizabeth never married, and the illegitimate birth of her daughter Susan ensured poverty and degraded status for both.

At age six, Susan Williford was apprenticed to a farmer, William Gordon. Growing up could not have been easy for children like her who were separated at very young ages—sometimes as young as one year—from their mothers. In Susan's case, separation was made worse by an abusive master. In November 1822, her mother charged Gordon with mistreating Susan, but not until February 1823 did the court remove the child from Gordon's home. Perhaps Susan's childhood apprenticeship experiences influenced her impassioned plea for custody of her children forty years later.

The court's treatment of women like Williford demonstrated that, despite southern leaders' idealistic vision of women's absorption within the family circle, state and local judges recognized that some women were neither the wives nor the slaves of white men. Such women had no place or function in southern society. Unmarried, propertyless women were not the vessels through which white male property and progeny passed. Instead, many were mothers of a troublesome white and black laboring class.

By contradicting society's cherished beliefs about women's natural delicacy, servility, and virtue, the behavior of some poor women compounded their inferior status. Besides violating prescribed norms of female behavior, poor women broke taboos against interracial social and sexual intercourse more often than did economically privileged women. Respected white southerners regarded deviant white women as "vile," "lewd," and "vicious" products of an inferior strain of humanity. They considered unmarried free black women naturally lascivious and amoral by virtue of their race. These attitudes in turn, legitimized the power of the courts to punish such behavior and limit the freedom of poor women.

Enforcement of laws governing bastardy, prostitution, fornication, and apprenticeship provided the chief means through which courts punished sexually active women and appropriated the labor of their children. Class, race, and marital status dictated which women were mostly likely to be summoned before county magistrates. An unmarried woman who did not remain celibate might frequently find herself in court throughout her childbearing years.

Despite the tremendous social and legal costs, some unmarried women led sexually active lives, entering into a subculture of mostly poor people who did not abide by the rules of polite society. This behavior allowed them a measure of personal choice in a world that otherwise restricted poor or unmarried women to lives spent serving others. Chart 1 reveals the connections that two deviant women—Susan Williford and Parthenia Melton—forged among yeoman, poor white, and free black members of the neighborhoods surrounding the township of Tally Ho in Granville County. The Hobgoods, Adcocks, Willifords, and Curtises had frequent contact with each other throughout the antebellum era. The Hobgoods and Adcocks intermarried, and many of the free black Curtises were apprenticed to, or worked for, their white neighbors. In addition, illicit liaisons created cross-class and interracial relationships.

Williford and Melton were pivotal to these kinships. So was John R. Hobgood, who fathered children by both women in 1836 and 1837, respectively. He probably concluded from Williford's déclassé status that no harm was done by impregnating her, but he clearly "ruined" Melton, who probably was his sixteen-year-old niece (see Chart 1). Hobgood seemed particularly addicted to dissolute living. Like Williford and Melton, whose legal problems began with their pregnancies by him, he was in and out of court all his adult life, eventually entering the county poorhouse. His immediate family was plagued by violence. Two men beat to death his brother Shelton in 1828, and Mary Meadows, his notorious sister, was accused in 1847 of arranging the murder of her husband. Despite the solid yeoman background of the Hobgoods, the behavior of John, Shelton, and Mary mired them in Granville's impoverished subculture.

The relationship between John R. Hobgood and Parthenia Melton was long-lasting, despite its illicit nature. By 1850, the couple had five children, although they never married and apparently never shared a home. Melton, like Susan Williford, lived in a world of poverty and violence, and her control over her children was precarious. She was charged with bastardy once and, along with John Hobgood, for fornication twice. In 1851, the court took custody of all of her children and apprenticed two of them. It placed the remaining three children in the county poorhouse to await further action regarding their custody. In 1860, thirty-nine-year-old Melton lived alone with her youngest child, Joanna, whose custody she regained, while sixty-seven-year-old Hobgood languished in the county poorhouse.

Williford's social status dropped even lower than Melton's and Hobgood's in the 1840s, when she entered into a permanent relationship with Peter Curtis, a free black man of her community. Denied by law the right to marry the partner of her choice, although she lived with him for at least fifteen years, Williford lost all her children by Curtis when the court ruled that they were subject to apprenticeship because they were illegitimate. In addition, the court regularly charged Williford and Curtis with fornication. Whereas free black couples found it extremely difficult to prosper in a white slaveholding society, interracial couples found it almost impossible to maintain a traditional family life.

Living with Curtis instead of alone probably enhanced the personal safety and economic security of Williford, despite increased harassment by the courts. In 1840, before taking up with Curtis, she was beaten up and her house was torn apart by a white man—an experience all too common for poor white women of outcast status. Joining the Curtis family, which had numerous relatives among Granville County's vital community of free black farmers and artisans, lessened her vulnerability. Living among the Curtises also provided a community in which her mulatto children were accepted. Three of her children married into black families of their neighborhood in the 1860s. Thus at the price of utter condemnation by white society, Williford gained greater physical protection—something outcast poor white women generally lacked—by crossing the color line.

Crossing the color line also reveals the larger connection of female sexuality and reproduction to issues of race and poverty. Because of the counties' significant free black populations, the Orange and Granville courts enforced laws against prostitution and fornication as often to punish miscegenation and limit sexual contact

Chart 1. The Creation of a Subculture

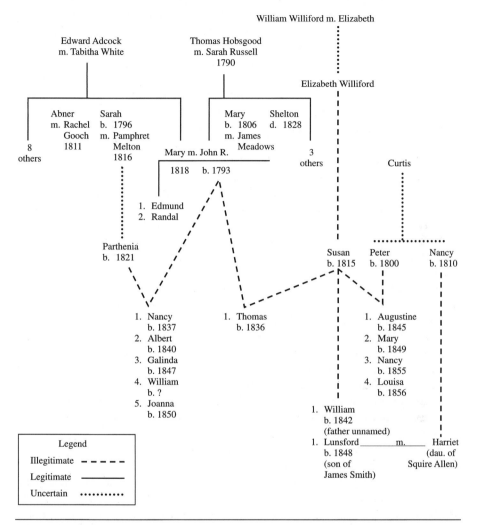

Legend

Illegitimate - - - - -

Legitimate ——————

Uncertain ··········

Sources: U.S. Federal Manuscript Censuses, 1850, 1860; Estate Records; Apprenticeship Bonds; Bastardy Bonds; Marriage Bonds; Granville County, NCDAH.

between free blacks and slaves as to punish white couples guilty of adultery (see Table 1). Indictments for prostitution particularly targeted women who engaged in interracial social activity or who operated taverns at which blacks and whites were suspected of gambling, drinking, and exchanging illegal goods. Prostitution was usually included within the general charge of operating a "disorderly house," rather than being the sole issue of an indictment.

Table 1. Charges of Sexual Misconduct and Larceny Brought Against Women in the Lower Courts, 1850–1860

	GRANVILLE	ORANGE	MONTGOMERY	TOTAL
Prostitution	8	11	0	19
Fornication	21	43	5	69
Bastardy	33	94	42	169
Larceny	5	2	1	8

Source: Criminal Action Papers and Bastardy Bonds, Granville, Orange, and Montgomery counties, Criminal Actions Concerning Slaves and Free Persons of Color, Granville County, NCDAH.

That court magistrates sought to control rather than eliminate prostitution is indicated by their general indifference toward white prostitutes who confined their services to white males. These women appear to have quietly plied their trade without legal challenge, perhaps because many white citizens believed that the availability of lower-class white prostitutes (as well as slave women) protected respectable women from defilement by lustful males. Few citizens seem to have thought much about the prostitute herself except to label her "vile," "dissolute," and the like. Respectable townspeople for the most part ignored prostitutes unless, if white, they crossed the color line or, as in the case of Nancy Glasgow who was caught milking the cow of Thomas Pleasants without his permission, they imposed upon more prosperous members of the community. . . .

Few owned any property of substance, and many were omitted by census takers in their enumeration of households. Consequently, most of the evidence that survives in the public records is negative, identifying such women as witnesses or victims of crimes. Criminal records, for example, record Nancy Glasgow's beating by well-to-do hotel keeper Simon G. Hayes—an incident suggesting that Glasgow perhaps tried to conduct business in Hayes's hotel. In Orange County, Emily King was subpoenaed as a witness to a murder that occurred during a drunken brawl at her place of business. Prostitutes and female tavern keepers clearly were visible figures in the shadowy social world denied to ladies of the community, a world in which violence and illicit sexual activity were commonplace. This and the fact that prostitutes were forced to cater to men who despised them even while they exploited their services left women of this underground subculture highly vulnerable.

In contrast to prostitution, indictments for fornication focused on women who gave rather than sold sexual favors. Targeted were those who cohabited with slaves (primarily free black women), participated in interracial sexual activity (mostly poor white women), or engaged in adulterous relationships with married men. The first two categories included some couples who considered themselves married but were legally forbidden to marry. . . .

In those indictments of fornication aimed at punishing miscegenation, magistrates prosecuted primarily white women and black men rather than white men and black women. This uneven application of the law reflected the structure of gender and racial relationships. White males claimed the right to govern all women, regardless of race. The sole sexual possession of white women by white men assured perpetuation of the dominant "pure" white race. Possession of a black woman by a white man, whether of her person, labor, or body, demonstrated the powerlessness of the black man, who could not claim sole rights of possession even to women of his own race. Black women were especially vulnerable. Subjected to sexual exploitation because of their gender, they were denied protection against sexual harassment on account of their race.

A white man might seek sexual activity with a black woman with little fear of censure from society provided he did not treat her in a manner that suggested the respect reserved for white women. Certainly, a white man should not appear at social gatherings with his black mistress. Just such behavior resulted in a rare case in which a white male was charged with fornication with a black female. By socializing publicly with Tabby Chavous (Chavis), a free mulatto woman, Thomas Peace so angered his brother Dickerson Peace that in 1844 the latter initiated charges of fornication against the couple. Undaunted by the charges, however, Thomas continued to escort Chavous to public gatherings well into the 1850s until Dickerson, unable to contain his rage, attacked and accidentally killed him at a neighborhood barbecue.

This violent end to a decade-long relationship illustrates the profound connections between sexual behavior and ordering of racial boundaries. The sexual possession of both white and black women symbolized men's power, but in very different ways. At a basic level, such possession signified the dominance of men over women. White women, however, were prizes; the higher a particular woman's family status, the better it spoke of the man who "won" her. Possession of black women, by contrast, symbolized a man's virility more than his honor, a virility manifested in racial domination. Thus a white man must never, as in the case of Thomas Peace, elevate a black woman to the status of a white woman.

Most white men treated their affairs with black women with the discretion required in antebellum society. Indictments of racially mixed couples for fornication usually targeted white women and black men. In a society steeped in the mythology of white female purity and black inferiority, such couplings, though rare, were disturbing. Most nineteenth-century Americans viewed sexual intercourse as an act done *to* women rather than one in which women participated. Thus a black man's sexual "conquest" of a white woman potentially empowered him and humiliated white men. A white woman who chose a black mate had to be lowered in status to prevent the elevation of the black male who possessed her and, of course, to confirm white males' cherished notion of themselves as the preferred sexual choice of any decent white woman.

White couples whose sexual behavior offended the community might also find themselves indicted for fornication. Many such cases involved poor white women and propertied (usually married) white men. An indictment for fornication could also serve as a prelude to a suit for divorce, or it might simply reflect feuding among members of a community. Many people routinely used the courts to punish and embarrass each other. . . .

The racial concerns that influenced the enforcement of civil and criminal laws also influenced the use of the apprenticeship system, which functioned as an instrument of racial control as well as an early attempt to institute a system of social welfare for the poor. Several categories of children were subject to apprenticeship: fatherless children "who have not sufficient estate to be educated on the profits"; children deserted without support for at least one year by their fathers; children not living with a father and living with a mother deemed by the court an improper parent; all free illegitimate children; and all children of "free negroes or mulattoes, where the parents do not employ their time in some industrious, honest occupation." The courts used the system most consistently to apprentice the children of free blacks.

County court officials removed poor children from their mothers through the apprenticeship system because women had no legal rights of guardianship over their children unless specifically endowed with them by courts. Fathers were by law the "natural" guardians of children. The courts defined as an orphan any child without a living or legitimate father. All minor orphans were legal wards of the court regardless of whether they had living mothers. In strict legal terms, the courts "allowed" a mother to raise her children by virtue of her marriage to the children's legal "owner," their father. Hence the law required that widowed mothers apply in court for legal guardianship over their "orphaned" children, though in cases involving propertied families, the court usually granted such guardianships routinely. The likelihood that the children of propertyless widows and unmarried mothers would be apprenticed was much greater.

As Table 2 shows, more free black than white women lost custody of their children through the apprenticeship system. An unmarried mother of a black or mulatto child could certainly expect her child to be apprenticed. Between 1850 and 1860, black and mulatto children accounted for 61 percent of the children apprenticed in Orange, Granville, and Montgomery counties even though free black women made up only 9 percent of female-headed households. . . .

Giving birth to a black man's child eliminated the racial advantage for white women. In an 1855 suit similar to Susan Williford's, Nancy Midgett, a white mother of two mulatto children, appealed to the state supreme court to rescind her children's apprenticeships on grounds that she was living an industrious life and able to support them. Judge Pearson denied the request and reminded her that the county court "has power to bind out *all* free base-born children of color, without reference to the occupation or condition of the mother.". . .

In some cases involving single or widowed women who were unable to provide decent homes for their children, the interests of the children would probably have

---

Table 2. Number and Race of Children Apprenticed Between 1850 and 1860

	GRANVILLE	ORANGE	MONTGOMERY	TOTAL
Black	60	71	13	144
White	34	40	17	91
Total	94	111	30	235

Source: Apprenticeship Bonds and Minutes of the county courts, Granville, Orange, and Montgomery counties, NCDAH.

been better served had the apprenticeship system removed them from the custody of their mothers. In 1860, Mary Ann Inscore, a twenty-three-year-old white woman, apparently still had not named her three- and two-year-old illegitimate children. She lived with William Ferrill, who had been charged in November 1857 with operating a "disorderly house" that included prostitution. It is no surprise that in a society that socialized women to be dependent on others and decreed marriage women's only viable vocation, those who failed to marry wisely or at all might lack the financial or emotional resources to raise their children. In such cases, the apprenticeship system provided an alternative to the poorhouse and, in theory at least, an opportunity for an indigent child to learn a skill. Most orders of apprenticeship, however, did not address a woman's ability to raise a child but merely cited the fatherlessness of a child as a priori evidence of that fact. . . .

Most women charged with bastardy in Granville, Montgomery, and Orange counties were, indeed, poor. Almost half of sixty-seven women so charged between 1850 and 1860 whose profiles I have constructed lived in propertyless households on the eve of the war. Most of these households were headed by the mother or another female. Just over half of the remaining thirty-five women who lived in propertied households lived in homes headed by males. All but one of the women who lived in households with property valued at more than $500 lived in male-headed households, usually those of their father. Usually unskilled and unlikely to marry, most mothers of illegitimate children lived in or on the edge of poverty. Fully half of them lived in households containing no apparent kin other than their illegitimate children. . . .

Despite their modest resources, relatively few unwed mothers became wards of county poorhouses during the antebellum era. The courts' policy of assigning financial responsibility to the fathers of bastards perhaps kept most unwed mothers off the county charity rolls. So, too, perhaps, did the lack of personal freedom, dreary surroundings, and general degradation associated with public charity. Officials closely monitored the work habits and behavior of poorhouse inmates.

The buildings that housed paupers were at best functional, and the food and clothing supplied were predictably monotonous and plain. In 1857, inspectors of the Orange County poorhouse found the building's walls almost entirely rotted behind its brick facade. Inside, they discovered that the portion of the floor where the paupers slept had "generally mouldered into [the] earth." The diet consisted primarily of chicken or pork, corn, oats, milk, and coffee, while clothing was made from "good, substantial linsey." To enter the poorhouse represented a final loss of individual autonomy, and only those women on the brink of starvation chose the security of food and shelter over remaining in their communities.

Although most women charged with bastardy were poor, this does not mean that only poor women gave birth outside of marriage. In their zeal to prevent illegitimate children from becoming charges upon county funds, court magistrates tried to force poor unmarried women to name the fathers of their children in court. The illegitimate children of wealthy women did not present the same economic burden to society. Yet, despite the courts' efforts to prosecute the fathers of poor women's bastards, many men nevertheless found ways to protect their identity or evade full financial responsibility for their illegitimate children. . . .

While some white men evaded financial responsibility for illegitimate children, those who fathered black or mulatto children were rarely charged with bastardy. For this reason, bastardy numbers in the records of Montgomery and Orange counties are far higher than in Granville, where many fathers of bastards may have been slaves, free blacks, or whites who wished to remain anonymous. Besides, court officials could show less interest in prosecuting the parents of free black bastards because the practice of apprenticing all such children from the age of five until twenty-one considerably lessened the need for county aid.

The inability of blacks to testify against whites in court further relieved the courts of prosecuting white fathers of mulatto children. Only a single bastardy case involving a free black mother and a white father reached the state supreme court in this period, and it was decided in favor of the father. In 1848, the high court ruled that free black mother Lucinda Simpson was by law "incompetent to give testimony against a white man," which the imputed father of her child happened to be. Two years after denying Simpson's suit, the state supreme court ordered William Haithcock, a free black of Orange County, to support his illegitimate child by a white woman. Consistent with social custom, the courts punished blacks and women, but seldom white men, who violated the taboo against interracial sexual relations.

White men profited from their ability to bribe court officials and coerce women into silence. For a woman, the extensiveness of her family roots was the most decisive factor in how she fared in court. Montgomery County's most notorious unmarried mothers—Hannah, Rosetta, and Ann Hurley—were from an extensive and long-standing yeoman family of the community. Hannah and Rosetta Hurley successfully sued their children's fathers for support when court-ordered payments were not forthcoming. Although the Hurley sisters' sexual conduct may have cost them their reputations, their strong roots in the community gave them the confidence and resources to demand their legal due. . . .

Poor kinless women . . . received little protection against sexual exploitation. Men considered lower class women, particularly African Americans, a sexual proving ground for those too "gentlemanly" to disturb the "finer" sensibilities of higher-class women. Women of loose reputation also risked blame for provoking the violence of men repulsed by their behavior. In 1851, thirty-six citizens of Halifax County petitioned Governor David Reid to pardon Lemuel Nevill and Davis Shearin, who had brutally beaten Polly Gaffin because she had committed adultery with the husband of Nevill's sister and had given birth to a mulatto baby. The legal right of husbands to "chastise" wives physically encouraged a general consensus that men at large could discipline women at large—much like the attitude of white men toward African American men.

Similarly, prosecutions for rape focused on the reputation of the victim as well as the evidence against the accused. Conventional nineteenth-century thought regarded rape as the theft of a woman's most prized possession—a body reserved exclusively for her future or present husband. Under these terms, protection of sexually active single women would have degraded the pure white women whom the law was designed to protect. Given the attitudes of most white southerners, it hardly occurred to them that a black woman could be raped.

Neither, apparently, could an unchaste white woman. In several cases involving charges of rape of white women by slaves, women of low, debased reputation—specifically, those guilty of miscegenation—were considered unworthy of the execution of a valuable slave. In such cases, white men admitted that some white women willingly had sexual intercourse with black men—and they were of course correct—but labeled such women "base prostitutes" whether they sold their services or not.

The existence of unmarried sexually active women, many of whom lived in female-headed households, provided a striking contradiction to the ideal of a woman's place as either wife, daughter, or slave within the patriarchal structure of southern society. Women who lived outside the family structure and lacked economic independence were a familiar sight in local courts, where they were summoned by judges empowered to regulate their sexual and reproductive behavior. Although apparently unburdened by paternalistic responsibilities, the state assumed the role of patriarch in governing the lives of women who lacked proper male figures of authority to control them.

Throughout the antebellum period, social leaders and lawmakers treated single, sexually active women as outlaws and outsiders. The frequent presence of deviant women in the local courts reminded all women of the price of misbehaving, and prosecution of such women probably did curb antisocial behavior to a certain extent. Thus on the eve of the Civil War, North Carolina had a well-developed, if unevenly applied, system of laws that, despite the persistent misbehavior of a small, distinct subculture of free black and white women, reinforced the structure of the white family and preserved at least the appearance of sexual separation of the races.

FURTHER READING

Fred Arthur Bailey, *Class and Tennessee's Confederate Generation* (1987)

Barbara Bellows, *Benevolence Among Slaveholders: Assisting the Poor in Charleston, 1670–1860* (1993)

Frederick A. Bode and Donald E. Ginter, eds., *Farm Tenancy and the Census in Antebellum Georgia* (1986)

Charles C. Bolton, *Poor Whites of the Antebellum South* (1994)

———, ed., *The Confessions of Edward Luham, A Poor White Life of the Old South* (1998)

Victoria Bynum, *Unruly Women: The Politics of Social and Sexual Control in the Old South* (1992)

Randolph B. Campbell, "Intermittent Slave Ownership: Texas as a Test Case," *Journal of Southern History* 51 (1985), 15–30

Bill Cecil-Fronsman, *Common Whites: Class and Culture in Antebellum North Carolina* (1992)

Bruce Collins, *White Society in the Antebellum South* (1985)

Paul D. Escott, *Many Excellent People: Power and Privilege in North Carolina, 1850–1900* (1985)

Lacy K. Ford, Jr., *Origins of Southern Radicalism: The South Carolina Upcountry, 1800–1860* (1988)

Eugene D. Genovese, "Yeoman Farmers in a Slaveholders' Democracy," in Elizabeth Fox-Genovese and Eugene Genovese, *Fruits of Merchant Capital* (1983)

Elliott J. Gorn, " 'Gouge and Bite, Pull Hair and Scratch': The Social Significance of Fighting in the Southern Backcountry," *American Historical Review* 90 (1985), 18–43

Steven Hahn, *The Roots of Southern Populism* (1983)

J. William Harris, *Plain Folk and Gentry in a Slave Society: White Liberty and Black Slavery in Augusta's Hinterlands* (1985)

Stephanie McCurry, *Masters of Small Worlds* (1995)

Forrest McDonald and Grady McWhiney, "The Antebellum Southern Herdsman: A Reinterpretation," *Journal of Southern History* 41 (1975), 147–166

Grady McWhiney, *Cracker Culture* (1988)

Frank L. Owsley, *Plain Folk of the Old South* (1949)

Gavin Wright, *The Political Economy of the Cotton South* (1978)

White Women's Culture and
Reality in the Old South

One of the most rapidly growing fields of scholarship in southern history has been
the study of women, both black and white. Initially oriented toward comparisons
with the North, research on southern women has generated its own models and theories, producing information valuable for a better understanding of southern
women and the role they played in southern society.

Southern white women lived in a variety of social environments divided by
class. Compared to the North, the South had more women living in a rural environment, cut off from the institutions and associations beyond family and church. They
existed within a circumscribed, prescribed role that idealized them as submissive,
domestic, frail, and pious. Yet as scholars have shown, few women lived according to
such ideals. Some privileged women began to move beyond the home to engage in
benevolent and reform activities, but the majority lived out their lives focused on
family, work, and church and constrained by legal limitations that prevented them
from occupying a position of equality with men.

DOCUMENTS

During the antebellum period, writers of prescriptive literature fashioned an idealized
vision of southern women and celebrated their weakness, piety, and legal and social
limitations. One of the earliest and best known of these authors was Thomas Roderick
Dew, president of William and Mary College, whose words in Document 1 reflect what
many other writers also articulated about southern white women. As Sarah McCulloch's words and Ann Ginn's tombstone show in Document 2, reality was far harsher.
Childbirth was a dangerous time for a parturient woman and her newborn, and southern
women anticipated each new birth with some foreboding. Document 3, a letter written
by a Galveston, Texas, woman, reveals the trials of Lucy Shaw as she raised her children and ran a boarding house. As an excerpt from the Whitsett diary in Document 4 reveals, childrearing could be a heartwrenching experience during a period when medical
knowledge was limited and in a region of the country where poor health was common.

Document 5 shows that women's situation was not merely a product of male dictates. Female writers like Louisa Cheves McCord, one of the South's most prolific and popular authors, articulated a domestic, submissive role for women. Document 6 includes various letters and writings by southern women, showing their relationships with female family members and friends, the importance of religion, and seemingly unending work demands.

1. Thomas Roderick Dew Idealizes Southern Women, 1835

The relative position of the sexes in the social and political world, may certainly be looked upon as the result of organization. The greater physical strength of man, enables him to occupy the foreground in the picture. He leaves the domestic scenes; he plunges into the turmoil and bustle of an active, selfish world; in his journey through life, he has to encounter innumerable difficulties, hardships and labors which constantly beset him. His mind must be nerved against them. Hence courage and boldness are his attributes. It is his province, undismayed, to stand against the rude shocks of the world; to meet with a lion's heart, the dangers which threaten him. He is the shield of woman, destined by nature to guard and protect her. Her inferior strength and sedentary habits confine her within the domestic circle; she is kept aloof from the bustle and storm of active life; she is not familiarized to the out of door dangers and hardships of a cold and scuffling world: timidity and modesty are her attributes. In the great strife which is constantly going forward around her, there are powers engaged which her inferior physical strength prevents her from encountering. She must rely upon the strength of others; man must be engaged in her cause. How is he to be drawn over to her side? Not by menace—not by force; for weakness cannot, by such means, be expected to triumph over might. No! It must be by conformity to that character which circumstances demand for the sphere in which she moves; by the exhibition of those qualities which delight and fascinate— which are calculated to win over to her side the proud lord of creation, and to make him an humble suppliant at her shrine. Grace, modesty and loveliness are the charms which constitute her power. By these, she creates the magic spell that subdues to her will the more mighty physical powers by which she is surrounded. Her attributes are rather of a passive than active character. Her power is more emblematical of that of divinity: it subdues without an effort, and almost creates by mere volition;—whilst man must wind his way through the difficult and intricate mazes of philosophy; with pain and toil, tracing effects to their causes, and unravelling the deep mysteries of nature—storing his mind with useful knowledge, and exercising, training and perfecting his intellectual powers, whilst he cultivates his strength and hardens and matures his courage; all with a view of enabling him to assert his rights, and exercise a greater sway over those around him. Woman we behold dependant and weak; but out of that very weakness and dependance springs an irresistible power. She may pursue her studies too—not however with a view of triumphing in the senate chamber—not with a view to forensic display—not with a view of leading armies to combat, or of enabling her to bring into more formidable

---

From Thomas Roderick Dew, "Dissertation on the Characteristic Differences Between the Sexes, and on the Position and Influence of Women in Society, No. III," *Literary Messenger,* August, 1835.

action the physical power which nature has conferred on her. No! It is but the better to perfect all those feminine graces, all those fascinating attributes, which render her the centre of attraction, and which delight and charm all those who breathe the atmosphere in which she moves; and, in the language of Mr. Burke, would make ten thousand swords leap from their scabbards to avenge the insult that might be offered to her. By her very meekness and beauty does she subdue all around her. . . .

. . . That woman is destined to the office of nursing and rearing her children, the arrangement of nature evidently demonstrates. It is she alone whom nature provides with the food adapted to the support of the fragile constitution of the newly born babe. She has known and felt all the solicitude, anxiety and pain pertaining to its existence. It is a law of our nature, to love that with most ardor, which has cost us most pain and most anxiety in the attainment. For this reason perhaps, it may be that even at birth, a mother's love for her babe is more intense than that of the father; and hence an additional reason of a moral character, why the office of tutoring and nursing should devolve more particularly on her. Let us now proceed, for a moment, to trace the consequences of this position of woman. It is evident that its tendency must be, to narrow the circle in which she moves; a considerable portion of her life must be spent in the nursery and the sick room. Here, at once, would be presented an insurmountable barrier against that ambition which would lead her into the field, into politics, or any of the regular professions. She never could compete with man. In fact, to succeed at all, she would be obliged to desert the station and defeat the ends for which nature intended her. A physician, a lawyer, or statesman, who should be obliged to attend to the suckling, clothing, and the thousand little wants of a helpless babe, would be distanced in the race by him, who with any thing like equal power of intellect, was unimpeded in his career by any of those embarrassing obstacles. . . .

Another cause, no doubt, of the more religious character of woman, is her greater feebleness and dependence upon the powers around her, than that felt by man. . . .

Do we not all know that there is something much more devotional in the love of woman than man—a something much more nearly allied to religion? Do we not know that this same weakness and consequent dependence, makes woman more confiding, more trusting, more submissive than man? She feels much greater veneration for the great and the powerful, and acquiesces much more readily in the tyranny and oppression of rulers. Even women of the very first order of intellect feel this reliance and trust on the greater powers around them. Mrs. Jameson says, in speaking of the Portia of Shakspeare, "I never yet met in real life, nor ever read in tale or history, of any woman distinguished for intellect of the highest order, who was not also remarkable for this *trustingness* of spirit, this hopefulness and cheerfulness of temper, which is compatible with the most serious habits of thought, and the most profound sensibility. Lady Wortley Montague was one instance; and Madame de Stael furnishes another much more memorable."

The physical weakness of woman and her consequent dependence on man, makes religion more necessary to her for another reason. It is her interest that every restraint should be imposed on the passions of man; that he should walk in the paths of virtue and morality; that his superior strength should be subdued and tempered by motives of humanity. He is then more kind, more attentive, and more loving to her. He is then a better father, a better economist,—in fine, a better citizen, fulfilling more perfectly all the relations of life. The Christian religion, as we shall soon see, is eminently calculated to produce this happy result, and consequently woman is deeply interested in its spread. Let no one start forward with the objection, that in this way she is the better enabled to *govern* her husband. I admit this, if, to govern him, means to restrain him from vice and immorality; but surely this is a government which no honest good citizen can object to. Every lady has a fearfully deep interest in the whole character and temperament of her husband's mind and feelings. Upon them depend, indeed, her weal or woe. Her condition may be deplorable, and sometimes irremediable, if a wicked husband choose to oppress her. But that is certainly a holy and a virtuous selfishness, if selfishness it can possibly be called, which secures our own welfare and happiness while adding to that of another, by curbing and controlling his more violent and malignant feelings and passions, and attuning the whole inner man is harmony and concord. . . .

Lastly, her physical organization renders her much more liable than man to constitutional derangements, to periodical sickness, and physical infirmities of all descriptions. Disease gradually inures the mind to resignation and patience, and at least teaches us to bear with fortitude all the ills we have. "We seldom," says Bulwer, "find men of great animal health and power, possessed of much delicacy of mind. That impetuous and reckless buoyancy of spirit which mostly accompanies a hardy and iron frame, is not made to enter into the infirmities of others;" and he might well have added, is not made to bear its own infirmities and calamities with resignation and fortitude, when at last overtaken by them.

2. The Sorrows of Childbirth, 1809, c. 1800

Sarah McCulloch Describes the Trials of Childbirth, 1809

I have had "much anxiety about the health of my dear little babe she is in good health well grown and will be three months old tomorrow her hair and eyes are extremely black and I think her perfectly beautifull. For my own health I cannot boast, as one well day is more than I have had since her birth but I am satisfied at having recovered so far which is more than was ever expected for a fortnight after and three days before her birth each day was thought to be my last but by the assistance of that all merciful God whose name you so often call I hope I shall soon be perfectly well but never expect to wear that appearance of health which was once my happy lot for never was there a constitution more injured than mine."

Epitaph on Ann Ginn's Tombstone, c. 1800

> Behold amidst the youthful bloom of life
> The tender mother, the beloved wife
> To death's unalterable call attends

McCulloch letter can be found in the Cameron Family Papers, Southern Historical Collection, Wilson Library, University of North Carolina at Chapel Hill, Chapel Hill, North Carolina. Epitaph can be found in Sally McMillen's *Motherhood in the Old South* (Baton Rouge: Louisiana State University Press, 1990).

And dies lamented by her numerous friends.
Her infant child had just received its breath
When to the parent mother sinks in death
Survivors, all this solemn lesson read
Prepare this life to rest among the dead.

3. Lucy Shaw Laments the Death of Her Child, 1841

Galveston, July 24, 1841

My Dear Mother and Sister:

You have several times had occasion to write to me of the death of those who were near and dear to me and though we have had death with us, yet not among our own. But our turn has come. God who gave him to us has seen fit to take to himself our beautiful little boy. Dear precious child, he died last Monday, the nineteenth of July and Tuesday afternoon we had him laid in a grave in our own garden out of town. I used to take great pleasure in anticipating the time when I should show you this lovely child. You would have loved him so dearly. He was uncommonly handsome, had large beautiful black eyes and beautiful features. He was small but fat and healthy and perfectly good. Mrs. Marston (Emily Shaw, sister of Clark) says she is very glad she came in time to see him alive and well for she could not have had an idea that he was half so lovely. He would have been nine months old yesterday. I always thought he looked more like you, mother, than anyone else, and when Emily first saw him she exclaimed, "He looks just like your mother, Lucy." And so he did. No stranger passed him without turning to look at him and both the last two months it seems as if both body and mind gained in beauty and expression every day. I often remarked to his Aunt that it seemed to me as if his mind expanded in a remarkable manner for several weeks before his death. He was one of the best children in the world. If he ever cried loud or long every one of the ladies in the house would come or send to see if he was not sick. Dear darling, I don't know how I can live without him. The little fellow was first attacked with croup on Tuesday, the 6th of July. I gave him Hive syrup which operated powerfully and he had a bad night. Wednesday he was better, but I did not take off his night gown. Towards night dear little Emily was taken quite sick and was all night in a violent fever. Thursday I washed and dressed my little darling as usual and he seemed quite recovered, so I gave up the care of him that day principally to the servants and administered an emetic to Emily, which had the effect of removing every bad symptom. I thought the baby did not seem well that night when I put him in bed, but he slept until 10 o'clock, when he awoke with a hoarse, croupy cough. Clark called in Dr. Wynne (who boards with us), who gave him half a teaspoonful of antimonial wine twice, which operated well and in two hours his Aunt Joann and the Dr. left him, thinking he would have a comfortable night, but the little darling slept but a few moments when he woke in great distress which continued to increase till near day, when we again called Dr. Wynne who said his complaint then was inflammation of the

Reprinted courtesy of the Rosenberg Library, Galveston, Texas.

bowels. He gave him 30 drops of paregoric and Clark called Mrs. Shaw who held him in a warm bath. He was relieved for a time but soon the complaint revived to such a degree that we feared he would not live through the day. This was Friday and that night his aunt, Mrs. Flood and Mrs. Edwards sat up with him and Mr. Chaulet (a French gentleman who boards with us) and Dr. Wynne were with him several hours. Clark and I went to bed but were often up through the night. That night was one of great distress to the baby and once, but for the immediate use of the warm bath he would certainly have died in a few minutes. Saturday was a comfortable day and Dr. Smith was called in to consult with Dr. Wynne, (who) the day before pronounced him to be "in sight of land" as he expressed it. Oh, how happy we were in the vain belief that our darling was to be spared to us. Miss Mussina watched that night but I took the baby into bed with me and he slept quietly until toward morning when he seemed in pain so great that James, who sat up too, called in Dr. Wynne, who gave him paregoric, which relieved him so that he slept well till morning. Sunday was a happy day for us. The sweet had a quiet day and even laughed and played something like himself. He was so well that we had no one to watch him and he slept well till towards 2 o'clock. I was so delighted that I spoke to Clark several times to look at him and see how fast he was getting well. At two the darling woke up again in distress and I walked the room with him till the servants got up and I then called Mrs. Shaw and the Dr. and then we found that he was attacked with the remittent chills and fever of the country. He had not a bad day and Mrs. Shaw and I took care of him through that night. Tuesday his illness increased and Dr. and Mrs. Wynne and Mrs. Shaw sat up till 2 o'clock and then James and I got up. Tuesday afternoon Dr. Monk (who is our family physician, but who had been confined to his house with rheumatism for six weeks) rode down and consulted with Drs. Wynne and Smith. Wednesday our darling's illness and Mrs. Flood and Mrs. Hinton sat up with him. He had a tolerable night. Thursday Dr. Monk rode down and spent the day and at night Mrs. Edmunds and Mrs. Taylor watched. No better, not so well on Friday, Miss Selma Savage watched and just before the hour for his chill I got up and called Dr. Wynne and James got a warm bath prepared and put him in. By giving him proper medicine and wrapping him in flannels we brought on a perspiration and we succeeded in breaking his chill. Saturday morning Dr. Wynne came down with his wife and said he would remain with us till the case was decided. Mrs. Shaw and Mrs. Monk sat up all night with him but that day and the next the disease steadily gained ground. Sabbath night Mrs. Flood and Mrs. Taylor watched with him and they thought several times that he was dying. On monday his fever left him and he was very much exhausted. We kept up his strength with wine till the middle of the afternoon, when he failed rapidly and between five and six "the o'er wearied wheels of life at length stood still". His death was so peaceful that it was not easy to tell when he finally ceased to breathe. Lovely most lovely he was both in life and death. There was nothing about him that seemed to have any affinity with earth except the beautiful little body that enclosed his still more pure and perfect spirit. He seemed perfectly patient and resigned and altogether unlike a sick child. If we had ever allowed ourselves to think of such a thing we might have known he was far too beautiful for this world. I know that He who made him so exceedingly lovely had a right to resume his gift, but my heart does rebel against his decree. It was not our partiality alone that made us think him beautiful. When I carried him to where the ladies were sitting, they used to say "there comes the splendid eyes". Mrs. Edmunds used to say she wished she could have his eyes put into her Mary's head and Mrs. Street said the white of his eyes even was handsomer than the eyes of any other child she ever saw. Mrs. Wynne said often that she never saw such a head upon any person in her life. Emily Marston used to say to her mother that she knew that child would not live long for she never saw anything that would compare with him. He was no trouble but I kept him almost constantly in my arms though he would lie a long time on the floor and could sit alone, too. Little Emily asked me a day or two since if I would give such and such things to brother if he was alive; certainly, I said, we would give him everything that is good. Oh, she said, God can give him gooder things as we can. The same day she said to me "Mother what do you be so sorry for? I know you are sorry for brother. Said I, you don't seem to be sorry for anything, dear. Well, said she, sorry isn't always crying. It is singular that he should have had three different diseases, one after the other, as he did. He had two and part of the time three good physicians and as kind friends to help us nurse him as could be found in the world. Mr. Flood, charge d'affaires from the United States to this Republic, boards with us and his wife has been as kind day and night as a friend could be. She watched with him three times, Mrs. Edmunds twice and Mrs. Street, who had at first a sick child of her own to take care of, was to have sat up with Mrs. Edmunds the night our precious baby died. Dr. Wynne, who has a wife and six daughters, boards with us. He and his wife sat up one night and was in a dozen times a day. Dr. Smith, whom I have mentioned to you before, called often and as soon as Dr. Monk was able to ride he came and stayed with us with his wife and watched the sweet little fellow to the last. Mr. Eaton, the Episcopalian clargyman, officiated at the funeral and read the church service in the house and at the grave. . . . Mr. Sargent of Calais who came out here when Mr. Swan first came is going home and will sail sometime next week. I shall write by him and send you some of our darling's hair, and little Emily's at the same time. I hope you will see Jane Delesdernier before she returns to Texas. The baby's name was William Nelson Weston. Sometimes we called him Willie, sometimes Nelson, but the ladies who board with us wanted us to call him Weston because they liked the name better than either of the others. Clark's mother, sister, sister's husband and two children have been here about six weeks. They came to New Orleans by land. Do write to me as soon as you can. I hope before I write again I shall feel differently from what I do now, for now I am wretched. I cannot go anywhere or see anything that does not remind me of the beloved one I have lost. Sweet precious little creature what a comfort it was to have him in my arms. I can't bear to go to bed or to get up again and wherever I go about the house there is something to remind me of him. What shall I do without him? Dear little Emily has been miserable but is getting better. She is a smart intelligent child and rather pretty but would not compare with the baby. We were just about hiring a girl to take care of him. I am glad we did not. I am very glad that I always took care of him myself. How many plans and hopes for the future is buried in his grave. I should have been in Eastport this summer if we could have raised the necessary funds and when I found it was impossible I said to myself, "Well then he will have grown and improved so much the more when mother does see him". How you would have loved him. Jane always was in hopes that Emily would have black eyes and the baby's were so beautiful. I ask Emily what shall I tell

Grandmother for you, she says tell her I've been good. She send her love to grand-mother and Aunt Jane. Do write to me very soon. Clark, his mother and sisters send much love to you. Mrs. Shaw says she hopes she shall never love any child as she has loved our darling. Write soon to your affectionate daughter and sister.

Lucy.

4. William Whitsitt Recounts the Death of His Daughter, 1848

Monday August 7 1848. Our little daughter Martha Jane was taken sick—For sev-eral weeks previous she had been afflicted with whooping cough, cough by which she was much reduced, and so severe was the whooping cough that we had a few weeks previous lost our little negro Charity from its influences. She died Saturday morning July 12th 1848. Monday evening, after Martha Jane was taken, this is, on the first day of her sickness, her mother gave her a dose of Calomel which Shegogg had left for her to take if the whooping cough should make her any worse, and Tues-day morning she gave her a dose of oil. The medicine operated well; but she grew no better.

Tuesday evening Dr. Shegogg was sent for. He came and gave her medicine but she grew worse. Her Grandfather and Grandmother came and staid during nearly the whole of her illness; scarcely a single day or night did they leave her. Kind friends came to assist us, and to sympathize with us, both day and night; and not a single moment after her first night's illness passed away, where there was not some kind friend at her bedside, strictly attentive to her every want.

Wednesday Shegogg bled her. She submitted to be bled as patiently as any grown person would have done. But still she grew worse. Shegogg came to see her every day and sometimes twice a day until August 19th.

He had been told time and again that she was salivated, but he examined her and said she was not. On the morning of the 19th he was told again that she was salivated, and that he was pursuing a wrong course of treatment, administering medicine for one disease when it was the disease which Mercury produces under which she was labouring. Again he examined [her] and said she was salivated and that badly. He then prescribed leeching and poulticing externally, and Iodine to be given internally. The leeches were twice applied, the poulticing frequently all on her left cheek, which was remarkably sore on the inside and inflamed on the out-side. The right one was not affected. The Iodine was given regularly according to prescription. But still the soreness increased and her jaw swelled amazingly. This course of treatment was pursued for above five days during which time Shegogg did not see her. Tho he was sent for once, and once I went to let him know how she was and to see if any alteration in the treatment was necessary.

Wednesday evening August 23rd a little black spot came on her cheek. We thought it had come to a head and was going to discharge matter. Shegogg was sent

From the William A. Whitsitt Journal from Davidson County, Tennessee, in the William Whitsitt Collec-tion, Special Collections Library, Duke University. Reprinted by permission.

for to come and lance it, but he was not at home. In the night we saw that the black spot had grown much larger and was spreading very fast. We saw it was mortification, became alarmed and sent for Shegogg immediately. He came. Looked at it. Lanced it. A little blood and water ran out but not matter. He prescribed a course of treatment and went away. Thursday by the middle of the day the black spot had increased to about the size of a half dollar and was still spreading.

Being convinced that Shegogg was doing no good, I went for Dr. Ezell. He came and prescribed a course of treatment. For a day or two, she took his medicine tolerably well. But she had become so wearied out and disgusted by taking so much medicine that she refused to take, and it was the utmost difficulty that she could be prevailed upon to take anything in the form of medicine. External applications was our only resort. These were insufficient. Still the mortification spread most fearfully. Ezell came to see her until we saw he was doing no good, when he was requested to cease his visits.

Still the mortification spread until it reached the corner of her mouth. I thought that surely it would then stop. But no. It took hold of her sweet little lips and day after day I saw them gradually giving way, blackening, putrefying.

At last it reached the middle of her dear little lips, and I fondly hoped it would then surely stop. But no. Still it pressed on to sure and certain dissolution. Not only did it spread upon her mouth, but also in every other direction. Towards her ear, nose, eye, chin, throat, under jaw, all, *all.* Her left eye became swollen and closed up. Her nose began to decay, her chin was nearly half destroyed, and her poor little mouth almost entirely gone. With difficulty it was, that she could even take a drink of water to cool her little tongue and throat. So intense were her sufferings that she often wished to die. She said that she wanted to die but could not die.

Many remarked that she bore her sufferings with as much patience as a grown person could have done. A few hours before her death, her mother, who was labouring under affliction and had been lying down trying to rest came into the room and sat down by her on her bed. She looked at her. Asked her where she had been, and she stretched her little emaciated arms, with her poor little hands even then cold and icy in death. She stretched them out I say toward her mother. But her mother did not comprehend her design until she said, "I want to hug you, but you won't let me.["]

Her mother then leaned forward over her when she threw her dear little arms around her neck. This caused her mother to burst into a flood of tears, at which the heart of the sufferer was touched. She looked at her and said, "Don't cry Ma.["] She then held her little arms toward her father who was near. He leaned forward and kissed her while she embraced him. Beholding her mother still weeping she was much grieved. And seeking to console her, time and time again she embraced her, exclaiming "Don't cry Ma, Don't cry, Ma.["]

For several days before her death, so great was her pain that she could not lie long contentedly in any one position but wished continually to be turned. Yet when she was turned, though the position was changed, the pain ceased not.

Sunday night Sept. 3rd about 10 o'clock it was observed that she had rested quietly in one position longer than usual but we concluded that while she was easy we would not disturb her. After a time she made some slight movement and said the rocks at her feet were too hot. They were moved a little farther from her feet and she was turned over. In a short time manifesting some little uneasiness she was asked if she did not want some water? She faintly ejaculated yes. Her Grandmother brought her some water and her father raised her up in bed. The water was placed to her mouth, but she could not drink. We then looked at her and saw she was dying. We made haste to call her friends who were in an adjoining room. Scarcely had they time to come in, before she ceased to breathe. She died without a struggle, without a groan, without a sigh. She died, as if it did her good to die.

She died as though it were not death. She only seemed to sink quietly, gently into deep, calm and sweet repose. For 28 long, *long* wearisome days and nights she suffered—how much, no tongue can tell. But when at last death *did* come, he gave a quick and gentle exit, while angelick bands wafted the little uncaged spirit to the bosom of that dear Saviour who loves little children, and who said, of such is the kingdom of heaven. Yes! She suffers no longer. She has gone to bloom in immortal youth in that glorious clime where there is no sickness, no pain and no death!!

But one consideration yet wrings the hearts of her bereaved parents with unutterable anguish. And that is the fact that she did not die a natural death. To die is natural. This is very true. But to be eaten up by calomel is not natural, but poor Martha Jane was killed by degrees, eaten, destroyed, murdered, butchered by calomel and that, too, administered by a regular bred physician.

Oh! She was a lovely girl! Her form was delicate, and she was not well grown, being less than her sister who is two years younger. She was weighed in the early part of the year. Her weight was then 32 pounds. She was remarkably fond of her parents and her sister, not abashed in the company of strangers like most children are, very sociable in her disposition, and seldom ever forgot any person whom she had once known. Her features were comely enough, and her keen penetrating eyes shone with unusual lustre and gave a just and true indication of the mind within, which certainly was of a superior mould. Her mind was that which made her an extraordinary child. This was what made her so justly the pride of her parents, who doted on her too fondly. At the time of her decease, she was aged 7 years, eleven months and 18 days.

5. Louisa Cheves McCord, "Woman's Progress," 1853

And is this progress—Are these noisy tongues—
In fierce contention raised and angry war—
Fit boast for womanhood? Yon shrewish things,
In wordy boisterous debate,—are these
Perfected woman's exponents to show
Her model virtues to a later age?
And shall our daughters cast their woman robes,
A useless cumbrance aside, to seize
Some freer imitation of the man,
Whose lordly strut and dashing stride attract
Their envious love for notoriety?
Shall they, with flashing eye and clanging tongue,

Louisa Susanna Cheves McCord, "Woman's Progress," *Southern Literary Messenger,* November, 1853.

Mount in the rostrum, lecture in the streets,
And, in the arena of election strife,
Claim with shrill voice, and rude dishevelled locks,
"Your votes! your votes!" ye loud-mouthed populace!
Nay;—should that peach-like cheek but feel the breath
Of yonder foul-mouthed crowd, methinks its bloom
Should wither in the contact. God hath made
A woman-nature holier than the man's—
Purer of impulse, and of gentler mould,—
Let her not stain it in the angry strife
Which these, our modern female Reverends,
Learned M. D's, and lecturing damsels, seek
To feed their hungry vanity, and bring
Unnoticed charms before the gaping crowd.
'Tis surely not for this that God hath given
That soothing voice so sweetly taught to whisper
Pity, and hope, and sympathy, and love,
And every holier thought, whose gospel tongue
Can preach its comfort to grief's riven heart!
Here, in the crowd, 'tis harsh and dissonant;
Its softer notes must struggle to a scream
Of impotently shrill, unmeaning effort.
'Tis surely not for this that God hath given
The soft light hand, whose velvet touch can soothe
The achings often both of head and heart.
Here, it would illy stand her in the strife;
And doubled fist, and tiny foot advanced
In attitude of combat were a mock,—
And oh! alas! how foul a mimicry!
Of man's contemptuous life. 'Tis not for this,
Sweet Sisters! not for this! that God hath given
That purer soul, whose impulse (like the flower
Instinct with life that ever seeks the sun
And in his rays doth live) turns to the truth
And loves, and hopes, and doth expand itself
Only to nobler instincts! Stronger to hope,
Loftier to bear than man's; yet meeker too
To patiently endure,—this soul methinks
To strife of grosser passions, God formed not.
The fallen woman is the viler man,
Even as her fall is greater. From the height
Of her own nature's lofty pedestal,
She flings herself with grovelling pride, as though
The nightingale should cease its chaunt, and turn
The aspiring wing which nature taught to rise,
Earthward again, stooping its course to spar
And jungle with some harsh, unnatural note,
In emulation of yon dunghill cock.

Sweet Sister! stoop not thou to be a man!
Man has his place as woman hers; and she
As made to comfort, minister and help;
Moulded for gentler duties, ill fulfils
His jarring destinies. Her mission is
To labour and to pray; to help, to heal,
To soothe, to bear; patient, with smiles, to suffer;
And with self-abnegation nobly lose
Her private interest in the dearer weal
Of those she loves and lives for. Call not this—
(The all-fulfilling of her destiny;
She the world's soothing mother)—call it not,
With scorn and mocking sneer, a drudgery.
The ribald tongue profanes Heaven's holiest things,
But holy still they are. The lowliest tasks
Are sanctified in nobly acting them.
Christ washed the apostles' feet, not thus cast shame
Upon the God-like in him. Woman lives
Man's constant prophet. If her life be true
And based upon the instincts of her being,
She is a living sermon of that truth
Which ever through her gentle actions speaks,
That life is given to labour and to love.
Through this rough world her angel ministry,
Like sweetest water bubbling through the sands
Of arid desert, cheers the weary heart,
And leads the restless soul which cursed its fate
To pause, to think, and learn to love that God
Who midst the parching waste of suffering,
Has dropped this comfort like a boon from Heaven
To bid him drink and live.

                  Sweet Sisters! thus
God wills that we should be; and who profanes
This, the last formed, so the most perfect work
Of His creative will,—this woman nature,—
Who seeks to drag it down, to smirch and blot
Its purer being with the tainting blight
Of passion's license,—doth profane the hope
Of God's creation; doth blot out the light;
Sully the purest beam of reasoning life,
And cast man's nature back upon the beast
To strive and grovel in the lowest lusts
Of passion's vile excess As God is love,
So reasoning nature lives in him through love;
And Woman in the trueness of her being
Is still the never-ceasing minister

Of love which wearies not, which toils and bears,
And sorrowing for the loved ones, doth forget
Her own life's anguish, soothing others' woes.
Then let our holy task be still to cleanse,
But not to change our natures. Let us strive
To be *more* woman,—never to be man.
These reverend Misses, doctors in mob caps,
And petticoated lecturers, are things
Which make us loathe, like strange unnatural births,
Nature's disordered works. You chirping thing
That with cracked voice, and mincing manners, prates
Of rights and duties, lecturing to the crowd,
And in strange nondescript of dress arrays
Unfettered limbs that modesty should hide;
Thus raising, as it were, rebellion's flag
Against her being's nature—call it not,
Sweet Sisters, call not that unsexed thing
By the pure name of Woman. Let us strive
With silent effort in the Woman's cause,
Perfecting in its destinies, our sex,
And cast aside this foul attempt which clings
To degradation as it were our pride.
Oh! let us be the woman of God's make;
No Mrs. Bloomer, Abby Kelly thing
Aping man's vices, while our weaker frame
Knows not his harsher virtues. Let us be
Strong,—but as Woman; resolute in right—
All woman—perfect woman—no false ape—
No monster birth—no female Caliban,
Mocking our nature with unnatural shades
Of strange and foul resemblance. Gentle, pure,
Kind, loving Woman, never can degrade
Her own God-given nature. Only then
When she distorts it to unnatural ends
Doth she degrade her being. Man may rail,
Or mock, or pity her; with tyrant strength
May trample on her weakness, or may sneer
As though his being were of higher mould;
But not for this is she degraded; rather
Ennobled, in the gently bearing it.
There is no degradation which springs not
From our own inmost being. Noble things
Are never trampled into meanness. Low
May be their uses, but vile purposes
Soil not the diamond's hue. Our inmost worth,
At our own heart's tribunal, rights itself,
And e'en midst persecution calmly rests

On its proud consciousness. A noble thing
Is woman's undistorted nature. Let
No taunt, nor jeer, sweet Sisters, shame us from it.
Woman, true Woman, is of larger worth
Than rank or power can fashion. Far above
All that the loud reformer ever dreamed,
Her virtues are no wordy theories,
But sky-born instincts touching on our earth
Still in full flower from Heaven.

6. Southern Women Write of Family, Friendship, Work, and Race, 1821–1853

Family

Will of Justina Maria Henrietta Campbell Taylor, 24 November 1828.

State of South Carolina
I Justina Maria Henrietta Campbell wife of John Taylor Junior of Cheraw in the said state Merchant under the power reserved to me in and by my marriage settlement before marriage dated the twenty-ninth day of December in the year of our Lord one thousand eight hundred and twenty one do make and publish this my last will and testament.

Imprimis whereas my dear and esteemed Husband has a life estate in all the property to which I am entitled and as by the blessing of God he is possessed of an ample fortune of his own I deem it of no consequence to him to leave him any of my property in perpetuity. I therefore give devise and bequeath direct limit and appoint all my Estate and property real and personal whatsoever to my dear daughter Anna Maria Coit her heirs and assigns forever to and for her own sole and separate use and without being in any manner liable to the debts contracts or control of any Husband who in she may have with full power and authority to my said Daughter notwithstanding coverture to dispose thereof or of any part or parts therefore in her life time by deed or instrument under her hand and seal executed in the presence of two witnesses or in and by her last will and testament in the same manner and to the same effect as if she were a feme sole.

Friendship

M. Hooper to her friend Julia Pickens, n.d. 1832, from "At Mrs. McLean's," in North Carolina, to Pittsborough, North Carolina.

Twere vain my Julia to attempt to describe the anguish of this day. Sad inexpressibly sad have been my reflections—and when again and again the truth the bitter truth

These documents can be found in Joan Cashin, ed., *Our Common Affairs: Texts from Women in the South* (Baltimore: Johns Hopkins University Press, 1996).

that we have parted, so far as we can judge, <u>forever</u>—arose, the blood has rushed to my heart until (<u>believe</u> me) I trembled and felt sick in body as well as mind.—

O' Julia Julia <u>now</u> my heart is throbbing with very agony—my tears are ever ready to overflow but what avail are they? Can they recall that dear embrace? those eyes of love? that brow (sweet brow) this very morning I kissed? the hand whose pressure now I feel—No oh no! now will they ever be recalled. O <u>this, this</u> is what breaks my heart—for it feels as if it was really breaking.

To look back <u>upon all your love</u> is vain to alleviate my sufferings. I can only say again and again in agony of Spirit,

> "<u>Jesus thy</u> timely aid impart
> And raise my heart and cheer my heart"

This does comfort me and when I recollect that <u>my Father</u> ordered it in <u>infinite love</u> for our <u>mutual</u> good I am comforted. It cannot be a thing of chance. So <u>much</u> suffering must be intended for some good. I do not give you a romantic exaggeration but the <u>real</u> and literal state of my feelings. Why is it? Is it that I am more capable of feeling more <u>keenly acutely</u> than others? I [illegible] O happy are they who have less. Tis a relief to tell you—oh it is—and this privilege is worth worlds to me.

We meet not here but above—oh <u>there</u> in that bright land—<u>we shall</u>—yes we <u>shall</u>—and these sorrow will <u>then</u> be forgotten—My Julia forget me not—my sister forget me not, forget not my last request. Love my Julia seek her society and the many hours that would otherwise be wasted in frivolous company will be gained in imitating one so estimable—so lovely. Heaven bless you both, asks your almost broken hearted friend & sister.

Miss J. Pickens & Miss M. Hooper

Love to all <u>every Girl</u>—each has in my heart a large place. Kiss the little girls—Adelaide Euphenia Susan Frances Betsy—Sister sends my [page torn]. I value them—my darling farewell!

Sunday morning. With whom dear sister did you sleep? Tell me were you resting placidly on another's arm while I wept in bitterness that mine was not your pillow and this sabbath morning <u>whose hand</u> usurps the sweet place that mine was wont to hold and whose is first in that heart <u>now</u>—Is it your sister whose matchless love for your makes her wretched—<u>oh forget me not.</u>

Do not show this be sure. send my [illegible] from you—

M. S. Rucker and Mary Jane Barton to Elizabeth Taylor, 7 October 1847, from Washington, Texas, to Readyville, Rutherford County, Tennessee.

Dear Mrs. Taylor,

I received your letter dated sept. 22nd and was happy to learn that you were all well. I was forced to believe that you was not a going to write to me, but you have explained it so satisfactorily that I cant complain. We were all truly delighted to hear what an excellent camp meeting you have had and would have been extremely happy to have been with you and participated in your enjoyment. We have had several excellent revivals in the county attended by the most desirable consequences. Indeed religion seems to have exerted an influence upon all there are but a few who does not seem impressed with the necessity of religion. We have church nearly ever sabbath and attended by a flourishing Sunday School. My dear friend you cant imagine how happy it would make me to visit my native land and to see my friends once more. I am very thankful to your father for his kind offer and would except of it but the children have become so attached to their Uncles and Aunts and also to the country that [they] do not wish to leave it; yet they all express their pleasure and happiness to visit their Grandfather and relatives and spend a year or so, but there is one part of your letter that I dont understand in reference to the company you keep. I have never doubted but you have kept the best of company. In response Mr. Ferel I have not seen him but once since last Christmas and then but a few moments. I just di——— to speak to him and that is all. I would be glad if you would explain it to me in your next letter.

Joshua was delighted to think that you a going to send him a present and ask us about a dozen times a day what we think it is. He says he will visit you when he receives it but cant think of spending a night with you unless I go with him. He is going to school. His uncle bought him a reading book. He was so delighted with it he memorized a piece directly to speak on Friday last. They are all going to school here, the two girls and Joshua. James is boarding at Brenham. Tell Mary Jane that we are all so much pleased to think we are to be at her wedding. We s[t]ill hold our selves ready to go. I am in hopes it will be very soon for I am desirous of visiting you and I know that I will never get there unless something of the kind happens. We are all well at this time. The county is generally healthy. We all join and send our love to you and Mother, Father, Husband, Children, and all. Your affectionate friend, M. S. Rucker.

P.S. I saw Bob last week. He was very sorry to hear of his Brother in law['s] death. He was delighted to hear from his Mother and wishes to be remembered to them all. I should [have] concluded my letter as Mary wishes to address her cousin a few lines.

My dear Cousin

It is has been a long time since I have written to you and I will state my reasons for neglecting to write. First I am going to school and have a number of difficult studies to attend and worst of all have a composition to write every other week which keeps me very busy. Secondly, I have been very unhealthy this summer and dilatory both mental and phisically but I have now regained my health and being at leisure I shall deliver you a short epistol and try to portray my thoughts to you as exactly as possible.

My dear Cousin it is useless of me to express my desire of seeing you seeing that it is impossible. We will content ourselves by imagining ourselves conversing with each other. When Aunt wrote how you were enjoying yourselves sitting by your fireside you know not how I wish to be with you and participate in your pleasure. I am rather confined at present having to attend school. I cannot get time to write you a long letter. I have no news to tell you No weddings no actves of importance from me was just a monotony of dullness. I wish you would write me a long letter with all the news you have. If you have nothing else describe your fathers residence and all pertaining to it and another thing I want you to eat a double portion of apples, one half for me and when you sit down by your fireside to eat apples think of me in Texas seating by a heeping log fire eating pecans for want of better. I have tasted an apple but three times since here I have been living and cider I have never taste a single drop since I left my native land. We have plenty of whisky and brandy and ale such as I care the least about yet for all that I do not think that I could leave Texas to live. Cousin you must come to see me. You will be pleased I am sure. I will give you as many beaus as you can take care of and as many beautiful flowers to press and fill your album as you can wish. Do come it would give me inexpressible happiness. I see nothing to prevent you. Elizabeth and Joshua are standing around the table fixing some hair for cousin Frances. Joshua says the short piece is his the middle E. and the outside mine. Elizabeth says that Frances must come with you. She sends her love to all. Tell Cousin Jane that it will not be long before our school is out and then I will—and you a long letter. In the meantime you must write to me every opportunity. Receive all our best love. Your affectionate cousin M. J. Barton.

WORK

Diary of Lucy Muse Walton Fletcher.

2 February 1857. Although I have Scarcely time or strength to write tonight I must write down an event that is altogether a new thing in our history among this people—Mr. Engle brought his wife over to spend the evening with us. It really did me good, although it placed me in quite a dilemma. Poor Sarah has been suffering dreadfully with a gathering on one of the fingers of her right hand, & had with difficulty succeeded in getting up our frugal dinner. (We have had but 2 meals a day since Christmas.) It was after 3 when they arrived, & we were just finishing off our dinner—table was to be cleared off, fires replenished in both rooms—the baby to nurse, company to be entertained, & <u>immediate</u> preparations made up for an early supper, as they had several miles to ride. I had been almost worn out by the exertions of the morning—after making up 2 beds, helping to clear off the breakfast table, cleaning out my own room, washing & dressing the children, I had cleaned up in the study & <u>Robert's</u> room which is always a <u>serious</u> undertaking, owing to the <u>quantity</u> & variety of litter (tobacco, ashes, &c) & the number & weight of books &c to be lifted & dusted—& I had to clear away the dust & dirt of plaster made by some men who came to cut a hole in the ceiling to the garrett. Stopping meanwhile to make up some light bread for dinner. (It was my first attempt at light rolls & I succeeded better than I expected.) As Nannie too was complaining I had the passages & stairs to swept & by the time I had finished I was aching from head to foot. When I seated myself to nurse the baby, I could scarcely raise myself up again. My back has been troubling me very much of late, indeed I have felt for the last month like a stiffened, over-worked horse. . . .

I do not wish to <u>complain</u> of any hardship or trial, but I so long for a <u>little sympathy</u> sometimes. My poor husband has so many demands on his time & patience in the performance of his responsibilities as man of all work, that I try to say as little as possible about my own trials of nerve & strength. It does trouble me to see so much of his time taken up with the care of horse cow & hogs, having to run thro' snow nearly up to his waist after an unruly cow, who has been more than usually well willed of late, or in full chase after some of the neighbor's hogs who have already ruined a large quantity of the fodder he was at so much pains to have put up, for the winter—

Our new cook is really very pleasant, more like a <u>human</u> being than any I have had. She is very careless in her habits, but not more so, than many, who are older, & as she seems conscious of her faults & wishes to have them corrected I hope to have some satisfaction in my Kitchen—which has always been a place of horror to me, except at intervals last year when Mary laid aside her contrariness for a time. Sarah has really had a hard time getting settled, for two or three weeks the weather was intensely cold, wells & springs nearly dry & it was almost impossible to hire any of the lazy negro men about here to bring wash water—one night, Antony a waggish black fellow belonging to Mrs. Neill took a large tub & a bucket in his hand, & returned from the Spring ¼ mile distant, over 2 or 3 fences, with the tub full of water—the next week no soap could be attained, after waiting as long as I could for some other opportunity to "turn up" I had to send Sarah off in a snowstorm 3 miles on a man's saddle—last week when Soap & water were plenty she was suffering so much with a gathering on the middle finger of her right hand that she could not wash at all or do much of any thing. I tried very hard to get a woman from one of the neighbors who has a number of servants about her, but was unsuccessful, & on Saturday had to set to work myself—as we had had so little washing done since Christmas, the children's wardrobes would not holdout—After making up bread to last over Sabbath, I washed on until Sarah seeing that I was very much exhausted <u>insisted</u> on washing (on the board) with her left hand while I rinsed, wrung them & hung them out, before bed time I had them all ironed aired & ready for use—The Sabbath fortunately for me was stormy & I could not go to Church, so that I had what I greatly needed a day of rest. . . .

Race

Judith Page Rives to her sister-in-law Mrs. J. F. Page, 23 June 1852, from Paris, France, to Albemarle County, Virginia.

. . . I have just been reading <u>"Uncle Tom's Cabin."</u> I dare say you have seen it and cannot fail as I do to admire the wonderful talent with which it is written. The author is a perfect artist, and her paintings however terrible are splendid. I am sure we have half a dozen <u>Mrs. Shelby's</u> and <u>Mas' Georges</u> in our own neighborhood, and one of our dear angels now in glory might well impersonate to us the faultless <u>Eva</u>. The dreadful part it is to be hoped is not every day occurrence but it is fearful to think that there are such abominations in our land, as I have too often heard from credible sources to doubt. The author slaps up and down, right and left, North and South, so that we cannot quarrel with her for telling us dreadful though wholesome truths—I was delyhted to find so powerful a writer an advocate of colonization in Africa, the only reasonable solution of this vexed and troublesome question. I feel quite "<u>curious</u>" to know what is generally thought of such a work in our country and neighborhood—do tell me when you write. . . .

Give our united and best love to each member of your dear family circle, and continue to remember us in your prayers as we never fail to remember you and yours. Offer our kindest rgards and best wishes to our neighbors and friends, and believe me as ever, my dearest sister, most affectionately yours, J. P. Rives.

⚶ *E S S A Y S*

In this excerpt from her book *Within the Plantation Household,* Elizabeth Fox-Genovese, a professor at Emory University, offers a rigorous conceptualization of women's status in the South, a status determined by class, race, and gender. Her essay outlines some of her basic concepts and delves more deeply into gender conventions that affected southern women. She demonstrates how the southern household was the center of productive and reproductive activities. Sally McMillen, a professor of history at Davidson College, exposes the realities, joys, and tragedies of women's lives through their experiences as mothers in an excerpt from her book *Motherhood in the Old South.* McMillen argues that childrearing was a wearing time in women's lives, and that because of limited medical knowledge, unsanitary conditions, and widespread diseases in the South, the illness and death of children were common.

Constraints of the Plantation Household

ELIZABETH FOX-GENOVESE

Southern women belonged to a slave society that differed decisively from the northern bourgeois society to which it was politically bound. Slavery as a social system shaped the experience of all its women, for slavery influenced the nature of the whole society, not least its persisting rural character. Southern slave society consisted largely of a network of households that contained within themselves the decisive relations of production and reproduction. In the South, in contrast to the North, the household retained a vigor that permitted southerners to ascribe many matters—notably labor relations, but also important aspects of gender relations—to the private sphere, whereas northerners would increasingly ascribe them to the public spheres of market and state. The household structure and social relations of southern society had multiple and far-reaching consequences for all spheres of southern life, including law, political economy, politics, and slaveholders' relations with yeomen and other nonslaveholding whites. And it had special consequences for gender relations in general and women's experience in particular.

The persistence in the South of the household as the dominant unit of production and reproduction guaranteed the power of men in society, even as measured by nineteenth-century bourgeois standards. During the period in which northern society was undergoing a reconversion of household into home and ideologically ascribing it to the female sphere, southern society was reinforcing the centrality of plantation and farm households that provided continuities and discontinuities in the experience of women of different classes and races. Variations in the wealth of households significantly differentiated women's experience, but the common structure as a unit of production and reproduction under men's dominance provided some basic similarity. Effectively, the practical and ideological importance of the household in southern society reinforced gender constraints by ascribing all women to the domination of the male heads of households and to the company of the women of their own households. In 1853 Mary Kendall, a transplanted New Englander, wrote to her sister of her special pleasure in receiving a letter from her, for "I seldom see any person aside from our own family, and those employed upon the plantation. For about three weeks I did not have the pleasure of seeing *one white female face,* there being no white family except our own upon the plantation." The experience of black slave women differed radically from that of all white women, for they belonged to households that were not governed by their own husbands, brothers, and fathers. But even black slave women shared with white women of different social classes some of the constraints of prevalent gender conventions.

As members of a slave society, southern women differed in essential respects from other American women, although their experience has not figured prominently in the development of American women's history, much less influenced the theory that informs generalizations about the experience of American women. Southern women's history should force us to think seriously about the relation between the experiences that unite women as members of a gender and those that divide them as members of specific communities, classes, and races. It should, in other words, challenge us to recognize class and race as central, rather than incidental to, women's identities and behavior—to their sense of themselves as women. . . .

Class and race deeply divided southern women, notwithstanding their shared experience of life in rural households under the domination of men. There is almost no evidence to suggest that slaveholding women envisioned themselves as the "sisters" of yeoman women, although there may have been some blurring at the margins when kin relations crossed class lines. In contrast, there is reason to believe that some slaveholding women felt minimal kinship with their female slaves, with whom they might have intimate, if tension-fraught, relations in everyday life. In general, but for women in particular, class relations in southern society remained essentially hierarchical. If anything, relations among women of different classes strengthened and reaffirmed class distance among free white families and served as an antidote to the elements of egalitarianism—or at least formal political democracy—that characterized relations among free white men. The relations among women also reaffirmed the special race relations of slave society, for the more established slaveholding women viewed their female slaves as somehow part of their affective universe in a way that they did not view yeoman women or even arrivistes. But they unavoidably viewed those slaves as social and racial inferiors whose station in life was that of perpetual servants. Thus, the arrivistes could in time "arrive," whereas the slaves had no prospects and the nonslaveholders could be perceived as having none.

Gender, race, and class relations constituted the grid that defined southern women's objective positions in their society, constituted the elements from which they fashioned their views of themselves and their world, constituted the relations of different groups of southern women to one another. The class relations that divided and interlocked southern women played a central role in their respective identities. Slaveholding, slave, yeoman, poor white, and middle-class town women, as members of a gender, shared the imposition of male dominance, but their experience of that dominance differed significantly according to class and race.

The forms of male prejudice and dominance differ among societies that assign specific purposes and forms to prejudice and domination. The distinctive forms of male dominance in the South developed in conjunction with the development of slavery as a social system and reflected the rural character that slavery reinforced in southern society. In the South, as in many other societies, church and state substantially reinforced the prevalent forms of male dominance, some of which were national and some regionally specific. Within the South, the forms varied considerably according to community. Like religion and the law, the rural character of southern slave society impinged upon women of all classes and races in innumerable, albeit different, ways. Above all, it circumscribed their mobility and the size of the communities to which they belonged or within which they developed their sense of themselves. For most women, male dominance appeared specifically as a direct manifestation of the social and gender relations of particular communities, however much accepted as a general law of life. . . .

Within the household, the everyday lives of slaveholding women, and in some measure those of slaves, conformed closely to prevailing notions of the appropriate division of labor by gender, following earlier British, European, and, to some extent, African conceptions of male and female spheres. Although some Euro-American and Afro-American views coincided, slaveholders and slaves did not contribute equally to the gradual crystallization of distinct southern patterns. With their power over slaves, slaveholders could set the terms of everyday life and could, if they chose, violate their slaves' notions of gender relations. Convention declared that the household responsibilities of slaveholding women were natural extensions of their personal relations as wives, mothers, and daughters, all of whom answered to a master who was husband or father. Slave women, in contrast, answered to a master who was not of their natural family, class, or race and who at any moment could exercise his power according to imperatives that had nothing to do with family feeling. They knew that he frequently exercised his power severely and might even make sexual demands that mocked the prevalent norms of gender relations to which he claimed to subscribe.

For slaveholding women, gender relations merged seamlessly with the sense of their own social roles and personal identities. Modern sensibilities may view them as the oppressed victims of male dominance, but few of them would have agreed, notwithstanding some bad moments. Their men's abuse of prerogatives, notably sexual philandering but also excessive drinking and the squandering of family resources, caused them untold distress. But their resentment of these abuses rarely passed into rejection of the system that established their sense of personal identity within a solid community.

For slave women, the power of masters over their lives and the lives of their men distorted their sense of the links between their relations with men and their roles and identities as women. For black women, social relations with black men did not necessarily mesh with work relations. They did not primarily devote themselves to the care of their own children and houses, and their gender roles did not necessarily emanate directly from their relations with black men or from African traditions. Within the big house, they performed the labor deemed appropriate to the gender roles of white women, but they worked as servants—the opposite of mistress. Even the exceptions—cook, mammy, and a few especially well-trained maids—did work that bore no necessary relation to their roles as mother or wife. Their field labor departed even further from Euro-American notions of women's gender roles, although it may have fit more comfortably with Afro-American traditions. From the perspective of the dominant culture, slave women were regularly assigned to men's work. White farm women, North and South, might work in the fields, but they were not expected to do the kind of heavy work routinely assigned to black women. The only concession to a notion of orderly gender roles for slave women lay in their being primarily assigned to work with other women rather than with men, and even that norm was frequently breached. Within the slave community women's activities were tied more directly to their personal relations with men, as, for example, when they cooked and sewed for their own families. But their roles as daughters, wives, and mothers depended upon the sufferance of a master who could always break up families. Under these conditions the slave's sense of herself as a woman—her gender identity—remained separable from the gender relations and roles that depended heavily on the vicissitudes of power in a slave society.

Both slave and slaveholding women lived in a world in which gender afforded a principle of the practical, political, and symbolic organization of society. Norms of appropriate gender conventions could be violated. Black women could be set to work considered unfit for white women. Slave women could be separated from their children and husbands and could be subject to a sexual violation that would have offended the honor and evoked the murderous retaliation of the husbands and fathers of white women. Violations of the norm painfully reminded slaves that they did not enjoy the full status of their gender, that they could not count on the "protection"—however constraining and sometimes hypocritical—that surrounded white women. Yet the norms also governed the opportunities available to slave women, for ruling men, like enslaved men, were unlikely to violate the norms in ways that would promote the independence of slave women. Slave women may not have had access to the privileges of slaveholding women, but they, too, remained excluded from a host of male prerogatives. In this respect, the gender conventions of slave society weighed equally on all women, regardless of race or class. Gender relations, in both their observance and their breach, constituted an essential aspect of the relations of power between classes and races.

The household worlds of slave and slaveholding women embodied and contributed to the dominant gender relations of southern society, forming a system of conventions that guided women's behavior and identities. Southern gender conventions simultaneously derived from and influenced social relations and operated like a language or discourse that helped individuals to make sense of their place in their world. The constant flux of relations between individual women and men, as with those among women of different classes and races, unfolded as discrete stories—the result of personality and circumstance—but gender conventions offered a way of interpreting those stories and linking them to society. The widespread acceptance of gender conventions limited a woman's freedom to write her life exactly as she might have chosen.

Gender conventions direct fundamental human impulses into socially accept-able and useful channels and thereby serve the needs of individuals as well as of so-ciety. They derive as much from custom and practice as from ideology. Influenced both by tradition and circumstances, they constitute compelling ideals disseminated through literate, visual, and oral cultures. They figure among society's most influ-ential and binding elements, for, in telling people how to be men and women, they tell them how to relate to society. Modern cynicism about the observance of social rules has celebrated the breach rather than the observance of conventions in past so-cieties. A healthy appreciation of people's determination to create their own lives and to resist the imprint of official values has led to doubts that official prescrip-tions had anything to do with life as it was actually lived.

Yet although the dominant gender conventions of the antebellum South reflected the values, aspirations, and anxieties of the dominant class, they also encoded a slave society's essential conditions of life for yeomen and slaves as well as for masters. The yeomen, not to mention the slaves, did not always share most of the slaveowners' concerns. They resisted many of their pretensions, not least because the slaveholders' conventions linked gender relations closely to attitudes toward class relations. But they could not readily forge alternate gender conventions, at least not in the great heartland dominated by the system of plantation households, whatever success they may have had in the yeoman-dominated upcountry. Slaveholders, slaves, and non-slaveholding whites—whatever their differences over specifics—shared an ideal of the universal division between women and men. They agreed that defined male and female spheres constituted the bedrock of society and community, even if they did not subscribe to emerging bourgeois notions about the nature of the spheres.

For southerners, gender spheres interlocked with networks of families and households; men represented those families and households in the larger worlds of politics and warfare, or, to reverse matters, women belonged within families and households under the governance and protection of their men. As Henry Wise wrote to his first wife, Anne: "My wife is not competent to advise the statesman or the politician—her knowledge, her advice, her ministry is in a kindlier sphere." Yet southerners, unlike northerners, did not view either families or households as pri-marily female preserves, but as terrain that contained woman's sphere. According to this view, women did not belong abroad alone; a woman alone on the public thor-oughfares was a woman at risk. Women had no business to bear arms and no place in politics. They were not fit to meet men on equal terms in the combat of public life and, should they attempt to, they would open themselves to being bested by supe-rior physical strength.

Rural women lived within the constraints of these fundamental attitudes to-ward gender relations and spheres—within a set of firmly entrenched expectations about appropriate behavior for women and for men. Although rooted in the specific conditions of their everyday lives in rural households in a slave society, these ex-pectations derived from longstanding Euro-American and Afro-American notions about the natural relations between women and men. At all levels, southern culture reflected and reinforced a view of the world in which women were subordinate to men. The view proved the more powerful because it conformed so closely to intu-itive notions about "natural" differences between women and men. . . .

The ideal of the lady constituted the highest condition to which women could aspire, but the lady, like other women, remained bound by a broad vision of appropriate gender relations. The activities of even the most prestigious lady remained carefully circumscribed by the conventions ordained for women in general, but southern culture placed a premium on her meeting her responsibilities in accordance with her station. The lady, like less privileged women, accepted the dominance of men but cultivated her own sense of honor, which depended heavily on her embodiment of the privileges of her class. In her case, the male dominance that weighed so heavily on black slave and many nonslaveholding white women was, in many respects, experienced as protection. Even as male prerogative hedged her in, it shielded her from direct contact with the disorderly folks who populated the world beyond her household.

A concern with locking women firmly into coverture and domesticity prevailed throughout the United States during the first half of the nineteenth century. No region encouraged divorce or the ownership, much less the effective control, of property by married women, but southerners and their courts proved especially intransigent, the precocious married woman's property act of Mississippi (1839) notwithstanding. As Wyatt-Brown has insisted, southern women's legal standing affected "not only their livelihood but also their sense of themselves." In his judgment, "the effect of the law upon gender relations" has been so little considered that "the hard economic and legal reasons for women's passivity have been hidden from historical view. Too often advances in church life, opening new vistas for usefulness, have obscured the implications of restraints in law."

In a world dominated by male strength, women could not aspire to be the head of a household. They might answer for the household as delegates of their families, but even then they required extensive support from male kin or friends. Slaveholding women might inherit households from their fathers or husbands, but they almost invariably turned the management over to men in practice, even if a will or marriage settlement had left them legally in the woman's control. In general, a widow's ability to assume command depended upon the age of her sons. Should they still be minors, she would have to make do, normally with the help of an overseer; should one son be an adult, he would probably try to assume control himself. Natalie de DeLage Sumter of South Carolina ranked as one of the few women who, as a widow, genuinely managed a plantation, and even she had ample assistance from overseers. Keziah Brevard, who was a widow, did the same, relying upon male advice and the everyday assistance of her difficult driver, Jim.

Whenever possible the male kin of heiresses assumed legal or de facto control. James Henry Hammond braved the wrath of the family of his bride, Catherine Fitzsimmons, to secure complete control of her large inheritance and made his "duties as plantation master . . . the focus of his existence." Anna Matilda King participated more actively than Catherine Fitzsimmons in the management of her extensive inheritance, for her husband, Thomas Butler King, was more often absent than present on the estate. Yet she always treated him as master of the household, consulting him on everything from the marketing of crops to the education of their children, and in everyday matters she relied heavily on the advice of male neighbors, factors, and kin. Eventually, to her delight and relief, her oldest son, Butler, took over completely. Margaret Campbell, who inherited Argyle Plantation in the

Mississippi Delta from her husband, ran the place with the assistance of an overseer and neighbors and on the basis of constant consultation with her cousin, Robert Campbell.

David Outlaw spent long periods fulfilling his obligations in the U.S. House of Representatives, leaving his wife, Emily, to preside over the household in Bertie County, North Carolina. He regularly wrote to her about the details of management but expected to provide her with male assistance for their execution. Emily Outlaw consulted him on everything, including the hiring of a governess and the appropriateness of letting their daughter give a party. "Really," he responded on the question of the governess, "I shall quarrel with you if you do not quit asking my advice and permission about matters of this kind." She was implying, whatever her intentions, "that I exact from you to do nothing without my permission." He did not deserve the reproach and had always considered theirs at least "a partnership of equals." He had the "most unlimited confidence in your prudence and discretion." Yet on the matter of the party, to which he had "no objection" and in which he could see no "impropriety," he admonished her "not to give your guest [*sic*] liquor enough to get drunk and get Joe Cherry or some other gentleman to assist you."

John Quitman did not take so tolerant a view. His wife, Eliza, reported that things were going badly on their Springfield Plantation, where the overseer "was in a constant state of intoxication," the "negroes were idle doing nothing whatever," the cotton had not been weighed, and the overseer had "shot some of the cattle for mere sport." She had requested Mr. Kent, who brought the news, to go up and discharge Rees, the delinquent overseer, at once. "I hope my dear John," she concluded, "that what I have done may meet your approbation. It appeared to me to be the only course to pursue in your absence." She hoped in vain. Quitman replied, "I fear you have done wrong in discharging Rees—These reports are generally exaggerated and at any rate no more harm could have been done before my return." He did not add that had he been present the harm might never have occurred at all.

Like Sarah Gayle, many women cared deeply about having a plantation household—a farm—as a basis for family security, and some, like Floride Calhoun, preferred to remain at home while their husbands were off attending to politics or business. Yet few had the training or taste to oversee the management of farming or business activities themselves. Mrs. James Polk insisted on keeping the family plantation when her husband became president, but she had a competent overseer to run it. She apparently possessed uncommon business sense. The overseer consulted her on the timing of the marketing of the crop, but she consulted him on the specifics of managing the slaves. When John Grimball was away, he meticulously instructed his wife, Meta, on innumerable details, from the feeding of mulch cows to care of the horses to distributing molasses to sick slaves. As a widow, Hugh Legaré's mother retained the family plantation, but she always begged her son to assume responsibility for its management. Legaré, although devoted to his mother, did not respond to her pleas. Rachel O'Connor, a widow who presided over a cotton plantation in Feliciana Parish, Louisiana, had terrible trouble with her overseers and regularly wrote to her brother, David, for advice.

A lack of business knowledge constituted only part of the problem for these southern women—romance aside—they could not exercise mastery of their own slaves, much less contribute to the control of the slaves in their communities.

Women who managed plantations were, like all other planters, responsible for contributing to the patrols and to other community responsibilities such as building and repairing the levees on the delta, but women could not meet those obligations in person. Some women, in fact, relied heavily on slave drivers to manage the other slaves and even the basic farm operations of the household. During the Civil War, with many overseers as well as slaveholders away, the use of drivers to run plantations became even more common. When the driver was accomplished and loyal the results could be excellent; when he chafed under the direction of a mistress they could leave a good deal to be desired. Keziah Brevard was at her wits' end with Jim, her driver. Jim enjoyed the requisite authority over the other slaves: "Every servant knuckles to him. If they do not his family will put them down." But he was also "an impudent negro," whom Keziah Brevard mistrusted yet dared not punish. She believed him to be "a self willed negro" who "wants every servant on the place to look to him as a superior & he certainly has great influence over my negroes." She could only hope that he "begins to cave a little" and that "his power is on the wane." As Keziah Brevard, like Sarah Gayle and many others, knew, slaveholding women could not, in their own persons, embody the physical attributes of a master, who could, if circumstances demanded, whip his strongest male field hand himself.

Thus, although some women owned plantations and more had to assume responsibility when their husbands were away, they "managed" them through men in all except the rarest of cases. Overseers exercised much wider authority when working for women than they would have dared to claim when working for men. Overseer or no, a woman planter almost always had a male relative or close friend in the neighborhood to look in on her plantation affairs. Not surprisingly, southern men assumed women's incapacity and discussed its consequences for the maintenance of community order. It will not do to dismiss their judgment as so much male prejudice, for the diaries and correspondence of these women with their husbands and others sustains it, and, more to the point, the evidence from the war years, when many women were put to the test, is overwhelming.

Motherhood in the Old South

SALLY G. McMILLEN

"James has been ill," wrote an Alabama mother of her infant son, "and my inexperience and fear of relying on my own judgment, together with the heartrending task of watching a little sufferer who cannot tell its wants, all convince me that I am now beginning as a Mother and wife to experience trials I have hitherto been a stranger to—I often feel like giving up under the responsibilities of my station." She added, though, that she would "look above for strength to assist" her. A Georgia physician understood such apprehensions. "There is no anxiety like that of the fond mother who clasps in her arms her sweet and tender babe," commented Dr. Joseph Wright, "which she has but recently struggled and travailed to bring into the world yet knows not how to minister to its wants." The care of children was what southern antebellum society regarded as women's sacred occupation. . . .

Steady good health escaped nearly all antebellum southern families. Almost all experienced epidemics, illnesses, accidents, and accompanying high mortality. Most southern parents saw the death of at least one child, and infant illnesses recurred seemingly without end. The poor health of young children was so common that references to sickness often described a relatively vigorous family. Anne Cameron was pleased that her children had "upon the whole enjoyed good health," although one youngster had a sore throat and another was suffering from a disordered stomach. More strikingly, Fanny Lawrence reassured her husband that their children were well. She went into the condition of each, mentioning that one son had an ear that was oozing, one child had worms, another had an inflamed foot, and their newborn had an enlarged navel and "has not looked so well for a day or so." From Fanny's perspective, things could apparently have been much worse. . . .

The ultimate responsibility for infant care usually rested on mothers. Sympathetic husbands, neighbors, relatives, domestic servants, and physicians provided assistance, but it was mothers who had their infants' needs at heart, could sensitively react to each mood and movement, and were deemed best suited to ensuring the soundness of the country's next generation. Society's glorified vision of motherhood notwithstanding, southern women found child rearing difficult, especially when their infants were ill. Mothers might spend days or even weeks attending sick children. Mahala Roach's diary chronicled ceaseless attention to her sickly family. On one occasion, with two children ill, she managed to find time for only a brief journal entry. "I have not been to bed at all," wrote the exhausted mother, "sat up and held John in my arms all night long." (This infant demanded constant care, for he had weighed only three and a half pounds at birth.) Several mothers mentioned all-night vigils, which could continue as long as two or three weeks. Nursing a sick child interfered with a mother's normal routine and sometimes absorbed her so totally that she had no time to herself even for sleep or writing letters. Typical of many young mothers was Letty Lewis, of Virginia, who wrote, "Today is the first time for near a week, my dear mother, that I have been able to put my poor little Letty out of my arms long enuf to commence a letter in reply to your last which I rec'd about ten days ago." Husbands might relate domestic news—as they often did after delivery—when their wives were burdened with a sick child. More likely, letters remained unwritten.

Even under the best of conditions, women approached their maternal tasks with a good deal of trepidation, particularly in the case of a firstborn. "I cannot tell you what a trial it was and how awkward I felt when I first undertook the management of my baby," confessed an Alabama woman in 1837, "but now I am learning to wash, dress, and undress her without suffering half as much anxiety." Though the family owned slaves, this mother apparently did not have, or did not use, domestic servants to assist with the tasks she spoke of. She probably learned what to do through trial and error, from sympathetic neighbors, or from advice books. Handling an illness was far more distressing but an almost constant concern. Hugh Clay, of Huntsville, Alabama, described the reaction of his wife, Celeste, to their newborn's bout with colic. "She has all a mother's apprehension—has had a cry or two—wishes her mother were here—and is nervous and unhappy," he admitted. . . .

A mother's own poor health could reduce her ability to nurse a sick infant. A weakened condition during a difficult pregnancy or following a delivery could make infant health care arduous or impossible. Anne Holmes commented that her cousin Ann Jones was again "in a family way" and so sick that she could not nurse her one-year-old daughter, who had whooping cough. G. A. Wyche, of Alabama, described the postnatal condition of his wife Bettie as "high fever and great soreness of the womb and violent pain in the womb and all her limbs, so much so that she was perfectly helpless." Bettie was unable to roll over in bed without assistance, much less attend her newborn.

The constant care of young children was often the very reason women's health declined. One husband sighed, "My wife's ill health has been much increased by the labours and cares and anxieties of a large family." Often other domestic duties added to the burdens of a mother with sick children. Mrs. P. M. Syme, of Petersburg, Virginia, nursed her baby, who had a severe case of croup. In a typical reaction of pure exhaustion, she confessed, "I am sometimes almost ready to give up, in despair, but a sense of duty urges me on." Her responsibilities had become heavier because her husband was incapacitated for three months and also required her attention.

Mothers often had to act on their own with regard to infant health. Husbands might be away tending to business or political matters, leaving their wives without another adult they could turn to for comfort and assistance. As a rule, husbands, when home, did not take charge of nursing a sick child but might be consulted on medical problems or perform in certain medical or child-care capacities. Just as important, they offered a strong shoulder when their wives felt overwhelmed or exhausted. In the more remote southern settlements, plantation women missed the support that neighbors and friends could provide, especially in an emergency. Locating a doctor was often difficult. In a crisis, women often acted alone, making important decisions about the proper medical attention for their children.

Mrs. Hall's efforts to raise her children on the family plantation were poignant. Rebecca worked under the disadvantage of an unstable mental condition, a dependence on drugs, and an unsupportive and absent husband. Maternal duties overwhelmed her, and she frequently complained that she had no nearby relatives or friends or reliable domestic servants. She admitted that she was "almost worried out" by constantly holding the newborn and that she never ventured off the plantation. Months later, she apologized to her sister for failing to write. "I am so engaged in nursing," she explained, "I cannot, and then after losing my sleep every night I have to be in attendance all day and no one to relieve me whilst I could take a few moments repose." The situation only worsened with time. Four years later, Rebecca was home alone with three young daughters. She blamed her "hysteria" on the "constant din of children." "Now I have to stand the fire and roar of their artillery, which I can never do without fleeing from them or trying to remedy their perturbed and violent passions," she wrote in a desperate vein. "I am almost worn out in the cause, when I have a baby, it can never lie like other people's, always must be in the arms or suckling, and the larger ones not much better." Rebecca's daughters suffered from worms and fevers, and except for occasional visits from a local physician, she saw to their health care. In the fall of 1841, her daughter Alice was fatally burned—in an accident that Rebecca's husband blamed on her inattention and carelessness. In her effort to save the child, she severely burned her own hand. For months thereafter, the frazzled mother left the family clothes unwashed and unmended. Rebecca herself died shortly after Alice's tragedy, never having achieved peace as wife and mother.

Each addition to a large southern family brought new burdens. A Virginia woman, F. Brockenbough, commenting on her domestic situation to a friend, wrote, "I can hardly say my time is my own—six small daughters, I assure you, make me a complete bond woman, every moment is theirs." Some mothers scarcely weaned a child before becoming pregnant with the next. In raising a large family, southern mothers often had neither the time nor the energy to do more than look after the children who were ill. Family size prevented southern mothers from lavishing time and attention on each child. Even so, they worked overtime, undermining their own physical and emotional well-being.

The southern climate, with its numerous epidemic and endemic diseases, made things worse. Typical were the Elliotts, of coastal South Carolina, who battled the unending parade of childhood illnesses and malarial fevers. Phoebe Elliott regretted the location of their plantation. "I begin now to feel great concern about the health of my family in the low country," she noted, as the family began its annual trek to cooling mountain springs. Southern mothers blamed the "mushetoes," "musketos," or yellow flies for bothering their babies' sleep at night and interfering with their own rest. Humid malarial regions could be particularly devastating to young children's health, and when possible, families relocated temporarily to healthier regions.

In accepting the miasmic explanation for diseases, southern mothers concluded that pure air was essential to good health. Trips to the mountains, the sea, and to cooling springs often figured in a privileged family's summer or fall plans. Mothers might leave home and husband temporarily to find an invigorating setting for their children. A North Carolina mother believed that city air might be more beneficial for her newborn than the malarial damp surrounding their plantation. When Anne Cameron's three-month-old daughter experienced severe chills and fever, the worried mother vowed to leave the family plantation to visit Raleigh, judging that "if she stays here, she will hardly get through this month." Southern mothers put their infant's health before other concerns, even if that meant dismantling part of the household and causing other inconvenience. Taking an active step probably eased a mother's anxiety as well.

The poor health of the young could persuade southern families to move permanently. Families like the Whittles, of Richmond, Virginia, relocated to the countryside where the situation was "much better for children." Israel Pickens, a North Carolinian, moved his family to St. Stephens, Alabama, in 1818, presumably to make his fortune in cotton. After his youngest son suffered prolonged diarrhea, Pickens realized that the change had an unacceptable cost for his family's health. "This admonition which so long threatened the life of a fine child," he wrote, "and the fair prospect of having more thrown on my hands, has induced me to look a little higher up the country for a permanent situation where the prospect of health may be surer." In another instance, Mrs. Howe announced that the children's chronic ill health determined her family to relocate "from our sickly place in Alabama," and she expressed optimism that in their new home, she would "see the children looking as rosy as the little ones in the country." Yet even after the Howes settled on the Mississippi prairies, good health escaped them. Within a few years, Julia persuaded her husband to move to Greensboro, North Carolina. She was thoroughly fed up with lonely frontier living and the children's illnesses. Julia at last realized her wish to be surrounded by "churches, physicians, and friends." . . .

Worms were an ever-present health concern. The *Charleston Medical Journal and Review* observed that worms were more common in warm climates and "notorious on our plantations." Census statistics reveal that worms occurred most often in children over two years of age. One Alabama doctor extracted three hundred from a two-year-old. Mothers and physicians noticed that suckling infants rarely had problems with worms—perhaps one more argument for breast-feeding. A newborn's exposure to worms was limited by its diet as well as its relative immobility. But once youngsters learned to walk and began to consume a variety of foods, they became hosts to several intestinal parasites.

In one particularly severe case, worms may have led to a young child's death. When two-year-old Duncan Cameron, of North Carolina, came down with chills and disordered bowels, his distraught father called him "hardly a good shadow of himself" and said that he was "without life." A week later, Paul Cameron diagnosed worms, purged the youngster with calomel, and urged his wife, Anne, to "commence the use of worm tea." After a week on medication, Duncan still remained "pale, feeble, and lifeless." The physicians and the parents continued their efforts to restore his health, but Duncan did not live to complete his third year. Worms were a serious concern, for they depleted young bodies of essential nutrients, weakened constitutions, led to anemia, and increased the susceptibility to other illnesses.

Southern parents treated worms in a variety of ways. Anna Garretson, of Virginia, suggested that "if Rosa complains of an itching in the anus, please to let one of your most careful female servants introduce the head of a pin and by twitching it around they will work out." She added that "Henry took out as many as seven" from the little girl. Mrs. Hall wrote of her daughter Betsy, "We have physicked her for worms and she has passed [one] and measured a foot in length." Eighteen months later, Rebecca recorded that another daughter had "discharged fifty odd worms." Still, Betsy's problem persisted, for she remained a "shadow, so pale and ematiated and under her clothes is a mere skeleton," according to her anxious mother. Rebecca finally consulted the family doctor, who employed heroic remedies including Pink Root, bleeding, and a body rub of turpentine. Nonetheless, the child remained "delirious with fever" three months later, still passing worms. . . .

Like infants today, southern babies suffered from colic. It was typically one of the first illnesses southern mothers had to treat. Clay declared that his child's fretfulness could hardly be "called a disease" but that his wife, Celeste, was in a mild state of panic, fearful that colic might lead to croup. She tried various treatments and finally covered the poor infant's chest with a plaster of suet and turpentine. Nealy Lenoir applied brandy to her colicky baby's stomach and also gave him alcohol to drink. The combination of colic and constipation received blame for the death of one six-week-old infant. Mrs. McCorkle wrote that her newborn "suffered excruciatingly" from the two medical problems. The baby's suffering was "evidenced first by wailings—then by moanings, till utterance failed." Two physicians attempted to bring relief with heavy doses of oil, calomel, and morphine, but to no avail. Heroic therapies were often as devastating to a tiny baby as the illness itself. What Clay felt scarcely deserved the appellation of sickness was considered the cause of the McCorkle child's death.

Of all the diseases surveyed in the federal census of 1850, croup caused the greatest number of deaths among young children, particularly among children under the age of one. Southern mothers mentioned the illness infrequently in their correspondence, and it may be that southern youngsters were less prone to it than children living in colder parts of the country. Nevertheless, southern parents were concerned. Mrs. Clay made every effort to prevent her infant from contracting a case. A North Carolina girl knew enough about croup's dangers to refer to it as "that dreaded disease" when her infant brother suffered from it. Virginia Shelton's five-month-old firstborn caught an apparent case of croup, and the Tennessee mother gave her baby nothing stronger than sweet oil. A neighbor who had more experience with domestic remedies "rubbed him all over with mutton suet and gave him a mixture of mutton suet and molasses," and the child recovered. Since the Sheltons had reservations about consulting doctors for infant health problems, Virginia was probably relieved that domestic remedies availed.

Whooping cough, or pertussis, a highly contagious bacterial disease characterized by a wheezing, rasping cough, was probably one of the most dramatic and frightening of all infant ailments. Frequently every young member of a family was affected, for its rate of contagion was 85 to 90 percent among children. The recovery rate was lowest for infants under the age of one. Whooping cough was a long-lasting disease, usually hanging on for six to ten weeks. One South Carolina woman believed that it was of even more protracted duration; she remarked that "if it is taken in the fall of the year, they don't get better of it until spring." When young children caught it, mothers spent anxious weeks in attentive nursing. But there was little that antebellum mothers could do apart from avoiding exposing their children and easing their suffering.

The diary of Mary Henderson, of North Carolina, underlines the seriousness of whooping cough. Mary's frenetic state and her sorrow, anger, and bewilderment often make it difficult to follow the details of the tragedy that whooping cough visited upon her young family. But her stream-of-consciousness writing and her mental disorder make the tale all the more moving. Apparently, when two of Mary's school-age sons caught whooping cough from a classmate, Mary did not remove them from school at once. After the deaths of the two youngsters, she reproached herself, saying, "My sad experience has taught me that whooping cough is one of the most formidable diseases." Unfortunately, the illness passed on to her infant daughter. Mary spent a total of eighteen months nursing the three of her children who caught the disease. In page after page of her journal, she poured out her despair, especially during the infant's suffering. When her efforts in behalf of the baby proved futile and the child died, Mary denounced everyone involved, including the attending nurse, whose teas and oils had produced no improvement. Not least did she censure herself, believing that "overanxiety and the dread of whooping cough" caused her to accept too readily the physician's heroic cures. The distraught mother criticized her own weakness in not forcing the doctor to stop medicating the infant. "I erred, erred, erred, terribly, fatally," she moaned. But the principal target of her anger was the physician himself, who had done nothing right in her eyes. She took exception to his dosing the baby with calomel and cupping her, and she decided that "a blister between shoulders with purgative and quinine" would have been far better, even if no less violent. She reproved the doctor for prescribing "depressing syrups" and "blue stone, which entirely destroyed her voice and I fear permanently injured her little palate." Mary assailed the "desperate and dangerous remedies" the physician thought suitable for a nine-month-old; she maintained that water, breast milk, flannel clothing, cool baths, and wool stockings would have served far better. "It is very wonderful that she lived a month under such treatment, actually taking poisons all the time," she charged. . . .

Young children often caught mumps and measles, which, like whooping cough, were recognized as having little, if any, effective treatment. Rarely was a fatal case of measles recorded, though Octavia Otey, of Alabama, claimed that her baby daughter "lay at the point of death" with the disease. Scarlet fever posed a greater risk. A form of this disease became more virulent by the first quarter of the nineteenth century, after existing in a milder form during the colonial period. Scarlet fever demanded constant nursing and could be a merciless killer of young children. Mary Custis, of Deep Creek, North Carolina, lost twins to the dreaded disease. Parents made every effort to keep healthy children from infected households to prevent exposure. When a Raleigh woman, Mary Polk, heard of neighboring children who had scarlet fever, she noted, "I live in constant dread that Catherine is to be the next victim" and did her best to keep her children at home. . . .

Southern infants were disposed to physical injury. Constant vigilance was needed. Especially recurrent were burns, falls, and accidental poisonings. Eliza Clitherall described a friend's infant who died by poison: "The sweet Babe was poison'd by the shameful mistake of the Apothecaries clerk, who sent a wrong phial— sent a Aconite, a deadly poison." Several southern mothers described their babies' near-fatal falls from beds and tables. Other infants swallowed foreign objects, ate unripe fruit and vegetables from the garden, received scaldings from hot water or burns from an open fire, and fell out of open windows.

Yet no illness, epidemic, or physical calamity proved to be so distressing as teething. Some of the problems connected with dentition and weaning have already become evident, but the impact of dentition went well beyond infant nourishment and cholera infantum. The period of dentition covered roughly the time between six months and two years of age and came to assume major importance as a stage of human development, much like puberty and menopause. At least until 1860, the federal census included teething as a cause of death. Few infants passed through this stage with ease. So critical was the period that some southern mothers kept written records of each child's progress—or lack of it. Sophia Watson, of Greensboro, Alabama, distraught that her six-and-a-half-month-old son still lacked teeth, poured out her distress to her absent husband. "I begin almost to despair of seeing one for some time to come," she lamented. But Ann Blank, of Leesburg, North Carolina, had cause for celebration. "Dear Henry . . . has two through and two almost through," noted the happy mother. Bringing infants through the period alive and in relative good health became a major challenge for southern physicians and mothers. As the most obvious and universal sign of bodily change during the early part of a child's life, teething was at one time or another held accountable for nearly every infant ill.

Mothers assumed that this stage of human development meant infant distress and illness, so they were prepared to worry and to provide attentive nursing. Margaret Cameron resigned herself to the task ahead, commiserating, "I shall feel most anxious for her until she is done teething." She later held teething responsible for her infant's bout with a ten-week-long siege of spasms, high fever, and irritable stomach. Mrs. Shelton described the ailments accompanying her son's dentition and bravely accepted the incommodity his teething imposed upon her. "Of course, I have much anxiety and have not slept for several nights," she wrote, knowing that her aunt would understand. When infants teethed without suffering, incredulity met their good fortune. Caroline Pinckney, of South Carolina, had the enviable experience of raising a daughter whom teething scarcely affected. "She looks so robust," wrote the puzzled mother, "that you would not suppose she had been cutting teeth thro' a Carolina summer."

Southern mothers were always looking for ways to ease their infants' distress. Mrs. Clay recommended the healing waters of a local Alabama spring, vouching that they would "afford instantaneous relief to teething children." Mrs. Shelton followed a suggestion in many advice books and purchased an India-rubber tooth cutter for her baby to chew. Lancing the gums was advocated by the majority of southern physicians, who felt that it created a freer passage for the growing tooth, relieved swollen gums of excess blood, and prevented irritation from reaching the brain. Parents often took matters into their own hands and lanced their infant's gums. Rebecca Cameron expressed gratitude to her husband for doing the job, noting that it "was of the greatest importance" to their son. Anne Cameron believed her daughter Mary was much "relieved by having her gums scarified."

But at times teething was so unpleasant that only medicines and physicians could provide relief. When Ann and William Elliott's son had three days of high fever while teething, the parents administered castor oil and then called in the local doctor, who lanced the boy's gums. When the fever persisted, the doctor returned and lanced the gums in four places. Margaret Devereux administered doses of calomel on the advice of her doctor and concluded that the purging was "decidedly beneficial" to her teething child. Mrs. Lenoir's baby vomited and suffered convulsions, and the doctor, certain that teething was the problem, lanced the baby's gums and administered morphine. Unfortunately, the poor child never recovered, but whether because of an undiagnosed illness or an overdose by the doctor is unclear. . . .

The role of southern fathers in nursing sick children is perhaps as variable as that of doctors. In some instances fathers became actively involved, but in other families they were reluctant child assistants. The time and energy of the father who appeared uninvolved may have been needed elsewhere, or he may have believed that child-care activities fell within the sphere of maternal responsibility. Some men found children bothersome and demanding and had no desire to be around them. In a letter written during one of his annual and lengthy sojourns in Saratoga Springs, New York, to restore his failing health, William Elliott questioned his wife about their plantation and crops, and then, as an afterthought, his children: "Tell me of my little ones that I love most at a distance—why? Can it be because they do not then plague me?" The peace that Elliott discovered away from juvenile noise may have been as soothing as the sulphur springs. The fathers who assumed parental duties normally believed their role a limited one. Frances Bumpas delineated the division of parental responsibility in her family. "I have taken charge of her for the first year," she wrote, "and Mr. Bumpas says he will afterwards take charge of her." *Taking charge* meant punishing the youngster, for Frances continued to attend to the girl's daily needs and nurse her illnesses when she was well beyond the age of one, but her husband assumed the duty of spanking the child. Any form of parenting at all embarrassed the father who perceived it as a maternal responsibility. Demonstrations of love and tenderness undermined the masculine image that southern men cultivated. Jean Syme told of visiting a friend and her new baby and inadvertently bursting in while the father was holding the newborn. "I went over last night and found him in the act of nursing it," she related, "and you can't think how much ashamed he was of being caught so effeminately employed, he instantly put it down and left himself."

But some fortunate mothers received loving support and steady assistance from their husbands. Isaac Avery sat up all night when a newborn suffered a sudden seizure of the "livid disease of infants." When a young daughter became partially paralyzed, James Gwynn—who appeared to be a particularly solicitous father—slept in a downstairs room with her while his wife cared for their baby. During one absence Gwynn worried about their young daughter to the point of issuing constant reminders to his wife. "Take good care of her," he urged Mary Ann, "mind her to stand up a great deal and try and get her to use her limbs; it's time now she was sitting alone—toss and tumble her about a great deal and don't let her be carried about in persons arms too much. She has been nursed too much for her good, I think." James had a well-defined view of proper infant care. . . .

The participation of other people who aided with infant nursing is less ambiguous. Female family members, friends, and neighbors proved to be an invaluable source of aid during difficult periods, particularly when infants were ill. Southern mothers wrote of friends and neighbors who sat with them during all-night vigils. Letty Lewis mentioned a neighbor, Mrs. Dunn, who spent four sleepless nights with her when her daughter had scarlet fever. She found it hard to "express the sympathy I felt, and feel, for the poor creature who seems never to weary in the discharge of kind offices towards myself and children." Mrs. Petigru described two neighbor women who "were very attentive and were a great deal with us" when her son suffered a case of worm fever. Susan Hutchinson's acquaintance, Mrs. Smelt, sat up with her baby until two one night. The women who helped were likely to be neighbors living near enough to provide a mother with immediate aid. Those who had prior experience in nursing specific illnesses were undoubtedly the greatest help. The sharing of time, emotion, and maternal advice proved to be an important way for women to support one another in moments of stress.

The position that black nurses achieved within the southern family structure and the extent to which they shared power with southern mothers must have varied from family to family. Personal relationships between mistress and slave could be close, but distrust and distaste from the standpoint of either race were also possible. From limited data in slave narratives and white women's correspondence, it appears that slave women rarely assumed a primary role when infants were ill or raised a child as long as the mother could tend to her duties. Healthy white mothers did not readily leave nursing duties to black domestic slaves, or if they did, they rarely admitted it. Like breast-feeding, nursing a sick child remained a prerogative of the mothers, and white women were unlikely to turn these duties over to a family servant, particularly when a child's life was in danger.

Perhaps the greatest contribution that black slaves made during a mother's nursing vigil was to look after other members of the household and to do domestic chores, thereby enabling the mother to concentrate on her ailing child. Slave narratives show too that a typical duty for slave children was as child-sitters or playmates for the master's children. Privileged southern mothers relied on black nurses and black children to assist mainly in the care of children who were well. Often youngsters of both races played and matured together on the plantation, though such interaction was mentioned more often in slave narratives than in white correspondence. Perhaps it was so common that it did not occur to women to write about it, or perhaps southern mothers were disinclined to admit their dependence on others' help.

Childrearing, touted as a joyful duty, was often worrisome, exhausting, and difficult for mothers. Doctors played an uncertain role during these early years, while mothers, as long as they were healthy, retained ultimate responsibility for the well-being of their infants. In most instances, their attentiveness paid off, but in other cases, the reality of death had to be faced. Not even deep love and devoted care could forestall the reality of infant mortality.

FURTHER READING

Carol Bleser, ed., *In Joy and In Sorrow: Women, Family, and Marriage in the Victorian South* (1991)

Jane Turner Censer, *North Carolina Planters and Their Children, 1800–1860* (1984)

Catherine Clinton, *The Plantation Mistress: Women's World in the Old South* (1982)

————, ed., *Half Sisters of History: Southern Women and the American Past* (1994)

Carl N. Degler, *At Odds: Women and the Family in America from the Revolution to the Present* (1980)

Christie Farnham, *The Education of the Southern Belle* (1994)

Elizabeth Fox-Genovese, *Within the Plantation Household* (1988)

Walter J. Fraser, Jr., R. Frank Saunders, Jr., and Jon L. Wakelyn, eds., *The Web of Southern Social Relations: Women, Family, and Education* (1985)

Jean E. Friedman, *The Enclosed Garden: Women and Community in the Evangelical South, 1830–1900* (1985)

Joanne V. Hawks and Sheila L. Skemp, eds., *Sex, Race, and the Role of Women in the South* (1983)

Suzanne Lebsock, *The Free Women of Petersburg: Status and Culture in a Southern Town, 1784–1860* (1984)

Anya Jabour, *Marriage in the Early Republic* (1998)

Sally G. McMillen, *Motherhood in the Old South: Pregnancy, Childbirth, and Infant Rearing* (1991)

————, *Southern Women: Black and White in the Old South* (1992)

Elizabeth Moss, *Domestic Novelists in the Old South: Defenders of Southern Culture* (1992)

Elisabeth Muhlenfeld, *Mary Boykin Chesnut* (1981)

Anne Firor Scott, *The Southern Lady: From Pedestal to Politics* (1970)

Elizabeth R. Varon, *We Mean to be Counted: White Women and Politics in Antebellum Virginia* (1998)

Marli Weiner, *Mistresses and Slaves: Plantation Women in South Carolina, 1830–1880* (1998)

Margaret Ripley Wolfe, *Daughters of Canaan: A Saga of Southern Women* (1995)

CHAPTER
10

Sectionalism and Secession

In the 1850s, the nation entered the period of its greatest crisis. Sectionalism had become a major theme in national politics, and southern challenges to federal authority were increasingly emotion-charged and serious. An unapologetic proslavery argument had emerged well before the 1850s, and it became an explicit theme of southern protest. Some white southerners began to debate the wisdom and desirability of leaving the Union. Ultimatums and threats of secession that were uttered in 1850 became a reality a decade later. The issue of slavery in the territories was troublesome from this point forward, as evidenced by the Compromise of 1850 and the Dred Scott *decision. Among the significant political events during this decade were the rise of the Republican Party and the splitting of the Democratic Party into a southern and northern wing.*

Historians ponder how and why the slavery issue came to the fore in southern politics and whether slaveholders or nonslaveholders were most responsible for pressing the issue. Slavery was becoming the dominant concern in southern politics, and southerners insisted that they had the right to take their property (slaves) into new territories out West. Historians also debate how widespread support for secession was and how views differed between the upper and lower South, and between urban and rural voters, between wealthy and poor, both overall and within the same state. They also continue to grapple with whether secession was forced upon a reluctant South or whether it garnered widespread support.

✘ D O C U M E N T S

The status of slavery in the territories convulsed the U.S. Congress for almost nine months in 1850. During that period, representatives from nine slave states met in Nashville to formulate southern demands. Although "moderates" controlled the Nashville convention, the convention's closing resolutions, in Document 1, state southerners' rights in the territories and the obligations of Congress. Many southern intellectuals developed religious and sociological defenses of slavery, especially between the 1830s and the outbreak of the Civil War. Thornton Stringfellow, a Virginia Baptist minister, penned one of the most popular and widely read scriptural defenses of the South's "peculiar institution"; it appears in Document 2. In 1857, the Supreme Court addressed the issue of slavery in the territories and congressional power and obligations on that issue. Dred Scott, a Missouri slave, had sued for his freedom on the grounds that previously he had been taken to live in a free territory. The Court's decision in *Dred Scott* v. *Sandford,* Document 3, attracted national attention and a strong response from northerners. Document 4 contains a famous statement of southern self-confidence voiced in 1858 by Senator James Henry Hammond of South Carolina. Hammond's declarations about King Cotton led into an analysis of slavery and the strengths of southern society. After the Democratic Party split in 1860, Kentucky's Senator John J. Crittenden devised a final compromise proposal. Although Lincoln and the Republicans rejected it, his proposal, in Document 5, seemed acceptable to southern leaders in the Senate. Document 6, taken from various southern newspapers, gives additional insight into how southern spokesmen viewed secession. But not all southerners were pro-secessionists. As Document 7 indicates, Andrew Johnson, Tennessee senator and Union supporter, gave an influential speech defending his views; these letters suggest voters' support for his position. Finally, in Document 8, members of the Jones family of Liberty County, Georgia, express hatred toward Yankees and support for their region.

1. Resolutions of the Nashville Convention, 1850

1. *Resolved,* That the territories of the United States belong to the people of the several States of this Union as their common property. That the citizens of the several States have equal rights to migrate with their property to these territories, and are equally entitled to the protection of the federal government in the enjoyment of that property so long as the territories remain under the charge of that government.

2. *Resolved,* That Congress has no power to exclude from the territory of the United States any property lawfully held in the States of the Union, and any act which may be passed by Congress to effect this result is a plain violation of the Constitution of the United States. . . .

4. *Resolved,* That to protect property existing in the several States of the Union the people of these States invested the federal government with the powers of war and negotiation and of sustaining armies and navies, and prohibited to State authorities the exercise of the same powers. They made no discrimination in the protection to be afforded or the description of the property to be defended, nor was it allowed to the federal government to determine what should be held as property. Whatever the States deal with as property the federal government is bound to recognize and defend as such. Therefore it is the sense of this Convention that all acts of the federal government which tend to denationalize property of any description recognized in the Constitution and laws of the States, or that discriminate in the degree and efficiency of the protection to be afforded to it, or which weaken or destroy the title of any citizen upon American territories, are plain and palpable violations of the fundamental law under which it exists.

5. *Resolved,* That the slaveholding States cannot and will not submit to the enactment by Congress of any law imposing onerous conditions or restraints upon the

This document can be found in Henry Steele Commager, ed., *Documents of American History,* vol. 1, Appleton-Century-Crofts, © 1948, pp. 324–325.

rights of masters to remove with their property into the territories of the United States, or to any law making discrimination in favor of the proprietors of other property against them. . . .

8. *Resolved,* That the performance of its duties, upon the principle we declare, would enable Congress to remove the embarrassments in which existed, everywhere, and in every country, where civilization has been established among men. Destroy them to-day, and they will spring up to-morrow; and we have no right to expect, or even to hope, that this Southern climate of ours, would be exempt from the operation of this Universal law.

Menial services have to be performed, by some one; and every where the world over, within the range of civilization, those persons, by whom the menial services have been performed, as a class, have been looked upon, as occupying, and are reduced to a state of inferiority. Wherever a distinction in color has not existed to draw the line, and mark the boundary, the line has been drawn, by *property,* between the rich and poor. *Wealth* and *poverty* have marked the boundary. The poor man stands in need of all his rights, and all his privileges, and therefore, this question is of the greatest, and the gravest importance to him; much more so than it is to the rich. The rich by siding with the party in power—the authorities that be, may always be safe. Not so with the poor. Their all is suspended upon their *superiority* to the *blacks*—their all of equality, in a political and social point of view—the social equality of their wives, daughters, and sons, are all suspended upon, and involved in this question. It will not do to say that this is a fancy sketch, or that these things are too far in the distance, to be seriously contemplated. The tendencies are all in that direction, and if they are not met, and met promptly, and rolled back, or stayed forever in their progress, the wheel of revolution will roll on until the institution is crushed, the great object of the freesoilers accomplished, and the negroes freed.

But they have, if possible, still higher grounds than these. The constitution, the palladium of the liberties of the people, in more respects than one, has been violated, and that violation is to be continued, under the *implied* invitation of the submissionists, if they succeed in the present contest. And when once it becomes an established principle, that repeated violations of that instrument will be tolerated by the people—that they will submit—the poor man's liberties are all gone, and gone forever.

2. Reverend Thornton Stringfellow Defends Slavery, 1856

Jesus Christ recognized this institution [slavery] as one that was lawful among men, and regulated its relative duties.

. . . I affirm then, first, (and no man denies,) that Jesus Christ has not abolished slavery by a prohibitory command: and second, I affirm, he has introduced no new moral principle which can work its destruction, under the gospel dispensation; and that the principle relied on for this purpose, is a fundamental principle of the Mosaic law, under which slavery was instituted by Jehovah himself: the third, with this

Reprinted with the permission of Simon & Schuster from *Slavery Defended: The Views of the Old South* by Eric L. McKitrick. Copyright © 1963 by Prentice-Hall, Inc.

absence of positive prohibition, and this absence of principle, to work its ruin, I affirm, that in all the Roman provinces, where churches were planted by the apostles, hereditary slavery existed, as it did among the Jews, and as it does now among us, (which admits of proof from history that no man will dispute who knows any thing of the matter,) and that in instructing such churches, the Holy Ghost by the apostles, has recognized the institution, as one *legally existing* among them, to be perpetuated in the church, and that its duties are prescribed.

Now for the proof: To the church planted at Ephesus, the capital of the lesser Asia, Paul ordains by letter, subordination in the fear of God,—first between wife and husband; second, child and parent; third, servant and master; *all, as states, or conditions, existing among the members.*

The relative duties of each state are pointed out; those between the servant and master in these words: "Servants be obedient to them who are your masters, according to the flesh, with fear and trembling, in singleness of your heart as unto Christ; not with eye service as men pleasers, but as the servants of Christ, doing the will of God from the heart, with goodwill, doing service, as to the Lord, and not to men, knowing that whatsoever good thing any man doeth, the same shall he receive of the Lord, whether he be bond or free. And ye masters do the same things to them, forbearing threatening, knowing that your master is also in heaven, neither is there respect of persons with him." Here, by the Roman law, the servant was property, and the control of the master unlimited, as we shall presently prove.

To the church at Colosse, a city of Phrygia, in the lesser Asia,—Paul in his letter to them, recognizes the three relations of wives and husbands, parents and children, servants and masters, as relations existing among the members; (here the Roman law was the same;) and to the servants and masters he thus writes: "Servants obey in all things your masters, according to the flesh: not with eye service, as men pleasers, but in singleness of heart, fearing God: and whatsoever you do, do it heartily, as to the Lord and not unto men; knowing that of the Lord ye shall receive the reward of the inheritance, for ye serve the Lord Christ. But he that doeth wrong shall receive for the wrong he has done; and there is no respect of persons with God. Masters give unto your servants that which is just and equal, knowing that you also have a master in heaven."

The same Apostle writes a letter to the church at Corinth;—a very important city, formerly called the eye of Greece, either from its location, or intelligence, or both, and consequently, an important point, for radiating light in all directions, in reference to subjects connected with the cause of Jesus Christ; and particularly, in the bearing of its practical precepts on civil society, and the political structure of nations. Under the direction of the Holy Ghost, he instructs the church, that, on this particular subject, *one general principle* was ordained of God, applicable alike in all countries and at all stages of the church's future history, and that it was this: *"as the Lord has called every one, so let him walk."* "Let every man abide in the same calling wherein he is called." "Let every man wherein he is called, therein abide with God."—1 Cor. vii: 17, 20, 24. *"And so ordain I in all churches;"* vii: 17. The Apostle thus explains his meaning:

"Is any man called being circumcised? Let him not become uncircumcised."

"Is any man called in uncircumcision? Let him not be circumcised."

"Art thou called, being a servant? Care not for it, but if thou mayest be made free, use it rather;" vii: 18, 21. Here, by the Roman law, slaves were property,—yet Paul ordains, in this, and all other churches, that Christianity gave them no title to freedom, but on the contrary, required them not to care for being slaves, or in other words, to be contented with their *state,* or *relation,* unless they could be *made free,* in a lawful way.

Again, we have a letter by Peter, who is the Apostle of the circumcision—addressed especially to the Jews, who were scattered through various provinces of the Roman empire; comprising those provinces especially, where were the theater of their dispersion, under the Assyrians and Babylonians. . . . He thus instructs them: "Submit yourselves to every ordinance of man for the Lord's sake." "For so is the will of God." "Servants, be subject to your masters with all fear, not only to the good and gentle, but also to the froward."—1 Peter ii: 11, 13, 15, 18. What an important document is this! enjoining political subjection to *governments of every form,* and Christian subjection on the part of servants to their masters, whether good or bad; for the purpose of showing forth to advantage, the *glory of the gospel,* and putting to silence the ignorance of foolish men, who might think it seditious.

By "every ordinance of man," as the context will show, is meant governmental regulations or laws, as was that of the Romans for enslaving their prisoners taken in war, instead of destroying their lives.

When such enslaved persons came into the church of Christ let them (says Peter) "be subject to their masters with all fear," whether such masters be good or bad. It is worthy of remark, that he says much to secure civil subordination to the State, and hearty and cheerful obedience to the masters, on the part of servants; yet he says nothing to masters in the whole letter. It would seem from this, that danger to the cause of Christ was on the side of *insubordination among the servants,* and a *want of humility with inferiors,* rather than *haughtiness among superiors* in the church. . . .

. . . It is taken for granted, on all hands pretty generally, that Jesus Christ has at least been silent, or that he has not personally spoken on the subject of slavery. Once for all, I deny it. Paul, after stating that a slave was to honor an unbelieving master, in the 1st verse of the 6th chapter, says, in the 2d verse, that to a believing master, he is the rather to do service, because he who partakes of the benefit is his brother. He then says, if any man teach otherwise, (as all abolitionists then did, and now do,) and consent not to wholesome words, "even the words of our Lord Jesus Christ." Now, if our Lord Jesus Christ uttered such words, how dare we say he has been silent? If he has been silent, how dare the Apostle say these are the words of our Lord Jesus Christ, if the Lord Jesus Christ never spoke them? . . . We will remark, in closing under this head, that we have shown from the text of the sacred volume, that when God entered into covenant with Abraham, it was with him as a slaveholder; that when he took his posterity by the hand in Egypt, five hundred years afterward to confirm the promise made to Abraham, it was done with them as slaveholders; that when he gave them a constitution of government, he gave them the right to perpetuate hereditary slavery; and that he did not for the fifteen hundred years of their national existence, express disapprobation toward the institution.

We have also shown from authentic history that the institution of slavery existed in every family, and in every province of the Roman Empire, at the time the gospel was published to them.

We have also shown from the New Testament, that all the churches are recognized as composed of masters and servants; and that they are instructed by Christ how to discharge their relative duties; and finally that in reference to the question which was then started, whether Christianity did not abolish the institution, or the right of one Christian to hold another Christian in bondage, we have shown, that "the words of our Lord Jesus Christ" are, that so far from this being the case, it adds to the obligation of the servant to render service with good-will to his master, and that gospel fellowship is not to be entertained with persons who will not consent to it!

3. *Dred Scott* v. *Sandford,* 1857

TANEY, C. J. . . . The question is simply this: Can a negro, whose ancestors were imported into this country, and sold as slaves, become a member of the political community formed and brought into existence by the Constitution of the United States, and as such become entitled to all the rights, and privileges, and immunities, guarantied by that instrument to the citizen? One of which rights is the privilege of suing in a court of the United States in the cases specified in the Constitution. . . .

The words "people of the United States" and "citizens" are synonymous terms, and mean the same thing. They both describe the political body who, according to our republican institutions, form the sovereignty, and who hold the power and conduct the government through their representatives. They are what we familiarly call the "sovereign people," and every citizen is one of this people, and a constituent member of this sovereignty. The question before us is, whether the class of persons described in the plea in abatement compose a portion of this people, and are constituent members of this sovereignty? We think they are not, and that they are not included, and were not intended to be included, under the word "citizens" in the Constitution, and can, therefore, claim none of the rights and privileges which that instrument provides for and secures to citizens of the United States. On the contrary, they were at that time considered as a subordinate and inferior class of beings, who had been subjugated by the dominant race, and whether emancipated or not, yet remained subject to their authority, and had no rights or privileges but such as those who held the power and the government might choose to grant them. . . .

In the opinion of the court, the legislation and histories of the times, and the language used in the Declaration of Independence, show, that neither the class of persons who had been imported as slaves, nor their descendants, whether they had become free or not, were then acknowledged as a part of the people, nor intended to be included in the general words used in that memorable instrument.

It is difficult at this day to realize the state of public opinion in relation to that unfortunate race, which prevailed in the civilized and enlightened portions of the world at the time of the Declaration of Independence, and when the Constitution of the United States was framed and adopted. . . .

They had for more than a century before been regarded as beings of an inferior order; and altogether unfit to associate with the white race, either in social or political relations; and so far inferior that they had no rights which the white man was

This document can also be found in Henry Steele Commager, ed., *Documents of American History,* vol. 1, Appleton-Century-Crofts, © 1948, pp. 340–345.

bound to respect; and that the negro might justly and lawfully be reduced to slavery for his benefit. . . . This opinion was at that time fixed and universal in the civilized portion of the white race. It was regarded as an axiom in morals as well as in politics, which no one thought of disputing, or supposed to be open to dispute; and men in every grade and position in society daily and habitually acted upon it in their private pursuits, as well as in matters of public concern, without doubting for a moment the correctness of this opinion. . . .

The legislation of the different Colonies furnishes positive and undisputable proof of this fact. . . .

The language of the Declaration of Independence is equally conclusive. . . .

And upon a full and careful consideration of the subject, the court is of opinion that, upon the facts stated in the plea in abatement, Dred Scott was not a citizen of Missouri within the meaning of the Constitution of the United States, and not entitled as such to sue in its courts; and, consequently, that the Circuit Court had no jurisdiction of the case, and that the judgment on the plea in abatement is erroneous. . . .

We proceed, therefore, to inquire whether the facts relied on by the plaintiff entitled him to his freedom. . . .

In considering this part of the controversy, two questions arise: 1st. Was he, together with his family, free in Missouri by reason of the stay in the territory of the United States hereinbefore mentioned? And 2d, If they were not, is Scott himself free by reason of his removal to Rock Island, in the State of Illinois, as stated in the above admissions?

We proceed to examine the first question.

The Act of Congress, upon which the plaintiff relies, declares that slavery and involuntary servitude, except as a punishment for crime, shall be forever prohibited in all that part of the territory ceded by France, under the name of Louisiana, which lies north of thirty-six degrees thirty minutes north latitude, and not included within the limits of Missouri. And the difficulty which meets us at the threshold of this part of the inquiry is, whether Congress was authorized to pass this law under any of the powers granted to it by the Constitution; for if the authority is not given by that instrument, it is the duty of this court to declare it void and inoperative, and incapable of conferring freedom upon any one who is held as a slave under the laws of any one of the States.

The counsel for the plaintiff has laid much stress upon that article in the Constitution which confers on Congress the power "to dispose of and make all needful rules and regulations respecting the territory or other property belonging to the United States;" but, in the judgment of the court, that provision has no bearing on the present controversy, and the power there given, whatever it may be, is confined, and was intended to be confined, to the territory which at that time belonged to, or was claimed by, the United States, and was within their boundaries as settled by the treaty with Great Britain, and can have no influence upon a territory afterwards acquired from a foreign Government. It was a special provision for a known and particular territory, and to meet a present emergency, and nothing more. . . .

. . . If the Constitution recognizes the right of property of the master in a slave, and makes no distinction between that description of property and other property owned by a citizen, no tribunal, acting under the authority of the United States, whether it be legislative, executive, or judicial, has a right to draw such a distinction, or deny to it the benefit of the provisions and guarantees which have been provided for the protection of private property against the encroachments of the Government.

Now . . . the right of property in a slave is distinctly and expressly affirmed in the Constitution. The right to traffic in it, like an ordinary article of merchandise and property, was guaranteed to the citizens of the United States, in every State that might desire it, for twenty years. And the Government in express terms is pledged to protect it in all future time, if the slave escapes from his owner. . . . And no word can be found in the Constitution which gives Congress a greater power over slave property, or which entitles property of that kind to less protection than property of any other description. The only power conferred is the power coupled with the duty of guarding and protecting the owner in his rights.

Upon these considerations, it is the opinion of the court that the Act of Congress which prohibited a citizen from holding and owning property of this kind in the territory of the United States north of the line therein mentioned, is not warranted by the Constitution, and is therefore void; and that neither Dred Scott himself, nor any of his family, were made free by being carried into this territory; even if they had been carried there by the owner, with the intention of becoming a permanent resident. . . .

Upon the whole, therefore, it is the judgment of this court, that it appears by the record before us that the plaintiff in error is not a citizen of Missouri, in the sense in which that word is used in the Constitution; and that the Circuit Court of the United States, for that reason, had no jurisdiction in the case, and could give no judgment in it.

Its judgment for the defendant must, consequently, be reversed, and a mandate issued directing the suit to be dismissed for want of jurisdiction. WAYNE, J., NELSON, J., GRIER, J., DANIEL, J., CAMPBELL, J., AND CATRON, J., filed separate concurring opinions. McCLEAN, J., and CURTIS, J. dissented.

4. James Henry Hammond Praises King Cotton, 1858

[W]ould any sane nation make war on cotton? Without firing a gun, without drawing a sword, should they make war on us we could bring the whole world to our feet. The South is perfectly competent to go on, one, two, or three years without planting a seed of cotton. I believe that if she was to plant but half her cotton, for three years to come, it would be an immense advantage to her. I am not so sure but that after three years' entire abstinence she would come out stronger than ever she was before, and better prepared to enter afresh upon her great career of enterprise. What would happen if no cotton was furnished for three years? I will not stop to depict what every one can imagine, but this is certain: England would topple headlong and carry the whole civilized world with her, save the South. No, you dare not make war on cotton. No power on earth dares to make war upon it. Cotton *is* king. Until

This document can also be found in the Congressional Globe, 35th Congress, First session, speech given on March 4, 1858, quoted sections on pp. 961–62.

lately the Bank of England was king; but she tried to put her screws as usual, the fall before the last, upon the cotton crop, and was utterly vanquished. The last power has been conquered. Who can doubt, that has looked at recent events, that cotton is supreme? When the abuse of credit had destroyed credit and annihilated confidence; when thousands of the strongest commercial houses in the world were coming down, and hundreds of millions of dollars of supposed property evaporating in thin air; when you [Northerners] came to a dead lock, and revolutions were threatened, what brought you up? Fortunately for you it was the commencement of the cotton season, and we have poured in upon you one million six hundred thousand bales of cotton just at the crisis to save you from destruction. That cotton, but for the bursting of your speculative bubbles in the North, which produced the whole of this convulsion, would have brought us $100,000,000. We have sold it for $65,000,000, and saved you. Thirty-five million dollars we, the slaveholders of the South, have put into the charity box for your magnificent financiers, your "cotton lords," your "merchant princes."

But, sir, the greatest strength of the South arises from the harmony of her political and social institutions. This harmony gives her a frame of society, the best in the world, and an extent of political freedom, combined with entire security, such as no other people ever enjoyed upon the face of the earth. Society precedes government; creates it, and ought to control it; but as far as we can look back in historic times we find the case different; for government is no sooner created than it becomes too strong for society, and shapes and moulds, as well as controls it. In later centuries the progress of civilization and of intelligence has made the divergence so great as to produce civil wars and revolutions; and it is nothing now but the want of harmony between governments and societies which occasions all the uneasiness and trouble and terror that we see abroad. It was this that brought on the American Revolution. We threw off a Government not adapted to our social system, and made one for ourselves. The question is, how far have we succeeded? The South, so far as that is concerned, is satisfied, harmonious, and prosperous, but demands to be let alone.

In all social systems there must be a class to do the menial duties, to perform the drudgery of life. That is, a class requiring but a low order of intellect and but little skill. Its requisites are vigor, docility, fidelity. Such a class you must have, or you would not have that other class which leads progress, civilization, and refinement. It constitutes the very mud-sill of society and of political government; and you might as well attempt to build a house in the air, as to build either the one or the other, except on this mud-sill. Fortunately for the South, she found a race adapted to that purpose to her hand. A race inferior to her own, but eminently qualified in temper, in vigor, in docility, in capacity to stand the climate, to answer all her purposes. We use them for our purpose, and call them slaves. We found them slaves by the common "consent of mankind," which, according to Cicero, *"lex naturæ est."* The highest proof of what is Nature's law. We are old-fashioned at the South yet; slave is a word discarded now by "ears polite;" I will not characterize that class at the North by that term; but you have it; it is there; it is everywhere; it is eternal.

The Senator from New York [William H. Seward] said yesterday that the whole world had abolished slavery. Aye, the *name,* but not the *thing;* all the powers of the earth cannot abolish that. God only can do it when he repeals the *fiat,* "the poor ye always have with you;" for the man who lives by daily labor, and scarcely lives at that, and who has to put out his labor in the market, and take the best he can get for it; in short, your whole hireling class of manual laborers and "operatives," as you call them, are essentially slaves. The difference between us is, that our slaves are hired for life and well compensated; there is no starvation, no begging, no want of employment among our people, and not too much employment either. Yours are hired by the day, not cared for, and scantily compensated, which may be proved in the most painful manner, at any hour in any street in any of your large towns. Why, you meet more beggars in one day, in any single street of the city of New York, than you would meet in a lifetime in the whole South. We do not think that whites should be slaves either by law or necessity. Our slaves are black, of another and inferior race.

5. The Proposed Crittenden Compromise, 1860

Whereas, serious and alarming dissensions have arisen between the Northern and Southern States, concerning the rights and security of the rights of the slave-holding States, and especially their rights in the common territory of the United States; and whereas it is eminently desirable and proper that these dissensions which now threaten the very existence of this Union, should be permanently quieted and settled, by constitutional provisions, which shall do equal justice to all sections, and thereby restore to the people that peace and good will which ought to prevail between all the citizens of the United States: Therefore,

Resolved by the Senate and House of Representatives of the United States of America in Congress Assembled, That the following articles be, and are hereby, proposed and submitted as amendments to the Constitution of the United States, . . .

Article 1. In all the territory of the United States now held, or hereafter acquired, situate North of Latitude 36° 30', slavery or involuntary servitude, except as a punishment for crime, is prohibited while such territory shall remain under territorial government. In all the territory south of said line of latitude, slavery of the African race is hereby recognized as existing, and shall not be interfered with by Congress, but shall be protected as property by all the departments of the territorial government during its continuance. And when any Territory, north or south of said line, within such boundaries as Congress may prescribe, shall contain the population requisite for a member of Congress according to the then Federal ratio, of representation of the people of the United States, it shall, if its form of government be republican, be admitted into the Union, on an equal footing with the original States, with or without slavery, as the constitution of such new State may provide.

Art. 2. Congress shall have no power to abolish slavery in places under its exclusive jurisdiction, and situate within the limits of States that permit the holding of slaves.

Art. 3. Congress shall have no power to abolish slavery within the district of Columbia so long as it exists in the adjoining States of Virginia and Maryland, or

---

This document can be found in Henry Steele Commager, ed., *Documents in American History,* 5th ed. (New York: Appleton-Century-Crofts, 1949), pp. 369–371.

either, not without the consent of the inhabitants, nor without just compensation first made to such owners of slaves as do not consent to such abolishment. Nor shall Congress at any time prohibit officers of the Federal Government, or members of Congress, whose duties require them to be in said District, from bringing with them their slaves, and holding them as such during the time their duties may require them to remain there, and afterwards taking them from the District.

Art. 4. Congress shall have no power to prohibit or hinder the transportation of slaves from one State to another, or to a Territory in which slaves are by law permitted to be held, whether that transportation be by land, navigable rivers, or by the sea. . . .

Art. 6. No future amendment of the Constitution shall affect the five preceding articles . . . and no amendment shall be made to the Constitution which shall authorize or give to Congress any power to abolish or interfere with slavery in any of the States by whose laws it is, or may be, allowed or permitted.

And whereas, also, besides these causes of dissension embraced in the foregoing amendments proposed to the Constitution of the United States, there are others which come within the jurisdiction of Congress, and may be remedied by its legislative power; Therefore

1. Resolved. . . . That the laws now in force for the recovery of fugitive slaves are in strict pursuance of the plain and mandatory provisions of the Constitution, and have been sanctioned as valid and constitutional by the judgment of the Supreme Court of the United States; that the slave-holding States are entitled to the faithful observance and execution of those laws, and that they ought not to be repealed, or so modified or changed as to impair their efficiency; and that laws ought to be made for the punishment of those who attempt by rescue of the slave, or other illegal means, to hinder or defeat the due execution of said laws.

2. That all State laws which conflict with the fugitive slave acts of Congress, or any other Constitutional acts of Congress, or which, in their operation, impede, hinder, or delay, the free course and due execution of any of said acts, are null and void by the present provisions of the Constitution of the United States; yet those State laws, void as they are, have given color to practices, and led to consequences which have obstructed the due administration and execution of acts of Congress, and especially the acts for the delivery of fugitive slaves, and have thereby contributed much to the discord and commotion now prevailing. Congress, therefore, in the present perilous juncture, does not deem it improper, respectfully and earnestly to recommend the repeal of those laws to the several States which have enacted them, or such legislative corrections or explanations of them as may prevent their being used or perverted to such mischievous purposes.

3. That the Act of the 18th of September, 1850, commonly called the fugitive slave law, . . . the last clause of the fifth section of said act, which authorizes a person holding a warrant for the arrest or detention of a fugitive slave, to summon to his aid the *posse comitatus,* and which declares it to be the duty of all good citizens to assist him in its execution, ought to be so amended as to expressly limit the authority and duty to cases in which there shall be resistance or danger of resistance or rescue.

4. That the laws for the suppression of the African slave trade, and especially those prohibiting the importation of slaves in the United States, ought to be made effectual, and ought to be thoroughly executed: and all further enactments necessary to those ends ought to be promptly made.

6. Southern Editors Speculate on Secession, 1860, 1861

Charleston Mercury, *November 3, 1860*

The issue before the country is the extinction of slavery. No man of common sense, who has observed the progress of events, and who is not prepared to surrender the institution, with the safety and independence of the South, can doubt that the time for action has come—now or never. The Southern States are now in the crisis of their fate; and, if we read aright the signs of the times, nothing is needed for our deliverance, but that the ball of revolution be set in motion. There is sufficient readiness among the people to make it entirely successful. Co-operation will follow the action of any State. The example of a forward movement only is requisite to unite Southern States in a common cause. Under these circumstances the Legislature of South Carolina is about to meet. It happens to assemble in advance of the Legislature of any other State. Being in session at this momentous juncture—the Legislature of that State which is most united in the policy or freeing the South from Black Republican domination—the eyes of the whole country, and most especially of the resistance party of the Southern States, is intently turned upon the conduct of this body. We have innumerable assurances that the men of action in each and all of the Southern States, earnestly desire South Carolina to exhibit promptitude and decision in this conjuncture. Other states are torn and divided, to a greater or less extent, by old party issues. South Carolina alone is not. Any practical move would enable the people of other States to rise above their past divisions, and lock shields on the broad ground of Southern security. The course of our Legislature will either greatly stimulate and strengthen, or unnerve the resistance elements of the whole South. A Convention is the point to which their attention will be chiefly directed.

The question of calling a Convention by our Legislature does not necessarily involve the question of separate or co-operative action. That is a question for the Convention when it assembles, under the circumstances which shall exist when it assembles. All desire the action of as many Southern States as possible, for the formation of a Southern Confederacy. But each should not delay and wait on the other. As these States are separate sovereignties, each must act separately. . . .

. . . What is really essential is this—that by the action of one or more States, there shall be the *reasonable probability* that a Southern Confederacy will be formed.

New Orleans Bee, *December 14, 1860*

The political charlatans of the North and the patriotic but mistaken public men of the border slave States appear to outvie each other in efforts to discover a remedy for existing evils. They do not perceive that the wound inflicted by the North upon the South is essentially incurable. They think, on the contrary, it may be plastered, and bandaged, and dressed in some sort of fashion and will do very well. The Union is broken in two, but the political doctors fancy that the ruptured extremities can be readily brought together, and that by the aid of the world-renowned "compromise" machine, the integrity of the fractured parts may be completely restored. Without further figure of speech, let us say that we hardly know whether to smile or sigh over the innumerable devices resorted to by members of Congress to save the Union. With just about as much hope of success might they expect to breathe life into a corpse, or look for green leaves, bright flowers, and savory fruit from the blackened and withered trunk of a blasted tree, as imagine that the Union may yet be preserved. This *might* have been done a few months ago. The Union might have received a new lease of life, had the Abolition party been overwhelmingly defeated in the recent contest; but after its signal triumph to seek to bolster up the Union is as fruitless a task as would be the attempt to teach [William Lloyd] Garrison moderation, [Charles] Sumner national patriotism, and [Henry] Wilson the feelings and instincts of a gentleman. . . .

But the grand, overwhelming objection to these feeble and fruitless projects is the absolute impossibility of revolutionizing Northern opinion in relation to slavery. Without a change of heart, radical and thorough, all guarantees which might be offered are not worth the paper on which they would be inscribed. As long as slavery is looked upon by the North with abhorrence; as long as the South is regarded as a mere slave-breeding and slave-driving community; as long as false and pernicious theories are cherished respecting the inherent equality and rights of every human being, there can be no satisfactory political union between the two sections. If one-half the people believe the other half to be deeply dyed in iniquity; to be daily and hourly in the perpetration of the most atrocious moral offense, and at the same time knowing them to be their countrymen and fellow-citizens, conceive themselves authorized and in some sort constrained to lecture them, to abuse them, to employ all possible means to break up their institutions, and to take from them what the Northern half consider property unrighteously held, or no property at all, how can two such antagonistic nationalities dwell together in fraternal concord under the same government? Is not the thing clearly impossible? Has not the experiment been tried for more than seventy years, and have not the final results demonstrated its failure? The feelings, customs, mode of thought and education of the two sections, are discrepant and often antagonistic. The North and South are heterogeneous and are better apart. Were we foreign to the North, that section would treat us as our Government now treats Mexico or England—abstaining from interference in the internal policy of a country with which we have nothing to do, and with which we are at peace. As it is, we are persuaded that while the South continues a part of the American confederacy, there is no power which can prevent her progressive degradation, humiliation and spoliation by the victorious North. We are doomed if we proclaim not our political independence.

Republican Banner, *Nashville, January 25, 1861*

The Resolutions adopted by the General Assembly, published in our paper a few days since, define the position of Tennessee satisfactorily, as we believe, to the great mass of the people. They substantially adopt the Crittenden Compromise as a basis of adjustment of the pending issues between the North and South, and Tennessee will say to the people of the North, not in a spirit of blustering defiance and braggadocio, but firmly and calmly, and with a sincere and honest desire that this adjustment may be accepted—we demand nothing more—*we will accept of nothing less.* This settlement can be agreed upon by the people of both sections without the sacrifice of a principle or of any material interest. It would be acceptable, we believe, to a majority of the people in the seceding States, and the State of Tennessee could take no course better calculated to befriend and conserve the interests of those States than by maintaining such a position as will enable her, in conjunction with other Southern States, to negotiate the adoption of this compromise with the North. That the sympathies of Tennessee are emphatically Southern, no one will deny. She will take no course, in any event, calculated to militate against the interests of her Southern sisters. But the question for her to decide—and it is a question upon which hangs her own and the destiny of the South and the Union—is what course is most judicious, most patriotic, and best calculated to conserve the interests of her Southern sisters, and if possible preserve the Union? Upon this question there is a difference of opinion. Some are for precipitate secession. Others for maintaining our present attitude, prepared, when the time comes, to act as mediators upon the basis of the Crittenden adjustment. If the policy of the former party is pursued, we lose the advantage of our position as pacificators, and gain nothing that we could not gain at any future time, when it shall be demonstrated, as it unfortunately may be, that a settlement is impracticable. We are therefore opposed to hasty action. We do not think the friends of a fair and honorable settlement, in the seceding States, desire Tennessee to follow their example until all honorable endeavors to secure such a settlement are exhausted. Doubtless there are many in those States who do not desire a settlement—who prefer disunion and a Southern Confederacy to any reconstruction of the Government. There are a few, even in Tennessee, who sympathize with these disunionists *per se,* but they are very few, and thus far have been very modest in the avowal of such sentiments. Tennessee is emphatically a Union State, if the Union can be preserved upon terms of equality and justice, and is for making an attempt to preserve it before abandoning the hope. The difference of opinion among her people is merely as to the best policy to be pursued to accomplish a given end, at which all seem to be driving. We should rejoice to see this difference of opinion reconciled or compromised, so that we might all move in solid phalanx, and as a unit. It would add immensely to our influence in the crisis, and might, indeed, be the means of securing what, under existing circumstances, may not be attained—a perpetuation of the Government.

7. Letters of Support to Senator Andrew Johnson 1860–1861

From A. Waldo Putnam

Nashville, December 22, 1860

Hon. Andrew Johnston
Senator in Congress

My dear Sir,

It is my *duty* and *pleasure* promptly to express to you,—and I rejoice in the opportunity to record,—my most hearty approbation of the sentiments uttered by you in the Senate on 18th inst.

I cannot but regard the course pursued by South Carolina as one of madness, demented folly, unparalleled in history only by that of the French Revolution—and that she has shown arrogance, dictation, disrespect and contempt of other States, which

From *The Papers of Andrew Johnson,* Vol. 4, © 1976, Leroy Graf and Ralph Haskins, eds. Reprinted by permission of The University of Tennessee Press.

should make them scorn her advice and abhor her example. . . . It is absolutely a post of degradation to ask Tennessee. Ky. & Va. to follow the haughty lead of such a State as S.C.— *At last*—Jackson and his patriotic Tennesseans are to bow down at the nullification, yea *Disunion Despotism* of Calhoun and his successors, the aristocrats of the least oppressed, least democratic and most anti-republican State on this continent!

God grant to multiply the number of wise, prudent course & patriotic men, & may they soon peaceably adjust the fearful troubles of the times.

Very respectfully   A. W. Putnam
Nashville Dec. 22/60

From William R. Hurley

Nashville Dec 23d 1860

Hon A. Johnson.

Dear Sir:

You will doubtless be surprised to receive a letter from me. My apology is the present danger to which our country is exposed. From telegraphic reports of your speech I am of opinion that it will have a good effect upon the public. I am anxious to have a copy for publication in the Democrat. I suppose that there will [be] a large number of your speeches circulated in pamphlet form. I am anxious that you shall send out large numbers to every point in Tennessee *especially*. All our papers or most of them in this state are *timid*. I shall fight a bold an[d] earnest fight, if I can sustain the Democrat. But as long as it can be sustained I will make an ea[r]nest contest in the union & for the union and our rights within the union. Secession is the short Cut to abolitionism especially in the border states and there is great danger of extermination of the African race from the continent. If our white people get the impression— that there is danger of establishing equality of the races, a war of extermination will set in at once. The Union & American and a few men of the *clique* are disposed to denounce you, but you will be sustained by a majority of men of all parties in this state, if you are reported correctly by telegraph. You and I differed very widely during the last can[v]ass, but when I see you stand up boldly for your cou[n]try, I say "well done good and faithful servant[.]" I am proud of a Representative who has the manliness to discharge his duty, and you will find the Democrat defending your position, boldly and earnestly, as long as it is sustained. Secession has been on the increase in this state but we calculate largely on the influence of your speech. My dear sir go on in the great work and save our bleeding country if possible.

I am yours in an effort to preserve the bonds of an everlasting Union.

W R Hurley

From Richard M. Edwards

Cleveland Tenn Jany 2nd 1861

Hon A. Johnson

Your late able speech in vindication of the constitution and the Union, has won back hundreds who have been temporarily estranged from you besides thousands who have never stood by you before. You have caused tremendous confusion among the seceders and disunionists; for there are disunionists even here. It afforded me great pleasure when I learned the position you had taken for there is no mistaking the fact that to the senators in Congress the great mass of the people are looking and upon the present senators most of the responsibility will attach for the events now transpiring and which will occur in the almost present portentous future. We are here taking the position that unless President Buchanan does his sworn duty by reinforcing fort Sumpter & retaking Fort Moultrie, that he should be impeached; and that should be done by some Southern senator, & a democrat. Believing that the Union can only be saved by decided prompt and energetic action of its friends; I believe that you ought to, at least enquire into the conduct of the president at once and show by your action that you intend to have the constitution of our country respected. The time is upon us for action. The controversy is already growing hot; and the issue is one involving the lives happiness and honor of us and our children; for already do secessionists talk glibly of the term "Tory" and it remains to be seen whether that term shall be applied to you and me & our children after us or shall that title with its attendant odium attach to those who from their position *of hostility to the present form of government,* are more legitimately entitled to it. However, the application of that or any other term of reproach depends upon the turn of affairs in the future. If the Revolutionists are successful we will bear all the odium; but if we are successful in maintaining the government then all the odium will attach to the other party. I have taken pains to sound the public mind here and at a large meeting here Union resolutions were passed notwithstanding Rowles Smith Harris Swan & others moved Heaven & earth to defeat them. With all their ability and long speaking they only succeeded in getting 35 on their side and *they* are not real disunionists. The Union sentiment will win here. Send us if possible a large lot of your speeches & we can break the disunion movement down entirely.

Dreadful consequences are just ahead of us and they can not be averted by timid persuasive policy— such a policy is but the nursing the viper to life to sting you afterwards.

No reason is given for breaking up the government except that those who are leading in the movement *want to form a different one.* The love of a *different* government from this was the guiding star of the "Tories" of the Revolution. I have written thus much simply to encourage you to do your duty as you have heretofore.

Your friend   R. M. Edwards

8. The Jones Family Responds to Republican Victory, 1860–1861

Mrs. Mary Jones to Hon. Charles C. Jones, Jr.

Montevideo, *Thursday,* November 15th, 1860

My dear Son,

We are happy to receive your affectionate favor by today's mail, and to know that you were well and again at the post of duty. No festive greetings were

---

Robert Manson Myers, *Children of Pride: A True Story of Georgia and the Civil War,* copyright © 1972 by Yale University Press. Reprinted by permission of the publisher.

ever mingled with more elevated feelings of friendship, honor, patriotism, and courage than those recently enjoyed by the citizens of Charleston and Savannah. We were much obliged to you for the *Mercury,* and felt honored that our son bore so high a place. Your opening speech at the Pulaski gave evidently a tone to the meeting.

Be assured, my dear child, of your parents' warmest sympathy at this time, and of our united and special prayer that you may be divinely guided and ever act with wisdom and fidelity in your sacred and responsible station. It is a new era in our country's history, and I trust the wise and patriotic leaders of the people will soon devise some united course of action throughout the Southern states. I cannot see a shadow of reason for civil war in the event of a Southern confederacy; but even that, *if it must come,* would be preferable to submission to Black Republicanism, involving as it would all that is horrible, degrading, and ruinous. "Forbearance has ceased to be a virtue"; and I believed we could meet with no evils out of the Union that would compare to those we will finally suffer if we continue in it; for we can no longer doubt that the settled policy of the North is to crush the South. . . .

Father has just returned from the chapel, and unites with me in best love to Ruth and yourself, and many kisses for our granddaughter.

Ever your affectionate mother,

Mary Jones.

Howdy for the servants.

Rev. C. C. Jones to Hon. Charles C. Jones, Jr.

Montevideo, *Thursday,* November 15th, 1860

Your position is a very responsible one. Go calmly and quietly about your duties, and discharge them with integrity and fidelity, and avoid excitements and too frequent speaking on public occasions. I was much gratified with your speech at the dinner to the Charlestonians in Savannah.

The times are remarkable; the questions before the people momentous. The final issues are with Him who rules among the nations. A nation to be born in a day, without a struggle, would be a wonder on earth. If the Southern states resolve on a separate confederacy, they must be prepared for any emergency, even that of war with the free states; as their arrogance and confidence in their power may urge them to attempt our subjugation—although I do not fear it if the Southern states are united. We have a heavy Northern element, and a Southern element Northernized, to contend with in our own borders, and may perhaps lead to some embarrassment; but the majority the other way is so decided that it cannot—at least it is so to be hoped—effect much. Certainly we do need "the prayers of the pious and the wisdom of the wise." Portions of Governor Brown's special message are excellent. Having no access to the leading spirits of the day, I cannot discern the drift of affairs beyond the light of the newspapers, which we read with interest. We have no knowledge of the course which Maryland, Virginia, North Carolina, Tennessee, Kentucky, and Missouri will pursue.

The Lord keep and bless you and yours, my dear son, and give you a place in that Kingdom which cannot be moved, is the prayer of

Your affectionate father,

C. C. Jones.

Hon. Charles C. Jones, Jr., to Rev. and Mrs. C. C. Jones

Savannah, *Wednesday,* April 17th, 1861

My very dear Father and Mother, . . .

Recent telegrams inform us of the probable passage of an ordinance of secession by the Virginia legislature. The North Carolinians are realizing the importance of decided action. A noble reply to Lincoln's demand for troops has been returned by Governor Magoffin of Kentucky. Thus act succeeds act in this wonderful drama. Lincoln has made requisitions upon the Northern states for one hundred and fifty thousand more troops. Every indication points to a prolonged and sanguinary struggle.

We are endeavoring to prepare for the conflict. Colonel Lawton has, as you have observed, been appointed a brigadier general of the Confederate States, and is charged specially with the defense of our city, harbor, and coast. Tybee Island is now occupied by more than two hundred troops. Batteries are soon to be erected there. Near two hundred men from the interior of the state arrived last night, and will take post also upon Tybee. Fort Pulaski is garrisoned by four hundred men, and Fort Jackson by one hundred and twenty. The volunteer corps of the city are at present held as a reserve—subject, however, to orders at any moment. When the plot thickens and the day of battle comes, they will be where stout hearts and brave hands are most needed.

The ladies of Savannah are not idle. They are daily engaged singly and in concert in the preparation of cartridges both for muskets and cannon. Thousands have been already made by them, and the labor is just begun. Others are cutting out and sewing flannel shirts. Others still are making bandages and preparing lint. Their interest and patriotic efforts in this our cause are worthy of all admiration.

We have now three full batteries of field pieces in the city—one in the possession of our company, another in the keeping of the Savannah Artillery, and a third at the barracks. Upon Tybee Island they have two six-pounders and two twelve-pound howitzers. Heavy guns are needed there, and I doubt not but that General Lawton is directing his immediate attention to the preparation of batteries both at the northern and southern extremities of the island. The work of mounting columbians at Fort Pulaski progresses slowly. Eighteen-pounders have arrived for Fort Jackson, are lying now upon the parade and upon the parapets of that fortification, and will be mounted so soon as carriages can be prepared. The workshops of the Central Railroad are busily occupied with their construction. Our company has been constantly engaged in putting our battery in thorough order, and in the manufacture of fuses (a very delicate and responsible duty) for the forts and for ourselves.

It is today officially announced that our mails are cut off, and that there will be henceforth no further communication through their agency with the Confederate States.

Can you imagine a more suicidal, outrageous, and exasperating policy than that inaugurated by the fanatical administration at Washington? The Black Republicans may rave among the cold hills of their native states, and grow mad with entertainment of infidelity, heresies, and false conceptions of a "higher law"; but Heaven forbid that they ever attempt to set foot upon this land of sunshine, of high-souled honor, and of liberty. It puzzles the imagination to conceive the stupidity, the fanaticism, and the unmitigated rascality which impel them to the course which they are now pursuing. I much mistake the policy of this Confederacy and the purposes of our worthy President (at once soldier and statesman) if in the event of our pure rivers and harbors being blockaded by Northern fleets, a great Southern army is not put in motion, attracting to itself the good and true men of every section, whose object it shall be to redeem the tomb of Washington from the dominion of this fanatical rule, and to plant the standard of this Confederacy even upon the dome of the capitol at Washington. This is a favorite scheme with President Davis, and he has brave men such as Major McCulloch and General Pillow to sustain him in carrying the idea into practical effect. . . .

Your affectionate son,

Charles C. Jones, Jr.

✳ E S S A Y S

Lacy K. Ford, Jr., a professor of history at the University of South Carolina, argues in his book *Origins of Radicalism* that South Carolina leaders saw slavery as an institution that enhanced a republican concept of liberty and would save the South from the evils of free-labor capitalism as practiced in the North. He suggests that eventually both the elite and yeomen saw secession as the only means to defend their way of life and slavery as the institution that would uphold republican values. Not all southerners were committed to defending slavery if that meant secession, however. In the second essay, historian Daniel W. Crofts, a professor at College of New Jersey, reminds us of the enormous political shifts that occurred in Virginia, North Carolina, and Tennessee as many Unionists and nonslaveholders mobilized to oppose secession. For many voters in these border states, secession became inevitable only after the war began.

South Carolina Leaders Defend Slavery and Secession

LACY K. FORD, JR.

By the late 1850s, South Carolinians clearly believed that they were living in a society under siege. Beneath the many tactical disputes and strategic disagreements lay general agreement that the South's right to exist as a slave society was in jeopardy. For more than two decades, the abolitionists had waged their psychological war on the region, encouraged insurrection, and convinced even conservative Southerners such as Beaufort planter William Elliott, a lifelong Unionist, that what the North wanted for the South was "an agricultural prosperity like that of Jamaica" and "such security as is found in St. Domingo." South Carolina slaveholders, and non-slaveholders for that matter, were not about to surrender their proud society, one wrested by their forefathers from wilderness and disease and Indians, to what they perceived as the "mawkish sentimentality" of Northern abolitionists. Yet although the fundamental right of the South to exist as a slave society always lay beneath the region's response to the abolitionists' attack and at the heart of the sectional conflict, the South's growing dissatisfaction with the Union was more than a primitive struggle for survival. Also at issue were other equally fundamental rights, rights stemming from the right of survival but also transcending and ennobling that right, which South Carolinians believed to be threatened by the increasingly militant anti-slavery and free-soil movements in the North.

As always, South Carolinians perceived threats through the lens of their gripping republican ideology and with a stubborn refusal to yield rights they believed to be guaranteed by the Constitution. From within this well-fortified frame of reference, the question of slavery in the territories involved a number of fundamental republican rights. First of all, South Carolinians believed that while Congress had the right to control the territories, Congress had no right to prevent slaveholders from taking slaves into the territories, since the slaveholder's property rights must be considered the equal of other citizens' property rights, as guaranteed by the Constitution. As early as 1852, Laurens's Zelotus Holmes told his Northern relatives that their "new and prevailing doctrine" of "no more slave territory" was "so different from that which the old States originally set out under the Constitution" and constituted "such bad faith in carrying out the original understanding" that the South was justified in its complaints about Northern tyranny and aggression. Southerners, Holmes argued, might accept *de facto* restrictions on the expansion of slavery arising from "natural causes" or "moral influences," but the Southern people were determined not to be "legislated out of the possible chances" to take their slaves into the territories. Moreover, if Congress did not have the power to exclude slavery from the territories, it certainly had no right to delegate such authority to territorial legislatures. Thus territories could only prohibit slavery when they drafted a constitution and applied for statehood. This position, though subject to considerable legal dispute throughout the antebellum period, was essentially that taken by the Supreme Court in the Dred Scott decision of 1857.

Yet more than mere legalism was involved in the controversy. If slaveholders were prohibited from taking their slave property into the territories, they were denied their full rights as citizens. Southerners were especially sensitive to what they regarded as the necessity of equality among republican citizens. If the slaveholder's rights were in any way circumscribed, he lost his equality within the Union. Such a reduction in status lowered the slaveholder to a position of shame and degradation, and forfeited his honor and independence. Moreover, as the number of free states continued to increase while the number of slave states remained constant, the slave South found itself in the same minority position in the Senate that it had long occupied in the House of Representatives. As a minority, Southern politicians were zealous in defense of the South's right to "equality" within the Union. Francis W.

Pickens summed up the position of most South Carolinians well in a speech on the crisis in Kansas at Anderson courthouse in 1855. "I trust in God that the watchword will always be, *Equality forever or Independence,*" Pickens declared, "and that it will ring over a thousand hills and start from their scabbards the swords of a hundred thousand freemen." . . .

By the middle of the 1850s, most South Carolinians were convinced that almost every aspect of the sectional conflict involved significant ideological disagreements between North and South. This ideological component of sectional conflict had been evident for a number of years, and was often painted in bold relief by Calhoun's relentless insistence that the South defend its moral and ideological values as well as its narrow political and economic interests. Moreover, as Southerners responded to incessant abolitionist attacks with an increasingly sophisticated defense of slavery, the region's moral and ideological commitment to slavery became both stronger and more visible. Yet despite the ideological overtones which were evident throughout the period of sectional conflict, the presence of pervasive, and perhaps fundamental, ideological antagonism did not become obvious until free-labor ideology gained widespread popularity in the North during the 1850s. To be sure, politicians and ideologues in both North and South used the inherited republican tradition as a prism through which to refract their respective visions of the good society, sometimes badly distorting republicanism itself in the process. But, as Eric Foner has demonstrated, the emergence of the Republican party in the North during the 1850s marked the triumph of an ideology devoted to the principles of "free soil, free labor, and free men." This Northern free-labor ideology was a dynamic version of republicanism adjusted to the peculiarities of nineteenth-century commercial capitalism. According to free-labor ideology, the good society was one dominated by independent, property-holding, petty producers, free to attain self-sufficiency and pursue the main chance in an expanding market economy. The ideal-typical North of free labor enthusiasts was a veritable republican utopia of "family farms, small shops, and village artisans," a competitive society of petty capitalists, where labor knew neither the oppression of alienation from capital nor the degradation of competition with slavery.

South Carolinians, as well as other Southerners, shared a republican heritage that was not, at first glance, very different from that of the North. For Southerners, the good society was also one dominated by independent, property-holding producers who sought both to maintain their autonomy and to enjoy the benefits of material accumulation. By the 1850s, however, many South Carolinians were convinced that the community of independent producers which provided the foundation for republican government could, ironically, only survive in a slave society. "[N]o social state, without slavery as its basis," asserted Iveson Brookes, "can permanently maintain a republican form of government." To Southerners, the marriage of republicanism and capitalism which seemed so natural at one time now threatened to pervert republicanism beyond recognition. The good republican citizen had to maintain his personal independence, and it was crucial that that personal independence rest on a proper economic base. Since ownership of productive property was considered the best economic guarantee of personal independence, republican values were easily corrupted and destroyed in a society whose population included hordes of propertyless, and therefore dependent, citizens. Thus, as the process of industrialization slowly began to transform an economy of independent proprietorships into one of capitalists and laborers, the economic foundation of republican values was threatened by invidious new dependencies and class distinctions. In a slave economy, however, the propertyless, dependent, laboring class was defined out of the body politic where it would remain forever beyond the reach of dangerous radicals, aspiring dictators, and scheming demagogues.

Throughout the sectional conflict, South Carolina leaders argued that the Southern experiment in slave-labor republicanism had better prospects for long-term success than did its Northern free-labor counterpart. As early as the writing of the *Exposition and Protest,* Calhoun argued that only slavery stood to prevent the conflict between labor and capital from destroying the Republic. "After we are exhausted," Calhoun observed, "the contest will be between the capitalists and operatives; for into these two classes it must, ultimately, divide society." A few years later, Calhoun again suggested that slavery could preserve republicanism in the South long after class struggle had destroyed it in the North. . . .

Although antislavery leaders dismissed the Southern critique of Northern society as merely a *tu quoque* response to their attacks on slavery, what emerged during the 1850s was not only a scathing indictment of "wage-slavery" but also a thorough-going defense of slave-labor republicanism. As it existed in South Carolina, chattel slavery enhanced republican liberty in a number of important ways. First, it allowed the economy to expand beyond the subsistence level without the creation of a vast proletariat which was economically dependent but politically dangerous. Since slaves were not citizens, the dependent laboring population in the South posed no challenge to the political rule of independent producers. Second, according to South Carolinians, slavery dampened the conflict between labor and capital not only by rendering labor politically impotent but also by introducing a "moral" dimension into capital's control of labor. In a slave society, labor (slaves) was dependent on capital, yet capital (the masters) was placed in a position where its responsibilities went far beyond mere contractual obligation. Instead, masters were charged with the entire physical and moral stewardship of their chattels. Finally, and most important, South Carolinians argued that slavery strengthened republican values by enhancing the "independence" of whites and creating a pervasive sense of equality among all whites, since all whites could claim membership in a privileged class simply on the basis of race. But black slavery did more for common whites in the South than simply allow them to enjoy whatever psychological satisfaction grew from a sense of belonging to a superior caste defined solely by race. By providing the labor necessary for large-scale commercial agriculture like that of Southern plantations, the so-called "factories in the fields," slavery insulated Southern yeomen from that which they feared most: the danger that they would one day be forced to become a laboring class dependent on capitalists for their livelihood. Though deeply rooted in the traditional ideal of personal independence, by the late 1850s, the yeomanry's fear of being proletarianized was fed by the growing power of capital and commerce in the region. Thus, while some planters doubtless saw the profoundly conservative implications of a pro-slavery republicanism which minimized class conflict by literally enslaving the working class, yeoman farmers and other whites saw that same ideology as profoundly egalitarian. Slavery liberated the

yeoman from his own potential dependency; slavery for blacks guaranteed the freedom of common whites.

Republican theorists had long argued that republics could not survive if the
great mass of citizens were cut off from control of productive property and forced
into economic dependency. In the late antebellum period, the Southern critique of
free-labor ideology focused on this issue. Southern thinkers argued that the North
was not headed toward a free-labor millennium of prosperous producers, but rather
toward an unfettered capitalism of rapacious robber barons, belligerent wage-labor-
ers, and corrupt political leaders. In free-labor societies, propertyless citizens were
forced to sell their labor in the marketplace, where it was necessarily placed under
the control of capital. "If money is power," noted Chester slaveholder Jonathan
Newland in 1856, "money must ultimately succeed in bringing all the laboring
classes into subjection to itself." As a result, the independence of the laborer was
sacrificed for profits for the capitalists and living wages for the laborers. "The capitalist sits alone in his easy chair, and learns to regard labor in the aggregate," noted
the *Carolina Spartan,* "[and] the individuality of the laborer is lost sight of." Having lost their independence, free laborers were no longer fit citizens for a republic,
and, in fact, were reduced to a form of subjugation that Southerners called "wage-
slavery." The man "who has to put out his labour in the market and take the best he
can get for it; in short, your whole hireling class of manual laborers and 'operatives,' " James Henry Hammond told Northern senators, ". . . are essentially
slaves." The North, according to Hammond, had not done away with slavery, it had
merely eliminated the "*name,* but not the *thing.*" Several years earlier, Louisa Mc-
Cord, daughter of Langdon Cheves, declared in a reply to abolitionist criticisms:

> He who has not the right to dispose of his own labour becomes consequently and
> necessarily, to a greater or lesser extent . . . the serf or bondsman of the individual or
> government, thus shackling or limiting his exchanges.

Moreover, a number of South Carolinians argued, the "wage-slavery" of the North
was more cruel and oppressive than the chattel slavery of the South. "Starvation is
not an *approach* towards slavery," McCord declared, "The Southern slave is . . .
well clothed, well fed, well treated, in every way comfortable beyond the labouring
class of any country, and, although not enjoying the luxuries of life, is as far from
starvation as his master." . . .

Supposedly, slavery saved the South from all [the] evils of free-labor capitalism. According to Edgefield's Iveson Brookes, slavery was "a main pillar to the
peace and safety of a republic." The South's peculiar institution, Brookes argued,
"unites labor and capital, and prevents the alienation of feeling and strife of opposing interests experienced where labor and capital stand in antagonistic relation to
each other." . . .

In antebellum America, North and South, the standard unit of production was
not the factory or the workshop but the household. Households whose members enjoyed control of productive property enjoyed the economic independence that
formed the bedrock of republican values. In a free-labor society, however, there
were fundamental constraints on the ability of a household to expand its productive
capacity. The most important of these constraints, of course, was the absolute limit
on the household supply of labor. To expand production beyond a certain point, the

household had to procure its labor in the marketplace. Once employees were hired in any significant number, the household was transformed into a workshop and the labor discipline of the marketplace replaced that of the family. Ultimately, as the shop and factory replaced the household as the standard unit of production, the relationship between capital and labor became that of employer and worker instead of that between the head of the household and his familial dependents.

In the South, however, chattel slavery allowed the household head (master) to expand production almost indefinitely without abandoning the household as the principal unit of production simply by expanding his definition of the household to include his extended "family" in the slave quarters. Doubtless the metaphors of the plantation as a vastly extended household and of the slaves as part of a much extended family were in part intellectual constructs designed to blunt the impact of the abolitionists' portrayal of the harsh relationship between master and slave. But it was a metaphor which grew logically from the nature of the master-slave relationship and which contained a great deal of meaning for Southern slaveholders. As the influence of evangelical Christianity expanded in the slave South during the nineteenth century, slaveholders increasingly came to view their responsibilities as moral as well as economic. The slave did not enjoy even the limited freedom of the labor market and, with a few exceptions, enjoyed little protection from the law. The power of the master over the slave, at least in theory, was nearly absolute. Yet the very scope of the master's responsibility for the slave, the completeness of his stewardship over his bondsmen, introduced a moral element into the relationship that was absent in the relations of capitalists and laborers in a free-labor society. . . .

The slaveholder's role as chief steward of his extended household established his credentials as a "paternalist," even if paternalism was a model relationship between master and slave which seldom if ever actually existed. As D. K. Roberts has shown in a study of Great Britain, paternalism was gaining acceptance in all parts of the transatlantic world as a method of softening the harsher aspects of free-market capitalism and slowing the erosion of traditional values during commercial and industrial revolutions. In Great Britain, traditional sources of authority such as the Crown, the nobility, and the Church of England attempted to shore up their position in a market society by actively shouldering more and more social responsibility. Paternalism appeared in the antebellum North when capitalists in the first industrial areas moved to promote community harmony and tranquility by accepting responsibility for preserving social order in the industrial community. Thus the rhetoric of paternalism and the idea that capitalists as well as more traditional figures of authority had to take an active role in the moral, spiritual, and physical uplift of their society flourished in free-labor societies as well as in the slave South. In both free and slave societies, paternalism was an idiom of social responsibility and moral uplift adopted with more or less sincerity by those who enjoyed economic and political power. By maintaining that masters were paternalistic in their control of slaves, South Carolinians adopted an idiom of enlightened social control which placed them clearly within the mainstream of the early Victorian intellectual world, yet they adapted that idiom to justify the persistence of a slave society in a world increasingly dominated by free labor.

To the extent that paternalism gained acceptance in South Carolina, it did so as a model for the relationships between a master class, which was, with a few exceptions, white, and slaves who were always black or colored. No one in South Carolina argued that paternalism did or should serve as a model for relations among whites. Indeed, the racial aspect of Southern slavery was crucial to the acceptance of slavery as the proper foundation for republican government. "I am sure no one would deny that if the slave had been of the same race as his master, slavery would have been long ago extinguished and forgotten," William Henry Trescot asserted. Indeed, slavery was seen as a buttress to republican liberty because it supplied dependent laborers to a growing economy without creating invidious class distinctions among whites. "In every community," observed Whitemarsh Seabrook, "where the institution of slavery is interwoven with its social system, the public tranquility and safety demand the toleration of only two classes, white men and colored slaves." James Henry Hammond claimed that any society must have its "mudsill" class "requiring but a low order of intellect and but little skill." Fortunately for the South, Hammond continued, "she found a race adapted to that purpose to her hand. A race inferior to her own, but eminently qualified in temper, in vigor, in docility, in capacity to stand the climate, to answer all her purposes." . . .

Black slavery, therefore, was portrayed as a bulwark of republican liberty for whites. It brought racial and class lines in antebellum South Carolina into close identification. One group was independent, enfranchised, white, and free, the other was dependent, politically impotent, black, and enslaved. With black slavery serving as a foundation for white liberty, the sentiments of kinship and democracy among whites were intensified. "In a country like the South, those invidious distinctions which prevail in all free-soil States must be to a very considerable extent unknown," claimed Chester's Jonathan Newland. . . .

Southern Rights advocates in South Carolina received unexpected help in October 1859, when John Brown's well-planned but ill-fated raid on the arsenal at Harper's Ferry, and the exposure of Brown's plan to incite major slave insurrections throughout the South, reminded white South Carolinians that some abolitionists were willing to resort to terrorism to achieve their goals. Moreover, the subsequent revelation that Brown's efforts were financed by the so-called "Secret Six" of Boston alarmed members of the South Carolina gentry who had long pinned their hopes for the nation's future on the desire of conservative Northern businessmen to restrain the most radical antislavery forces in their region. As soon as the first reports of Brown's raid reached South Carolina, a brief panic swept the state. Almost immediately, vigilance committees were formed in nearly every beat in the Upcountry. For most of the next year, all strangers were suspected of being abolitionists, any hint of slave revolt met with a strong show of force, and the siege mentality in the state capital grew so intense that William Campbell Preston described Columbia as "a focus of slave traders, disunionists and lynching societies." Beat-level vigilance committees were officially organized "for the purpose of protecting our homes, families, and property, and for the general welfare of the community," but were also important in mobilizing the white population politically. "Vigilance is everywhere needed," noted the Yorkville *Enquirer.* "The roving mendicant, the tobacco-wagoner, the whisky peddler, the sample trader may be honest and reliable, but in such like disguise abolitionists have prowled about elsewhere and may do so here."

The general alarm that followed Harper's Ferry led to the harassment of suspicious whites, uncovered a few abolitionists and abolition sympathizers, and led to closer supervision of slaves in many parts of the state, but it also brought new urgency to calls for a more lasting remedy to the South's problems. Entering the critical election year of 1860, the grip of fear on the state was still tight, and the radicals had just the sort of emotional issue they needed to win popular support for secession. . . .

Throughout the secession campaign, Upcountry leaders insisted that they were defending republican values, and that secession was not the radical, but rather the conservative, course of action. "We are upholding the great principles which our fathers bequeathed us," maintained the Presbyterian theologian James Henley Thornwell. "We shall perpetuate and diffuse the very liberty for which Washington bled, and which the heroes of the Revolution achieved." In York district, radical Jonathan L. Miller claimed that Lincoln's election would leave South Carolina with a clear choice. "We must be content with the mere shadow of a Republic, with every feature of republicanism completely obliterated," Miller asserted, "or we must reaffirm and re-establish the fundamental principles of our government in building up a Southern Confederacy." The Yorkville *Enquirer* claimed that the South only wanted to preserve "simple republicanism." The question of secession was the major issue in the fall campaigns for the state legislature, and politicians found public opinion strongly in favor of secession if Lincoln were elected. Candidates such as Unionist A. S. Wallace of York, who advocated "patriotic forbearance" if Lincoln won, were, as a rule, soundly defeated. When news of Lincoln's victory finally reached the state on November 7, the legislature immediately called for a special convention to meet on December 17. Minutemen chapters quickly formed in every Upcountry district, and public meetings were called to select delegates to the secession convention. . . .

It was easy to ignore cautionary voices in the winter of 1860. Secession feeling was high. Men of all ages sported the blue cockade of resistance proudly. As military companies were organized, the state found itself flooded with more volunteers than it could use. Wade Hampton III, the wealthy Richland planter, outfitted an entire legion out of his personal fortune. Others made similar sacrifices. To be sure, this enthusiasm for sacrifice and harmony among all citizens did not last long once the fighting actually began, but in December 1860, most Upcountrymen agreed with the sentiments of David Harris. "She [South Carolina] has taken a bold and noble stand, she must and will maintain it let it cost as much blood and money as it may," the Spartanburg farmer confided to his journal. "I for one am glad she has committed herself, and do not fear the consequences." . . .

. . . South Carolina seceded not because her citizens were looking for a more perfect confederacy, but because they believed they no longer had any choice. The only alternative appeared to be submission to Black Republican rule and the sacrifice of republican independence and equality. "Secession is a desperate remedy," acknowledged David Harris, "but of the two evils I do think it is the lesser."

Late in the 1850s, the bloody struggle in Kansas and the suggestive horror of John Brown's raid on the arsenal at Harper's Ferry made the political warfare with the Republicans and abolitionists seem like a struggle to the death. Enemies willing to incite insurrection and wage campaigns of terror were enemies real and danger-ous enough to curdle the blood of the bravest Upcountryman. Moreover, these ex-ternal threats appeared at a time when most Upcountrymen were increasingly uneasy about their own experiment in republicanism. The sweeping commercial revolution of the 1850s, an increasingly active and spendthrift state government, the growing power of bank and railroad corporations, and the vicissitudes of staple agriculture all posed serious threats to the fictive republican elysium which most South Carolinians believed that they had inherited from their forefathers. The tri-umph of an avowedly antislavery President pushed an already anxious citizenry to rebellion. Yeoman joined planter to make a revolution.

Almost literally, Upcountrymen saw secession as the required defense of basic republican values. The republican citizen's most cherished possession, his own independence and that of his household, was threatened by powerful external forces. One set of those forces threatened to force him into slavery and degradation through the loss of his economic independence. The other set of forces threatened to free the entire black slave population to violate his home and family. Secession of-fered the independent citizen a chance to meet this challenge at the threshold, to de-fend the autonomy of his household by literally throwing himself across the doorway in defiance. This was the secessionist appeal that reached not just planters and slaveholders but all whites who considered themselves entitled to liberty and personal independence.

In the final analysis, a unified South Carolina could secede because the domi-nant ideal in her society was not the planter ideal or the slaveholding ideal, but the old "country-republican" ideal of personal independence, given peculiar fortifica-tion by the use of black slaves as a mud-sill class. Yeoman rose with planter to de-fend this ideal because it was not merely the planter's ideal, but his as well.

The Unionist Groundswell in the Upper South

DANIEL W. CROFTS

One must take into account both slaveholding and previous patterns of party alle-giance to understand why the upper and lower South took such different stances during the months after Lincoln's election. High-slaveowning areas across the South generally displayed more support for secession, and slaveowning was more concentrated in the lower than the upper South. Deep South secessionists also bene-fited from virtually unchallenged statewide Democratic majorities. The party's rad-ical Southern Rights wing planted seeds of poisonous suspicion that suddenly sprouted in late 1860. . . . Closer two-party competition in the upper South, how-ever, gave Whiggish opponents of secession a substantial nucleus from which to build. Antisecessionists there, using a new "Union party" label, could thus over-whelm the initial secessionist challenge.

Three waves of change, each successively larger than the other, washed over and fundamentally reshaped political contours in Virginia, North Carolina, and Ten-nessee during the brief six-month interval between November 1860 and April 1861.

Promoters of secession tried to spur the upper South to follow the example of the lower South. At first it appeared they might succeed. Those favoring secession were active, ardent, and outspoken after Lincoln's election. They had a program to confront northern menace and insult. And, not least among their assets, they had leverage in the Democratic party, which maintained a modest majority in all three states. Many Democrats, especially the officeholding elite, either supported secession overtly or allowed disunionists to lead. For perhaps two months, secession strength grew, creating a wave that surged formidably as it crested in late December and early January. In parts of "lower Virginia" and the Democratic plantation counties of North Carolina, the initial secessionist wave looked irresistible.

But in the upper South—unlike the lower South—the first wave did not dislodge any state from the Union. Instead, the push for secession created an explicitly antisecession countermobilization. Upper South Unionists organized, campaigned, and deeply stirred popular feeling, especially in nonplantation areas. They generated a second wave, greater than the first, that appeared to sweep away the popular underpinnings of secession in February 1861. Voters in all three states decisively rejected southern independence. To be sure, Unionists usually attached conditions to their allegiance, pledging to resist federal "coercion" of the seceding states. They nevertheless expected that secessionists would reconsider their rash action, thereby allowing peaceful restoration of the Union.

The Unionist coalition in the upper South was composed primarily of Whigs, often simply called "Opposition" by the late 1850s, after the collapse of their national party. The survival of competitive Opposition parties in the upper South, in contrast to the experience of the lower South during the 1850s, provided institutional barriers against secession. In nonplantation areas of the upper South, substantial increments of Union Democrats and previous nonvoters also voted against secession. Many other Democrats, uneasy about secession and about alliance with Whiggish Unionists, did not vote at all, thereby further depressing prosecession vote totals.

The action of the upper South stunned secessionists, as one famous example will illustrate. Edmund Ruffin, the elderly prophet of southern nationalism, fled from his native Virginia to South Carolina in early March 1861. He arrived just before Lincoln's inauguration, to avoid living "even for an hour" in a country with a Republican president. Ruffin had reason to feel frustrated as he traveled south. Lincoln's election had not united the South, as Ruffin had hoped. On February 4, 1861, the very day that representatives from the seven seceding states met in Montgomery, Alabama, to organize the Confederate States of America, Ruffin's home state delivered a crippling blow against upper South secession. Strongly affirming their hopes for peaceful restoration of the Union, Virginia voters rejected most prosecession candidates for the state convention. More than two out of three of those voting also specified that any convention action be made subject to popular referendum, a provision secessionists bitterly opposed. Just before leaving Virginia, Ruffin visited the convention, by then in session in Richmond. "The majority of this Convention is more basely submissive than I had supposed possible," he fumed.

The ability of Unionists to prevent the upper South from seceding gave legitimacy to the efforts of conciliatory Republicans, headed by the incoming secretary of state, William H. Seward. He tried to persuade President Lincoln that a noncoercive "hands-off" policy toward the seceded states would maintain the dominance of Unionists in the upper South and lead eventually to peaceful restoration of the Union. During March and early April, upper South Unionists believed Lincoln had agreed to the conciliatory plan.

Lincoln's proclamation calling for seventy-five thousand troops on April 15, in effect asking the upper South to fight the lower South, stirred the third and greatest wave. It immediately engulfed upper South Unionism. The three states studied here seceded in a frenzy of patriotic enthusiasm. Only in northwestern Virginia and East Tennessee did an unconditionally Unionist leadership and electorate resist the majority current. Elsewhere, original secessionists rolled out the red carpet for new converts. Believing they had been betrayed by the Lincoln administration, countless thousands who had earlier rejected secession embraced the cause of southern independence. Original and converted secessionists joined hands to defend southern honor and constitutional principles against what they perceived as corrupt, tyrannical oppression. They believed themselves fighting for the same cause as the patriots of 1776. So it was that Edmund Ruffin could return in triumph to Richmond on April 23. By then, a common resolve to resist "northern domination" had undermined Virginia's earlier Unionism, and the "submissive' convention had voted for secession. "There has been a complete and wonderful change here since I left," Ruffin exulted. . . .

Upper South Unionism coalesced during the first two months of 1861. Though confronted by grave obstacles, Unionists possessed one key advantage: popular support for secession had grown since November but had not yet gained a majority in any upper South state. Unionists faced the task of arresting and reversing the growth of secession sentiment in their home states, while also urging Congress to enact Union-saving measures. . . .

The great Unionist achievement, during a winter otherwise marked by frustration and failure, was the mobilizing of popular majorities across the upper South to thwart secession. Why did the upper South refuse to follow the lead of the lower South? That crucial question requires a two-pronged answer, involving both slavery and party. Relatively smaller concentrations of slaves and slaveowners, plus statewide political arenas in which the two major parties competed on close terms, made the upper South less receptive to secessionist appeals. The combination of fewer slaveowners and more formidable political opposition to the secession-leaning Democratic party kept Virginia, North Carolina, and Tennessee in the Union during early 1861.

Plantation regions dominated the seven seceding states in the deep South. It was no coincidence that the first states to leave the Union had the greatest commitment to slavery. Support for secession, both in the upper and lower South, tended to be strongest in high-slaveowning areas and weakest in the low-slaveowning regions of the upcountry. However formidable the slaveowning interest in Virginia, North Carolina, and Tennessee, a larger share of each state's electorate resided in the upcountry than anywhere in the lower South.

Somewhat less well known, but of comparable importance in understanding the relative weakness of secession in the upper South, was a set of partisan arrangements that differed markedly from those in the lower South. Competitive two-party politics in the upper South gave antisecessionists an indispensable base. The Whig party organization and electorate provided the foundation for what would soon be called the Union party in Virginia, North Carolina, and Tennessee.

Whig and Opposition parties throughout the lower South were much weaker and generally weakest in the upcountry. The tendency for lower South Whigs to reside in the "black belts" enervated whatever latent Unionism they possessed. But in the Upper South, Whigs had greater residual strength, which was by no means confined to plantation regions. In North Carolina, notably, a cluster of low-slaveowning counties in the piedmont regularly provided the largest Whig margins in the state. Voters in this Whiggish "Quaker Belt" spearheaded statewide opposition to secession. They gained reinforcements from party loyalists in the mountains and the northeast. Each Tennessee party received comparable support from high- and low-slaveowning regions. But a bloc of strong Whig counties around Knoxville provided a militantly antisecession nucleus for the broader East Tennessee region, and Whiggish counties in the fertile Cumberland Valley of Middle Tennessee proved especially hospitable to a qualified wait-and-see conditional Unionism. Western Virginia was slightly more Democratic than eastern Virginia, but the unique geographical position of the trans-Allegheny, coupled with its long history of estrangement from the east, made the west almost unanimously pro-Union. Whig strongholds in the Virginia valley and western piedmont also rejected secession, including, for example, Jefferson County, the site of John Brown's assault in October 1859. Even in Southampton County, the Virginia tidewater locale where the slave rebel Nat Turner had rampaged thirty years before, Whigs voted overwhelmingly pro-Union. The inability of secessionists to carry even a bare majority in Southampton well illustrated the linkage between Unionism and Whig party loyalties.

Upper South Unionism thus had both a regional and a party base. A popular outpouring of antisecession sentiment among upcountry nonslaveowners provided the most conspicuous element of Union strength. But Unionism had the potential to become a dominant political force because it extended beyond the upcountry to draw support from the Whig rank and file. The latter included a broad spectrum of southerners, among them more than a few slaveowners from the fertile lowlands. Thomas P. Devereux, one of the wealthiest plantation owners in North Carolina, berated South Carolina for her "folly" and confidently awaited a Union-saving compromise. A conservative orientation was especially pronounced among Union Whigs in eastern Virginia, many of whom deplored the democratic revisions in the 1851 Virginia constitution. They blamed secession on the new breed of "worthless, disgusting politicians" who pandered to popular fears.

Although some embraced Unionism to preserve or rebuild existing social hierarchies, the antisecession insurgency in the upper South had unmistakable egalitarian overtones. Far more than in the lower South, class resentments surfaced in late 1860 and early 1861. One of Edmund Ruffin's correspondents told him in late November that secession sentiment in the Southside Virginia counties of Lunenburg and Nottoway had increased greatly since the election but that "disaffection" among "the poorer class of non slaveholders" had also appeared. Some antisecessionists stated flatly that "in the event of civil war or even servile insurrection, they would not lift a finger in defense of the rights of slaveholders." An observer in Hertford County, North Carolina, a tidewater area just below the Virginia border, was similarly "mortified" to find many nonslaveowning "plain country people" unwilling to fight "to protect rich men's negroes." Nor were nonslaveowning Virginians in the Shenandoah Valley willing "to break up the government for the mere loss of an election." Similar reports emanated from West Tennessee, where "the nonslave holders (or a large majority of them) when approached on the subject declare that they will not fight if war fol[l]ows a dissolution of the union." And in towns and cities across the upper South, "workingmen" organized and demonstrated against secession.

Sensitive to the egalitarian stirrings, some secession sympathizers cautioned against trying to rush the states of the upper South out of the Union prematurely. "You cannot unite the *masses* of any southern State much less those of North Carolina against the Union and in favor [of] slavery *alone*," surmised an astute secessionist. Nonslaveowners would resist any movement that appeared controlled by "the *avarice* and the *selfishness* of *Negro Slavocracy*." But by prudently waiting until the federal government attacked the seceding states, secessionists could "change the issue" to "a question of popular liberty." Once the second consideration was introduced, nothing could hold North Carolina in the Union. A Southern Rights supporter from Virginia reasoned along the same lines. "You can't make the great mass of the people, especially the non slaveholders understand . . . the nice principles on which the secessionists are now attempting to act," he observed. Indeed, he feared that secessionist clamor ran the potential danger "of creating a party with sympathies for the incoming administration, here in our midst." He therefore thought it best "to *prepare* for resistance" without seeming to follow the lead of "disunionists *per se*." He foresaw, too, that "the non slaveholder will fight for his section as soon as the slaveholder if you can convince him that *his* political rights are really threatened."

Such caution was appropriate. Large regions of Virginia, North Carolina, and Tennessee opposed secession with at least as much fervor and with even greater unanimity than it was supported in other areas of those states. Spontaneous Union meetings gathered in upcountry locations at the same time secessionists seized the organizational initiative in many plantation districts. For example, a well-attended public meeting on November 29 in Hawkins County, East Tennessee, resolved that "the doctrine of secession" was "subversive of all just principles of government." The meeting reaffirmed Andrew Jackson's view that secession was "treason." An estimated eight hundred to a thousand people likewise gathered on December 28 in intensely Unionist Randolph County, in the North Carolina piedmont, to condemn secession as "unwise and suicidal" and to deplore the "folly and madness" of extremists North and South.

For the Breckinridge wing of the Democratic party, which provided the political backbone for the secession movement, the antisecession groundswell in parts of Virginia, North Carolina, and Tennessee posed a deadly threat. Breckinridge had readily carried most Democratic areas of the upcountry. Any significant slippage of Democratic loyalties there, when coupled with the already manifest disaffection from the party of those who voted for Douglas in 1860, seriously endangered the prospects for statewide secession. It likewise threatened the narrow statewide Democratic majorities in all three states. . . .

. . . The majority of Unionist politicians and newspapers supported calling state conventions in North Carolina and Tennessee, for fear of alienating conditional

Unionists who were willing to support antisecession delegates but who still wanted a convention held. The election results suggested, however, that "the people determined for once to think and act for themselves" and that in so doing they discovered "*their power* over politicians, and party organizations." The high turnouts in Union strongholds in Tennessee and North Carolina revealed an unusual intensity of popular feeling. Randolph County, North Carolina, in the heart of the Quaker Belt, normally cast fewer than 2,000 votes but voted against a convention by a majority of 2,466 to 45. The county sheriff, J. W. Steed, reported: "The people of Randolph believed that all the warm advocates of a Convention wanted to withdraw this State from the Union, and voted accordingly. Not quite all of the 45 who voted 'Convention' are disunionists. Every one of the 2,466 are Union men. We regarded the question as of infinitely greater moment than any on which we had ever before been called upon to vote, and large numbers went to the polls who often neglect the privilege of voting."

Many slaveowners in the upper South reacted nervously to the triumph of "the people." The recent furor about Hinton Helper's book *The Impending Crisis* had revealed a large reservoir of anxiety about the loyalty of nonslaveowning southern whites. The secession crisis rekindled such doubts. Observers noted with dismay "a disposition on the part of the *non* slave holders to back out." Pessimistic secessionists predicted that the convention elections would give "bright visions of coming glory" to Unionist leaders, whose political ambitions would inevitably lead them to sacrifice "the rights of the slaveholder" by creating "a party with supporters for the incoming administration here in our midst." Former Secretary of War John B. Floyd bitterly condemned the willingness of Virginia voters to submit "to the long continued aggressions of the North" and to value "peace and quiet" over an assertion of southern rights. "Far seeing and sagacious men begin already to see symptoms of a coming contest in Virginia for the emancipation of the slaves," he noted. Virginia had dealt "the Southern cause" a "fearful defeat." Historian Roy Franklin Nichols shrewdly assessed the motives of powerful southern Democrats: their "very real and often overlooked fear was loss of power at home" and a "shift of power to poorer farmers and artisans," who would reject the extreme proslavery politics of the 1850s.

A specific case nicely illustrates why upper South slaveowners could become alarmed about the nonslaveowning majority during the secession crisis. William S. Pettigrew, of Washington County, North Carolina, on Albemarle Sound—an eminent large slaveowner, conservative Whig, and heir to one of the great family names in his state—decided to run for the convention as a conditional Unionist, expecting that "he would unite the vote of all parties and not have the shadow of an opposition." Instead, local Unionists challenged Pettigrew by nominating incumbent state legislator Charles Latham. The latter "avowed himself as the poor man's candidate" and circulated rumors that Pettigrew, "the property-holders candidate," would not permit the poor to enter his house, "but would send a servant to meet them at the gate to ask their business." Latham and his friends also spread word that Pettigrew was a secret secessionist who had been urged to run for office by his brother in the South Carolina army. The whispering campaign, conducted behind Pettigrew's back on election day and the day before, gave him no chance to respond. Having aroused what Pettigrew considered "a furious agrarian spirit" in the upper part of the county, Latham handily carried the election 396 to 276. The convention lost even more decisively, 418 to 238.

Hysterical Southern Rights fulminations about the rise of a Black Republican–abolitionist-submissionist and pro-Lincoln party in the upper South were based upon a kernel of truth. In Tennessee, for example, secessionists tried to woo nonslaveowners by insisting that a Republican president threatened their interests too. Secessionists contended that slavery prevented class antagonisms among whites, thereby making the social and economic status of nonslaveowning southerners enviably better than that of northern workers. Southern white artisans were better paid, secessionists asserted; they were treated with dignity and respect. Secessionists furthermore predicted that Tennessee's material prosperity would be enhanced by joining the Confederacy. The already well-established pattern of selling grain and livestock to the cotton states would expand, and Tennessee would become "the chief manufacturer for the South."

The voting results baffled and frustrated Southern Rights supporters. As they saw it, Unionist nonslaveowners had been misled and had failed to perceive their own best interests. Memphis secessionists, especially, complained bitterly that their city faced a miserable future if isolated economically from the planters of Alabama and Mississippi. The two secessionist newspapers in Memphis warned that economic calamity would "fall most heavily" on the "laboring men" and "artisans," who had "voted in a solid phalanx for the Union ticket." Memphis secessionists attempted to reassure Alabama and Mississippi customers that "the great mass of our property-holders" and "the solid, substantial and reliable business men" had voted secessionist and therefore deserved continued patronage. But the initial response from the deep South was not encouraging. One Alabama newspaper proposed an economic boycott of Tennessee products. Mississippi secessionists sneered that people in Tennessee were "too cowardly" to stand up for their rights and were "willing to be treated as inferiors—*as serfs.*" The "dastard Tennesseans," having submitted their necks "to a yoke worse than death to an honorable people," were "trotting like a cur to the beck and call of Lincoln." The *Memphis Avalanche* despondently agreed that Tennessee had been "plunged" into "disgrace" and "shame." Warning that Unionists had resurrected the heresy of Hinton Helper, the *Avalanche* predicted editorially that "the germ of Abolitionism is budding in our midst and will soon blossom."

Secessionists may well have exaggerated the dangers of internal disunity, but the upper South in 1861 was no monolith and never had been. The survival of a competitive two-party system there institutionalized the means to challenge existing power relationships. Of course, no serious challenge occurred before 1861. But during the preceding decade, popular discontents had spilled decisively into the arena of party politics in the North. There, Know-Nothings and subsequently Republicans had incorporated most of the old Whig party and given the new grouping a politically appealing antiaristocratic ethos; Unionists in the upper South in early 1861 were moving in a parallel direction. The Union party thus threatened to disrupt the ground rules for political competition. For the first time nonslaveholders in the upper South would have found a political framework within which to develop a consciousness of separate interests. . . .

The pro-Union mobilization of nonslaveowners in the upper South certainly did not, by itself, signal an overt challenge to planter hegemony, let alone opposition to slavery. Most upper South Unionists were not trying to subvert the social order in the style of Hinton Helper. They were, however, rejecting the program of Southern Rights Democrats who claimed to champion the slave interest. They were also broadly hinting that they intended to extinguish the political power of the secession-tainted Democratic party at the first possible opportunity. And by refusing even to countenance a state convention, nonslaveowners in North Carolina and Tennessee defied the upper-class slaveowning leadership in the Union coalition itself, thereby alerting aspiring new political entrepreneurs to potential opportunity.

Most fundamentally, the February 1861 elections in Virginia, North Carolina, and Tennessee created a situation within each state very much like what had happened nationally in November 1860. A gnawing sense of political irrelevance was one of the principal sources of southern distress following Lincoln's election. By sweeping the North, Lincoln had accomplished the unprecedented feat of winning the presidency without needing southern support. That stunning demonstration of apparent southern political powerlessness in the Union probably fueled the secession movement as much as any other single factor. For the proud, assertive leaders of the Southern Rights wing of the Democratic party, Lincoln's election was too great a humiliation to bear. Even those who had private doubts about secession soon found that their core constituencies—the substantial slaveowning areas that voted for Breckinridge—demanded radical action.

But then, to the surprise and horror of the Southern Rights leaders in the upper South, the Unionist groundswell in January and February 1861 jeopardized their power at home just as Lincoln had jeopardized their power in the nation. The secession stigma suddenly crippled the Democratic parties of the upper South, the instruments through which Southern Rights leaders had long wielded power. To make matters worse, the challenge to the Democrats came from new political entities, the emerging Union parties, whose most distinguishing characteristic was a base of support in which slaveowners were incidental and irrelevant. Union victories could easily have been achieved in all three states without the vote of a single slaveowner. Stung by Lincoln's victory, the self-designated custodians of southern interests found themselves facing a situation in the upper South which, to say the least, added insult to injury. And because nobody had demonstrated very conclusively how Lincoln might injure the South—his victory was more of an insult than an injury—the rise of Union party power and the eclipse of Democratic party power was perhaps the true injury.

All things considered, the Union party of 1861 contained in embryo something as close to the outer limits of change in the social basis of political power as could ever be expected from electoral politics. That was its strength and also its weakness. It threatened not only to thwart secession but also to overthrow the structure of power Southern Rights Democrats had amassed in the upper South, while isolating most slaveowners in a minority party. Though led for the most part by a comfortable elite of Whig politicians whose property-holding and social position better fit the secessionist profile, the Union party constituency came closer to being non-planter, if not yet antiplanter, than any political coalition ever to hold power in a slaveowning state. To flourish, the Union party desperately needed to bring about a peaceful resolution to the crisis that had spawned it. Failing that, it was peculiarly vulnerable to disruption. Leading Unionists well knew that war could destroy their new party even more quickly than it had been formed.

人 *F U R T H E R   R E A D I N G*

Thomas B. Alexander, *Sectional Stress and Party Strength* (1967)

William L. Barney, *The Secessionist Impulse: Alabama and Mississippi in 1860* (1974)

Randolph B. Campbell, *An Empire for Slavery: The Peculiar Institution in Texas, 1821–1865* (1989)

Steven A. Channing, *Crisis of Fear: Secession in South Carolina* (1970)

William J. Cooper, Jr., *The South and the Politics of Slavery, 1828–1856* (1978)

———, *Liberty and Slavery* (1983)

Avery O. Craven, *The Growth of Southern Nationalism, 1848–1861* (1953)

Daniel W. Crofts, *Reluctant Confederates: Upper South Unionists in the Secession Crisis* (1989)

Drew Gilpin Faust, *James Henry Hammond and the Old South* (1982)

———, *A Sacred Circle: The Dilemma of the Intellectual in the Old South, 1840–1860* (1977)

Lacy K. Ford, Jr., *Origins of Southern Radicalism: The South Carolina Upcountry, 1800–1860* (1988)

William W. Freehling, *The Road to Disunion* (1990)

William W. Freehling and Craig M. Simpson, eds., *Secession Debated: Georgia's Showdown in 1860* (1992)

Eugene D. Genovese, *The Political Economy of Slavery* (1965)

Fletcher M. Green, *Constitutional Development in the South Atlantic States, 1776–1860:A Study in the Evolution of Democracy* (1930)

Holman Hamilton, *Prologue to Conflict: The Crisis and Compromise of 1850* (1964)

Michael F. Holt, *The Political Crisis of the 1850s* (1978)

John C. Inscoe, *Mountain Masters: Slavery and the Sectional Crisis in Western North Carolina* (1989)

Michael P. Johnson, *Toward a Patriarchal Republic: The Secession of Georgia* (1977)

Marc W. Kruman, *Parties and Politics in North Carolina, 1836–1865* (1983)

Ernest M. Lander, Jr., *Reluctant Imperialists: Calhoun, the South Carolinians, and the Mexican War* (1980)

John McCardell, *The Idea of a Southern Nation* (1979)

Chaplain W. Morrison, *Democratic Politics and Sectionalism: The Wilmot Proviso Controversy* (1967)

John Niven, *John C. Calhoun and the Price of Union* (1988)

David M. Potter, *The Impending Crisis, 1849–1861* (1976)

Charles S. Sydnor, *The Development of Southern Sectionalism, 1819–1848* (1948)

J. Mills Thornton III, *Politics and Power in a Slave Society: Alabama, 1800–1860* (1978)

Eric H. Walther, *The Fire-Eaters* (1992)

Ralph Wooster, *The Secession Conventions of the South* (1962)

Gavin Wright, *The Political Economy of the Cotton South* (1978)

CHAPTER
11

The Confederate Experience

*The Civil War was an unprecedented event in this nation, massive in scale and af-
fecting nearly everyone. However, it had its greatest effect in the South, where it
brought about profound changes. The fact that most of the battles took place on
southern soil was only one factor contributing to the war's effect. More fundamental
was the need to organize and mobilize the South's resources to fight a contest on this
scale. Eleven southern states had seceded in order to avoid altering their institutions
and way of life, but the realities of war compelled the Confederacy to make and accept sweeping transformations in almost all areas.*

*Such alterations occasioned intense conflict. Controversies raged over such issues
as the importance of state rights versus the need for an effective central government,
and the sanctity of slavery versus the necessity of making better use of southern
blacks in the war effort. Conflicts between slaveholders and nonslaveholders and between rich and poor reached unaccustomed proportions. Hunger and suffering
among the civilian population affected women and children who were left at home
to run their farms or plantations. As the military and home situation worsened, desertions among soldiers increased.*

*These striking changes and struggles have also produced controversies among
historians. Scholars continue to explore the depth of the transformation in the South
and to debate the degree to which changes elicited acceptance or resistance. The sense
of Confederate nationalism versus a defense of states' rights and the rights of the individual brought conflict between Confederate authorities, states, and individuals.
Historians debate the sources of division. Two of the most intriguing aspects of the
Confederate struggle were the effort to emancipate the slaves at the end of the war
and the question of why the Confederacy ultimately failed. Historians also study the
ultimate impact of war on the civilian population, especially the role of women and
whether females emerged emboldened by their experience or desired to return to
their prewar situation.*

D O C U M E N T S

One of the most outspoken critics of the Confederate administration was Governor
Joseph E. Brown of Georgia. He felt that it was taking too much power into its own
hands and threatening states' rights. Brown's letter to President Jefferson Davis,

Document 1, is only one example of his frequent protests and indicates the seriousness of these confrontations. The two letters in Document 2, one to a Georgia newspaper and the other from a North Carolina private to his governor, exemplify another kind of discontent—that of nonslaveholders. Injustices perceived by ordinary soldiers and concerns about the welfare of their families threatened the ability of the Confederacy to keep troops in the field. Letters to the Confederate secretary of war, which appear in Document 3, testify to the seriousness of the problems of desertion and resistance to Confederate authority. The excerpts in Document 4 from the diaries and letters of southern women suggest the privations and hardship that faced women on the home-front. Suffering and need drove them to take actions that affected Confederate strength. As the letters of Dick and Tally Simpson in Document 5 show, life for Confederate soldiers was difficult and frustrating, despite the initial enthusiasm on the part of many men who wanted to "whip" the Yankees. Document 6 shows a few of President Jefferson Davis's efforts to rally his people and inspire greater commitment, admitting the need for sacrifices but insisting that God was on the side of the South. Document 7 presents thoughts on the Davis administration's proposal to enlist slaves as soldiers and subsequently reward them for their service with emancipation. Robert E. Lee's letters to a Confederate congressman make the case for the administration's proposal, and Richmond and Charleston newspapers respond to the idea.

1. Joseph E. Brown Attacks Conscription, 1862

Canton, Ga., Oct. 18, 1862.

His Excellency Jefferson Davis:

Dear Sir: The act of Congress passed at its late session extending the Conscription Act, unlike its predecessor, of which it is amendatory, gives you power, in certain contingencies, of the happening of which you must be the judge, to suspend its operation, and accept troops from the States under any of the former acts upon that subject. By former acts you were authorized to accept troops from the States organized into companies, battalions and regiments. The Conscription Act of 16th April last, repealed these acts, but the late act revives them when you suspend it.

For the reasons then given, I entered my protest against the first conscription act on account of its unconstitutionality, and refused to permit the enrollment of any State officer, civil or military, who was necessary to the integrity of the State government. But on account of the emergencies of the country, growing out of the neglect of the Confederate authorities to call upon the States for a sufficient amount of additional force to supply the places of the twelve months' troops, and on account of the repeal of the formal laws upon that subject having, for the time, placed it out of your power to accept troops organized by the States in the constitutional mode, I interposed no active resistance to the enrollment of persons in this State between 18 and 35, who were not officers necessary to the maintenance of the government of the State.

The first Conscription Act took from the State only part of her military force. She retained her officers and all her militia between 35 and 45. Her military organi-

This document can be found in Allen D. Candler, ed., *The Confederate Records of the State of Georgia* (Atlanta: Charles P. Byrd, State Printer, 1910), vol. II, pp. 294–296, 299–302.

zation was neither disbanded nor destroyed. She had permitted a heavy draft to be made upon it, without Constitutional authority, rather than her fidelity to our cause should be questioned, or the enemy should gain any advantage growing out of what her authorities might consider unwise councils. But she still retained an organization subject to the command of her constituted authorities, which she could use for the protection of her public property, the execution of her laws, the repulsion of invasion, or the suppression of servile insurrection which our insidious foe now proclaims to the world that it is his intention to incite, which if done may result in an indiscriminate massacre of helpless women and children.

At this critical period in our public affairs, when it is absolutely necessary that each State keep an *organization* for home protection, Congress, with your sanction, has extended the Conscription Act to embrace all between 35 and 45 subject to military duty, giving you the power to suspend the Act as above stated. If you refuse to exercise this power, and are permitted to take all between 35 and 45 as conscripts, you *disband and destroy* all military organization in this State, and leave her people utterly powerless to protect their own families even against their own slaves. Not only so, but you deny to those between 35 and 45 a privilege of electing the officers to command them, to which, under the Constitution of the Confederacy and the laws of this State, they are clearly entitled, which has been allowed to other troops from the State, and was to a limited extent allowed even to those between 18 and 35 under the Act of 16th of April, as that Act did allow them thirty days within which to volunteer under such officers as they might select, who chanced at the time to have commissions from the War Department to raise regiments.

If you deny this rightful privilege to those between 35 and 45, and refuse to accept them as *volunteers* with officers selected by them in accordance with the laws of their State, and attempt to compel them to enter the service as *conscripts,* my opinion is, your order will only be obeyed by many of them when backed by an armed force which they have no power to resist. . . .

The late act of Congress, if executed in this State, not only does gross injustice to a large class of her citizens, utterly destroys all State military organizations, and encroaches upon the reserved rights of the State, but strikes down her sovereignty at a single blow, and tears from her the right arm of strength, by which she alone can maintain her existence, and protect those most dear to her and most dependent upon her. The representatives of the people will meet in General Assembly on the 6th day of next month, and I feel that I should be recreant to the high trust reposed in me, were I to permit the virtual destruction of the government of the State, before they shall have had time to convene, deliberate and act.

. . . I can no longer avoid the responsibility of discharging a duty which I owe to the people of this State, by informing you that I cannot permit the enrollment of conscripts, under the late act of Congress entitled "An act to amend the act further to provide for the common defence," until the General Assembly of this State shall have convened and taken action in the premises.

The plea of necessity set up for conscription last spring, when I withheld active resistance to a heavy drain upon the military organization of the State under the first conscription act, cannot be pleaded, after the brilliant successes of our gallant armies during the summer and fall campaign, which have been achieved by troops who entered the service, not as conscripts but as volunteers. If more troops are needed to meet coming emergencies, call upon the State, and you shall have them as *volunteers* much more rapidly than your enrolling officers can drag *conscripts,* like slaves, "in chains," to camps of instruction. And who that is not blinded by prejudice or ambition, can doubt that they will be much more effective as volunteers than as conscripts? The volunteer enters the service of his own free will. He regards the war as much his own as the government's war, and is ready, if need be, to offer his life a willing sacrifice upon his country's altar. Hence it is that our *volunteer armies* have been invincible when contending against vastly superior numbers with every advantage which the best equipments and supplies can afford. Not so with the conscript. He may be as ready as any citizen of the State to volunteer, if permitted to enjoy the constitutional rights which have been allowed to others, in the choice of his officers and associates. But if these are denied him, and he is seized like a serf and hurried into an association repulsive to his feelings, and placed under officers in whom he has no confidence, he then feels that this is the Government's war, not his; that he is the mere instrument of arbitrary power, and that he is no longer laboring to establish constitutional liberty, but to build up a military despotism for its ultimate but certain overthrow. Georgians will never refuse to volunteer as long as there is an enemy upon our soil, and a call for their services. But if I mistake not the signs of the times, they will require the government to respect their constitutional rights.

Surely no just reason exists why you should refuse to accept volunteers when tendered, and insist on replenishing your armies by conscription and coercion of free-men.

The question then is, not whether you shall have Georgia's quota of troops, for they are freely offered—*tendered in advance*—but it is whether you shall accept them when tendered as volunteers, organized as the Constitution and laws direct, or shall, when the decision is left with you, insist on rejecting volunteers and dragging the free citizen of this State into your armies as conscripts. No act of the government of the United States prior to the secession of Georgia struck a blow at constitutional liberty, so fell, as has been stricken by the conscription acts. The people of this State had ample cause, however, to justify their separation from the old government. They acted cooly and deliberately in view of all the responsibilities, and they stand ready to day to sustain their action, at all hazards; and to resist submission to the Lincoln government, and the reconstruction of the old Union, to the expenditure of their last dollar and the sacrifice of their last life. Having entered into the revolution freemen, they intend to emerge from it freemen. And if I mistake not the character of the sons, judged by the action of their fathers against Federal encroachments under Jackson, Troup, and Gilmer, respectively, as executive officers, they will refuse to yield their sovereignty to usurpation, and will require the government, which is the common agent of all the States, to move within the sphere assigned it by the constitution.

Very respectfully, your obedient servant,

Joseph E. Brown.

2. Nonslaveholders Protest Wartime
Inequities, 1861, 1863

Letter to the Candidates of Floyd County

Rome (Georgia) Weekly Courier, *September 27, 1861*

Please give your views concerning our present condition—about the war, and the cause of said war, the Stay Law, and our present condition of taxation for the support of the war. Is it right that the poor man should be taxed for the support of the war, when the war was brought about on the slave question, and the slave at home accumulating for the benefit of his master, and the poor man's farm left uncultivated, and a chance for his wife to be a widow, and his children orphans? Now, in justice, would it not be right to levy a direct tax on that species of property that brought about the war, to support it?

Now, we have many candidates out, will they give their views on these questions?

MANY ANXIOUS TO HEAR.

Letter from Confederate Soldier to Governor
Zebulon Vance of North Carolina

Fayetteville NC 27th Feb/63

Gov Vance

Dr Sir

Please pardon the liberty which a poor soldier takes in thus addressing you as when he *volunteered* he left a wife with four children to go to fight for his country. He cheerfully made the sacrifices thinking that the Govt. would protect his family, and keep them from starvation. In this he has been disappointed for the Govt. has made a distinction between the rich man (who had something to fight for) and the poor man who fights for that he never will have. The exemption of the owners of 20 regroes & the allowing of substitutes clearly proves it. Healthy and active men who have furnished substitutes are grinding the poor by speculation while their substitutes have been discharged after a month's service as being too old or as invalids. By taking too many men from their farms they have not left enough to cultivate the land thus making a scarcity of provisions and this with unrestrained speculation has put provs. up in this market as follows Meal $4 to 5 per Bus, flour $50 to 60 per Brl, Lard 70¢ per lb by the brl, Bacon 75¢ per lb by the load and every thing else in proportion.

Now Govr. do tell me how we poor soldiers who are fighting for the "rich mans negro" can support our families at $11 per month? How can the poor live? I dread to see summer as I am fearful there will be much suffering and probably many deaths from starvation. They are suffering now. A poor little factory girl begged for a piece of bread the other day & said she had not had anything to eat since the day before when she eat a small piece of Bread for her Breakfast.

First letter can be found in the *Rome* (Georgia) *Weekly Courier,* September 27, 1861. Second letter can be found in the Governors' Papers, North Carolina Division of Archives and History, Raleigh, North Carolina.

I am fearful we will have a revolution unless something is done as the majority of our soldiers are poor men with families who say they are tired of the rich mans war & poor mans fight, they wish to get to their families & fully believe some settlement could be made were it not that our authorities have made up their minds to prosecute the war regardless of all suffering since they receive large pay & they and their families are kept from suffering & exposure and can have their own ends served. There is great dissatisfaction in the army and as a mans first duty is to provide for his own household the soldiers wont be imposed upon much longer. If we hear our families are suffering & apply for a furlough to go to them we are denied & if we go without authority we are arrested & punished as deserters. Besides not being able to get provs. the factories wont let us have cloth for love or money & are charging much over 75 per ct profit. Now Govr you are looked upon as the soldiers friend and you know something of his trials & exposures by experience. But you do not know how it is to be a poor man serving your country faithfully while your family are crying for bread because those who are enjoying their property for which you are fighting are charging such high prices for provs & the necessaries of life and still holding on for higher prices.

I would also request in behalf of the soldiers generally (for I know it is popular with the army) for you to instruct our representatives in Congress to introduce a resolution as follows. That all single young men now occupying salaried positions as Clerks Conductors or Messengers in the Depts of Govt & State & Rail Road & Express Cos. be discharged immediately & sent into the services and their places filled by married men & men of families who are competent to fill the positions.

Such a move as this would enable many a poor man to support his wife & family & prevent them from becoming public charges & at the same time it would fill our ranks with a very large no. of young active men who have no one dependent upon them for a support and who are shirking service. This would be very acceptable to the army generally. Our soldiers cant understand why so many young magistrates are permitted to remain at home and especially so many militia officers there being no militia and two sets of officers.

Respy your obt svt

O. GODDIN
Private Co D. 51st Regt. N.C.T. on detached service

3. The Confederacy Struggles with Desertion and Disaffection, 1863

STATE OF NORTH CAROLINA, EXECUTIVE DEPT.,

Raleigh, July 25, 1863

Hon. J. A. SEDDON,

Secretary of War:

DEAR SIR: A large number of deserters, say 1,200, are in the mountains and inaccessible wilds of the west. I have found it impossible to get them out, and they are

These documents can be found in *The War of Rebellion: A Compilation of the Official Records of the Union and Confederate Armies,* 130 Volumes, Government Printing Office; Series IV, Volume 2, pp. 674 and pp. 783–86.

plundering and robbing the people. Through their friends they have made me propositions to come out and enlist for defense of this State alone. Shall I accept it? The effect on the Army might be injurious, but they can never otherwise be made of service or kept from devastating the country. If you advise favorably, I think I can get at least 1,000 effective men. Please answer soon.

Very respectfully, your obedient servant,

Z. B. VANCE.

[Indorsement.]

SECRETARY OF WAR:

There is a great necessity for some practical dealing with the crime of desertion, if so general a habit is to be considered a crime.

There are from 50,000 to 100,000 men who are in some form or other evading duty. Probably there are 40,000 or 50,000 of absentees without leave. The accommodation of the Department to the necessity of the case is, in my judgment, the best policy. To allow those who belong to other organizations than those in which they enlisted to remain, to allow all persons not in the Army to connect themselves with new organizations, to pronounce a general amnesty, and to make a new departure seems to me a measure of prudence under the existing circumstances. I notice that desertion during the French Revolution was a great source of complaint. There were at one time 12,000 on furlough, and there had been ten times that number of desertions.

[J. A. CAMPBELL.]

OFFICE OF INSPECTOR OF CONSCRIPTION,
Salisbury, N. C., September 2, 1863.

Col. J. S. PRESTON,
Superintendent of Conscription:

SIR: When the conscript service was organized the direction that among its duties should be embraced that of collecting and forwarding deserters and skulkers by the use of force was doubtless based on the supposition that such characters would be found lurking about singly, unarmed, acting in no concert, and supported by no local public opinion or party. Even for such work our means at command have been inadequate in many parts of the country, and whatever auxiliary force time may prove to be available under the special efforts indicated in my letter of July ————, approved and adopted by the War Department, cannot be expected to accomplish more than to meet the condition of things above described.

The utter inadequacy now of any force that we can command without potential aid from armies in the field will become apparent when it is realized that desertion has assumed (in some regions, especially the central and western portions of this State) a very different and more formidable shape and development than could have been anticipated. It is difficult to arrive at any exact statistics on the subject. The unquestionable facts are these: Deserters now leave the Army with arms and ammunition in hand. They act in concert to force by superior numbers a passage against bridge or ferry guards, if such are encountered. Arriving at their selected localities of refuge, they organize in bands variously estimated at from fifty up to hundreds at various points. These estimates are perhaps exaggerated in some cases. The patrols sent out from the conscript guard and bringing back a few prisoners each report that they have only captured these by surprise, and have been compelled to make good their retreat in returning by circuitous routes to avoid arrangements made to intercept them by superior force. His Excellency Governor Vance credits official information received by him, that in Cherokee County a large body of deserters (with whom I class also those in resistance to conscription) have assumed a sort of military occupation, taking a town, and that in Wilkes County they are organized, drilling regularly, and intrenched in a camp to the number of 500. Indeed, the whole number of deserters in the latter county is said to be much larger. The reports of our patrols indicate 300 or 400 organized in Randolph County, and they are said to be in large numbers in Catawba and Yadkin, and not a few in the patriotic county of Iredell. These men are not only determined to kill in avoiding apprehension (having just put to death yet another of our enrolling officers), but their esprit de corps extends to killing in revenge as well as in prevention of the capture of each other. So far they seem to have had no trouble for subsistence. While the disaffected feed them from sympathy, the loyal do so from fear. The latter class (and the militia) are afraid to aid the conscript service lest they draw revenge upon themselves and their property.

The present quiet of such lawless characters of course cannot be expected to continue, and the people look for a reign of marauding and terror, protection against which is loudly called for. Letters are being sent to the Army stimulating desertion and inviting the men home, promising them aid and comforts. County meetings are declaring in the same spirit and to hold back conscripts. As desertion spreads and enjoys impunity, in the same proportion do the enrolled conscripts hang back from reporting where there is not force enough to compel them, and the more dangerous and difficult becomes the position of our enrolling officers. All this trouble is of very rapid, recent growth, and is intimately connected with—indeed, mainly originates in and has been fostered by—the newly developed but active intrigues of political malcontents, having the Raleigh Standard for their leader, and, it is said, a majority in the capital itself. The resolutions of the several county meetings, central and western, have evidently issued from the same mint, the common stamp being that North Carolina has not received due justice or credit, that she has done more than her share, and that her people ought to contribute no further. I allude to the political aspect only to show that there is danger of marked political division and something like civil war if the military evils reported be not at once met by strong measures of military repression. Such appears the calm opinion, without panic, of loyal and substantial men, and such are my own impressions from observation. They all think the evil is spreading, and such are likely to find themselves in a bad position in some regions—for the balance of physical force is on the wrong side, the loyal having contributed most freely to the Army, even their sons still in early boyhood and not liable to serve. So far it does not appear that men of political weight have come forward publicly to any great extent to meet the intriguing demagogues on their own arena and prevent the ignorant masses from following their lead in ovine style. A reference to the faithful reports of Colonel Mallett, the vigilant State commander of conscripts, will show that he has been anticipating such evils, though their rapid increase has surpassed expectation.

In considering the remedies to be applied but two appear feasible of sufficient promptness to be effective—the one consisting of detachments of troops by the nearest local commanders, the other in like detachments from the larger armies depleted by desertion and demanding re-enforcement.

. . . Your attention is invited to the inclosed proclamation addressed to the public at large by Colonel Mallett at my instance. He had already instructed his subordinates in a like sense. All other details of our efforts to invigorate the conscript service here I reserve for a future report. Assuming that it is of vital import to crush out without the least delay the evils I have described as threatening to develop indefinitely, I am led by the foregoing exhaustive discussion to tender boldly, though reluctantly, an unpalatable conclusion. It is that the sort of success demanded by the crisis can only be attained by a prompt detachment of effective force (say two or three selected regiments of fidelity) from the main army which suffers most from desertion and evasion of service, and which it is to be hoped can best spare the remedial agencies. Such a force should proceed to occupy the infected districts, surround the traitors, bring the disloyal to punishment, fortify the loyal, and decide the wavering. The adoption of this plan, if practicable, may be rendered more palatable by the reflection that its rejection will probably involve a loss of numbers at least equal to those proposed to be detached under a system which would secure not only their own return, but that of large re-enforcements in, say, probably five or six weeks.

I am, sir, very respectfully, your obedient servant,

GEO W. LAY,
Lieutenant-Colonel and Inspector.

4. Women React to Suffering at Home, 1862–1864

Excerpts from the Diary of Margaret Junkin Preston

April 3d, 1862: . . .

Darkness seems gathering over the Southern land; disaster follows disaster; where is it all to end? My very soul is sick of carnage. I loathe the word—*War.* It is destroying and paralyzing all before it. Our schools are closed—all the able-bodied men gone—stores shut up, or only here and there one open; goods not to be bought, or so exorbitant that we are obliged to do without. I actually dressed my baby all winter in calico dresses made out of the lining of an old dressing-gown; and G. in clothes concocted out of old castaways. As to myself, I rigidly abstained from getting a single article of dress in the entire past year, except shoes and stockings. Calico is not to be had; a few pieces had been offered at 40 cents per yard. Coarse, unbleached cottons are very occasionally to be met with, and are caught up eagerly at 40 cents per yard. Such material as we used to give ninepence for (common blue twill) is a bargain now at 40 cents, and then of a very inferior quality. Soda, if to be had at all, is 75 cents per lb. Coffee is not to be bought. We have some on hand, and

Preston letter can also be found in Elizabeth Preston Allan, *The Life and Letters of Margaret Junkin Preston,* pp. 134–35, 146–47. Copyright © 1903 by Houghton Mifflin Company.

Revis letter can be found in *The War of the Rebellion: A Compilation of the Official Records of the Union and Confederate Armies,* 130 Volumes, Government Printing Office. Series 1, Vol. 23, Part 2, p. 951. Miller County and Hinolin letters can be found in Letters Received, Confederate Secretary of War, in Record Group 109, National Archives, National Archives Microfilm Publication M437, Roll 80, pp. 700–705, 730–32. Mangum letter can be found in Governors' Papers, North Carolina Division of Archives and History, Raleigh, North Carolina.

for eight months have drunk a poor mixture, half wheat, half coffee. Many persons have nothing but wheat or rye.

These are some of the *very trifling* effects of this horrid and senseless war. Just now I am bound down under the apprehension of having my husband again enter the service; and if he goes, he says he will not return until the war closes, if indeed he come back alive. May God's providence interpose to prevent his going! His presence is surely needed at home; his hands are taken away by the militia draught, and he has almost despaired of having his farms cultivated this year. His overseer is draughted, and will have to go, unless the plea of sickness will avail to release him, as he has been seriously unwell. The [Virginia Military] Institute is full, two hundred and fifty cadets being in it; but they may disperse at any time, so uncertain is the tenure of everything now. The College [Washington College] has five students; boys too young to enter the army.

April 10th: Ground white with snow; no mails still: Mr. P. consents to postpone his going to the army, till there is a more decided change in George (an ill child). How this unnatural war affects everything! Mr. P. asks me for some old pants of Willy's or Randolph's, for a boy at the farm. I tell him that on them I am relying wholly to clothe John and George this summer.

August 2d: . . . What straits war reduces us to! I carried a lb. or so of sugar and coffee to Sister Agnes lest she should not have any, and she gave me a great treasure—a *pound of soda!* When it can be had, it is $1.25 per lb.

August 23d: . . . Willy Preston has been in a battle (Cedar Run), and we hear behaved with remarkable gallantry—rallied a disorganized regiment, or rather parts of many companies, and with a lieutenant led them to the charge.

Sept. 3d: . . . Yesterday asked the price of a calico dress; "Fifteen dollars and sixty cents!" Tea is $20. per lb. A merchant told me he gave $50. for a pound of sewing silk! The other day our sister, Mrs. Cocke, purchased 5 gallons of whiskey, for which, by way of favor, she only paid $50.! It is selling for $15. per gallon. Very coarse unbleached cotton (ten cent cotton) I was asked 75 cts. for yesterday. Eight dollars a pair for servants' coarse shoes. Mr. P. paid $11. for a pair for Willy. These prices will do to wonder over after a while.

10 o'clock P. M. Little did I think, when I wrote the above, that such sorrow would overtake this family so soon! News came this afternoon of the late fearful fight on Manassas Plains, and of Willy Preston *being mortally wounded*—in the opinion of the surgeons! His Father was not at home, and did not hear the news for some time. Oh! the anguish of the father-heart! This evening he has gone to Staunton; will travel all night in order to take the cars tomorrow morning. I am afraid to go to bed, lest I be roused by some messenger of evil tidings, or (terrible to dread) the possible arrival of the dear boy—dead! Father in Heaven! Be merciful to us, and spare us this bitterness!

Sept. 4th: The worst has happened—our fearful suspense is over: Willy, the gentle, tender-hearted, brave boy, lies in a soldier's grave on the Plains of Manassas! This has been a day of weeping and of woe to this household. I did not know how I loved the dear boy. My heart is wrung with grief to think that his sweet face, his genial smile, his sympathetic heart are gone. My eyes ache with weeping. But what is the loss to me, compared to the loss to his Father, his sisters, his brothers! Oh! his precious stricken Father! God support him to bear the blow! The carriage has returned, bringing me a note from Mr. P. saying he had heard there was faint hope. Alas! The beloved son has been five days in his grave. My poor husband! Oh! if he were only here, to groan out his anguish on my bosom. I can't write more.

Letter of Martha Revis to Her Husband

Marshall, Madison County, North Carolina
July 20 [?], 1863

H. W. Revis:

Dear Husband: I seat myself to drop you a few lines to let you know that me and Sally is well as common, and I hope these few lines will come to hand and find you well and doing well. I have no news to write to you at this, only I am done laying by my corn. I worked it all four times. My wheat is good; my oats is good. I haven't got my wheat stacked yet. My oats I have got a part of them cut, and Tom Hunter and John Roberts is cutting to-day. They will git them cut to-day.

I got the first letter yesterday that I have received from you since you left. I got five from you yesterday; they all come together. This is the first one I have wrote, for I didn't know where to write to you. You said you hadn't anything to eat. I wish you was here to get some beans for dinner. I have plenty to eat as yet. I haven't saw any of your pap's folks since you left home. The people is generally well hereat. The people is all turning to Union here since the Yankees has got Vicksburg. I want you to come home as soon as you can after you git this letter. Jane Elkins is living with me yet. That is all I can think of, only I want you to come home the worst that I ever did. The conscripts is all at home yet, and I don't know what they will do with them. The folks is leaving here, and going North as fast as they can, so I will close.

Your wife, till death,

MARTHA REVIS

Petition from Women of Miller County, Georgia, to Secretary of War James Seddon and President Jefferson Davis, September 8, 1863

Our crops is limited and so short . . . cannot reach the first day of march next . . . our fencing is unanamosly allmost decayed . . . But little [illegible] of any sort to Rescue us and our children from a unanamus starveation. . . . We can seldom find [bacon] for non has got But those that are exzempt from service by office holding and old age and they have no humane feelinging nor patraotic prinsables. . . . An allwise god ho is slow to anger and full of grace and murcy and without Respect of persons and full of love and charity that he will send down his fury and judgement in a very grate manar [on] all those our leading men and those that are in power ef thare is no more favors shone to those the mothers and wives and of those hwo in poverty has with patrootism stood the fence Battles . . . I tell you that with out som grate and speadly alterating in the conduckting of afares in this our little nation god will frown on it and that speadly.

Plea by Mrs. R. H. Hinolin of Clarksville, Virginia, to Secretary of War James Seddon, October 27, 1864

I have felt so dieply the wrongs and sufferings of our people . . . the wail of the widows and orphans, the poor and oppressed . . . that I can stand it no longer, and am induced to say to you that if you will grant my Husband a 60 day furlough, I will go on to Washington and see if I can penetrate those hard hearts. Do you believe a *Lady* could do anything with them? . . .

My own deplorable condition will cause me to exhaust every effort in paving the way to peace.

Letter from Nancy Mangum to Governor Zebulon Vance of North Carolina

Mcleanesville N c
Aprile 9th 1863

Gov Vance

I have threatend for some time to write you a letter—a crowd of we Poor we-men went to Greenesborough yestarday for something to eat as we had not a mouth-ful meet nor bread in my house what did they do but put us in gail Jim Slone, Linsey Hilleshemer and several others I will not mention—thes are the one that put us to gail in plase of giveing us aney thing to eat and I had to com hom without aney-thing—I have 6 little children and my husband in the armey and what am I to do Slone wont let we Poor wemen have thread when he has it we know he has evry thing plenty he say he has not got it to spair when we go but just let thes big men go they can git it withou aney trouble. when we go for aney thing they will not hardley notis us Harper Linsey has money for the Poor weman it was put in his handes for the Poor weman I have not got one sent of it yet since my husband has bin gon he has bin gon most 2 years I have went to Linsey for money he told me to go to a nother man and he said . . . he could not do nothing for me—Lindsey would grum-ble at him for him takeing such a big bil if you dont take thes yankys a way from greenesborough we wemen will write for our husbans to come . . . home and help us we cant stand it the way they are treating us they charge $11.00 Per bunch for their thread and $2.50 for their calico—They threatend to shoot us and drawed their pis-tols over us that is hard.

Jim Slone sid he would feed we poor weman on dog meet and Roten egges. I tel you if you dont put Slone and Linsey out of offis the Poor weman will perish for the want of something to eat my brother sent home for some shirtes I went to Slone for bunch coten he would not let me have one thread and he had plenty their is bound to be a fammon if I dont git help soon.

if their ant beter better times in greenesborough the waar will end in in that plase The young men has runaway from newburn and come to this plase about to take the country they are speclating evry day their is old Ed. Holt where has a fac-tory on alamance he has maid his Creiges [?] if this war holds on 2 years longer he would own all of alamance county he has cloth and thread and wont let no body have it without wheat or Corn or meet what am I to do I cant git it to eat—three and four men gatherd hold of one woman and took thir armes away from them and led them all up to gail—you have no ide how the men in Greenesborough has treated we poor weman we have to pay $3.50 per bushel for goverment corn and half mea-sure and have the exact change or dont git the corn for the meel we dont git nun they seling sugar sugar at $1.50 per pound and black peper $9.00 per pound and say it not half as much as a soldier wife ought to pay and asking $50.00 for a barel of flour so no more

Yours very Respectfuly

NANCY MANGUM

5. Dick and Tally Simpson Describe the Life of Confederate Soldiers, 1861–1863

TNS to Richard Franklin Simpson

Bull's Run
4 miles above Manassas Junction
June 29th 1861

Dear Pa

As yet I have heard nothing from home by mail since I left Columbia. Cousin Jim brought me a letter from you; but since, I have heard nothing, either through mail or any other way. Buddie wrote home a day or so ago, and it is our intention to keep you posted regularly with reference to our health, movements, et cetera, whether letters are received from home or not.

The present condition of our camp is very good, and from all I can see and hear, the health of the soldiers is excellent. Several constantly report themselves for medical aid, but none are seriously ill. But I am sorry to say that we were called to mourn the loss of a fellow soldier who died yesterday morning. His name was Hipp. His complaint, congestive fever. I know nothing of him—only that he belonged to Nunamaker's company and his name.

Yesterday five out of eight of our mess were sick—Buddie, Osh, Cas, Bill Gunnels, and Cousin Jim. Today all better, but none on duty. Col Williams is not the man he was cracked up to be. He is firm and decisive, but entirely too slow and says too little on nearly all occasions. The regiment is not satisfied with him. . . .

We get enough to eat and that is all. If it were not for the little delicacies we buy out of our own purses, the fare would be miserable—grease biscuit (occasionally they are very good) and the very rankest meat, together with rice, which we hardly ever eat, and coffee. But by putting ourselves to some trouble and expense, [we] feast on butter, honey, chicken pie, mutton, and sometimes—or rather one time—cherry pies. Such luxuries do not, however, last long, for we can't get a great deal at a time, and when out, it is some time before we can come across any more of the same kind.

Our regiment is very well drilled, and in my opinion the companies are the best drilled of any companies from our state or from any other state. . . .

Your affectionate son

T. N. Simpson

RWS to Caroline Virginia Taliaferro Miller

Fairfax CH Va
July 4th 1861

My dear Aunt . . .

From the above you see that we are now at Farifax CH, the advanced regt of all, having taken Col Gregg's position. We can distinctly hear the drum and cannon of the enemy, and last night even fire works were seen at Falls Church, the place where the enemy are now stationed. This morning we could hear the cannon at Washington fired to celebrate the anniversary of the independence of America. What mocking it, that celebrating their independence and at the same time striving to deprive their assistants in the strife of the very boon which they estimate so highly. No doubt but what they'll yet conquer free born Southern men.

Yesterday a dispatch was received stating that the advanced portion of Lincoln's army was ordered to occupy Fairfax, now held by us, and that they had already advanced a mile and a half toward us. Our Gen (Bonham) was not slow to action but doubled the pickets, making in all something over a thousand, and had several companies of artillery brought to our assistance, and besides ordered us all to sleep on our loaded guns, which we did all night. Talking about arms, here I am way out here and to my surprise have forgotten my pistol and knife, a thing I have never done before.

Yesterday I was (just then I heard one of Lincoln's guns fire) kept hard at work throwing up breastworks, and I can tell you it is no child's play. This morning some pickets from Kershaw's Regt were out and some Va pickets came by them. They were ordered to halt, but not hearing them, the S.C. pickets fired into them, killing two and mortally wounding another.

The day we marched from the Run I had been on the sick list and was told I either had to stay there or march and carry my baggage, but was told at the same time I could put it on the wagon if I could, but this all despaired of doing but myself. I got up on the wheel, and as soon as I saw a place, I dropped it in, and as soon as I saw it covered up, I left. . . .

We had to march ten (10) miles, and it rained all the way, and the roads were as slick as glass. That night we camped in a clover patch, or I should say a mud hole. That night also our company, although cold, wet, and nothing to eat, were ordered on four (4) miles further on picket duty and had to stay up all night. When Gregg left, we took his place. Many were the longing hearts among our men when they passed us with bright faces on their way home in the land of Dixie. For several days after you could hear our men singing with plaintive notes as if it came from their very soul, "I wish I was in Dixie." But now that is passed, and all they wish for is to hear "the clash of resounding arms."

When we went to bed last night you could see many crawling in with even their hats and boots on and with their guns close by their sides. All expected that the time had come when the strength of the contending parties would be fairly measured, but we awoke this morning to find all quiet. Yet no one knows when the long expected hour will come.

There is a report in camp that a battle took place at Winchester in which 10,000 of Lincoln's men and 7,000 of ours were engaged, also that we killed 500, but not how many we lost. I can't say how true this is.

We are now in the land of danger, far, far from home, fighting for our homes and those near our hearts. I have been from home for months at a time, but I never wished to be back as bad in my life. How memory recalls every little spot, and how vividly every little scene flashes before my mind. Oh! if there is one place dear to me it is home sweet home. How many joys cluster there. To join once more our family circle (I mean you all) and talk of times gone by would be more to me than all else besides. . . .

Most affectionate nephew

R W S

TNS to Mary Simpson

Freder'sburg Va
April 10th /63

My dear Sister

As I wrote you only a short note the last time, I will write again to make up the deficiency.

Our regiment and James' old battalion are now on picket in town. We are scattered all over the place, some quartered in one place and some another. Capt Richardson's co[mpany] occupies a four-roomed cabin in the suburbs of the town. Tis a wretched place, but much better than in the open air. The window glasses are nearly all broken out, plastering torn down, and a cannon shot passing through joist, rafters, & shingles almost from one end of the house to the other, making a sad wreck of an ancient, ugly house.

Our picket posts are along the banks of the river at night but in the day time they are withdrawn and one only out of every three that were on post during the night is made to keep watch. Our regt has four posts to keep up, twelve men each on two, and fifteen each on the other two, making in all fifty-four men, exclusive of seven noncommissioned officers under the command of two lieutenants. We came down Monday morning and will return next Sunday.

I tell you we are pushed for something to eat. Our rations, which should have lasted till this evening, gave out yesterday at noon. I borrowed meat for my yesterday's meal at dinner and have not smelt any since. I had dry bread without grease or soda, and a little coffee for breakfast. The day we came down our meat gave out, and the next morning Bakes McDowell and myself obtained permission to go down town to get breakfast, as nothing was to be drawn till late in the evening. We went to a "Snack House" (What an appropriate name!) and called for a "snack." It came, and what do you think it was? Two biscuits, a little piece of beef as big as your two fingers, and cup of coffee. This passed very well, except the biscuits, which were as tough as the heel of a forty year old milch cow——

Says I to the boy in attendance, "What's the damages?" One dollar a piece, answered he. . . .

I was on guard or picket night before last and spent a very pleasant time indeed. A Mississippian had a small boat about three inches deep and two feet long, with rudder and sails affixed and every thing in trim. We took it down to the river, waved our hand [at the Yankees], and received the same signal in return. We then laded her with papers and sent her across. She landed safely and was sent back with a cargo of coffee. The officer of the day is very strict with them (the Yankees), and whenever he is about, they have to keep close. The first time the boat was sent over, he was not there, and every thing passed off very well. But the next morning when we sent it over, they were detected, and the boat was captured, greatly to the mortification of us all. Before the officer detected them, however, they had taken the papers and tobacco which we sent them and concealed them. . . .

The news from So Ca is truly cheering. I trust we may thrash them decently at Charleston, and then they will let that place alone. Tis rumored in camp today that it has been telegraphed to Genl Lee that we had sunk seven iron clad vessels in the harbor of Charleston. This is too good to be true, and I will not believe it till it is positively confirmed. . . .

The revival still continues, and several hundred of Barksdale's men have been converted, and many more are still anxious about their soul's salvation. I saw, the other day, about twelve young men baptized in [the] Baptist faith. The pool is under the pulpit, and all to be done is to lift off the floor of the pulpit, where the preacher stands every Sunday, and there is the pool of the proper size. The evening was very cold, and it went very hard with the poor fellows. It was a touching sight, and I could not help thinking of the account given in the New Testament when Jesus was baptized by John. My prayers ascended to Heaven in behalf of the young converts, and Oh! how I wish we all, friends and relatives, and in fact every one, were in the Arc of Safety at this moment. I believe if we were all Christians this moment the war would close immediately. But as our nation is wicked, God will chastise it severely ere He stays his hand.

A good many citizens are living in town at present. Occasionally I meet up with a pretty gal, and it does my soul good. You have no idea how it makes a fellow feel. If I were instantly transferred to the streets of old P and [could] gaze upon some of the gals that I know and have heard so much about, it would nearly run me crazy. There is not a woman that passes camp but there are a hundred men, more or less, huddled together, gazing with all their eyes. When you write, tell me about some of those pretty ones. Sister Anna doesn't like it, at least it seems so. So I will have to ask you to do all the talking about the women.

I am about getting out of soap as you see, so let's close, agreed? Look here, you must excuse this closely and badly written piece of composition. But necessity compels me to be close. I gave one dollar for four sheets of paper like this and four envelopes. Remember me kindly to all friends, especially Col P's family and that of Mr Ligon. Give my love to all. Write soon to

Your affec bro

T. N. Simpson

6. President Jefferson Davis Rallies His People, 1863

By the President of the Confederate States

A PROCLAMATION.

Again do I call upon the people of the Confederacy—a people who believe that the Lord reigneth and that his overruling providence ordereth all things—to unite in prayer and humble submission under his chastening hand, and to beseech his favor on our suffering country.

It is meet that when trials and reverses befall us we should seek to take home to our hearts and consciences the lessons which they teach, and profit by the self-examination for which they prepare us. Had not our successes on land and sea made us self-confident and forgetful of our reliance on him; had not love of lucre eaten like a gangrene into the very heart of the land, converting too many among us into worshipers of gain and rendering them unmindful of their duty to their country, to their fellow-men, and to their God—who, then, will presume to complain that we have been chastened or to despair of our just cause and the protection of our Heavenly Father?

Let us rather receive in humble thankfulness the lesson which he has taught in our recent reverses, devoutly acknowledging that to him, and not to our own feeble arms, are due the honor and glory of victory; that from him, in his paternal providence, come the anguish and sufferings of defeat, and that, whether in victory or defeat, our humble supplications are due at his footstool.

Now, therefore, I, Jefferson Davis, President of these Confederate States, do issue this, my proclamation, setting apart Friday, the twenty-first day of August ensuing, as a day of fasting, humiliation, and prayer; and I do hereby invite the people of the Confederate States to repair on that day to their respective places of public worship, and to unite in supplication for the favor and protection of that God who has hitherto conducted us safely through all the dangers that environed us.

[SEAL.] In faith whereof, I have hereunto set my hand and the seal of the Confederate States, at Richmond, this twenty-fifth day of July, in the year of our Lord one thousand eight hundred and sixty-three.

By the President: JEFFERSON DAVIS.

J. P. BENJAMIN, *Secretary of State.*

By the President of the Confederate States.

A PROCLAMATION.

The Soldiers of the Confederate States.

After more than two years of warfare scarcely equaled in the number, magnitude, and fearful carnage of its battles, a warfare in which your courage and

Material from *Jefferson Davis: Constitutionalist,* Dunbar Rowland, ed. Quoted courtesy of Mississippi Department of Archives and History, Jackson, Mississippi.

fortitude have illustrated your country and attracted not only gratitude at home, but admiration abroad, your enemies continue a struggle in which our final triumph must be inevitable. Unduly elated with their recent successes, they imagine that temporary reverses can quell your spirit or shake your determination, and they are now gathering heavy masses for a general invasion in the vain hope that by a desperate effort success may at length be reached.

You know too well, my countrymen, what they mean by success. Their malignant rage aims at nothing less than the extermination of yourselves, your wives, and children. They seek to destroy what they cannot plunder. They purpose as the spoils of victory that your homes shall be partitioned among the wretches whose atrocious cruelties have stamped infamy on their Government. They design to incite servile insurrection and light the fires of incendiarism wherever they can reach your homes, and they debauch the inferior race, hitherto docile and contented, by promising indulgence of the vilest passions as the price of treachery. Conscious of their inability to prevail by legitimate warfare, not daring to make peace lest they should be hurled from their seats of power, the men who now rule in Washington refuse even to confer on the subject of putting an end to outrages which disgrace our age, or to listen to a suggestion for conducting the war according to the usages of civilization.

Fellow-citizens, no alternative is left you but victory or subjugation, slavery, and the utter ruin of yourselves, your families, and your country. The victory is within your reach. You need but stretch forth your hands to grasp it. For this end all that is necessary is that those who are called to the field by every motive that can move the human heart should promptly repair to the post of duty, should stand by their comrades now in front of the foe, and thus so strengthen the armies of the Confederacy as to insure success. The men now absent from their posts would, if present in the field, suffice to create numerical equality between our force and that of the invaders; and when with any approach to such equality have we failed to be victorious? I believe that but few of those absent are actuated by unwillingness to serve their country, but that many have found it difficult to resist the temptation of a visit to their homes and the loved ones from whom they have been so long separated; that others have left for temporary attention to their affairs with the intention of returning, and then have shrunk from the consequence of the violation of duty; that others again have left their posts from mere restlessness and desire of change, each quieting the upbraidings of his conscience by persuading himself that his individual services could have no influence on the general result. These and other causes (although far less disgraceful than the desire to avoid danger or to escape from the sacrifices required by patriotism) are, nevertheless, grievous faults, and place the cause of our beloved country and of everything we hold dear in imminent peril.

I repeat that the men who now owe duty to their country, who have been called out and have not yet reported for duty, or who have absented themselves from their posts are sufficient in number to secure us victory in the struggle now impending. I call on you, then, my countrymen, to hasten to your camps in obedience to the dictates of honor and of duty, and I summon those who have absented themselves without leave, or who have remained absent beyond the period allowed by their furloughs, to repair without delay to their respective commands; and I do hereby declare that I grant a general pardon and amnesty to all officers and men within the Confederacy now absent without leave who shall with the least possible delay return to their proper posts of duty; but no excuse will be received for any delay beyond twenty days after the first publication of this proclamation in the State in which the absentee may be at the date of publication. This amnesty and pardon shall extend to all who have been accused, or who have been convicted and are undergoing sentence for absence without leave or desertion, excepting only those who have been twice convicted of desertion.

Finally, I conjure my countrywomen, the wives, mothers, sisters, and daughters of the Confederacy, to use their all-powerful influence in aid of this call, to add one crowning sacrifice to those which their patriotism has so freely and constantly offered on their country's altar, and to take care that none who owe service in the field shall be sheltered at home from the disgrace of having deserted their duty to their families, to their country, and to their God.

[SEAL.]   Given under my hand and the seal of the Confederate States, at Richmond, the first day of August, in the year of our Lord one thousand eight hundred and sixty-three.

JEFFERSON DAVIS.

By the President:

J. P. BENJAMIN, *Secretary of State.*

7. The Confederacy Debates Emancipation, 1865

Robert E. Lee to Congressman Ethelbert Barksdale, February 18, 1865

I have the honor to acknowledge the receipt of your letter of the 12th instant [February], with reference to the employment of negroes as soldiers. I think the measure not only expedient but necessary. The enemy will certainly use them against us if he can get possession of them; and, as his present numerical superiority will enable him to penetrate many parts of the country, I cannot see the wisdom of the policy of holding them to await his arrival, when we may, by timely action and judicious management, use them to arrest his progress. I do not think that our white population can supply the necessities of a long war without overtaxing its capacity, and imposing great suffering upon our people; and I believe we should provide resources for a protracted struggle,—not merely for a battle or a campaign.

In answer to your second question, I can only say that, in my opinion, the negroes, under proper circumstances, will make efficient soldiers. I think we could at least do as well with them as the enemy, and he attaches great importance to their assistance. Under good officers and good instructions, I do not see why they should not become soldiers. They possess all the physical qualifications, and their habits of obedience constitute a good foundation for discipline. They furnish a more promising material than many armies of which we read in history, which owed their efficiency to discipline alone. I think those who are employed should be freed. It would be neither just nor wise, in my opinion, to require them to serve as slaves. The best

This document can be found in James D. McCabe, Jr., *Life and Campaigns of General Robert E. Lee* (Atlanta, 1866), pp. 574–575.

course to pursue, it seems to me, would be to call for such as are willing to come with the consent of their owners. An impressment or draft would not be likely to bring out the best class, and the use of coercion would make the measure distasteful to them and to their owners.

I have no doubt that if Congress would authorize their reception into service, and empower the President to call upon individuals or States for such as they are willing to contribute, with the condition of emancipation to all enrolled, a sufficient number would be forthcoming to enable us to try the experiment. If it proved successful, most of the objections to the measure would disappear, and if individuals still remained unwilling to send their negroes to the army, the force of public opinion in the States would soon bring about such legislation as would remove all obstacles. I think the matter should be left, as far as possible, to the people and to the States, which alone can legislate as the necessities of this particular service may require. As to the mode of organizing them, it should be left as free from restraint as possible. Experience will suggest the best course, and it would be inexpedient to trammel the subject with provisions that might, in the end, prevent the adoption of reforms suggested by actual trial.

Richmond Examiner, *February 25, 1865*

The question of employing negroes in the army is by no means set at rest by the Senate majority of one. The debates having been secret, the publick can have no knowledge of the reasons and arguments urged on either side. Undoubtedly the arming of negroes, whether as slaves or not, is a very serious step; justifies earnest deliberation, and accounts for honest differences of opinion. It is a great thing which General Lee asks us to do, and directly opposite to all the sentiments and principles which have heretofore governed the Southern people. Nothing, in fact, but the loud and repeated demand of the leader to whom we already owe so much, on whose shoulders we rest so great a responsibility for the future, could induce, or rather coerce, this people and this army to consent to so essential an innovation. But still the question recurs—can we hope to fight successfully through a long war without using the black population? Evidently General Lee thinks not; because at the same moment that he makes new efforts to recall the absentees and deserters to their posts, he also urgently demands that Congress and the several States pass at once such legislation as will enable him to fill his ranks with negro troops. On this point of military necessity, there are few in the Confederacy who would not defer to the judgment of the General.

There is another very material consideration. If we arm negroes can they be made serviceable soldiers? This journal has heretofore opposed the whole project upon the last named ground; and has not changed its opinion. Yet General Lee has, on this question also, very decidedly expressed a different judgment in his letter to a member of Congress. And this is another question purely military; upon which, therefore, the whole country will be disposed to acquiesce silently in the opinion of the commander who undertakes to use that species of force efficiently for our defence. There are many other considerations, which are not military, but moral, political and social, relating to the future of the black race as well as of the white,—all of which oppose themselves strongly to the revolutionary measure now recommended. On these General Lee cannot be admitted as an authority without appeal:

indeed, his earnestness in providing that "those who are employed should be freed," and "that it would be neither just nor wise to require them to serve as slaves," suggests a doubt whether he is what used to be called a "good Southerner"; that is, whether he is thoroughly satisfied of the justice and beneficence of negro slavery as a sound, permanent basis of our national polity. Yet all these considerations must also give way, if it be true that, to save our country from Yankee conquest and domination it is "not only expedient but necessary" to employ negroes as soldiers. *He* is the good Southerner who will guaranty us against that shameful and dreadful doom. To save ourselves from that, we should of course be willing not only to give up property and sacrifice comfort, but to put in abeyance political and social theories, which in principle we cannot alter.

The whole matter depends practically on the question—Is this necessary, or not necessary, to the defeat of the Yankee invaders and the establishment of Confederate independence? The Senators who voted against the measure are entitled to credit for purity of purpose. It would be very invidious, and is unnecessary, to assume that any of them refuse the aid of negroes in this war from any silly and sneaking sort of a lingering secret hope that if the country is subdued they will not perhaps be deprived of their slaves by the Yankee conquerers. If any Senator, or any constituent of any Senator, is at this day so hopelessly idiotick as to imagine that in case of subjugation the enemy will not take from him both his negroes and his plantation to boot, that Senator, or constituent, is not to be argued with. Leaving that out of the question, then, it may be assumed that the majority of the Senate objected to the employment of negro soldiers, either because they think the "Necessity" spoken of by General Lee does not exist—or because they are of opinion that negroes would make bad soldiers; and that if the whites confess themselves unable to continue the contest, negroes would not save them; or because they are inflexibly opposed in principle to altering the relative *status* of white and black from these moral, political and social considerations alluded to before. As to the two first objections, the only answer that can be made is that General Lee is of a different opinion; he thinks he can make efficient soldiers of negroes, and he thinks the time has come when it is necessary to take and use them. It is one thing to be quite converted to his opinion, and another to acquiesce in his decision. As to those other and larger considerations, which do not depend upon military necessity, nor on the present exigency, but go down to the foundations of society and the natural relation of races, those Senators who hold that it would be a cruel injury, both to white and black, to sever their present relation of master and slave; that to make "freedom" a reward for service, is at war with the first principles of this relation, and is the beginning of abolition, and that abolition means the abandonment of the black race to inevitable destruction upon this continent, those Senators are undoubtedly right. This is the true Southern principle, and the only righteous principle. But what then? What good will our principle do if the Yankees come in over us? Will there be any comfort in going down to perdition carrying our principles with us intact? The principle of slavery is a sound one; but is it so dear to us that rather than give it up we would be slaves ourselves? Slavery, like the Sabbath, was made for man; not man for slavery. On this point also, as well as all the others, the only practical question now ought to be: Is it necessary, in order to defend our country successfully, to use negroes as soldiers—not abandoning any principle, but reserving for quieter times the definitive arrangements which may thus become needful? If it is necessary, as General Lee has said—that is, if the alternative is submission to the enemy—then no good Southern man will hesitate. It may be under protest that we yield to this imperious necessity; but still we yield.

Charleston [S.C.] Mercury, *January 13, 1865*

In 1860 South Carolina seceded alone from the old union of States. Her people, in Convention assembled, invited the *slaveholding* States (none others) of the old Union to join her in erecting a separate Government of *Slave States,* for the protection of their common interests. All of the slave states, with the exception of Maryland and Kentucky, responded to her invitation. The Southern Confederacy of slave States was formed.

It was on account of encroachments upon the institution of *slavery* by the sectional majority of the old Union, that South Carolina seceded from that Union. It is not at this late day, after the loss of thirty thousand of her best and bravest men in battle, that she will suffer it to be bartered away; or ground between the upper and nether mill stones, by the madness of Congress, or the counsels of shallow men elsewhere.

By the compact we made with Virginia and the other States of this Confederacy, South Carolina will stand to the bitter end of destruction. By that compact she intends to stand or to fall. Neither Congress, nor certain make-shift men in Virginia, can force upon her their mad schemes of weakness and surrender. She stands upon her institutions—and there she will fall in their defence. *We want no Confederate Government without our institutions.* And we will have none. Sink or swim, live or die, we stand by them, and are fighting for them this day. That is the ground of our fight—it is well that all should understand it at once. Thousands and tens of thousands of the bravest men, and the best blood of this State, fighting in the ranks, have left their bones whitening on the bleak hills of Virginia in this cause. We are fighting for our system of civilization—not for buncomb, or for Jeff Davis. We intend to fight for *that,* or nothing. We expect Virginia to stand beside us in that fight, as of old, as we have stood beside her in this war up to this time. But such talk coming from such a source is destructive to the cause. Let it cease at once, in God's name, and in behalf of our common cause! It is paralizing [*sic*] to every man here to hear it. It throws a pall over the hearts of the soldiers from this State to hear it. The soldiers of South Carolina will not fight beside a nigger—to talk of emancipation is to disband our army. We are free men, and we chose to fight for ourselves—we want no slaves to fight for us. Skulkers, money lenders, money makers, and bloodsuckers, alone will tolerate the idea. It is the man who won[']t fight himself, who wants his nigger to fight for him, and to take his place in the ranks. Put that man in the ranks. And do it at once. Control your armies—put men of capacity in command, re-establish confidence—enforce thorough discipline—and there will be found men enough, and brave men enough, to defeat a dozen Sherman's. Falter and hack at the root of the Confederacy—our institutions—our civilization—and you kill the cause as dead as a boiled crab.

The straight and narrow path of our deliverance is in the reform of our government, and the discipline of our armies. Will Virginia stand by us as of old in this rugged pathway? We will not fail her in the shadow of a hair. But South Carolina will fight upon no other platform, than that she laid down in 1860.

⚔ *E S S A Y S*

Historian Emory M. Thomas of the University of Georgia has done more than any other scholar to show the extent of the changes that swept over Confederate society. In the first essay, from his book *The Confederate Nation,* he describes the dimensions of this wartime transformation. Paul D. Escott of Wake Forest University argues in the second essay that the South's class system generated considerable opposition to the changes that occurred, and that this opposition damaged Confederate nationalism. In the third essay, from her book *Mothers of Invention,* Drew Gilpin Faust of the University of Pennsylvania shows how the war affected privileged southern women and the profound alterations it created in their lives, and she also suggests what happened to them at the war's end.

The Revolution Brings Revolutionary Change

EMORY M. THOMAS

Southerners since 1865 have been peculiarly squeamish about the terms "rebel" and "revolution." Long ago they convinced the nation at large to drop "War of Rebellion" as the name of their Confederate experience. Even now many Southerners recoil at the use of "Civil War." They prefer "War between the States," which implies, it would seem, some kind of sterile conflict over antique political principles. Perhaps Reconstruction was never so successful as in the realm of semantics. For even otherwise "unreconstructed" Southerners have in the years since Appomattox outdone themselves to become 100 percent Americans. The recent South has been a bastion of American orthodoxy in which revolution is a nasty word. Corporately Americans remember the Confederacy as the vehicle through which brave men fought a gallant though tragic war. Somehow the dust and smoke of battles, real and reenacted, has obscured the revolutionary nature of the struggle.

The time has come to recognize anew that Southern Confederates made a revolution in 1861. They made a "conservative revolution" to preserve the antebellum status quo, but they made a revolution just the same. The "fire-eaters" employed classic revolutionary tactics in their agitation for secession. And the Confederates were no less rebels than their grandfathers had been in 1776.

The supreme irony was that the Confederate revolution was scarcely consummated when the radicals lost control. Moderate elements of the Southern political leadership took charge and attempted to carry out the radicals' program. In the process, however, the Confederacy underwent an internal revolution—one revolution became two. In the name of independence the Southerners reversed or severely undermined virtually every tenet of the way of life they were supposedly defending. The substantive revolution came only after the Confederacy was engaged in a fight for its life. That fight itself was in part characterized by revolutionary strategy and guerrilla tactics.

The Confederates sacrificed a state rights polity and embraced centralized nationalism. The Davis administration outdid its Northern counterpart in organizing for total war. Economically, the nation founded by planters to preserve commercial, plantation agrarianism became, within the limits of its ability, urbanized and industrialized. A nation of farmers knew the frustration of going hungry, but Southern industry made great strides. And Southern cities swelled in size and importance. Cotton, once king, became a pawn in the Confederate South. The emphasis on manufacturing and urbanization came too little, too late. But compared to the antebellum South, the Confederate South underwent nothing short of an economic revolution.

Pre-Confederate Southerners had thought themselves stable people. The Confederacy and its war changed their minds. Wartime brought varieties of experience hitherto unknown below the Potomac. Riot and disaffection rocked the nation. An incipient proletariat exhibited a marked degree of class awareness. Southern women climbed down from their pedestals and became refugees, went to work in factories, or assumed responsibility for managing farms. The upheaval of war severely tested the aristocracy and brought "new people" to financial and social prominence. The military and governmental hierarchies created new avenues to social status and to a large extent democratized Southern social mores. Southerners, some of them for the first time, became aware of their corporate as well as their individual identities. Organized religion underwent structural and doctrinal change. And the war rudely shocked the Confederates out of many of their romantic self-delusions.

Ultimately even racial slavery changed. Although the Confederates "used" free and bonded black people in ways unknown in the Old South, the institution of slavery underwent a fundamental change in the wartime South. White mastery declined and in turn black dependence faded. In the cities and in the countryside slavery was a "dying institution." Finally the Confederates were willing to sacrifice their "peculiar institution" for the sake of independence. The Congress provided for black troops, and the administration was willing to exchange emancipation for foreign recognition.

By 1865, under the pressure of total war, the Confederate South had surrendered most of its cherished way of life. Independence became an end, not a means. The South had revolutionized itself. This is not to say that the origins of the Confederate revolution were not present in the antebellum South, or that all the tendencies in Confederate national life came to full flower. Rather, the movement of the Confederate South in so many new directions in so short a time constituted a genuine revolution in Southern life.

Ironically the internal revolution went to completion at the very time that the external revolution collapsed. Both died at Appomattox. In 1865 the Confederacy did more than surrender—it disintegrated. The Union not only destroyed and devastated; it eradicated the rebel nation. All that was positive in the Confederate experience went down with all that was negative. The Davis administration and Southern nationalism were no more. Southern industry and cities were largely rubble. Social structure disappeared in individual struggles for survival. Slaves were freedmen by fiat of the Yankee. Few "nations" have suffered defeat more thorough than that of the rebel South.

The Confederate revolutionary experience did not survive the total defeat and destruction of the Confederate state. And Reconstruction finished the job. The program of the radical Republicans may have failed to restructure Southern society. It may, in the end, have "sold out" the freedmen in the South. Yet Reconstruction did succeed in frustrating the positive elements of the revolutionary Southern experience. In 1865 Southerners, while accepting military defeat, were blind to its implications. They hoped to rejoin the Union and continue "business as usual," and they found the presidential plans for Reconstruction encouraging. But then Congress took a hand in Reconstruction. Northern legislators were understandably displeased by the ease with which the rebel states reentered the Union. The "black codes" enacted by Southern state legislatures alarmed Northern solons, and the race riots in Southern cities appalled them. Senators and congressmen from these unrepentant states were ex-Confederate leaders, grinning and primed to pick up the old sectional quarrels where they had left off in 1860. The Republican majority would have none of it. The South had fulfilled the president's conditions for rejoining the Union without fulfilling the war aims of that Union. The radical Republicans imposed new conditions, sent troops to occupy the Southern states, and hoped for genuine repentance. The South yielded only bitterness. The bitterness of Reconstruction outlasted the bitterness of the war. It survives still in the persistent myth of "black Reconstruction."

From Reconstruction and its aftermath arose the New South. Yet nothing is so striking about the New South as its resemblance to the Old South. The New South rhetoric preached reunion and economic progress. But beginning with the "Redeemers," those men who credited themselves with restoring white, conservative rule, the New Southerners reasserted state rights, racial bondage, agrarianism, and all the rest of those conditions rejected by Confederate Southerners. The New South was the thermidor of the Confederate revolutions—the conservative reaction. "Freed" black men belonged to company stores and landlords. The issue of race submerged class awareness on the part of poor and middle-class white men. The South remained predominantly rural and agricultural. Money and land raised up a New South aristocracy who longed for nothing so much as the brave old world, that mythical South that existed before the "late unpleasantness." In short, most of the positive, substantive changes wrought during the Confederate experience drowned in a sea of "Bourbonism."

There are some far-reaching implications here. If indeed the Confederacy was a revolutionary experience, however much it failed, it should stand at the center of Southern historical consciousness. The Confederacy was not simply the end of the Old South, nor simply the beginning of the New South. It was a unique experience in and of itself. For four brief years Southerners took charge of their own destiny. In so doing they tested their institutions and sacred cows, found them wanting, and redefined them. In a sense the Confederacy was the crucible of Southernism. And as such it provides a far better source of Southern identity than the never-never world of agrarian paradise in the Old South or the never-quite-new world of the New South. In the context of the Confederate revolutionary experience, when "unreconstructed" Southerners venerate the Confederacy, they are right for the wrong reasons. And when liberated Southerners vilify the Confederacy, they are wrong for the right reasons.

There are broader implications still. It is a truism that history, the process of human development, enslaves its products. No people should be more aware of this than Southerners. No other Americans seem to have so thoroughly bound themselves to the past. The study of history, however, can liberate. An honest awareness of the past can sever the bonds of that past. An honest awareness of the past can reveal to us who we are, and enable us to live with the past in the present.

The challenge here is to be honest to the Confederate past. Honesty requires that myths and historical apology be put to rest, along with many of the negative clichés about the Confederate South. To be honest to the Confederate experience requires that we accept its revolutionary aspects and rethink many outworn judgments of its positive and negative accomplishments.

The task is not simple. But the rewards are rich. Present Americans have much in common with the Confederate past. Both people have experienced revolution. Both have known corporate guilt and shame amid triumph. The Confederate experience is "usable past."

The Failure of Confederate Nationalism

PAUL D. ESCOTT

For Southerners the Confederacy was an unwelcome experience, a change that the majority of Southerners came to oppose. A spirit of Confederate nationalism failed to develop, and voluntary support for the war effort progressively disintegrated. The roots of this failure lay in the Southern class system as it responded to the stresses of war. The nation did not cohere; and the Old South was not fundamentally changed. It retained a class system based on contradiction and a regional identity that was inescapable, even though it was insufficient to constitute a nation-state.

On the eve of the Civil War the South had attained a regional identity, a sense of itself as a place and as a distinct social system. The creation of the Confederacy, however, was an assertion of something more, a declaration of a sense of nationalism that was not yet present. In 1860 most southerners felt they belonged to the American nation. Some new bond, some sense of Confederate purpose was required to efface those loyalties and establish a Confederate identity. Moreover, in terms of the harsh realities of war, a sense of Confederate nationalism *had* to grow and inspire southerners if they were to emerge from their ordeal as an independent nation.

The responsibility for fostering commitment to the nation fell to Jefferson Davis, who, as a determined but distant personality, was both well and poorly qualified for the task. Davis devoted himself irrevocably to Confederate independence, and initially he nurtured the frail spirit of nationalism with skill. He organized a government and articulated an ideology that avoided potential disagreements. By emphasizing that the Confederacy was the embodiment and continuation of American political principles, his ideology invited the many southerners who still had affection for the United States to transfer their loyalty to the new government.

From Paul D. Escott, "The Failure of Confederate Nationalism" in Harry P. Owens and James J. Cooke, eds., *The Old South in the Crucible of War,* 1983. Published by permission of University Press of Mississippi.

Collisions with Northern armies stimulated an outpouring of regional loyalty for the sake of self-defense. In the late summer of 1861 Southern unity was at its zenith, and the prospects for growth of a national spirit seemed bright.

By early 1862, however, "the spirit of volunteering had died out," and serious problems multiplied thereafter—long before the military situation became hopeless. The next year, 1863, brought further deterioration and calamities that put the growth of disaffection beyond the government's control; by 1864 the Davis administration was struggling against disintegration. What had happened? The sources of these ills provide a clue to their cause.

The Confederacy's internal problems appeared at the top and bottom levels of white society—at the extremes of the class system. The centralizing efforts of the Davis administration offended prominent state rightists, who began a continuing attack on the policies, and even legitimacy, of their own government. Opposition from planters grew as the Richmond government impressed slaves and interfered with plantation routines. Meanwhile poverty invaded the homes of ordinary Southerners who had reason to wonder whether they had as much at stake as the wealthy planters. Worse, Congress' unpopular conscription law discriminated against the poor by giving exemptions to those who managed twenty or more slaves, and the stringent tax-in-kind added to the burdens of an "unequal and odious" impressment law.

In the face of such troubles, Davis' ideology degenerated into little more than racial scare tactics, a desperate effort (often repeated in Southern history) to force white Southerners to pull together out of fear. During 1864 a lack of consensus over war aims and widespread reluctance to continue the war were painfully evident. Despite the absence of a two-party system, which tarnished those who proposed alternate policies with the taint of treason, a variety of peace movements appeared. Long before the end of the war (in 1863 or certainly in 1864) most Confederates knew the feeling voiced by one bitter farmer: "The sooner this damned Goverment [falls] to pieces the better it [will] be for us." . . .

. . . As hundreds of thousands of yeomen sank rapidly into poverty, class tensions flared. The proud individualism and democratic outlook of the yeomen stirred them to demand justice (in no uncertain terms). Why was it, asked even a supporter of the government, that "nine tenths of the youngsters of the land whose relatives are conspicuous in society, wealthy, or influential obtain some safe perch where they can doze with their heads under their wings?" A Georgian denounced the "notorious fact [that] if a man has influential friends—or a little money to spare he will never be enrolled." The yeomen believed, as a hill-country newspaper put it, that, "*All classes of the community* MUST *do their share of the fighting,* the high, the low, the rich and poor, and those who have *the means* MUST *pay the expense. . . .*" Hundreds of letters to the War Department echoed this warning: "the people will not *always* submit to this *unequal, unjust,* and partial distribution of favor. . . ."

In response to these angry protests the aristocrats of the South too often answered with assertive individualism of their own. Consider these phenomena: Robert Toomb's defiant refusal to grow less cotton, the wealthy men who "spent a fortune in substitutes," Congress' refusal to end substitution until the start of 1864, and the arrogant opinion of the *Richmond Examiner* that "this ability to pay [for a substitute] is, in most cases, the best proof of the citizen's social and industrial value." Planters continued to expect privileged treatment, as shown by men like North Carolina's Patrick Edmondston who declined to serve unless given a high command and by the fact that in September, 1864, when the army was desperately short of mules and horses, the War Department was lending them to prominent citizens.

Such self-serving, callous acts by the elite were a slap in the face to the yeomen, and they responded with quiet rebellion. Men who saw themselves as "we poor soldiers who are fighting for the 'rich mans [N]egro' " stopped fighting. Wives urged husbands to "desert again. . . . come back to your wife and children." With calm determination and self-assurance in their course, "many deserters . . . just pat[ted] their guns and . . . sa[id], 'This is my furlough.' " Thousands of others refused to cooperate with tax collectors, enrollment officers and other officials or went into open opposition.

As for the slaveowners, they too had a frustrating and bitter experience, but one they had brought on themselves. For as political leaders they had made a profound mistake. They had launched a revolution to secure conservative ends, and they found that their means and ends were incompatible. To keep their lives and plantations unchanged, they had plunged into a vortex of change. The gamble that secession might be peaceful or war brief was lost, and with it went any hope of attaining their goal amid total war.

To this fact they could not, as a class, adjust. Reality required strong measures, changes of many kinds. Jefferson Davis understood the situation and inaugurated change, but the planter class was frozen in the past and inflexible. As Davis responded to reality, his unpopularity with slaveowners grew. They had used the shibboleth of state rights so often, and resisted central power so long, that they fought against their own government and opposed measures necessary for survival. Their capacity for creative statesmanship had withered, and they ended the war hostile and uncooperative prisoners of their own initiative.

Moreover, the planter class failed to offer a vision for the society it wished to lead and the nation it attempted to create. The planters had no unifying goal in mind and little inclination to seek one; they merely wanted to be left undisturbed in their way of life, their privileges, and their possession of slaves. When the debate over Confederate emancipation occurred, the response of slaveowners was overwhelmingly negative. Thus, they revealed that they valued slavery above independence and had led their society into a cataclysm for nothing beyond a selfish reason: to safeguard their class interests. . . .

The failure of Confederate nationalism is apparent in this sequence of events and has been documented in various ways. Thomas Alexander and Richard Beringer have shown that Congress' spirit was marked by a declining willingness to sacrifice, rather than by revolutionary zeal. They confirmed, as well, Buck Yearns' finding that as opposition grew the Davis administration relied more and more heavily on the votes of congressmen whose districts lay in enemy hands. Popular governors like North Carolina's Zeb Vance and Georgia's Joe Brown won people's loyalty by expressing the dissatisfactions of poor and rich alike and by shielding all their citizens, as far as they were able, from the Confederacy's relentless demands for sacrifice. Successful politics became the art of playing on dissatisfactions without offering a solution. Politicians who sought solutions by making the hard choices necessary for survival became unpopular, while those who denounced stern but necessary policies of the Confederacy won gratitude and devotion.

The Confederacy did not fall apart. Some ardent secessionists—like Robert B. Rhett of the Charleston *Mercury*—swallowed their hatred of Davis to support his insistence on independence. Many Southerners endured their dislike of the Confederacy because their dislike of Yankees was growing even more rapidly. Because the army rounded up deserters and the bureaucracy enforced war measures, because Jefferson Davis was unbending and many soldiers were gritty and courageous, the South doggedly stayed in the fight until Appomattox. But no sense of unity or purpose had emerged to turn southern society into a nation.

"We Shall Never . . . Be the Same": How War Affected Southern Women

DREW GILPIN FAUST

Mary Greenhow Lee never returned to Winchester after her expulsion by the Union army. She resettled in Baltimore, where she passed the remainder of a long life, taking in boarders and dedicating herself to church work and to the activities of the United Daughters of the Confederacy. "Political reconstruction," she observed late in 1865, "might be unavoidable now, but social reconstruction we hold in our hands & might prevent."

Lizzie Neblett described "seven years of struggle" shared with her husband, Will, after the war as they tried to adapt to free labor on their Texas cotton land. The value of the Nebletts' real estate had fallen 60 percent by 1870, and their personal property, with the emancipation of the slaves, was 5½ percent of its former value. In the spring of 1871 Will died of pneumonia, leaving his wife five months pregnant with a third daughter. Widowed at thirty-eight, Lizzie had more than half her life to live. She survived until 1917, emerging briefly in the public eye as a temperance columnist in the 1880s. Ironically, she would pass the last decades of her life in the Austin household of her second daughter, Bettie, the unwelcome war baby.

Jo Gillis of Alabama turned to teaching to support her family at the end of the war, for her husband's income as an itinerant minister did not even cover his board. Yet it was her household responsibilities that she found most demanding. "Sometimes I have a cook," she wrote in 1866, "and sometimes I don't and everything I do is done by guesswork. My ignorance and inexperience is a great trial." Often she cried all night contemplating her hardships and her husband's lack of support and understanding. In November 1868 Jo Gillis died from complications following the delivery of her second child.

After Confederate defeat, Emma and Will Crutcher returned to Vicksburg from San Antonio, where they had gone to live as refugees in 1863 after Will's health had prompted him to withdraw from the army. Mother of two young sons, Emma contributed to her family's income by teaching at a girls' high school in Vicksburg.

In 1869 Kate Stone of Louisiana married a Confederate officer she had met during the war. He first worked as a plantation manager, then eventually acquired land of his own. They produced four children, only two of whom lived to adulthood. Kate became active in the United Daughters of the Confederacy and in local book and literary clubs, reflecting, no doubt, her unsatisfied hunger for reading material all through the war.

Impatient as she had been to see the war's end, Gertrude Thomas found life even more trying in its aftermath. Her husband, Jeff, proved financially incompetent and irresponsible, wasting what little remained of her inherited fortune in a series of disastrous business ventures. Gertrude took up teaching to support her children. By the end of the century she had emerged as a leader in the new southern temperance crusade and had been selected president of the Georgia Woman's Suffrage Association and national treasurer of the United Daughters of the Confederacy.

Lucy Buck had been prescient indeed when she had observed as early as 1862, "We shall never any of us be the same as we have been." For each of these women, as for the thousands of others who, like them, had been part of the Old South's master class, Appomattox brought a new world, inaugurating lives unlike those they had anticipated or desired. Perhaps most conspicuously, this was a world without slaves. Loss of the property that had provided the foundation for privilege undermined the wealth and position of formerly slaveowning families. For the white women within these households, however, emancipation had a more personal significance. The daily work of domestic life and the routines of white women's lives were revolutionized by the coming of free labor. "All the talk, everywhere now," Emma Mordecai noted just after the cessation of military hostilities, "is servants." More than a generation later, the "servant problem" continued to preoccupy southern ladies. Asked by a Vanderbilt social scientist in the early 1890s to specify the most significant impact of the war on the lives of white southern women of her class, a Carolina matron old enough to have memories of "better days" before emancipation did not hesitate. "From being queens in social life," she replied, ladies had become "after the war, in many instances, mere domestic drudges."

But the increased labors of white women were not exclusively domestic. The disappearance of slave-based wealth left many formerly prosperous families struggling to make ends meet and dependent on women's work outside the home. Like Emma Crutcher, Jo Gillis, and Gertrude Thomas, many of these women turned to teaching. By 1880 the majority of southern schoolteachers had for the first time become female. The necessity for growing numbers of respectable women to find employment prompted southerners to direct more serious attention to women's education. In the 1890s the president of a southern women's college observed that nearly a quarter of his graduates now supported themselves. This expectation, he explained, led students to prosecute their studies with far greater earnestness and diligence than had their antebellum counterparts. Several southern state universities introduced coeducation in the 1880s, and women's colleges, such as Sophie Newcomb at Tulane in 1886, were established to offer women opportunities paralleling those of men. By the 1890s the Vanderbilt researcher noted the "growing respectability of self support" emerging from conditions of economic necessity, and one of his interviewees applauded the abandonment of prewar beliefs in "the nobility of dependence and helplessness in woman."

After their experiences of war, southern women found it difficult any longer to celebrate helplessness. When male protection had disappeared, female dependence had proved far too costly and too painful. Women had not been prepared to manage slaves and farms, control children, and even work to provide their own basic support. The desperate plight in which the war had placed so many females proved an unforgettable lesson, one only reinforced by the postbellum lives of many women of the formerly slaveowning classes. The absolute necessities of widowhood imposed independence on many, but the erosion of slave-based wealth and political power often left even those whose husbands returned from war unable to rely on male support. The actions of white women in a wide range of postwar arenas and their frequent appearances in the public spheres of work and reform can perhaps best be understood as a determination never to be entirely helpless or dependent again. The enhancement of opportunities for female education, women's advocacy of reforms in married property law, and the movement for female suffrage emerging by the 1890s all represented women's efforts to define and defend their own interests. A mistrust of men fueled many of these women's zeal.

In large measure, female dependence seemed dangerous because of the desperate condition of so many white southern men. Economic instability in the postwar environment enhanced the logic of the movement for married women's property laws. In a time of enormous financial uncertainty white men could protect the larger interests of their families by separating their wives' property from their own. Both Gertrude and Jeff Thomas would have fared far better had her wealth been immune from his indebtedness. New postbellum women's property laws, securing support from conservative men as well as most female suffragists, thus served both traditional and seemingly progressive interests. The implications of these new measures for domestic power and marital relationships were profound, however, for the laws embodied, as historian Suzanne Lebsock has written, a new "vision of masculine irresponsibility." Instead of playing its customary role in support of men's right and duty to serve as the protectors of women, the law here represented the intervention of the state to protect women from men.

For many white southern males, difficulties were far more than simply financial. From Vietnam we have gained an appreciation of the depth and persistence of war's wounds that may help us to understand other postwar generations. It is not unrealistic to think that many former Confederate soldiers must have suffered from posttraumatic stress disorders in the years after Appomattox. Certainly family papers hint at such distress among white southern men. Nearly two years after the end of the war, Amanda Sims of South Carolina described her father as "shattered mentally and physically." Kate Stone remarked that her brother "rarely talks at all" and her grandfather was "much depressed." Jeff Thomas described himself as a "fit subject for the Lunatic Asylum," and his wife, Gertrude, hinted at the alcoholism and the outbursts of rage that compounded his depression. Women were confronted not just with the delicate task of defending their own interests in the face of the failures and incompetence of their traditional "protectors"; they had to deal as well with these injured and broken men. For all the pain women had suffered in war, they had not so directly confronted the horrors of four years on the battlefield, nor did they bear the same accountability for failure and defeat. The rehabilitation of southern white men became a central postwar responsibility for Confederate women.

The United Daughters of the Confederacy, the Ladies Memorial Associations, and celebrations of the Lost Cause were designed in considerable measure to accomplish this restoration. Beginning in the years immediately after Appomattox, women began to organize to honor the dead with cemeteries, monuments, and annual memorial day observances. By the 1880s the United Daughters of the Confederacy had broadened women's concerns to a more general celebration of the Confederate struggle as well as its martyrs. On a personal and psychological level these efforts were meant to reassure defeated Confederates about their honor, courage, and manhood and to bury the pain of failure by redefining it as noble sacrifice and ultimate moral victory. But the Lost Cause operated on a broader social and political level as well, for it was intended to rehabilitate the larger system of patriarchy as well as the egos of individual southern men.

Doubting the competence of their men and recognizing the necessity of defending their own interests, women were at the same time reluctant, especially in the face of postwar racial upheaval, to abandon the possibility of white male power and protection entirely and forever. As Emily Harris had written in 1863 when her husband returned from furlough to the front, "I shall never get used to being left as the head of affairs at home. I am constituted so as to crave a guide and protector." Daunted by the experience of wartime responsibility, many women hoped to shift some of those burdens back to their husbands, brothers, and sons. They knew they could no longer entirely trust these men, but they wanted at least to avoid assuming all of their obligations. "Trying to do a man's business," as Lizzie Neblett put it, had proved for many Confederate women an almost overwhelming task. Thus, in what seems to our late twentieth-century eyes an almost inexplicable paradox of progressivism and reaction, Gertrude Thomas—and many southern women like her—could logically work for both female suffrage and the Lost Cause.

Through the experiences of war, white southern women had come to a new understanding of themselves and their interests as women. Their new postwar environment would yield a continued enhancement of female consciousness through the women's organizations that now flourished in the South as they never had in antebellum years. Not just associations to support suffrage or the Lost Cause, but temperance societies, educational and civic reform groups, church and missionary organizations, literary leagues, and women's clubs involved ladies in a variety of efforts aimed at personal and social uplift. The power of association, Anne Scott has written, "had its own inner dynamic," propelling women into public life as well as into closer bonds with one another.

These gendered identities, however, could not be separated from the prerogatives of class and race on which "ladyhood" rested. Inevitably the omnipresent issue of race tied white men and women together and undermined white southern females' willingness to challenge patriarchy. Black freedom seemed to pose an immediate and dangerous threat to the lady's status and to her long cherished privileges. In a tellingly symbolic civic gathering in turn-of-the-century North Carolina, for example, young white girls appeared on a float inscribed with the words *Protect Us* as part of a parade in support of a candidate committed to black disfranchisement. Even during the war itself, elite women had recognized the urgency of retaining "at least one good negro to wait upon" them. The much discussed late nineteenth-century "servant problem" was essentially the postemancipation expression of southern ladies' commitment to reestablishing the authority and benefits of whiteness. The men of their race would naturally serve as important allies in this struggle. Prerogatives of race thus undermined the imperatives and commonalities of gender in the postwar South, separating black and white women, weakening and retarding the development of southern feminism, and subordinating its agenda to the seemingly more pressing concerns of reestablishing class and racial privilege.

When some southern women began actively to advocate female suffrage in the 1890s, their movement displayed a regionally distinctive and racist cast. Their arguments for women's votes emphasized not female empowerment but the potential for privileged white women's suffrage to serve as an instrument to blunt the impact of black enfranchisement. The women seemed not to seek validation of their equality with white men so much as their superiority to black men. The letterhead of the Southern States Woman Suffrage Conference represented its adherents' sense of their rightful preeminence of both race and class, declaring "A government is not yet complete that withholds from its most enlightened women what it freely gives to its most benighted men." "Never before," proclaimed a speaker at a southern suffrage convention, "in the history of the world have men made former slaves the political masters of their former mistresses." In a calculated effort to create an alliance that would at once serve the interests of white women and white men, southern suffragists attempted to forge white unity through the definition of common class and racial goals and the adoption of a shared white supremacist rhetoric. In their elitism, in their emphasis on white superiority, and in their complementary concerns with protecting women and rehabilitating men, the suffrage movement and the celebration of the Lost Cause embodied the paradoxical interplay of old and new in the postwar South.

White women of the postwar South were new people living in a new world. Yet for those who remembered the rewards of class and racial power in the Old South, the desire to cling to eroding status remained strong. The ladies of the late nineteenth-century South understood all too well what Mary Lee had perceived as early as 1865: "social reconstruction we hold in our hands & might prevent." The necessities of changed economic and social circumstances and the self-knowledge gained from four years of crisis gave white southern women the bases for inventing new selves erected firmly upon the elitist assumptions of the old.

FURTHER READING

Thomas B. Alexander and Richard E. Beringer, *The Anatomy of the Confederate Congress* (1972)

Fred Arthur Bailey, *Class and Tennessee's Confederate Generation* (1987)

Richard E. Beringer, Herman Hattaway, Archer Jones, and William N. Still, Jr., *Why the South Lost the Civil War* (1986)

James H. Brewer, *The Confederate Negro* (1969)

Catherine Clinton, *Tara Revisited: Women, War and the Plantation Legend* (1995)

Thomas L. Connelly and Archer Jones, *The Politics of Command* (1973)

David P. Crook, *The North, the South, and the Powers, 1861–1865* (1974)

Charles P. Cullop, *Confederate Propaganda in Europe* (1969)

Robert F. Durden, *The Gray and the Black: The Confederate Debate on Emancipation* (1972)

Clement Eaton, *A History of the Southern Confederacy* (1954)

Paul D. Escott, *After Secession: Jefferson Davis and the Failure of Confederate Nationalism* (1978)

Drew Gilpin Faust, *Mothers of Invention: Women of the Slaveholding South in the American Civil War* (1996)

Shelby Foote, *The Civil War, a Narrative,* 3 vols. (1958–1974)

Joseph T. Glatthaar, *The March to the Sea and Beyond* (1985)

Winthrop D. Jordan, *Tumult and Silence at Second Creek: An Inquiry into a Civil War Slave Conspiracy* (1993)

Ella Lonn, *Desertion During the Civil War* (1928)

Mary Elizabeth Massey, *Bonnet Brigades* (1966)

———, *Refugee Life in the Confederacy* (1964)

Malcolm C. McMillan, *The Disintegration of a Confederate State* (1986)

James. M. McPherson, *Battle Cry of Freedom* (1988)

Grady McWhiney and Perry D. Jamieson, *Attack and Die: Civil War Military Tactics and the Southern Heritage* (1982)

Clarence L. Mohr, *On the Threshold of Freedom: Masters and Slaves in Civil War Georgia* (1986)

Museum of the Confederacy (Richmond, Va.), *A Woman's War: Southern Women, Civil War and the Confederate Legacy* (1996)

Harry P. Owens and James J. Cooke, eds., *The Old South in the Crucible of War* (1983)

Benjamin Quarles, *The Negro in the Civil War* (1953)

George Rable, *Civil Wars: Women and the Crisis of Southern Nationalism* (1989)

Emory M. Thomas, *The Confederacy as a Revolutionary Experience* (1971)

———, *The Confederate Nation* (1979)

C. Vann Woodward ed., *Mary Chesnut's Civil War* (1981)

LeeAnn Whites, *The Civil War as a Crisis in Gender: Augusta, Georgia, 1860–1890* (1995)

Bell Irvin Wiley, *The Life of Johnny Reb: The Common Soldier of the Confederacy* (1943)

———- - *The Plain People of the Confederacy* (1943)

W. Buck Yearns, *The Confederate Congress* (1960)

———, ed., *The Confederate Governors* (1985)

Emancipation and Reconstruction

The emancipation of four million slaves promised momentous changes in American politics, American society, and the American economy. For the men, women, and children who had endured bondage and prayed for freedom, emancipation had profound implications. The traditional dominance-subservience relationship between masters and slaves had to give way to a relationship between free citizens—between resentful whites and hopeful blacks. Landowners and laborers had to devise arrangements under which crops could be cultivated and workers compensated. As black aspirations and white resistance collided in the South, a victorious North began to establish ground rules through federal policies on how to reconstruct and rebuild the South.

Historians have approached Reconstruction from a wide range of perspectives. Decades ago, they saw this period as a disastrous episode during which unscrupulous northern carpetbaggers, aided by acquisitive scalawags and unskilled blacks, wrested power from southern governments and inaugurated an orgy of corruption and misrule. Since the 1960s, historians have revised this interpretation and presented a much more balanced approach to Reconstruction. They have investigated carefully the political debates in Washington over land distribution and land reform, the administrations of Johnson and Grant, the meaning of Radical Reconstruction and what motivated its vindictive policies, the developing violence and virulent racism in the South, and the return to Democratic rule in the region by the 1870s.

⅄ D O C U M E N T S

In the 1930s, the Federal Writers' Project conducted interviews with elderly ex-slaves who recalled their experiences in slavery and freedom. Document 1 records the reaction of three slaves to the news of freedom. An affidavit from the federal archives, reprinted in Document 2, describes what one female slave suffered because her husband fought for the Union army and how she eventually ran away, leaving her children behind. Certain "Radical Republicans" urged strong measures to deal with the South. Thaddeus Stevens, a leading Republican in Congress, was the principal, and one of the few, advocates of land confiscation and redistribution. Note that the features in his proposal, outlined in Document 3, are designed to make it appealing to the many who disapproved of this. Negroes' desire for better treatment and land and the prejudice that they faced are prominent subjects discussed in the journal and family letter of Mrs. Mary Jones of Georgia in Document 4. President Andrew Johnson, despite statements to the contrary, began to issue wholesale pardons of leading Confederates, even those who had ignored his proclamations and sought office without a pardon. Alarmed by the return of former Confederate leaders to power and upset by state laws that restricted southern blacks' liberty—the Black Codes—Congress stepped in. Its involvement in Reconstruction is summarized in the Fourteenth Amendment and in the Military Reconstruction Act of 1867, which appears in Document 5. George Fitzhugh, a former defender of slavery, reveals southern whites' fears, in his article "Cui Bono?" (Document 6), as blacks gained political power and the right to vote under the policies of Radical Reconstruction. In Document 7, congressional testimony of the Ku Klux Klan shows how southern Conservatives, or Democrats, typically blamed violence on Republicans and southern blacks. One of the few black congressmen sent to Washington, Robert B. Elliott of South Carolina, expresses his desires in Document 8 to see Congress pass a civil rights bill to ensure the equality of his race.

1. Ex-Slaves Recall Their First Taste of Freedom, 1937

Betty Jones, b. 1863, Charlottesville, Virginia

Gramma used to tell dis story to ev'ybody dat would lissen, an' I spec' I heered it a hundred times. Gramma say she was hired out to de Randolphs during de war. One day whilst she was weedin' corn another slave, Mamie Tolliver, come up to her an' whisper, "Sarah, dey tell me dat Marse Lincum done set all us slaves free." Gramma say, "Is dat so?" an' she dropped her hoe an' run all de way to de Thacker's place—seben miles it was—an run to ole Missus an' looked at her real hard. Den she yelled, "I'se free! Yes, I'se free! Ain't got to work fo' you no mo'. You can't put me in yo' pocket now!" Gramma say Missus Thacker started boohooin' an' threw her apron over her face an' run in de house. Gramma knew it was true den.

Charlotte Brown, b. c. 1855, Woods Crossing, Virginia

De news come on a Thursday, an' all de slaves been shoutin' an' carryin' on tell ev'ybody was all tired out. 'Member de fust Sunday of freedom. We was all sittin' roun' restin' an' tryin' to think what freedom meant an' ev'ybody was quiet an' peaceful. All at once ole Sister Carrie who was near 'bout a hundred started in to talkin':

> Tain't no mo' sellin' today,
> Tain't no mo' hirin' today,
> Tain't no pullin' off shirts today,
> Its stomp down freedom today.
> Stomp it down!

An' when she says, "Stomp it down," all de slaves commence to shoutin' wid her:

Interviews with ex-slaves conducted by the Federal Writers' Project in the 1930s. First published in *Negro In Virginia,* republished in Charles L. Perdue Jr., Thomas E. Barden, and Robert K. Phillips, *Weevils in the Wheat* (Charlottesville: University Press of Virginia, 1976), pp. 58–59, 180, 233–234.

> Stomp down Freedom today—
> Stomp it down!
> Stomp down Freedom today.

Wasn't no mo' peace dat Sunday. Ev'ybody started in to sing an' shout once mo'. Fust thing you know dey done made up music to Sister Carrie's stomp song an' sang an' shouted dat song all de res' de day. Chile, dat was one glorious time!

Georgianna Preston, b. c. 1855, Residence Unspecified

Us young folks carried on somep'n awful [that first night of freedom]. Ole Marse let us stay up all night, an' didn't seem to mind it at all. Saw de sun sot an' befo' we know it, it was a-risin' again. Ole folks was shoutin' an' singin' songs. Dar's one dey sung purty nigh all night. Don't know who started it, but soon's dey stopped, 'nother one took it up an' made up some mo' verses. Lawdy, chile, I kin hear dat song a-ringin' in my haid now:

> Ain't no mo' blowin' dat fo' day horn,
> Will sing, chillun, will sing,
> Ain't no mo' crackin' dat whip over John,
> Will sing, chillun, will sing.

2. Clarissa Burdett Recounts the Difficulties of a Black Soldier's Wife, 1865

Camp Nelson Ky 27th of March 1865

Personally appeared before me J M Kelley Notary Public in and for the County of Jessamine State of Kentucky Clarissa Burdett a woman of color who being duly sworn according to law doth despose and say

I am a married woman and have four children. My husband Elijah Burdett is a soldier in the 12" U.S.C.H. Arty. I and my children belonged to Smith Alford Garrard County Ky. When my husband enlisted my master beat me over the head with an axe handle saying as he did so that he beat me for letting Ely Burdett go off. He bruised my head so that I could not lay it against a pillow without the greatest pain. Last week my niece who lived with me went to Camp Nelson. This made my master very angry and last monday March 20" 1865 he asked me where the girl had gone. I could not tell him He then whipped me over the head and said he would give me two hundred lashes if I did not get the girl back before the next day. On Wednesday last March 22" he said that he had not time to beat me on Tuesday but now he had time and he would give it to me. He then tied my hands threw the rope over a joist stripped me entirely naked and gave me about three hundred lashes. I cried out. He then caught me by the throat and almost choked me then continued to lash me with switches until my back was all cut up. The marks of the switches are now very visible and my back is still very sore. My master was a very cruel man and strongly sympathizes with the rebels. He went with the Rebel General Bragg when the latter

---

This document can be found in Ira Berlin et al., eds., *Freedom: A Documentary History of Emancipation, 1861–1867* (Cambridge: Cambridge University Press, 1985).

retreated from the State. He took me and my children to Beans Station and send the parents and two sisters of my niece to Knoxville where he sold them. After he whipped me on Wednesday last he said he would give me until next morning to bring the girl back, and if I did not get her back by that time he would give me as much more. I knew that I would be whipped so I ran away. My master frequently said that he would be jailed before one of his niggers would go to Camp. I therefore knew he would not permit any of my children to come with me. So when I ran away I had to leave my children with my master. I have four children there at present and I want to get them but I cannot go there for them knowing that master who would whip me would not let any of my children go nor would he suffer me to get away

her

HDcSr   (Signed) Clarissa Burdett

mark

3. Thaddeus Stevens Advocates the Redistribution of Land, 1865

Reformation *must* be effected; the foundation of their institutions, both political, municipal and social *must* be broken up and *relaid,* or all our blood and treasure have been spent in vain. This can only be done by treating and holding them as a conquered people. Then all things which we can desire to do, follow with logical and legitimate authority. As conquered territory Congress would have full power to legislate for them; for the territories are not under the Constitution except so far as the express power to govern them is given to Congress. They would be held in a territorial condition until they are fit to form State Constitutions, republican in fact not in form only, and ask admission into the Union as new States. If Congress approve of their Constitutions, and think they have done works meet for repentance they would be admitted as new States. If their Constitutions are not approved of, they would be sent back, until they have become wise enough so to purge their old laws as to eradicate every despotic and revolutionary principle—until they shall have learned to venerate the Declaration of Independence. . . .

We propose to confiscate all the estate of every rebel belligerent whose estate was worth $10,000, or whose land exceeded two hundred acres in quantity. Policy if not justice would require that the poor, the ignorant, and the coerced should be forgiven. They followed the example and teachings of their wealthy and intelligent neighbors. The rebellion would never have originated with them. Fortunately those who would thus escape form a large majority of the people, though possessing but a small portion of the wealth. The proportion of those exempt compared with the punished would be I believe about nine tenths.

There are about six millions of freemen in the South. The number of acres of land is 465,000,000. Of this those who own above two hundred acres each, number

This document is from a speech given by Thaddeus Stevens in Lancaster, Pennsylvania, September 7, 1865.

about 70,000 persons, holding in the aggregate (together with the States) about 394,000,000 acres, leaving for all the others below 200 each about 71,000,000 of acres. By thus forfeiting the estates of the leading rebels, the Government would have 394,000,000 of acres beside their town property, and yet nine tenths of the people would remain untouched. Divide this land into convenient farms. Give if you please forty acres to each adult male freed man. Suppose there are one million of them. That would require 40,000,000 of acres, which deducted from 394,000,000 leaves three hundred and fifty-four millions of acres for sale. Divide it into suitable farms and sell it to the highest bidders. I think it, including town property, would average at least ten dollars per acre. That would produce $3,540,000,000,—Three billions, five hundred and forty millions of dollars.

Let that be applied as follows to wit:

1. Invest $300,000,000 in six per cent. government bonds, and add the interest semi-annually to the pensions of those who have become entitled by this villainous war.
2. Appropriate $200,000,000 to pay the damages done to loyal men North and South by the rebellion.
3. Pay the residue being $3,040,000,000 towards the payment of the National debt. . . .

But, it is said, by those who have more sympathy with rebel wives and children than for the widows and orphans of loyal men, that this stripping the rebels of their estates and driving them to exile or to honest labor would be harsh and severe upon innocent women and children. It may be so; but that is the result of the necessary laws of war. But it is revolutionary, say they. This plan would, no doubt, work a radical reorganization in southern institutions, habits and manners. It is intended to revolutionize their principles and feelings. This may startle feeble minds and shake weak nerves. So do all great improvements in the political and moral world. It requires a heavy impetus to drive forward a sluggish people. When it was first proposed to free the slaves, and arm the blacks, did not half the nation tremble? The prim conservatives, the snobs, and the male waiting maids in Congress, were in hysterics.

The whole fabric of southern society *must* be changed, and never can it be done if this opportunity is lost. Without this, this Government can never be, as it never has been, a true republic. Heretofore, it had more the features of aristocracy than of democracy.—The Southern States have been despotisms, not governments of the people. It is impossible that any practical equality of rights can exist where a few thousand men monopolize the whole landed property. The larger the number of small proprietors the more safe and stable the government. As the landed interest must govern, the more it is subdivided and held by independent owners, the better. What would be the condition of the State of New York if it were not for her independent yeomanry? She would be overwhelmed and demoralized by the Jews, Milesians and vagabonds of licentious cities. How can republican institutions, free schools, free churches, free social intercourse exist in a mingled community of nabobs and serfs; of the owners of twenty thousand acre manors with lordly palaces, and the occupants of narrow huts inhabited by "low white trash?"—If the south is ever to be made a safe republic let her lands be cultivated by the toil of the owners or the free labor of intelligent citizens. This must be done even though it drive her nobility into exile. If they go, all the better.

It will be hard to persuade the owner of ten thousand acres of land, who drives a coach and four, that he is not degraded by sitting at the same table, or in the same pew, with the embrowned and hard-handed farmer who has himself cultivated his own thriving homestead of 150 acres. This subdivision of the lands will yield ten bales of cotton to one that is made now, and he who produced it will own it and *feel himself a man. . . .*

This doctrine of restoration shocks me.—We have a duty to perform which our fathers were incapable of, which will be required at our hands by God and our Country. When our ancestors found a "more perfect Union" necessary, they found it impossible to agree upon a Constitution without tolerating, nay guaranteeing Slavery. They were obliged to acquiesce, trusting to time to work a speedy cure, in which they were disappointed. *They* had some excuse, some justification. But we can have none if we do not thoroughly eradicate Slavery and render it forever impossible in this republic. The Slave power made war upon the nation. They declared the "more perfect Union" dissolved. Solemnly declared themselves a foreign nation, alien to this republic; for four years were in fact what they claimed to be, We accepted the war which they tendered and treated them as a government capable of making war. We have conquered them, and as a conquered enemy we can give them laws; can abolish all their municipal institutions and form new ones. If we do not make those institutions fit to last through generations of free men, a heavy curse will be on us. Our glorious, but tainted republic has been born to new life through bloody, agonizing pains. But this frightful "Restoration" has thrown it into "cold obstruction, and to death." If the rebel states have never been out of the Union, any attempt to reform their State institutions either by Congress or the President, is rank usurpation.

4. Mary Jones Describes the Concerns of Ex-Slaves, 1865

Mary Jones in Her Journal, 1865

Friday, January 6th. No enemy appeared here today, but we have heard firing around on different places.

The people are all idle on the plantations, most of them seeking their own pleasure. Many servants have proven faithful, others false and rebellious against all authority or restraint. Susan, a Virginia Negro and nurse to my little Mary Ruth, went off with Mac, her husband, to Arcadia the night after the first day the Yankees appeared, with whom she took every opportunity of conversing, informing them that the baby's father was Colonel Jones. She has acted a faithless part as soon as she could. Porter left three weeks since, and has never returned to give any report of Patience or himself or anyone at Arcadia. Little Andrew went to Flemington and re-

Letters of the C. C. Jones family as found in Robert Manson Myers, editor, *The Children of Pride,* 1972, Yale University Press. Charles Colock Jones Papers, Howard-Tilton Memorial Library, Tulane University, reprinted with permission.

turned. I sent him back to wait on our dear sister and family and to be with his own. I hope he will prove faithful. Gilbert, Flora, Tenah, Sue, Rosetta, Fanny, Little Gilbert, Charles, Milton and Elsie and Kate have been faithful to us. . . .

Tuesday, January 10th. We have been free from the presence of the enemy thus far today, although in great apprehension for several hours, as Sue came in at dinner time and advised us to hasten the meal, as she heard firing in the woods between this and White Oak, which is not much over a mile distant. It was reported they would return today with a large forage train of several hundred wagons going on to the Altamaha.

One thing is evident: they are now enlisting the Negroes here in their service. As one of the officers said to me, "We do not want your women, but we mean to take the able-bodied men to dredge out the river and harbor at Savannah, to hew timber, make roads, build bridges, and throw up batteries." They offer twelve dollars per month. Many are going off with them. Some few sensible ones calculate the value of twelve dollars per month in furnishing food, clothing, fuel, lodging, etc., etc. Up to this time none from this place has joined them. I have told some of those indisposed to help in any way and to wander off at pleasure that as they were perfectly useless here it would be best for me and for the good of their fellow servants if they would leave and go at once with the Yankees. They had seen what their conduct was to the black people—stealing from them, searching their houses, cursing and abusing and insulting their wives and daughters; and if they chose such for their masters to obey and follow, then the sooner they went with them the better; and I had quite a mind to send in a request that they be carried off. . . .

Thursday and Friday, January 12th and 13th. . . . Everything confirms the raid south. The enemy are in full possession of Savannah; Negroes in large numbers are flocking to them. . . .

Saturday Night, January 21st. On Thursday Mr. L. J. Mallard visited us. He is now with his family. Gave us various accounts of the enemy. They encamped near his house; at one time on his premises over a thousand. They entered his dwelling day and night. They were forced to obtain a guard from the commander of the post, who was stationed at Midway, to protect his family. The house was repeatedly fired into under pretense of shooting rebels, although they knew that none but defenseless women and children were within. And Mrs. Mallard, who is almost blind, was then in her confinement. They rifled the house of every article of food or clothing which they wished. Mr. Mallard had nothing left but the suit of clothes he wore. . . .

Kate, Daughter's servant who has been cooking for us, took herself off today— influenced, as we believe, by her father. Sent for Cook Kate to Arcadia; she refuses to come.

Their condition is one of perfect anarchy and rebellion. They have placed themselves in perfect antagonism to their owners and to all government and control. We dare not predict the end of all this, if the Lord in mercy does not restrain the hearts and wills of this deluded people. They are certainly prepared for any measures. What we are to do becomes daily more and more perplexing. It is evident if my dwelling is left unoccupied, everything within it will be sacrificed. Wherever owners have gone away, the Negroes have taken away all the furniture, bedding, and household articles.

Mary Jones to Her Daughter, Mary S. Mallard, November 17, 1865

As I wrote you, Sue had left. She is still at the Boro, and I am told has hired Elizabeth to work at Dr. Samuel Jones's. Flora is in a most unhappy and uncomfortable condition, doing very little, and that poorly. . . . I think Flora will certainly leave when she is ready. I overheard an amusing conversation between Cook Kate and herself: they are looking forward to gold watches and chains, bracelets, and *blue veils* and silk dresses! Jack has entered a boardinghouse in Savannah, where I presume he will practice attitudes and act the Congo gentleman to perfection. Porter and Patience will provide for themselves. I shall cease my anxieties for the race. My life long (I mean since I had a home) I have been laboring and caring for them, and since the war have labored with all my might to supply their wants, and expended everything I had upon their support, directly or indirectly; and this is their return.

You can have no conception of the condition of things. I understand Dr. Harris and Mr. Varnedoe will rent their lands to the Negroes! The conduct of some of the citizens has been very injurious to the best interest of the community. At times my heart is so heavy I feel as if it would give way, and that I cannot remain. But I have no other home, and if I desert it, everything will go to ruin. Mr. Fennell has done all he could to protect my interest; but he is feeble physically, and I do not know that he has any special gift at management. I believe him to be an honest and excellent man. We planted only a half-crop of provisions here, and they did not work one-fourth of their time. Judge the results: not a pod of cotton planted, and all I had stolen, and the whole of that at Arcadia gone. You know I wished Little Andrew to return to Montevideo after Mr. Buttolph decided not to go to Baker, as he was our best plowman. He did not do so. Wanting help at this time in grinding cane, I wished him to come down. He did so, stayed part of a day, and walked off. I have not heard of him since. This is a specimen of their conduct. It is thought there will be a great many returning to the county; I do not believe so.

I have mentioned all the news I could collect in Aunty's letter, and refer you to that.

I hope Robert received your brother's letter in reference to the circulars. All we want at present is to obtain subscribers. The work probably cannot be published under a year. I have requested Joseph to confer with Mr. Rogers about the paper he so generously and kindly offered to give for printing the first edition. Do let him know where Mr. Rogers is.

I have just called Charles and asked if he had any messages. "He sends love to Lucy and Tenah, and begs to be remembered to you, and says he will make an opportunity to come and see them before long." This is the sum and substance of his message. It is impossible to get at any of their intentions, and it is useless to ask them. I see only a dark future for the whole race. . . . Do write me all about yourself and the dear children and Robert and the church. . . . Kiss my precious grandchildren. If they were here they should eat sugar cane all day and boil candy at night. . . . The Lord bless you, my dear child!

Ever your affectionate mother,

Mary Jones.

5. The Military Reconstruction Act, 1867

Whereas no legal State governments or adequate protection for life or property now exists in the rebel States of Virginia, North Carolina, South Carolina, Georgia, Mississippi, Alabama, Louisiana, Florida, Texas, and Arkansas; and whereas it is necessary that peace and good order should be enforced in said States until loyalty and republican State governments can be legally established: Therefore

Be it enacted, . . . That said rebel States shall be divided into military districts and made subject to the military authority of the United States . . .

Sec. 2. . . . It shall be the duty of the President to assign to the command of each of said districts an officer of the army, not below the rank of brigadier general, and to detail a sufficient military force to enable such officer to perform his duties and enforce his authority within the district to which he is assigned.

Sec. 3. . . . It shall be the duty of each officer assigned as aforesaid to protect all persons in their rights of person and property, to suppress insurrection, disorder, and violence, and to punish, or cause to be punished, all disturbers of the public peace and criminals, and to this end he may allow local civil tribunals to take jurisdiction of and to try offenders, or, when in his judgment it may be necessary for the trial of offenders, he shall have power to organize military commissions or tribunals for that purpose; and all interference under color of State authority with the exercise of military authority under this act shall be null and void. . . .

Sec. 5. . . . When the people of any one of said rebel States shall have formed a constitution of government in conformity with the Constitution of the United States in all respects, framed by a convention of delegates elected by the male citizens of said State twenty-one years old and upward, of whatever race, color, or previous condition, . . . and when such constitution shall provide that the elective franchise shall be enjoyed by all such persons as have the qualifications herein stated for electors of delegates, and when such constitution shall be ratified by a majority of the persons voting on the question of ratification who are qualified as electors of delegates, and when such constitution shall have been submitted to Congress for examination and approval, and Congress shall have approved the same, and when said State, by a vote of its legislature elected under said constitution, shall have adopted the amendment to the Constitution of the United States, proposed by the thirty-ninth Congress, and known as article fourteen, and when said article shall have become a part of the Constitution of the United States, said State shall be declared entitled to representation in Congress, and senators and representatives shall be admitted therefrom on their taking oaths prescribed by law, and then and thereafter the preceding sections of this act shall be inoperative in said State: *Provided,* That no person excluded from the privilege of holding office by said proposed amendment to the Constitution of the United States shall be eligible to election as a member of the convention to frame a constitution for any of said rebel States, nor shall any such person vote for members of such convention.

This document can be found in the United States of America Statutes at Large, Volume 13, pp. 428–29.

Sec. 6. . . . Until the people of said rebel States shall be by law admitted to representation in the Congress of the United States, any civil governments which may exist therein shall be deemed provisional only, and in all respects subject to the paramount authority of the United States at any time to abolish, modify or control, or supersede the same; and in all elections to any office under such provisional governments all persons shall be entitled to vote, and none others, who are entitled to vote under the provisions of the fifth section of this act; and no person shall be eligible to any office under any such provisional governments who would be disqualified from holding office under the provisions of the third article of said constitutional amendment.

6. George Fitzhugh Reveals Southern White Fears of the Negro Vote, 1867

Port Royal, Va., September 17th, 1867

Messrs. Editors—The Radicals have overreached themselves. The negroes throughout the South are determined not to become their allies and supple tools, but to set up a party of their own, and to vote for none but negro candidates for office. They naturally reject with scorn and contempt the Radical proposition that henceforth there shall be no distinctions of color or race, but that all men shall stand on their own merits. They see, that under a thin disguise, this is a proposition that the negroes shall do the voting, and the Radicals fill all the offices. Four millions of negroes in the South, they insist, by virtue of their numbers and their loyalty, are entitled to fill most of the Federal and State offices at the South, and not to become mere hewers of wood and drawers of water for a handful of false, hypocritical, newly-converted white Unionists. Thrown upon their individual merit regardless of color or race, and they know that no negroes would be elected or appointed to office, for more capable white men are everywhere to be found. Obliterate all distinctions of race, and the negroes at the South, like those at the North, would become outcasts, pariahs, paupers and criminals. They would be confined to the most loathsome and least lucrative employments, and spend half their time in prisons, workhouses and poor-houses. They know that mere political equality would at once condemn them to social slavery—and they see at the North, that this social slavery, or slavery to skill and capital, of an inferior to a superior race, is the worst possible condition in which human beings can be placed. You, and your readers, must see that the negroes will not be satisfied with a nominal, but deceptive equality, but are everywhere determined to become masters of those who lately owned them as slaves. We admire their pluck. They are all armed and ready; all burning for a fight. They are impatient at the tedious process of reconstruction, and lavish much more abuse upon the Federal soldiers, the Freedman's Bureau and the Radicals, than upon the Secessionists. So soon as invested with the voting franchise, they will be full masters of the situation, for they constitute a majority on every acre of good

Reprinted by permission of Louisiana State University Press from *The Cause of the South: Selections from De Bow's Review,* edited by Paul F. Paskoff and Daniel J. Wilson. Copyright © 1982 by Louisiana State University Press.

land (except a little about the mountains) from Maryland to Florida, from the Atlantic to the Mississippi, and from the Rio Grande to Memphis. By mere voting, and selecting none but negroes as county, state and federal officers, in the favored regions where they constitute the majority, in two or three years they might expel the whites from all the fertile sections of the South, and turn those sections into hunting, ranging, fowling and fishing grounds, just as they were held, or infested by the Indians. Nature seems to have intended all the fertile portions of the South for mere roaming grounds for savages, for no where else on the globe would bountiful Nature enable savages to live with so little labor. It would be far easier for negro savages to live without labor on the sea, gulf and river coasts in the South, than in any parts of Africa. Wild fruits are ten-times as abundant in these favored sections of the South as in any parts of Africa; and so are fish, oysters, water fowl, and forest game. Give the negroes the right of suffrage, and at once they become masters of the situation throughout every acre of good land in the South, except about the mountains. They would only have to elect negro judges, sheriffs, justices of the peace, constables, jurors, etc., in order to expel the whole white population, except here and there a few old, infirm, silly, infatuated landholders. Our mechanics have nothing to do, and are rapidly emigrating. White common laborers or hirelings have all disappeared. We have not seen a single one since the war. There is nothing for our educated, enterprising young men to do here, and they are all removing. We have no industrial pursuits, except farming, and that is carelessly, lazily and languidly pursued by a few white landowners, and by troops of freedmen, who work occasionally, in a desultory way—say, on the average, three days in the week. The negro tenants, next year, will claim half of our lands, and negro judges, jurors, justices, etc., will sustain their claims—that is, provided, negro suffrage turns over the South to negro rule. It is a monstrous absurdity, cruelty and attempted deception, to invite white men from the North to settle in the South, subject themselves to negro rule, and probably ere long, to be massacred by negroes. No! Let the whites at the North first expel the Radicals from power, deny to the negro the rights of citizenship, make him a subordinate, or mere coarse, common laborer, as God and Nature designed he should be, and these white men from the North will find the South a delightful residence. Now, no sane man would live here longer than he could make arrangements to quit but for the hope and expectation that Radical rule is nearly ended, and that the Northern Democrats, soon to come into power, will do justice to the whites of the South, and the whites of the North, by putting the negro to work, and leaving voting, legislating, and governing, to the whites.

We have said that the negroes, so soon as they become invested with the right of suffrage, will become masters of the situation, and may seize on and hold all of the property of the whites, without redress on their parts; for negro jurors, justices and judges, taught by Northern Abolition emissaries that they (the negroes) are the rightful owners of all Southern lands and other property, would be sure to profit by the lessons they have thus learned. But they are impatient. This is too slow a process for them. We assure you, and your readers, and the entire North, that the freedmen (with very few exceptions) are anxious, impatient, burning with desire to begin the fight—the war of races—at once. They hold incendiary meetings, caucuses and conventions every day. They are all around; they are continually drilling in defiance of law. They have every where secret military organizations; they daily defy and insult the Federal troops and the Freedman's Bureau. They are ready and anxious to fight all the whites both North and South. They believe themselves far better soldiers than the whites, and are ready to attempt the expulsion or extermination of the whites. Unless the elections at the North, this fall, show a decided Democratic gain, the war of the races will begin ere the commencement of another year. And what will be the consequences? Why, a few hundreds or thousands, whites, men, women and children, will be massacred by the negroes; and then, in retaliation, hundreds of thousands negroes will be exterminated by the infuriated whites. This war of races will brutalize whites as well as blacks. Yet, knowingly, willfully, premeditatedly and advisedly, the Radical leaders are bringing about this inhuman and bloody result. And for why? Not to make allies of the negroes, for the negroes hate and despise them, and are everywhere busy in building up a negro party and in nominating negro candidates for office. They are equally the enemies of radical measures and radical men. In all their meetings in the cotton states, they denounce the direct tax on cotton, and will be sure to oppose the protective tariff; or indirect tax on cotton and other necessaries of life; for such taxes fall most heavily on the laboring classes. They will, for like reasons, be sure to advocate the repudiation of the National debt; whilst white representatives from the South would vote for its payment to the uttermost cent; for such payment would obviously be part of the terms of Reconstruction, which no honest Southron would attempt to violate. Besides, this war of races would involve the North also in war, increase the National debt, greatly increase Federal taxation, destroy altogether the Northern market for her merchandise and manufactures at the South; put a stop to the production of cotton, rice, sugar and tobacco; render reconstruction equally hopeless and undesirable; divide, probably, the Union into a half dozen separate nations, and involve the whole country, without distinction of race or section, in one common, irremediable ruin. But we hope and believe that Northern men begin to see that the continuance of radical rule is rapidly bringing about these disastrous results, and that they will soon hurl these cruel, dishonest and disorganizing rulers from the seats of power, do justice to the South, restore the Union on constitutional terms, and renew amicable and profitable relations between the lately hostile sections.

With us in tidewater Virginia, and I presume the same is true every where south of us, all is indecision, confusion, chaos. Men live from day to day, from year to year, from hand to mouth, without any settled or fixed plans of future life. Houses innumerable have been burnt or destroyed, and not one is rebuilt. Dilapidated houses are not repaired. Fences and enclosures of all kinds have gone down, and no one thinks of renewing them. Lands are cultivated merely for present profit, without a thought or purpose or improving them, for no one knows how soon his lands may be confiscated by the Radicals, or seized upon by the negroes. Our native white population is deserting, and no immigrants coming in. Before, and up to the time of the war, our rivers were alive with Northern vessels, every family in tolerable circumstances had its Northern teacher, male or female, and our roads and court-yards swarmed with agents and drummers, peddlers, etc., from the North. Now, all this is changed, and not a single individual, male or female, visits us by land or water from the North. A "Live Yankee" has not been seen in these parts for the last six months. And why come to be subjected to negro competition,—and soon—still worse,—to negro rule? No! Let the Northern men stay at home, and first put down the negroes and the Radicals. Then, the South, and not till then, will be a place fit to live in. Then, we will find room and extend the most cordial welcome to five millions of Northerners, if they will come among us,—without regard to their opinions, political, social, or religious. We know, when they see things here with their own eyes, and become identified with us in interest, that they will all make most valuable citizens. But at present, none but a negro amalgamationist should remove to the South.

7. Congressional Testimony on the Ku Klux Klan, 1871

General John B. Gordon on the Loyal Leagues and the Origin of the Ku Klux Klan

The instinct of self-protection prompted that organization; the sense of insecurity and danger, particularly in those neighborhoods were the negro population largely predominated. The reasons which led to this organization were three or four. The first and main reason was the organization of the Union League, as they called it, about which we knew nothing more than this: that the negroes would desert the plantations, and go off at night in large numbers; and on being asked where they had been, would reply, sometimes, "We have been to the muster;" sometimes, "We have been to the lodge;" sometimes, "We have been to the meeting." These things were observed for a great length of time. We knew that the "carpetbaggers," as the people of Georgia called these men who came from a distance and had no interest at all with us; who were unknown to us entirely; who from all we could learn about them did not have any very exalted position at their homes—these men were organizing the colored people. We knew that beyond all question. We knew of certain instances where great crime had been committed; where overseers had been driven from plantations, and the negroes had asserted their right to hold the property for their own benefit. Apprehension took possession of the entire public mind of the State. Men were in many instances afraid to go away from their homes and leave their wives and children for fear of outrage. Rapes were already being committed in the country. There was this general organization of the black race on the one hand, and an entire disorganization of the white race on the other hand. . . . It was therefore necessary, in order to protect our families from outrage and preserve our own lives, to have something that we could regard as a brotherhood—a combination of the best men of the country, to act purely in self-defense. . . .

Ben Hill on the Klan

Question. You have not studied this organization?

Answer. I have only investigated a few cases for the purpose of ascertaining who were the guilty offenders. One reason for investigating the few cases was upon the attempt to reconstruct Georgia some time ago, and these Ku-Klux outrages were made to bear very, very heavily against even Union parties [who opposed returning Georgia to military rule]. I wanted to know if that was the case, and if so, I wanted

---

This document can be found as part of the United States of America's Congress testimony taken by the Joint Select Committee to inquire into the Condition of Affairs: Georgia, volume I, p. 308, volume II, pp. 770–71.

the people to put down the Ku-Klux. In the second place, I arrived at the conclusion that a great many of these outrages were committed by gentlemen who wanted a reconstruction of the State, and committed those outrages to give an excuse for it. I have always thought that two or three of the most outrageous murders committed in the State were really committed by persons of the same political faith of the parties slain. . . .

Question. So far as I have observed your papers, (and I have examined them both before I came into the State and since, I mean the democratic papers,) two lines of thought on this subject seem to run along through them; one is to deny the existence of this organization, and the other is to discountenance with unmeasured abuse every effort to punish such offenses, and even to inquire and ascertain whether in fact they exist. . . . Why is that?

Answer. I am unable to give you a very satisfactory reason. I think myself that the great body of our people are really anxious to put down anything of this sort, the great body of our people of the best class, almost without exception. There are a very few, however, who, as you have stated, have denied unconditionally the existence of such things at all, even in the local and sporadic form I have mentioned, for I do not myself believe that they have existed in any other form. I think they have discountenanced the effort of some people to investigate them, first, because they professed to believe that they did not exist; second, because I think a great many of them have honestly been actuated by a simple desire to pander to what was considered sectional prejudice on this subject. I think we have a class of people in our State, and democrats, too, who are willing to use this occasion, as a great many politicians use all occasions to make themselves popular, by simply pandering to what they consider the sectional prejudices of the hour. I think some have been extreme and ultra in denouncing all pretense of lawlessness, merely for the purpose of making political capital for themselves individually.

Question. We hear from a great many witnesses about the "impudence" of negroes. What is considered in your section of the country "impudence" on the part of a negro?

Answer. Well, it is considered impudence for a negro not to be polite to a white man—not to pull of his hat and bow and scrape to a white man, as was always done formerly.

Question. Do the white people generally expect or require now that kind of submissive deportment on the part of the negroes that they did while the negroes were slaves?

Answer. I do not think they do as a general thing; a great many do.

Question. Are there many white people who do require it?

Answer. Yes, sir; I think there are a great many who do require it, and are not satisfied unless the negroes do it.

Question. Suppose that a negro man has been working for a white man, and they have some difference or dispute in relation to wages, will your people generally allow a negro man to stand up and assert his rights in the same way and in the same language which they would allow to a white man without objection?

Answer. O, no sir, that is not expected at all.

Question. If the colored man does stand up and assert his rights in language which would be considered pardonable and allowable in a white man, that is considered "impudence" in a negro?

Answer. Yes, sir; gross impudence.

Question. Is that species of "impudence" on the part of the negro considered a sufficient excuse by many of your people for chastising a negro, or "dealing with him?"

Answer. Well, some think so. . . .

Question. In your judgment, from what you have seen and heard, is there something of a political character about this organization?

Answer. I think it is entirely political.

Question. What makes you think so?

Answer. Because the parties who are maltreated by these men are generally republicans. I have never known a democrat to be assaulted. . . .

Question. What, in your opinion, is the object of keeping up the Ku-Klux organization and operating it as they do? What do they intend to produce or effect by it?

Answer. My opinion is, that the purpose was to break down the reconstruction acts; that they were dissatisfied with negro suffrage and the reconstruction measures and everybody that was in favor of them.

Question. Do you think this organization was intended to neutralize the votes of the negroes after suffrage had been extended to them?

Answer. Yes, sir, I think so.

Question. How? By intimidating them?

Answer. Any way. Yes, sir, by intimidation.

Question. Making them afraid to exercise the right of suffrage?

Answer. Yes, sir.

Question. Do you believe that the organization and its operations have, in fact, produced that effect?

Answer. I think they have to some extent.

Question. What is the state of feeling which has been produced among the colored people by this armed, disguised organization, and the acts they have committed?

Answer. Well, in my section of the country, the colored people, generally, are afraid now, and have been for some time, to turn out at an election. They are afraid to say much, or to have anything to do with public affairs. I own a plantation on Coosa River, upon which I have, perhaps, about 40 negroes, and some of them have been pretty badly alarmed, afraid to say much. Some have lain out in the woods, afraid to stay at home.

8. Representative Robert B. Elliott of South Carolina Demands Federal Civil Rights, January 1874

. . . Sir, it is scarcely twelve years since that gentleman [Alexander H. Stephens of Georgia] shocked the civilized world by announcing the birth of a government which rested on human slavery as its corner-stone. The progress of events has swept away that *pseudo*-government which rested on greed, pride, and tyranny; and the race whom he then ruthlessly spurned and trampled on are here to meet him in debate, and to demand that the rights which are enjoyed by their former oppressors—

This speech is found in the Congressional Record, 43rd Congress, 1st Session, Volume II, pp. 407–410. It was delivered on January 6, 1874.

who vainly sought to overthrow a Government which they could not prostitute to the base uses of slavery—shall be accorded to those who even in the darkness of slavery kept their allegiance true to freedom and the Union. Sir, the gentleman from Georgia has learned much since 1861; but he is still a laggard. Let him put away entirely the false and fatal theories which have so greatly marred an otherwise enviable record. Let him accept, in its fullness and beneficence, the great doctrine that American citizenship carries with it every civil and political right which manhood can confer. Let him lend his influence, with all his masterly ability, to complete the proud structure of legislation which makes this nation worthy of the great declaration which heralded its birth, and he will have done that which will most nearly redeem his reputation in the eyes of the world, and best vindicate the wisdom of that policy which has permitted him to regain his seat upon this floor.

To the diatribe of the gentleman from Virginia, [Mr. Harris,] who spoke on yesterday, and who so far transcended the limits of decency and propriety as to announce upon this floor that his remarks were addressed to white men alone, I shall have no word of reply. Let him feel that a negro was not only too magnanimous to smite him in his weakness, but was even charitable enough to grant him the mercy of his silence. [Laughter and applause on the floor and in the galleries.] I shall, sir, leave to others less charitable the unenviable and fatiguing task of sifting out of that mass of chaff the few grains of sense that may, perchance, deserve notice. Assuring the gentleman that the negro in this country aims at a higher degree of intellect than that exhibited by him in this debate, I cheerfully commend him to the commiseration of all intelligent men the world over—black men as well as white men.

Sir, equality before the law is now the broad, universal, glorious rule and mandate of the Republic. No State can violate that. Kentucky and Georgia may crowd their statute-books with retrograde and barbarous legislation; they may rejoice in the odious eminence of their consistent hostility to all the great steps of human progress which have marked our national history since slavery tore down the stars and stripes on Fort Sumter; but, if Congress shall do its duty, if Congress shall enforce the great guarantees which the Supreme Court has declared to be the one pervading purpose of all the recent amendments, then their unwise and unenlightened conduct will fall with the same weight upon the gentlemen from those States who now lend their influence to defeat this bill, as upon the poorest slave who once had no rights which the honorable gentlemen were bound to respect.

But, sir, not only does the decision in the Slaughter-house cases [a Supreme Court decision of 1873 limiting federal jurisdiction over the citizens of individual states] contain nothing which suggests a doubt of the power of Congress to pass the pending bill, but it contains an express recognition and affirmance of such power. I quote now from page 81 of the volume:

> "Nor shall any State deny to any person within its jurisdiction the equal protection of the laws."
>
> In the light of the history of these amendments, and the pervading purpose of them, which we have already discussed, it is not difficult to give a meaning to this clause. The existence of laws in the States where the newly emancipated negroes resided, which discriminated with gross injustice and hardship against them as a class, was the evil to be remedied by this clause, and by it such laws are forbidden.

> If, however, the States did not conform their laws to its requirements, then, by the
> fifth section of the [fourteenth] article of amendment, Congress was authorized to en-
> force it by suitable legislation. We doubt very much whether any action of a State not di-
> rected by way of discrimination against the negroes as a class, or on account of their
> race, will ever be held to come within the purview of this provision. It is so clearly a
> provision for that race and that emergency, that a strong case would be necessary for its
> application to any other. But as it is a State that is to be dealt with, and not alone the va-
> lidity of its laws, we may safely leave that matter until Congress shall have exercised its
> power, or some case of State oppression, by denial of equal justice in its courts shall,
> have claimed a decision at our hands.

No language could convey a more complete assertion of the power of Congress
over the subject embraced in the present bill than is here expressed. If the States do
not conform to the requirements of this clause, if they continue to deny to any person within their jurisdiction the equal protection of the laws, or as the Supreme
Court had said, "deny equal justice in its courts," then Congress is here said to have
power to enforce the constitutional guarantee by appropriate legislation. That is the
power which this bill now seeks to put in exercise. It proposes to enforce the constitutional guarantee against inequality and discrimination by appropriate legislation.
It does not seek to confer new rights, nor to place rights conferred by State citizenship under the protection of the United States, but simply to prevent and forbid inequality and discrimination on account of race, color, or previous condition of
servitude. Never was there a bill more completely within the constitutional power
of Congress. Never was there a bill which appealed for support more strongly to
that sense of justice and fair-play which has been said, and in the main with justice,
to be a characteristic of the Anglo-Saxon race. The Constitution warrants it; the
Supreme Court sanctions it; justice demands it.

Sir, I have replied to the extent of my ability to the arguments which have been
presented by the opponents of this measure. I have replied also to some of the legal
propositions advanced by gentlemen on the other side; and now that I am about to
conclude, I am deeply sensible of the imperfect manner in which I have performed
the task. Technically, this bill is to decide upon the civil status of the colored American citizen; a point disputed at the very formation of our present Government,
when by a short-sighted policy, a policy repugnant to true republican government,
one negro counted as three-fifths of a man. The logical result of this mistake of the
framers of the Constitution strengthened the cancer of slavery, which finally spread
its poisonous tentacles over the southern portion of the body-politic. To arrest its
growth and save the nation we have passed through the harrowing operation of in-
testine war, dreaded at all times, resorted to at the last extremity, like the surgeon's
knife, but absolutely necessary to extirpate the disease which threatened with the
life of the nation the overthrow of civil and political liberty on this continent. In that
dire extremity the members of the race which I have the honor in part to represent—
the race which pleads for justice at your hands to-day, forgetful of their inhuman
and brutalizing servitude at the South, their degradation and ostracism at the
North—flew willingly and gallantly to the support of the national Government.
Their sufferings, assistance, privations, and trials in the swamps and in the rice-
fields, their valor on the land and on the sea, is a part of the ever-glorious record
which makes up the history of a nation preserved, and might, should I urge the

claim, incline you to respect and guarantee their rights and privileges as citizens of our common Republic. But I remember that valor, devotion, and loyalty are not always rewarded according to their just deserts, and that after the battle some who have borne the brunt of the fray may, through neglect or contempt, be assigned to a subordinate place, while the enemies in war may be preferred to the sufferers.

The results of the war, as seen in reconstruction, have settled forever the political status of my race. The passage of this bill will determine the civil status, not only of the negro, but of any other class of citizens who may feel themselves discriminated against. It will form the cap-stone of that temple of liberty, begun on this continent under discouraging circumstances, carried on in spite of the sneers of monarchists and the cavils of pretended friends of freedom, until at last it stands in all its beautiful symmetry and proportions, a building the grandest which the world has ever seen, realizing the most sanguine expectations and the highest hopes of those who, in the name of equal, impartial, and universal liberty, laid the foundation stones. . . .

⚐ *E S S A Y S*

James Roark, a historian at Emory University, in an excerpt from his book *Masters Without Slaves,* shows the effect that emancipation had on elite southern whites and how they dealt with what to them seemed a world turned upside down. One of the leading experts on Reconstruction is historian Eric Foner of Columbia University, who has written extensively on this chaotic and difficult period. Here he delineates the role that blacks played in Reconstruction and the resistance to their freedom that emerged.

The Effect of Emancipation on Elite Southern Whites

JAMES ROARK

Although the political aspects of Reconstruction have often dominated modern perceptions of the period, politics did not fill the life of the average Southern planter. Economic survival was his first priority. Energy was funneled into his effort to salvage a living from the ruins of his plantation. In this battle to save himself, the front lines were the cotton, rice, and sugar fields. Politics remained on the periphery. In 1866, an Alabama planter reported that his neighbors remained aloof from political affairs because they had "too many private and domestic troubles to think about." A year later another Alabaman said, "The subject which most concerns us here is how to manage to keep famine from the door." Summing up the attitude of many, Ella Clanton Thomas declared, "With most of us the present duty—the duty of the hour—is to provide for our familys and *avoid politics.*"

The disengagement of planters from politics was not simply a function of their economic difficulties, however. For some, political inactivity stemmed from a profound alienation from the postbellum South. To these individuals, the North's victory and emancipation meant that nothing of value was at stake any longer in the political arena. "As I fought the Radicalism of N. England to preserve the Slave power (which I esteemed of inestimable value)," Thomas S. Watson of Virginia declared in 1868, "I am convinced that the loss of that issue by battle makes it impossible . . . to raise any other issue that could eventuate in good to us." Given the failure "to preserve the only thing that was of interest to us" and the impossibility of retrieving what was lost, Watson believed it was foolish to engage "in thwarting the plans of the North." From his perspective, Reconstruction applied "not to the *South that I loved,* but to a new & strange & terribly vicious system." Without slavery, in other words, politics had become hollow and irrelevant. All that remained for Watson was his private battle to protect "persons and property."

And yet, most planters could not ignore political developments after Appomattox. To forfeit meekly their power would have been uncharacteristic of the antebellum ruling class. In addition, most planters recognized that politics impinged directly on their primary postwar objective—the reorganization and economic recovery of the plantations. Continued control of labor, land, and other resources was crucial in restoring the plantations and in maintaining a planter-dominated economic and social structure in the South. To lose control permanently was to risk complete destruction. Southern agriculture had never functioned independently of politics, and after the war, planters' workplaces remained squarely in the middle of the political struggle. Because politics and plantations were still linked, therefore, the battle to preserve plantation agriculture and planter power became a political as well as an economic affair.

Defeat had brought a revolution to the lives of Southern planters, but in the summer of 1865 they did not yet know how deeply it would cut. Planters had obviously lost slavery and national independence, but vital decisions were still to be made in Washington. How heavy a yoke would the Republicans decide to fashion? Would the sequel to war be a quick restoration or a thoroughgoing reconstruction? Planters were liable to a variety of charges, including treason, and numerous penalties, including confiscation. Could they expect sympathy or compassion from the victorious North? "Rumours innumerable of Yankee plans, the Yankee intentions toward us," Catherine Edmondston noted hurriedly in her diary a few weeks after the end of the war. "What will be the fate of Virginia is beyond my ken," sighed George W. Munford. "Whether the Yankees will permit us to have any rights or property is more than I can say." The soul-eroding war had ended, but apprehension and anxiety continued unabated, and planters still stared northward.

Despite the confusion surrounding Abraham Lincoln's assassination, answers to the planters' questions were not long in coming. Andrew Johnson rapidly revealed a plan of reunion that rested more on Southern conciliation and consent than upon coercion and reconstruction. Hoping to stimulate renewed loyalty among the South's traditional leaders and to build a national coalition of conservatives, the new president requested the minimum—renunciation of secession, slavery, and the Confederate debt. Instead of implementing the Confiscation Acts, under which the lands of every supporter of the Confederacy were subject to forfeiture, he halted all proceedings and issued a sweeping proclamation of amnesty and pardon, restoring most planters' political rights and land titles. Early fears that the maverick

Southerner would unleash a social revolution in the South were largely dispelled. In the cause of reunion, the president promised to leave land, blacks, and political power in the hands of the old rulers.

The moods and aspirations of Southern planters found expression in their responses to Johnson's program. Some simply assumed that absolute submission was the inevitable consequence of total military defeat. But considerably more urged minimal compliance as practical wisdom. Realizing the impossibility of victory on the old issues of slavery and national self-determination, yet still resolved to protect their vital interests, planters believed that acceptance of Johnson's program was a strategic necessity. Accommodation to harsh realities was not the same as servile submission. Practical conservatives rather than doctrinaire reactionaries, they sought speedy reunion in order to restore autonomy and self-determination to the South. With the reinstatement of the South's traditional rulers and the reestablishment of order and stability, they could set about rebuilding plantation society. In the autumn of 1865, a wife argued with her irreconcilable husband that he must learn to live under "the new order of things." Her message was the realistic one that the sooner Southerners "can manage to be restored to civil rights, the better it will be for their interests and future prospects." Putting her finger on her husband's greatest worry, she explained that reunion would mean that white Southerners, through their state legislatures, could create "a new system" to control black labor. Without political power, she reminded him, the key to the planters' future would remain "in unfriendly hands."

Advocates of rapid reintegration usually saw a clear choice between Johnson and the Radical Republicans. "If the movement of Sumner in the Senate and Thad Stevens in the House foreshadow the future of the Govt. then indeed are our darkest days yet to come," declared Howell Cobb. The Southerners' only hope, he asserted, was "the willingness and ability of President Johnson to rescue them from the fate that bigotry, hatred and passion would bring upon them." Without Southern cooperation, Henry Watson, Jr., argued, Johnson would surely lose to the Radicals. The ex–Confederate governor of Virginia, John Letcher, said that in his personal meeting with President Johnson, he had found him both "liberal and conciliatory," and he suggested that it was "both politic and wise to meet him in the same spirit." In the opinion of these realists, considerations of power, not outdated formal principles, needed to govern action. Through minimal compliance, the South could reassert its mastery.

Others, however, saw the political situation in 1865 quite differently. For them, the emotions and issues of the war were still very much alive. They refused to accept the victory of Northern arms as final and continued to assert their allegiance to the values and institutions of the Old South. Because they were unwilling to accept as permanent any rupture in Southern continuity, they were unwilling to become participants in a political debate in which union and emancipation were taken for granted. It was useless to seek allies in the North, they reasoned, because no Northerner was willing to offer Southerners the restoration of the master-slave relationship. Old patterns could be perpetuated or restored intact only if Southerners would remain loyal to their traditions and affirm their total resistance to change. Even slavery in some form was not beyond their grasp, they thought, if Southerners would stand firm on principle and conviction. . . .

In the autumn of 1865, former Confederates, in accordance with the restoration plans of President Andrew Johnson, met in state conventions, drew up constitutions, and held elections. New state legislatures convened and enacted legislation to meet pressing problems. Even though a significant number of planters were still too unreconstructed to join the constituencies the Johnson legislatures represented, a good deal of the early legislation was designed to facilitate the reconstruction of Southern agriculture along familiar lines. In several states, the Black Codes promised planters a disciplined, immobile, and productive labor force. Stay laws helped protect plantations from immediate foreclosure. "Confederate Brigadiers," heavily represented in the newly elected congressional delegation, were expected to fulfill the traditional role of Southern political leaders—that of looking after the plantation interests. In addition, several states even resisted Johnson's minimum recommendations, refusing to ratify the Thirteenth Amendment, to repudiate the Confederate debt, or to admit the illegality of secession. . . .

The South's response to Johnson's plan of Reconstruction revealed that although militarily defeated, economically crippled, and politically weakened, its leaders were not prepared to ignore what they perceived as their vital interests in pursuit of reunion. Essentially unrepentant, the South adopted a public stance of acquiescence that was superficial and misleading, occasioned only by military necessity. As Michael Perman has recently demonstrated, Johnson's insistence that Southern reorganization take place with the co-operation of the region's traditional leaders meant that their wishes and aspirations were allowed to surface. Seeking renewed sectional harmony, Johnson could not present demands; he could only offer recommendations. When Southerners balked, Johnson retreated, and Southerners simply took as much easy ground as they could. New state legislatures moved swiftly to retrieve as much as possible of the traditional order and to protect themselves from any further unreasonable demands.

When Congress reconvened in December, 1865, Republican legislators responded sharply to the South's Black Codes and Brigadiers. Searching for contrite and reformed ex-Confederates, they found very few, and refused to seat the Southerners. Instead, they began to shape Reconstruction in their own way. They extended the life of the Freedmen's Bureau and passed the Civil Rights Act and the Fourteenth Amendment, each of which sent a chill down the spines of Southern planters. In 1866, Ella Clanton Thomas tersely described the congressional program as one of "extermination, confiscation, and annihilation." She could only hope that her champion, Andrew Johnson, could muster enough power to keep the Radicals from carrying out their plans. "Should the Stevens, Sumner & Phil[l]ips party succeed," said another witness to the struggle between the president and Congress, "God save the South, for she will be in the jaws of wolves and tigers."

In March, 1867, Southerners believed Republicans had actually taken them by the throat. When the South continued to follow Johnson's lead and rejected the Fourteenth Amendment, Congress took charge of Reconstruction altogether. It reorganized the ten obstreperous states under military rule, enfranchised blacks, and disenfranchised substantial numbers of whites, including many planters. The gentry was shocked and dismayed. Hopes that had been kindled under Johnson were extinguished. One Louisiana planter said in May that while things had not been easy under Johnson, they had been tolerable, "but now this new move to enfranchise the blacks places the whole matter once more in the cloud of doubt." The congressional program jeopardized the precarious system of white control. Yankees had "disenfranchised her best citizens & enfranchised the blacks," a planter from Virginia moaned when he heard the news, and "we are destined to have negro officers of government from the highest to the lowest." Everything was adrift, and the situation was more ominous than at any time since Grant had besieged Lee outside Richmond.

When a South Carolina planter heard the news in mid-March, he poured out his anger and frustration. Of "all the miserable & wretched men on Earth I am the most so," he cried. "Just look at the horrid condition our Country is in—all civil government suspended & naught but Military Rule." The military commander would be "a perfect monarch," he predicted, with "all things at his will." He could even "divide out our lands." In fact, the plantations would be "confiscated just as certain as we live." In truth, he said, "we are subjugated to the negroes completely & all of our offices will be filled by them & Sumner says he hopes to see a black man President— that damnable rascal. Brooks ought to have killed him." From the bottom of his soul he "wished the whole North & all the blacks were in hell & never to get out." . . .

One response was simply to drop out of politics entirely. Abstention was prompted by a variety of motives. Some white Southerners, of course, had no choice, being barred from participation by Reconstruction legislation. But eligible ex-rebels were sometimes unwilling to bend principle, and refused to participate again in Yankee-dominated politics. Others were so incensed at the enfranchisement of former slaves that they divorced themselves from political affairs. "I shall never cast another vote so long as I live," vowed an angry and humiliated South Carolinian. And some were simply politically adrift, appalled by the policies of the Republicans and sickened by the past record of the Democracy. A Mississippi planter who had suffered heavy damage during the war called for a pox on both their houses. It was "emphatically an age of small men," he observed, "men dwarfed in principle and intellect." He was disgusted with Republicans, and as for the old Confederate leaders, they were "political mad caps, who have destroyed our once prosperous & happy people. . . ." Who knows, he asked helplessly, "where we are drifting, where we shall make harbor?"

Probably a more important consideration in the detachment of planters from politics was their sense of powerlessness. The planting counties, with their large concentration of blacks, consistently returned Republicans on election day. Since blacks voted the party of their emancipators rather than that of their former masters, the outlook was grim. Many planters decided to sit out the political struggle and wait for Northerners to come to their senses. Some had no choice, for in several black-belt counties, the Democrats did not put forward a slate of candidates, and conservative planters were left without even a continuous minority party organization they could accept. "We are certainly . . . entirely powerless," a Lowndes County, Mississippi, planter remarked in 1867, "and it is as well for us . . . to eschew politics altogether and endeavor to advance our own interests." Agriculturalists in Alabama's black belt felt "that they can do nothing to help themselves politically but must wait for a change of opinion elsewhere." A Virginian declared, "In matters political we have large interest but no active part. . . . we have to 'stand & wait.' " In South Carolina, almost the only native whites active in politics after 1867 were allied with the conservative wing of the Republican party.

The Republican party did offer an alternative political avenue for some Southern planters. Before Congress threw its weight behind Radical Reconstruction, formal Republican organizations existed in only three Southern states, but after 1867, they sprouted everywhere. Planters could be attracted to Republicanism for any number of reasons—persistent Whiggery, consistent Unionism, hope for economic recovery and the end of lawlessness, disillusionment with the Democracy, a realization that the war made old issues irrelevant, and so on. Despite the diversity of their motives, the planters active in Republican politics usually pursued approximately the same course, seeking to control their party, moderate its apparent radicalism, and promote nationalism and economic recovery. . . .

The majority of Southern planters neither retreated from politics entirely nor joined the enemy's ranks. They enlisted in the motley coalition of white conservatives which struggled to defeat Republican rule in the Southern states. But whether politically active or merely fireside politicians, planters were generally agreed that the caldron of Reconstruction politics threatened to boil over with anarchy and ruin. The danger emanated from three sources, a Mississippi planter declared. Ranking the evils, he declared that the South was "accursed with (2) carpetbag, (1) Negro & (3) scalawag rule—(1) bad, (2) worse, (3) worst, & then cotton has fallen to ten cents." Though not always agreeing with this particular gradation, planters generally did agree that he had, indeed, identified the devils.

Each offered its own special threat. Carpetbaggers and their Radical sponsors in the North, planters believed, despised the plantation aristocracy and were eager to destroy it through a program of free labor, confiscation, and disfranchisement. Blacks were unpredictable and potentially dangerous. They might laze about, quietly die out, or lapse into barbarism. And no one doubted that they might also be wooed by unscrupulous whites and led on a rampage against their former masters. Scalawags, whom planters increasingly characterized as native poor whites, might join with blacks and carpetbaggers to inaugurate a sweeping program of political, social, and economic democracy, completely leveling the plantation gentry and the traditional hierarchy of the South. Clearly, the planters' wartime preoccupation, almost obsession, with class and racial revolution had not died with the Confederacy.

Apparently threatened with multiple dangers, both internally and externally, planters had difficulty agreeing on a single political strategy. What, if any, political alliance to strike was difficult to decide. Since white Southerners were "saddled" with black voters, one planter reasoned in June, 1867, "we must hope to divide them and thus rule." And in the period 1868–74, the Democracy, often running under the flag of the Conservative party in an effort to broaden its appeal, did follow an electoral strategy of seeking the support of black voters and dissident white Republicans. Although not without divisions in their ranks, planters made mighty efforts to see that blacks voted correctly. Donelson Caffery of Louisiana hoped to woo freedmen to his party, where they could work against Radical rule and for the "re-establishment of constitutional liberty." "I shall make speeches to the negroes at the Barbecues," he announced optimistically in 1868, and "hope they will be of service to the cause." A Virginian considered running for office because his party was in desperate need of "decent gentlemen" and because he had "some strength with the darkies." Still, he feared that "the Yankees will cause the negro vote to go, in mass, for their candidate." Others tried more direct means of influencing black voters. Believing that freedmen voted with "the same intelligence that a drove of cattle would," a Tennessee planter simply rounded up his laborers, gave them the right ballot, and herded them to the polls.

Planters who had not yet accepted blacks as free laborers suddenly found them active as citizens, voters, and legislators. To seek after their votes was more than some could stomach. They responded to black enfranchisement as to a racial slur. Black suffrage "debased and degraded" white men and was an intolerable "humiliation," a North Carolinian asserted. So long as Negroes were politically active, Ella Clanton Thomas declared in 1870, "just so long will the feeling of resentment linger in our minds." Joseph Buckner Killebrew of Tennessee remembered, "I had fully made up my mind that to be governed by my former slaves was an ignominy which I should not and would not endure."

More often, however, planters were less concerned with racial humiliation than they were with the consequences of black power. In 1866, John Moore predicted that black voters would "be nothing but the tools of leud and designing men, as proven in the late riot in New Orleans." Stability and social order were crumbling under black rule, declared an Alabaman in September, 1867. "I am willing to do almost anything and submit to anything in preference to nigger domination," he said, "because they have neither the intelligence [n]or virtue to rule properly." Even that minority of planters who expressed relatively liberal attitudes toward black suffrage usually agreed that it was an idea whose time had not come. "I say negroes are *not going to vote until we,* the *States,* give them the right, or they win it by a fight," shouted a Georgian in September, 1867. "Negroes who get able to read & write, & pay taxes of $250 real property," he explained, "may get leave to vote, bye & bye. . . ." An Alabama planter agreed. "The African, in his present condition in the South, I do not consider capable of exercising the franchise discretely and prudently." Without substantial inducements to acquire learning and accumulate property, he predicted, "he will go down to his native ignorance, poverty, and barbarism." Most believed blacks had already fallen to their natural level. "Our state is in a horrible condition," a South Carolina woman cried in 1871. "The negro's [*sic*] are making laws perfectly distruction [*sic*] of all property[,] order and peace."

From the beginning, some conservative ex-slaveholders had sought to end their political troubles by emphasizing race and calling for a white man's party. Although it did not usually become the basic anti-Republican strategy until the mid-1870s, some Southerners in the late 1860s already thought it made eminently more sense to tighten party and color lines than to seek co-operation with blacks and dissident whites. In December, 1867, George W. Munford concluded that "the only thing that could be done was to establish a white man's party." When whites resumed control, "the Blacks will be made to know their places, or be driven from the State." Six months later, William H. Heyward declared that "with a white man's civil government again," the Negroes would "be more slaves than they ever were," and white laborers would also step back into harness. Radical Republicans were hammering away at class issues, and planters were frightened of a revolution from below. Racism and opposition to black suffrage would attack the threat directly, and would also erode any alliance that was in the making between poor whites and blacks. The gentry had traditionally used antagonism toward blacks as a means of manipulating poor whites, and some planters argued for continuation of the tactic after the war. . . .

What terrified the gentry was the specter of a fusion of "negroes and Tories." Together, they could completely overwhelm the men of "intelligence," the "good men." If scalawags and Negroes ever took charge of the state of Georgia, C. S. Sutton announced in 1867, "repudiation—the abolition of [the] poll tax—a general division of land, & disfranchisement of Rebels will probably follow, with laws regulating the price of labor and the rent of lands—All to benefit the negro & the poor." William M. Byrd of Alabama noted that a "people, white or black, to reach any exalted scale of refinement and civilization must first be taught to respect labor, learning and property." He feared that "ignorance and poverty" had gotten such a hold on Southerners that there would soon be *a more bloody revolution.*" Another Alabaman agreed that they were "bound to have another revolution of *some sort.*" He believed that "seven tenths of the people of the south would vote for . . . confiscation of Southern *property.* Every negro would vote for such a proposition and a vast number of the whites." And, he added, the "masses of the north would doubtless favor such a proposition." You can form no idea how very reckless our people have become," he told his correspondent, Henry Watson, Jr. And Watson himself agreed that "no tyranny can compare with that of a mob."

In time, the planters' image of the Southern white Republican became almost entirely that of a mean, opportunistic poor white. Sympathetic relationships between poor whites and planters had deteriorated with the Civil War and emancipation. The destruction of slavery had meant the destruction of the poor white's dream of slaveholding, and the rise of white sharecropping had meant that class differences in the rural South were sharpened and made dangerously visible. With the stability of the antebellum social order destroyed, the gentry believed that poor whites, like blacks, had become volatile and unreliable. They feared that poor whites would respond to the Radicals' constant plea that they vote their class, not their race. Scalawags sprang from every element of Southern society, of course, but native white Republican strength was concentrated, as planters believed, in the nonplanting counties and states of the South.

The potential catalyst of revolution, the element which threatened to fuse blacks and poor whites and lead them in an assault upon property and person, was the interloping Northern Republican, the carpetbagger. And carpetbaggers were everywhere, Donelson Caffery of Louisiana complained in 1868, tampering with the lower classes, preaching democracy and egalitarianism, appealing to "the sovereign freedmen & the 'white trash.' " Blatant manipulation of blacks by Radicals enraged James M. Willcox of Virginia. "Congress has placed those Southern States under Negro rule and the Negroes led on by a set of wild, mean Yankees, *Carpet Baggers,* who incite them to all wicked and vicious acts, make tools of the poor deluded creatures to advance their own purposes." They shouted such nonsense as, "The black man is the equal of the white and the white the inferior race, and we of the North the only men fit to govern the Rebs. . . ." In the planters' eyes, blacks, scalawags, and carpetbaggers made up a formidable coalition, one powerful enough perhaps to raise a full-blown social revolution.

The issue around which the three challenging groups were most likely to coalesce, planters believed, was the confiscation of plantations. No political topic was more consistently on planters' lips. Confiscation was an old fear, dating back to the early years of the war, when the Northern Congress passed the Confiscation Acts and Confederate propagandists argued that loss of the plantations would be the price of defeat. A year after Appomattox, on the eve of the registration of black voters in his county, William H. B. Richardson concluded, "Confiscation is inevitable in my opinion." In 1867, a Mississippi man reported that the freedmen ran to the county seat "every week to know something about when the time will be they expect to have the lands & stock devied out amongst them." In 1868, Henry Watson, Jr., said that the tendency in Alabama was "for a subdividing of property rather than for its aggregation." With only gradual abatement, the worry persisted through the early years of the next decade, even though confiscation was last broached in Congress in March, 1867 (and then the proposal did not even reach the floor), and no black legislator ever proposed a plan of confiscation during the years of Republican government in the South. The explanation for the persistence of this fear perhaps lies in the fact that on this one matter planters clearly did "know the Negro." The black man, an Alabama gentleman observed, "wants the white man's property."

Black field hands did not get their ex-masters' lands, however. Land remained in the possession of whites, if not always planters. And eventually, state by state, political power returned to conservative white Southerners. But many planters did endure for as many as ten years what they considered intolerable "Radical rule." "We are so oppressed with carpetbag & negro rule," a Mississippi planter moaned in 1872, "that we the Southern people feel we have quite gone out of existence except to work very hard for bare subsistence." It is incredible, another Mississippian declared two years later, that the "North is so ignorant of the bad rule their party established in [the] South." The "outlook from here is worse than ever before," he asserted, "labor demoralized, taxes high, provisions high & this country making nothing. . . . Do not see nothing but universal Bankruptcy—of both negro and white." But in the end, instead of suffering a revolution from below, white Southerners of all classes joined hands to end Republican rule. Rallying around the standard of white supremacy and applying large doses of white terrorism, they smashed the fragile Republican coalition in the South, ending the era of Reconstruction.

To what degree the restoration of home rule meant a return to power of the antebellum ruling class is not entirely clear. A quarter of a century ago, C. Vann Woodward argued brilliantly that after Reconstruction the ex-Confederate states were dominated by an elite in which new men from the middle classes had a disproportionate influence. Wartime destruction, emancipation, proscription, and economic decay had eroded the planters' political base, while the new urban middle class, with its Whiggish-industrial outlook, was in touch with the dynamic forces of the age. But just how complete the rupture was, just how separated agricultural interests were from post-Reconstruction political power, has never been adequately measured. That some planters were agile enough to resume political careers in the new governments is obvious. That the owners of land in a society still predominately agricultural would have considerable political leverage is likely. Nevertheless, we know that in several states in the 1880s government policies drove planters out of the Democratic party and into agricultural insurgency. Only a thorough study of the social origins and social ideas of post-Reconstruction Southern leadership can answer the question satisfactorily. What we can say with confidence is that after Reconstruction, planters faced powerful, often unprecedented, challenges from small farmers, middle-class professionals, and the new urban, industrial class. The antebellum equation of planters and political power was no longer automatically valid.

Black Life During Reconstruction

ERIC FONER

Early in 1873 a northern correspondent in Mississippi commented on the remarkable changes the previous decade had wrought in the behavior and self-image of southern blacks. "One hardly realizes the fact," he wrote, "that the many negroes one sees here . . . have been slaves a few short years ago, at least as far as their demeanor goes as individuals newly invested with all the rights and privileges of an American citizen. They appreciate their new condition thoroughly, and flaunt their independence." As the writer intimated, the conception of themselves as equal citizens of the American republic galvanized blacks' political and social activity during Reconstruction. Recent studies have made clear how the persistent agitation of Radical Republicans and abolitionists, and the political crisis created by the impasse between Andrew Johnson and Congress over Reconstruction policy, produced the Civil Rights Act of 1866 and the Fourteenth and Fifteenth amendments—measures that embodied a new national commitment to the principle of equality before the law. But the conception of citizens' rights enshrined in national law and the federal Constitution during Reconstruction also came, as it were, from below. In seeking to invest emancipation with a broad definition of equal rights, blacks challenged the nation to live up to the full implications of its democratic creed and helped set in motion events that fundamentally altered the definition of citizenship for all Americans. . . .

. . . [T]he second session of the Thirty-eighth Congress was indeed a historic occasion, for in January Congress gave final approval to the Thirteenth Amendment, abolishing slavery throughout the Union. "The one question of the age is *settled*," exulted Congressman Cornelius Cole of California. But the amendment closed one question only to open a host of others. Did emancipation imply any additional rights for the former slaves? "What is freedom?" James A. Garfield would soon ask. "Is it the bare privilege of not being chained? . . . If this is all, then freedom is a bitter mockery, a cruel delusion." Rather than being a predetermined category or static concept, however, "freedom" itself became a terrain of conflict in the aftermath of emancipation, its substance open to different and sometimes contradictory interpretations, its content changing for both blacks and whites in the years following the Civil War. And as the former slaves entered the nation's public life after the war, they sought to breathe life into the promise of freedom.

"The Negroes are to be pitied," wrote a South Carolina educator and minister. "They do not understand the liberty which has been conferred upon them." In fact, blacks carried out of bondage an understanding of their new condition shaped both by their experience as slaves and by observation of the free society around them.

What one planter called their "wild notions of right and freedom" encompassed first of all an end to the myriad injustices associated with slavery—separation of families, punishment by the lash, denial of access to education. To some, like Georgia black leader Rev. Henry M. Turner, freedom meant the enjoyment of "our rights in common with other men." "If I cannot do like a white man I am not free," Henry Adams told his former master in 1865. "I see how the poor white people do. I ought to do so too, or else I am a slave."

Underpinning blacks' individual aspirations lay a broader theme: their quest for independence from white control, for autonomy both as individuals and as members of a community itself being transformed as a result of emancipation. In countless ways, blacks in 1865 sought to "throw off the badge of servitude," to overturn the real and symbolic authority whites had exercised over every aspect of their lives. Some took new names that reflected the lofty hopes inspired by emancipation— Deliverance Belin, Hope Mitchell, Chance Great. Others relished opportunities to flaunt their liberation from the infinite regulations, significant and trivial, associated with slavery. Freedmen held mass meetings unrestrained by white surveillance; they acquired dogs, guns, and liquor (all forbidden them under slavery); and they refused to yield the sidewalk to whites. Blacks dressed as they pleased and left plantations when they desired. They withdrew from churches controlled by whites and created autonomous churches, stabilized and strengthened the families they had brought out of slavery, and established a network of independent schools and benevolent societies.

In no other realm of southern life did blacks' effort to define the terms of their own freedom or to identify the "rights" arising from emancipation with independence from white control have implications so explosive for the entire society as in the economy. Blacks brought out of slavery a conception of themselves as a "Working Class of People," in the words of a group of Georgia freedmen who had been unjustly deprived of the fruits of their labor. In January 1865 Gen. William T. Sherman and Secretary of War Edwin M. Stanton met with a group of black leaders in Savannah, Georgia, recently occupied by the Union army. Asked what he understood by slavery, Baptist minister Garrison Frazier responded that it meant one man's "receiving . . . the work of another man, and not by his consent." Freedom he defined as "placing us where we could reap the fruit of our own labor." Yet more than simply receiving wages, blacks demanded the right to control the conditions under which they worked, to free themselves from subordination to white authority, and to carve out the greatest possible measure of economic autonomy.

The desire to escape from white supervision and to establish a modicum of economic independence profoundly shaped blacks' economic choices during Reconstruction. It led them to resist working in gangs under overseers and to prefer leasing land for a fixed rent to working for wages. Above all, it inspired their quest for land of their own. Without land, there could be no economic autonomy, blacks believed, for their labor would continue to be subject to exploitation by their former owners. "Gib us our own land and we take care ourselves," a Charleston black told northern correspondent Whitelaw Reid, "but widout land, de ole massas can hire or starve us, as dey please."

Numerous freedmen emerged from slavery convinced they had a "right" to a portion of their former owners' land. In part, their belief stemmed from actions of the federal government—the Freedmen's Bureau Act of early 1865, which held out the prospect of the division of confiscated and abandoned land among blacks and white refugees, and General Sherman's Field Order 15, which set aside a portion of the South Carolina and Georgia Lowcountry for exclusive settlement by blacks. In addition, blacks insisted it was only fair that "the land ought to belong to the man who (alone) could work it," as one former slave told rice planter Edward B. Hey-ward. Most often, however, blacks insisted their past labor entitled them to a por-tion of their owners' estates. "They have an idea that they have a certain right to the property of their former masters, that they have earned it," reported a North Car-olina Freedmen's Bureau official. In its most sophisticated form, the claim to land rested on an appreciation of the role of black labor in the evolution of the nation's economy. . . .

If the goal of autonomy inspired blacks to withdraw from religious and other institutions controlled by whites and to attempt to work out their own economic destinies, in the polity freedom implied inclusion rather than separation. Indeed, the attempt to win recognition of their equal rights as citizens quickly emerged as the animating impulse of black politics during Reconstruction. Achieving a measure of political power seemed indispensable to attaining the other goals of the black com-munity, including access to the South's economic resources, equal treatment in the courts, and protection against violence. But apart from its specific uses, in the United States the ballot was itself an emblem of citizenship. In a professedly demo-cratic political culture, the ballot did more than identify who could vote—it defined a collective public life, as woman suffrage advocates so tirelessly pointed out. (For most postwar Americans, to be sure, "black suffrage" meant black male suffrage. Few black men argued that women should exercise political rights; yet most black women seem to have agreed that the enfranchisement of black men would represent a major step forward for the entire black community.) Democrats were repelled by the very idea of including blacks in the common public life defined by the suffrage. "Without reference to the question of equality," declared Senator Thomas Hen-dricks of Indiana, "I say we are not of the same race; we are so different that we ought not to compose one political community." The United States, Frederick Dou-glass reminded the nation, differed profoundly from societies accustomed to fixed social classes and historically defined gradations of civil and political rights:

> If I were in a monarchial government, . . . where the few bore rule and the many were subject, there would be no special stigma resting upon me, because I did not exercise the elective franchise. . . . But here, where universal suffrage is the fundamental idea of the Government, to rule us out is to make us an exception, to brand us with the stigma of in-feriority.

The statewide conventions held throughout the South during 1865 and early 1866 offered evidence of the early spread of political mobilization among the South's freedmen. Several hundred delegates attended the gatherings, some selected by local meetings specially convened for the purpose, others by churches, fraternal societies, and black army units, still others simply self-appointed. Although the dele-gates "ranged all colors and apparently all conditions," urban free mulattoes took the most prominent roles, whereas former slaves, although in attendance, were almost entirely absent from positions of leadership. Numerous black soldiers, ministers, and artisans also took part, as well as a significant number of recent black arrivals from the North.

The conventions' major preoccupations proved to be the suffrage and equality before the law. In justifying the demand for the vote, the delegates invoked the nation's republican traditions, especially the Declaration of Independence, "the broadest, the deepest, the most comprehensive and truthful definition of human freedom that was ever given to the world," as black Freedmen's Bureau official John M. Langston put it. "The colored people," Rev. James Hood would declare in 1868, "had read the Declaration until it had become part of their natures." The North Carolina convention he chaired in 1865 portrayed the Civil War and emancipation as chapters in the onward march of "progressive civilization," embodiments of "the fundamental truths laid down in the great charter of Republican liberty, the Declaration of Independence." Such language was not confined to convention delegates. Eleven Alabama blacks complaining in 1865 of contract frauds, injustice before the courts, and other abuses concluded their petition with a revealing masterpiece of understatement: "this is not the persuit of happiness." . . .

Like their northern counterparts during the Civil War, southern blacks now proclaimed their identification with the nation's history, destiny, and political system. The very abundance of letters and petitions addressed by black gatherings and ordinary freedmen to officials of the army, to the Freedmen's Bureau, and to state and federal authorities, revealed a belief that the political order was at least partially open to black influence. "We are Americans," declared an address from a Norfolk black meeting, "we know no other country, we love the land of our birth." It went on to remind white Virginians that in 1619 "our fathers as well as yours were toiling in the plantations on James River" and that a black man, Crispus Attucks, shed "the first blood" in the American Revolution. And, of course, blacks had fought and died to save the Union. America, resolved another Virginia meeting, was "now *our* country—made emphatically so by the blood of our brethren" in the Union army.

Despite the insistent language of individual speeches, the conventions' resolutions and public addresses generally adopted a moderate tone, revealing both a realistic assessment of the political situation during Presidential Reconstruction and the fact that political mobilization had proceeded more quickly in southern cities than in the Black Belt where most freedmen lived. Similarly, economic concerns figured only marginally in the proceedings. The ferment rippling through the southern countryside found little echo at the state conventions of 1865 and 1866, a reflection of the paucity of Black Belt representation. Far different was the situation in 1867 when, in the aftermath of the Reconstruction Act, a wave of political mobilization swept the rural South.

Like emancipation, the advent of black suffrage inspired freedmen with a millennial sense of living at the dawn of a new era. Former slaves now stood on an equal footing with whites, a black speaker told a Savannah mass meeting, and before them lay "a field, too vast for contemplation." As in 1865 blacks found countless ways of pursuing aspirations for autonomy and equality and of seizing the opportunity to press for further change. Strikes broke out during the spring of 1867 among black longshoremen in the South's major port cities and quickly spread to other workers, including Richmond, Virginia, coopers and Selma, Alabama, restaurant workers. Hundreds of South Carolina blacks refused to pay taxes to the existing state government, and there was an unsuccessful attempt to rescue chain gang prisoners at work on Mobile, Alabama's streets. Three blacks refused to leave a whites-only Richmond streetcar, and crowds flocked to the scene shouting, "let's have our rights." In New Orleans, groups commandeered segregated horse-drawn streetcars and drove them around the city in triumph. By midsummer, integrated transportation had come to these and other cities.

But in 1867 politics emerged as the principal focus of black aspirations. Itinerant lecturers, black and white, brought the message of equality to the heart of the rural South. In Monroe County, Alabama, where no black political meeting had occurred before, freedmen crowded around the speaker shouting "God bless you, bless God for this." Richmond's tobacco factories were forced to close on August 1 because so many black laborers quit work to attend the Republican state convention. Black churches, schools, and indeed, every other institution of the black community became highly politicized. Every African Methodist Episcopal minister in Georgia was said to be engaged in Republican organizing, and political materials were read aloud at "churches, societies, leagues, clubs, balls, picnics, and all other gatherings." One plantation manager summed up the situation: "You never saw a people more excited on the subject of politics than are the negroes of the South. They are perfectly wild."

In Union Leagues, Republican gatherings, and impromptu local meetings, ordinary blacks in 1867 and 1868 staked their claim to equal citizenship in the American republic. A black organizer in Georgia voiced the prevailing sentiment: "He was no nigger now. He was a citizen and was going to have all the rights of the white man, and would take no less."

At their most utopian, blacks now envisioned a society purged of all racial distinctions. That does not mean they lacked a sense of racial identity, for blacks remained proud of the accomplishments of black soldiers and preferred black teachers for their children and black churches in which to worship. But in the polity, those who had so long been proscribed because of color, defined equality as colorblind. "I heard a white man say," black teacher Robert G. Fitzgerald recorded in his diary, "today is the black man's day; tommorrow will be the white man's. I thought, poor man, those days of distinction between colors is about over, in this (now) free country." . . .

Nor did blacks evince much interest in emigration during Radical Reconstruction. Over twelve hundred emigrants from Georgia and South Carolina had sailed for Liberia under American Colonization Society auspices during 1866 and 1867, "tired of the unprovoked scorn and prejudice we daily and hourly suffer." But the optimism kindled in 1867 brought the emigration movement to an abrupt halt. "You could not get one of them to think of going to Liberia now," wrote a white colonizationist. Blacks probably considered themselves more fully American then than at any time in the nineteenth century; some even echoed the exuberant nationalism and Manifest Destiny expansionism of what one called "our civilization." Throughout Reconstruction, blacks took pride in parading on July 4, "the day," a Charleston, South Carolina, diarist observed, "the Niggers now celebrate, and the whites stay home." As late as 1876, a speaker at a black convention aroused "positive signs of disapproval" by mentioning emigration. "Damn Africa," one delegate declared. "If Smith wants to go let him; we'll stay in America."

Blacks' secular claim to equality was, in part, underpinned by a religious messianism deeply rooted in the black experience. As slaves, blacks had come to think of themselves as analogous to the Jews in Egypt, an oppressed people whom God, in the fullness of time, would deliver from bondage. And they endowed the Civil War and emancipation with spiritual import, comprehending those events through the language of Christian faith. A Tennessee newspaper commented in 1869 that freedmen habitually referred to slavery as "Paul's Time" and to Reconstruction as "Isaiah's Time"—referring perhaps to Paul's message of obedience and humility and to Isaiah's prophecy of cataclysmic change, a "new heaven and a new earth" brought about by violence. Black religion reinforced black republicanism, for as Rev. J. M. P. Williams, a Mississippi legislator, put it in 1871, "of one blood God did make all men to dwell upon the face of the earth . . . hence their common origin, destiny and equal rights." Even nonclerics used secular and religious vocabulary interchang[e]ably, as in one 1867 speech recorded by a North Carolina justice of the peace:

> He said it was not now like it used to be, that . . . the negro was about to get his equal rights. . . . That the negroes owed their freedom to the courage of the negro soldiers and to God. . . . He made frequent references to the II and IV chapters of Joshua for a full accomplishment of the principles and destiny of the race. It was concluded that the race have a destiny in view similar to the Children of Israel. . . .

The land issue animated grass-roots black politics in 1867. The Reconstruction Act rekindled the belief that the federal government intended to provide freedmen with homesteads. In Alabama freedmen delivered "inflammatory" speeches asserting that "all the wealth of the white man has been made by negro labor, and that the negroes were entitled to their fair share of all these accumulations." "Didn't you clear the white folks' land," asked one orator. "Yes," voices answered from the crowd, "and we have a right to it!" There seemed a great deal more danger, wrote former South Carolina governor Benjamin F. Perry, "of 'Cuffee' than Thad Stevens taking over lands."

By mid-1867, planter William Henry Trescot observed, blacks had become convinced that membership in the Union League "will in some way, they do not exactly know how, secure them the possession of the land." Yet that was only one among the multiplicity of purposes blacks sought to achieve through Reconstruction politics. In a society marked by vast economic disparities and by a growing racial separation in social and religious life, the polity became the only area where black and white encountered each other on a basis of equality—sitting alongside one another on juries, in legislatures, and at political conventions; voting together on election day. For individuals, politics offered a rare opportunity for respectable, financially rewarding employment. And although elective office and the vote remained male preserves, black women shared in the political mobilization. They took part in rallies, parades, and mass meetings, voted on resolutions (to the consternation of some male participants), and formed their own auxiliaries to aid in electioneering. During the 1868 campaign, Yazoo, Mississippi, whites found their homes invaded by buttons depicting Gen. Ulysses S. Grant that were defiantly worn by black maids and cooks. There were also reports of women ostracizing black Democrats (one threatened to "burn his damned arse off") and refusing conjugal relations with husbands who abandoned the Republican party.

Throughout Reconstruction, blacks remained "irrepressible democrats." "Negroes all crazy on politics again," noted a Mississippi plantation manager in the fall of 1873. "Every tenth negro a candidate for office." And the Republican party—the party of emancipation and black suffrage—became as central an institution of the black community as the church and the school. When not deterred by violence, blacks eagerly attended political gatherings and voted in extraordinary numbers; their turnout in many elections exceeded 90 percent. Despite the failure of land distribution, the end of Reconstruction would come not because propertyless blacks succumbed to economic coercion but because a politically tenacious black community fell victim to violence, fraud, and national abandonment. Long after they had been stripped of the franchise, blacks would recall the act of voting as a defiance of inherited norms of white superiority and would regard "the loss of suffrage as being the loss of freedom."

The precise uses to which blacks put the political power they achieved during Radical Reconstruction lie beyond the scope of this essay. But it is clear that with wealth, political experience, and tradition all mobilized against them in the South, blacks saw in political authority a countervailing power. "They look to legislation," commented an Alabama newspaper, "because in the very nature of things, they can look nowhere else." Although political realities (especially the opposition of northern Republicans and divisions among southern Republicans) prevented direct action on the land issue except in South Carolina, black legislators successfully advocated crop lien, tax, and other measures advantageous to plantation laborers. Their success marked a remarkable departure from the days of slavery and Presidential Reconstruction, when public authority was geared to upholding the interests of the planter class. On the local and state levels, black officials also pressed for the expansion of such public institutions as schools, hospitals, and asylums. They insisted, moreover, that the newly expanded state must be color-blind, demanding and often achieving laws prohibiting racial discrimination in public transportation and accommodations and, although generally amenable to separate schools for black and white, insisting that such segregation be a matter of choice, rather than being required by law. Black lawmakers also unsuccessfully advanced proposals to expand public responsibility even further to include regulation of private markets and insurance companies, restrictions on the sale of liquor, and even prohibition of fairs, gambling, and horse racing on Sundays. In those ways and more, they revealed a vision of a democratic state actively promoting the social and moral well-being of its citizens.

Ultimately, however, blacks viewed the national government as the guarantor of their rights. Before 1860 blacks and their white allies had generally feared federal power, since the government at Washington seemed under the control of the "Slave Power," and after 1850 they looked to state authorities to nullify the federal Fugitive Slave Act. But blacks who had come to freedom through an unprecedented exercise of national power and who then had seen whites restored to local hegemony by President Johnson attempt to make a mockery of that freedom became increasingly hostile to ideas of states' rights and local autonomy. Until Americans abandoned the idea of "the right of each State to control its own affairs. . . ," wrote Frederick Douglass, "no general assertion of human rights can be of any practical value." Black political leaders did not share fears of "centralism" common even in Republican circles, and throughout Reconstruction they supported proposals for such vast expansions of federal authority as Alabama black congressman James T. Rapier's plan for a national educational system complete with federally mandated textbooks.

As Reconstruction progressed, the national Constitution took its place alongside the Declaration of Independence as a central reference point in black political discourse. . . .

But more than any other issue, racial violence led blacks to identify the federal government as the ultimate guarantor of their rights. Increasingly, it became clear that local and state authorities, even those elected by blacks, were either unwilling or unable to put down the Ku Klux Klan and kindred organizations. "We are more slave today in the hand of the wicked than we were before," read a desperate plea from Alabama freedmen. "We need protection . . . only a standing army in this place can give us our right and life." "Dear sir," read a letter written during Mississippi's violent Redemption campaign of 1875, "did not the 14th Article . . . say that no person shall be deprived of life nor property without due process of law? It said all persons have equal protection of the laws but I say we colored men don't get it at all. . . . Is that right, or is it not? No, sir, it is wrong." Blacks enthusiastically supported the Enforcement Acts of 1870 and 1871, which effectively put an end to the Klan, and the Reconstruction era expansion of the powers of the federal judiciary. One black convention went so far as to insist that virtually all civil and criminal cases involving blacks be removable from state to federal courts, a mind-boggling enhancement of federal judicial authority.

Throughout Reconstruction, blacks insisted that "those who freed them shall protect that freedom." Increasingly, however, blacks' expansive definition of federal authority put them at odds with mainstream white Republicans, who by the 1870s were retreating from the war-inspired vision of a powerful national state. Indeed, even among abolitionists, the persistent demands of blacks for federal action on their behalf raised fears that the freedmen were somehow not acting as autonomous citizens capable of defending their own interests. Frederick Douglass himself had concluded in 1865 that the persistent question "What shall we do with the Negro?" had only one answer: "Do nothing. . . . Give him a chance to stand on his own legs! Let him alone!" Douglass realized that the other face of benevolence is often paternalism and that in a society resting, if only rhetorically, on the principle of equality, "special efforts" on the freedmen's behalf might "serve to keep up the very prejudices, which it is so desirable to banish." It was precisely that image to which President Johnson had appealed in justifying his vetoes of the Freedmen's Bureau and Civil Rights bills in 1866. Douglass, of course, and most Republicans, believed equal civil rights and the vote were essential to enabling blacks to protect themselves. But by the 1870s, with those rights granted, blacks' demands for protection struck many whites, including reformers, as reflecting a desire to become privileged "wards of the nation."

The fate of Charles Sumner's federal Civil Rights Bill, prohibiting racial discrimination in public accommodations, transportation, schools, churches, and cemeteries, illustrated how much black and white Republicans differed regarding what obligations the federal government had incurred by emancipating the slaves. Before galleries crowded with black spectators, black congressmen invoked both the personal experience of having been evicted from inns, hotels, and railroads and the black political ideology that had matured during Reconstruction. To James T. Rapier, discrimination was "anti-republican," recalling the class and religious inequalities of other lands—in Europe "they have princes, dukes, lords"; in India "brahmans or priests, who rank above the sudras or laborers"; in the United States "our distinction is color." Richard H. Cain reminded the House that "the black man's labor" has enriched the country; Robert B. Elliott recalled the sacrifices of black soldiers. But white Republicans considered the bill an embarrassment to the party. Not until 1875 did a watered-down version pass Congress. It contained only weak provisions for enforcement and remained largely a dead letter until the Supreme Court ruled it unconstitutional in 1883.

In the end, the broad conception of "rights" with which blacks attempted to imbue the social revolution of emancipation proved tragically insecure. Although some of the autonomy blacks had wrested for themselves in the early days of freedom was irreversible (control of their religious life, for example), the dream of economic independence had been dashed even before the end of Reconstruction. By the end of the century, the Fourteenth and Fifteenth amendments had been effectively nullified in the South. As Supreme Court Justice John Marshall Harlan put in 1883, the United States entered on "an era of constitutional law when the rights of freedom and American citizenship cannot receive from the nation that efficient protection which heretofore was unhesitatingly accorded to slavery and the rights of the master." During Reconstruction, political involvement, economic self-help, and family and institution building had all formed parts of a coherent ideology of black community advancement. After the South's "Redemption," that ideology separated into its component parts, and blacks' conception of their "rights" turned inward. Assuming a defensive posture, blacks concentrated on strengthening their community and surviving in the face of a patently unjust political and social order, rather than directly challenging the new status quo.

A disaster for blacks, the collapse of Reconstruction was also a tragedy that deeply affected the future development of the nation as a whole. If racism contributed to the undoing of Reconstruction, by the same token Reconstruction's demise and the emergence of blacks as a disfranchised class of dependent laborers greatly facilitated racism's further spread, so that by the early twentieth century it had become more deeply embedded in the [nation's] culture and politics than at any time since the beginning of the antislavery crusade. Meanwhile, the activist state's association with the aspirations of blacks discredited it in the eyes of many white Americans. And the removal of a significant portion of the laboring population from public life shifted the center of gravity of American politics to the right, complicating the tasks of reformers for generations to come. Long into the twentieth century, the South remained a one-party region under the control of a reactionary ruling elite whose national power weakened the prospects not simply of change in racial matters but of progressive legislation in many other realms.

⚹ *F U R T H E R   R E A D I N G*

Eric Anderson and Alfred A. Moss, Jr., eds., *The Facts of Reconstruction* (1991)

Michael Les Benedict, *A Compromise of Principle* (1974)

Carol Bleser, *The Promised Land: The History of the South Carolina Land Commission, 1869–1890* (1969)

Orville Vernon Burton, *In My Father's House Are Many Mansions* (1985)

Dan T. Carter, *When the War Was Over: The Failure of Self-Reconstruction in the South* (1985)

John Cimprich, *Slavery's End in Tennessee* (1985)

Edmund L. Drago, *Black Politicians and Reconstruction in Georgia: A Splendid Failure* (1982)

W. E. B. Du Bois, *Black Reconstruction* (1935)

Katharine L. Dvorak, *An African-American Exodus: The Segregation of the Southern Churches* (1991)

Laura F. Edwards, *Gendered Strife and Confusion: The Political Culture of Reconstruction* (1997)

Barbara Jeanne Fields, *Slavery and Freedom on the Middle Ground* (1985)

Eric Foner, *Reconstruction: America's Unfinished Revolution, 1863–1877* (1988)

William Gillette, *Retreat from Reconstruction, 1869–1879* (1979)

William C. Harris, *The Day of the Carpetbagger* (1979)

Janet Sharp Hermann, *The Pursuit of a Dream* (1981)

Reginald Francis Hildebrand, *The Times Were Strange and Stirring: Methodist Preachers and the Crisis of Emancipation* (1995)

Thomas Holt, *Black over White: Negro Political Leadership in South Carolina During Reconstruction* (1977)

Elizabeth Jacoway, *Yankee Missionaries in the South: The Penn School Experiment* (1980)

Jacqueline Jones, *Soldiers of Light and Love: Northern Teachers and Georgia Blacks, 1865–1873* (1980)

J. Morgan Kousser and James M. McPherson, eds., *Region, Race, and Reconstruction* (1982)

Leon Litwack, *Been in the Storm So Long: The Aftermath of Slavery* (1979)

Edward Magdol, *A Right to the Land* (1977)

William S. McFeely, *Yankee Stepfather: General O.O. Howard and the Freedmen* (1968)

Robert C. Morris, *Reading, 'Riting, and Reconstruction* (1981)

Elizabeth Studley Nathans, *Losing the Peace: Georgia Republicans and Reconstruction, 1865–1871* (1968)

Otto H. Olsen, ed., *Reconstruction and Redemption in the South* (1980)

Claude F. Oubre, *Forty Acres and a Mule* (1978)

Joseph H. Parks, *Joseph E. Brown of Georgia* (1977)

Michael Perman, *Reunion Without Compromise* (1973)

———, *The Road to Redemption: Southern Politics, 1869–1879* (1984)

Lawrence N. Powell, *New Masters: Northern Planters During the Civil War and Reconstruction* (1980)

Howard N. Rabinowitz, *Race Relations in the Urban South, 1865–1890* (1978)

———, ed., *Southern Black Leaders of the Reconstruction Era* (1982)

George C. Rable, *But There Was No Peace: The Role of Violence in the Politics of Reconstruction* (1984)

James Roark, *Masters Without Slaves: Southern Planters in the Civil War and Reconstruction* (1977)

Willie Lee Rose, *Rehearsal for Reconstruction: The Port Royal Experiment* (1964)

Julie Saville, *The Work of Reconstruction: From Slave to Wage Laborer in South Carolina, 1860–1870* (1994)

Mark W. Summers, *Railroads, Reconstruction, and the Gospel of Prosperity* (1984)

Daniel E. Sutherland, *The Confederate Carpetbaggers* (1988)

Joe Gray Taylor, *Louisiana Reconstructed, 1863–1877* (1974)

Allen W. Trelease, *White Terror: The Ku Klux Klan Conspiracy and Southern Reconstruction* (1971)

Ted Tunnell, *Crucible of Reconstruction: War, Radicalism, and Race in Louisiana, 1862–1877* (1984)

Clarence E. Walker, *A Rock in a Weary Land: The African Methodist Episcopal Church During the Civil War and Reconstruction* (1982)

Sarah Woolfolk Wiggins, *The Scalawag in Alabama Politics, 1865–1881* (1977)

Lou Falkner Williams, *The Great South Carolina Ku Klux Klan Trials* (1996)

Joel Williamson, *The Crucible of Race: Black/White Relations in the American South Since Emancipation* (1984)